ISBN: 978-1-964079-59-2

Table of Contents

Intro:

Imagine standing at the helm of a complex, high-stakes project at a leading technology firm, tasked with launching an innovative new software product designed to revolutionize the way small businesses manage their operations. The atmosphere is electric, buzzing with the energy of cross-functional teams from engineering, marketing, and customer support, all coordinated by a skilled project manager—let's call her Maya. Maya's challenge is formidable. She faces tight deadlines, technical hurdles, and the daunting task of keeping a diverse team aligned and motivated. Three months into the project, a major technical issue threatens to derail the entire timeline. The integration of the software with existing platforms isn't working as planned, leading to frustration across teams and mounting pressure from senior management. With her CAPM certification knowledge at her fingertips, Maya demonstrates why effective project management is more art than science. She convenes emergency meetings, fostering an environment where every voice is heard and every suggestion is valued. Through a series of strategic decisions, grounded in methodologies she mastered during her CAPM training—such as risk management and conflict resolution—Maya navigates the team through this storm. Under her leadership, the team not only identifies a creative workaround but also enhances the product's functionality, turning a near-catastrophe into a groundbreaking feature that sets the company apart in the market. The launch is a resounding success. Sales exceed projections, customer satisfaction scores soar, and the company solidifies its position as an industry innovator. This success story is not just about overcoming project challenges; it's about how a certified project manager like Maya can drive growth, spur innovation, and positively impact the bottom line. Her story illustrates the profound effect that skilled project management can have on an organization's trajectory. Now, imagine yourself in Maya's shoes. With the CAPM certification, you are equipped with the tools, techniques, and methodologies to lead with confidence. You can see beyond the complexity and chaos, identify opportunities for innovation, and steer your projects to successful completion. The CAPM certification isn't just a mark of your expertise; it's a gateway to new opportunities and a career that makes a tangible difference in your organization and your professional life. Embrace this journey, and let the CAPM be your guide to becoming a pivotal player in your organization's success. The Certified Associate in Project Management (CAPM)® is a globally recognized entry-level certification that endorses an individual's understanding of the fundamental knowledge, terminology, and processes of effective project management. This certification, offered by the Project Management Institute (PMI)®, is designed for those who are looking to advance or start a career in project management, as well as project team members who wish to demonstrate their project management knowledge.

Why CAPM Certification?

The CAPM certification is ideal for less experienced professionals who want to enhance their ability to manage larger projects, gain more responsibility, or add project management skills into their current role. It's particularly valuable for those who are not yet ready to commit to the more rigorous Project Management Professional (PMP)® certification but still wish to gain a solid grounding in the project management processes and best practices.

Eligibility Requirements

To apply for the CAPM, candidates need to have a secondary degree (high school diploma, associate's degree, or the global equivalent) and either 1,500 hours of project experience or 23 hours of project management education by the time they sit for the exam.

Exam Details

The CAPM exam consists of 150 multiple-choice questions, which cover the principles and terminology within the Project Management Institute's A Guide to the Project Management Body of Knowledge (PMBOK® Guide). Candidates have three hours to complete the exam. The questions are structured to test the candidate's knowledge of the five process groups: Initiating, Planning, Executing, Monitoring and Controlling, and Closing.

Maintaining Certification

To maintain the CAPM certification, individuals must retake the exam every five years. This requirement ensures that CAPM holders keep up with changes in the field of project management and continuously refresh their knowledge.

Benefits of CAPM Certification

1. **Increased Employment Opportunities**: The CAPM certification is recognized internationally, greatly expanding job opportunities. It distinguishes individuals in the job market and enhances credibility with employers.
2. **Higher Salary Potential**: CAPM certification can lead to improved salary prospects. According to PMI, those with a certification garner a higher salary than those without a PMI certification.
3. **Recognition of Knowledge and Skills**: CAPM certification demonstrates to employers, peers, and stakeholders that an individual has a solid foundation of knowledge in project management.
4. **Foundation for Future Growth**: The CAPM also provides a stepping stone to the more advanced PMP certification, allowing professionals to embark on a progressive path in project management.
5. **Enhanced Skills and Confidence**: The preparation for the CAPM exam itself helps candidates develop their understanding of PMI's project management processes and best practices, leading to greater confidence in their professional abilities.

Whether you are new to project management or looking to solidify your skills, the CAPM certification is a valuable asset that can enhance your career, increase your job opportunities, and provide you with the tools necessary to execute large-scale projects effectively.

Obtaining the Certified Associate in Project Management (CAPM)® certification offers a multitude of benefits that can significantly enhance your career in project management. Here's a closer look at the key advantages of achieving this certification:

1. Recognition of Expertise:

The CAPM certification is acknowledged globally and showcases your commitment to project management as a profession. Holding this certification communicates to employers, peers, and clients that you possess a standardized level of understanding of project management principles, based on the PMI framework.

2. Increased Job Opportunities:

As businesses increasingly recognize the importance of structured project management, the demand for certified professionals continues to grow. The CAPM certification can open doors to new job roles, particularly for those entering the field or looking to transition into project management from another career.

3. Enhanced Credibility:

With a CAPM certification, you gain credibility among your peers and within your organization. It serves as evidence of your dedication to following industry-recognized project management practices and enhances your professional reputation.

4. Foundation for Career Progression:

The CAPM certification is an excellent starting point for project management professionals. It lays the groundwork for further development and is a stepping stone toward more advanced certifications, such as the Project Management Professional (PMP)®. For many, the CAPM is the first milestone in a long-term career in project management.

5. Improved Earning Potential:

Certification in a specialized field typically leads to higher salary prospects. According to surveys conducted by the Project Management Institute, individuals with a CAPM certification tend to enjoy better remuneration compared to their non-certified counterparts.

6. Broader Understanding of Project Management:

Preparing for the CAPM exam forces candidates to thoroughly understand and apply the terminologies and processes described in PMI's PMBOK® Guide. This comprehensive knowledge allows individuals to manage larger and more complex projects more effectively.

7. Confidence Boost:

Achieving the CAPM certification can significantly boost your confidence in handling project management tasks. Knowing that you have mastered the tools and techniques essential for project management can increase your confidence in making decisions and leading projects.

8. Networking Opportunities:

Being a CAPM holder also grants you membership to PMI, providing opportunities to attend meetings, conferences, and seminars that can enhance your networking circle. This network can be invaluable for career growth, learning best practices, and staying updated with industry trends.

9. Organizational Impact:

CAPM-certified employees bring a higher level of competence to their projects, potentially leading to more successful project outcomes and contributing positively to the organization's bottom line. This can lead to greater internal recognition and opportunities for advancement within the company.

10. Commitment to Professional Growth:

Pursuing and maintaining a CAPM certification requires a commitment to continuous learning and professional development. This dedication not only helps in personal growth but also demonstrates to employers your initiative in staying relevant and up-to-date in the field.

Obtaining the CAPM certification can be a transformative step for anyone looking to establish or advance their career in project management. It not only improves your job prospects and potential earnings but also equips you with the knowledge and skills to effectively contribute to and lead projects within any industry. To sit for the Certified Associate in Project Management (CAPM)® exam, candidates must meet specific eligibility requirements set by the Project Management Institute (PMI)®. These requirements are designed to ensure that individuals have the basic knowledge and educational background necessary to understand the fundamental principles of project management. Here's a detailed look at the eligibility criteria for the CAPM exam:

1. Educational Background

- **Secondary Degree**: Candidates must have a high school diploma, associate's degree, or the global equivalent. This requirement ensures that all applicants have a foundational level of education that supports the comprehension of the project management concepts covered in the exam.

2. Project Management Education

- **23 Contact Hours**: Candidates must complete 23 contact hours of formal education in project management. This education must cover the fundamental knowledge areas of project management as outlined in PMI's A Guide to the Project Management Body of Knowledge (PMBOK® Guide). These hours can be obtained through PMI-recognized Registered Education Providers (REPs) or through programs offered by other accredited educational institutions. The coursework must be completed before the candidate submits the application for the exam.

Alternative to Project Management Experience:

- While not a requirement, having practical experience in project management can be beneficial. Candidates who have 1,500 hours of project team experience will also meet the eligibility criteria. This experience allows candidates to relate the theoretical knowledge learned through education to real-world project activities.

3. Application Process

- Candidates must submit an application detailing their educational background and any project management experience. PMI reviews these applications for completeness and accuracy. If the application is selected for audit, candidates will be required to provide supporting documentation, such as copies of diplomas and records of project management education.

4. Maintaining Certification

- Once obtained, the CAPM certification is valid for five years. To maintain certification, holders must retake and pass the CAPM exam every five years. This requirement ensures that certified professionals stay current with project management practices and continue to develop their skills.

Why These Requirements Matter:

The eligibility criteria for the CAPM exam ensure that all candidates have a sufficient understanding of basic project management concepts before they undertake the certification. This baseline knowledge is essential for grasping the more complex topics covered in the exam and for applying these concepts in practical project management scenarios. Moreover, the educational and experience requirements help standardize the knowledge base among certified professionals, enhancing the credibility and reliability of the CAPM certification in the global job market. By meeting these eligibility requirements, candidates demonstrate their commitment to professional development and their dedication to advancing their careers in project management. The preparation involved in meeting these requirements also ensures that candidates are well-prepared to contribute effectively to project teams and achieve successful project outcomes in their professional roles.

The Certified Associate in Project Management (CAPM)® exam is meticulously structured to assess a candidate's understanding of project management principles aligned with the Project Management Institute's (PMI)® A Guide to the Project Management Body of Knowledge (PMBOK® Guide). Understanding the exam's structure and format is crucial for candidates preparing to take the test, as it helps in devising effective study and test-taking strategies. Here's a detailed breakdown of the CAPM exam structure and format:

1. Exam Composition

- The CAPM exam consists of 150 multiple-choice questions. Each question has one correct answer and three incorrect answers (distractors).
- Out of these 150 questions, 135 are scored questions, and 15 are pretest questions. Pretest questions are not scored and are used by PMI to gather data on question effectiveness. Candidates will not know which questions are scored and which are not.

2. Exam Content

- The questions are based on the content outlined in the PMBOK® Guide and are distributed across various chapters of the guide. The exam tests the candidate's knowledge of the 12 chapters of the PMBOK® Guide, which encompass the knowledge areas and process groups of project management:
    - Introduction to Project Management
    - Project Environment
    - Role of the Project Manager
    - Project Integration Management
    - Project Scope Management
    - Project Schedule Management
    - Project Cost Management
    - Project Quality Management
    - Project Resource Management
    - Project Communication Management
    - Project Risk Management
    - Project Procurement Management
    - Project Stakeholder Management

3. Duration and Passing Score

- Candidates are allotted three hours to complete the exam. There is no scheduled break during this time.
- PMI does not publicly disclose the exact passing score or percentage as it uses a psychometric analysis to determine passing standards. The score is believed to be a function of the difficulty of the questions presented to each test taker.

4. Exam Administration

- The CAPM exam is offered as a computer-based test at PMI-approved testing centers around the world.
- Candidates also have the option to take the exam online via a proctored format, which allows for more flexibility in scheduling and location.

5. Exam Preparation

- Thorough preparation is essential for success on the CAPM exam. Candidates should familiarize themselves with the PMBOK® Guide and consider additional study resources such as CAPM prep courses, study guides, practice questions, and flashcards.
- Developing a study plan that covers all the knowledge areas and understanding the underlying concepts rather than just memorizing terms is highly recommended.

6. Retaking the Exam

- Candidates who do not pass the exam on their first attempt have the opportunity to retake it up to two more times within one year from the eligibility period start date. There is a re-examination fee associated with each subsequent attempt.

Conclusion The structure of the CAPM exam demands rigorous preparation and a deep understanding of project management principles as outlined in the PMBOK® Guide. By thoroughly preparing and understanding the exam format, candidates can enhance their chances of passing the exam and earning this esteemed credential, which can significantly impact their professional life in the project management field.

II. Project Management Fundamentals:

Projects and ongoing operations are two fundamental, yet distinctly different components within organizations. Understanding the characteristics that distinguish a project from ongoing operations is essential for any project manager or professional working in the field of project management. Here are the key characteristics that set them apart:

1. Temporality (Duration)

- **Projects**: Projects are temporary in nature. They have a defined start and end date. The temporary nature is crucial as it determines the scope and resources allocated to achieving the project goals. Once the project's specific objectives are achieved, the project concludes.
  - *Example*: Developing a new software application is a project that begins with the design phase and ends after the software is fully deployed and accepted by the user.
- **Ongoing Operations**: These are continuous and do not have an end date. Operations are repetitive and involve activities that are crucial to the daily functions of an organization.
  - *Example*: The daily production of an automobile manufacturing plant or the continuous operation of customer support services.

2. Objectives and Output

- **Projects**: Projects aim to achieve specific goals and produce unique products, services, or results. Each project is unique in terms of its deliverables and execution.
  - *Example*: Construction of a new office building or launching a new marketing campaign for a product launch.
- **Ongoing Operations**: The objective of ongoing operations is to sustain the business by performing routine activities that support the organization's business model and strategy. The outputs are usually repetitive and similar.
  - *Example*: Annual software updates and maintenance, regular manufacturing of consumer goods like smartphones or TVs.

3. Scope of Change and Innovation

- **Projects**: Projects often involve a high degree of change or innovation. They are typically implemented to solve a specific problem, fulfill a requirement, or capitalize on an opportunity, often leading to changes in processes, products, or the introduction of new methodologies.
    - *Example*: Implementing a new IT system to improve productivity or re-designing a website to enhance user experience.
- **Ongoing Operations**: Operations focus on stability and efficiency, with changes occurring incrementally if at all. These tasks are critical for maintaining the status quo and ensuring the continuous function of the organization.
    - *Example*: Routine maintenance of IT systems or ongoing quality control in manufacturing.

4. Management and Processes

- **Projects**: Project management processes are used, which involve initiating, planning, executing, monitoring, and closing. These processes help manage the temporary and unique aspects of projects.
    - *Example*: A project to integrate renewable energy solutions into an existing power grid will involve a clear project lifecycle, including feasibility studies, design, installation, and project closeout.
- **Ongoing Operations**: Operations management focuses on ongoing activities that are repetitive and often use process optimization and quality management methodologies to improve efficiency and effectiveness.
    - *Example*: Daily operations in a call center, including handling calls, customer service, and issue resolution.

By recognizing these distinctions, organizations can better allocate resources, manage activities, and achieve both short-term project goals and long-term operational success. Understanding these differences also aids in strategic planning and helps in setting realistic goals and expectations for project outcomes versus operational outputs.

Understanding the five phases of the project life cycle is crucial for effective project management, as each phase has distinct objectives, deliverables, and involves different stakeholders. Here's a detailed look at each phase:

1. Initiation Phase

- **Main Objectives**: The initiation phase is where the project starts. The primary objective is to define the project at a broad level, identify its purpose, and evaluate its feasibility through a feasibility study or business case. This phase involves the initial gathering of project requirements and needs.
- **Deliverables**: Key deliverables include the Project Charter, which officially authorizes the existence of the project, and preliminary project scope definition. Stakeholder identification is also a crucial deliverable.
- **Stakeholders Involved**: Key stakeholders include project sponsors, project managers, and initial key project team members. Other stakeholders may include clients or customers, and high-level organizational leaders.

2. Planning Phase

- **Main Objectives**: This phase aims to define clear, actionable plans to achieve the project objectives. It involves setting the project's scope, defining and refining objectives, and developing the course of action required to attain those objectives.
- **Deliverables**: Major deliverables include the Project Management Plan, which encompasses the project scope, cost management plan, schedule management plan, quality management plan, resource plan, stakeholder engagement plan, risk management plan, and communications plan. Other deliverables can include work breakdown structures (WBS), schedules, and budget documents.
- **Stakeholders Involved**: Project managers, the project team, and possibly external consultants play key roles in this phase. Other stakeholders can include functional managers and, potentially, regulatory bodies, depending on the project's nature.

3. Execution Phase

- **Main Objectives**: During the execution phase, the plans created during the planning phase are put into action. The main objective is to complete the work defined in the project management plan to satisfy project specifications and stakeholders.
- **Deliverables**: Deliverables are the actual project outputs—products, services, or results. This phase also includes project deliverables such as status reports, project modifications, updates to the project plan, and performance metrics.
- **Stakeholders Involved**: This phase involves all project team members, suppliers, contractors, and direct stakeholders who are actively working on the project. Project managers spend the majority of their time in this phase, coordinating and communicating with these stakeholders.

4. Monitoring and Controlling Phase

- **Main Objectives**: This phase occurs concurrently with the execution phase and involves tracking, reviewing, and regulating the progress and performance of the project. Objectives include ensuring project resources are being used efficiently, project deliverables meet quality standards and compliance requirements, and everything is on time and within budget.
- **Deliverables**: Performance reports, change requests, and updates to the project plan are key deliverables. This phase ensures corrective actions are taken when necessary to keep the project on track.
- **Stakeholders Involved**: Project managers, project teams, quality assurance personnel, and any stakeholder involved in project governance (e.g., steering committees) are key players in this phase.

5. Closing Phase

- **Main Objectives**: The closing phase finalizes all project activities across all groups to formally close the project or a project phase. The main objectives are to complete and settle each contract, including the resolution of any open items, and formally close the project.
- **Deliverables**: Final product, service, or result transition, project closure report, and lessons learned documentation are key deliverables. This phase also involves the release of project resources and the termination of supplier contracts.
- **Stakeholders Involved**: Project managers, project sponsors, higher management, and clients or end-users are primarily involved. Legal and financial representatives may also play roles, especially in administrative closure involving contractual obligations.

Each phase of the project life cycle is critical for the success of a project. Effective management of each phase, considering its specific objectives, deliverables, and stakeholders, ensures the project is completed on time, within budget, and to the required quality standards.

Project Charter: Foundation of the Initiating Phase

Purpose and Importance of the Project Charter At the heart of any project, especially during the crucial Initiating phase, lies the project charter. This document is not merely administrative but foundational, serving as a formal authorization for the project to commence. The project charter sets the stage for the project's definition and boundaries, ensuring every team member has a clear understanding of the objectives, scope, and participants involved.

The importance of a project charter can be summarized through its primary functions:

1. **Authorization**: It provides the project manager with the authority to allocate organizational resources to project activities.
2. **Alignment**: It aligns the project with the organization's strategic objectives, ensuring that the project supports broader business goals.
3. **Clarity and Direction**: It clarifies the project's purpose and objectives, providing a preliminary delineation of roles and responsibilities.
4. **Boundary Setting**: It defines what is included and excluded from the project, helping manage stakeholders' expectations.
5. **Conflict Resolution**: It serves as a reference document that can be consulted to resolve conflicts and confusion throughout the project lifecycle.

Essential Elements of a Project Charter

Creating a project charter involves careful consideration of several key components that contribute to its effectiveness and clarity. These essential elements include:

- **Project Title and Description**: A concise title and a brief description providing an overview of the project, including its nature and what it intends to achieve.
- **Project Objectives**: Clear, measurable, and achievable objectives that the project seeks to fulfill. These are often aligned with the SMART criteria (Specific, Measurable, Achievable, Relevant, Time-bound).
- **Business Case**: A justification for the project, outlining the need it addresses and the value it adds to the organization. This section often includes an analysis of expected benefits, costs, and risks.
- **Budget Information**: An initial budget estimate that provides a financial framework for the project. This section outlines the financial resources allocated for the project's completion.
- **Project Scope**: This defines the boundaries of the project, detailing what will and will not be included, thus preventing scope creep.
- **Project Sponsor and Stakeholders**: Identification of the project sponsor—who champions the project at the executive level—and the main stakeholders affected by the project.
- **Project Manager and Authority Level**: The name and details of the project manager, and the extent of their authority within the project, are crucial for defining leadership and decision-making power.
- **Milestone Schedule**: Key milestones and approximate timelines to guide the project's progression and help in tracking critical achievements.
- **Risk Management**: An initial assessment of potential risks that might impact the project, with strategies for managing these risks effectively.

- **Approval Signatures**: Signatures from all key stakeholders and the project sponsor to signify agreement on the project's scope, budget, and administrative arrangements.

By encapsulating these elements, the project charter acts as both a contract and a guide, facilitating the smooth initiation and execution of the project. It's a vital tool that lays down the groundwork, ensuring all parties are on the same page from day one. With a robust charter, the project is poised for structured and organized progression, ideally minimizing misunderstandings and maximizing clarity and direction.

Project Management Plan: Navigating through the Planning Phase

Significance of the Project Management Plan The project management plan emerges during the Planning phase of a project and stands as a comprehensive document that outlines how the project will be executed, monitored, and closed. It encompasses all aspects of planning, serving as a roadmap for project execution and management, setting the stage for the methodologies to be used and the metrics by which success will be measured.

The significance of this plan is multifaceted and profound:

1. **Comprehensive Guide**: It consolidates all subsidiary plans and baselines, including scope, cost, schedule, quality, resource, communications, risk, procurement, and stakeholder engagement plans.
2. **Baseline for Performance Measurement**: It serves as a baseline to measure project performance. By comparing actual performance against the plan, deviations are identified early, allowing for prompt corrective actions.
3. **Communication Tool**: It acts as a critical communication tool that informs stakeholders of how the project will be managed and what to expect regarding project delivery.
4. **Strategic Alignment**: Ensures that the project remains aligned with the business goals and objectives, providing a clear link between project activities and expected outcomes.
5. **Flexibility and Governance**: While it provides detailed guidance, it also allows for governance processes to handle changes effectively, ensuring that the project can adapt to new information or external changes without losing direction.

Guidance Provided by the Project Management Plan throughout the Project Life Cycle

The project management plan is not merely a document created for compliance; it is actively used throughout the project to guide actions and decisions. Here's how it facilitates project management across different phases of the project life cycle:

- **Initiation**: In this phase, the project management plan helps in aligning the project's strategic objectives with organizational goals, setting the stage for detailed planning.
- **Planning**: During the planning itself, this document is developed to capture and articulate the approach to scope, schedule, cost management, quality, resources, communications, and risks. It details how the project will be planned, executed, and monitored.
- **Execution**: As the project moves into execution, the plan acts as a handbook for the project team, guiding them on processes, procedures, and protocols. It ensures that every team member understands their role, responsibilities, and the standards to which they must adhere.
- **Monitoring and Controlling**: The project management plan is crucial in this phase for comparing actual progress and performance against the planned objectives. It provides the procedures for managing changes and controlling the quality of deliverables, enabling the project manager to make informed decisions to steer the project toward its defined objectives.
- **Closing**: Finally, the project management plan outlines the criteria for project closure. It ensures that all project tasks have been completed and that the project has met its objectives and

stakeholders' expectations. It also provides a framework for finalizing outstanding contracts, conducting post-project reviews, and documenting lessons learned.

The project management plan is a dynamic document that evolves with the project's needs and external factors. It is referenced regularly, updated as needed, and serves as the spine of the project management effort, keeping the project aligned with its intended outcomes while accommodating the inherent changes that occur during the project lifecycle. By setting a clear path initially and adapting as necessary, it helps the project team navigate through challenges and changes, ultimately leading to a successful project delivery. The Executing phase of a project life cycle is where the plans prepared during earlier phases are put into action. It's a critical stage that largely determines the success of the project through the actual implementation of the planned activities. Here's a detailed look at the key activities and outputs of this phase and how they contribute to the successful completion of the project.

Key Activities of the Executing Phase:

1. **Resource Allocation and Management**: This involves mobilizing and managing the team members and other resources (materials, equipment, technology) outlined in the project management plan. Effective allocation ensures that resources are used efficiently and are available as needed throughout the project.
2. **Team Development and Leadership**: This includes conducting training sessions, team-building exercises, and establishing clear communication channels. The project manager must also provide leadership by motivating the team, resolving conflicts, and fostering a productive work environment.
3. **Quality Assurance and Quality Control**: These activities ensure that the project's deliverables meet the quality standards established in the planning phase. This includes ongoing quality control processes to measure output against standards and implementing necessary changes through quality improvement processes.
4. **Task Execution and Technical Work**: The actual performance of the tasks that lead to the project deliverables. This is the core of the execution phase and involves the direct application of the team's skills and resources to complete the project activities as outlined in the work breakdown structure (WBS).
5. **Stakeholder Engagement and Communication**: Keeping all stakeholders informed and involved through regular updates and feedback sessions. This helps manage expectations, ensures alignment with the project objectives, and fosters stakeholder support throughout the project lifecycle.
6. **Implementation of Approved Changes**: Any changes approved during the monitoring and controlling phase must be implemented. This requires revisiting the project plans and ensuring that the changes are executed effectively.

Key Outputs of the Executing Phase:

1. **Project Deliverables**: The tangible or intangible outputs generated as a result of project tasks. These are the products, services, or results that the project was undertaken to produce.
2. **Performance Data**: This includes work performance data that provides information about project progress, such as which tasks have been completed, the time spent on each task, and resources utilized.
3. **Change Requests**: Although typically identified during the monitoring and controlling phase, change requests may also arise during execution and need to be documented and processed accordingly.

4. **Project Updates**: Adjustments to the project management plan and project documents to reflect actual project performance and any changes to the project scope, schedule, costs, or resources.
5. **Issue Logs and Risk Registers**: Updated logs of issues and risks that have emerged during execution, along with their status and any mitigation measures taken.

Contribution to Project Success:

The activities of the Executing phase contribute to the successful completion of the project by:

- **Ensuring that project deliverables are produced as planned**, which is critical for achieving the project objectives.
- **Maintaining stakeholder engagement and communication** to ensure continuous support and alignment with project goals.
- **Effectively managing resources** to avoid any wastage and ensuring optimal productivity.
- **Monitoring quality** throughout the process to ensure the final product meets the required standards and stakeholder expectations.
- **Implementing changes effectively**, which helps the project remain flexible and responsive to any necessary adjustments, thereby maintaining its relevance and feasibility.

By focusing on these activities and ensuring the production of their corresponding outputs, the Executing phase drives the project toward its defined objectives, keeping it on track both in terms of timeline and budget, while also adapting to any changes or challenges that arise.

Monitoring and Controlling Phase: Ensuring Project Alignment and Success

Overview of the Monitoring and Controlling Phase The Monitoring and Controlling phase of project management is where the planned versus actual progress of the project is continuously observed and adjusted. This phase is vital for the successful delivery of the project as it ensures that the project stays on track, within scope, on budget, and is aligned with quality standards. This phase spans the entire life cycle of the project, overlapping with execution activities, and involves various processes to assess performance, identify variances, and implement corrective actions when necessary.

Main Processes in the Monitoring and Controlling Phase

1. **Performance Measurement**: This involves tracking project variables (cost, time, scope, quality) against the project management plan and the project performance baseline. Techniques like Earned Value Management (EVM) provide quantifiable data on performance efficiencies and variances.
2. **Scope Verification and Control**: Ensures the project scope is accurately followed and controlled. Any requested changes or additional activities are evaluated and managed to prevent scope creep.
3. **Schedule Control**: Techniques such as critical path method and schedule compression are employed to monitor the project schedule and make adjustments to ensure timely project completion.
4. **Cost Control**: Involves monitoring expenditures and cost performance to detect and understand variances from the cost baseline. It often uses cost management tools like EVM to ensure the project remains on budget.
5. **Quality Control**: Consists of periodic inspections and audits to ensure that the project outputs meet the quality standards established in the quality management plan. Tools like statistical sampling and Six Sigma methodologies are commonly used.

6. **Risk Monitoring and Control**: This involves tracking identified risks, identifying new risks, and evaluating risk process effectiveness throughout the project life cycle. Contingency plans are enacted, and risk mitigation strategies are adjusted as needed.

Tools and Techniques Used in Monitoring and Controlling

- **Earned Value Management (EVM)**: An essential tool that integrates project scope, cost, and schedule measures to help assess project performance and progress.
- **Gantt Charts and Project Schedules**: Visual tools to track progress and timelines. They help in identifying which tasks have been completed and which are lagging.
- **Dashboards and Status Reports**: Provide a quick snapshot of project health across various parameters—scope, schedule, cost, and quality. These tools facilitate transparency and communication among stakeholders and team members.
- **Change Control Systems**: Essential for managing changes to the project scope, ensuring all changes are recorded, evaluated, and approved before implementation.
- **Performance Reviews**: Meetings and sessions conducted to evaluate the progress and performance of the project against the baselines.
- **Variance Analysis**: Used to determine the cause of deviations from the baseline and the impact on the project.
- **Risk Audit and Reviews**: Regular reviews of the risk management process to assess the effectiveness of risk strategies and the accuracy of risk identification.

Through these processes and tools, the Monitoring and Controlling phase plays a crucial role in keeping the project aligned with its goals. By continuously measuring performance and implementing necessary changes, project managers can ensure efficient resource utilization, adherence to the project plan, and achievement of project objectives. This phase not only helps in avoiding surprises at the end of the project but also provides ongoing visibility and control over the project, enabling proactive management and decision-making. The Closing phase of a project life cycle is critical because it ensures that all project activities are completed properly, all project objectives are met, and the project's outcome is accepted by the stakeholders. This phase is essential not only for administrative closure but also for the successful transition of the project's deliverables to operations or to another maintenance entity, ensuring the project's long-term success and sustainability. Here's a detailed exploration of the importance of this phase, its key activities, and deliverables:

Importance of the Closing Phase:

1. **Ensures Completion**: It verifies that all defined project deliverables are completed satisfactorily, aligning with the initial project scope and stakeholders' expectations.
2. **Facilitates Formal Acceptance**: By obtaining formal acceptance from the client or project sponsor, the Closing phase ensures all parties agree that project requirements have been met.
3. **Provides Documentation**: This phase helps in documenting the outcomes, experiences, and lessons learned from the project, providing valuable insights for future projects.
4. **Releases Resources**: Ensures that resources are released in an orderly manner, freeing up project team members, equipment, and materials for allocation to other initiatives.
5. **Fulfills Contractual Obligations**: By addressing all contractual closures and ensuring that all terms of the contract have been met, it helps avoid legal complications post-project.

Key Activities of the Closing Phase:

1. **Final Deliverables**: Ensure all project deliverables have been completed and are approved by the client or stakeholders. This may involve a final presentation or demonstration of the project's product.
2. **Documentation**: Gather and archive all project documents, including contracts, plans, financial records, and correspondence. This activity is crucial for maintaining records that might be referred to in future projects or audits.
3. **Contract Closure**: Includes the completion of any remaining contractual obligations, finalizing terms with suppliers or partners, and resolving any claims or disputes.
4. **Performance Reviews**: Conduct performance evaluations of team members and the overall project performance. This helps in recognizing contributions and identifying areas for improvement.
5. **Lessons Learned**: Conduct a lessons learned session to document what went well and what did not. This activity is vital for continuous improvement and helps organizations refine their project management processes for future projects.
6. **Resource Release**: Systematically release project resources, both human and material. Ensure that project team members are recognized for their efforts and reassigned appropriately.

Key Deliverables of the Closing Phase:

1. **Project Close-Out Report**: This report includes a summary of the project, the outcomes, the final budget status, and the performance against the objectives. It might also include stakeholder feedback and an assessment of the project's success.
2. **Lessons Learned Documentation**: This document is a compilation of the insights gained during the project, intended to inform and improve the execution of future projects.
3. **Archived Project Documentation**: Includes all contracts, plans, schedules, reports, and correspondence, stored in a manner that they can be accessed when needed in the future.
4. **Release Forms**: Documentations confirming that all project resources have been released and that all administrative tasks have been completed.

Ensuring a Smooth Transition to Operations:

The activities and deliverables of the Closing phase play a crucial role in ensuring a smooth transition to operations by:

- **Providing Complete and Functional Deliverables**: Ensuring that the project outputs are fully operational and acceptable to the end-users or stakeholders.
- **Establishing Ongoing Support and Maintenance**: Setting up support structures or handover to an operational team to manage and maintain the project deliverables.
- **Ensuring Availability of Documentation**: Making sure that operational teams have access to all necessary documentation to operate, maintain, and troubleshoot the project outputs.

By effectively managing these aspects, the Closing phase not only marks the completion of the project but also sets the stage for the successful ongoing utilization of the project's results.

Organizational Structures: Functional, Matrix, and Projectized
Functional Organizational Structure

In a functional organizational structure, the organization is divided into departments based on functions such as marketing, finance, human resources, and IT. Each department is managed independently by a department head.

- **Impact on Project Management**: In functional organizations, project management often takes a back seat as the focus is on departmental functions. Projects are usually managed within the department, and the department head acts as the project manager. This can limit the scope of project management to specific functional areas rather than integrating across the enterprise.
- **Resource Allocation**: Resources are allocated within each department, and their availability for projects typically depends on their primary functional responsibilities. This can sometimes result in resource conflicts between departmental duties and project needs.
- **Communication**: Communication tends to be vertical, flowing up and down within each department. This siloed communication can lead to challenges in cross-departmental information sharing and collaboration on projects.

Matrix Organizational Structure

Matrix structures blend features of functional and projectized structures, categorizing staff by both function and project, creating a dual reporting system.

- **Impact on Project Management**: Matrix organizations allow for more dynamic and balanced decision-making regarding project management, as employees report to both the project manager and the functional manager. This structure supports stronger project focus while retaining functional expertise.
- **Resource Allocation**: Resources are shared across functional departments and projects, which can optimize their use but may also lead to conflicts regarding prioritization. Effective resource management and conflict resolution skills are crucial in matrix environments.
- **Communication**: Communication in a matrix can be complex due to the dual reporting lines. However, this complexity can foster better collaboration and information flow between functions and projects, provided that there is clear communication from leadership.

Projectized Organizational Structure

In projectized organizations, the entire structure is arranged to prioritize projects. Teams are assembled specifically for projects, and team members report directly to the project manager.

- **Impact on Project Management**: Project management is the central focus of projectized organizations. Project managers have significant authority and autonomy, which can enhance responsiveness and flexibility in project execution.
- **Resource Allocation**: Resources are allocated to projects, often with greater flexibility compared to functional structures. Project managers typically have greater control over their teams and budgets, which can lead to more efficient project execution.
- **Communication**: Communication tends to be highly cohesive and streamlined around project goals. Since team members are primarily dedicated to projects, there is less risk of conflicting priorities, leading to more efficient decision-making and problem-solving within the project team.

Contrasting the Structures

- **Authority and Control**: Projectized structures offer the most authority to project managers, followed by matrix, and then functional structures.
- **Resource Flexibility**: Projectized organizations provide the most flexibility in resource management, whereas functional structures are the most restrictive.
- **Communication Efficiency**: Communication tends to be more efficient and project-focused in projectized and matrix structures due to the alignment of team members' goals and roles around specific projects.

Each structure offers different advantages and challenges. The choice of organizational structure should align with the organization's goals, projects' nature, and the degree of flexibility needed in managing projects and resources. Understanding these differences is crucial for tailoring project management approaches to fit the organizational context, thereby enhancing the effectiveness of project delivery and organizational success.

The five project management process groups are a fundamental aspect of the Project Management Body of Knowledge (PMBOK® Guide) and are essential for managing any project through its lifecycle. Each process group interacts with project lifecycle phases, ensuring a structured approach to project management. Here's an overview of each process group and how they relate to the project life cycle phases:

1. Initiating Process Group

- **Relationship to Life Cycle**: This process group aligns with the initiation phase of the project life cycle. It involves defining and authorizing the project or a project phase.
- **Examples of Processes**:
    - **Develop Project Charter**: Formalizing the initiation of a new project or a new phase of an existing project by documenting the initial requirements that satisfy the stakeholder's expectations and needs.
    - **Identify Stakeholders**: Identifying all people or organizations impacted by the project, and documenting their interests, involvement, and impact on project success.

2. Planning Process Group

- **Relationship to Life Cycle**: Corresponds with the planning phase. This group's processes are crucial for establishing the scope, objectives, and course of action required to achieve the project goals.
- **Examples of Processes**:
    - **Develop Project Management Plan**: Integrating and coordinating all project plans to create a consistent, coherent document outlining the project's path.
    - **Define Scope**: Developing a detailed description of the project and its products, which forms the basis for future project decisions.
    - **Create WBS (Work Breakdown Structure)**: Dividing project deliverables and project work into smaller, more manageable components.

3. Executing Process Group

- **Relationship to Life Cycle**: This group is associated with the execution phase where the project plan is implemented to accomplish the project's defined objectives.
- **Examples of Processes**:
    - **Direct and Manage Project Work**: Leading and performing the work defined in the project management plan and implementing changes to achieve the project's objectives.
    - **Acquire Resources**: Obtaining team members, facilities, equipment, materials, and supplies.
    - **Develop Team**: Improving competencies, team member interaction, and overall team environment to enhance project performance.

4. Monitoring and Controlling Process Group

- **Relationship to Life Cycle**: Overlaps with all phases but is most prominently linked with the execution phase. This group aims to track, review, and regulate the progress and performance of the project; identifying any areas in which changes to the plan are required.
- **Examples of Processes**:

- **Monitor and Control Project Work**: Tracking, reviewing, and reporting the progress to meet the performance objectives defined in the project management plan.
- **Perform Integrated Change Control**: Reviewing all change requests, approving changes, and managing changes to the deliverables, organizational process assets, project documents, and the project management plan.
- **Control Scope**: Monitoring the status of the project and product scope and managing changes to the scope baseline.

5. Closing Process Group
- **Relationship to Life Cycle**: Corresponds with the closing phase of the project life cycle, concluding all activities across all process groups to formally complete the project, phase, or contractual obligations.
- **Examples of Processes**:
  - **Close Project or Phase**: Finalizing all activities across all of the project management process groups to formally close the project or phase.
  - **Close Procurements**: Completing each project procurement.

These process groups are not strictly linear but are often iterative; for example, planning may continue during the execution phase as new information emerges and circumstances change. Each process group interacts with others throughout the project, ensuring that the project remains aligned with its objectives, can adapt to changes, and successfully moves through each phase toward its completion. Understanding these relationships is key to managing a project efficiently and effectively, from initiation through to closure.

Project Management Knowledge Areas: Integrating for Effective Project Delivery

The ten project management knowledge areas, as defined by the Project Management Institute (PMI), encompass a comprehensive framework that guides the project management process. Each area contributes a specific facet of project management expertise, essential for managing projects effectively. Understanding how these areas interact and complement each other can significantly enhance the project's chances of success.

1. Project Integration Management

This area involves making choices about resource allocation, balancing competing demands, and integrating the inputs and outputs from the other knowledge areas. It ensures that the project parts are coordinated effectively to achieve the project objectives.

2. Project Scope Management

It focuses on ensuring the project includes all the necessary work, and only the necessary work, to complete the project successfully. Scope management helps define and control what is included and excluded in the project.

3. Project Schedule Management

This area focuses on managing the project timeline, including the sequencing and duration of tasks required to complete the project. Effective schedule management helps ensure that the project is completed on time.

4. Project Cost Management

Cost management involves planning, estimating, budgeting, and controlling costs so that the project can be completed within the approved budget. It's crucial for keeping the project financially viable and managing funding throughout its lifecycle.

5. Project Quality Management

Quality management ensures that the project's deliverables meet the necessary quality standards and stakeholder expectations. This area is closely linked to customer satisfaction and can influence the project's overall success.

6. Project Resource Management

Resource management involves planning, estimating, and acquiring resources, including people, equipment, and materials, to ensure that they are available when needed and used effectively.

7. Project Communications Management

This area ensures timely and appropriate generation, collection, distribution, storage, retrieval, and ultimate disposition of project information. Effective communication is vital for ensuring that stakeholders are engaged and informed.

8. Project Risk Management

Risk management involves identifying, analyzing, and responding to project risks, which includes maximizing the results of positive events and minimizing the consequences of adverse events.

9. Project Procurement Management

Procurement management is about acquiring goods and services from outside the performing organization. It involves managing bidding, selection, and contract management processes.

10. Project Stakeholder Management

Stakeholder management involves engaging all individuals affected by the project, assessing their needs and expectations, and integrating their input at appropriate project stages.

Interaction and Influence Among Knowledge Areas

These knowledge areas are not isolated; they interact and influence one another throughout the project lifecycle:

- **Integration and Scope**: Effective integration management helps to manage changes to the project scope, ensuring all aspects of the project remain aligned with the project objectives.
- **Cost, Schedule, and Resources**: These areas are deeply interconnected. For example, a delay in the schedule can increase costs and alter resource allocation.
- **Quality and Risk**: Managing quality often involves identifying and mitigating risks that can impact the quality of deliverables.
- **Stakeholder and Communications**: Effective stakeholder management depends on good communication strategies to ensure stakeholders are informed, engaged, and satisfied.
- **Procurement and Resources**: Procurement activities must be coordinated with resource management to ensure that external services and materials meet project needs and timing.

Understanding and managing the interdependencies between these knowledge areas can lead to more strategic decision-making and efficient project management. This integration ensures that changes in one area are reflected in others, maintaining project alignment with its goals, which is crucial for achieving project success. The "Develop Project Charter" process is the first step in the project management lifecycle, laying the foundation for defining the scope of the project and guiding its execution and closure. Understanding the key inputs, tools and techniques, and outputs (ITTOs) of this process is crucial for creating a comprehensive and effective project charter. Here's a detailed explanation of these elements:

Key Inputs

1. **Business Case**: This document provides the necessary information from a business standpoint to determine whether or not the project is worth the required investment. Typically, it includes the business needs, cost-benefit analysis, and potential return on investment.
2. **Agreements**: Formal or informal agreements that define the initial intentions of a project. This can include contracts, memorandums of understanding (MOUs), service level agreements (SLAs), and other types of agreements.
3. **Enterprise Environmental Factors (EEFs)**: These are conditions, not under the immediate control of the team, that influence, constrain, or direct the project. EEFs can include organizational culture, infrastructure, existing human resources, market conditions, and project management software.
4. **Organizational Process Assets (OPAs)**: Plans, processes, policies, procedures, and knowledge bases specific to and used by the performing organization. These include but are not limited to, standardized processes, templates for a project charter, and historical information.

Tools and Techniques

1. **Expert Judgment**: Engaging individuals or groups with specialized knowledge or training in the areas relevant to project charter development. These experts can provide insights into the scope, objectives, and potential risks of the project.
2. **Brainstorming**: Employed to generate and collect multiple ideas related to project boundaries, requirements, and even potential risks.
3. **Conflict Resolution Techniques**: Used to address and resolve conflicts from different stakeholders with potentially divergent interests and opinions about the project.
4. **Facilitation Techniques**: Used to effectively lead a group event to a successful decision, solution, or conclusion that brings together the collective knowledge of the group members (e.g., workshops, meetings).
5. **Data Gathering Techniques**: Techniques such as interviews, focus groups, and surveys to collect data from stakeholders and experts to define project scope, risks, milestones, and objectives.

Key Outputs

1. **Project Charter**: The primary output of this process, the project charter, is a document that formally authorizes the existence of the project and provides the project manager with the authority to apply organizational resources to project activities. It includes the project purpose or justification, measurable project objectives and related success criteria, high-level requirements, high-level project description, boundaries, and key deliverables, overall project risk, summary milestone schedule, pre-approved financial resources, key stakeholder list, project approval requirements, assigned project manager and authority level, and name and authority of the sponsor or other person(s) authorizing the project charter.
2. **Assumption Log**: Captures the assumptions and constraints that are identified during the process. Assumptions are things that are assumed to be true but that may not be true (and hence, carry risk), and constraints are restrictions that will limit the project team's options.

The comprehensive use of these ITTOs contributes significantly to the creation of a project charter that accurately defines the vision and boundaries of a project, sets expectations, and allocates resources and authority appropriately. This foundation is critical for guiding subsequent project activities and decisions, ensuring alignment with business goals, and facilitating communication among all stakeholders.

Work Breakdown Structure (WBS): Essential for Detailed Project Planning

Creating a Work Breakdown Structure (WBS) The Work Breakdown Structure (WBS) is a pivotal tool used during the Planning phase of project management. It serves as a hierarchical decomposition of the total scope of work to be carried out by the project team to accomplish the project objectives and create the required deliverables. The process of developing a WBS involves several key steps:

1. **Define Project Vision**: Start with a clear understanding of the project's objectives and deliverables, usually derived from the project charter and scope statement.
2. **Identification of Major Deliverables**: Break the project deliverables into smaller, more manageable parts. This step involves collaborating with key stakeholders and team members to ensure all deliverables are included.
3. **Decomposition of Deliverables**: Each major deliverable is further broken down into smaller, more detailed components of work. This decomposition continues until the deliverables are divided into workable components, which can be easily managed and estimated. These smaller components are often called work packages.
4. **Assign Identification Codes**: Assign a unique identifier to each element of the WBS. This helps in tracking project progress and facilitates communication about specific parts of the project.
5. **Verification of the WBS**: Review the WBS to ensure it meets the needs of the project. This includes checking for completeness, the appropriate level of detail, and ensuring that no deliverables are overlooked. The 100% rule—that the WBS includes 100% of the work defined by the project scope and captures all deliverables, internal, external, and interim—should be applied.

Benefits of Using a WBS

- **Clarifies Project Scope**: The WBS is a dynamic tool for scope management, as it provides a detailed and visual representation of what is to be delivered. By defining the project scope at a granular level, it helps ensure that all project work is identified and properly managed.
- **Facilitates Planning and Organization**: Helps in organizing team assignments, creating a schedule, and planning resources more effectively. It provides a structured view of the project and helps break down complex project activities into manageable tasks.
- **Enhances Communication**: Serves as a reference point for project team members and stakeholders, enhancing clarity and understanding regarding project work and responsibilities.
- **Improves Cost Estimation**: By breaking down the project into smaller parts, the WBS allows for more accurate cost estimation and control.
- **Risk Management**: Helps in identifying risks at different levels of the project, allowing for more effective mitigation strategies.

Impact on Defining Project Scope

The creation of the WBS directly influences the definition and understanding of the project scope by detailing what needs to be done for each part of the project. It ensures that all team members and stakeholders have a clear understanding of the project's tasks and deliverables, thereby minimizing the potential for scope creep—where the scope of a project gradually increases beyond its original intentions without corresponding increases in resources, time, and budget.

By providing a clear, visual map of all tasks necessary for project completion, the WBS is instrumental in ensuring effective scope management. It supports the detailed planning, execution, monitoring, and control of project work, aligning every task with the project objectives. This alignment is crucial not just for project success but also for maintaining stakeholder alignment and satisfaction throughout the project lifecycle. Understanding the distinction between project management processes and project management process groups is essential for effective project management. Both concepts are fundamental to the Project Management Institute's (PMI)® A Guide to the Project Management Body of Knowledge (PMBOK® Guide), yet they serve different organizational functions within the framework of managing a project.

Project Management Processes

Project management processes are a series of activities performed to achieve a specific project objective. These processes are generally described in terms of:

- **Inputs** (documents, plans, designs, etc.)
- **Tools and Techniques** (mechanisms applied to inputs)
- **Outputs** (documents, products, or services resulting from the process).

There are 49 project management processes in the PMBOK® Guide, divided across ten knowledge areas, such as Scope Management, Schedule Management, Cost Management, Quality Management, etc. Each process is a specific action designed to contribute a particular facet of project management. For example:

- **Define Scope** (from Scope Management): Involves detailing the project and product description, deliverables, and acceptance criteria.
- **Estimate Costs** (from Cost Management): Involves developing an approximation of the monetary resources needed to complete project activities.

Project Management Process Groups

Project management process groups, on the other hand, are a logical grouping of project management processes to achieve project objectives. They reflect the phase of the project life cycle and include:

1. **Initiating**
2. **Planning**
3. **Executing**
4. **Monitoring and Controlling**
5. **Closing**

Each process group consists of processes that occur at various points in the project lifecycle and are iterative, often repeated during the project. The processes within these groups are linked by the outputs they produce, which serve as inputs to other processes in a sequential manner. For example:

- **Executing Process Group**: Includes processes like 'Direct and Manage Project Work' and 'Acquire Resources', which involve carrying out the project plan and obtaining the team necessary to complete the work.

Interaction of Processes Across Different Knowledge Areas within Process Groups

Within each process group, processes from different knowledge areas interact to move the project forward. Here's how processes from different knowledge areas can interact within the Planning Process Group:

- **Collect Requirements** (from Scope Management): Involves determining, documenting, and managing stakeholder needs and requirements to meet project objectives. The output from this process, the requirements documentation, becomes an input to the **Define Scope** process.
- **Define Scope** (also from Scope Management): Uses the requirements documentation to produce the project scope statement. This scope statement is crucial for the **Create WBS** (Work Breakdown Structure) process.
- **Create WBS** (from Scope Management): Utilizes the project scope statement to break down project deliverables into smaller, manageable components, which help in planning costs, time, and resource allocation in processes such as **Estimate Costs** (from Cost Management) and **Develop Schedule** (from Schedule Management).

These interactions show how integration is maintained between different knowledge areas within a single process group to ensure cohesive and comprehensive project management. This systemic interaction enables the project manager and the team to align project objectives with organizational goals effectively, ensuring a streamlined approach to achieving project deliverables.

While project management processes are specific actions within defined knowledge areas, process groups are a way of organizing these processes to effectively manage the project through its life cycle. The interaction between processes across different knowledge areas within each process group ensures that the project progresses logically towards its defined goals.

A project management plan is a comprehensive document that delineates how a project will be executed, monitored, and controlled. It integrates and consolidates all subsidiary plans and baselines from the various knowledge areas of project management. Understanding the main components of a project management plan and their significance is crucial for successful project delivery. Here's an overview of these components and their roles:

Main Components of a Project Management Plan

1. **Scope Management Plan**
   - **Importance**: Defines how the scope will be developed, validated, and controlled. It ensures that the project includes only the work required to complete the project successfully, preventing scope creep and unapproved changes.
2. **Schedule Management Plan**
   - **Importance**: Establishes criteria and activities for developing, monitoring, and controlling the project schedule. This plan helps to ensure timely completion of the project.
3. **Cost Management Plan**
   - **Importance**: Details the methodology and processes for planning, estimating, budgeting, financing, funding, managing, and controlling project costs. This ensures the project is completed within the approved budget.
4. **Quality Management Plan**
   - **Importance**: Provides guidance on how the project will demonstrate compliance with quality requirements. It ensures the project deliverables are of satisfactory quality and fit for purpose.
5. **Resource Management Plan**
   - **Importance**: Outlines how project resources should be categorized, allocated, managed, and released. It ensures efficient and effective utilization of physical and human resources.
6. **Communications Management Plan**

- **Importance**: Details the project's structure and methods of information collection, screening, formatting, and dissemination of project information. It ensures that timely and appropriate communication happens throughout the life of the project.

7. **Risk Management Plan**
   - **Importance**: Defines how risk management activities will be structured and performed. This plan helps to identify, analyze, and respond to project risks, which increases the likelihood of project success.

8. **Procurement Management Plan**
   - **Importance**: Outlines how the procurement processes will be managed from developing procurement documentation through contract closure. It ensures that all procurements are conducted in a timely and cost-effective manner.

9. **Stakeholder Engagement Plan**
   - **Importance**: Provides strategies and actions to effectively engage stakeholders throughout the project life cycle. Managing stakeholder engagement helps in fulfilling their expectations and needs, gaining support for the project, and creating a positive project environment.

10. **Change Management Plan**
    - **Importance**: Details the process of managing changes to the project scope, schedule, and costs. This ensures that changes are controlled and only approved changes are implemented.

11. **Configuration Management Plan**
    - **Importance**: Details how configuration management will be performed regarding the specification of deliverables and processes, which supports the management of products, service, or system life cycles.

12. **Performance Measurement Baseline**
    - **Importance**: Integrates scope, schedule, and cost baselines. It provides a reference against which project performance can be monitored and managed.

Collective Importance in Project Execution, Monitoring, and Control

The integration of these components into a single, coherent document guides project execution by providing a roadmap that aligns the project's objectives with operational activities. This comprehensive document facilitates decision-making processes and serves as a reference point throughout the project lifecycle. During project execution, the management plans included in the project management plan help to ensure that the project proceeds as envisioned. They provide guidelines and processes to address issues and manage project activities effectively. For monitoring and controlling, the project management plan acts as a baseline against which project performance is measured. This comparison helps to identify deviations from the plan and initiate corrective and preventive actions to realign the project with its planned objectives. Overall, the project management plan is indispensable for guiding, executing, monitoring, and controlling a project. It ensures project alignment with business goals, effective utilization of resources, and that project outcomes meet stakeholder requirements and expectations.

Project Life Cycle and Product Life Cycle: Interconnected Frameworks

Understanding the Relationship The project life cycle and the product life cycle are interconnected concepts that, while distinct, often overlap and influence each other in business operations. The project life cycle refers to the sequence of phases that a project undergoes from initiation to closure. These phases typically include initiating, planning, executing, monitoring and controlling, and closing.

The product life cycle, on the other hand, describes the stages a product goes through from its introduction to the market through its growth, maturity, and eventual decline. These stages are development, introduction, growth, maturity, and decline.

Relationship and Interaction

- **Development and Initiation/Planning**: The development phase of the product life cycle often coincides with the initiating and planning phases of the project life cycle. During this time, projects are defined and planned to bring the product concept to reality.
- **Introduction and Execution**: As a product moves into the introduction stage in the market, the corresponding projects typically are in the execution phase, where the product is actually built, tested, and launched.
- **Growth, Maturity, and Monitoring/Controlling**: During the growth and maturity stages of the product, multiple projects may be initiated to handle expansions, modifications, or improvements to the product. These projects will generally be in the monitoring and controlling phases, ensuring that the product continues to meet market needs effectively.
- **Decline and Closing**: In the decline phase, projects might be initiated to phase out the product, such as projects aimed at reducing costs, discontinuing services, or transitioning customers to a new product.

Examples and Applications

1. **Smartphone Development and Launch**: The development of a new smartphone model represents a project within the larger product life cycle of the smartphone category. The project begins with designing and manufacturing (project life cycle) and transitions through introduction, growth, and maturity as the product gains market share and acceptance (product life cycle).
2. **Software Development**: A new software application development is a project that includes planning, development (coding), testing, and deployment phases (project life cycle). Once launched, the software enters the product life cycle phases of introduction, growth, maturity, and potentially decline, during which updates, upgrades, or new features might be introduced through subsequent projects.
3. **Automotive Industry**: The design and manufacture of a new car model is a project. This project begins with concept designs and prototypes and moves into full-scale production. The car then enters the product life cycle stages, where it might undergo various projects aimed at facelifts or technological updates as it moves through introduction, growth, maturity, and eventually decline.

Impact of the Relationship

Understanding the relationship between the project life cycle and the product life cycle is crucial for organizations to effectively manage not just the individual projects but the entire portfolio of products and services. Projects need to be aligned with the stage of the product life cycle to ensure appropriate resource allocation and strategy implementation. This alignment helps in optimizing performance, maximizing ROI, and ensuring the longevity and success of both the projects and the products they aim to deliver while projects are temporary endeavors aimed at creating a unique product or service, the product life cycle focuses on the management and strategic positioning of the product over time. Recognizing how projects support different stages of the product life cycle can lead to more strategic decision-making and better overall management of both projects and products.

Role of the Project Manager Across the Project Life Cycle

The project manager plays a crucial role in steering a project through its various phases, each requiring a unique set of skills and actions. Here's a breakdown of their role in each phase of the project life cycle, along with the key skills and competencies required.

1. Initiating Phase

- **Role**: The project manager is responsible for defining the project at a high level, securing project sponsorship, and ensuring that the project is feasible and aligned with organizational goals. They also facilitate the development of the project charter, which outlines the project's objectives, scope, and stakeholders.
- **Key Skills**: Leadership, communication, stakeholder analysis, negotiation.

2. Planning Phase

- **Role**: This phase is critical, as the project manager develops the project management plan, detailing how the project will be executed, monitored, and controlled. They define the scope, budget, schedule, resources, and plans for risk, procurement, quality, and communication.
- **Key Skills**: Strategic thinking, detail orientation, risk management, budgeting, scheduling, resource management.

3. Executing Phase

- **Role**: The project manager leads the execution of the project management plan, coordinates team activities, manages resources, and ensures that project deliverables meet quality standards. They also engage stakeholders and manage communications.
- **Key Skills**: Leadership, team management, effective communication, problem-solving, quality control.

4. Monitoring and Controlling Phase

- **Role**: Concurrent with the executing phase, the project manager monitors project progress against the project management plan, making adjustments as necessary to handle issues, scope changes, risks, and variances. They ensure the project stays on track with respect to time, cost, scope, and quality.
- **Key Skills**: Analytical skills, attention to detail, risk management, change management, problem-solving.

5. Closing Phase

- **Role**: The project manager finalizes all activities across all project management process groups to formally close the project or phase. They ensure project documents are complete and stored appropriately and that project outcomes are accepted by the stakeholders.
- **Key Skills**: Organizational skills, communication, stakeholder management, contract management.

Key Competencies Required Across All Phases

- **Leadership and Motivation**: The ability to lead, inspire, and motivate a team is crucial across all phases of the project.
- **Communication**: Effective communication is essential for negotiating resources, managing stakeholder expectations, and ensuring clear understanding among team members.

- **Organizational and Multi-tasking Skills**: The project manager must effectively juggle multiple tasks and priorities, keeping the project organized and on track.
- **Problem-solving and Decision-making**: The ability to quickly identify problems and make informed, effective decisions is critical to addressing the challenges that arise during a project.
- **Flexibility and Adaptability**: Projects rarely go exactly as planned, so the ability to adapt to changes and manage the unexpected is crucial.
- **Risk Management**: Identifying, analyzing, and managing risks effectively ensures that the project can overcome obstacles and reach successful completion.
- **Technical Project Management**: Knowledge of methodologies, tools, and techniques specific to project management is essential for planning, execution, and monitoring.

The project manager's role is both expansive and dynamic, requiring a balance of technical project management skills and soft skills. Effective project managers not only drive their projects to successful completions but also foster a positive environment that empowers and motivates their teams. By mastering these skills and fulfilling their roles diligently across each phase, project managers significantly enhance the likelihood of project success.

Stakeholder Identification and Engagement: Crucial for Project Success

Importance of Stakeholder Engagement Stakeholder identification and engagement are critical processes that significantly influence the success of a project. Stakeholders are individuals, groups, or organizations that may affect or be affected by the project's outcomes. The process of identifying and engaging stakeholders needs to begin early in the project life cycle and continue throughout to ensure the project's objectives are aligned with the needs and expectations of these key players.

1. During the Initiating Phase

- **Role**: The project manager identifies all possible stakeholders, assessing their potential impact, influence, and interest regarding the project. Early engagement helps in garnering support, identifying requirements, and understanding expectations, which are crucial for defining project scope and objectives.
- **Techniques**: Stakeholder analysis matrices and power/interest grids can be used to categorize stakeholders based on their level of interest and influence on the project.

2. During the Planning Phase

- **Role**: The project manager works to develop a stakeholder engagement plan that outlines strategies for communication and interaction with each stakeholder or group. This plan is vital for planning how to keep stakeholders informed and involved throughout the project.
- **Techniques**: Regular meetings, updates, and inclusion in planning sessions ensure stakeholders are aware of the project plans and are provided opportunities to provide feedback.

3. During the Executing Phase

- **Role**: Active engagement involves keeping stakeholders informed through regular updates and actively soliciting their feedback on deliverables. This phase often requires balancing differing stakeholder interests and managing conflicts effectively.
- **Techniques**: Utilizing communication plans that detail when and how to provide updates (e.g., newsletters, emails, presentations) ensures stakeholders remain supportive and engaged.

4. During the Monitoring and Controlling Phase

- **Role**: Stakeholders are continuously informed about the project's progress and any issues that arise. The project manager assesses stakeholder engagement levels and adjusts strategies as necessary to address concerns and manage expectations.
- **Techniques**: Performance reports, review meetings, and feedback sessions help in adjusting strategies and resolving any issues stakeholders might have.

5. During the Closing Phase

- **Role**: Ensuring stakeholders are satisfied with the project outcomes and that all contractual and communication commitments have been fulfilled. Feedback is gathered to evaluate the project's success from the stakeholder's perspective.
- **Techniques**: Final project reports, debriefing sessions, and satisfaction surveys are used to confirm that all stakeholder expectations have been met and to gather insights for future projects.

Ensuring Stakeholder Needs and Expectations Are Met

To ensure that stakeholder needs and expectations are effectively met, project managers can adopt several strategies:

- **Early and Regular Communication**: Keeping stakeholders informed from the start and throughout the project lifecycle helps prevent surprises and builds trust.
- **Feedback Mechanisms**: Implementing robust mechanisms for collecting and responding to stakeholder feedback ensures that their concerns and suggestions are heard and addressed promptly.
- **Adaptability**: Being responsive to stakeholder input and willing to adjust project plans as necessary can help align project outputs more closely with stakeholder expectations.
- **Conflict Resolution**: Developing and utilizing effective conflict resolution strategies to handle disagreements among stakeholders is essential for maintaining project harmony and progress.
- **Transparency**: Maintaining transparency about project challenges, progress, and changes helps manage stakeholders' expectations realistically.

By recognizing the critical role of stakeholders in the success of the project and maintaining systematic engagement, project managers can foster a positive environment conducive to successful project completion. This active involvement helps in building a strong rapport with stakeholders, ensuring their continuous support, and significantly enhancing the project's overall success rate.

Challenges and Risks Across the Project Life Cycle

Each phase of the project life cycle presents unique challenges and risks that can affect the outcome of a project. Understanding these risks and implementing strategies to mitigate them is crucial for project success. Here, we delve into common risks associated with each phase and suggest strategies for addressing them.

1. Initiating Phase

- **Challenges and Risks**: Inadequate project definition and stakeholder identification can lead to unclear objectives and expectations. There is also a risk of not securing sufficient resources or commitment from stakeholders.
- **Mitigation Strategies**:

- **Thorough Stakeholder Analysis**: Ensure all potential stakeholders are identified and their needs and influences are understood.
- **Clear Project Charter**: Develop a comprehensive project charter that outlines the project's scope, objectives, and key stakeholders, securing formal approval from all necessary parties.

2. Planning Phase

- **Challenges and Risks**: Poorly defined scope, unrealistic timeframes, and inadequate risk assessments can lead to project failure. Underestimating resources and costs are also common pitfalls.
- **Mitigation Strategies**:
  - **Detailed Project Plan**: Create detailed schedules, budget forecasts, and resource allocations that are realistic and flexible.
  - **Risk Management Plan**: Develop a risk management plan that identifies potential risks, their impact, and contingency plans.

3. Executing Phase

- **Challenges and Risks**: Miscommunication, scope creep, resource shortages, and lack of stakeholder engagement can derail a project. Quality issues with deliverables are also a significant risk.
- **Mitigation Strategies**:
  - **Effective Communication**: Implement a communication plan that keeps all project members and stakeholders regularly informed and engaged.
  - **Scope Management**: Use change control processes to manage requests for changes and ensure they are properly evaluated and approved.

4. Monitoring and Controlling Phase

- **Challenges and Risks**: Deviations from the plan regarding time, cost, and quality can occur. There is also a risk of failing to detect issues early enough, leading to significant impacts.
- **Mitigation Strategies**:
  - **Regular Monitoring**: Use tools like Earned Value Management (EVM) to monitor project performance and progress effectively.
  - **Flexible Response to Issues**: Quickly address any deviations by adjusting plans and resource allocations as needed.

5. Closing Phase

- **Challenges and Risks**: Incomplete documentation and unresolved project components can lead to stakeholder dissatisfaction. There is also a risk of inadequate post-project reviews.
- **Mitigation Strategies**:
  - **Comprehensive Close-Out Documentation**: Ensure that all project documents are completed and stored, and that all project outcomes are formally accepted by stakeholders.
  - **Lessons Learned**: Conduct a lessons learned session to document what went well and what didn't, to improve future projects.

Best Practices Across All Phases

- **Proactive Planning**: Engage in thorough planning at every phase, revisiting and adjusting plans as necessary.
- **Stakeholder Engagement**: Maintain strong and regular communication with stakeholders to ensure their needs are met and to foster support for the project.
- **Quality Assurance**: Implement continuous quality assurance processes to ensure deliverables meet the required standards.
- **Team Management**: Build, maintain, and support a competent project team to ensure all project requirements are met with the highest standards.

By anticipating these common challenges and risks and employing strategic mitigation practices, project managers can significantly enhance their ability to deliver projects successfully. Each phase requires careful attention and proactive management to navigate the risks effectively and ensure the project stays on track from inception to closure.

Integration of Project Management Processes and Knowledge Areas in the Project Life Cycle

The project management processes and knowledge areas are designed to interlock and support each phase of the project life cycle, ensuring systematic progress towards the project's objectives. Each knowledge area contributes specific expertise and processes that are critical at various stages of the project, enhancing both efficiency and effectiveness.

1. Initiating Phase

- **Integration Management**: Initiating processes are supported by developing the project charter, which formally authorizes the project.
- **Stakeholder Management**: Identifying stakeholders and understanding their influence and needs are crucial to ensure their expectations are met.
- **Example**: For a new software development project, the project manager creates a project charter and conducts stakeholder analysis to align the project objectives with organizational goals and stakeholder expectations.

2. Planning Phase

- **Scope Management**: Defining the scope, creating the Work Breakdown Structure (WBS), and ensuring detailed task identification.
- **Schedule Management**: Developing a detailed timeline, identifying the critical path, and estimating activity durations.
- **Cost Management**: Estimating costs and setting a budget baseline.
- **Risk Management**: Identifying potential risks and planning mitigation strategies.
- **Example**: In constructing a new building, the project manager will outline the project's scope using a WBS, schedule tasks using Gantt charts, budget the total costs, and prepare for risks like delayed material supply or regulatory changes.

3. Executing Phase

- **Quality Management**: Implementing the quality management plan to ensure that project deliverables meet the required standards.
- **Resource Management**: Mobilizing team members and physical resources to execute project tasks according to the plan.

- **Communications Management**: Ensuring that information is effectively exchanged among project stakeholders.
- **Example**: During a marketing campaign launch, the project manager coordinates with graphic designers, content writers, and digital marketers to produce high-quality content, ensures resources are available as needed, and maintains regular updates to all stakeholders.

4. Monitoring and Controlling Phase

- **Performance Monitoring**: Using tools like Earned Value Management (EVM) to measure project performance against the scope, schedule, and cost baselines.
- **Change Control**: Managing changes systematically through an integrated change control process to ensure that changes are beneficial and do not derail the project.
- **Example**: In an IT project, the project manager continuously tracks software development progress against the timeline and budget, evaluates performance reports, and handles scope changes with a formal change control system.

5. Closing Phase

- **Procurement Management**: Closing out vendor contracts and confirming that all contractual terms have been met.
- **Integration Management**: Finalizing all project activities across all process groups to formally close the project.
- **Stakeholder Management**: Ensuring stakeholder approval of final deliverables and addressing any remaining concerns.
- **Example**: At the end of a conference event project, the project manager ensures that all suppliers are paid, all objectives are met, feedback is collected from participants, and a final project report is distributed to sponsors and stakeholders.

Interdependencies and Support Mechanisms

The project management knowledge areas are interconnected; for example, effective scope management influences quality management, and good communication enhances stakeholder management. These interdependencies mean that processes in one area can support or enhance processes in another, creating a cohesive system that supports the project's success. By applying these processes and utilizing knowledge across different areas, project managers can adapt to changing project demands and environments, ensuring a strategic approach to project management that maximizes the likelihood of achieving project goals. The systematic application of these principles across the project life cycle not only supports successful project completion but also enhances organizational value and stakeholder satisfaction.

Project Management Practice Questions and Quizzes

Here is a set of practice questions designed to test and reinforce understanding of key concepts in project management, including the project life cycle, organizational structures, project management processes, and knowledge areas. Each question is followed by a detailed explanation to enhance learning.

Quiz 1: Project Life Cycle

1. **What are the five phases of the project life cycle?**
   - A) Initiating, Planning, Executing, Monitoring and Controlling, Closing
   - B) Planning, Analysis, Design, Implementation, Maintenance
   - C) Analysis, Design, Coding, Testing, Maintenance

- D) Concept, Development, Realization, Benefit-Cost Analysis, Termination

Correct Answer: A) Initiating, Planning, Executing, Monitoring and Controlling, Closing

- **Explanation**: These five phases represent the project life cycle in project management, providing a structured approach to managing projects from start to finish. Each phase focuses on different aspects of the project, from establishing its objectives and plans to executing the plan and closing the project.

Quiz 2: Organizational Structures

2. **Which organizational structure allows team members to report to both a functional manager and a project manager?**
   - A) Functional
   - B) Matrix
   - C) Projectized
   - D) Hybrid

Correct Answer: B) Matrix

- **Explanation**: In a matrix organizational structure, team members have dual reporting relationships – typically to both a functional manager and a project manager. This structure is designed to combine the benefits of functional and projectized structures, facilitating better resource allocation and flexibility in project management.

Quiz 3: Project Management Processes

3. **Which process involves defining and managing the work necessary to complete the project successfully?**
   - A) Scope Management
   - B) Cost Management
   - C) Quality Management
   - D) Risk Management

Correct Answer: A) Scope Management

- **Explanation**: Scope management is crucial as it involves defining all the work required and only the work required to complete the project successfully. It helps ensure that the project includes all necessary tasks while avoiding scope creep, where uncontrolled changes or continuous growth in project scope occur.

Quiz 4: Knowledge Areas

4. **Earned Value Management (EVM) is a tool primarily used in which knowledge area?**
   - A) Cost Management
   - B) Schedule Management
   - C) Risk Management
   - D) Integration Management

Correct Answer: A) Cost Management

- **Explanation**: EVM is a valuable tool used in cost management to measure project performance. It integrates project scope, schedule, and resource measurements to help project managers assess project performance and progress in an integrated manner, thus aiding in effective decision-making about resource allocation and corrective actions.

5. **How does effective stakeholder management support risk management in projects?**
    - A) By ensuring all project deliverables meet quality standards
    - B) By improving the allocation and use of resources
    - C) By identifying potential risks through stakeholder feedback
    - D) By guaranteeing project costs are kept under control

Correct Answer: C) By identifying potential risks through stakeholder feedback

- **Explanation**: Effective stakeholder management helps in risk management by engaging stakeholders to provide feedback and insights, which can reveal potential risks early in the project. This proactive approach allows for earlier mitigation planning and can significantly reduce the impact of these risks on the project.

These practice questions are designed to challenge and deepen your understanding of project management concepts, preparing you for real-world application and professional examinations.

III. Project Integration Management:

Develop Project Charter: Establishing Project Foundation

Purpose of the Develop Project Charter Process The Develop Project Charter process is fundamental to the initiation of any project. This process serves the critical function of officially authorizing the existence of a project, thereby granting the project manager the authority to apply organizational resources to project activities. Here are several key purposes of the project charter:

1. **Formal Authorization**: It provides formal approval from senior management, officially starting the project and ensuring that it is aligned with strategic organizational goals.
2. **Project Boundaries**: It defines the preliminary boundaries of the project scope, objectives, and major deliverables, which helps to set expectations and guide subsequent planning and decision-making.
3. **Resource Allocation**: It enables resources to be allocated to the project, highlighting the commitment of the organization to support the project with necessary personnel, budget, and materials.
4. **Stakeholder Identification**: It identifies the initial stakeholders, including the project sponsor, customers, and other key participants, which is crucial for communication planning and stakeholder engagement.

Key Components of a Project Charter and Their Significance

1. **Project Title and Description**: This provides a brief overview of the project, offering an easy reference to understand what the project is about. The title and description set the tone and direction for the project.
2. **Project Objectives**: Clearly stated objectives are critical as they define the criteria for success of the project. They must be measurable and align with business goals, providing a target for the project team to aim for.
3. **Project Scope**: Outlines the boundaries of the project, indicating what will be delivered. Defining the scope helps prevent scope creep and sets clear expectations for what the project will and will not cover.
4. **Budget Information**: An initial budget estimate is included to give an idea of the financial resources allocated. This helps in assessing the feasibility and constraints of the project.

5. **Project Sponsor and Stakeholders**: The charter should clearly identify the project sponsor who champions the project at an executive level, along with other key stakeholders. Their involvement is essential for providing guidance and making pivotal decisions.
6. **Project Manager and Authority Level**: This specifies who will lead the project and outlines their level of authority within the project. This clarity is crucial for empowering the project manager and clarifying their role to all project participants.
7. **Milestone Schedule**: Key milestones and their target dates are outlined to provide a timeline perspective of major project phases and deliverables. This helps in setting realistic expectations and planning purposes.
8. **Risk Assessment**: An initial assessment of potential risks gives an early focus on possible challenges that could impact the project, allowing for preliminary mitigation strategies to be considered.
9. **Success Criteria**: Defines how the success of the project will be measured. These criteria are essential for evaluating whether the project has achieved its objectives upon completion.
10. **Approval Signatures**: Includes the signatures of all key stakeholders and the project sponsor. This formalizes their agreement and commitment to the project as defined in the charter.

The project charter is not just an administrative requirement; it is a strategic document that lays the foundation for effective project governance and management. By setting clear objectives, defining the scope, and establishing roles and responsibilities, the project charter ensures that the project is set up for success from the outset. This initial clarity and structure are indispensable for guiding the entire project management process.

Project Statement of Work (SOW) vs. Business Case: Foundations for Project Charter Development

Understanding the differences between a Project Statement of Work (SOW) and a Business Case is crucial as both play pivotal roles in the initial stages of project planning and directly influence the development of the Project Charter.

Project Statement of Work (SOW)

The Statement of Work is a detailed document that describes the specific services or products to be delivered by a project. It outlines the:

- **Scope of Work**: Clearly defines what will be done in the project. This includes the tasks, deliverables, and activities that constitute the project.
- **Purpose of the Project**: Explains why the project has been initiated, detailing the specific needs the project will meet.
- **Objectives**: Sets out what the project aims to achieve, often with specific, measurable targets.
- **Deliverables**: Describes the expected outputs of the project. These can include products, services, or other tangible results.
- **Timeline**: Specifies the expected duration of the project and key milestones.
- **Resources Required**: Lists the materials, tools, and human resources necessary for the project.

The SOW is typically used as a direct input into the project charter. It helps define the scope and deliverables that the charter will authorize the project team to achieve.

Business Case

The Business Case, on the other hand, is a justification for the project based on its expected benefits, costs, and risks. It often includes:

- **Analysis of Business Needs**: Identifies and explains the problem or opportunity the project aims to address.

- **Options Evaluation**: Describes various solutions considered and the rationale for selecting the preferred solution that the project will implement.
- **Cost-Benefit Analysis**: Provides a detailed analysis of the financial and strategic benefits compared to the costs involved. This often includes projections of return on investment (ROI), payback period, and intangible benefits.
- **Risk Assessment**: Identifies potential risks associated with the project's implementation and suggests mitigating strategies.
- **Impact on Business Operations**: Outlines how the project will affect existing business processes and operations.
- **Strategic Alignment**: Shows how the project aligns with the organization's strategic objectives.

The business case is essential for decision-makers to assess whether the project is worth investing in. It provides the rationale for the project and helps secure the necessary approvals and funding.

Influence on the Development of the Project Charter

The project charter is developed using information from both the SOW and the business case:

- **From the SOW**: The detailed descriptions of the project's scope, objectives, and deliverables are incorporated into the project charter. This ensures that the project has clearly defined goals and a detailed plan for achieving them.
- **From the Business Case**: The justification provided in the business case, including the strategic alignment, financial analysis, and risk assessment, supports the authorization of the project. It helps stakeholders understand the value of the project and why it should be pursued.

Together, these documents ensure that the project charter is comprehensive and grounded in both the practicalities of the project's execution (SOW) and its strategic and financial justification (business case). The project charter then acts as a key document that formally authorizes the project, providing the project manager with the authority to utilize resources and directing the project team toward achieving the project's objectives.

Develop Project Charter: Essential ITTOs (Inputs, Tools and Techniques, Outputs)

The "Develop Project Charter" process is fundamental in establishing the initial framework of what the project is intended to accomplish, and authorizing its commencement. Understanding the Inputs, Tools and Techniques, and Outputs (ITTOs) involved in this process is crucial for effectively launching any project.

Inputs

1. **Business Case**: Provides the justification for undertaking the project based on the expected benefits, costs, and risks.
   - **Example**: A business case for a new customer relationship management (CRM) system may highlight improved customer satisfaction, increased sales efficiency, and better data management as benefits.
2. **Agreements**: Any type of contractual agreements relevant to the project which may include contracts, memorandums of understanding (MOUs), service level agreements (SLAs), etc.
   - **Example**: A contract with a software development firm to build the CRM system, outlining deliverables, timelines, and payment terms.
3. **Enterprise Environmental Factors (EEFs)**: Conditions not under the control of the project team that influence, constrain, or direct the project. EEFs include organizational culture, infrastructure, market conditions, and regulatory requirements.

- **Example**: Regulatory requirements in the banking sector that might impact how customer data is handled and stored in the new CRM system.
4. **Organizational Process Assets (OPAs)**: Plans, processes, policies, procedures, and knowledge bases specific to and used by the performing organization.
    - **Example**: The organization's project management templates, historical project data, and lessons learned repository.

Tools and Techniques
1. **Expert Judgment**: Using knowledge and expertise from individuals or groups to enhance the project charter.
    - **Example**: Consulting with senior IT managers and CRM implementation specialists to ensure the project scope and objectives are accurately defined in the charter.
2. **Data Gathering Techniques**: Techniques such as brainstorming, focus groups, interviews, or conflict resolution techniques used to prepare the project charter.
    - **Example**: Facilitating a brainstorming session with future users of the CRM system to understand their needs and expectations.
3. **Interpersonal and Team Skills**: Skills such as negotiation, conflict management, and meeting management are essential in forming the project charter.
    - **Example**: Using conflict resolution skills to address differing opinions among department heads about the CRM system's features during the charter development.
4. **Meetings**: Conduct meetings with key stakeholders to discuss project objectives, high-level requirements, and project boundaries.
    - **Example**: A kickoff meeting with all stakeholders to agree on the project's primary objectives and the approach.

Outputs
1. **Project Charter**: The primary output of the process, which formally authorizes the existence of a project and provides the project manager with the authority to apply organizational resources to project activities.
    - **Example**: The project charter for the CRM system project would include background of the project, project purpose and objectives, high-level requirements, summary milestone schedule, risks, summary budget, project approval requirements, assigned project manager, authority level, and stakeholder list.
2. **Assumption Log**: Captures the assumptions and constraints throughout the project life cycle.
    - **Example**: An assumption might be that the necessary IT infrastructure for the new CRM system will be in place by a specific date.

Importance of ITTOs in Developing the Project Charter
- **Inputs**: Provide the foundational information needed to define the project and its alignment with organizational strategic goals.
- **Tools and Techniques**: Facilitate the efficient development and integration of project information to craft a comprehensive and robust project charter.
- **Outputs**: The project charter is critical as it officially launches the project, while the assumption log helps manage potential future risks and clarifications.

By leveraging these ITTOs effectively, project managers can ensure that the project charter is well-crafted, serving as a solid foundation for all subsequent project activities.

Project Charter: Authorizing Project Resources and Implications of Inadequacy
Authorizing the Project Manager through the Project Charter

The project charter plays a crucial role in the project management lifecycle by formally authorizing a project's existence and providing the project manager with the authority to allocate and utilize organizational resources. This authorization is critical for several reasons:

1. **Empowerment**: The project charter empowers the project manager to lead the project and make decisions regarding the use of resources, including human resources, budget, equipment, and technology. It establishes the project manager's role and responsibilities clearly within the organizational context, enabling them to act with authority in project-related matters.
2. **Access to Resources**: By explicitly stating the project manager's authority, the charter facilitates smoother interactions when acquiring resources. This can include securing the right personnel for the project team, accessing technology, allocating budgetary funds, and scheduling facilities or equipment.
3. **Stakeholder Alignment**: The charter helps align various stakeholders and departments within the organization to support the project. It ensures that all parties understand the project's goals, the importance of the resources required, and the project manager's role in steering the project.
4. **Risk Management**: Authorization through the charter also includes the ability to manage risks appropriately by allocating resources to risk mitigation activities as needed.

Implications of Not Having a Properly Approved Project Charter

The absence of a properly approved project charter can lead to significant challenges in project management and execution:

1. **Lack of Clarity and Direction**: Without a charter, the project may lack clear objectives and defined scope, leading to confusion and misalignment among project team members and stakeholders about what the project is intended to achieve.
2. **Resource Allocation Issues**: Without formal authorization, the project manager may face difficulties in securing necessary resources. Departments may be reluctant to allocate their resources without formal approval, leading to delays and inefficiencies.
3. **Stakeholder Engagement Problems**: Without a charter, stakeholders may not be fully engaged or committed to the project. This lack of commitment can result in reduced support, which can critically impact project success.
4. **Authority and Decision-Making Challenges**: A project manager without the backing of a formally approved charter may struggle to enforce decisions and actions. This can lead to a lack of respect for their role, making it difficult to lead the project effectively.
5. **Project Scope Creep**: Without a well-defined scope as part of a formal charter, projects are more susceptible to scope creep. This occurs when the project's scope expands beyond the original objectives without proper evaluation of impacts on time, costs, and resources.
6. **Increased Project Risk**: Without a charter to outline preliminary risks and the approaches to managing them, projects can be exposed to higher levels of uncertainty and risk, potentially compromising project outcomes.

Conclusion

A project charter is not merely a formality; it is a foundational document that sets the stage for effective project management and execution. It provides the project manager with the necessary authority to effectively utilize resources, manage the project team, and make critical decisions that drive the project towards its objectives. The implications of not having a properly approved project charter can be far-reaching, potentially jeopardizing the project's success from the outset. Ensuring that the project charter is well-crafted and formally approved should be a top priority for any organization initiating a new project.

Develop Project Management Plan: Cornerstone of Effective Project Execution
Importance of the Develop Project Management Plan Process

The Develop Project Management Plan process is crucial in project management as it consolidates all individual project plans into a coherent, integrated document that defines how the project is executed, monitored, controlled, and closed. The importance of this process lies in its ability to:

1. **Provide a Roadmap**: The project management plan serves as a roadmap for project execution and control, detailing the actions needed to ensure the project progresses from initiation to closure successfully.
2. **Establish Consistency**: It integrates and harmonizes all project subsidiary plans, ensuring consistency in how the project will manage various aspects such as scope, schedule, cost, quality, resources, and risks.
3. **Facilitate Communication**: It acts as a key communication tool that informs all stakeholders of how the project will be managed and what to expect in terms of deliverables and timelines.
4. **Enable Stakeholder Alignment**: By documenting project strategies and plans, it ensures all stakeholders are aligned with the project's objectives and approach, minimizing misunderstandings and conflicts.
5. **Guide Decision-Making**: The plan provides a basis for making informed decisions throughout the project lifecycle and is used to guide corrective actions when project performance deviates from the plan.

Key Components of a Comprehensive Project Management Plan

A comprehensive project management plan typically includes the following components:

1. **Project Scope Management Plan**: Details how the scope will be defined, validated, and controlled. It helps prevent scope creep and ensures all project work is authorized and aligned with project objectives.
2. **Schedule Management Plan**: Outlines how project schedules will be developed, managed, and controlled. It includes information on scheduling methodologies, tools, and techniques to be used throughout the project.
3. **Cost Management Plan**: Specifies how project costs will be estimated, budgeted, and controlled. This plan is crucial for ensuring the project is completed within the approved budget.
4. **Quality Management Plan**: Defines how the project will ensure that deliverables meet the required standards and satisfy customer requirements. It includes quality policies, objectives, and criteria.
5. **Resource Management Plan**: Details the physical and human resource requirements, including how resources will be estimated, acquired, managed, and released. It ensures optimal use of resources for project success.
6. **Communications Management Plan**: Specifies the project's internal and external communication requirements, outlining how information will be disseminated among stakeholders.
7. **Risk Management Plan**: Identifies potential project risks, their impact, and outlines strategies for managing these risks. It is essential for proactive project management.
8. **Procurement Management Plan**: Describes how procurement will be handled, including contract types, suppliers, and procurement timelines. It ensures that all project procurement is aligned with project needs and legal requirements.

9. **Stakeholder Engagement Plan**: Details strategies for engaging stakeholders throughout the project lifecycle based on their needs, expectations, interests, and potential impact on the project.
10. **Change Management Plan**: Defines the process by which the project scope, plans, and deliverables can be changed. It includes how changes will be managed and controlled to prevent unauthorized changes.

How These Components Guide Project Execution

Each component of the project management plan provides specific guidance that helps project teams navigate the complexities of project execution. They serve to:

- Ensure that all project activities are aligned with the project's strategic objectives.
- Provide criteria for measuring project performance and triggering corrective actions.
- Facilitate effective communication and stakeholder engagement to maintain project support and alignment.
- Manage resources efficiently to meet project timelines and budget constraints.

The project management plan is not just a document, but a dynamic tool that guides every aspect of project execution. By detailing how various elements of the project will be managed, it ensures that the project team has a clear understanding of their roles and responsibilities, the methodologies to be employed, and the criteria for project success. This comprehensive guide is indispensable for navigating project challenges and ensuring successful project delivery. The "Develop Project Management Plan" process is central to the discipline of project management, serving as the framework that guides how the project will be executed, monitored, controlled, and closed. The process's Inputs, Tools and Techniques, and Outputs (ITTOs) are essential for creating a comprehensive and effective project management plan. Here's an in-depth look at each component:

Inputs

1. **Project Charter**: Provides the initial scope, objectives, and participants, including the project manager. It acts as the primary input, defining the direction and boundaries of the project.
2. **Outputs from Other Processes**: Inputs such as risk registers, scope baselines, and stakeholder registers from other planning processes provide detailed information necessary for integrating various aspects of the project management plan.
3. **Enterprise Environmental Factors (EEFs)**: Include organizational culture, infrastructure, market conditions, and regulatory standards that influence how the project is managed.
4. **Organizational Process Assets (OPAs)**: Include existing policies, procedures, and templates from within the organization that influence the project's management plans. Historical data and lessons learned from similar projects also fall under this category.

Tools and Techniques
1. Expert Judgment:

Utilizing the experience and knowledge of subject matter experts in project management or the project's specific industry is crucial for making informed decisions about project planning.

2. Data Gathering Techniques:

- **Brainstorming**: Used to generate ideas and solutions during the planning process.
- **Checklists**: Ensure that all necessary components of the project management plan are considered.

- **Focus Groups**: Engage stakeholders and subject matter experts to discuss and refine project aspects.

3.   **Data Analysis Techniques**:
- **Alternatives Analysis**: Involves evaluating different ways to accomplish project objectives and deliverables, leading to more effective planning decisions.

4.   **Interpersonal and Team Skills**:
- **Conflict Management**: Ensures that differences of opinion do not derail the planning process.
- **Facilitation**: Effective facilitation skills help to lead planning sessions that involve diverse group inputs.

5.   **Meetings**:
Conducted to discuss and integrate various aspects of the project management plans, including integration management, scope, risk, and other areas of concern.

Outputs
1.   **Project Management Plan**:
The primary output, this document integrates all subsidiary plans and baselines, such as:
- **Scope Management Plan**
- **Requirements Management Plan**
- **Schedule Management Plan**
- **Cost Management Plan**
- **Quality Management Plan**
- **Resource Management Plan**
- **Communications Management Plan**
- **Risk Management Plan**
- **Procurement Management Plan**
- **Stakeholder Engagement Plan**

2.   **Baselines**:
Part of the project management plan, these include scope, schedule, and cost baselines, which are used to measure and control project performance.

Contribution to a Robust and Effective Project Management Plan
The ITTOs contribute significantly to crafting a robust and effective project management plan in several ways:

Comprehensive Integration:
By integrating inputs from various sources, including the project charter and outputs from other processes, the project management plan covers all necessary aspects of project execution comprehensively.

Expert Insights:
The use of expert judgment and various data gathering and analysis techniques ensures that the plan is based on informed decisions that consider the best practices and tailored solutions for specific project challenges.

Collaboration and Alignment:
Interpersonal and team skills, along with structured meetings, ensure that the project team and stakeholders are aligned and committed to the project's goals, enhancing collaborative efforts and overall project cohesion.

Flexibility and Control:
The development of subsidiary plans and baselines provides a flexible yet controlled approach to managing the project, allowing adjustments as necessary while ensuring project objectives are met efficiently.

The ITTOs of the Develop Project Management Plan process ensure that the plan is not only comprehensive and integrated but also dynamic and adaptable to project changes, thereby setting the stage for successful project execution and delivery. The project management plan plays a pivotal role in defining and communicating the project scope, objectives, and stakeholder expectations. It serves as the primary reference document for the project team and stakeholders, outlining the project's roadmap and ensuring all parties are aligned with the project goals and processes. Here's a closer look at how the project management plan facilitates communication and ensures alignment:

Role of the Project Management Plan
1. **Defining Project Scope and Objectives**:
- The plan provides a detailed description of the project scope, including the boundaries of the project and the major deliverables. It specifies what is included and what is excluded, helping team members understand the extent of their responsibilities.
- Clear objectives are set within the plan, often outlined with specific, measurable, achievable, relevant, and time-bound (SMART) criteria. This clarity helps team members focus their efforts on what needs to be accomplished to consider the project successful.

2. **Communicating Stakeholder Expectations**:
- The plan includes a stakeholder engagement plan which identifies all stakeholders, their influence, and their interests in relation to the project. It also outlines strategies for engaging stakeholders throughout the project lifecycle, ensuring their needs and expectations are met.
- This engagement plan helps in managing and aligning stakeholder expectations with the project's progress and outcomes, preventing miscommunications and conflicts.

Ensuring the Plan is Understood and Followed
To ensure that the project management plan is effectively understood and adhered to by the project team, project managers can employ several strategies:

1. **Comprehensive Onboarding and Training**:
- Conduct detailed onboarding sessions for all project team members to walk them through the project management plan. This includes discussing the scope, objectives, key deliverables, timelines, and individual roles and responsibilities.
- Provide training or workshops to address specific areas of the plan, such as risk management procedures, quality standards, or change control processes, ensuring everyone understands how these should be managed according to the plan.

2. **Regular Communication and Updates**:
- Hold regular meetings (e.g., daily stand-ups, weekly team meetings) to discuss project progress, address any discrepancies from the plan, and reinforce the importance of following the established procedures.
- Use these meetings to solicit feedback from the team on the project management plan and make adjustments as necessary to ensure it remains effective and relevant.

3. **Accessibility of the Plan**:
- Ensure that the project management plan is easily accessible to all team members, ideally in a digital format that can be referenced at any point. Tools like project management software can be used to share documents and updates efficiently.
- Regularly update the plan to reflect any approved changes, and notify the team of these updates to keep everyone informed.

4. **Monitoring and Reinforcement**:
- Continuously monitor the adherence to the project management plan through regular check-ins and the use of performance metrics.
- Reinforce the importance of the plan through recognition of team members who effectively follow the plan and contribute to meeting project objectives.

5. **Stakeholder Engagement**:
- Keep stakeholders informed about the project's progress in relation to the plan and actively involve them in reviews and decision-making processes. This helps maintain their support and ensures their expectations are continuously aligned with the project's direction.

By effectively communicating and ensuring adherence to the project management plan, project managers can foster a well-informed and cohesive team environment. This proactive approach not only facilitates smoother project execution but also enhances the likelihood of project success, meeting or exceeding stakeholder expectations.

Overview of the Direct and Manage Project Work Process

The Direct and Manage Project Work process is a critical component of the project management lifecycle, primarily executed during the project's execution phase. This process involves overseeing and performing the work defined in the project management plan, ensuring that the project's deliverables are produced as specified. It is the core function where the project plan is turned into tangible outputs.

Key Activities Performed by the Project Manager

1. **Implementation of the Project Management Plan**: The project manager is responsible for implementing the project management plan, ensuring that every aspect of the project is carried out according to the defined processes, schedules, budgets, and resources.
2. **Resource Allocation**: Efficient allocation and management of resources (human resources, materials, equipment) is crucial. The project manager ensures that resources are available as needed and are being used effectively to achieve project objectives.
3. **Quality Assurance**: Throughout the project execution, the project manager must ensure that the work meets the quality standards established in the quality management plan. This includes overseeing the execution of quality policies and procedures to maintain the quality of project outputs.
4. **Communication Management**: Managing communications is vital. The project manager facilitates appropriate generation, collection, dissemination, and storage of project information. This ensures all stakeholders are kept informed and engaged throughout the project lifecycle.
5. **Performance Reporting**: Monitoring and reporting on project progress and performance relative to the plan is essential. This includes tracking milestones, deliverables, and any variances in schedule and budget, using tools such as earned value management (EVM).
6. **Risk and Issue Management**: Identifying and responding to risks and issues as they arise is a key responsibility. The project manager must implement the risk response plans and adapt as necessary to address new or evolving project risks and issues.
7. **Change Management**: Managing changes to the project scope, schedule, and costs through a formal change control system. This involves assessing the impact of changes, obtaining approvals, and updating the project plans accordingly.
8. **Stakeholder Engagement**: Actively working to engage stakeholders by addressing their concerns and expectations, resolving issues, and coordinating their participation in project activities.

Contribution to Project Success
Plan Implementation:

By effectively implementing the project management plan, the project manager ensures that the project stays aligned with its goals and objectives, which is crucial for meeting the project's expected outcomes.

Resource Efficiency:

Proper resource allocation prevents resource wastage and optimizes project performance, contributing significantly to project success by ensuring that the project can be completed within the allocated budget and timeline.

Quality Control:

Quality assurance activities ensure that the project deliverables meet the required standards and stakeholder expectations, which is vital for the project's acceptance and success.

Effective Communication:

Keeping all stakeholders informed and engaged reduces misunderstandings and increases support, thereby facilitating smoother project execution and increasing the likelihood of project success.

Performance Tracking:

Regular performance reporting allows for timely detection of issues and variances, enabling corrective actions to be taken before they can derail the project.

Proactive Risk and Issue Management:

By managing risks and issues proactively, the project manager minimizes their potential negative impact on the project, thereby safeguarding the project objectives.

Change Control:

Effective change management ensures that the project remains flexible and adaptable without compromising its defined scope and objectives, which helps in accommodating necessary changes while still delivering value.

Stakeholder Satisfaction:

By maintaining high levels of stakeholder engagement and satisfaction, the project manager fosters a positive environment that supports project objectives and enhances collaborative effort.

The Direct and Manage Project Work process is where the project manager takes active steps to ensure that the project's work is performed according to the plan, adapting to challenges and changes as needed. This process is foundational to translating the project plan into the actual, tangible outcomes that define project success. Project kickoff meetings and work performance information are crucial components in the "Direct and Manage Project Work" process of project management. They play vital roles in setting the stage for project execution and providing continuous feedback on the project's progress and challenges. Let's explore each element in detail and discuss how project managers can utilize them effectively to ensure project progress.

Significance of Project Kickoff Meetings
1.   Setting Expectations and Aligning the Team:

- **Purpose**: The kickoff meeting is the first formal gathering of all project stakeholders and team members. It serves to align everyone's understanding of the project objectives, scope, and the roles and responsibilities of each team member.
- **Impact**: By setting clear expectations from the start, the project manager can ensure that all team members are on the same page, reducing confusion and misalignment that could derail the project later on.

2. Building Team Cohesion and Commitment:

- **Purpose**: This meeting also serves as a platform to build team rapport and foster relationships among team members who may be working together for the first time. It's an opportunity to encourage open communication and collaborative teamwork.
- **Impact**: Establishing a positive team dynamic early on can enhance teamwork throughout the project lifecycle, leading to more effective problem-solving and innovation.

2.   Reviewing Key Project Management Plans:

- **Purpose**: The kickoff meeting allows the project manager to review the project management plan, including the scope, timeline, risk management strategies, and communication plans with the team.
- **Impact**: Reinforcing these plans ensures that every team member understands how the project will be managed and what the key deliverables and milestones are.

Significance of Work Performance Information
1. Real-Time Project Monitoring:

- **Purpose**: Work performance information involves the collection of data regarding the status of project activities being performed to produce project deliverables. It includes details about project progress, resource usage, task completion, and compliance with project standards.
- **Impact**: This information is critical for assessing whether the project is on track, within budget, and in alignment with the quality standards.

3. Basis for Decision Making:

- **Purpose**: Work performance information provides the empirical evidence needed to make informed decisions regarding project changes, resource re-allocation, and other adjustments.
- **Impact**: Effective use of this data helps prevent or mitigate project issues, ensuring the project meets its objectives efficiently.

Effective Use of These Elements to Ensure Project Progress
1. Conducting Effective Kickoff Meetings:

- **Preparation**: Ensure all relevant stakeholders are invited, create a detailed agenda, and prepare to discuss the project's scope, objectives, and expectations clearly.
- **Engagement**: Encourage participation from all attendees to foster a sense of ownership and accountability. Use this opportunity to address any questions or concerns.

3. Leveraging Work Performance Information:

- **Regular Updates**: Schedule regular check-ins and status update meetings to gather and discuss work performance information. This keeps the project on track and allows for timely adjustments.
- **Transparent Communication**: Share performance reports with the team and stakeholders regularly to maintain transparency and adjust expectations as needed.
- **Adaptive Management**: Use performance information to adapt project plans and strategies proactively. Address discrepancies and implement corrective actions swiftly to mitigate risks.

By effectively conducting kickoff meetings and utilizing work performance information, project managers can establish a strong foundation for project execution and maintain tight control over the project's progress. These elements are instrumental in ensuring that the project remains aligned with its goals, adequately resourced, and adaptable to changes and challenges that arise during its execution. Capturing and documenting lessons learned throughout the project life cycle is a crucial practice in project management that helps ensure continuous improvement in processes and outcomes. This practice not only benefits the project at hand by identifying what works and what doesn't but also informs future projects by providing actionable insights that can prevent repetition of past mistakes and leverage successful strategies.

Importance of Lessons Learned
1. Improving Project Performance:

By regularly capturing lessons learned, project teams can quickly adapt and make necessary adjustments during the project. This proactive approach to problem-solving and optimization can lead to more efficient project execution and higher quality outcomes.

2. Risk Mitigation:

Documenting challenges and obstacles encountered during a project provides future projects with a roadmap of potential risks and effective mitigation strategies. This preparedness can significantly reduce the likelihood and impact of similar risks in future projects.

3. Cost Efficiency:

Learning from past projects can lead to cost savings by avoiding the repetition of errors, optimizing resource allocation, and streamlining processes based on proven successes.

4. Team Development and Empowerment:

Engaging the project team in the process of gathering and analyzing lessons learned fosters a culture of learning and continuous improvement. It empowers team members to contribute to the growth and success of the organization actively.

5. Organizational Knowledge and Growth:

Lessons learned contribute to the organization's knowledge base, enhancing its intellectual capital. They provide invaluable insights that can influence strategic decisions and long-term planning.

Facilitating Knowledge Sharing and Reuse

Project managers can play a pivotal role in facilitating effective knowledge sharing and reuse across the organization through several strategies:

Structured Lessons Learned Sessions:

Conduct regular lessons learned meetings throughout the project lifecycle, not just at the end. This allows the team to reflect on what has been effective and what could be improved while the project activities are fresh in their minds.

Creating Accessible Documentation:

Store lessons learned in a centralized, accessible repository that is easy for other teams and projects within the organization to access. This could be a digital database, an intranet site, or a dedicated section within the organization's knowledge management system.

Integration into Training Programs:

Incorporate lessons learned into onboarding and training programs for new employees. This can help inculcate a culture of learning from past projects from the very beginning of an employee's journey within the organization.

Promoting a Learning Culture:

Encourage a culture that values not only success but also learning from failures. This can be fostered by leadership through recognizing and rewarding teams that effectively document and share lessons learned.

Cross-Project Reviews:

Organize cross-project review sessions where teams from different projects can share successes and challenges. This not only helps in disseminating lessons learned but also fosters a sense of community and collaborative growth among different teams.

Use of Technology:

Leverage technology to facilitate easier capture, storage, and dissemination of lessons learned. Tools such as project management software, collaboration platforms, or AI-driven analytics can help in identifying trends and insights that may not be immediately apparent. By systematically capturing, documenting, and sharing lessons learned, project managers can significantly enhance the knowledge base of the organization. This ongoing process helps build a proactive, reflective, and continually improving organizational culture, crucial for staying competitive and effective in today's dynamic business environment. The Manage Project Knowledge process is designed to ensure that the knowledge generated over the course of a project is captured and integrated with organizational knowledge assets. The main purposes of this process are to:

Capture Knowledge:
Both explicit (documented) and tacit (undocumented or intuitive) knowledge are captured from project team members throughout the project lifecycle. This includes lessons learned, insights gained, and innovative solutions developed during the project.

Share Knowledge:
Facilitate the distribution of knowledge among current project team members and other organizational stakeholders to enhance individual and team performance in current and future projects.

Integrate Knowledge:
Ensure that the knowledge gained from a specific project contributes to the organization's broader knowledge base, improving future projects and strategic decision-making.

Promote Organizational Learning:
By systematically managing knowledge, organizations can create a culture of continuous learning and improvement, adapting more effectively to new challenges and opportunities.

Contribution to Organizational Learning and Continuous Improvement
The Manage Project Knowledge process contributes to organizational learning and continuous improvement by:

- **Avoiding Repeated Mistakes**: By capturing lessons learned from each project, the organization can avoid repeating past mistakes, thereby reducing costs and improving project efficiency over time.
- **Leveraging Past Successes**: Similarly, documenting and sharing effective practices and successes ensures that these can be replicated and adapted in future projects, continuously improving project outcomes.
- **Enhancing Skills and Competencies**: Knowledge sharing helps in upskilling team members by exposing them to new ideas, techniques, and experiences from diverse projects within the organization.
- **Building a Knowledge Repository**: Creating a centralized repository of project documents, templates, and lessons learned makes it easier for project teams to access and utilize valuable resources, speeding up project initiation and planning phases.
- **Fostering Innovation**: By encouraging the free flow of information and ideas, organizations can foster a culture of innovation, where new ideas are valued and can be tested and implemented in projects.

Examples of Knowledge Management Techniques Used in Project Management

1. **Lessons Learned Repositories**:

These are databases where information on both successes and failures of past projects is stored. This information can include what was planned, what actually happened, why it happened, and how future projects can plan effectively to replicate successes or avoid failures.

- **Example**: After completing a software development project, a project manager documents the challenges faced during the integration phase and the solutions that helped overcome them. This information is stored in the organization's lessons learned repository.

2. **Knowledge Sharing Sessions**:

Regularly scheduled meetings or workshops where team members present findings, discuss project challenges, and share best practices and new knowledge gained during the project.

- **Example**: Monthly 'knowledge cafes' where project teams gather informally to discuss recent projects and share insights that could benefit ongoing or future projects.

3. **Communities of Practice (CoPs)**:

These are groups of people who share a concern or a passion for something they do and interact regularly to learn how to do it better.

- **Example**: A community of practice for project managers within a large organization where they share tools, techniques, and experiences to enhance their project management skills.

4. **Digital Collaboration Tools**:

Platforms such as wikis, forums, and online dashboards that allow for the dynamic sharing and updating of project information and documentation.

- **Example**: Using a project management software tool that allows for real-time updates and information sharing among project team members and stakeholders.

Through these techniques and processes, the Manage Project Knowledge process plays a critical role in capturing valuable project insights and disseminating them throughout the organization. This systematic approach to knowledge management not only enhances individual project outcomes but also contributes significantly to the broader goals of organizational learning and continuous improvement. The "Monitor and Control Project Work" process is integral to project management, as it involves tracking, reviewing, and reporting the project's progress to meet the performance objectives defined in the project management plan. This ongoing process allows project managers to ensure that the project remains on track, within scope, within budget, and in alignment with quality standards.

Key Activities of the Monitor and Control Project Work Process
Performance Measurement:

This involves comparing actual project performance against the project management plan. Performance indicators such as cost performance index (CPI), schedule performance index (SPI), actual cost (AC), and earned value (EV) are commonly used to measure the performance of the project.

Scope Verification and Control:

Monitoring scope is critical to ensure that the project includes only the work required. This involves reviewing deliverables and work results to ensure compliance with the scope and making adjustments as necessary to control any scope creep.

Schedule and Cost Control:

Monitoring the timeline and budget involves assessing the progress of the project against its planned schedule and budget. This includes updating project schedules, modifying strategies, and re-allocating resources to address any deviations.

Quality Assurance:

Quality control measurements are compared against quality standards to ensure that the project outputs meet the desired standards. Any discrepancies are addressed through corrective measures.

Risk Monitoring and Response Implementation:

Identifying new risks and reassessing existing risks throughout the project lifecycle is crucial. Effective risk management involves implementing risk response plans and taking corrective actions to mitigate their impact.

Stakeholder Communication:

Regular updates and communications with stakeholders are essential to maintain trust and engagement. This activity ensures that stakeholders are kept informed of progress and any issues that may affect them.

Tools Used to Track Project Progress, Identify Issues, and Make Adjustments
Project Management Software:

Tools like Microsoft Project, Asana, and Trello help track tasks, schedules, resources, budgets, and risks. These tools provide dashboards and real-time data that aid in monitoring the various aspects of the project.

Earned Value Management (EVM):

EVM is a systematic process that integrates scope, schedule, and resource measurements to assess project performance and progress. It provides a set of formulas that help in evaluating the cost variance, schedule variance, cost performance index, and schedule performance index.

Gantt Charts and S-Curves:

These visual tools help track project progress against the baseline plan. Gantt charts display the duration of tasks and their sequences, while S-curves show the growth of project variables over time, which is useful for understanding the rate of progress.

Change Control Systems:

These systems help manage all requests for changes from their inception to decision making and eventual implementation. Effective change control ensures that no unnecessary changes are made and that all changes are documented.

Performance Reviews:

These involve periodic evaluation meetings where project progress is discussed, and performance data is reviewed. Performance reviews help identify variances from the plan and facilitate the discussion of necessary adjustments.

Risk Registers:

Updated continuously, risk registers track identified risks and their status, along with strategies for their mitigation. Monitoring risks involves reviewing the likelihood and impact of risks and adjusting mitigation strategies accordingly.

Status and Progress Reports:

Regularly scheduled reports that provide insights into various aspects of the project, such as current status, achievements, challenges, and forecasts. These reports are essential for keeping stakeholders informed and involved.

By effectively employing these activities and tools, project managers can ensure that the project adapts to any internal or external changes, remains aligned with its objectives, and is positioned for success. The Monitor and Control Project Work process is vital for making informed decisions that facilitate timely and appropriate management actions throughout the project lifecycle. The Monitor and Control Project Work process is a vital phase in project management, encompassing activities necessary to track, review, and regulate the progress and performance of a project. It ensures the project remains on track with its objectives, budget, and timeline, and adapts to any issues or changes required. Key elements within this process are change requests and performance reports.

Role of Change Requests

Change requests are formal proposals for modifications to any aspect of the project—such as the scope, schedule, or cost—and can include corrective or preventive actions or efforts to address defects.

1. **Adaptation to New Information or Requirements**: Change requests allow the project to adapt to new information, stakeholder feedback, or changes in external conditions. This adaptability is crucial for maintaining the relevance and viability of the project in dynamic environments.
2. **Formal Approval Process**: By requiring formal approval, change requests help ensure that any modifications to the project are well-considered and align with overall project goals and stakeholder expectations. This process prevents unauthorized changes that could lead to scope creep or project misalignment.
3. **Documentation and Traceability**: Change requests provide a documented trail of what changes were proposed, why they were necessary, who approved them, and how they were implemented. This traceability is essential for audits, historical records, and lessons learned.

Role of Performance Reports
Performance reports

are documents that capture the current status of the project, including metrics on scope, schedule, cost, resources, risks, and other critical factors.

1. **Visibility into Project Health**: Performance reports offer visibility into the health and progress of the project, allowing stakeholders and the project team to understand whether the project is on track.
2. **Basis for Decision Making**: These reports provide the data necessary for informed decision-making. They allow project managers and stakeholders to identify areas that may require attention or adjustment, such as deviations from the schedule or budget overruns.
3. **Communication Tool**: Performance reports serve as a critical communication tool between the project team, sponsors, and other stakeholders. They ensure everyone is informed about the project's status and can align their expectations and actions accordingly.

Maintaining Project Alignment with Objectives and Stakeholder Expectations
Change Requests and Performance Reports

work synergistically within the Monitor and Control Project Work process to ensure the project remains aligned with its objectives and meets stakeholder expectations:

Dynamic Adjustment:

Change requests provide a mechanism to adjust plans and align the project with changing requirements or environments. By managing these requests systematically, project managers can ensure that changes are beneficial and do not derail the project.

Performance Tracking and Correction:

Performance reports help track the efficacy of the project's strategies and the achievement of its objectives. By continuously monitoring performance, project managers can quickly identify and correct deviations, thereby aligning the project more closely with its intended goals.

Stakeholder Confidence and Engagement:

Regular and transparent communication through performance reports and structured change requests maintains stakeholder confidence and engagement. Stakeholders are more likely to support a project when they are kept informed and their inputs are considered in decision-making.

Change requests and performance reports are indispensable tools in the Monitor and Control Project Work process. They enable project managers to maintain control over the project, ensuring it adapts to changes responsibly while staying aligned with its objectives and stakeholder expectations. This dynamic balance between control and flexibility is crucial for the successful completion of any project. The "Perform Integrated Change Control" process is a critical component of project management, overseeing all requests for changes or modifications to the project's scope, schedule, cost, and resources. This process ensures that no changes are made without proper review, approval, and integration into the overall project plan, thereby maintaining the project's integrity and coherence.

Purpose of the Perform Integrated Change Control Process

1. **Review All Change Requests**: All requests for changes, whether they originate from within the project team or from external stakeholders, are formally documented, reviewed, and either approved, rejected, or deferred. This includes changes to project documents, deliverables, baselines, or any aspect detailed in the project management plan.
2. **Assess Impact of Changes**: Before any change is approved, its impact on the project's scope, schedule, budget, quality, and resources is thoroughly analyzed. This ensures that the implications of the change are understood and that the project remains aligned with its objectives.
3. **Approve or Reject Changes**: Decision-making authority lies with the Change Control Board or project manager, depending on the project's governance structure. Approved changes must be managed and monitored as they are implemented.
4. **Update Project Documents and Plans**: Upon approval, changes need to be reflected in the project's documents and plans to ensure that all project information remains current and accurate.
5. **Communicate Changes**: It's essential that all approved changes are communicated to relevant stakeholders to ensure that everyone involved with the project understands the new requirements, timelines, and tasks.

Change Control Board (CCB)

A Change Control Board (CCB) is a formally constituted group of stakeholders responsible for reviewing, evaluating, approving, or rejecting changes to the project, and for recording and communicating such decisions. Here's how the CCB facilitates effective decision-making regarding project changes:

Structured Decision-Making:

The CCB provides a systematic approach to assess and decide on proposed changes. This structured process helps ensure that each change is considered carefully and that the decisions are balanced, taking into account the project's best interests.

Expertise and Representation:
Typically, a CCB includes members who represent diverse areas of expertise relevant to the project. This ensures that decisions are made based on a wide range of insights, which include technical, financial, and operational perspectives.

Impartiality:
By involving members from various disciplines and possibly independent stakeholders, the CCB can maintain impartiality in decision-making, which is crucial for the objective assessment of changes.

Transparency:
The operations of the CCB are transparent, with formal documentation and communication of decisions. This transparency builds trust and maintains accountability among stakeholders.

Risk Management:
The CCB plays a critical role in risk management by assessing the potential risks associated with implementing changes. Their expertise helps in devising strategies to mitigate risks while harnessing the potential benefits of the change.

Consistency:
The CCB ensures that all changes are reviewed and handled in a consistent manner, regardless of their origin or nature. This consistency helps in maintaining the project's scope, quality, and objectives.
The "Perform Integrated Change Control" process and the Change Control Board are essential for managing changes systematically and efficiently. They ensure that all changes are thoughtfully considered and integrated into the project plan while aligning with the project's goals and deliverables. This process is vital for the project's adaptability and success, helping to manage the complexities and dynamics of project execution.

Significance of the Change Log
The change log is an essential component of the Perform Integrated Change Control process in project management. This process is crucial for assessing, approving, or rejecting changes to the project baseline, which includes the scope, schedule, and cost. The change log plays a significant role in maintaining the integrity and traceability of these changes.

Roles and Benefits of a Change Log
1. **Documentation of All Change Requests**: The change log records every change request submitted during the project's lifecycle, including details about the request, the evaluation process, and the approval or rejection status. This comprehensive record ensures that all changes are considered systematically and transparently.
2. **Tracking Status and Decisions**: It provides an ongoing record of the status of each change request, including whether it is under review, approved, rejected, or implemented. This tracking is crucial for ensuring that no requested change is overlooked and that all changes are processed in a timely manner.

3. **Accountability and Traceability**: The change log helps in maintaining accountability as it includes information on who requested the change, who approved it, and the rationale for the decision. This traceability is essential for audits, dispute resolution, and for understanding the impact of changes on the project.

4. **Communication Tool**: As a centralized source of information on changes, the change log serves as a key communication tool. It helps project managers keep stakeholders informed about how changes are affecting the project and ensures transparency.

Using the Change Log to Track and Communicate Project Changes
For Project Managers

- **Proactive Management**: Project managers can use the change log to monitor the status and impact of each change request. By keeping an eye on this log, they can proactively manage resources and adjust project plans to accommodate approved changes, thereby maintaining project alignment with its objectives.
- **Decision-Making Support**: The detailed documentation in the change log supports informed decision-making. Project managers can review past decisions and their outcomes, which can provide valuable insights for handling current and future change requests.

For Communicating with Stakeholders

- **Regular Updates**: Project managers can provide regular updates to stakeholders by sharing the current state of the change log. This can be done during stakeholder meetings or through project update reports, ensuring that stakeholders are always aware of changes and their status.
- **Transparency and Trust**: By openly sharing the change log with stakeholders, project managers foster a sense of transparency and trust. Stakeholders appreciate visibility into how changes are being managed and are more likely to support the decision-making process.
- **Conflict Resolution**: The change log can be used to resolve conflicts by providing a clear, documented trail of decisions and actions. This can help clarify misunderstandings and justify why certain decisions were made, thus helping to align disparate stakeholder views.

Conclusion
The change log is not just a record-keeping tool but a dynamic part of project governance that supports the effective management of changes within a project. It helps ensure that changes are made thoughtfully and with consideration of their broader impact on the project's goals and deliverables. For project managers, the change log is indispensable for maintaining control over the project scope, schedule, and costs, and for communicating effectively with stakeholders, thereby playing a crucial role in the project's success. The "Close Project or Phase" process is a critical component of project management, marking the formal conclusion of a project or a project phase. This process ensures that all aspects of the project are appropriately finalized to avoid leaving any tasks incomplete and to ensure a smooth handover of deliverables. Here's a detailed look at the key activities and deliverables of this process and how they contribute to a smooth transition to operations and support organizational learning.

Key Activities of the Close Project or Phase Process
1. Confirm Work is Completed to Requirements:
- Ensuring all project work has been completed according to the contractual agreements and project documents. This includes a thorough review to confirm that all specifications have been met and that deliverables are acceptable to the stakeholders.

2. Finalize All Procurements:

- Closing all contracts associated with the project, ensuring that all terms have been met, final payments have been processed, and any claims have been settled. This activity is essential to maintain good relationships with suppliers and vendors.

3. Complete Final Performance Reporting:

- Documenting the performance of the project, including successes, challenges, and the degree of achievement of project goals. This report provides a benchmark for evaluating the overall success of the project.

4. Obtain Final Acceptance of Deliverables:

- Securing formal acceptance of the project's results from the client or sponsor. This is crucial for the formal closure of the project and transitions the deliverables for operational use.

5. Conduct Post-Project Review:

- Organizing a meeting with the project team and relevant stakeholders to discuss what went well and what could be improved. This review is a vital part of capturing lessons learned.

6. Document Lessons Learned:

- Documenting insights and integrating them into the organization's knowledge base. Lessons learned include challenges, project anomalies, successes, and areas for improvement.

7. Release Project Resources:

- Releasing project resources, including team members, equipment, and facilities. This involves ensuring that all human resources are appropriately acknowledged for their efforts and reassigned to other projects or roles within the organization.

8. Archive Project Documents:

- Ensuring all project documents are finalized and stored in an organizational knowledge repository for future reference. This includes all contractual documents, project plans, reports, creative files, and correspondence.

Key Deliverables of the Close Project or Phase Process

1. Final Project Report:

- A comprehensive summary of the project, encapsulating all critical aspects of performance, including scope, quality, cost, and schedule adherence. It also includes an evaluation of the project management processes used and their effectiveness.

2. Accepted Deliverables:

- Documented acceptance of the project's final outputs by the client or sponsor. This formal acceptance is necessary to transition the deliverables for practical use or for benefits realization.

3. Lessons Learned Report:

- A detailed document that records the knowledge gained during the project, providing valuable insights for future projects. This report includes what was learned about project management processes, technology usage, and team dynamics.

Ensuring a Smooth Transition to Operations and Supporting Organizational Learning
Transition to Operations:

- By obtaining formal acceptance of the deliverables and documenting all project activities and outcomes in the final project report, the process ensures that the transition to operations is seamless. Operations teams receive all the necessary information to effectively utilize and maintain the project outputs.

Support Organizational Learning:

- The lessons learned report and the archival of project documents enhance organizational knowledge and maturity. These activities ensure that successes can be replicated and that past mistakes are avoided in future projects.

Overall, the "Close Project or Phase" process not only marks the project's conclusion but also ensures that the project's benefits are realized, risks are mitigated, and the organization continues to evolve and improve its project management capabilities.

Importance of Administrative Closure

Administrative closure is a critical component of the Close Project or Phase process in project management. It involves the formal conclusion of project activities, ensuring all contractual and administrative responsibilities are finalized. This closure process is crucial for several reasons:

1. **Documentation and Record Keeping**: Ensures that all project documentation is complete, archived, and accessible for future reference. This is important for legal compliance, audit trails, and historical data for future projects.
2. **Release of Resources**: Ensures that resources, including staff, equipment, and materials, are formally released from the project. This allows for the efficient reallocation of resources to other projects or operational uses.
3. **Stakeholder Satisfaction**: By formally closing the project, stakeholders are assured that all objectives have been met and that there are no outstanding obligations or issues. This helps in maintaining good relationships and trust.
4. **Learning and Improvement**: Administrative closure includes the completion of lessons learned sessions, which are vital for capturing insights and knowledge gained during the project. These lessons are crucial for continuous improvement in future projects.

Main Tasks in Administrative Closure
1. Documenting and Archiving Project Information

- **Task**: Collect and finalize all project documents, including plans, performance reports, deliverables, and correspondence.
- **Purpose**: Ensures that all documentation is organized and stored in an accessible manner for compliance, reference, and historical analysis.

2. Completing Financial Closure

- **Task**: Confirm that all financial accounts related to the project have been closed, all invoices have been processed, and final payments have been made.
- **Purpose**: Prevents ongoing financial liabilities and ensures all financial transactions are accounted for and audited.

3. Conducting Lessons Learned

- **Task**: Organize sessions to discuss what went well and what could be improved. Document these insights in a lessons learned repository.
- **Purpose**: Improves organizational practices and project management methodologies, enhancing the success of future projects.

5. Releasing Project Resources
- **Task**: Formally release team members, contractors, and rented equipment.
- **Purpose**: Frees up resources for other projects and reduces ongoing project costs.

5. Delivering Final Product, Service, or Result
- **Task**: Ensure the project's outputs are formally handed over to the client or sponsor, with all necessary training and documentation.
- **Purpose**: Guarantees that the deliverables are accepted and operational, marking the formal end of the project.

6. Stakeholder Communication
- **Task**: Communicate the closure of the project to all stakeholders, providing final reports and closure statements.
- **Purpose**: Ensures that all stakeholders are aware of the project completion, understand the outcomes, and have an opportunity to provide feedback.

Documentation Requirements for Effective Closure
1. Project Closure Report
- Includes a summary of the project, confirmation of project deliverables, performance metrics, and any unresolved issues or risks.
2. Lessons Learned Document
- Captures insights and experiences from the project, detailing what was successful and what needs improvement.
3. Final Project Performance Report
- Provides a comprehensive review of the project's performance against the initial baselines of scope, schedule, and budget.
4. Resource Release Forms
- Documentation confirming that all resources have been properly released from the project.
5. Stakeholder Acceptance Forms
- Signed forms from stakeholders acknowledging the receipt and acceptance of the project's deliverables.

Conclusion
Administrative closure is more than just a formality; it is a crucial phase that ensures projects are concluded with a focus on compliance, learning, and resource optimization. By effectively managing this phase, project managers can uphold the integrity of their project management practices and contribute positively to the organization's reputation and knowledge base. Here is a set of practice questions designed to test and reinforce understanding of Project Integration Management processes, their Inputs, Tools and Techniques, Outputs (ITTOs), and their application in real-world project scenarios. Each question is followed by a detailed explanation to enhance learning.

Question 1: What is the primary purpose of the Develop Project Charter process in Project Integration Management?

- A) To track project performance and make necessary adjustments
- B) To formally authorize the existence of a project
- C) To close the project and finalize all activities
- D) To manage stakeholders' expectations and engagement

Correct Answer: B) To formally authorize the existence of a project

- **Explanation**: The Develop Project Charter process is crucial as it provides the project manager with the authority to allocate organizational resources to project activities. It formally authorizes the existence of a project, setting the initial scope, identifying stakeholders, and defining the roles and responsibilities of the project team.

Question 2: Which document is NOT typically an input to the Develop Project Management Plan process?

- A) Project Charter
- B) Stakeholder Register
- C) Project Funding Requirements
- D) Enterprise Environmental Factors

Correct Answer: C) Project Funding Requirements

- **Explanation**: Project Funding Requirements are typically outputs of the planning processes that determine budget needs, not direct inputs to the Develop Project Management Plan process. Inputs generally include the Project Charter, outputs from other processes (such as the Stakeholder Register), and Enterprise Environmental Factors that influence how the project is managed.

Question 3: In Project Integration Management, what tool or technique is essential for the Direct and Manage Project Work process?

- A) Expert Judgment
- B) Change Control Tools
- C) Variance Analysis
- D) Project Management Information System (PMIS)

Correct Answer: D) Project Management Information System (PMIS)

- **Explanation**: PMIS is crucial in the Direct and Manage Project Work process as it supports the project team in executing the tasks defined in the project management plan. This system helps in facilitating communication, integrating project components, and providing tools to assist in scheduling, managing resources, and performing other project management activities efficiently.

Question 4: What is a key output of the Perform Integrated Change Control process?

- A) Change log
- B) Project schedule
- C) Cost forecasts
- D) Quality metrics

Correct Answer: A) Change log

- **Explanation**: A key output of the Perform Integrated Change Control process is the change log. This document records all changes requested, approved, and denied. It's essential for tracking changes and ensuring transparency in how alterations to the project scope, timeline, and costs are managed.

Question 5: How does the Closing Process in Project Integration Management contribute to project success?
- A) It provides a structured procedure for verifying that all project work is completed satisfactorily.
- B) It ensures that all project funds are used appropriately.
- C) It assists in the ongoing management of project team resources.
- D) It extends the project schedule to accommodate additional scope.

Correct Answer: A) It provides a structured procedure for verifying that all project work is completed satisfactorily.
- **Explanation**: The Closing Process is vital for confirming that all project phases have been completed successfully, all contractual obligations have been met, and that project deliverables are accepted. This formal closure helps in documenting project outcomes, lessons learned, and releases project resources, contributing to the overall success and organizational learning.

These questions are designed to challenge the understanding of Project Integration Management and provide a comprehensive insight into how these processes contribute to successful project execution. By examining these areas, learners can deepen their knowledge and apply these concepts effectively in real-world project scenarios. Project Integration Management is a critical knowledge area in project management as it involves making decisions about resource allocation, balancing competing demands, and integrating and reconciling the various elements of the project. The processes within this knowledge area interact extensively with processes from other knowledge areas to ensure a seamless, coherent workflow and successful project outcomes. Below, we explore these interactions with examples to illustrate their relationships and dependencies:

Key Processes of Project Integration Management
1. **Develop Project Charter**
2. **Develop Project Management Plan**
3. **Direct and Manage Project Work**
4. **Monitor and Control Project Work**
5. **Perform Integrated Change Control**
6. **Close Project or Phase**

Interactions with Other Knowledge Areas
1. **Develop Project Charter and Scope Management**:
- **Interaction**: The project charter, developed as part of Project Integration Management, is directly influenced by the initial scope definition from Scope Management.
- **Example**: When the project scope is initially defined, it provides the necessary information regarding project objectives, deliverables, and boundaries that are essential for drafting the project charter.

2. **Develop Project Management Plan and All Knowledge Areas**:
- **Interaction**: The project management plan integrates all subsidiary plans from various knowledge areas, including scope, schedule, cost, quality, resource, communications, risk, procurement, and stakeholder engagement plans.

- **Example**: The integration of the schedule management plan (Schedule Management) and the cost management plan (Cost Management) into the project management plan ensures that the planning for time and budget are aligned and coherent.

3. Direct and Manage Project Work and Quality Management:
- **Interaction**: While directing and managing project work, compliance with the quality management plan is crucial.
- **Example**: As the project execution unfolds, quality assurance activities are conducted to ensure that the deliverables are in line with the quality standards defined in the Quality Management plan.

4. Monitor and Control Project Work and Risk Management:
- **Interaction**: Monitoring and controlling project work involves assessing performance and implementing necessary changes, which often require revisiting the risk management plan.
- **Example**: Continuous monitoring might identify new risks or changes in existing risks, prompting updates to the risk responses in the Risk Management plan.

5. Perform Integrated Change Control and All Knowledge Areas:
- **Interaction**: This process involves reviewing all change requests, approving changes, and managing changes to the deliverables or project baselines across all project aspects, which include scope, schedule, cost, and quality.
- **Example**: A change request to extend the project schedule will require adjustments not only in the Schedule Management plan but may also affect the Cost Management and Resource Management plans.

6. Close Project or Phase and Procurement Management:
- **Interaction**: Closing the project or a project phase involves confirming that all contracted work is completed as per the agreement, which is an aspect of Procurement Management.
- **Example**: Final audits of the procurement contracts to ensure all deliverables are received and payments are complete before officially closing the project phase.

Conclusion

The processes within Project Integration Management are designed to ensure that project management is not conducted in silos; instead, they guarantee that there is coordination and alignment among all aspects of the project. By managing these interactions effectively, project managers can ensure that the project progresses smoothly, meets its objectives, aligns with stakeholder expectations, and adheres to its constraints and requirements. This integrated approach is vital for managing complex projects where multiple variables and changes can significantly impact the project outcome. The construction of a multi-functional sports complex represented a complex, multi-year project undertaken by a major construction company. The project aimed to deliver a state-of-the-art facility with multiple sports arenas, commercial spaces, and a community center. The budget was estimated at $150 million, with a timeline of three years for completion.

Challenges Faced
1. **Scope Management**: Balancing the diverse needs of stakeholders including sports teams, community groups, and commercial tenants.
2. **Schedule Delays**: Initial delays due to land acquisition disputes and later unforeseen geological challenges that required redesigning foundational structures.

3. **Budget Overruns**: Increased costs arising from delays and changes in building materials prices.
4. **Stakeholder Conflicts**: Differing priorities among stakeholders led to numerous change requests, complicating project execution.

Strategies Employed
Robust Project Charter Development:
The project began with a well-defined project charter, which included clear project objectives, identified all key stakeholders, and outlined the authority of the project manager. This charter proved crucial in aligning expectations and authorizing resource allocation.

Comprehensive Project Management Plan:
The project management plan was developed meticulously to integrate and coordinate all areas of the project. This plan included detailed scope, schedule, cost, quality, resource, communication, risk, procurement, and stakeholder management plans.

Dynamic Change Control System:
A robust integrated change control system was implemented to manage changes systematically. Each change request was logged, assessed for impact on scope, schedule, and budget, and then approved, rejected, or deferred by a change control board comprising key stakeholders.

Effective Communication Channels:
Regular stakeholder meetings and updates were institutionalized to ensure all parties were kept informed about project progress, decisions, and changes. This helped in managing stakeholder expectations and resolving conflicts effectively.

Lessons Learned
1. **Importance of Early Stakeholder Engagement**: Engaging stakeholders early in the project helped identify potential conflicts and align expectations. Future projects should invest more time in stakeholder analysis during the early phases.
2. **Flexibility in Project Plans**: The need for adaptability in managing large-scale projects was evident. Future projects should plan for contingencies more robustly, allocating resources for potential delays and changes.
3. **Value of an Integrated Approach**: The integrated nature of the project management processes ensured that changes in one area (like scope or schedule) were evaluated concerning their impact on other areas (like budget and resources). This holistic view prevented many potential issues from becoming critical problems.
4. **Documentation and Records Are Critical**: Maintaining detailed records and documentation, especially concerning change requests and project decisions, was invaluable for transparency and for resolving discrepancies and claims.

Conclusion
The construction of the multi-functional sports complex, though fraught with challenges, was ultimately successful and delivered within a revised schedule and budget. The application of Project Integration Management processes proved vital in navigating the complexities of the project. The lessons learned from this project have since been incorporated into the company's project management methodology, enhancing its capability to manage large-scale, multifaceted projects more effectively.

IV. Project Scope Management:

The "Plan Scope Management" process is foundational within project management as it sets the groundwork for defining, managing, and controlling the project's scope. This process is critical because it ensures that the scope is accurately defined and measured, and that the project includes only the work required to complete the project successfully.

Purpose of the Plan Scope Management Process

The primary purpose of the Plan Scope Management process is to create a scope management plan that documents how the project scope will be defined, validated, and controlled throughout the project lifecycle. By establishing clear guidelines and procedures for scope management, this process helps prevent scope creep, ensures project objectives are met, and maintains project alignment with business goals.

Contribution to Project Success

Effective scope management is integral to the overall success of any project. It helps to ensure that all project work is aligned with the project objectives and that all necessary work (and only the necessary work) is included in the project. This precision in defining and managing scope aids in resource allocation, guides project decisions, and helps manage stakeholder expectations, thereby contributing significantly to project efficiency and effectiveness.

Key Components of a Scope Management Plan
1. Scope Definition:

- **Significance**: Clearly defines what is included and excluded in the project. This clarity helps all team members and stakeholders understand the boundaries of the project and what the project aims to deliver, thus preventing misunderstandings and scope creep.
- **Component Detail**: The scope definition will typically include project boundaries, deliverables, and the processes used to prepare the detailed project scope statement.

2. Work Breakdown Structure (WBS) Development:

- **Significance**: The WBS breaks down the scope into manageable sections, making it easier for team members to organize and implement project tasks. This breakdown helps in monitoring and controlling the project scope, schedule, and budget.
- **Component Detail**: This includes the methodology used to develop the WBS and the level of detail required.

3. Scope Verification:

- **Significance**: Involves formalizing acceptance of the completed project deliverables. This step is crucial to ensure that the deliverables meet the agreed-upon project scope and are accepted by the stakeholders.
- **Component Detail**: It outlines the process by which the project deliverables will be accepted and the criteria that must be met for acceptance.

4. Scope Control:

- **Significance**: Provides the process for managing changes to the scope. Effective scope control ensures that any changes to the scope are carefully evaluated and approved before being implemented, helping to manage costs and schedule impacts.
- **Component Detail**: Details the procedures for how scope changes will be performed, including how changes will be identified, classified, and whether they will impact the project baselines.

Conclusion

The Plan Scope Management process is essential for defining a clear framework and criteria for managing the project scope from start to finish. By meticulously planning how scope will be managed, project managers can significantly enhance the project's ability to meet its objectives, stay within budget, and adhere to its timeline, all of which are critical for the project's success. This process not only helps in effectively managing the project but also in aligning project objectives with business goals, thereby maximizing project value and stakeholder satisfaction.

The process of collecting requirements is fundamental in project management as it determines and documents the needs and expectations of the stakeholders for achieving project objectives. Accurately collecting and agreeing on these requirements ensures the project scope is clearly understood and managed.

Key Importance of Collecting Requirements:

1. **Defining Scope**: Proper collection of requirements is crucial for defining the project scope. This clarity helps prevent scope creep, which occurs when the project's scope is not accurately defined or controlled.
2. **Stakeholder Satisfaction**: By capturing all relevant stakeholder requirements, the project is more likely to meet or exceed stakeholder expectations, leading to higher satisfaction and support.
3. **Project Efficiency and Effectiveness**: Accurate requirements gathering helps in planning the project more effectively, ensuring resources are appropriately allocated, reducing waste, and increasing the likelihood of project success.
4. **Risk Reduction**: Thoroughly understanding requirements early in the project helps identify potential risks and ambiguities, allowing for earlier mitigation strategies.
5. **Baseline for Validation and Verification**: Requirements serve as a baseline against which project deliverables are developed, tested, and validated. This ensures the final products or services meet the intended purpose and solve the right problems.

Techniques Used to Gather and Prioritize Project Requirements
Gathering Techniques

1. **Interviews**: Conducting one-on-one or group interviews with stakeholders to gather detailed information about their needs and expectations.
2. **Focus Groups**: Bringing together pre-qualified stakeholders and subject matter experts to learn about their expectations and attitudes regarding the project's product, service, or result.
3. **Workshops**: Facilitative sessions that help bring various stakeholders together to define product requirements collectively.
4. **Surveys/Questionnaires**: Distributing surveys or questionnaires to a large group of people to gather quantitative and qualitative information about requirements.
5. **Observation**: Directly observing the work being performed by the end-users and gathering insights into the system, process, or product requirements.

6. **Prototypes**: Developing a working model of the expected product or system to clarify requirements by allowing stakeholders to interact with the prototype.
7. **Document Analysis**: Reviewing existing documentation and files to identify requirements from previously captured data.

Prioritization Techniques

1. **MoSCoW Method**: Categorizing requirements into Must have, Should have, Could have, and Won't have. This method helps stakeholders understand the priority of each requirement.
2. **100-Point Method**: Giving stakeholders 100 points each to distribute among the requirements. The more points a requirement receives, the higher its priority.
3. **Pairwise Comparison**: Comparing each requirement against all others to prioritize them based on their relative importance.
4. **Nominal Group Technique (NGT)**: A structured form of brainstorming that helps prioritize issues by letting participants vote on the importance of each requirement.

Conclusion

Collecting and prioritizing project requirements are critical steps in the project management process. They ensure that the project deliverables are aligned with stakeholder needs and expectations, provide a foundation for project planning, and set the stage for project success. Techniques for gathering and prioritizing requirements should be chosen based on the project context, the nature of the requirements, the number of stakeholders, and available resources. By effectively managing this process, project managers can significantly reduce project risks and increase the likelihood of delivering a successful project. The "Collect Requirements" process is a crucial step in project management, particularly in the planning phase, where stakeholders' needs and expectations are identified and documented. These requirements form the foundation for project scope, deliverables, and the work required to deliver the project. Understanding the Inputs, Tools and Techniques, and Outputs (ITTOs) of this process is essential for creating comprehensive and traceable requirements documentation that accurately reflects stakeholder needs and supports successful project delivery.

Inputs

1. **Project Charter**: Provides a high-level description of the project, including its objectives and constraints, which guides the requirements gathering process.
2. **Stakeholder Register**: Contains all information regarding the stakeholders, including their interests, influence, and potential impact on the project. This register is crucial for identifying who will provide requirements.
3. **Business Documents**: May include business case documents and benefits management plan, which give context to the business need and the expected benefits from the project, influencing requirement priorities.

Tools and Techniques

1. **Interviews**: Conducting direct discussions with stakeholders to elicit requirements. This technique allows for a deep understanding of stakeholder needs and expectations.
2. **Focus Groups**: Gathering pre-qualified stakeholders and subject matter experts to learn about their expectations and attitudes about a proposed product, service, or result.
3. **Facilitated Workshops**: Bringing key cross-functional stakeholders together to define product requirements. Workshops like JAD (Joint Application Development) sessions are particularly effective for this.

4. **Brainstorming**: Generating a broad list of ideas, which are then narrowed down to the best options to be developed into a set of actionable and achievable requirements.
5. **Observation**: Also known as job shadowing, this involves watching stakeholders work to discover requirements based on their work processes.
6. **Surveys/Questionnaires**: Distributing written sets of questions to various stakeholders to quickly gather information from a large number of people.
7. **Prototypes**: Creating a working model of the expected product to help stakeholders better understand and refine requirements.
8. **Benchmarking**: Comparing current project practices against those of similar projects within or outside the performing organization to generate ideas for improvement and provide a basis upon which performance standards can be measured.
9. **Context Diagrams**: Visual depictions of the product scope showing a business system and how people and other systems interact with it.
10. **Document Analysis**: Reviewing available documentation to elicit requirements like contracts, marketing literature, or agreements provided by the customer.

Outputs
Requirements Documentation:
This document includes detailed descriptions of project and product requirements, which include business requirements, stakeholder requirements, solution requirements, transition requirements, and assumptions and constraints. It is comprehensive and describes what needs to be delivered and the conditions of acceptance.

Requirements Traceability Matrix:
A grid that links requirements from their origin through the life of the project. It provides a means to track requirements, ensures they are addressed throughout the project lifecycle, and helps manage changes to requirements.

Contribution to Comprehensive and Traceable Requirements Documentation
Comprehensive Requirements:
By employing diverse techniques such as interviews, workshops, and observation, the process ensures that all possible requirements are captured, not only from the perspective of what stakeholders say they want but also from what can be inferred through behavior and operational needs.

Traceability:
The Requirements Traceability Matrix (RTM) plays a key role in ensuring each requirement's traceability back to its source, whether it's a stakeholder, a document, or an observation. This traceability ensures that every requirement can be justified and aligned with business objectives and stakeholder expectations. It also facilitates changes in requirements as the project progresses, ensuring that changes are well-documented and their impacts thoroughly analyzed.

The "Collect Requirements" process, through its structured approach using various tools and techniques, ensures that requirements are not only gathered comprehensively but are also well-documented and traceable. This meticulous documentation aids in managing stakeholder expectations, guiding design and implementation, and ensuring a successful project delivery aligned with the defined objectives.

Overview of the Requirements Traceability Matrix (RTM)

The Requirements Traceability Matrix (RTM) is a document used to ensure that all project requirements are linked to their origins and tracked throughout the project lifecycle. It is a critical tool in project scope management, helping to monitor and control the scope by ensuring that all requirements are accounted for, met, and validated.

Purpose of the Requirements Traceability Matrix

1. **Verification and Validation**: Ensures that each requirement is clearly defined, agreed upon, and tested, verifying that all are included in the final deliverables.
2. **Scope Control**: Helps in managing changes to the project scope. By providing a clear linkage between requirements and their fulfillment in specific deliverables, the RTM helps in assessing the impact of any proposed changes.
3. **Enhanced Communication**: Facilitates better communication among team members by providing a clear reference of what needs to be achieved and the basis for these requirements.
4. **Documentation and Compliance**: Assists in documenting the traceability of requirements for audit purposes and ensures compliance with the defined processes and standards.

Key Components of a Requirements Traceability Matrix

A typical RTM includes several columns, each detailing aspects of project requirements and their traceability:

Example of a Requirements Traceability Matrix

Here's an example of how an RTM might look for a software development project:

- **Requirement ID**: A unique identifier for each requirement.
- **Requirement Description**: A detailed description of what the requirement entails.
- **Source**: The origin of the requirement, which could be a stakeholder, existing system, regulatory requirement, etc.
- **Priority**: Indicates the relative importance of the requirement (e.g., high, medium, low).
- **Baseline Document**: Refers to the document or documents where the requirement is originally described and approved.
- **Assigned To**: The person or team responsible for implementing the requirement.
- **Status**: The current status of the requirement (e.g., under review, approved, implemented, tested).

Requirement ID	Description	Source	Priority	Baseline Document	Assigned To	Status	Deliverable(s)
REQ-001	User login functionality	Client	High	SRS Document	Dev Team	Completed	Login Module
REQ-002	Email notification feature	Stakeholder Feedback	Medium	Project Charter	Dev Team	In Progress	Notification System
REQ-003	Data encryption at rest	Regulatory Requirement	High	Compliance Document	Security Team	Planned	Security Enhancements
REQ-004	Mobile responsiveness	User Survey	Medium	SRS Document	UI/UX Team	Testing	Mobile Interface

- **Deliverable(s)**: Links to specific project deliverables that satisfy the requirement.

Using the RTM to Monitor and Control Project Scope

- **Identifying Scope Changes**: The RTM can be used to identify when new requirements are added or existing ones are modified or removed, helping project managers assess and manage scope changes effectively.
- **Impact Analysis**: Before approving changes, project managers can use the RTM to analyze the impact of changes on project deliverables and other related requirements, ensuring that all implications are considered.
- **Tracking Progress and Compliance**: By updating the status of each requirement as the project progresses, the RTM provides a visual representation of project progress and compliance with the requirements.
- **Ensuring Deliverable Completeness**: By linking requirements to specific deliverables, the RTM helps ensure that all project outputs meet the agreed-upon requirements, thus avoiding scope creep and ensuring project quality.

The Requirements Traceability Matrix is an essential tool in project management. It not only aids in managing and controlling the project scope but also ensures that the final deliverables are compliant with the requirements, thus contributing to project success. The "Define Scope" process is a critical component of project planning that involves developing a detailed description of the project and its deliverables. It builds on the foundational information provided by the "Collect Requirements" process and refines it into a precise project scope statement. This process is essential for setting the boundaries of the project, which guides all subsequent project activities and decisions, ensuring that the project team and stakeholders have a clear understanding of what needs to be accomplished.

Significance of the Define Scope Process

1. **Clear Project Boundaries**: Define Scope establishes precise boundaries for what the project will and will not include, helping to manage stakeholders' expectations and preventing scope creep by clearly defining the limits of project work.
2. **Guidance for Decision Making**: A well-defined scope provides a basis for making project decisions throughout its lifecycle, supporting the project team in focusing their efforts on required tasks and deliverables.
3. **Basis for Future Project Planning**: The project scope statement serves as a reference for all future project planning processes, including time management, cost estimation, risk analysis, and resource allocation.
4. **Enhanced Stakeholder Alignment**: By clearly defining the scope, the process helps ensure that all stakeholders are aligned in their understanding of the project objectives and deliverables, reducing conflicts and misunderstandings.

Key Elements of a Project Scope Statement

The project scope statement is a critical document that outlines the detailed scope of work and is used throughout the project to make decisions about what is and isn't included in the project. Key elements typically included in the project scope statement are:

1. **Project Objectives**: Describes the project's purpose and its expected outcomes. Objectives should be specific, measurable, achievable, realistic, and time-bound (SMART).

2. **Project Deliverables**: Lists and describes the specific products, services, or results that the project is expected to produce. This includes both the final project deliverables and the key interim deliverables.
3. **Milestones**: Important checkpoints or interim deadlines that help to track project progress. Milestones are significant events within the project's timeline that are used to measure the progress of work.
4. **Technical Requirements**: Specifies the technical issues and other specialized details that must be considered to execute the project effectively. This may include limitations or standards that must be met as part of project delivery.
5. **Exclusions**: Explicitly states what is out of scope for the project. This section is crucial for preventing scope creep by clarifying what will not be addressed or produced by the project.
6. **Acceptance Criteria**: Defines the process and criteria for accepting completed project deliverables. These criteria are used to determine whether the work completed satisfies the project requirements and deliverables are fit for use.
7. **Project Constraints**: Identifies the restrictions that must be considered during project planning and execution, such as budget limitations, time constraints, or available resources.
8. **Assumptions**: States the assumptions on which the project scope and planning are based. These assumptions are considered to be true for planning purposes, although they may later prove to be incorrect.

The "Define Scope" process and the project scope statement together form a cornerstone of effective project management. They ensure all team members and stakeholders have a shared understanding of the project's scope and deliverables, which is critical for project success. This clarity and structure help manage expectations and guide the project through its completion, keeping it on track and aligned with the originally established objectives. The project scope statement and the project charter are foundational documents in project management, each playing a crucial role in defining the project's boundaries and objectives. Though they are related and interconnected, they serve distinct purposes and are used at different stages of the project management process.

Project Charter

The **project charter** is a document issued at the very beginning of the project. It formally authorizes the existence of a project and provides the project manager with the authority to allocate organizational resources to project activities. It is typically created during the project initiation phase.

Key Components of the Project Charter:
- **Project purpose or justification**: Explains why the project is necessary.
- **High-level project description and requirements**: Provides a brief description of the project and its requirements.
- **Assigned project manager and authority level**: Names the project manager and outlines their authority.
- **Summary milestone schedule**: Lists major project milestones and their anticipated completion dates.
- **Preapproved financial resources**: Indicates the budget allocated to the project.
- **Stakeholder list**: Identifies the project's stakeholders.
- **Initial risks**: Outlines potential risks at the outset of the project.

The project charter sets the stage for defining the project by outlining its general scope, identifying its stakeholders, and linking the project to the ongoing work of the organization.

Project Scope Statement

The **project scope statement**, developed during the project planning phase, provides a detailed description of the project and its deliverables. It builds upon the initial information provided in the project charter and describes the project scope in greater detail.

Key Components of the Project Scope Statement:

- **Detailed description of the project scope**: More comprehensive than the outline provided in the charter.
- **Product acceptance criteria**: Specific conditions that must be met for the project deliverables to be accepted.
- **Deliverables**: A detailed list of outcomes to be provided by the project.
- **Project exclusions**: Explicitly states what is out of scope, clarifying what will not be addressed by the project.
- **Constraints**: Lists and describes the restrictions that apply to the project.
- **Assumptions**: Documents the assumptions that are being made in planning the project.

Relationship and Roles in Defining Project Scope

The relationship between the project charter and the project scope statement is one of progression and refinement:

Initiation to Planning:

The project charter initiates the project by defining its broad objectives and authorizing work to begin, thereby setting the framework. The project scope statement, developed during the subsequent planning phase, refines and elaborates on this framework.

General to Detailed:

The charter provides a high-level overview of project needs and expected deliverables, while the scope statement details the specific work to be done, how it will be accomplished, and what will be achieved.

Authorization to Execution:

The charter grants the project manager the authority to proceed and manage the project resources. In contrast, the scope statement helps the project manager and the team understand exactly what needs to be done and serves as a critical reference document to guide project execution and help measure project performance.

The project charter and the project scope statement work in tandem: the charter kicks off the project with necessary approvals and resources, while the scope statement details the path the project will take, ensuring that everyone involved has a clear understanding of the project's objectives and limitations. Together, they provide a comprehensive outline and plan for achieving the project goals, crucial for effective scope management. The "Create WBS" (Work Breakdown Structure) process is fundamental in project management as it provides a structured way of dividing the project scope and deliverables into smaller, more manageable components called work packages. The WBS is a key project deliverable that organizes the team's work into manageable sections, ensuring that the entire scope of the project is covered and nothing is overlooked.

<h1 style="text-align:center">Purpose of Creating a Work Breakdown Structure (WBS)</h1>

1. **Clarification of Project Scope**: The WBS visually breaks down the scope of the project into manageable chunks that can be understood and managed more effectively. It translates project scope and deliverables into a hierarchy of deliverable-oriented elements.
2. **Foundation for Planning**: It serves as the foundation for project planning activities, providing a structured vision of what has to be delivered. Using the WBS, project managers can create a more accurate schedule, cost estimation, and resource plan.
3. **Assignment of Responsibilities**: The WBS facilitates the assignment of responsibilities, allocation of resources, and budgeting as each element of the WBS can be assigned to specific teams or individuals.
4. **Risk Identification**: By breaking down the project into smaller parts, it is easier to identify potential risks at different levels of the project. Each segment can be analyzed for possible problems, allowing for more targeted risk management.
5. **Improved Communication**: The WBS helps improve communication among stakeholders by providing a clear picture of project deliverables and the work required. It serves as a reference point for discussions about project progress and scope changes.
6. **Enhanced Tracking and Control**: The WBS allows for better tracking of project progress and performance by comparing planned outcomes with actual results at various stages of the project. This structure supports effective project monitoring and controlling processes.

How a WBS Helps in Decomposing Project Scope into Manageable Work Packages
Hierarchical Decomposition:

The WBS breaks down the project scope into a hierarchical structure, starting from the highest level, which encapsulates the total deliverables of the project, down to the lowest level components or work packages that are sufficiently detailed to be scheduled, cost estimated, executed, and monitored.

Definition of Work Packages:

At the lowest level of the WBS, the work is segmented into work packages that define specific tasks or activities that are required to produce each deliverable. These work packages are the fundamental building blocks of project planning and execution.

Clear Deliverable Outlines:

Each element of the WBS is a deliverable or an outcome. This outcome-oriented approach ensures that every piece of work is focused on producing a specific output, which cumulatively leads to achieving the project's final objectives.

Integration and Overlap Identification:

As the project is broken down, overlaps and dependencies between different parts of the project become clearer. This helps in integrating various project efforts and aligning them more closely with the project's objectives.

The WBS is an essential tool for managing projects efficiently. It systematically breaks down the overwhelming complexity of a project into smaller, more manageable parts, ensuring thorough planning, effective execution, risk management, and overall project control. It not only supports project managers in organizing and defining the total scope of the project but also provides teams with a clear roadmap and focused deliverables to work towards, thereby enhancing project coherence and team alignment. The "Create WBS" process is a core function in project scope management. It involves subdividing the major project deliverables and project work into smaller, more manageable components. Understanding the

Inputs, Tools and Techniques, and Outputs (ITTOs) of this process is essential for creating a detailed and structured Work Breakdown Structure (WBS) that organizes and defines the total scope of the project.

Inputs

1. **Scope Management Plan**: Provides guidance on how the WBS should be structured and outlines the process for its approval.
2. **Project Scope Statement**: Offers a detailed description of the project scope, deliverables, and boundaries that serve as the basis for developing the WBS.
3. **Requirements Documentation**: Contains detailed descriptions of project and product requirements which are essential for ensuring that all aspects of these requirements are captured in the WBS.
4. **Enterprise Environmental Factors (EEFs)**: Might include organizational culture and structure, industry-specific WBS standards that could influence the WBS development.
5. **Organizational Process Assets (OPAs)**: Include policies, procedures, and templates from previous projects that can be leveraged to construct the WBS.

Tools and Techniques

1. **Decomposition**: The primary technique used in the Create WBS process. It involves breaking down project deliverables and work into smaller components. The decomposition is guided by the scope statement and requirements documentation, ensuring completeness in capturing all work.
2. **Expert Judgment**: Engaging with subject matter experts who provide insights based on their experience to ensure that the WBS is comprehensive and all-encompassing.
3. **Graphic Representation**: Tools such as organizational charts or WBS software are often used to visually represent the breakdown of work, making it easier to understand and manage.

Outputs

1. **Scope Baseline**:

This includes the WBS, WBS Dictionary, and the Project Scope Statement. The WBS forms part of the scope baseline and is used as a reference to monitor and control the project scope.

- **Work Breakdown Structure (WBS)**: A hierarchical decomposition of the total scope of work to be carried out by the project team to accomplish the project objectives and create the required deliverables.
- **WBS Dictionary**: Accompanies the WBS and provides detailed descriptions of each component of the WBS, including work packages and control accounts.

2. **Project Documents Updates**:

Documents that might be updated include the assumption log and requirements documentation, reflecting changes or clarifications resulting from the WBS development process.

Contribution to Project Management

The Create WBS process is vital for several reasons:

- **Clarity and Direction**: The WBS provides a clear and precise structure that outlines and organizes the work to be done, breaking complex projects into manageable tasks.
- **Foundation for Planning**: It serves as the basis for many other project planning processes, such as scheduling, cost estimating, and resource allocation.

- **Control and Monitoring**: The WBS allows for the effective monitoring and control of the project scope, facilitating easier management of scope creep and ensuring all project work is authorized and aligned with project objectives.
- **Accountability**: By defining clear work packages, the WBS assigns responsibility and accountability for tasks, facilitating better communication and coordination among team members.

The ITTOs of the Create WBS process collectively ensure that the WBS is comprehensive and aligns with the project scope and requirements. This structured breakdown is essential for ensuring that the project is delivered successfully, meeting all its objectives and deliverables within the agreed scope. The Work Breakdown Structure (WBS) dictionary is an essential document that provides detailed information about each element within the Work Breakdown Structure. While the WBS visually decomposes the project into smaller components, the WBS dictionary offers a descriptive backing to each component, ensuring that everyone involved has a clear understanding of the tasks and deliverables.

Purpose of the WBS Dictionary

The WBS dictionary serves as a complementary document to the WBS by providing detailed descriptions of the work content of each WBS element. It clarifies the deliverables and defines the work scope at each level of the WBS, thereby minimizing ambiguity and enhancing clarity. This detailed description helps all project team members understand what needs to be done, who is responsible, and the criteria for completing each component satisfactorily.

How the WBS Dictionary Complements the WBS

The WBS provides a structured decomposition of the project into deliverable-oriented elements, usually represented in a hierarchical tree structure. However, it often lacks detailed descriptions of each element. The WBS dictionary fills this gap by providing comprehensive information about each WBS component, including:

1. **Detailed Descriptions**: Explains what each component of the WBS actually involves, detailing the work required to complete each part of the project.
2. **Ownership Information**: Identifies who is responsible for the delivery of each component. This helps in accountability and resource allocation.
3. **Cost Estimates**: Provides estimated costs for each element, which is crucial for budget planning and control.
4. **Time Estimates**: Includes duration and scheduling information for each task, aiding in overall project scheduling.
5. **Resources Required**: Lists the resources needed to complete each element, whether these are human resources, technology, or materials.
6. **Quality Criteria**: Specifies the quality requirements and acceptance criteria for each deliverable, ensuring that outputs meet the required standards.
7. **Dependencies**: Details the dependencies between WBS elements, which is vital for scheduling and risk management.

Example of Information Included in a WBS Dictionary

Consider a project to develop a new software application. A component of the WBS might be "1.3 User Interface Design." The corresponding entry in the WBS dictionary might include:

- **Description**: Design and prototype the user interface for the application, based on user requirements and feedback.
- **Responsible**: John Doe, UI/UX Designer.

- **Estimated Cost**: $15,000.
- **Estimated Duration**: 3 weeks.
- **Resources**: UX design tools, access to user testing panels.
- **Quality Criteria**: The interface must pass usability testing with a score of at least 85% on user satisfaction.
- **Dependencies**: Requires completion of "1.2 User Requirements Analysis."

Importance in Scope Management

The WBS dictionary is vital in scope management as it provides the necessary details to ensure that all project stakeholders have a clear, shared understanding of what each part of the project entails. This understanding helps to manage expectations, facilitate communication, and ensure that each component of the project is completed as planned. It acts as a reference that can be consulted to resolve ambiguities and confirm scope details throughout the project lifecycle.

The WBS and the WBS dictionary are instrumental in providing a dual-layered structural and descriptive foundation for effective project management, ensuring each task within the project is executed with clarity and precision.

Concept of Scope Baseline

The scope baseline is a component of the project management plan and includes three key elements:

1. **Project Scope Statement**: This document details the project's deliverables, boundaries, assumptions, and constraints. It provides a clear definition of what is included in the project and what is not.
2. **Work Breakdown Structure (WBS)**: A hierarchical decomposition of the total scope of work to be executed by the project team to accomplish the project objectives and create the required deliverables.
3. **WBS Dictionary**: Provides detailed information about each element of the WBS, including the definition of work, the assignment of responsibilities, milestones, and resources.

Role in Monitoring and Controlling Project Scope

The scope baseline is vital for monitoring and controlling the scope of a project throughout its lifecycle. Here's how it is used:

- **Performance Measurement**: It serves as a standard against which actual performance is measured. This is crucial for identifying variances from the planned scope and determining whether corrective or preventive actions are needed.
- **Change Control**: The scope baseline is integral to the change control process. Any proposed changes to the project scope must be evaluated against the baseline to assess their impact on the project's time, cost, resources, and quality. Only approved changes can modify the scope baseline, ensuring that all changes are controlled and documented.
- **Preventing Scope Creep**: By providing a clear definition of what is included in the project scope and what is not, the scope baseline helps to manage and prevent scope creep, which can lead to project delays, budget overruns, and other issues.

Integration with Other Project Baselines

The scope baseline does not operate in isolation but is used in conjunction with other project baselines, particularly the schedule and cost baselines. Here's how they interact:

Schedule Baseline:

This baseline details the planned start and finish dates for the project activities. Changes in the project scope often affect the project schedule, as additional tasks may require more time, or changes may streamline processes and reduce the time needed. The integration of the scope baseline with the schedule baseline allows for coordinated adjustments that align with the project's time objectives.

Cost Baseline:

This is a budgeted allocation of the funds necessary to complete the project tasks as defined in the scope baseline. Any change to the project scope usually has a financial impact. Therefore, adjustments to the scope baseline necessitate corresponding adjustments in the cost baseline to ensure the project remains financially viable.

Performance Monitoring:

Using tools like Earned Value Management (EVM), project managers can integrate scope, schedule, and cost baselines to assess project performance. This comprehensive view helps in identifying whether the project is ahead, on track, or behind the planned progress and budget, allowing for timely corrective actions.

Conclusion

The scope baseline is a critical tool for ensuring that a project adheres to its defined scope throughout its duration. By integrating the scope baseline with the schedule and cost baselines, project managers can maintain better control over the project, ensuring that it meets its objectives efficiently and effectively. This integration is key to successful project management, as it allows for a holistic view of project performance and facilitates proactive management of changes and challenges. The "Validate Scope" process is a crucial phase in project management that involves formalizing acceptance of the project's completed deliverables. This process is critical because it ensures that deliverables meet the defined requirements and acceptance criteria agreed upon by the project stakeholders. It is distinct from quality control, which is concerned with the correctness of the deliverables and meeting the quality requirements specified for the products.

Importance of Validate Scope Process
1. Stakeholder Satisfaction:

Validate Scope is essential for confirming that the project deliverables satisfy the stakeholders' requirements as initially agreed upon. By involving stakeholders in the evaluation process, it helps ensure their expectations are met, thus maintaining their support and satisfaction.

2. Project Alignment:

This process ensures that the project remains aligned with its objectives throughout its lifecycle. It provides an opportunity to make adjustments based on stakeholder feedback before the project moves further along, which can prevent costly changes later.

3. Progress Measurement:

Validating scope helps in objectively measuring project progress by marking milestones when deliverables are formally accepted. This aids in performance reporting and gives stakeholders a clear view of where the project stands in terms of its schedule and budget.

4. Change Management:

During scope validation, if the deliverables are found not to meet the agreed-upon requirements, the necessary changes can be identified and managed through the Perform Integrated Change Control process. This helps in keeping the project on track and aligned with stakeholder expectations.

Key Activities Performed During Scope Validation
Review Deliverables:
The first step in the Validate Scope process is to inspect the completed project deliverables against the documented requirements and acceptance criteria. This review is typically conducted by the project team along with the stakeholders.

Gather Stakeholder Acceptance:
Once the deliverables have been reviewed and deemed to meet the specified requirements, formal acceptance is obtained from the stakeholders. This acceptance is often documented in the form of signed acceptance forms or through a formal approval in project management software.

Identify and Document Variances:
If discrepancies or variances are found between the completed deliverables and the acceptance criteria, these issues are documented. The documentation is crucial for the change control process, where decisions are made on whether to adjust the scope, schedule, or costs to accommodate the changes needed to meet the acceptance criteria.

Update Records and Adjust Plans:
Following stakeholder feedback and acceptance, project records are updated to reflect the validated status of the deliverables. If necessary, the project management plan and other project documents are adjusted to align with any agreed changes or updates resulting from the validation process.

Communicate with Stakeholders:
Communication is a vital part of the Validate Scope process. The results of the validation, including stakeholder feedback and final decisions, are communicated to all relevant stakeholders to ensure transparency and maintain trust. The Validate Scope process is essential for controlling project scope and ensuring that the project delivers the value that was intended. By systematically reviewing and obtaining formal acceptance of project deliverables, this process not only confirms that deliverables meet stakeholder requirements but also plays a crucial role in maintaining project governance and stakeholder satisfaction throughout the project lifecycle.

Validate Scope Process Overview
The Validate Scope process is essential in project management as it involves the formal acceptance of the project deliverables by the stakeholders. This process occurs at the end of each phase or upon the completion of set deliverable milestones and is crucial for ensuring that the deliverables meet the agreed-upon project requirements and stakeholders' expectations.

Accepted Deliverables
Definition: Accepted deliverables are those outputs that have been completed and formally approved by the stakeholders or clients. They have been reviewed and have met the acceptance criteria defined in the project scope statement.

Role in Validate Scope:

- **Formal Acceptance**: The core of the Validate Scope process is the formal acceptance of deliverables. This acceptance is crucial as it signifies that the deliverables meet stakeholders' needs and expectations, as per the agreed-upon project requirements.
- **Documentation**: Accepted deliverables are documented as part of the project records. This documentation is critical for closing out project phases, releasing funding, and providing evidence in case of disputes or audits.

Work Performance Data

Definition: Work performance data includes raw observations and measurements identified during the activities performed to carry out the project work. Examples include timesheets, completed tasks, resource utilization rates, and technical performance measures.

Role in Validate Scope:

- **Evaluation Basis**: Work performance data provides a factual basis for evaluating the deliverables against the scope baseline. This data helps to ascertain if the work was done correctly and in alignment with the planned activities.
- **Quality Assurance**: It plays a significant role in quality control processes that feed into scope validation. By analyzing this data, project teams can correct or improve work processes and outputs before they are presented to stakeholders for acceptance.
- **Progress Tracking**: This data helps in tracking progress against the schedule and scope baselines, identifying variances that might affect deliverable quality or timeliness, which are then addressed in the scope validation meetings.

Contribution to Formal Acceptance of Project Scope

Both accepted deliverables and work performance data are integral to the formal acceptance of the project scope:

Ensuring Deliverable Conformity:

By using work performance data to track and measure deliverable development, project teams can ensure that each deliverable conforms to the predefined acceptance criteria. This rigorous tracking facilitates the acceptance process when stakeholders review the deliverables.

Building Stakeholder Confidence:

Regularly presenting stakeholders with work performance data and accepted deliverables builds confidence in the project team's ability to deliver as per the scope. This transparency helps in maintaining good stakeholder relations and facilitates smoother acceptance phases.

Feedback Mechanism:

The Validate Scope process, supported by deliverable acceptance and work performance data, provides a critical feedback mechanism for the project. It allows stakeholders to suggest necessary changes or confirm that the project can proceed as planned, thus ensuring that the project remains aligned with its objectives and stakeholders' expectations.

Mitigating Scope Creep:

Through the formal documentation and acceptance of each deliverable, and the continual analysis of work performance data, scope creep can be effectively mitigated. This ensures that all changes are controlled and approved, maintaining the integrity of the original project scope.

Conclusion

Accepted deliverables and work performance data are crucial in the Validate Scope process, enabling effective monitoring, control, and formal acceptance of project outputs. These elements ensure that the project delivers value as defined by the stakeholders' requirements, maintaining alignment with the project's defined scope and objectives throughout its lifecycle. The "Control Scope" process is crucial for ensuring that the project remains within its defined scope throughout its lifecycle. This process involves monitoring the status of the project and managing changes to the scope baseline, which helps to ensure that all authorized work is completed while preventing unauthorized work from creeping into the project.

Significance of the Control Scope Process

1. **Prevents Scope Creep**: Scope creep is one of the major risks in project management, referring to uncontrolled changes or continuous growth in a project's scope without adjustments to time, cost, and resources. Control Scope helps in identifying and preventing scope creep, ensuring the project stays aligned with agreed objectives.
2. **Ensures Project Objectives Are Met**: By keeping the project aligned with its initial scope, the Control Scope process ensures that the project objectives set during the planning phase are met. This alignment is critical for the successful delivery of the project as per stakeholder expectations.
3. **Optimizes Resource Use**: Effective scope control ensures that resources are not wasted on unapproved and unplanned work. This optimization of resources contributes to the overall efficiency and effectiveness of the project.
4. **Enhances Stakeholder Satisfaction**: Maintaining a clear and controlled scope helps manage stakeholder expectations throughout the project. Regularly involving stakeholders in scope reviews increases transparency and builds trust.

Key Activities in the Control Scope Process

1. **Scope Tracking**: Regular monitoring of project scope against the project baseline. This involves assessing performance to detect any scope variances.
2. **Change Request Management**: Handling requests for changes or additions to the project scope. This includes reviewing, analyzing, and approving change requests through the Integrated Change Control process. Each change request must be evaluated for its impact on the project's scope, time, cost, quality, and resources.
3. **Rebaselineing**: If significant changes are approved, the scope baseline may need to be updated (rebaselined) to reflect the new scope of the project. This ensures that project monitoring and control activities are based on accurate and up-to-date information.
4. **Stakeholder Communication**: Keeping all stakeholders informed about the current scope status and any changes approved or proposed. This continuous communication helps ensure that all stakeholders have a clear understanding of the project scope and any changes that affect it.

Tools Used to Monitor and Control Project Scope

1. **Variance Analysis**: A technique used to determine the cause and degree of difference between the baseline and the actual performance. Variance analysis helps in identifying the magnitude of scope changes and deciding on necessary corrective actions.

2. **Trend Analysis**: Examining project performance over time to detect whether performance is improving or deteriorating. This analysis can provide early indications of scope issues that could become more significant if not addressed.
3. **Configuration Management Systems**: These systems ensure that the configuration of project deliverables and the information about them are consistent and maintained. They help manage the scope by controlling how changes to the deliverables are introduced and communicated.
4. **Scope Change Control System**: A formal process by which the project scope is changed, including the paperwork, tracking systems, and approval levels necessary for authorizing changes. This system is integral to maintaining control over the scope throughout the project.

By effectively managing and controlling project scope, project managers can mitigate risks associated with scope creep, ensure resource efficiency, and maintain stakeholder satisfaction. The Control Scope process is thus essential for guiding the project successfully to its completion according to the planned objectives and constraints.

Definition of Scope Creep

Scope creep refers to the uncontrolled expansion to project scope without adjustments to time, resources, and costs, which can occur when the scope of a project is not accurately defined, documented, or controlled. It is typically caused by the project team taking on additional work beyond the agreed-upon project objectives and deliverables without proper change control processes.

Impact on Project Success

Scope creep can have several negative impacts on project success:
1. **Resource Drain**: Additional work requires more resources, potentially leading to resource shortages and increased costs that were not accounted for in the initial budget.
2. **Schedule Delays**: Additional tasks can delay the project timeline, impacting project milestones and potentially leading to missed deadlines.
3. **Reduced Quality**: Spreading resources thinner to cover more tasks can result in lower quality of deliverables.
4. **Stakeholder Dissatisfaction**: Continual changes can frustrate stakeholders, especially if changes lead to delays, increased costs, or reduced deliverable quality.
5. **Increased Risk**: Unplanned changes add uncertainty and increase the risk of project failure.

Strategies and Best Practices for Preventing and Managing Scope Creep
Clear Definition of Scope

- **Detailed Scope Statement**: Develop a comprehensive project scope statement that clearly defines what is included and excluded from the project. This document should be agreed upon by all key stakeholders.
- **Requirements Documentation**: Ensure all project requirements are well-documented, understood, and approved by stakeholders. Requirements should be specific, measurable, achievable, relevant, and time-bound (SMART).

Strong Change Control Processes

- **Formal Change Control System**: Implement a formal process to manage changes. This includes a change control board, documentation for every change request, and a clear procedure for approving or rejecting changes.
- **Change Log**: Maintain a change log to track all changes, including who requested the change, the reason for the change, and the impact on the project.

Effective Communication

- **Regular Stakeholder Engagement**: Keep stakeholders engaged and informed throughout the project. Regular communication can help manage expectations and ensure that stakeholders are aligned with the project's progress and objectives.
- **Feedback Loops**: Establish feedback mechanisms where team members and stakeholders can discuss project progress and potential scope adjustments. Use these discussions to reaffirm the project's scope and objectives.

Project Management Tools and Techniques

- **Work Breakdown Structure (WBS)**: Use a WBS to break down the project scope into manageable parts, ensuring each element of the project's deliverables is accounted for and no unauthorized work is undertaken.
- **Requirements Traceability Matrix (RTM)**: Utilize an RTM to link requirements to their delivery through the project lifecycle, ensuring all requirements are met without adding extras that are out of scope.

Education and Training

- **Educate Team and Stakeholders**: Ensure that all team members and stakeholders understand the impact of scope creep and the importance of adhering to the defined project scope. Training on change management processes is also beneficial.

Frequent Scope Reviews

- **Regular Scope Audits**: Conduct regular scope reviews to ensure that the project remains on track with the defined scope. These reviews can help identify potential scope creep early before it becomes a significant issue.

Conclusion

Managing scope creep is vital for maintaining project integrity and ensuring successful outcomes. By setting clear project boundaries, maintaining rigorous change control processes, and ensuring regular communication and stakeholder engagement, project managers can mitigate the risks associated with scope creep. These practices help ensure that the project delivers the agreed-upon deliverables within the approved budget and timeline, ultimately satisfying stakeholder expectations and achieving project objectives. Variance analysis is a critical tool in the Control Scope process, vital for ensuring that a project adheres to its defined scope and objectives. It involves quantitatively comparing planned project performance (often outlined in the project management plan and scope baseline) against actual performance. This analysis is fundamental in detecting deviations that might affect the project's scope, timeline, budget, or quality.

Importance of Variance Analysis in the Control Scope Process

1. **Early Detection of Scope Deviations**: Variance analysis helps in identifying discrepancies between the planned and actual scope early in the project lifecycle. Early detection allows project managers to take corrective actions before these deviations lead to significant impacts or become more costly to address.
2. **Ensuring Project Objectives Are Met**: By continuously monitoring scope variance, project managers can ensure that the project remains aligned with its objectives. This alignment is crucial for delivering the project as per the stakeholder's expectations and requirements.

3. **Maintaining Budget and Schedule Control**: Scope variances often affect a project's budget and schedule. By understanding these variances, project managers can make informed decisions about necessary adjustments to resource allocation, scheduling, and budgeting to keep the project on track.
4. **Enhancing Decision-Making Quality**: Variance analysis provides data-driven insights that improve the quality of decision-making. Project managers can use these insights to justify decisions and communicate effectively with stakeholders about the status and health of the project.
5. **Minimizing Risks**: Scope variances can be indicative of underlying risks and issues. Regular variance analysis allows project managers to identify and mitigate these risks proactively.

Using Variance Analysis to Identify and Address Scope Deviations

1. **Establishing a Baseline**: Before variance analysis can be effectively used, a clear, detailed scope baseline must be established. This baseline should include specific, measurable deliverables and milestones against which actual performance can be compared.
2. **Regular Monitoring**: Project managers should regularly collect data on project performance, including task completion statuses, deliverable quality, and resource usage. This data is then compared against the baseline to identify variances.
3. **Analyzing Variance Causes**: When variances are identified, project managers need to analyze the root causes. Understanding why a variance has occurred is crucial for determining the appropriate corrective or preventive actions. Causes could range from estimation errors to unforeseen external factors or changes in project requirements.
4. **Taking Corrective Actions**: Depending on the nature and impact of the variance, corrective actions may involve adjusting project scope, re-estimating time and costs, reallocating resources, or modifying project strategies and plans.
5. **Communicating with Stakeholders**: Variance analysis results and subsequent actions should be communicated to all relevant stakeholders. Transparent communication helps in managing expectations and maintaining stakeholder engagement and trust.
6. **Updating Project Documentation**: After taking corrective actions, project documentation, including the project management plan and scope baseline, should be updated to reflect the new state of the project. This ensures that ongoing monitoring is based on accurate, current information.
7. **Review and Learn**: Post-project, it's important to review the variance analysis performed during the project to identify lessons learned and potential improvements in processes and execution for future projects.

Variance analysis is an essential component of effective project management. It not only helps in maintaining control over the project scope but also supports the overall management of the project by providing a mechanism for continuous evaluation and improvement. The Project Scope Management knowledge area is inherently interlinked with various other knowledge areas, particularly Project Integration Management and Project Quality Management. These interdependencies are crucial for ensuring the overall success and alignment of the project with its objectives and stakeholder expectations.

Project Scope Management and Project Integration Management

Interaction:
- **Develop Project Charter** (Integration Management) provides the initial scope and objectives that feed into the **Plan Scope Management** process.

- **Develop Project Management Plan** (Integration Management) incorporates the scope management plan, which is developed in the Scope Management processes. This plan outlines how the scope will be defined, validated, and controlled.
- **Direct and Manage Project Work** (Integration Management) involves executing the work according to the project management plan, where changes to the project scope are identified and necessary adjustments are made.
- **Monitor and Control Project Work** and **Perform Integrated Change Control** (Integration Management) evaluate the impact of scope changes and coordinate across the entire project to maintain alignment and integrate changes.

Example:
- During the execution of a software development project, a change request is made to add new features based on user feedback. The **Perform Integrated Change Control** process reviews and approves these changes, which are then incorporated into the scope baseline. The project's scope management plan, part of the overall project management plan, dictates how these changes are incorporated and communicated.

Project Scope Management and Project Quality Management

Interaction:
- **Plan Quality Management** (Quality Management) relies on the project scope to define quality requirements and standards for project deliverables that align with customer or stakeholder requirements.
- **Manage Quality** (Quality Management) involves quality assurance activities that ensure the quality management plan is being followed, directly influencing how the project scope is delivered.
- **Control Quality** (Quality Management) is closely tied to **Validate Scope** (Scope Management). Both processes ensure that the project deliverables meet the required standards and stakeholder approval, respectively.

Example:
- In a construction project, the **Control Quality** process checks if the materials used meet the quality standards defined in relation to the project scope, such as using a specific type of concrete. Simultaneously, **Validate Scope** ensures these materials and the completed structure meet the agreed-upon project deliverables and receive formal stakeholder acceptance.

Conclusion: The effectiveness of scope management is enhanced when integrated with other knowledge areas:
- **Integration Management** ensures that scope changes are well-managed and communicated across the project, aligning various project aspects with updated directives.
- **Quality Management** ensures that the deliverables produced meet the requirements set out in the scope and are of a quality that satisfies the stakeholders.

This integration across knowledge areas ensures that scope management does not occur in isolation but is a part of a broader effort to manage the project holistically, aligning with overall project objectives, managing stakeholder expectations, and ensuring high-quality outputs. Greenway Technologies embarked on an ambitious project to expand their main tech campus to accommodate rapid growth. The project included the construction of two new office buildings, additional parking facilities, and enhanced recreational areas. With an estimated project duration of 18 months and a budget of $45 million, it was essential that the Project Scope Management processes were meticulously applied to ensure the project's success.

Challenges Faced:

1. **Scope Creep**: As the project progressed, various stakeholders began requesting additional features, such as advanced security systems in buildings and more sophisticated landscaping, which were not included in the initial scope.
2. **Stakeholder Misalignment**: Diverse stakeholder groups had different priorities and expectations, making it challenging to define and agree on the project scope.
3. **Resource Constraints**: Midway through the project, it became apparent that the allocated resources were insufficient to cover the unexpected expansion of scope due to enhanced security and aesthetic features.

Strategies Employed:
Rigorous Scope Definition:

During the initial phases, the project team developed a detailed scope statement that clearly defined what was included and excluded in the project. This statement was revisited and adjusted as necessary with stakeholder consultation to ensure alignment.

Creation and Use of WBS:

The Work Breakdown Structure (WBS) was meticulously crafted to break down all deliverables into manageable components. This tool proved invaluable in organizing team efforts and clarifying deliverable ownership.

Implementation of a Formal Change Control Process:

To manage scope creep, a strict change control process was established. All change requests were required to undergo a thorough impact analysis demonstrating the necessity, benefits, and potential risks before any approval.

Regular Stakeholder Engagement:

Frequent communication with all stakeholders was prioritized to manage expectations and gather feedback. This proactive engagement helped in mitigating misalignments and refining the project scope to better suit stakeholder needs.

Lessons Learned:

1. **Anticipate and Plan for Changes**: The project manager learned that changes are inevitable, especially in large-scale projects. Future projects would benefit from allocating a contingency budget and resources specifically for scope changes that are likely to occur.
2. **The Value of Early and Ongoing Stakeholder Involvement**: Engaging stakeholders early and continuously was crucial in aligning diverse interests and expectations with the project's goals and capabilities.
3. **Importance of Rigorous Scope Documentation**: Comprehensive documentation, including a detailed scope statement and a well-defined WBS, was essential in maintaining clarity and focus, preventing scope creep, and managing the project efficiently.

Project Outcome:

Despite initial challenges with scope creep and stakeholder alignment, the effective application of Project Scope Management processes led to the successful completion of the Greenway Tech Campus expansion. The project was delivered within the revised schedule and budget, meeting all the critical requirements and achieving high stakeholder satisfaction.

Conclusion:

This case study of Greenway Technologies demonstrates that thorough and proactive scope management is critical to managing complex projects effectively. By employing detailed planning, rigorous change control processes, and regular stakeholder engagement, project managers can navigate the challenges of scope creep and stakeholder misalignment to deliver successful project outcomes. The lessons learned highlight the importance of flexibility, detailed documentation, and stakeholder involvement in project success. Effective project scope management is critical for the success of any project. However, there are several common pitfalls and misconceptions that can undermine this process. Understanding these challenges is essential for project managers to avoid potential issues and ensure a smooth progression throughout the project lifecycle.

Pitfalls in Scope Management

1. **Insufficient Stakeholder Involvement**: One of the most common mistakes is not involving stakeholders sufficiently during the scope definition and throughout the project. This can lead to misunderstandings about project goals and deliverables.
2. **Inadequate Requirements Gathering**: Collecting requirements is a meticulous task, and failing to capture all necessary requirements can lead to scope creep or project deliverables that do not meet stakeholder needs.
3. **Poor Change Control**: Without a robust change control process, scope creep becomes a significant risk. Uncontrolled changes can lead to budget overruns, delayed timelines, and resource strain.
4. **Lack of Clear Scope Documentation**: Failing to clearly define and document the project scope can lead to ambiguity and misunderstandings. This often results in scope creep or misaligned project outputs.
5. **Underestimating the Complexity of the Project**: Often, project managers might overlook or underestimate certain complexities that affect the project scope, leading to inadequate planning and resource allocation.

Misconceptions in Scope Management

1. **Scope Management is a One-Time Task**: A common misconception is that scope management is only relevant at the beginning of the project. In reality, it is an ongoing activity that needs continuous attention throughout the project lifecycle.
2. **Change Is Always Negative**: Changes in scope are often viewed negatively, but they can be beneficial if managed correctly. Changes can lead to better project outcomes if they are the result of enhanced stakeholder understanding or necessary adjustments to project realities.
3. **Complete Flexibility in Scope is Possible**: While flexibility is important, excessive flexibility without proper controls can lead to scope creep. It's crucial to balance adaptability with adherence to agreed-upon objectives and requirements.

Guidance for Effective Scope Management

To avoid these pitfalls and overcome misconceptions, project managers should consider the following guidance:

1. **Engage Stakeholders Early and Often**: Ensure that all relevant stakeholders are involved from the beginning and throughout the project. Regular communication helps to manage expectations and gather continuous feedback.

2. **Thorough Requirements Analysis**: Spend adequate time during the initial phases of the project to thoroughly gather and analyze requirements. Use various techniques like interviews, focus groups, and surveys to capture a comprehensive set of requirements.
3. **Implement a Strong Change Control Process**: Develop and maintain a formal change control process. This should include a clear procedure for submitting, evaluating, and approving changes. Ensure that all changes are documented and communicated to relevant stakeholders.
4. **Document Scope Clearly**: Create a detailed project scope statement and use tools like the Work Breakdown Structure (WBS) to ensure all team members and stakeholders have a clear understanding of what is included in the project scope.
5. **Regular Scope Reviews**: Conduct regular scope reviews to assess the impact of any changes and ensure alignment with project goals. This helps in managing scope creep and ensures the project remains on track.
6. **Educate on Scope Management**: Train project teams and stakeholders on the importance of scope management and the processes involved. Understanding the implications of scope changes can foster a more disciplined approach to managing them.

Conclusion

By recognizing and addressing these common pitfalls and misconceptions, project managers can enhance their scope management practices. Effective scope management not only prevents project overruns and failures but also ensures that the project meets its intended objectives and delivers value to stakeholders. Here's a set of practice questions designed to assess and reinforce understanding of Project Scope Management processes, their ITTOs, and their practical application in real-world project scenarios. Each question includes a detailed explanation for the answer, enhancing the learning experience.

Practice Questions on Project Scope Management
Question 1:

What is the primary purpose of the 'Create WBS' process in project management?

A) To allocate the project budget across tasks
B) To define and organize the team structure
C) To break down the project deliverables into manageable sections
D) To identify project risks

Correct Answer: C) To break down the project deliverables into manageable sections

Explanation:
The Work Breakdown Structure (WBS) is a key project management tool that decomposes the project scope into manageable sections, each of which can be scheduled, costed, and assigned. This helps in organizing and defining the total work scope of the project.

Question 2:

Which document would you primarily refer to for understanding the detailed requirements and acceptance criteria of project deliverables?

A) Project Charter
B) Scope Statement
C) Risk Management Plan
D) Stakeholder Register

Correct Answer: B) Scope Statement

Explanation:
The scope statement is part of the project scope management process and provides detailed information

about the project's deliverables, including the requirements and acceptance criteria. It is essential for understanding what the project will deliver and how success will be measured.

Question 3:
Which of the following is NOT typically included in a WBS dictionary?
A) Detailed work descriptions
B) Cost estimates
C) List of project team members
D) Quality requirements
Correct Answer: C) List of project team members
Explanation:
The WBS dictionary supports the WBS by providing detailed descriptions of each component, including descriptions of work, associated cost estimates, and quality requirements. While it details resources needed, it does not typically list project team members by name.

Question 4:
In the scope management process, what is the role of variance analysis?
A) To determine the project's profitability
B) To compare planned performance with actual performance
C) To allocate resources across project tasks
D) To finalize the project schedule
Correct Answer: B) To compare planned performance with actual performance
Explanation:
Variance analysis is a tool used in the 'Control Scope' process to measure performance deviations from the scope baseline. It helps identify where performance is not aligning with the plan, enabling corrective actions to be taken.

Question 5:
What is a primary function of the scope baseline in project management?
A) To serve as a standard for comparison of actual project performance
B) To provide a summary of the project budget
C) To list all the project stakeholders and their interests
D) To schedule the project tasks
Correct Answer: A) To serve as a standard for comparison of actual project performance
Explanation:
The scope baseline includes the approved version of the scope statement, WBS, and WBS dictionary. It is used throughout the project to compare against actual results to detect scope creep, ensure alignment with project goals, and facilitate the control of the project scope.

Quiz Explanation
These questions are designed to test a range of knowledge from basic definitions and purposes of the tools and documents used in scope management to their practical application in monitoring and controlling the project scope. By understanding these concepts, project managers can ensure that their projects remain on track and meet the defined objectives and stakeholder expectations. Stakeholder involvement is crucial in project scope management, playing a pivotal role in defining, validating, and controlling the project scope throughout its lifecycle. Effective stakeholder engagement ensures that the project meets its intended objectives while aligning with stakeholder expectations and requirements.

Why Stakeholder Involvement is Important

1. **Defining Project Requirements**: Stakeholders are often the source of project requirements. Their input is crucial in defining what needs to be delivered, ensuring the project outcomes align with their needs and expectations.
2. **Validating Project Scope**: Stakeholders validate the project scope by confirming that the defined scope matches their expectations and meets the project's objectives. Their approval is essential for moving forward with planning and execution.
3. **Enhancing Project Buy-in and Support**: Engaging stakeholders throughout the scope management process helps build trust, secures buy-in, and fosters a collaborative environment. This support is crucial for navigating challenges and securing resources.
4. **Identifying and Resolving Issues Early**: Regular interaction with stakeholders can help identify potential issues or misunderstandings about the project scope early, allowing for timely resolutions that prevent costly changes later in the project.
5. **Managing Changes Effectively**: Stakeholders are often the drivers of change. Their involvement is essential in assessing the impact of changes, making informed decisions, and managing scope creep effectively.

Strategies for Effective Stakeholder Engagement

To effectively engage stakeholders in the scope definition and validation processes, project managers can employ several strategies:

Identify and Analyze Stakeholders:

Use tools like stakeholder analysis matrices to identify who needs to be involved in the project scope management process. Understand their level of influence, interest, and how the project impacts them.

Develop a Communication Plan:

Create a stakeholder communication plan that details how and when stakeholders will be engaged throughout the project. Tailor communication methods and frequencies to the needs and preferences of different stakeholders.

Involve Stakeholders in Requirement Gathering:

Actively involve stakeholders in requirement gathering sessions such as interviews, surveys, workshops, and focus groups. This direct involvement helps capture comprehensive and accurate requirements from the start.

Use Collaborative Tools and Techniques:

Utilize collaborative tools such as joint application development (JAD) sessions or collaborative software that allows stakeholders to provide input on project documents in real-time.

Establish a Formal Change Control Process:

Implement a formal change control process and involve key stakeholders in evaluating the impact of scope changes. This process should include mechanisms for submitting change requests, assessing impacts, and making decisions transparently.

Regular Review and Validation Meetings:

Schedule regular meetings where stakeholders can review progress and validate that the scope and deliverables still meet the project requirements. These reviews are critical checkpoints to ensure alignment and consensus.

Provide Transparency and Foster Trust:

Keep stakeholders informed about project progress and any issues that arise. Transparency helps build trust and reduces resistance to change, making it easier to manage scope modifications.

Educate Stakeholders on Scope Management:

Help stakeholders understand the importance of scope management, the implications of scope creep, and the benefits of adhering to the defined project scope.

Conclusion

Stakeholder involvement is integral to successful project scope management. By actively engaging stakeholders in defining and validating the project scope, project managers can ensure that the project delivers the intended value and meets stakeholder needs. Effective stakeholder engagement not only enhances project alignment but also facilitates smoother project execution and increases the likelihood of project success.

V. Project Schedule Management:

The "Plan Schedule Management" process is a critical initial step in the planning phase of project management. This process establishes the policies, procedures, and documentation for planning, executing, and monitoring the project schedule. It sets the guidelines on how the project schedule will be managed throughout the project, ensuring consistency and understanding among stakeholders.

Purpose of Plan Schedule Management Process
Establishing Framework:

It provides a structured framework for how schedule activities will be managed and controlled. This includes defining how to plan, execute, and monitor the project schedule, ensuring all team members are on the same page.

Guiding Execution and Monitoring:

The process sets out the methods and tools to be used throughout the project for managing the schedule. This guidance helps in maintaining a consistent approach to handling schedule changes, updates, and communications.

Enhancing Decision Making:

By establishing standard procedures for scheduling activities, this process aids project managers and stakeholders in making informed decisions based on the project timeline and progress. It defines the roles and responsibilities related to schedule management, ensuring clear accountability.

Facilitating Communication:

The process outlines how schedule changes and information will be communicated to stakeholders. Effective communication plans included in the schedule management plan ensure timely and appropriate dissemination of schedule-related information.

Key Components of a Schedule Management Plan

1. **Schedule Methodology**: Defines the approach and tools that will be used to create and manage the project schedule. This might involve specific project management software, scheduling techniques like critical path method (CPM), or agile sprints, depending on the project's nature.

2. **Scheduling Tools**: Specifies the tools that will be used for schedule development and tracking. Common tools include software like Microsoft Project, Primavera, or simpler tools such as Gantt charts in Excel, depending on the project's complexity.
3. **Frequency of Updates**: Details how often the project schedule should be reviewed and updated. Regular updates are crucial to reflect true project progress and any changes impacting the timeline.
4. **Performance Measurement**: Outlines how schedule performance will be measured. This often involves earned value management (EVM) metrics such as Schedule Performance Index (SPI) and Schedule Variance (SV) to track progress against the baseline schedule.
5. **Roles and Responsibilities**: Clearly defines who is responsible for developing, maintaining, and approving changes to the schedule. This clarity helps in ensuring that all schedule-related tasks are appropriately managed.
6. **Schedule Baseline**: Establishes the original approved project schedule, which serves as a basis for comparison to actual progress. The baseline is critical for measuring performance and managing any deviations.
7. **Change Control**: Describes the process for managing changes to the schedule. This includes how changes are documented, analyzed for impact, approved, and communicated. It ensures that only approved changes are implemented, helping to control scope creep and schedule slippage.
8. **Reporting Formats**: Specifies the format, content, and frequency of schedule reports. This ensures stakeholders receive consistent, timely, and relevant information regarding project progress and potential schedule issues.

Conclusion

The "Plan Schedule Management" process plays a foundational role in project schedule management. By setting clear guidelines, methods, and tools for managing the project schedule, it helps ensure that the project remains on track and meets its deadlines. Effective schedule management is essential not only for tracking project progress but also for providing critical information that influences decision-making throughout the project lifecycle. This process, therefore, not only helps in executing the project according to plan but also in adapting to changes and challenges that arise during the project duration. The process of defining activities is a crucial step in project planning, following the development of the Work Breakdown Structure (WBS). It involves identifying and documenting the specific actions that need to be performed to produce the project deliverables. This detailed planning helps in organizing and managing the project efficiently.

Importance of Defining Activities

1. **Detailed Planning**: Defining activities transforms the work packages outlined in the WBS into actionable steps. This level of detail is essential for precise scheduling, resource allocation, and cost estimation.
2. **Resource Management**: By clearly defining the activities, project managers can more effectively assign resources to specific tasks, ensuring that resources are used efficiently and that capabilities match the task requirements.
3. **Improved Accuracy**: Detailed activity definitions improve the accuracy of project duration and cost estimates. Clear descriptions of what each task involves help to foresee potential issues and plan mitigations.
4. **Enhanced Accountability**: When activities are clearly defined, it is easier to assign responsibility to team members, enhancing accountability and clarity in roles and expectations.

5. **Tracking and Monitoring**: Clearly defined activities make it easier to monitor progress and measure project performance against the project plan. This facilitates early detection of variances and timely corrective actions.

Techniques Used to Identify and Document Project Activities

Several techniques can be employed to identify and document the specific activities necessary for completing each work package in the WBS:

1. **Decomposition**: In continuation from the WBS, decomposition involves breaking down work packages into finer granular activities. This is done until the activities are manageable and can be assigned, scheduled, and monitored.
2. **Templates**: Utilizing standard templates for activity lists from previous projects can speed up the process and ensure consistency. Templates might include typical project tasks, estimated durations, and common dependencies.
3. **Expert Judgment**: Consulting with subject matter experts who have experience in similar projects can provide insights into necessary activities and potential challenges. Experts can help refine activity definitions based on real-world experiences.
4. **Brainstorming Sessions**: Organizing sessions with the project team and stakeholders to collectively identify activities can lead to a more comprehensive activity list. This collaborative approach can also foster team cohesion and buy-in.
5. **Rolling Wave Planning**: This is a form of progressive elaboration where the work to be done in the near term is planned in detail, while work in the future is planned at a higher level. As the project progresses and more information becomes available, the details of future work are defined.
6. **Milestone Charts**: Identifying major milestones first and then determining the activities required to achieve these milestones can help in structuring the activity list.

Documentation of Project Activities

The output of the Define Activities process is typically an activity list, which includes:

- **Activity Name and ID**: A unique identifier and brief name for each activity.
- **Scope of Work**: A description of what each activity involves.
- **Predecessors and Successors**: Information on dependencies between activities.
- **Assigned Resources**: Details of who is responsible for executing the activity.
- **Duration Estimates**: Initial estimates of how long each activity will take.
- **Resource Requirements**: Specific resources needed to complete each activity.
- **Constraints and Assumptions**: Any constraints that affect the activity and assumptions made during the planning phase.

Conclusion

Defining project activities is a critical step in translating project scope and deliverables into actionable and manageable components. Using various techniques to identify and document activities ensures a thorough and practical project plan. This detailed planning is foundational for effective project execution, enabling better control over scope, schedule, resources, and costs.

The "Define Activities" process in project management involves identifying and documenting the specific actions necessary to produce the project deliverables that were defined in the Work Breakdown Structure (WBS). This detailed listing of activities is essential for effective project planning, scheduling, executing, and monitoring. Understanding the Inputs, Tools and Techniques, and Outputs (ITTOs) of this process helps ensure that the activities are comprehensive and align with the project scope and objectives.

Inputs to Define Activities

1. **Scope Baseline**: This includes the project scope statement, the WBS, and the WBS dictionary. The scope baseline provides the foundation for defining activities by detailing what needs to be achieved and the deliverables at each level of the WBS.
2. **Enterprise Environmental Factors (EEFs)**: These include organizational culture and existing systems that can influence the definition of activities. For example, the availability of project management software or historical information on similar projects can aid in activity definition.
3. **Organizational Process Assets (OPAs)**: These assets may include guidelines, procedures, templates, and lessons learned from previous projects that can guide the activity definition process.

Tools and Techniques for Define Activities

1. **Decomposition**: This technique involves breaking down work package components of the WBS into smaller, more manageable parts or activities that can be scheduled, estimated, executed, and monitored.
2. **Rolling Wave Planning**: A form of progressive elaboration planning where work to be accomplished in the near term is planned in detail, while work in the future is planned at a higher level. It is particularly useful in projects where you cannot define all activities at the start.
3. **Expert Judgment**: Consulting with experienced project team members, subject matter experts, or other stakeholders to better define the necessary activities based on their expertise and experience.
4. **Meetings**: Project teams may hold planning meetings involving team members who will be responsible for executing and managing the work to discuss and develop the activity list.

Outputs from Define Activities
Activity List:
This is a comprehensive list including all scheduled activities required for the project. Each activity provides a unique scope of work that will contribute directly to completing project deliverables.

Activity Attributes:
Extends the description of the activity by identifying multiple components associated with each activity, such as predecessors, successors, logical relationships, leads and lags, resource requirements, constraints, and assumptions associated with the activity. Activity attributes provide a richer and more detailed schedule management base, helping project managers to effectively oversee and coordinate project tasks.

Milestone List:
Identifies all milestones and indicates whether the milestone is mandatory, such as those required by contract, or optional, based on project team decisions. This list helps in tracking progress toward significant project points and is crucial for stakeholder communication.

Contribution to Project Management
The Define Activities process transforms the project scope and deliverables into actionable steps that are necessary for project team members to follow. It creates a clear pathway towards the completion of project goals by detailing the specific work that needs to be performed. The activity list and activity

attributes form the backbone of project scheduling and resource planning, enabling more accurate estimations of duration and costs. Additionally, these detailed definitions help in identifying relationships among activities, which is essential for developing a reliable project schedule. The Define Activities process, with its structured approach and detailed outputs, ensures that project planning is thorough and all-encompassing, contributing significantly to project success by providing clarity and direction for all team members involved. Understanding the distinction between milestones and activities is fundamental in project management, particularly in planning and tracking the project schedule. Each serves unique purposes and offers different insights into the project's progress and achievements.

What is an Activity?

Definition: An activity is a distinct, scheduled portion of work performed during the course of a project. Activities represent tasks or sets of tasks that are required to produce project deliverables.

Characteristics:
- Activities are actionable and specific tasks.
- They consume resources and time.
- Activities can be further broken down into subtasks.
- They are the basic units used in the development of the project schedule.

Example of Activities:
- **Software Development Project**: Writing code for a new software feature.
- **Construction Project**: Pouring concrete for a building's foundation.
- **Event Planning**: Organizing and conducting a vendor meeting.

What is a Milestone?

Definition: A milestone is a significant point or event in the project schedule. It typically represents a major achievement or a critical decision point that marks the completion of key project phases or activities.

Characteristics:
- Milestones are specific points along the project timeline.
- They do not have a duration but indicate a moment of achievement or a deadline.
- Milestones are used to monitor project progress and are often linked to payment schedules or other contractual obligations.
- They can help in aligning team efforts and are useful in stakeholder communications.

Example of Milestones:
- **Software Development Project**: Completion of the beta version of the software.
- **Construction Project**: Completion of the structural framework of a building.
- **Event Planning**: Finalizing the event's program schedule.

Roles in Project Schedule Management

Activities:
- **Detailed Planning**: Activities form the backbone of the project schedule. They are sequenced, resourced, and estimated in terms of duration, forming a detailed plan of how the project will be executed.
- **Tracking and Control**: Monitoring the completion of activities is essential for tracking project progress. The actual performance of these activities is compared against the plan to identify variances and implement corrective actions.

Milestones:

- **Monitoring Key Points**: Milestones are used to monitor significant points throughout the project, offering a high-level overview of project progress. They are often checkpoints for go/no-go decisions.
- **Communication and Reporting**: Milestones provide clear targets that can be communicated to stakeholders, helping to demonstrate progress and justify continued investment. They are particularly useful in status reports and executive briefings.
- **Synchronization and Alignment**: Milestones help synchronize different parts of the project and ensure alignment with the project's objectives. They are critical in projects where multiple streams or teams work independently but need to integrate their outputs at specific points.

Conclusion

Both activities and milestones are essential elements in project schedule management. While activities focus on the detailed aspects of 'doing the work,' milestones are key indicators of 'significant achievements' throughout the project. Effective management of both is crucial for keeping the project on track and meeting its objectives. Project managers must adeptly define and use both activities and milestones to navigate the project toward successful completion.

The "Sequence Activities" process in project management involves arranging all the identified activities in the order they need to be carried out to complete the project successfully. This process is essential because it establishes the logical relationships among project activities, which is crucial for developing a realistic and effective project schedule.

Significance of the Sequence Activities Process
Establishing Project Timeline:

Sequencing helps in mapping out the path activities will take from the start to the end of the project, clarifying how long the project will take by determining the critical path, which is the longest sequence of activities from start to finish that dictates the project duration.

Resource Allocation:

By understanding the sequence of activities, project managers can plan and allocate resources more efficiently. Knowing which activities follow or precede others helps in optimizing resource usage without overallocation or conflicts.

Risk Management:

Effective sequencing can help identify potential risks associated with the timing and dependencies of activities. This awareness allows for the development of more informed risk mitigation strategies.

Enhanced Coordination and Communication:

Clear sequencing of activities facilitates better communication and coordination among team members, as everyone understands the order of operations and dependencies. This clarity can improve teamwork and productivity.

Types of Dependencies in Activity Sequencing

Dependencies determine the sequence in which project activities must occur. There are four primary types of dependencies:

Finish-to-Start (FS):
The most common type of dependency. The start of one activity depends on the completion of another. For example, you cannot start painting a wall (successor activity) until the wall has been constructed (predecessor activity).

Start-to-Start (SS):
The start of one activity depends on the start of another, but both can continue concurrently. For instance, you can start installing software (successor activity) as soon as the installation of the hardware begins (predecessor activity), though both activities continue simultaneously.

Finish-to-Finish (FF):
The completion of one activity depends on the completion of another. An example would be that a quality inspection (successor activity) can finish only after the last unit of production (predecessor activity) is completed.

Start-to-Finish (SF):
The least common type; the completion of one activity depends on the start of another. For example, the current shift (successor activity) can only finish once the next shift (predecessor activity) begins. These dependencies can be further classified as:
- **Mandatory Dependencies (Hard Logic)**: Inherent in the nature of the work, such as you must build a foundation before erecting the walls.
- **Discretionary Dependencies (Preferred, Preferential, or Soft Logic)**: Established based on best practices or some desired sequence, such as the preferred order of tasks for efficiency or convenience, often defined based on historical data.
- **External Dependencies**: Involve a relationship between project activities and non-project activities. These dependencies are usually outside the team's control, such as waiting for government permits or delivered materials.

Conclusion
The Sequence Activities process is crucial for project planning and management as it directly impacts the project's timeline, resource allocation, risk management, and team coordination. Understanding and applying the correct types of dependencies allows for a realistic and efficient project schedule, ultimately supporting the successful completion of the project. The Sequence Activities process in project management involves identifying and documenting the relationships among project activities. This process is crucial for developing a comprehensive project schedule that accurately reflects how tasks are interrelated, the order in which they need to be performed, and their dependencies. Project schedule network diagrams are essential tools used in this process.

Purpose of Project Schedule Network Diagrams
1. **Visual Representation**: Network diagrams provide a visual representation of the project's activities and their sequential relationships. This visual layout helps project managers and team members understand the workflow and identify the best path to follow for project completion.
2. **Dependency Identification**: Diagrams highlight the dependencies between activities. Understanding these dependencies is crucial for realistic scheduling and helps in anticipating potential bottlenecks.

3. **Critical Path Analysis**: Network diagrams enable the identification of the critical path, which is the longest path through the network and shows the shortest time in which the project can be completed. This is vital for effective project time management.
4. **Resource Planning**: By laying out the sequence and interdependencies of tasks, network diagrams help in efficient resource allocation and management.
5. **Risk Management**: Network diagrams aid in identifying high-risk activities that may impact the project schedule, allowing for better risk assessment and mitigation planning.

Commonly Used Network Diagramming Techniques
1. Precedence Diagramming Method (PDM)

- **Description**: PDM, also known as the activity-on-node (AON) method, is one of the most commonly used techniques in project scheduling. In PDM, each activity is represented by a node (box), and dependencies between activities are shown with arrows.
- **Dependencies**: PDM supports four types of dependencies or logical relationships: Finish-to-Start (FS), Start-to-Start (SS), Finish-to-Finish (FF), and Start-to-Finish (SF).
- **Example**: In a software development project, the activity "Code Module A" must finish before "Test Module A" can start (FS relationship). Meanwhile, "Document Module A" can start simultaneously with "Code Module A" (SS relationship).

3. Arrow Diagramming Method (ADM)

- **Description**: Known as the activity-on-arrow (AOA) method, ADM represents activities on the arrows and milestones on the nodes. This method is less common than PDM but is used in certain types of projects.
- **Dependencies**: ADM primarily uses only one type of dependency, which is Finish-to-Start (FS). Because of its structure, it sometimes requires the use of dummy activities to accurately represent complex relationships.
- **Example**: In a construction project, the activity "Lay Foundation" (represented by an arrow) must finish before "Erect Walls" can begin (nodes at the start and end of the arrow). If there's a need to show a parallel path that only starts after "Lay Foundation" but does not directly depend on "Erect Walls," a dummy activity (represented by a dashed arrow) may be used to depict this relationship.

Benefits of Using Network Diagrams

- **Enhanced Team Understanding and Communication**: Visual representations help teams understand the project scope and sequence, improving communication and coordination.
- **Improved Schedule Accuracy**: By clearly illustrating dependencies and the critical path, network diagrams enhance the accuracy of the project schedule.
- **Effective Monitoring and Control**: Network diagrams make it easier to monitor progress and make adjustments as needed, ensuring the project remains on track.

Conclusion

Project schedule network diagrams are vital tools in project management, especially during the Sequence Activities process. They provide essential insights into project scheduling, help manage dependencies, and are instrumental in planning and controlling the project. Techniques like PDM and ADM are foundational in creating these diagrams, each serving specific project needs and preferences. Leads and lags are essential scheduling tools used in project management to fine-tune the timing of activities within the project schedule. They help manage the relationships and dependencies between tasks more precisely, enabling better control over the project timeline.

Understanding Leads and Lags

Leads: A lead is a modification to a logical relationship that allows an activity to start earlier than it otherwise would. It is effectively speeding up the successor activity. A lead is used in situations where activities can overlap.

Lags: A lag introduces a delay between predecessor and successor activities. It represents a time waiting period inserted between tasks, often necessary to accommodate physical constraints, required waiting periods, or prerequisites that must be fulfilled before subsequent activities can commence.

Impact on Sequencing of Activities

Leads and lags can significantly impact the sequencing of activities by altering the start or end times of subsequent activities based on non-linear or non-sequential requirements. This can affect the overall project duration, either compressing it (with leads) or extending it (with lags).

Examples of Leads and Lags
1. Example of Using a Lead:

- **Scenario**: You are managing a software development project. The design phase is scheduled to finish before coding begins. However, to expedite the project, you decide to start coding some modules that do not depend on the full design being complete.
- **Application**: You apply a two-week lead to the coding activity. This means that coding starts two weeks before the design phase is officially completed, overlapping the final stages of the design.
- **Impact**: This lead can reduce the overall project duration and allow earlier testing and integration phases.

2. Example of Using a Lag:

- **Scenario**: In a construction project, after pouring concrete, a certain period must elapse for curing before beginning the next phase of construction, such as framing.
- **Application**: You introduce a lag of seven days between the end of the concrete pouring and the start of the framing.
- **Impact**: The lag ensures that the concrete has sufficiently set to support the next construction phase, thereby preventing structural failures and ensuring safety.

How Leads and Lags Can Optimize the Project Schedule

- **Improving Resource Allocation**: By adjusting leads and lags, project managers can better align resource usage with availability, preventing resource bottlenecks and idleness.
- **Enhancing Flexibility**: Leads can be used to overlap activities where possible, offering flexibility in scheduling and potential acceleration of the project timeline.
- **Managing Interdependencies**: Lags ensure that necessary wait times between dependent tasks are respected, which is crucial for activities requiring drying, curing, or other time-based prerequisites.
- **Reducing Downtime and Delays**: Strategic use of leads can reduce downtime between tasks, keeping the project momentum going and potentially bringing forward the project completion date.

Conclusion

Leads and lags are critical for effective project scheduling. They provide project managers with the flexibility to adjust activity start and end times based on practical considerations and interdependencies between tasks. By understanding and applying leads and lags appropriately, project managers can optimize the project schedule, ensuring that the project progresses efficiently while meeting all necessary operational constraints and prerequisites. The Estimate Activity Durations process in project management is essential for developing a realistic and effective project schedule. This process involves assessing the number of work periods needed to complete individual activities with estimated resources. Accurate duration estimates are crucial for planning project timelines, scheduling work, and managing expectations.

Importance of Estimating Activity Durations

1. **Project Planning Accuracy**: Precise duration estimates are fundamental to creating a reliable project schedule. They affect the planning and coordination of project phases, resource allocation, and budgeting.
2. **Resource Management**: Understanding how long activities will take helps in the efficient allocation and utilization of resources, preventing overallocation or idle resources.
3. **Critical Path Analysis**: Duration estimates are crucial for determining the project's critical path—the sequence of dependent tasks with the longest cumulative duration. This analysis highlights tasks that directly impact the project completion date.
4. **Risk Management**: Accurate duration estimates help identify high-risk activities (e.g., those with long durations or significant complexity), allowing for targeted risk mitigation strategies.
5. **Stakeholder Communication and Confidence**: Realistic timelines based on sound duration estimates improve communication with stakeholders and build their confidence in project management.

Key Factors Influencing Activity Duration Estimates

Several factors impact the accuracy of activity duration estimates, including:

1. **Resource Availability and Capability**: The skills, availability, and productivity of assigned resources significantly influence how long activities will take. Limited resource availability or lower skill levels can extend activity durations.
2. **Project Scope and Task Complexity**: More complex tasks generally take longer to complete. Understanding the technical and logistical complexities involved in each activity is crucial for accurate estimation.
3. **Historical Information**: Past project performance and historical data provide valuable insights into how long similar tasks have taken under comparable circumstances.
4. **Project Environment Factors**: External conditions such as weather (in construction projects), regulatory approvals, or market conditions can affect the duration of activities.
5. **Dependency Relationships**: The sequence in which activities must be performed, especially where outputs of one activity are inputs for another, can affect duration estimates. Overlapping activities (lead and lag) can also modify durations.
6. **Tools and Techniques**: The availability and efficiency of tools and technology used in executing the project work can significantly impact the speed and effectiveness of activity completion.
7. **Team Performance and Workload**: The overall team performance, morale, and current workload can influence the time it takes to complete tasks.

Estimating Techniques

To effectively estimate activity durations, project managers often use several techniques:

1. **Expert Judgment**: Leveraging the experience and knowledge of team members or consultants who are familiar with similar projects.
2. **Analogous Estimating**: Using duration data from similar past projects as the basis for estimating the duration of future activities. This method is quicker but less accurate.
3. **Parametric Estimating**: Involves using statistical relationships between historical data and other variables (e.g., installing 100 square feet of brick wall per hour) to calculate activity durations.
4. **Three-Point Estimating**: Considering three scenarios—most likely, optimistic, and pessimistic—to derive an estimate that accounts for uncertainty.
5. **Bottom-Up Estimating**: Breaking down activities into smaller components and estimating the duration of each component. These are then aggregated to give an overall duration estimate for larger activities.

Conclusion

The Estimate Activity Durations process is critical for creating a realistic project schedule that is essential for project success. By considering various influencing factors and using appropriate estimating techniques, project managers can develop more accurate schedules, effectively manage resources, and increase the likelihood of project completion within the planned time frame. In project management, estimating the duration of activities is crucial for effective scheduling and planning. Various techniques can be used to estimate these durations, each with its own strengths and suitable applications. Three common techniques include analogous estimating, parametric estimating, and three-point estimating. Each of these methods offers different approaches based on the project data available and the complexity of the tasks.

Analogous Estimating

Description: Analogous estimating involves using the actual duration of similar past activities as the basis for estimating the duration of future activities. It is often used when there is limited information available and relies heavily on expert judgment.

Example of Use: A project manager is overseeing the construction of a small office building. Having managed several similar construction projects, the manager estimates the duration based on how long previous projects took to complete similar phases.

Appropriateness: This method is most appropriate when projects are similar in fact and not much detailed information is available about the new project. It's quick and less costly but can be less accurate unless the previous projects are very similar to the current project.

Parametric Estimating

Description: Parametric estimating uses a statistical relationship between historical data and other variables (e.g., square footage in construction, lines of code in software development) to calculate an estimate for activity durations. It involves using a rate or a parameter to calculate estimates, based on the quantities of work and the productivity rate.

Example of Use: A software development project can use parametric estimating by calculating the average number of lines of code that programmers can write per hour and applying this rate to the estimated lines of code for the new system.

Appropriateness: This technique is useful when you can quantify the project and effectively apply a unit rate. It tends to be more accurate than analogous estimating if the underlying data is reliable and scalable.

Three-Point Estimating

Description: Three-point estimating takes into account uncertainty and risk by making three estimates: most likely (M), optimistic (O), and pessimistic (P). The final estimate is calculated using a formula like the triangular distribution $(O+M+P)/3$ or a weighted average, as used in PERT (Program Evaluation and Review Technique): $(O+4M+P)/6$.

Example of Use: When planning a new marketing campaign, a project manager may not be sure how long it will take to complete certain creative tasks. They estimate durations based on best-case scenarios (optimistic), most likely scenarios, and worst-case scenarios (pessimistic) to find a balanced estimate.

Appropriateness: This method is particularly suited for projects with a high level of uncertainty or when the tasks are unique and have no historical precedents. It provides a more refined estimate by considering different scenarios, thus reducing the risk of surprises.

Conclusion

Choosing the right estimating technique often depends on the nature of the project, the accuracy of the data available, and the specific risks associated with project tasks. Analogous estimating is quick and easy but relies heavily on similar past projects. Parametric estimating is data-driven and can be highly accurate if good quality data is available. Three-point estimating is useful for addressing the uncertainty inherent in project estimates, providing a range that accommodates various risk scenarios. Each method has its strengths and can be chosen based on the project's needs, the environment, and the manager's experience with similar projects.

The Program Evaluation and Review Technique (PERT) is a valuable tool used in project management for planning and coordinating large, complex projects. One of its applications includes the PERT formula in three-point estimating, which is used to estimate activity durations when there is uncertainty about the precise length of time an activity will take.

Understanding the PERT Formula in Three-Point Estimating

The PERT formula is designed to calculate a weighted average of three estimated durations to determine an expected activity duration:

- **Optimistic Time (O)**: The shortest time in which the activity can be completed, assuming everything proceeds better than is normally expected.
- **Most Likely Time (M)**: The best estimate of the duration required to complete the activity, assuming everything proceeds as normal.
- **Pessimistic Time (P)**: The longest time the activity might take, assuming everything goes wrong but excluding major catastrophes.

The formula for the PERT estimate is often given as: $TE = \frac{(O+4M+P)}{6}$

Where TE is the Expected Time for the activity.

Purpose of the PERT Formula

1. **Incorporate Uncertainty**: The PERT formula takes into account the uncertainty inherent in estimating durations, providing a more realistic and statistically probable estimate by considering the best, worst, and most likely scenarios.
2. **Risk Management**: By accounting for the most optimistic and pessimistic scenarios, the PERT formula helps in risk management. It allows project managers to prepare for the worst while planning for the best.
3. **Improve Accuracy**: The weighting in the formula gives more influence to the most likely duration, improving the accuracy of the estimate by acknowledging that while extreme cases can occur, they are less likely.

4. **Balanced Approach**: This method provides a balanced view of potential future events, helping stakeholders and project managers make better-informed decisions regarding time allocations and schedules.

How PERT Helps in Calculating Expected Activity Duration

The PERT formula's approach to calculating the expected activity duration is beneficial for several reasons:

1. **Statistical Rationale**: The formula is based on the Beta Distribution, which is useful when there is limited data but known minimum and maximum times. The distribution allows the estimate to reflect the asymmetry in the duration likelihoods.
2. **Focus on the Most Likely Scenario**: By multiplying the most likely time by four, the PERT formula emphasizes the realistic estimate while still considering the outer limits of optimistic and pessimistic estimates. This helps in centering the duration around the most probable outcome.
3. **Comprehensive Estimation**: Including all three time estimates ensures that the calculation reflects a range of potential outcomes, which can be crucial for planning and buffer management in project scheduling.

Example of PERT in Action

Suppose a project task has an optimistic estimate of 3 days, a most likely estimate of 5 days, and a pessimistic estimate of 8 days. Using the PERT formula:

$TE = \frac{(3 + 4 \times 5 + 8)}{6} = \frac{(3 + 20 + 8)}{6} = \frac{31}{6} \approx 5.17$ days

This calculation shows that, considering uncertainty, the expected duration of the task is approximately 5.17 days. This helps in setting more realistic schedules and preparing for potential deviations in project timelines.

Conclusion

Using the PERT formula in three-point estimating is a powerful approach to handle the inherent uncertainty in project activities' durations. It provides a comprehensive, balanced estimation that aids in effective project planning, risk management, and decision-making. This method is particularly useful in complex projects where the time to complete tasks cannot be precisely known and where flexibility in planning is crucial. The "Develop Schedule" process is a critical step in project management that involves analyzing activity sequences, durations, resource requirements, and schedule constraints to create a project schedule that outlines how and when the project's objectives are to be achieved. This process enables the integration of all the individual activity estimates and resource plans into a cohesive, actionable project plan.

Significance of the Develop Schedule Process

1. **Time Management and Planning**: The development of a project schedule allows project managers to plan the timing of project activities, ensuring that tasks are completed in the most logical and efficient order.
2. **Resource Allocation**: The schedule helps in identifying the resource needs and optimizing the allocation of resources throughout the duration of the project, preventing resource overallocation and ensuring efficient use of resources.
3. **Stakeholder Communication**: A well-developed schedule serves as a communication tool that provides stakeholders with visibility into the project's timeline and critical milestones, facilitating better decision-making and engagement.

4. **Performance Measurement**: The schedule provides a baseline for tracking project progress and performance, allowing for corrective actions to be taken in response to delays or early task completions.
5. **Risk Management**: By identifying critical path activities and schedule flexibilities (float), project managers can focus risk management efforts on critical areas, enhancing the overall risk response strategies.

Key Inputs to the Develop Schedule Process

1. **Activity List and Attributes**: Provides detailed information about each activity necessary for completing the project, including dependencies, requirements, and constraints associated with them.
2. **Project Scope Statement**: Offers a detailed description of the project deliverables and the work required to create those deliverables, influencing how the schedule is planned.
3. **Resource Calendars**: Detail the availability and working hours of project resources, which are crucial for accurate scheduling.
4. **Activity Duration Estimates**: These are assessments of the work periods needed to complete individual tasks, forming the basis for scheduling the activities.
5. **Project Schedule Network Diagrams**: Visual representations of the project activities and their logical relationships, which are essential for understanding task dependencies.
6. **Risk Register**: Contains information about potential risks which could impact the schedule, requiring integration into the planning process to mitigate possible delays.

Tools Used in the Develop Schedule Process

1. **Critical Path Method (CPM)**: Identifies the longest path of planned activities to the end of the project and the shortest time possible to complete the project. Activities on this path cannot be delayed without delaying the project.
2. **Resource Leveling**: Adjusts the start and finish dates based on resource constraints with the goal of minimizing periods of underuse or overuse of resources.
3. **What-If Scenario Analysis**: This tool involves analyzing different scenarios to assess their potential impacts on the project schedule, helping in identifying the feasibility of the project deadlines under varying conditions.
4. **Schedule Compression**: Techniques such as crashing (adding resources) or fast tracking (rearranging activities to overlap) are used to decrease the project duration without changing the project scope.
5. **Gantt Charts**: Visual tools that provide a graphical representation of a schedule that helps in tracking project progress and understanding the relationship between activities.
6. **Scheduling Software**: Used to automate the scheduling, updating, and monitoring of project activities. Common tools include Microsoft Project, Primavera P6, and others.

Conclusion

Developing a comprehensive project schedule through the "Develop Schedule" process is essential for effective project management. It not only provides a roadmap for project execution but also serves as a critical tool for managing time, resources, stakeholder expectations, and risks. By integrating various inputs and applying appropriate scheduling techniques, project managers can create realistic, flexible, and robust plans to guide the project to successful completion. The Critical Path Method (CPM) is a fundamental project management technique used to schedule project activities. It identifies the longest stretch of dependent activities and measures the time required to complete them from start to finish, determining the project's shortest possible duration. This longest path through the network of activities is known as the critical path.

Understanding the Critical Path Method (CPM)
Role of CPM:
1. **Project Duration**: CPM helps in determining the minimum project duration by identifying the longest path of planned activities to the end of the project and the earliest and latest that each activity can start and finish without making the project longer.
2. **Schedule Management**: By highlighting the critical path, CPM enables project managers to see which activities have zero float (i.e., no spare time) and are crucial for timely project completion.
3. **Priority Setting**: Activities on the critical path must be prioritized because any delay in these activities directly impacts the project completion date.

Steps in Applying the Critical Path Method
1. **List of Activities**: Start with a complete list of all activities required to complete the project.
2. **Sequencing Activities**: Determine the dependencies between these activities, noting which activities depend on others for their start.
3. **Drawing the Network Diagram**: Plot these activities and dependencies in a network diagram using nodes for activities and arrows for dependencies.
4. **Estimating Duration**: Assign an estimated duration to each activity based on the best information available.
5. **Identifying the Critical Path**: Calculate the earliest start and finish times (forward pass) and the latest start and finish times (backward pass) for each activity. The critical path is identified as the path with the longest duration through the network, where any delay in the activities will delay the project.

Using CPM to Prioritize Activities and Manage Risks
Prioritizing Activities:
- **Resource Allocation**: Project managers can allocate resources more efficiently by prioritizing activities on the critical path to ensure they are adequately resourced to avoid delays.
- **Monitoring and Control**: Focus monitoring efforts on critical path activities, as these require the most attention to keep the project on schedule.

Managing Project Risks:
- **Risk Identification**: Activities on the critical path should be the focus of intensive risk analysis because any delay in these activities poses a risk to the project schedule.
- **Developing Contingency Plans**: Prepare contingency plans specifically for critical path activities. Consider options like fast tracking (overlapping activities that normally would be sequential) or crashing (adding resources to decrease the time needed to complete a critical task).
- **Regular Reviews**: Conduct regular critical path analyses as project conditions change. Updating the critical path can help identify new risks or shifts in project priorities.

Example of Critical Path Application
Imagine a project that involves building a small bridge, which includes the following key activities:
- **A (Excavate)**: 3 days
- **B (Pour Foundation)**: 2 days (depends on A)

- **C (Cure Concrete)**: 5 days (depends on B)
- **D (Build Supports)**: 3 days (depends on C)
- **E (Lay Decking)**: 2 days (depends on D)

After creating a network diagram and applying the CPM, it's determined that the critical path is A-B-C-D-E, totaling 15 days. Since this is the critical path, no delays can be afforded on any of these activities without affecting the overall project duration.

Conclusion

CPM is a powerful tool that helps project managers plan and execute projects efficiently. By focusing on the critical path, project managers can effectively prioritize activities that impact the project timeline, better allocate resources, and proactively manage potential risks that could derail project success. Resource leveling is a technique used in project management to address the allocation of necessary resources to the project without over-allocating any single resource. It involves adjusting the project schedule to balance the demand for resources with the available supply. This technique is crucial in scenarios where the resource availability is constrained or varies over the duration of the project.

Significance of Resource Leveling in the Develop Schedule Process

Resource leveling is significant because it directly impacts the efficiency and feasibility of a project schedule. It ensures that resources are not over-extended, which can lead to burnout and reduced productivity. It also helps in:

1. **Avoiding Resource Over-Allocation**: Ensures that no resource is scheduled for more than their available hours, preventing delays and disruptions in the project workflow.
2. **Smoothing Resource Usage**: Evens out the demands on resources, avoiding peaks and troughs in resource utilization, which can help maintain a steady project pace.
3. **Extending Project Duration**: Sometimes, leveling will extend the project's duration because activities may need to be delayed to match resource availability. This extension needs to be managed carefully against project deadlines.

Resource Leveling Techniques
1. Delaying Non-Critical Activities:

- **Technique**: Activities that have free slack can be delayed without affecting the project's critical path. This delay can help in managing the availability of resources more evenly across the project.
- **Example**: If an IT specialist is scheduled to work on two modules simultaneously and the completion of one module does not impact other critical tasks, one module can be rescheduled to start after the other ends.
- **Benefit**: This helps in reducing the burden on the IT specialist and ensures quality work is maintained by focusing on one task at a time.

3. Allocating Resources Based on Priority:

- **Technique**: Prioritizing project tasks based on their strategic importance or criticality and then allocating resources accordingly.
- **Example**: In a software development project, coding the login feature may be prioritized over developing an optional user profile customization feature. Resources would first be allocated to the login feature.
- **Benefit**: Ensures critical project components are resourced adequately, reducing the risk of project delays.

3. Using Substitute Resources:

- **Technique**: Identifying alternative resources that can be used if the primary resources are over-allocated.
- **Example**: If a particular software developer is overbooked, another developer with similar skills but lower current utilization might be assigned some tasks.
- **Benefit**: Helps maintain the project schedule by utilizing all available talent without waiting for specific individuals to become available.

4. Adjusting Working Hours:

- **Technique**: Temporarily increasing or adjusting the working hours to meet project demands without changing the project scope.
- **Example**: Offering overtime to workers or shifting work to weekends to cope with a particular spike in activity without delaying subsequent activities.
- **Benefit**: Provides flexibility in meeting project deadlines when critical activities must be completed within a fixed time frame.

Conclusion

Resource leveling is an essential tool in the Develop Schedule process, especially in projects where resource availability is limited or highly variable. It helps optimize the use of personnel, equipment, and materials, ensuring that the project progresses smoothly without unnecessary stops and starts. While resource leveling may sometimes extend the overall project duration, the benefits of better resource utilization and reduced risk of over-allocation often outweigh the potential drawbacks. By effectively using resource leveling techniques, project managers can create more realistic and achievable schedules, enhancing overall project success. A project calendar plays a pivotal role in the process of developing a project schedule. It is an essential tool that helps project managers define the working days, non-working days, holidays, and other factors that impact how the project tasks are scheduled. This calendar is specific to the project and is used to ensure that the schedule accurately reflects when project activities and resources are available.

Role of the Project Calendar in Schedule Development

1. **Accurate Time Planning**: The project calendar allows for the precise planning of activity start and end dates based on actual working days, ensuring that the project timeline is realistic and achievable.
2. **Resource Allocation**: It helps in resource planning by outlining when resources are available. For projects that span multiple locations or include resources from different organizations, this becomes particularly important.
3. **Coordination Across Teams and Locations**: For projects involving multiple teams or stakeholders across different geographical locations, project calendars are crucial for synchronizing work amidst varying local holidays and working hours.
4. **Avoiding Scheduling Conflicts**: By marking out non-working days and public holidays, the project calendar helps avoid scheduling critical work during times when staff or resources are not available.
5. **Efficiency and Productivity**: Proper use of a project calendar helps in optimizing the allocation of work, avoiding downtime, and improving overall project efficiency and productivity.

How the Project Calendar Accounts for Various Factors
1. Working and Non-Working Days

- The project calendar clearly defines which days of the week are considered working days. For instance, while a standard calendar might assume a Monday-Friday workweek, project calendars can be adjusted for industries or countries where the norm might be different.
- Non-working days are blocked out to prevent the scheduling of tasks on weekends, evenings, or other times when work is not planned.

2. Holidays

- All relevant public holidays that affect project activity are incorporated into the project calendar. This includes local, national, and possibly international holidays, depending on the project's scope and locations involved.
- For global projects, the calendar may need to account for different holiday schedules in different countries, which can affect the availability of shared resources or stakeholders.

2. Resource Availability

- Project calendars are adjusted to reflect the availability of specific resources, including human resources (e.g., vacations, personal leaves) and physical resources (e.g., equipment downtime for maintenance).
- For projects depending on external vendors or contractors, the calendar might also need to reflect the times when these external parties are available or operational.

Example of a Project Calendar in Use

Consider a construction project that needs to account for various working conditions:

- **Standard Work Hours**: 7 AM to 3 PM, Monday to Friday.
- **Holidays and Non-Working Days**: All national public holidays, plus every Saturday and Sunday.
- **Special Non-Working Periods**: Two weeks in December for year-end holidays, one week in spring for local festivities.
- **Resource Specific Non-availability**: The crane needed for the project is scheduled for maintenance for the first week of every third month.

Using this information, the project manager develops a project calendar that ensures all planning respects these constraints. Tasks requiring the crane are not scheduled during its maintenance periods, and no critical work is planned during the holiday breaks or weekends.

The "Control Schedule" process is a fundamental aspect of project management, focusing on monitoring the project schedule's progress and managing changes to the schedule baseline. This process ensures that the project remains on track, meets deadlines, and adheres to its timeline, all of which are crucial for successful project delivery.

Significance of the Control Schedule Process

1. **Project Tracking**: Control Schedule allows project managers to track actual project progress against the planned schedule. This ongoing monitoring is essential for detecting deviations early, which can then be addressed before they lead to significant impacts.
2. **Performance Management**: It provides a framework for assessing the efficiency of project execution. Timely information about potential schedule slippages or advancements enables managers to make informed decisions to bring project execution back in line with planned progress.

3. **Change Management**: As changes occur, the Control Schedule process ensures that all impacts on the schedule are considered, and necessary adjustments are made. It helps maintain the current schedule by integrating approved changes in a controlled manner, thereby aligning the project with its goals.
4. **Stakeholder Communication**: Regular schedule reviews as part of this process provide transparency and keep all stakeholders informed about the project's status. This communication is vital for maintaining stakeholder confidence and support.

Key Activities in the Control Schedule Process

1. **Comparative Analysis**: Regularly comparing the planned schedule to actual progress. This involves reviewing progress reports, updating project schedules with actual data, and analyzing variations.
2. **Identifying Variations**: Determining the cause and degree of variance relative to the schedule baseline. If activities are ahead or behind schedule, it is crucial to understand why, so appropriate actions can be taken.
3. **Taking Corrective Actions**: Implementing actions necessary to realign the project schedule. This may involve accelerating activities, reassigning resources, or modifying dependencies and task durations.
4. **Updating Schedule Baseline**: If significant changes are approved that impact the schedule, updating the baseline is necessary for future tracking and comparisons.
5. **Forecasting**: Using current schedule performance to predict future schedule trends. This can involve estimating when particular project milestones will be achieved.

Tools Used to Measure and Manage Schedule Performance

1. **Gantt Charts**: Visual tools that show the schedule of activities against time. They are useful for tracking progress and understanding the relationship between activities.
2. **Critical Path Method (CPM)**: Identifies the longest path of dependent activities and measures the time necessary to complete the project. It helps project managers focus on critical activities that directly impact the project completion date.
3. **Earned Value Management (EVM)**: Integrates scope, schedule, and cost measurements. Key metrics from EVM, such as Schedule Variance (SV) and Schedule Performance Index (SPI), provide quantitative data on schedule performance, helping to assess how well the project is adhering to the schedule.
4. **Trend Analysis**: Analyzing performance over time to detect whether performance is improving, worsening, or staying constant. This analysis helps predict future project performance based on past trends.
5. **What-if Scenario Analysis**: Using project simulation techniques to explore the effects of changing project conditions or decisions. This can help identify potential problems before they occur and plan how best to use available resources or adjust timelines accordingly.

Conclusion

The Control Schedule process plays a critical role in ensuring that projects are completed on time. By effectively monitoring, analyzing, and adjusting the schedule as needed, project managers can significantly increase the likelihood of meeting project deadlines and achieving project goals. This process is integral not just for the project's tactical management but also for strategic decision-making regarding resource allocation, stakeholder management, and risk mitigation. Schedule compression is a technique used in project management to shorten the project schedule without altering the project scope. It becomes crucial when a project must meet a deadline earlier than originally planned or when unexpected delays jeopardize the original schedule. Schedule compression is often used during the Control Schedule process to bring a project back on track.

Main Techniques of Schedule Compression
1. Crashing

- **Description**: Crashing involves adding additional resources to critical path activities without necessarily increasing the scope of the work. This may mean adding more labor, increasing working hours (overtime), or employing more efficient technology.
- **Advantages**:
    - **Effectiveness**: Crashing can significantly reduce the time needed to complete critical path activities, directly impacting the overall project duration.
    - **Quantifiable Impact**: The time savings are generally predictable if the relationship between resource addition and schedule reduction is well understood.
- **Disadvantages**:
    - **Increased Costs**: Crashing often leads to higher project costs due to overtime, additional manpower, or higher costs of more efficient methods or technologies.
    - **Diminishing Returns**: There is a limit to how much time can be saved by simply adding resources, beyond which additional resources may not lead to further time savings (Law of Diminishing Returns).
    - **Resource Fatigue**: Increased workload can lead to worker fatigue, potentially affecting productivity or increasing the likelihood of errors.

2. Fast-Tracking

- **Description**: Fast-tracking involves rearranging tasks to be done in parallel that were originally planned in sequence, as long as the activities can be overlapped without affecting the subsequent tasks.
- **Advantages**:
    - **No Additional Costs**: Generally, fast-tracking does not involve additional costs as it doesn't require extra resources, just a reorganization of existing workflows.
    - **Flexibility**: Offers flexibility in managing the schedule and can be implemented quickly without significant disruptions.
- **Disadvantages**:
    - **Increased Risk**: Performing tasks simultaneously, which were initially planned to be done sequentially, can increase risks due to a lack of information from pending tasks.
    - **Quality Issues**: Overlapping tasks might compromise quality if the hurried completion of activities leads to errors or omissions.
    - **Coordination Challenges**: Requires excellent coordination and communication; missteps can lead to delays rather than time savings.

Using Schedule Compression in the Control Schedule Process

In the Control Schedule process, project managers monitor the project's progress against the schedule baseline. If the project is lagging, schedule compression techniques may be employed to align the project with its planned completion date. The choice between crashing and fast-tracking often depends on the specific circumstances of the project, such as the available budget, risk tolerance, and flexibility of task sequences.

107

For example, if a software development project is behind schedule but has available budget, the project manager might decide to crash the schedule by hiring additional developers. Alternatively, if the budget is tight, the project manager might opt to fast-track the development by overlapping the design phase with the early stages of coding.

Conclusion

Schedule compression is a vital strategy for project managers needing to accelerate project timelines. Both crashing and fast-tracking have their places, depending on the project's specific needs, risks, and resource availability. Effective use of these techniques can help ensure project success even when original timelines are no longer feasible due to unforeseen delays or changes in project requirements. However, each technique carries inherent risks, particularly related to costs, quality, and team performance, which must be carefully managed. Schedule Variance (SV) and Schedule Performance Index (SPI) are two critical metrics used in Earned Value Management (EVM), a method that integrates scope, schedule, and cost measurements. These metrics are essential for the Control Schedule process as they provide quantitative data to assess and manage the schedule performance of a project.

Purpose of SV and SPI
Schedule Variance (SV):

- **Purpose**: SV measures the schedule performance by comparing the amount of work actually completed to the amount of work planned to be completed by a given time. It tells project managers whether they are ahead or behind the planned schedule.
- **Calculation**:

$$SV = EV - PV$$

Where EV (Earned Value) is the budgeted amount for the work actually completed to date, and PV (Planned Value) is the budgeted amount for the work planned to be completed by now.

Schedule Performance Index (SPI):

- **Purpose**: SPI is a ratio that gives a quick snapshot of the schedule efficiency. It helps in understanding how efficiently the team is using its time. An SPI greater than 1 indicates better than expected performance, whereas less than 1 indicates poor performance concerning the schedule.
- **Calculation**:

$$SPI = \frac{EV}{PV}$$

Using SV and SPI to Assess Schedule Performance
Assessing Project Health:

- Both SV and SPI can be used to quantitatively assess how well the project is adhering to the schedule. Positive SV and SPI greater than 1 suggest that the project is ahead of schedule, while negative SV and SPI less than 1 indicate a delay relative to the plan.

Forecasting Project Trends:

- These metrics are not only diagnostic but also predictive. They can help forecast future performance trends based on current data. If SPI is consistently below 1, project managers can anticipate potential delays and adjust the project plan accordingly.

Making Informed Decisions:

- By understanding SV and SPI, project managers can make informed decisions about resource reallocation, process adjustments, and corrective actions. For example, if SPI is low, additional resources might be allocated to critical tasks to bring the project back on track.

Examples of Using SV and SPI

1. **Example Scenario**: Suppose a project with a budget at completion (BAC) of $100,000 is supposed to have 50% of the work completed ($50,000 of PV) by a certain milestone. However, only $40,000 worth of work (EV) has been completed.
   - **SV Calculation**: $40,000 - $50,000 = -$10,000
   - **SPI Calculation**: $40,000 / $50,000 = 0.8
   - **Interpretation**: The project is behind schedule, as indicated by an SV of -$10,000 and an SPI of 0.8. The project is only achieving 80% of the work planned for this period.
2. **Corrective Actions**: Based on the SV and SPI values, the project manager might decide to implement overtime work, shift resources from less critical tasks to more urgent ones, or re-baseline the schedule if delays are unavoidable.

Conclusion

SV and SPI are powerful tools in the arsenal of a project manager for monitoring and controlling the schedule of a project. These metrics provide critical insights into the schedule performance, allowing project managers to identify issues early and apply corrective measures to keep the project on track. Through the effective use of SV and SPI, managers can maintain better control over project timelines, ultimately leading to more successful project outcomes. Project Schedule Management is deeply interwoven with several other knowledge areas in project management, particularly Project Scope Management and Project Resource Management. Understanding these interactions is crucial for comprehensive project planning and execution.

Interaction with Project Scope Management

Scope Management Processes:
- **Collect Requirements**: Determines what the stakeholders need, which directly influences the project's activities.
- **Define Scope**: Outlines what is to be accomplished in the project, forming the basis for all scheduled activities.
- **Create WBS (Work Breakdown Structure)**: Breaks down project deliverables into smaller, manageable components or work packages, which are essential for defining activities in the schedule.

Schedule Management Dependencies:
- Activities in the **Define Activities** process of Schedule Management are derived directly from the WBS created in Scope Management. The WBS provides the structure and detail needed to identify all the tasks that must be scheduled.
- The **Sequence Activities** process, where dependencies between activities are identified, relies on the detailed understanding of the project scope to determine the logical order of operations.

Example: In a building construction project, the scope might define a need for foundation, framing, roofing, and interior work. Each of these broad areas will be broken down in the WBS, and subsequently, specific activities such as "pour concrete", "install frames", etc., are scheduled. The project scope dictates the sequencing because certain tasks (like roofing) cannot begin until others (like framing) are complete.

Interaction with Project Resource Management

Resource Management Processes:

- **Estimate Resource Requirements**: Identifies the types and quantities of materials, people, equipment, or supplies required to perform project work.
- **Acquire Resources**: Involves obtaining the team members and physical resources necessary to complete project work.
- **Develop Team** and **Manage Team**: Focus on optimizing team performance through training, team-building, and conflict resolution.

Schedule Management Dependencies:

- The **Estimate Activity Durations** process in Schedule Management depends heavily on input from Resource Management, particularly regarding resource capabilities and availability. The accuracy of duration estimates improves with detailed knowledge of the resources assigned to each task.
- The **Develop Schedule** process must align with resource availability, ensuring that resources are not overallocated and that activities are planned for when resources are available.

Example: For a software development project, the schedule might require specific skilled developers to work on critical modules. Resource Management processes will ensure these developers are available and not assigned to other overlapping tasks. If a key team member is available only part-time, the schedule must accommodate this limitation, potentially extending the duration of related tasks.

Conclusion

Effective project management requires a holistic approach where processes from different knowledge areas interact seamlessly. The integration between Schedule Management, Scope Management, and Resource Management is particularly critical. This synergy ensures that the project progresses as planned, with activities well-defined, properly sequenced, and adequately resourced. Each element—scope, schedule, and resources—must be aligned to ensure that the project meets its objectives efficiently and effectively. Riverdale Regional Hospital embarked on an ambitious project to expand its facilities to accommodate increased patient intake and enhance its medical services. The project involved constructing a new wing, which included an advanced surgical unit, additional patient rooms, and updated medical technology systems. The project was budgeted at $25 million with a planned duration of 24 months.

Challenges Faced:

1. **Resource Constraints**: Midway through the project, there was a shortage of specialized labor due to overlapping projects in the region.
2. **Unexpected Delays**: Archaeological findings during the excavation phase required halting construction, causing significant project delays.
3. **Schedule Overruns**: Initial estimates proved optimistic as integration of new medical technology systems required more time than planned.

Strategies Employed:

1. **Adaptive Scheduling Techniques:**

- Employed rolling wave planning to detail work as the project progressed and more information became available, particularly in areas affected by uncertain archaeological findings.
- Used resource leveling to address the shortage of skilled labor by adjusting work sequences and reallocating resources from non-critical to critical path activities to mitigate delays.

2.   Enhanced Monitoring and Control:

- Implemented rigorous monitoring using Earned Value Management (EVM) to track project progress against the schedule and budget baselines. This included calculating Schedule Variance (SV) and Schedule Performance Index (SPI) to assess performance and make necessary adjustments.
- Conducted bi-weekly review meetings with stakeholders to discuss progress, issues, and corrective actions, maintaining transparency and ensuring all were informed and engaged.

3.   Proactive Risk Management:

- Developed a detailed risk management plan that included contingency strategies for potential delays due to archaeological findings. This proactive planning included engaging with local archaeological experts and regulatory bodies to expedite necessary procedures.
- Regularly updated the risk register and adjusted project plans as risks materialized, using what-if scenario analysis to predict the impact of potential changes and delays.

Lessons Learned:

1. **Importance of Flexible Planning**: The project manager noted the importance of flexibility in project planning and execution. Adaptive scheduling techniques like rolling wave planning proved crucial in managing complexities and uncertainties inherent in the project.
2. **Value of Proactive Risk Management**: Early identification and management of risks associated with archaeological findings prevented longer delays. Engaging experts and authorities early in the project facilitated smoother resolution of unexpected issues.
3. **Effective Stakeholder Communication**: Regular and transparent communication with all stakeholders, including the hospital administration, medical staff, and regulatory authorities, was essential. This ensured that all parties were aligned with the project's progress and any necessary adjustments.
4. **Robust Monitoring and Control**: Continuous monitoring using EVM enabled the project team to keep a close watch on schedule and cost deviations. This allowed for timely corrective actions, which were critical in keeping the project on track despite several challenges.

Project Outcome:

Despite initial setbacks and challenges, the Riverdale Regional Hospital expansion was completed with a four-month delay but remained within the original budget, thanks to effective schedule management and control practices. The new facilities were well-received, enhancing the hospital's capacity and service quality.

Conclusion:

This case study demonstrates the critical role of effective project schedule management in handling complex projects. It highlights how adaptive scheduling, proactive risk management, and robust project monitoring and control can address and mitigate project challenges, leading to successful project outcomes. Here's a set of practice questions designed to test and reinforce understanding of Project Schedule Management processes, their Inputs, Tools and Techniques, Outputs (ITTOs), and their application in real-world project scenarios. Each question includes a detailed explanation to enhance learning.

Question 1: What is the primary purpose of the "Define Activities" process in Project Schedule Management?

- A) To identify the project team and assign tasks
- B) To establish the amount of time each task will take to complete
- C) To determine the logical order of work required to complete the project tasks
- D) To decompose work packages into manageable activities

Correct Answer: D) To decompose work packages into manageable activities

- **Explanation**: The "Define Activities" process involves breaking down work packages from the Work Breakdown Structure (WBS) into smaller, more manageable components. This detail is crucial for further planning in the scheduling processes, such as estimating durations and sequencing activities.

Question 2: Which technique is NOT typically used in the "Sequence Activities" process?

- A) Precedence Diagramming Method (PDM)
- B) Critical Path Method (CPM)
- C) Bottom-Up Estimating
- D) Dependency Determination

Correct Answer: C) Bottom-Up Estimating

- **Explanation**: Bottom-Up Estimating is a technique used in estimating costs or durations by aggregating the estimates of lower-level components of the WBS. It is not used for sequencing activities, which instead utilizes methods like Precedence Diagramming Method (PDM) and tools like Dependency Determination to establish the order of activities.

Question 3: What is the main output of the "Develop Schedule" process?

- A) Project schedule
- B) Activity list
- C) Resource calendars
- D) Work performance data

Correct Answer: A) Project schedule

- **Explanation**: The main output of the "Develop Schedule" process is the project schedule, which integrates all the schedule activities, their durations, resources, and dependencies into a calendar. This comprehensive timeline reflects planned start and finish dates for project activities and is essential for executing, monitoring, and controlling the project.

Question 4: Which of the following statements best describes the role of the Critical Path Method (CPM) in project management?

- A) CPM is used to increase the project budget to accelerate the completion schedule.
- B) CPM is a technique to estimate the shortest path and duration through a project, determining the activities that cannot be delayed without affecting the project end date.
- C) CPM is utilized to distribute project communications.
- D) CPM focuses on risk management and mitigation strategies.

Correct Answer: B) CPM is a technique to estimate the shortest path and duration through a project, determining the activities that cannot be delayed without affecting the project end date.

- **Explanation**: The Critical Path Method (CPM) is crucial for identifying the longest sequence of dependent tasks in a project. Activities on this path form the critical path, which determines the shortest possible duration to complete the project. Any delay in these activities will directly impact the project completion date, making it a key focus for schedule management.

Question 5: How does the "Control Schedule" process contribute to project management?
- A) It involves developing the project team to ensure that they are effective in their roles.
- B) It is concerned with identifying changes to the project scope.
- C) It focuses on monitoring the status of the project to update project progress and manage changes to the schedule baseline.
- D) It ensures that quality standards are met for project deliverables.

Correct Answer: C) It focuses on monitoring the status of the project to update project progress and manage changes to the schedule baseline.
- **Explanation**: The "Control Schedule" process is essential for monitoring the progress of the project against the planned schedule baseline. It involves updating project progress, managing changes to the schedule, and adjusting forecasts based on performance. This process helps ensure that the project remains on track and can meet its deadlines, despite any necessary adjustments along the way.

These questions are designed to challenge the reader's understanding of Project Schedule Management and its practical applications in managing projects effectively. Each explanation helps reinforce the learning by clarifying how the processes and their outputs contribute to successful project execution.

VI. Project Cost Management:

The "Plan Cost Management" process is a crucial step in project management, which involves establishing policies, procedures, and documentation for planning, managing, spending, and controlling project costs. This process ensures that all project expenditures are planned, structured, and controlled. It sets the groundwork for how costs will be managed throughout the project lifecycle, from initial planning through to project completion.

Purpose and Importance of the Plan Cost Management Process
1. **Cost Efficiency and Budget Control**: The process enables project managers to define the methods and means to manage costs efficiently. This is crucial for keeping the project within the approved budget.
2. **Financial Planning**: It helps in the accurate estimation of costs, ensuring that the project financials are viable and aligned with the funding available.
3. **Decision Making**: Effective cost management planning provides the project manager and stakeholders with a clear picture of financial resources, enhancing decision-making related to project expenses and investments.
4. **Performance Measurement**: Establishes the criteria for measuring project performance against the allocated budget. This helps in identifying variances and taking corrective actions timely to avoid budget overruns.
5. **Risk Management**: Proper cost management planning helps identify financial risks early in the project, allowing for the development of risk mitigation strategies.

Key Components of a Cost Management Plan
Cost Estimation Methods:
This component details the techniques and tools that will be used to estimate project costs. Methods may include analogous estimating, parametric estimating, bottom-up estimating, and three-point estimating. Choosing the right estimation method is critical for developing accurate cost forecasts.

Budgeting Procedures:
Outlines the process for aggregating estimated costs to establish a total project budget. This often involves cost baseline development, which sets the benchmark for measuring project performance and managing changes to the cost baseline.

Cost Control Procedures:
Specifies how cost variances will be managed and controlled throughout the project. This includes tracking actual costs against the budget, forecasting potential overruns, and describing the steps for reporting and approving changes to the budget.

Funding Process:
Details the process for funding the project costs, including the timing of fund releases. This component is critical for cash flow management, ensuring that sufficient funds are available as needed to meet project milestones.

Reporting Formats:
Defines how and when cost information will be communicated to stakeholders. This includes specifying the types and formats of cost reports that will be used, such as cost variance reports and cost performance reports, which are essential for ongoing cost management and stakeholder communication.

Change Control Procedures:
Describes the process for managing changes in project costs and the budget. It outlines how such changes should be integrated into the overall project cost baseline and reported to stakeholders.

How These Components Guide Effective Cost Management
The components of the cost management plan work together to ensure that every dollar spent on the project is accounted for and wisely used. For instance:

- **Cost Estimation Methods** and **Budgeting Procedures** provide a framework for preparing a realistic and comprehensive budget, which is crucial for tracking financial performance.
- **Cost Control Procedures** help maintain control over expenditures, ensuring that the project remains within budget or that deviations are managed proactively.
- **Reporting Formats** ensure transparency, keeping stakeholders informed and involved in the financial aspect of the project, which aids in trust and collaborative decision-making.
- **Change Control Procedures** ensure that any changes that impact the project's costs are thoroughly evaluated and approved before being implemented, thus maintaining financial discipline and alignment with project goals.

The Plan Cost Management process is essential for ensuring that a project can be completed within the approved budget. It provides a structured approach to cost estimation, allocation, and control, guiding the project team in making informed financial decisions and taking corrective actions as necessary. This process is integral to the financial health of the project and its ultimate success. The Cost Management Plan is an integral component of the project management process, closely intertwined with other key management plans, particularly the Scope Management Plan and the Schedule Management Plan.

Understanding these relationships is crucial for ensuring that project planning and execution are coherent and aligned across all areas.

Cost Management Plan and Its Relationship with Scope and Schedule Plans
1. Scope Management Plan:

- **Influence on Cost Management**: The Scope Management Plan defines what is to be accomplished in the project. It outlines the project deliverables and the work required to complete those deliverables. Since the cost management plan focuses on estimating, budgeting, and controlling costs, the defined scope directly influences these elements. The more detailed and clear the project scope, the more accurate and effective the cost estimation and control can be.
- **Impact Example**: If the Scope Management Plan is expanded, the Cost Management Plan must be adjusted to accommodate increased costs associated with broader work requirements, additional resources, and possibly extended project timelines.
-

2. Schedule Management Plan:

- **Influence on Cost Management**: The Schedule Management Plan lays out the timeline for project activities, including when resources are needed. Since many costs in a project are time-dependent (such as labor rates, equipment rentals, and facility costs), the schedule significantly impacts cost estimations and expenditures over the project's lifecycle. The duration of scheduled activities can affect the project's cash flow and budget allocation.
- **Impact Example**: Delays in the schedule can increase costs due to longer resource utilization, extended operational expenditures, and potentially higher costs for rush orders or overtime. Conversely, accelerating the schedule might save money on some fronts but could increase costs on others, such as higher labor rates for overtime.

Development of the Cost Management Plan Influenced by Scope and Schedule
Integrating Scope and Schedule into Cost Management:

- **Cost Estimation**: Begins with detailed requirements from the Scope Management Plan. Cost estimators use the work breakdown structure (WBS) from the scope plan to itemize costs for materials, labor, equipment, and any other expenses necessary to complete the work.
- **Budgeting**: Once costs are estimated, the budgeting process allocates financial resources across the project's schedule, detailed in the Schedule Management Plan. This step involves distributing the total project budget over the planned duration according to scheduled activities and milestones.
- **Cost Control**: Involves tracking the project expenses against the budgeted costs over time, as dictated by the Schedule Management Plan. This process ensures that the project remains financially on track and provides a mechanism for adjusting the budget or schedule as the project progresses.

Example of Plan Integration in a Project
Imagine a construction project where the Scope Management Plan specifies building a new facility, including dimensions and materials required. The Schedule Management Plan outlines the project timeline, specifying key milestones such as completion of the foundation, main structure, and interior fittings. The Cost Management Plan will use the scope details to estimate costs for materials (like concrete and steel), labor (from construction workers to architects), and other direct costs (like equipment rental). It will then allocate the overall budget according to the timeline specified in the Schedule Management

Plan, perhaps setting specific budgets for each phase of construction. The plan will also include methods for monitoring costs as the project progresses, ensuring that spending aligns with the planned budget and schedule.

Conclusion

The development of a Cost Management Plan is heavily influenced by the project's scope and schedule. A well-integrated approach to managing scope, schedule, and costs leads to more accurate planning, efficient resource utilization, and better overall project control. Each plan should not be developed in isolation but rather as a coordinated effort to ensure project success. This integration ensures that changes in any area—scope, schedule, or cost—are reflected across all aspects of project management, maintaining alignment and facilitating effective decision-making. The "Plan Cost Management" process is a critical part of project management, serving as the blueprint for how costs will be managed throughout the project's lifecycle. Understanding its essential inputs, tools and techniques, and outputs (ITTOs) helps in establishing a systematic and effective approach to managing project costs.

Essential Inputs

1. **Project Charter**: This document provides the project's initial defined scope and financial resources, setting the stage for detailed cost management planning. It includes the total budget at a high level and any pre-approved financial resources.
2. **Project Management Plan**: Elements of the overall plan that influence cost management include the scope baseline, schedule baseline, and quality management plan. Each of these can affect how costs are estimated, budgeted, and controlled.
3. **Enterprise Environmental Factors (EEFs)**: These might include commercial databases of cost estimating data, standard cost estimating tools, and established financial policies and procedures that the project must adhere to.
4. **Organizational Process Assets (OPAs)**: Historical data and lessons learned from similar projects, financial tracking systems, and budgeting and financial policies of the organization.

Tools and Techniques

1. **Expert Judgment**: Utilizing experience and knowledge from individuals or groups, typically from finance or from past projects with similar scope, to inform the planning of cost management.
2. **Analogous Estimating**: Using the actual costs from previous, similar projects as the basis for estimating costs for the current project. This technique is quicker but less accurate, used when there is limited detailed information available.
3. **Parametric Estimating**: Involves using statistical relationships between historical data and other variables (e.g., cost per square meter of construction) to estimate costs, which can be more accurate than analogous estimating if the underlying data is reliable.
4. **Cost Aggregation**: Summing the lower-level cost estimates to produce a total estimate for the project at a higher level. This aggregation is typically done by work packages in the WBS and rolled up to higher levels for total project cost estimates.
5. **Historical Information Review**: Analyzing cost data from previous projects to identify relevant baselines, estimating data, and achieved costs, which can help improve the accuracy of cost predictions.
6. **Funding Limit Reconciliation**: Ensuring that the project's expenditure does not exceed the authorized funding by period. It involves comparing planned expenditure with actual funding over time, adjusting activities as necessary to adhere to the funding.

Outputs
1. Cost Management Plan:
The primary output, this plan details how project costs will be planned, structured, budgeted, and controlled. It includes:

- **Units of Measure**: Defined for each resource type, such as staff hours, days, or lump sum.
- **Precision Level**: Specifies the degree to which costs will be quantified (e.g., rounded to the nearest hundred dollars).
- **Thresholds**: Identified variances that will be tolerated in monitoring project cost performance, which may trigger actions.
- **Reporting Formats**: Defines how the reports will be structured, what they will include, and how often they will be produced.
- **Process Descriptions**: Detailed procedures for managing costs throughout the project.

Significance in Establishing a Comprehensive Cost Management Approach
Each component plays a vital role in ensuring effective cost management:

- **Inputs** provide the foundational information and contextual background necessary for accurate cost planning.
- **Tools and Techniques** are mechanisms through which cost planning, estimation, and control are executed, ensuring that cost management is both realistic and adherent to organizational practices.
- **Outputs**, primarily the Cost Management Plan, provide a roadmap for cost control throughout the project, ensuring that costs are transparently managed and reported.

By integrating these elements effectively, the Plan Cost Management process helps ensure that the project can be completed within the approved budget, thereby enhancing the project's likelihood of success and financial viability. The "Estimate Costs" process is crucial in project management as it involves developing an approximation of the monetary resources needed to complete project activities. This process is fundamental to establishing a project budget that reflects the expected costs of the project's tasks and resources.

Role of the Estimate Costs Process
1. **Budget Preparation**: The primary role of estimating costs is to provide a detailed, quantitative basis for preparing the project budget. Accurate cost estimates ensure that the project has adequate funding to reach completion without financial overruns.
2. **Decision Making**: Cost estimates are used to make informed decisions about resource allocation, project scope, and operational planning. They also help in determining the feasibility and viability of the project.
3. **Baseline for Cost Control**: Once approved, the cost estimates serve as a baseline for cost control. This allows project managers to monitor actual spend against the forecasted costs and take corrective action when variances occur.
4. **Stakeholder Communication**: Detailed cost estimates facilitate clear communication with stakeholders regarding financial needs and constraints, which helps in securing funding, approvals, and continued stakeholder support throughout the project lifecycle.

Primary Inputs of the Estimate Costs Process

1. **Cost Management Plan**: Provides guidelines on how costs will be managed and controlled throughout the project. It includes methodologies and procedures for estimating, budgeting, and controlling project costs.
2. **Human Resource Management Plan**: Outlines team resource management, including labor rates, which are necessary for calculating labor costs for project activities.
3. **Scope Baseline**: Includes the project scope statement, WBS, and WBS dictionary. These documents offer a detailed breakdown of the work to be performed, which is essential for accurate cost estimation.
4. **Project Schedule**: Contains information on the planned start and finish of project activities. The schedule helps in estimating costs related to project duration, such as labor costs, equipment rentals, and facility charges over time.
5. **Risk Register**: Provides insights into potential risks that could impact project costs. Including risk-related costs in the estimates helps in preparing for uncertainties.
6. **Enterprise Environmental Factors (EEFs)**: Factors such as market conditions, currency exchange rates, and commercial databases of cost estimating data can influence cost estimates.
7. **Organizational Process Assets (OPAs)**: Historical data and lessons learned from previous projects assist in creating more accurate and reliable cost estimates.

Primary Outputs of the Estimate Costs Process

1. **Activity Cost Estimates**: These are quantitative assessments of the likely costs of resources required to complete project work. These estimates cover all necessary funding for materials, equipment, services, labor, and reserves.
2. **Basis of Estimates**: This document provides a detailed explanation of how the cost estimates were derived. It includes details about the scope of work, assumptions made, constraints considered, range of possible estimates (e.g., ±10%), and the confidence level of the final estimates.
3. **Project Document Updates**: As cost estimates are developed, several project documents may be updated, including the risk register and the project schedule to reflect the latest cost-related insights and data.

Conclusion

The Estimate Costs process is pivotal in creating a financial framework for project management. Accurate cost estimation not only ensures that the project is financially feasible but also supports effective project control and management. By considering various inputs and carefully deriving outputs, project managers can maintain a firm grasp on the financial aspects of the project, ensuring that it progresses within the allocated budget. The "Estimate Costs" process in project management involves predicting the total cost of completing all project activities. It's crucial for budget planning, securing funding, and controlling spending. Several tools and techniques can be employed in this process, each with specific scenarios where they are most suitable, and each with distinct advantages and limitations.

1. Analogous Estimating

Description: This involves using the actual costs from previous, similar projects as a basis for estimating the costs of the current project.

Example: If a project manager previously built a bridge of similar size and complexity under comparable conditions for $2 million, they might estimate that a current bridge project will cost approximately the same.

Appropriateness: It's most suitable when there is limited detailed information about the project or when project details are still being defined. It's quick and less expensive to implement.

Advantages:
- Quick and cost-effective.
- Useful when limited data is available.

Limitations:
- Less accurate, as it relies on the assumption that current projects are similar to past projects.
- Can be misleading if past projects are not truly comparable.

2. Bottom-Up Estimating

Description: This technique involves estimating the cost of individual activities or work packages in detail and summing them to get the total project cost.

Example: In constructing a building, the project manager estimates the costs for foundation work, framing, electrical, plumbing, finishing, etc., separately and then aggregates these to form the total cost.

Appropriateness: Most appropriate for projects where detailed information about the project's tasks is available, and a high degree of accuracy is required.

Advantages:
- Highly accurate when detailed information is available.
- Provides a detailed view of where money is spent, which aids in monitoring and controlling project costs.

Limitations:
- Time-consuming and expensive to develop because it requires detailed information.
- Can be over-complicated if too much detail is unnecessary.

3. Parametric Estimating

Description: This technique uses statistical relationships between historical data and other variables (such as square footage or installation per unit) to calculate estimates.

Example: In software development, if historical data suggests that coding a certain type of software typically costs $100 per function point, and the project is estimated to require 800 function points, the total cost for coding would be estimated at $80,000.

Appropriateness: Useful when there is reliable data for the parameters being used and when the model or formula is scalable and applicable to the specific project context.

Advantages:
- More accurate than analogous estimating if the underlying data and model are robust.
- Efficient for projects with standard, repetitive tasks or components.

Limitations:
- Dependence on the availability of high-quality, relevant historical data.
- The accuracy is contingent on the mathematical model's applicability to the specific project circumstances.

Conclusion

Each cost estimating technique offers unique benefits and has specific scenarios where it is most effective. Choosing the right method depends on the project's requirements, the availability and reliability of data, the project's complexity, and how precise the cost estimate needs to be. In practice, project managers often use a combination of these techniques to leverage their respective strengths and mitigate their limitations, ensuring a more comprehensive and accurate project cost estimate. The Cost Breakdown

Structure (CBS) is a systematic categorization of the costs involved in a project, organized in a way that aligns with the way the project work is executed. It is fundamentally a financial representation of the project's Work Breakdown Structure (WBS), breaking down all project costs into manageable, identifiable parts.

Understanding the Cost Breakdown Structure (CBS)

Definition and Purpose:
- **Definition**: A CBS is a hierarchical decomposition of costs that mirrors the WBS. It categorizes and aggregates costs by the components of the WBS, including all phases, deliverables, and work packages involved in a project.
- **Purpose**: The main purpose of the CBS is to facilitate the effective management and control of project costs. It helps in tracking, reporting, and analyzing project expenditures, ensuring that the project remains on budget.

Relationship between CBS and WBS

- **Direct Correlation**: Each element of the WBS has a corresponding element in the CBS. This alignment ensures that costs are tracked and managed in parallel with the project work.
- **Detailed Cost Tracking**: By mirroring the WBS, the CBS allows project managers to track the costs associated with specific deliverables or work packages, making it easier to identify areas where the project may be over or under budget.
- **Simplified Communication and Analysis**: Having a structured breakdown that corresponds to the WBS simplifies communication about costs with stakeholders and facilitates detailed financial analysis and reporting.

Example of a Cost Breakdown Structure

Consider a software development project organized via a WBS. Below is an example of how the CBS might be structured corresponding to the WBS elements:
- **WBS 1.0 Software Development Project**
  - **WBS 1.1 Requirements Gathering**
    - **CBS 1.1.1 Personnel Costs (salaries for business analysts)**
    - **CBS 1.1.2 Travel Expenses (stakeholder interviews)**
  - **WBS 1.2 Software Design**
    - **CBS 1.2.1 Personnel Costs (salaries for software designers)**
    - **CBS 1.2.2 Software Tools (licensing fees for design tools)**
  - **WBS 1.3 Coding and Implementation**
    - **CBS 1.3.1 Personnel Costs (salaries for developers)**
    - **CBS 1.3.2 Hardware/Software (servers and development environments)**
  - **WBS 1.4 Testing**
    - **CBS 1.4.1 Personnel Costs (salaries for QA engineers)**
    - **CBS 1.4.2 Testing Tools (automation tools and services)**

Role of the CBS in Organizing and Tracking Project Costs

- **Budget Allocation**: The CBS allows project managers to allocate the budget specifically and suitably across different categories as per the project requirements detailed in the WBS.
- **Cost Monitoring**: It enables continuous monitoring of actual spending against budgeted costs for each element of the WBS, thus providing clear visibility into financial performance.

- **Financial Control**: By organizing costs according to the detailed structure of the WBS, the CBS supports stringent financial control, enabling quick adjustments in case of budget overruns or reallocation of funds based on project evolution.

Conclusion

The Cost Breakdown Structure is a critical tool in cost management that, when effectively utilized, ensures comprehensive tracking and control of project expenditures. By directly relating to the Work Breakdown Structure, the CBS enhances transparency and accountability in managing project costs, making it an indispensable component of successful project management. In project cost management, the concepts of **contingency reserves** and **management reserves** play crucial roles in addressing financial uncertainties and risks throughout the duration of a project. Both types of reserves provide buffers to the project budget but are intended for different types of uncertainties.

Contingency Reserves

Description: Contingency reserves, also known as contingency allowances, are budgetary provisions specifically set aside for "known-unknowns" — risks that are identified and analyzed for their potential impact. These reserves are part of the cost baseline.

Purpose: The primary purpose of contingency reserves is to address cost overruns for individual tasks or work packages due to identified risks. They provide a financial buffer that allows the project to respond to unforeseen issues without immediately impacting the overall project budget.

Determination: Contingency reserves are typically determined based on risk analysis and the cost impacts of identified risks. Techniques such as expected monetary value analysis, Monte Carlo simulation, or expert judgment can be used. The amount reserved is often a percentage of the estimated costs, based on historical data and risk assessments.

Management Reserves

Description: Management reserves are funds set aside for "unknown-unknowns" — unforeseen work that is within the scope of the project but was not identified and planned at the time of cost estimating and budgeting. These reserves are not included in the baseline but are part of the overall project budget.

Purpose: The purpose of management reserves is to ensure that the project has funds available to address completely unforeseen events or changes in scope. They are meant for use when something changes fundamentally about what the project needs to deliver, or an entirely unexpected situation arises.

Determination: Management reserves are generally determined based on organizational policies and past project experiences. They are typically set as a percentage of the total project budget, taking into account the project's complexity, the environment's volatility, and the project manager's or organization's risk tolerance.

Role in Addressing Project Risks and Uncertainties

Both types of reserves are critical in risk management and financial planning for projects:

Contingency Reserves:

These are used first when issues arise during the project. For example, if a project task is delayed due to a supplier issue and this delay costs extra money that was not in the original estimate, contingency funds can be used to cover this without needing to re-allocate funds from other parts of the project.

Management Reserves:

These funds are used for significant unforeseen changes that go beyond the original scope or risk assumptions of the project. For example, if new legislation requires additional compliance measures not originally planned for, management reserves might be tapped to cover these new requirements.

By effectively using these reserves, project managers can ensure that they have the financial flexibility to handle both expected and unexpected challenges, thereby maintaining control over the project's budget and schedule. This proactive financial planning helps in achieving project objectives, even in the face of uncertainty and risks, thus contributing to the overall success of the project. The "Determine Budget" process is a critical step in project management where the estimated costs of individual activities are aggregated to establish an authorized cost baseline. This baseline serves as the reference point against which all project spending is monitored and controlled, making it central to effective financial management and project success.

Significance of Establishing a Cost Baseline

1. **Financial Planning and Control**: The cost baseline provides a formal measure against which project performance can be compared in terms of financial expenditure. It enables project managers to gauge financial health and take corrective actions if expenditures deviate from the planned budget.
2. **Stakeholder Assurance**: By establishing a detailed budget, stakeholders have a clear understanding of the financial resources required for the project. It reassures funders and senior management of prudent financial planning and governance.
3. **Resource Allocation**: A well-defined budget ensures that resources are allocated efficiently across all project activities, supporting optimal resource utilization without overspending.
4. **Performance Measurement**: The cost baseline is essential for performance measurement techniques such as Earned Value Management (EVM), which uses the baseline to assess project performance and forecast future performance trends.

Key Steps in the Determine Budget Process
1. Aggregation of Cost Estimates

- **Activity Level Estimation**: Start by compiling the cost estimates for each individual activity within the project. These are detailed estimates derived from the "Estimate Costs" process, which considers resources, labor, materials, equipment, and any contingencies.
- **Work Package Aggregation**: Aggregate the activity cost estimates at the work package level. This involves summing up all the costs associated with the activities that make up each work package as defined in the Work Breakdown Structure (WBS).

2. Account for Contingency Reserves

- **Identification of Risks**: Review the risk register to identify potential risks that could impact the project budget.
- **Contingency Reserves**: Allocate contingency reserves to account for identified risks. These reserves are typically calculated based on the risk analysis and are intended to cover unforeseen costs directly associated with the execution of the planned scope.

3. Incorporation of Management Reserves

- **Management Reserves**: In addition to contingency reserves, management reserves are set aside for unforeseeable work that is not part of the project scope but may impact the project. These are generally controlled by higher management and are not included in the cost baseline but are part of the overall project budget.

4. Approval and Baseline Establishment

- **Consolidation and Approval**: Consolidate all costs, including base costs and reserves, and present the total project budget for approval by project stakeholders or sponsors.
- **Baseline Establishment**: Once approved, establish the cost baseline, which includes all authorized budgets allocated to the project excluding the management reserves.

5.   Update Project Documents

- **Documentation**: Update all relevant project documents to reflect the approved budget and baseline. This includes updating cost management plans, funding requirements, and cash flow statements.

Example of the Determine Budget Process

Imagine a project to upgrade IT infrastructure. Here's how the budget determination might unfold:

- **Activity Costs**: Costs are estimated for hardware upgrades, software licenses, and labor.
- **Work Package Aggregation**: These estimates are aggregated at the level of major deliverables, such as server installation, network configuration, and system testing.
- **Contingency Reserves**: Additional funds are allocated for risks identified, such as potential delays in hardware delivery or unexpected software incompatibility issues.
- **Management Reserves**: Further reserves are set aside for unforeseeable issues like sudden changes in technology standards.
- **Approval and Baseline**: The total budget, including all reserves, is consolidated and presented for approval. Once approved, it is set as the cost baseline.

Conclusion

The "Determine Budget" process is foundational in setting a realistic financial framework for the project. By meticulously aggregating cost estimates and accounting for both known and unknown risks, the process ensures that the project is financially well-planned, enhancing the probability of successful project delivery within the approved budget. In the context of project management, understanding the distinction between funding requirements and the cost baseline is crucial for effective financial planning and management. Each serves a distinct role in the Determine Budget process, which involves aggregating the estimated costs of individual activities or work packages to establish a total project budget.

Cost Baseline

Definition: The cost baseline is an approved version of the project budget, which includes all authorized project costs and is used as a fixed reference for measuring project performance against costs. It includes both the direct costs of tasks and indirect costs associated with completing the project.

Purpose: The cost baseline provides a benchmark for financial monitoring and controlling throughout the project. It's used to measure and report the actual cost performance against the planned budget, helping to identify variances that might impact the project's financial health.

Funding Requirements

Definition: Funding requirements refer to the projected total financial resources needed to carry out the project. This includes the total cost baseline plus any additional reserves, such as management reserves.

Purpose: Unlike the cost baseline, which is static and used for performance measurement, funding requirements consider the actual flow of funds needed to support the project. They reflect when funds will need to be available to ensure the project progresses without financial interruptions.

Differences and Relationship

- **Composition**: The cost baseline includes all budgeted amounts that will be spent directly on completing the project tasks, along with allocated indirect costs. Funding requirements encompass the cost baseline plus all reserves that might be needed, including contingency reserves and management reserves.
- **Usage**: The cost baseline is used for tracking and reporting project performance and financial health. Funding requirements are used to ensure that adequate funding is available when needed throughout the project lifecycle.
- **Adjustments**: The cost baseline is typically static once approved unless a formal change control process justifies a baseline change. In contrast, funding requirements might be adjusted more frequently as the project progresses and as funds are disbursed.

Ensuring Sufficient Funding

To ensure that sufficient funding is available throughout the project lifecycle, project managers can employ several strategies:

1. **Detailed Financial Planning**: During the budgeting phase, project managers need to develop a detailed understanding of the project's financial needs, including timing for specific expenditures. This involves creating detailed cost estimates and defining the schedule for funding requirements.
2. **Phased Funding**: In many cases, especially in long or complex projects, funding might be allocated in phases rather than all at once. Project managers need to plan for these phases and ensure that each phase of the project is funded appropriately before proceeding.
3. **Cash Flow Analysis**: Regular cash flow analyses can help project managers understand the inflows and outflows of project funds. This analysis helps in managing the liquidity needs of the project and ensuring that funds are available when critical payments need to be made.
4. **Management and Contingency Reserves**: By establishing and maintaining management and contingency reserves, project managers can ensure they have additional buffers that can be used if project costs exceed initial estimates due to unforeseen circumstances.
5. **Stakeholder Communication**: Keeping stakeholders informed about financial needs and the status of the project budget is crucial. Regular updates can help in securing additional funding or making necessary adjustments in a timely manner.

While the cost baseline is essential for measuring and controlling costs during the project, funding requirements ensure that the project has enough financial resources at the right times. Effective management of both elements is crucial to the successful financial execution of a project. The "Control Costs" process is a fundamental component of project management, focused on monitoring and regulating the project's expenditures to ensure that the actual spend does not exceed the budgeted costs. This process is essential for maintaining financial control over the project, making informed decisions, and ensuring project profitability.

Importance of the Control Costs Process

1. **Budget Compliance**: Ensures that project spending is kept within the approved budget. Regular monitoring helps detect and correct any deviations from the cost baseline early, preventing budget overruns.

2. **Financial Performance**: Provides continuous oversight of financial performance against the cost baseline, enabling project managers to evaluate the financial health of the project and take corrective actions when necessary.
3. **Decision Support**: Real-time cost data supports decision-making regarding resource allocation, scope adjustments, and other project variables that can impact costs.
4. **Stakeholder Confidence**: Maintaining control over costs enhances stakeholder trust and confidence in the project management team's ability to deliver the project within the financial constraints set out.
5. **Value Maximization**: By controlling costs, project managers can maximize the project's value by optimizing the use of resources and ensuring that financial resources are spent judiciously.

Primary Tools and Techniques for Controlling Costs
1. Earned Value Management (EVM)

- **Description**: EVM is a powerful analytical tool that integrates scope, schedule, and resource measurements to assess project performance and progress. It provides key metrics such as Cost Variance (CV), Schedule Variance (SV), Cost Performance Index (CPI), and Schedule Performance Index (SPI).
- **Application**: By comparing the Planned Value (PV), Earned Value (EV), and Actual Cost (AC), project managers can determine whether the project is ahead, on, or behind schedule and budget.

2. Forecasting

- **Description**: Techniques used to predict future project performance based on current cost performance trends. This includes estimating future project costs at completion (EAC) and estimating the time required to complete remaining work.
- **Application**: Forecasting helps in predicting where the project will end concerning the budget and schedule, allowing project managers to make informed decisions about resource reallocation or scope adjustments to stay within budget.

2. To-Complete Performance Index (TCPI)

- **Description**: An EVM measure used to calculate the cost performance efficiency that must be achieved on the remaining work to meet a specific management goal, such as the budget at completion (BAC) or the estimated at completion (EAC).
- **Application**: TCPI provides a reality check on the feasibility of achieving the project budget objectives, given the current project performance.

4. Variance Analysis

- **Description**: Involves determining the cause and degree of variance relative to the baseline plan. Cost variance analysis is critical for identifying the root cause of variances and implementing corrective actions.
- **Application**: Regularly performed, variance analysis helps maintain control over costs by providing early warning signs of possible cost overruns.

5. Performance Reviews

- **Description**: Involves assessing the project team's performance against the budget, schedule, and scope baselines.

- **Application**: These reviews are crucial for ensuring that project execution aligns with the plan and for making adjustments where necessary to bring project performance back on track.

6. Reserve Analysis

- **Description**: Evaluates the status and utilization of contingency and management reserves.
- **Application**: Helps determine whether remaining reserves are adequate to cover future risks and uncertainties, ensuring that the project remains financially viable.

Conclusion

The "Control Costs" process is crucial for effective financial management within project management. Utilizing sophisticated tools and techniques such as Earned Value Management, forecasting, variance analysis, and others ensures that project managers have the necessary information and analytical capability to keep the project financially on track. By effectively controlling costs, projects can meet their objectives without unnecessary financial waste, thereby enhancing their success and profitability. Earned Value Management (EVM) is a systematic project management process used to measure and evaluate the performance and progress of a project. EVM integrates scope, schedule, and cost data, providing an objective snapshot of project performance and its current and future status. This integration allows project managers to forecast project outcomes more reliably based on trends and provides an early warning of performance issues.

Fundamentals of Earned Value Management (EVM)

EVM operates primarily on three key data points:

1. **Planned Value (PV)**: Also known as the Budgeted Cost of Work Scheduled (BCWS), this is the budgeted cost for work planned to be done by a specified time. It represents the baseline of the costs for the project tasks that should have been completed by the measurement date.
2. **Earned Value (EV)**: Also known as the Budgeted Cost of Work Performed (BCWP), this is the budgeted cost for the work actually completed by the specified time. It measures the work performed in terms of the budget authorized for that work.
3. **Actual Cost (AC)**: Also known as the Actual Cost of Work Performed (ACWP), this is the actual cost incurred for the work completed by the specified date. It represents the true financial resources that have been consumed for the work performed.

EVM Metrics

Using these data points, several critical EVM metrics are calculated:

- **Cost Variance (CV)**: $CV=EV-AC$ – Measures cost performance by comparing the work done to the actual cost. A positive value indicates under budget, while a negative value indicates over budget.
- **Schedule Variance (SV)**: $SV=EV-PV$ – Measures schedule performance by comparing the work performed to the work planned. A positive value indicates ahead of schedule, while a negative value means behind schedule.
- **Cost Performance Index (CPI)**: $CPI=\frac{EV}{AC}$ – Shows the cost efficiency of the work performed. It is a critical factor for cost forecasting.
- **Schedule Performance Index (SPI)**: $SPI=\frac{EV}{PV}$ – Indicates the efficiency of time usage per plan.

Role of EVM in Control Costs Process

EVM provides a quantitative method to assess and control the overall cost performance of the project. Here's how it plays a pivotal role:

1. **Performance Measurement**: EVM provides a comprehensive and accurate method for measuring project performance against the original scope, schedule, and budget, allowing for performance analysis at a glance.
2. **Forecasting**: Through CPI and SPI, EVM helps predict future project performance scenarios. Project managers can forecast the estimated cost at completion (EAC) and determine if the current budget is sufficient to complete the project.
3. **Decision Making**: By identifying cost and schedule variances, EVM supports informed decision-making regarding resource reallocation, corrective actions, and efforts needed to meet project objectives.
4. **Risk Management**: Regular EVM analysis helps identify trends that may indicate potential risks in terms of scope delivery, schedule slippage, or budget overruns. It facilitates proactive management and mitigation strategies.

Integrating Scope, Schedule, and Cost

EVM effectively combines scope, schedule, and cost data:

- **Scope**: Earned value (EV) provides a quantifiable measure of the physical work accomplished, integrating scope verification into cost management.
- **Schedule**: Comparing EV against PV gives a clear picture of whether project tasks are on schedule, integrating the time dimension.
- **Cost**: Comparing EV against AC highlights how much more, or less, the project has cost than planned when achieving the actual work, integrating the cost dimension.

This integration ensures that project performance is not evaluated based solely on spending or task completion but on a holistic view of all three critical dimensions, thereby enhancing the control and success of the project. Earned Value Management (EVM) is a project management technique used for measuring project performance and progress in an objective manner. It integrates project scope, cost, and schedule measures to help project managers assess the project's performance and predict future trends. The key metrics in EVM are Planned Value (PV), Actual Cost (AC), and Earned Value (EV).

1. Planned Value (PV)

- **Definition**: Planned Value, also known as Budgeted Cost of Work Scheduled (BCWS), is the approved budget allocated for the work scheduled to be completed by a specified date.
- **Formula**: PV = Budget at Completion (BAC) × Percentage of Planned Work
- **Significance**: PV acts as a benchmark for assessing how much work should have been completed, given the plan up to a certain point in time. It is essential for comparing what has been spent to what should have been done according to the original plan.

2. Actual Cost (AC)

- **Definition**: Actual Cost, also known as Actual Cost of Work Performed (ACWP), is the total cost incurred for the work completed to date.
- **Formula**: AC = Total Direct Costs + Total Indirect Costs for the work completed
- **Significance**: AC provides a snapshot of the total expenses of the project to date. It is used to compare against the EV to determine cost efficiency and identify any cost overruns early in the process.

3. Earned Value (EV)

- **Definition**: Earned Value, also known as Budgeted Cost of Work Performed (BCWP), is the value of work actually completed to date, measured against the approved budget.
- **Formula**: EV = BAC × Percentage of Actual Work Completed
- **Significance**: EV is a critical metric that shows whether the budgeted cost of work completed is aligning with the pre-planned costs. It provides a quantitative measure of project performance and progress.

Using EVM Metrics to Assess Project Performance

These three metrics (PV, AC, EV) are foundational to performing further EVM calculations that help assess project health and efficiency:

- **Cost Variance (CV)**: CV = EV - AC. This metric shows whether the work completed is under or over the budget. A positive value indicates under budget, and a negative value indicates an overrun.
- **Schedule Variance (SV)**: SV = EV - PV. This metric indicates whether the project is ahead of or behind the planned schedule. Positive values signify ahead of schedule, and negative values signify delays.
- **Cost Performance Index (CPI)**: CPI = EV / AC. This index measures the cost efficiency of the work completed. Values greater than 1.0 indicate better than expected performance concerning the budget.
- **Schedule Performance Index (SPI)**: SPI = EV / PV. This index measures the efficiency of time usage. Values greater than 1.0 indicate faster progress than planned.

Example Application of EVM Metrics

Consider a project with a BAC of $100,000 planned to last 10 months. By the end of month 5:

- Planned Value (PV) would be $50,000 (50% of $100,000)
- If the Actual Cost (AC) of work performed by the end of month 5 is $55,000,
- And the Earned Value (EV) based on work actually completed is $45,000,

Then,

- CV = $45,000 - $55,000 = -$10,000 (over budget)
- SV = $45,000 - $50,000 = -$5,000 (behind schedule)
- CPI = $45,000 / $55,000 ≈ 0.82 (cost inefficiency)
- SPI = $45,000 / $50,000 = 0.90 (schedule inefficiency)

Conclusion

EVM metrics like PV, AC, and EV are essential for providing a comprehensive picture of project health, allowing project managers to make informed decisions about resource allocation, corrective actions, and future planning to steer the project towards its goals efficiently. Schedule Variance (SV) and Cost Variance (CV) are two fundamental metrics derived from Earned Value Management (EVM), a comprehensive project management technique that integrates scope, schedule, and cost data. These variances are critical for assessing a project's health and ensuring that it remains on track both financially and temporally.

Schedule Variance (SV)

Definition: Schedule Variance is a measure of the difference between the Earned Value (EV) and the Planned Value (PV) of work. It provides insight into whether a project is ahead or behind the schedule that was originally planned.

Calculation: $SV = EV - PV$

- **EV (Earned Value)**: The value of the work actually performed expressed in terms of the budget assigned to that work.
- **PV (Planned Value)**: The expected value of the work scheduled to be completed by a certain date.

Interpretation:

- A **positive SV** indicates that more work has been completed than was planned at this point in time, suggesting the project is ahead of schedule.
- A **negative SV** indicates that less work has been completed than was planned, suggesting the project is behind schedule.
- An SV of zero indicates that the project is exactly on schedule.

Cost Variance (CV)

Definition: Cost Variance is a measure of the difference between the Earned Value (EV) and the Actual Cost (AC) of work performed. It reflects how much over or under budget the project is in terms of the work completed to date.

Calculation: $CV = EV - AC$

- **AC (Actual Cost)**: The actual cost incurred for the work performed up to a given point in time.

Interpretation:

- A **positive CV** indicates that the project is under budget (the cost of the work performed is less than planned).
- A **negative CV** means that the project is over budget (the cost of the work performed is greater than planned).
- A CV of zero indicates that the project is on budget.

Implications for Project Performance
Project Schedule and Cost Control:

- **Schedule Variance (SV)**: Provides immediate feedback on time performance. Project managers can use this information to adjust task sequences, allocate additional resources, or take other corrective actions to bring the project back on schedule. Continuously negative SV values may signal deeper issues with project planning or execution.
- **Cost Variance (CV)**: Acts as an early warning system for cost overrun issues. It allows project managers to scrutinize specific tasks or processes that are costing more than expected and to implement cost-saving measures where feasible. Persistent negative CV values might necessitate a reevaluation of the project budget or scope.

Comprehensive Project Evaluation:

- Together, SV and CV offer a robust evaluation of a project's health, highlighting where issues may be occurring in terms of timing and finances. These metrics are particularly useful for upper management and stakeholders for making informed decisions about project continuation, adjustments, or additional oversight requirements.

By regularly monitoring SV and CV, project managers can maintain better control over projects, ensuring that they meet their objectives within the allocated time and budget constraints. This proactive approach to project management helps mitigate risks, avoid surprises, and deliver projects successfully. In the realm of project management, the Earned Value Management (EVM) system provides robust metrics to evaluate the efficiency and effectiveness with which project teams utilize time and resources. Two critical indices in this system are the Schedule Performance Index (SPI) and Cost Performance Index (CPI), which serve as key indicators of project health in terms of schedule and budget respectively.

Schedule Performance Index (SPI)

Calculation: $SPI = \dfrac{\text{Earned Value (EV)}}{\text{Planned Value (PV)}}$ $SPI = \dfrac{\text{Planned Value (PV)}}{\text{Earned Value (EV)}}$

Significance:

- **SPI > 1**: Indicates that more work has been completed than was planned for at this stage. The project is ahead of schedule.
- **SPI < 1**: Indicates that less work has been completed than was planned for at this stage. The project is behind schedule.
- **SPI = 1**: Indicates that the work is proceeding exactly as planned.

Role in Project Management:

- SPI is crucial for assessing the time efficiency of a project. It provides a quick snapshot of schedule adherence, allowing project managers to gauge whether adjustments are needed to catch up to or maintain the project timeline. It helps in forecasting the completion dates and taking proactive measures to address scheduling issues.

Cost Performance Index (CPI)

Calculation: $CPI = \dfrac{\text{Earned Value (EV)}}{\text{Actual Cost (AC)}}$ $CPI = \dfrac{\text{Actual Cost (AC)}}{\text{Earned Value (EV)}}$

Significance:

- **CPI > 1**: The project is under budget relative to the work completed. This is an indicator of cost efficiency.
- **CPI < 1**: The project is over budget relative to the work completed. This signals cost inefficiency.
- **CPI = 1**: The project is on budget, with spending exactly as planned relative to the work performed.

Role in Project Management:

- CPI is essential for managing project costs effectively. It allows project managers to understand how efficiently the allocated funds are being utilized to generate project value. This index helps in financial forecasting, budget adjustments, and provides insights into financial management practices that may need improvement to enhance cost efficiency.

Combined Insight from SPI and CPI

Using both SPI and CPI together provides a comprehensive view of project performance concerning time and cost:

- **High SPI and CPI**: The project is performing well, both ahead of schedule and under budget.
- **Low SPI and CPI**: The project is in trouble, lagging behind schedule and over budget.
- **High SPI and Low CPI**: The project is ahead of schedule but over budget, possibly due to rushing tasks that incur higher costs.
- **Low SPI and High CPI**: The project is behind schedule but under budget, possibly because tasks are not being completed as quickly as planned despite efficient spending.

Example Application: Suppose a project with a Budget at Completion (BAC) of $100,000 is halfway through its timeline. At this point:

- Planned Value (PV) = $50,000 (50% of BAC)
- Earned Value (EV) = $40,000 (the work completed is worth $40,000)

- Actual Cost (AC) = \$45,000 (the project has spent \$45,000)

Calculations: $SPI = \frac{EV}{PV} = \frac{40,000}{50,000} = 0.8$ $SPI = \frac{PV}{EV} = \frac{50,000}{40,000} = 0.8$
$CPI = \frac{EV}{AC} = \frac{40,000}{45,000} \approx 0.89$ $CPI = \frac{AC}{EV} = \frac{45,000}{40,000} \approx 0.89$

Interpretation:

- **SPI (0.8)** suggests the project is behind schedule.
- **CPI (0.89)** indicates the project is over budget.

Conclusion: Both SPI and CPI are indispensable for monitoring and controlling project performance. They provide actionable insights that enable project managers to make informed decisions to guide the project toward successful completion, ensuring both timely delivery and optimal use of financial resources.

Estimate at Completion (EAC) is a critical Earned Value Management (EVM) metric that forecasts the expected total cost of a project based on current performance. It provides project managers and stakeholders with a projected final cost, helping them to make informed decisions about resource allocation, budget adjustments, and project feasibility. The EAC is particularly useful for understanding the financial health of a project and anticipating potential budget overruns or savings.

Role of EAC in Project Management

The primary role of the EAC is to provide a realistic projection of project costs at completion. This projection helps in:

1. **Identifying Variance**: Understanding how much the actual project will cost compared to the original budget.
2. **Resource Management**: Adjusting resource allocation to control costs.
3. **Decision Making**: Assisting stakeholders in making decisions regarding project continuation, adjustments, or re-evaluation.
4. **Financial Planning**: Helping organizations plan financially for current and future project requirements.

Formula for Calculating EAC

The basic formula for EAC is: $EAC = AC + ETC$ Where:

- **AC (Actual Cost)**: The actual cost incurred for the work performed on the project to date.
- **ETC (Estimate to Complete)**: The estimated cost to complete the remaining project work.

However, the calculation of ETC can vary based on the assumption made regarding the nature of the cost variance encountered. Here are the different methods used to determine EAC:

1. **EAC based on original budgeted rates**: $EAC = AC + (BAC - EV)$
   - This formula assumes that the original budget is fundamentally sound and that past cost performance (whether over or under budget) was anomalous and won't repeat.
2. **EAC assuming current variances will continue**: $EAC = BAC / CPI$
   - This approach uses the Cost Performance Index (CPI) and assumes that the cost performance reflected in the CPI will continue throughout the remainder of the project.
3. **EAC considering both cost and schedule performance**:
   $EAC = AC + \left(\frac{BAC - EV}{CPI \times SPI}\right)$
   - This method is used when both cost and schedule performance influence the remaining work. It factors in the Schedule Performance Index (SPI) along with the CPI, assuming that the interplay between cost and schedule variances will affect the final cost.
4. **EAC for atypical variances**:
   $EAC = AC + (BAC - EV) + Management Reserve$

- This formula assumes that past variances were atypical and that future expenditures will be at the budgeted amount. Management reserves may also be added to cover unexpected costs.

Explanation of Methods

- **EAC based on original budgeted rates**: Best used when variances are seen as non-recurring.
- **EAC assuming current variances will continue**: Appropriate when the project's current performance is seen as indicative of future performance.
- **EAC considering both cost and schedule performance**: Useful in scenarios where delays impact resource usage and increase costs.
- **EAC for atypical variances**: Suitable for projects where specific events caused variances that are not expected to occur again.

By choosing the appropriate EAC calculation method, project managers can more accurately predict the end costs and take proactive measures to steer the project toward its budget and performance goals. Understanding these different forecasting techniques allows for better financial management and project control, critical for the successful completion of any project. The To-Complete Performance Index (TCPI) is an important Earned Value Management (EVM) metric that provides a projection of the cost performance that must be achieved on the remaining portion of the project to meet a specified financial goal, such as the Budget at Completion (BAC) or the Estimate at Completion (EAC). TCPI helps project managers understand how efficiently resources must be used going forward to stay within the project's financial targets.

Calculation of TCPI

The TCPI can be calculated using two different formulas depending on whether the original budget (BAC) is still considered achievable or if a new forecast (EAC) needs to be used due to performance to date.

1. To meet the original budget (BAC):

$$TCPI = \frac{BAC - EV}{BAC - AC}$$

- **BAC** (Budget at Completion): The total budget allocated for the project.
- **EV** (Earned Value): The value of the work actually completed.
- **AC** (Actual Cost): The actual costs incurred for the completed work.

2. To meet a new forecasted budget (EAC):

$$TCPI = \frac{BAC - EV}{EAC - AC}$$

- **EAC** (Estimate at Completion): The new forecasted total cost of the project based on project performance and risk analysis.

Significance of TCPI

- **Performance Benchmark**: TCPI provides a clear benchmark for the future cost performance required to meet specific financial objectives. It tells project managers how efficiently the project needs to use its resources going forward.
- **Future Cost Control**: By indicating the necessary cost performance for the remainder of the project, TCPI serves as a critical tool for making adjustments in cost control strategies, resource allocation, and operational plans.

- **Risk Assessment**: TCPI also helps in assessing the risk associated with achieving the project's financial objectives. A high TCPI value could indicate a significant challenge in meeting the budget, triggering a need for reassessment of project scope, resources, or strategies.
- **Decision Making**: It aids in decision-making by providing quantifiable data on whether additional measures such as scope reduction, schedule adjustments, or performance improvements are necessary to meet the budget targets.

Example of TCPI in Action

Suppose a project has a Budget at Completion (BAC) of $100,000. At a status review, the Earned Value (EV) is $40,000, and the Actual Cost (AC) is $50,000. The project is currently underperforming, and a new Estimate at Completion (EAC) is calculated to be $125,000.

- **To meet the original budget (BAC):**

$TCPI = \dfrac{100{,}000 - 40{,}000}{100{,}000 - 50{,}000} = \dfrac{60{,}000}{50{,}000} = 1.2$ $TCPI = \dfrac{100{,}000 - 50{,}000}{100{,}000 - 40{,}000} = \dfrac{50{,}000}{60{,}000} = 1.2$

- **To meet the new forecasted budget (EAC):**

$TCPI = \dfrac{100{,}000 - 40{,}000}{125{,}000 - 50{,}000} = \dfrac{60{,}000}{75{,}000} \approx 0.8$ $TCPI = \dfrac{125{,}000 - 50{,}000}{100{,}000 - 40{,}000} = \dfrac{75{,}000}{60{,}000} \approx 0.8$

Interpretation:

- **TCPI = 1.2 to meet BAC**: This suggests that the project needs to perform 20% more efficiently than planned in the remaining work to meet the original budget, which might be challenging.
- **TCPI = 0.8 to meet EAC**: This indicates that the project needs to perform at 80% of the planned rate to meet the new forecasted budget, suggesting a more manageable scenario if the EAC is accepted.

Conclusion

TCPI is a vital EVM tool in the Control Costs process, providing essential insights into the financial efficiency required to meet project objectives. By calculating and understanding TCPI, project managers can effectively guide their projects towards financial success or make necessary adjustments in strategy to accommodate evolving project dynamics. Effective communication of cost performance to stakeholders is crucial in project management, especially when using complex data derived from Earned Value Management (EVM). Clear and concise visual presentations can help stakeholders understand the project's financial health, foresee potential issues, and make informed decisions. Here are ways project managers can utilize EVM data along with examples of visual tools that can be employed to communicate this information effectively:

Key EVM Metrics for Communication

Before delving into the visuals, it's important to note the core EVM metrics that are typically communicated:

1. **Cost Variance (CV)** - Indicates whether the project is over or under budget.
2. **Schedule Variance (SV)** - Shows if the project is ahead or behind schedule.
3. **Cost Performance Index (CPI)** - Reflects the cost efficiency of the project.
4. **Schedule Performance Index (SPI)** - Indicates the efficiency of time usage against the plan.
5. **Estimate at Completion (EAC)** - Forecasts the projected total cost at the project's end.

Visual Tools for Presenting EVM Data
1. Cumulative Cost Curves:
- **Description**: This graph plots cumulative budgeted costs (BCWS), actual costs (ACWP), and earned value (BCWP) over time. It visually displays how actual spending compares to what has been budgeted and what value has been earned.
- **Example**: A line graph showing three lines, one each for BCWS, ACWP, and BCWP, plotted against the project timeline.
- **Utility**: Helps stakeholders quickly see cost trends, identify when costs are diverging from the plan, and assess whether corrective actions are needed.

2. Cost Performance Dashboard:
- **Description**: A dashboard that includes several EVM metrics such as CPI, CV, EAC, and other related financial indicators.
- **Example**: A dashboard with dials for CPI and SPI, a bar graph for CV and SV, and a line graph forecasting EAC based on current trends.
- **Utility**: Provides a comprehensive snapshot of all critical cost and schedule performance metrics, allowing stakeholders to assess project health at a glance.

3. S-Curve Graph:
- **Description**: An S-curve graphically represents the cumulative costs or work over time, showing planned versus actual expenditures.
- **Example**: A graph where the X-axis represents time, and the Y-axis represents cumulative costs, with two S-shaped curves showing planned and actual cost accumulation.
- **Utility**: Effective for visualizing the overall progress of project expenditures against the baseline, highlighting deviations, and forecasting future trends.

4. Variance Analysis Table:
- **Description**: A table that lists planned, actual, and earned values along with their variances and performance indexes.
- **Example**: A table format where each row represents a reporting period or a project phase, columns include PV, AC, EV, CV, SV, CPI, and SPI.
- **Utility**: Offers a detailed, period-by-period view of performance, allowing for a deeper analysis of trends and variances.

5. Earned Value Trend Chart:
- **Description**: This chart tracks CPI and SPI over time to identify trends in cost and schedule performance.
- **Example**: A dual-axis line chart where one axis represents CPI and another SPI, both plotted over the project timeline.
- **Utility**: Useful for spotting trends in performance indices, helping predict future performance and potential areas needing attention.

Best Practices for Communicating EVM Data
- **Regular Updates**: Provide EVM reports at regular intervals to keep all stakeholders informed and engaged.

- **Tailor Information**: Customize the information and visuals to suit the specific interests and expertise levels of different stakeholders.
- **Use Clear, Simple Visuals**: Avoid overly complex visuals that may confuse stakeholders; clarity is key.
- **Explain Context and Implications**: Always provide context for the data presented and discuss the potential implications on the project's trajectory and objectives.

By effectively using these visual tools and practices, project managers can ensure that stakeholders are well-informed about the project's cost performance, enhancing transparency, fostering trust, and facilitating better decision-making. This case study focuses on the construction of a regional airport designed to handle 2 million passengers annually. The project had an initial budget of $500 million and a timeline of 3 years. Due to the project's complexity, involving multiple contractors and stringent regulatory standards, effective cost management was critical.

Challenges Faced

1. **Scope Creep**: Changes in aviation regulations required unexpected modifications to runway designs, which increased the scope and, consequently, the costs.
2. **Resource Fluctuations**: Volatile prices for raw materials such as steel and concrete led to fluctuations in cost estimates.
3. **Scheduling Delays**: Delays in the delivery of custom components for the air traffic control tower pushed back the schedule, incurring additional holding costs.

Cost Management Strategies Employed
1. Detailed Cost Estimation

- **Initial Estimations**: Comprehensive initial cost estimations were performed, using historical data and parametric models.
- **Continuous Revisions**: As the project progressed and challenges emerged, cost estimations were regularly updated to reflect changes in scope and market conditions.

2. Establishment of a Cost Baseline

- **Baseline Setup**: Following the initial estimations, a cost baseline was established, which included direct and indirect costs, along with provisions for contingencies.
- **Baseline Reviews**: Regular reviews of the cost baseline were conducted during project status meetings to ensure alignment with the project's progress and external factors.

3. Implementation of Earned Value Management (EVM)

- **EVM Setup**: An EVM system was set up to integrate cost, schedule, and scope measures, providing a comprehensive view of project performance.
- **Performance Monitoring**: EVM metrics such as CPI and SPI were monitored to detect variances from the baseline and adjust forecasts and strategies accordingly.

4. Proactive Scope and Change Control

- **Change Control System**: A robust change control system was implemented to evaluate the impact of any proposed changes on the project's cost and schedule.
- **Stakeholder Engagement**: Regular engagement with stakeholders ensured that all changes were communicated, justified, and documented.

4. Strategic Sourcing and Procurement

- **Supplier Contracts**: Fixed-price contracts were negotiated with suppliers for key materials to mitigate the risk of price volatility.
- **Bulk Purchasing**: Where possible, bulk purchasing agreements were made to capitalize on discounts and ensure price stability.

Lessons Learned
1. Importance of Flexibility in Cost Baselines

- The project manager noted that while a detailed cost baseline is crucial, flexibility in managing this baseline is equally important to accommodate unforeseen changes without derailing the project.

2. Benefits of Integrated Cost Management Tools

- The use of EVM proved invaluable not only in tracking performance against budget but also in providing predictive insights, which helped in making proactive adjustments.

3. Effective Change Management is Critical

- Rigorous change management processes were essential in controlling scope creep and its associated costs. This involved clear communication channels and documented approvals for all scope changes.

4. Early Stakeholder Engagement Reduces Financial Surprises

- Engaging stakeholders early in the decision-making process helped in managing expectations and reducing last-minute changes that could impact the budget.

5. Anticipate and Plan for Regulatory Changes

- Given the regulatory environment surrounding aviation infrastructure, allocating additional contingency funds for compliance with future regulations was necessary.

Conclusion

The construction of the regional airport, despite its challenges, was successful in maintaining control over its finances through meticulous cost management practices. The strategies employed, particularly in scope and change management, not only kept the project within a reasonable budget threshold but also highlighted the importance of adaptive planning in complex projects. This case study underscores the value of proactive and integrated cost management in achieving project success, even under challenging circumstances. Project cost management is a crucial area in project management that demands meticulous planning and execution. However, several pitfalls and misconceptions can hinder effective cost management, leading to budget overruns, project delays, and even failure. Understanding these pitfalls and adopting strategic measures to mitigate them is essential for successful project execution.

Common Pitfalls and Misconceptions
1. Over-Optimism in Cost Estimating:

- **Misconception**: Project costs can be aggressively minimized in planning to make the project appear cost-effective or to win stakeholder approval.
- **Pitfall**: Leads to unrealistic budgets that are difficult to adhere to, causing significant overruns and project stress.

2. **Ignoring Risks in Budget Planning**:
- **Misconception**: Risk management is separate from cost management and doesn't need to be integrated into budgeting.
- **Pitfall**: Unexpected issues arise without allocated funds to manage them, disrupting project financials and timelines.

3. **Inadequate Contingency Reserves**:
- **Misconception**: Contingency reserves are an optional cushion that can be minimized to keep the initial budget low.
- **Pitfall**: Insufficient reserves lead to challenges in addressing project deviations, potentially stalling the project.

4. **Failure to Revisit and Revise Budgets**:
- **Misconception**: Once a budget is set, it should not change unless absolutely necessary.
- **Pitfall**: This rigid approach can prevent necessary adjustments in response to project changes, harming the project's adaptability and success.

5. **Poor Communication of Financial Status**:
- **Misconception**: Detailed financial data is only relevant for project managers, not for the wider project team or stakeholders.
- **Pitfall**: Stakeholders and team members may make uninformed decisions or fail to understand the implications of their actions on the project budget.

Guidance on Avoiding These Pitfalls
1. **Implement Rigorous Cost Estimating Techniques**:
- Use a combination of estimating techniques (e.g., analogous, parametric, and bottom-up estimating) to ensure accuracy and realism in cost forecasts.
- Involve experienced team members in the estimating process to leverage expert judgment.

2. **Integrate Risk Management with Cost Management**:
- Conduct thorough risk assessments during the cost planning phase and allocate appropriate contingency reserves based on identified risks.
- Regularly review and update the risk analysis to reflect new risks and changes in the project environment.

3. **Maintain Flexible Budgeting Practices**:
- Establish a change control process that includes financial impact assessment and budget adjustments.
- Encourage periodic reviews of the budget and cost performance to make timely corrections.

4. **Communicate Financial Information Effectively**:
- Develop regular financial reports tailored to the needs of different stakeholders to keep everyone informed and engaged.
- Use clear visuals and dashboards to present cost performance data, making it accessible and understandable.

5. **Utilize Earned Value Management (EVM)**:

- Implement EVM to integrate scope, schedule, and cost measurements, providing a comprehensive view of project health and facilitating early detection of potential issues.
- Train project team members on EVM principles to enhance their understanding and ability to manage project costs effectively.

Conclusion

By recognizing and addressing these common pitfalls and misconceptions in project cost management, project managers can enhance their ability to manage budgets effectively. This involves not only meticulous initial planning but also adaptive management throughout the project lifecycle to accommodate changes and unforeseen challenges. Effective cost management, coupled with clear communication and proactive adjustments, forms the backbone of successful project execution. Here's a set of practice questions designed to test and reinforce understanding of Project Cost Management processes, Earned Value Management (EVM) concepts, and their application in real-world scenarios. These questions can help prepare readers for the CAPM exam or enhance their project management skills.

Question 1: What is the primary purpose of the Cost Management Plan?
- A) To estimate the project's total costs
- B) To outline how costs will be managed throughout the project
- C) To document all project expenses after they occur
- D) To allocate tasks to project team members

Correct Answer: B) To outline how costs will be managed throughout the project
- **Explanation**: The Cost Management Plan is crucial as it establishes the processes and procedures used to manage costs throughout the project lifecycle. It includes methodologies for planning, estimating, budgeting, and controlling project costs.

Question 2: How is Earned Value (EV) calculated in a project?
- A) EV = Actual Cost (AC) – Planned Value (PV)
- B) EV = Budget at Completion (BAC) x % of work completed
- C) EV = Planned Value (PV) x Cost Performance Index (CPI)
- D) EV = Actual Cost (AC) + Planned Value (PV)

Correct Answer: B) EV = Budget at Completion (BAC) x % of work completed
- **Explanation**: Earned Value (EV) is calculated by multiplying the Budget at Completion (BAC) by the percentage of completed work. This calculation gives the value of the work actually completed to date, providing a measure of project performance against the budget.

Question 3: What does a Cost Performance Index (CPI) less than 1 signify?
- A) The project is under budget.
- B) The project is exactly on budget.
- C) The project is over budget.
- D) The project schedule is behind.

Correct Answer: C) The project is over budget.
- **Explanation**: The CPI is calculated as EV divided by AC (CPI = EV/AC). A CPI less than 1 indicates that the costs are exceeding the earned value, meaning the project is spending more than planned for the work completed and is therefore over budget.

Question 4: Which of the following best describes the To-Complete Performance Index (TCPI)?

- A) It measures past cost performance.
- B) It forecasts the future cost performance needed to complete the project within the budget.
- C) It calculates the total cost at the end of the project.
- D) It determines the percentage of completed tasks.

Correct Answer: B) It forecasts the future cost performance needed to complete the project within the budget.

- **Explanation**: TCPI is an EVM metric that forecasts the cost performance efficiency required to complete the remaining project work within the authorized budget. It provides insight into whether current spending efficiency is sufficient to meet the financial goals or if adjustments are needed.

Question 5: What is the formula for calculating the Schedule Performance Index (SPI)?
- A) SPI = EV / PV
- B) SPI = AC / PV
- C) SPI = EV / AC
- D) SPI = PV / EV

Correct Answer: A) SPI = EV / PV

- **Explanation**: The Schedule Performance Index (SPI) is calculated by dividing the Earned Value (EV) by the Planned Value (PV). This index indicates how well the project is adhering to the scheduled timeline. An SPI greater than 1 means the project is ahead of schedule, while an SPI less than 1 indicates a delay.

Question 6: What action should a project manager take if the CPI is 0.8 and the SPI is 0.9?
- A) Decrease the project scope.
- B) Increase the budget and reassess the project timeline.
- C) Continue the project without changes.
- D) Shorten the project schedule to save costs.

Correct Answer: B) Increase the budget and reassess the project timeline.

- **Explanation**: With a CPI of 0.8 and an SPI of 0.9, the project is both over budget and behind schedule. The project manager needs to consider increasing the budget to accommodate the higher costs and reassessing the project timeline to account for the delays, possibly through re-baselining or applying corrective actions.

These practice questions provide insight into the fundamentals and applications of Project Cost Management and EVM, helping readers deepen their understanding and prepare for project management examinations.

VII. Project Quality Management:

The **Plan Quality Management** process is an essential part of project management, focusing on defining quality standards and determining how those standards will be met throughout the project lifecycle. This process is critical because it ensures that the project deliverables and the final outcomes meet the necessary quality requirements and stakeholder expectations.

Purpose and Importance of Plan Quality Management

1. **Define Quality Standards**: The process establishes the quality standards relevant to the project. These standards are based on stakeholder expectations, regulatory requirements, and internal benchmarks that the project must adhere to.
2. **Ensure Customer Satisfaction**: By planning for and integrating quality management throughout the project, you increase the likelihood of meeting or exceeding customer expectations, which is critical for project success and stakeholder satisfaction.
3. **Prevent Defects**: Effective quality management helps in identifying potential quality issues early in the project, allowing for preventive measures to be implemented before these issues result in defects or require costly corrections.
4. **Reduce Waste and Increase Efficiency**: By focusing on quality from the beginning, the project can avoid rework and delays, thereby saving costs and enhancing operational efficiency.
5. **Provide a Systematic Approach**: The Plan Quality Management process offers a structured approach to managing quality, which includes specific practices, resources, and timelines to ensure quality objectives are achieved.

Key Components of a Quality Management Plan

1. **Quality Standards**: Identifies and defines the specific quality standards that the project deliverables must meet. These can be derived from industry standards, regulatory requirements, or stakeholder expectations.
2. **Quality Metrics**: Specifies how the quality of project deliverables will be quantified. Metrics might include error rates, compliance rates, performance benchmarks, or specific test results that the deliverables must achieve.
3. **Quality Assurance Activities**: Outlines the processes and activities that will be implemented to ensure that the project adheres to the defined quality standards. This might include scheduled quality audits, process reviews, and various quality assurance methodologies like Six Sigma or Total Quality Management.
4. **Quality Control Activities**: Describes the specific activities used to verify that the project deliverables meet the quality requirements. This includes testing, peer reviews, inspections, and the use of specific quality control tools like control charts, Pareto diagrams, or fishbone diagrams.
5. **Roles and Responsibilities**: Clearly defines who is responsible for quality management within the project team. This section details the responsibilities of each team member in ensuring quality, from the project manager to the quality inspectors and operational staff.
6. **Quality Improvement**: Details the procedures for handling quality issues that arise during project execution. This includes the process for managing non-conformities, implementing corrective actions, and making continuous quality improvements.
7. **Documentation**: Specifies the records that will be kept to track quality management efforts. These records are essential for auditing purposes and for validating the quality of the project deliverables.

How These Components Guide the Project Team

The components of the quality management plan provide a blueprint for managing quality throughout the project. By clearly defining what needs to be done, who will do it, and how it will be measured, the plan ensures that everyone on the project team understands their role in achieving quality. This comprehensive guidance helps the team work more efficiently and effectively, focusing their efforts on critical quality-related activities and making informed decisions about quality management. Additionally, it fosters a culture of quality within the team, encouraging continuous improvement and attention to detail, which are crucial for delivering high-quality project outcomes.

The Plan Quality Management process sets the foundation for delivering products and services that meet or exceed the required quality standards, thereby enhancing customer satisfaction and project success. Understanding the relationship between quality, grade, and precision is crucial for successful project quality management. Each term has a distinct meaning and implication for project outcomes, and it's important to grasp these differences to ensure that project deliverables meet stakeholder expectations and standards.

Quality

Definition: Quality refers to the degree to which a set of inherent characteristics fulfills requirements. In project management, quality is primarily about meeting or exceeding the expectations of stakeholders as defined by the project's requirements and standards.

- **Example**: If a software development project is expected to deliver an app that operates with 99.99% uptime, achieving or surpassing this standard reflects high quality.

Grade

Definition: Grade is a category or rank given to products or services having the same functional use but different technical characteristics. Unlike quality, grade does not imply better or worse but different levels of complexity or durability.

- **Example**: An automobile manufacturer might produce a basic car model and a luxury model. Both can be of high quality (free of defects, fulfilling their respective requirements) but of different grades due to variations in features and luxury elements.

Precision

Definition: Precision relates to the consistency of outputs and the absence of variation in deliverables. High precision in project management means that the processes produce results that are consistently close to each other, though not necessarily close to the target or true value (which would be accuracy).

- **Example**: In manufacturing, a machine that produces components with minimal variance between products demonstrates high precision. If the components are all within 0.01 millimeters of each other in dimension, the process is precise.

Relationship and Implications for Project Success

Quality vs. Grade:
- Quality and grade are independent but related aspects of a product or service. You can have a high-grade product with poor quality if the product has many features (high grade) but does not meet the functional requirements (low quality). Similarly, a low-grade product might still be of high quality if it meets its fewer, simpler functional requirements very well.
- **Project Implication**: Projects must clearly define and understand the required grade and ensure that the quality management processes can deliver this grade to the required quality standards.

Quality and Precision:
- High precision does not guarantee high quality, but it often contributes to it, especially in projects where consistent performance is critical. Quality, in the broader sense, will include both the conformity to requirements (accuracy) and the reduction of unwanted variation (precision).

- **Project Implication**: In many technical and manufacturing projects, precise execution of tasks and production processes can significantly enhance overall quality by reducing defects and ensuring uniformity, which in turn increases customer satisfaction.

Example in Practice
- **Construction Project**: A residential building project can have different grades of apartments – luxury and standard. Both grades can achieve high quality by meeting all respective building standards and customer expectations. Precision might come into play in the uniformity of installation work, paint finishes, and the consistency in the quality of fixtures used across all apartments.
- **Software Development**: Developing a high-grade enterprise software solution involves integrating advanced features like AI and machine learning. Achieving high quality in this context means the software meets specified performance benchmarks and user requirements, while precision might refer to the consistency in user experience across different devices and operating environments.

Conclusion
Quality, grade, and precision are distinct yet interconnected concepts in project management. A thorough understanding and effective management of these aspects are critical for delivering products or services that fulfill project objectives and stakeholder expectations. Each plays a unique role in defining the overall success of the project, influencing everything from customer satisfaction to product functionality and performance. The "Plan Quality Management" process is vital for ensuring that the project delivers outputs that meet the necessary quality standards and stakeholder expectations. Understanding the Inputs, Tools and Techniques, and Outputs (ITTOs) of this process helps in crafting a detailed and actionable plan that guides the entire project team towards achieving the desired quality levels.

Essential Inputs
1. **Project Management Plan**: Includes relevant information from the project's scope, schedule, and cost baselines, which provide insights into the project objectives, resources, constraints, and stakeholder expectations related to quality.
2. **Stakeholder Register**: Contains information about project stakeholders, including their interests, expectations, and influence levels. This input is crucial for understanding their quality expectations and requirements.
3. **Risk Register**: Offers insights into potential risks that could impact the quality of project deliverables, helping to integrate risk management into the quality planning process.
4. **Enterprise Environmental Factors (EEFs)**: Includes organizational culture and existing systems that influence quality management practices, such as industry standards, regulatory requirements, and quality policies of the organization.
5. **Organizational Process Assets (OPAs)**: Consists of historical data and lessons learned from previous projects, quality policies, procedures, and any existing quality management templates that can be utilized for the current project.

Tools and Techniques
1. **Cost-Benefit Analysis**: Used to evaluate the costs of implementing quality activities against the benefits expected from achieving quality objectives. This analysis helps justify the investment in quality initiatives.

2. **Benchmarking**: Involves comparing actual or planned project practices to those of comparable projects to identify best practices, generate ideas for improvement, and provide a basis for measuring performance.
3. **Design of Experiments (DOE)**: A statistical method used to identify which factors may influence specific variables of a product or process under development. It is used in the quality management process to systematically change all of the important factors in an experiment instead of changing the factors one at a time.
4. **Cost of Quality (COQ)**: Involves analyzing costs incurred to prevent poor quality (preventive costs), costs incurred to evaluate products or services for conformance to quality requirements (appraisal costs), and the costs resulting from non-conforming products or services (failure costs, both internal and external).
5. **Seven Basic Quality Tools**: Include tools like Cause-and-effect diagrams, Flowcharts, Checksheets, Pareto diagrams, Histograms, Control charts, and Scatter diagrams, which are used for quality problem-solving and monitoring.

Outputs

1. **Quality Management Plan**: A component of the project management plan that describes how the organization's quality policies will be implemented and how the project will ensure that the deliverables are fit for purpose. This plan includes quality standards, quality objectives, quality roles and responsibilities, and compliance documentation.
2. **Quality Metrics**: Specific descriptions of a project or product attribute and how the quality control process will measure these attributes with specified tolerances.
3. **Quality Checklists**: Used during the quality control process to verify that a set of required steps has been performed or to check if a list of specified requirements has been satisfied.
4. **Process Improvement Plan**: Details the steps for analyzing processes that will facilitate the identification of waste and non-value added activities, and the steps for improving process efficiency.

Significance in Establishing a Comprehensive Quality Management Approach

These ITTOs collectively ensure that a comprehensive quality management approach is developed, which is crucial for:

- Aligning project outputs with defined quality requirements and stakeholder expectations.
- Ensuring efficient use of resources by preventing defects and minimizing rework.
- Facilitating continuous process improvement and maintaining compliance with applicable standards and regulations.

By leveraging these inputs, tools and techniques, and outputs effectively, project managers can establish a robust quality management system that not only meets but exceeds the quality expectations of stakeholders, thereby enhancing the overall success of the project. Quality metrics are specific measures that are used in project management to describe a project's attributes and the processes by which they will be measured and controlled to meet the specified quality standards. These metrics are fundamental in the Plan Quality Management process as they provide a clear, quantifiable means to assess whether the project's deliverables and processes meet the defined quality requirements.

Role of Quality Metrics in Plan Quality Management

1. **Defining Quality Standards**: Quality metrics help in setting clear, measurable standards that reflect the project's quality requirements. These standards guide the project team on what needs to be achieved to satisfy stakeholder expectations.

2. **Monitoring and Control**: Metrics provide a basis for monitoring the quality of project outputs and processes. They enable the project team to measure performance systematically, identify deviations from the planned quality standards, and implement corrective actions.
3. **Continuous Improvement**: By analyzing the performance data collected through these metrics, project teams can identify opportunities for improving project processes and outputs, contributing to the overall quality improvement over the project lifecycle.
4. **Stakeholder Assurance and Communication**: Quality metrics serve as a transparent method for communicating with stakeholders about how quality is being managed and achieved. This builds trust and confidence in the project management process.

Identifying and Defining Appropriate Quality Metrics

1. Understand Project Requirements and Stakeholder Expectations:
- Project managers start by thoroughly understanding the project requirements and stakeholder expectations. These form the basis of what aspects of the project need to be measured.

2. Determine Measurable Attributes:
- Identify which attributes of the project deliverables or processes can be measured quantitatively or qualitatively. Common attributes include timeliness, compliance, reliability, and performance.

3. Develop Specific Metrics:
- Develop specific metrics that are relevant to the critical success factors of the project. For instance, for a software development project, metrics might include defect frequencies, system uptime, or response times.

4. Set Baselines and Targets:
- For each metric, set a baseline value and target values. The baseline provides a starting point against which improvements or deteriorations can be measured, while targets set the quality levels that need to be achieved.

5. Document and Communicate:
- Document the quality metrics in the project quality management plan. Communicate these metrics and their importance to all team members and relevant stakeholders to ensure everyone understands how quality will be measured and managed.

Using Quality Metrics to Measure and Control Quality
1. Implementation in Quality Assurance (QA):
- During the project execution phase, implement the quality metrics in QA processes to continuously measure the quality of project outputs. This is usually done through regular inspections, testing, and reviews.

2. Tracking and Reporting:
- Regularly track these metrics and report the findings in status meetings or through formal reports. This tracking helps identify trends and pinpoint areas where the project may not be meeting its quality objectives.

3. Corrective Actions:
- If quality metrics indicate that project deliverables or processes are not meeting the established standards, use corrective actions to address these deviations. This might involve additional training, process adjustments, or rework.

4. Quality Control (QC):

- Use the metrics in QC processes to verify that the final deliverables meet the quality requirements set by the client or primary stakeholders. This often involves extensive testing and validation against the quality metrics.

Example of Quality Metrics in Practice

For a construction project, quality metrics might include:

- **Concrete strength**: Measured in PSI, with specific sampling and testing intervals.
- **Adherence to schedule**: Measured by the percentage of tasks completed on time.
- **Client satisfaction**: Measured through client feedback scores at key project milestones.

Conclusion

Quality metrics are essential tools in the Plan Quality Management process, providing a methodological approach to ensuring, measuring, and controlling the quality of project deliverables and processes. By effectively identifying, defining, and implementing these metrics, project managers can substantially enhance the likelihood of project success, delivering outputs that meet or exceed stakeholder expectations. The **Manage Quality** process, formerly known as **Quality Assurance**, is crucial in the execution phase of project management. It involves the application of planned, systematic quality activities to ensure that the project employs all processes needed to meet requirements. This process is vital for ensuring that the project deliverables meet the specified quality standards, thereby enhancing stakeholder satisfaction and minimizing the cost of rework.

Role of the Manage Quality Process

1. **Ensures Consistency**: The process ensures that the project consistently uses appropriate quality standards and operational definitions that are part of the quality management plan.
2. **Improves Performance**: By applying quality assurance practices, the process aims to increase the efficiency and effectiveness of project performance, often through process optimization and identification of inefficiencies.
3. **Facilitates Stakeholder Confidence**: Regularly demonstrating adherence to quality standards helps to maintain confidence among project stakeholders, including clients, sponsors, and team members.
4. **Prevents Defects**: Manage Quality is proactive; it focuses on preventing defects by ensuring that the work is done right the first time. This is more cost-effective than identifying defects later in the project lifecycle.

Primary Tools and Techniques Used in the Manage Quality Process
1. Quality Audits:

- **Description**: These are structured and independent reviews to determine whether project activities comply with organizational and project policies, processes, and procedures.
- **Benefits**: Quality audits identify inefficiencies and non-conformities in the processes, provide an opportunity for improvement, and share good practices across the organization.

2. Process Analysis:

- **Description**: Process analysis follows the steps outlined in the process improvement plan to identify needed improvements. This technique involves evaluating processes to identify inefficiencies, constraints, and unnecessary activities.

- **Benefits**: Helps in optimizing process performance and ensuring each process effectively contributes to the quality objectives.

3. Quality Improvement Methods:

- **Description**: This includes various methodologies like Six Sigma, Lean, Total Quality Management (TQM), and Continuous Improvement. Each method provides a structured approach to quality improvement by focusing on reducing waste, improving process control, and striving for perfection.
- **Benefits**: These methodologies foster a culture of continuous improvement within the team and help in achieving higher efficiency and better quality outcomes.

4. Data Gathering and Analysis Tools:

- **Tools Include**: Check sheets, fishbone (Ishikawa) diagrams, histograms, Pareto charts, and scatter diagrams.
- **Benefits**: These tools help in collecting and analyzing data to identify the root causes of defects or issues, enabling effective decision-making to enhance quality.
  5.

6. Statistical Sampling:

- **Description**: Involves selecting a part of the total population of data or products for inspection, based on random sampling or other sampling methods, to draw conclusions about the quality of the entire product lot.
- **Benefits**: Provides a cost-effective means to gain insights into overall project quality, reducing the time and resources needed for quality inspections.

Conclusion

The Manage Quality process plays a pivotal role in executing the quality management plan by applying systematic quality activities to ensure that the project processes are adequate and capable of delivering project deliverables that meet specified quality requirements. By using the appropriate tools and techniques, project managers can maintain high-quality standards throughout the project, ensuring that the final deliverables are of the highest quality, thereby increasing customer satisfaction and reducing costs associated with non-conformance. The Seven Basic Quality Tools are fundamental techniques used to identify, analyze, and improve quality issues in project management. Each tool has specific applications that contribute to managing and enhancing project quality. Here's an overview of each tool and its application:

1. Check Sheets (Tally Sheets)

- **Description**: A check sheet is a structured, prepared form for collecting and analyzing data. It is a simple but effective tool for gathering data in real-time at the location where the data is generated.
- **Application**: Use check sheets to track the frequency of occurrences of specific issues or defects in a process. For example, in a construction project, a check sheet might be used to record the number of times a particular type of equipment fails.

2. Histograms

- **Description**: A histogram is a bar chart that shows the frequency distribution of numerical data.
- **Application**: Histograms help in identifying the distribution of quality data points, such as the frequency of defects or variances in a product dimension. For instance, in manufacturing, a

histogram could show the distribution of dimensions of a component like screws being produced, highlighting if many are out of specification.

3. Pareto Diagrams

- **Description**: A Pareto diagram is a type of chart that contains both bars and a line graph, where individual values are represented in descending order by bars, and the cumulative total is represented by the line.
- **Application**: Use Pareto diagrams to prioritize problems or defects to focus on the most significant issues first. In software development, a Pareto diagram could be used to identify the most frequently reported bugs by users to address the biggest issues quickly.

4. Cause and Effect Diagrams (Ishikawa/Fishbone Diagrams)

- **Description**: Cause and effect diagrams help in brainstorming to identify potential causes of a problem and sort ideas into useful categories.
- **Application**: A project team might use a fishbone diagram to explore the root causes of a delay in project schedule, categorizing potential causes under headings like People, Processes, Technology, and Materials.

5. Control Charts

- **Description**: Control charts are used to study how a process changes over time. These charts display data in a time sequence and show upper and lower control limits.
- **Application**: In a project involving repetitive processes, such as a call center implementation, control charts could monitor call handling times to ensure they are within acceptable control limits. Any deviations might indicate a need for process or training improvements.

6. Scatter Diagrams

- **Description**: Scatter diagrams are used to show the relationship between two variables, helping to identify the potential relationships between causes and effects.
- **Application**: A project team might use a scatter diagram to analyze the relationship between the number of hours spent on a task and the quality of the output, helping to optimize both factors for better productivity and quality.

7. Flowcharts

- **Description**: Flowcharts are graphical representations of a process. They show the steps in a workflow and how they are connected, which is helpful for understanding and analyzing a process.
- **Application**: Use flowcharts to map the process of document approvals in a project to identify bottlenecks or unnecessary steps that can be streamlined for efficiency.

Examples of Practical Application

- **Check Sheets**: During a quality inspection phase, inspectors could use check sheets to mark the occurrence of different types of defects in product batches.
- **Histograms**: A project team could analyze the time taken to complete various project tasks using a histogram to identify any tasks that are taking an unusually long or short amount of time.
- **Pareto Diagrams**: If a software project is experiencing numerous bugs, a Pareto diagram could help focus on the most common types that affect the most users or critical functions.

- **Cause and Effect Diagrams**: When a new product fails initial quality tests, a team might use a cause and effect diagram to trace issues back to their roots, such as materials, environmental factors, or operator errors.
- **Control Charts**: During the production phase, control charts could be used to monitor the consistency of production items, ensuring all are within designed tolerance limits.
- **Scatter Diagrams**: Investigating correlation between the skill level of workers and the incidence of errors in a project, helping to decide if more training is required.
- **Flowcharts**: In process improvement, flowcharts could detail the steps of a procurement process to identify delays in procurement and approval.

Conclusion

Each of these Seven Basic Quality Tools offers distinct benefits for identifying, analyzing, and solving quality-related issues in projects. By effectively utilizing these tools, project managers can ensure higher quality outcomes, meet customer satisfaction, and enhance overall project performance. Quality audits are a critical component of the Manage Quality process in project management. They serve to ensure that project activities comply with organizational and project policies, processes, and procedures, and they play a crucial role in maintaining the quality standards throughout the project's lifecycle.

Purpose of Quality Audits

1. **Ensure Compliance**: Quality audits check for adherence to internal and external standards and regulations. This compliance ensures that the project meets all required quality and regulatory requirements, which is crucial for project success and credibility.
2. **Identify Improvement Areas**: Audits help identify inefficiencies and non-conformities in project processes. These insights provide valuable opportunities for process improvements, contributing to better performance and outcomes.
3. **Share Best Practices**: Through the examination of different areas and functions of the project, quality audits can uncover best practices that can be documented and shared across the organization, enhancing overall productivity and quality.
4. **Enhance Stakeholder Confidence**: Regular audits reassure stakeholders that the project is not only compliant with quality standards but is also committed to continuous quality improvement.

Planning, Conducting, and Documenting Quality Audits

Planning:
- **Scheduling**: Quality audits are typically scheduled at specific intervals during the project lifecycle, detailed in the project's quality management plan. The frequency of these audits depends on the project's complexity, compliance requirements, and past performance.
- **Scope and Criteria**: Define what processes, areas, or deliverables will be audited and establish the criteria against which these will be evaluated. This scope should align with the project's most critical quality aspects.

Conducting:
- **Preparation**: Gather necessary documentation and records, such as process documents, previous audit reports, and compliance records. The audit team reviews these documents to understand the procedures and expected standards.
- **Execution**: The audit involves examining and questioning methods and quality processes to ensure they comply with the laid down procedures. It typically includes interviews with team members, observations of processes, and review of compliance documentation.

- **Findings**: Auditors note any discrepancies, non-conformities, and opportunities for improvement. They also highlight areas of compliance and any practices that exceed expectations.

Documenting:
- **Audit Report**: The findings from the audit are compiled into a detailed report. This report includes a description of the audit scope, criteria, observations, the evidence reviewed, and the conclusions drawn.
- **Recommendations**: Based on the findings, the audit report will recommend corrective actions for non-conformities and suggest areas for improvement.
- **Review and Approval**: The audit report is reviewed and approved by project management and relevant stakeholders. This approval is crucial for ensuring the objectivity and accuracy of the audit process.

Role in Identifying Improvements and Ensuring Compliance

Quality audits are instrumental in driving improvements and ensuring compliance:
- **Continuous Improvement**: Audits identify gaps and inefficiencies in processes, providing a foundation for ongoing improvements. Implementing audit recommendations helps in refining processes and enhancing project outcomes.
- **Compliance Assurance**: Regular audits verify that the project adheres to required quality standards and regulations, thus preventing compliance issues that could lead to penalties, legal problems, or reputational damage.
- **Feedback Mechanism**: Audits provide feedback to the project team and stakeholders about how well the project is performing against its quality objectives, which can be used to make informed decisions about future project directions and priorities.

Quality audits are an essential mechanism for maintaining rigorous quality control in projects. They ensure that the project not only meets the specified standards but also continuously improves in its execution and output, thereby maximizing project success and stakeholder satisfaction. Statistical sampling is a technique used in quality management to analyze a subset of data from a larger population to draw conclusions about the quality of the entire population. This method is particularly valuable in projects where inspecting every item or result is impractical due to time, cost, or feasibility constraints.

Use of Statistical Sampling in Manage Quality

Statistical sampling allows project managers to assess and control quality by examining a representative group selected from a production or process lot. By evaluating this sample, conclusions can be made about the overall quality of the entire lot without needing to check every item. This approach is efficient and cost-effective, especially in large-scale projects or those with high production volumes.

How Sampling Helps in Quality Assessment

1. **Efficiency**: Sampling reduces the time and resources needed for quality inspections. By inspecting a smaller, manageable set of items, project teams can quickly identify potential issues without the need for exhaustive examination.
2. **Cost-Effectiveness**: It lowers costs associated with quality control by reducing the manpower and material resources needed for testing every unit.
3. **Risk Management**: Sampling can help identify systematic errors or trends in quality defects, allowing corrective actions to be taken proactively to mitigate risks associated with poor quality.

4. **Decision Making**: Provides statistical evidence to support decision making in quality assurance and control processes. This data-driven approach enhances the credibility and effectiveness of quality management efforts.

Key Considerations When Designing a Sampling Plan

1. Define the Population: Clearly define the population from which the sample will be drawn. Understanding the total population helps in determining an adequate sample size that will represent the population accurately.

2. Determine Sample Size: The sample size should be large enough to give statistically valid results but not so large as to waste resources. Factors influencing sample size include the criticality of quality, the variability of the process, and the acceptable risk of errors.

3. Selection Method: Choose a method for selecting samples. Random sampling is often preferred because it minimizes bias and ensures each member of the population has an equal chance of being chosen. However, other methods like stratified sampling or systematic sampling might be appropriate depending on the project specifics.

4. Sampling Frequency: Decide how frequently samples should be taken. This could be based on time (e.g., every hour), production volume (e.g., every 100 units produced), or following significant changes in the process or materials.

5. Data Analysis Techniques: Plan how to analyze the data collected from the samples. Statistical tests, control charts, and other analytical tools can help interpret the results, identify trends, or detect anomalies.

6. Acceptance Criteria: Establish criteria for accepting or rejecting the lot based on the sample results. This includes setting thresholds for the number of defects that are acceptable before action is taken.

Example of Sampling in Practice

Consider a project to manufacture electronic components where each component must undergo electrical and safety testing. Testing every unit may be prohibitively expensive and time-consuming. Instead, the project manager decides to use statistical sampling by testing every 50th unit produced. The results from these tests are then used to infer the quality of the entire production batch. If more than 2% of the sampled units fail, the entire batch is reviewed for potential production issues.

Conclusion

Statistical sampling is a crucial component of the Manage Quality process in project management, enabling teams to ensure product or service quality efficiently and effectively. By carefully planning the sampling approach and considering factors such as sample size, selection method, and frequency, project managers can effectively manage quality and ensure project deliverables meet the required standards. This strategic approach not only saves resources but also helps in maintaining high-quality outputs consistently. Process analysis in the Manage Quality process is pivotal for enhancing the efficiency and effectiveness of project operations. It involves a detailed examination of project processes to identify areas of inefficiency, potential bottlenecks, and opportunities for improvement. By using various analytical tools and techniques, project managers can streamline processes, reduce waste, and enhance the overall quality and productivity of the project.

Importance of Process Analysis

1. **Identifying Inefficiencies**: Process analysis helps in pinpointing the stages in a process that cause delays, unnecessary costs, or quality issues, enabling targeted interventions.

2. **Optimizing Resources**: By analyzing processes, project managers can make better use of resources, ensuring that time, budget, and human resources are employed effectively.
3. **Enhancing Quality**: Continuous improvement in processes typically leads to higher quality outputs by reducing the chances of errors and rework.
4. **Increasing Stakeholder Satisfaction**: Streamlined processes that deliver quality outputs on time and within budget can significantly increase customer and stakeholder satisfaction.

Tools and Techniques for Process Analysis
1. Flowcharting

- **Description**: Flowcharting involves creating a diagram that depicts the sequence of steps in a project process. It visually represents the flow of activities and decision points from start to finish.
- **Application**: Flowcharts help in identifying redundancies, unnecessary loops, or bottlenecks in a process. For example, a flowchart might reveal that approvals are routed through multiple departments redundantly, causing delays.
- **Benefits**: Simplifies understanding of complex processes and aids in communication and discussion about process improvements.

2. Value Stream Mapping

- **Description**: Value stream mapping is a lean management tool that helps visualize the entire process flow to deliver a product or service from start to finish. It maps out all actions and decision points in a process and categorizes them into value-adding and non-value-adding activities.
- **Application**: This tool is used to identify waste in the form of delays, restrictions, or any steps that do not add value to the customer. For instance, it can show where inventory accumulates, indicating a lack of synchronization between process steps.
- **Benefits**: Focuses improvement efforts on areas that will most significantly enhance value to the customer, ensuring efficient use of resources.

2. Lean Techniques

- **Description**: Lean techniques aim to maximize customer value by minimizing waste, without sacrificing productivity. They focus on improving overall quality by streamlining operations and optimizing efficiency.
- **Application**: Techniques like 'Just-in-Time' production (reducing inventory waste), 'Kaizen' (continuous improvement), and 'Poka-yoke' (error-proofing) are employed to enhance process efficiency. For example, applying Kaizen can encourage ongoing incremental improvements in a software development project, enhancing agility and responsiveness.
- **Benefits**: Increases process speed and efficiency, reduces costs, and improves quality. Lean techniques foster a culture of continuous improvement and employee empowerment within the project team.

Conclusion

Process analysis is a critical activity within the Manage Quality process, providing the insights needed to make informed decisions about where and how to improve project processes. Tools like flowcharting, value stream mapping, and lean techniques are instrumental in identifying inefficiencies and ensuring that processes are as lean and effective as possible. By applying these tools, project managers can not only meet but exceed quality expectations, ultimately leading to projects that are more successful and deliver greater value to stakeholders. The Control Quality process is a critical component of project quality management, focusing on monitoring and recording the results of executing quality activities. This process ensures that the project's deliverables meet the quality standards established in the quality management plan and that the project effectively implements its designed quality processes.

Significance of the Control Quality Process

1. **Ensure Compliance with Standards**: The Control Quality process ensures that project outputs, both product and processes, comply with the quality standards, organizational procedures, and customer satisfaction requirements. This compliance is essential for the project's acceptance and success.
2. **Identify Causes of Issues**: It helps in identifying the causes of poor product quality and process inefficiencies, which can then be addressed to prevent recurrence.
3. **Increase Stakeholder Confidence**: Regularly demonstrating that the project meets quality requirements increases confidence among stakeholders and customers, which is critical for project continuation and reputation.
4. **Validate Deliverable Fitness for Use**: The process validates that the project deliverables are complete and function according to the requirements specified by the stakeholders, ensuring that the products are fit for use.
5. **Facilitate Continuous Improvement**: By monitoring outcomes and improving processes, the Control Quality process drives the continuous improvement that is essential for maintaining competitiveness and effectiveness in project execution.

Primary Tools and Techniques for Measuring and Analyzing Quality Performance
1. Inspection

- **Description**: Inspections involve examining a work product to determine if it conforms to documented standards. Inspections might include measuring, examining, testing, or gauging one or more characteristics of a product or process and comparing the results with specified requirements.
- **Application**: Used to identify defects or non-conformities in the project deliverables, such as inspecting a batch of manufactured components for physical defects.

2. Statistical Sampling

- **Description**: This technique involves selecting a part of a population of interest for inspection to draw conclusions about the whole population. Statistical sampling determines the need for corrective actions and ensures that the process outputs meet quality standards.
- **Application**: Sampling a subset of all code modules developed in a software project to test for defects.

3. Control Charts

- **Description**: Control charts are used to determine whether a process is stable or has predictable performance. These charts help to monitor performance and detect any trends, variations, or irregularities that might indicate issues.
- **Application**: Monitoring the number of defects identified in each phase of the project to ensure that the process remains within acceptable limits.

4. Pareto Diagrams

- **Description**: Pareto diagrams are based on the Pareto principle, which states that a small number of causes typically lead to a large portion of the problems. It helps in prioritizing problem-solving efforts.
- **Application**: Identifying the most common types of defects occurring in project deliverables and focusing quality improvement efforts on these areas.

5. Cause and Effect Diagrams

- **Description**: Also known as fishbone diagrams or Ishikawa diagrams, these tools help in brainstorming to identify potential causes of defects and categorize them into logical groups.
- **Application**: Analyzing the root causes of a recurring issue in product assembly to identify process adjustments.

6. Scatter Diagrams

- **Description**: Scatter diagrams are used to investigate the possible relationship between two variables.
- **Application**: Examining the relationship between the amount of testing and the number of defects found, helping to determine if increased testing results in fewer defects.

Conclusion

The Control Quality process is essential in maintaining the integrity of a project's outputs and ensuring that all project activities result in products that meet predefined standards. By using effective tools and techniques to measure and analyze quality performance, project managers can maintain control over the quality of deliverables, leading to improved project outcomes and stakeholder satisfaction. This vigilant monitoring and adjustment facilitate a dynamic approach to quality, ensuring project standards are upheld throughout its lifecycle. Inspections are a critical component of the Control Quality process in project management. They involve the methodical examination of a product, service, or process against agreed-upon standards to ensure it meets quality expectations. The effectiveness of inspections can significantly impact the project's ability to meet its objectives and customer satisfaction levels.

Role of Inspections in Control Quality

1. **Verification of Compliance**: Inspections verify that the project outputs comply with the specifications, standards, and other regulatory requirements. They ensure that all elements of the project are executed correctly, from materials and components to final products.
2. **Identification of Defects**: Through inspections, defects and non-conformities can be identified early before the product or service is delivered to the customer. Early detection allows for timely corrective actions, reducing rework and waste.
3. **Assurance of Quality**: Regular inspections reinforce the commitment to quality throughout the project lifecycle, providing stakeholders with assurance that quality control processes are effectively being applied.
4. **Feedback for Improvement**: Inspections provide critical feedback on the effectiveness of the project processes and offer insights into areas that may require improvements.

Planning and Conducting Inspections

Planning:

- **Develop Inspection Criteria**: Define clear, measurable criteria that the products or processes must meet. These criteria should be derived from the project requirements, regulatory standards, and customer expectations.
- **Schedule Inspections**: Determine the timing and frequency of inspections. Critical milestones, such as the completion of major phases or the integration of key components, are typical points where inspections might be scheduled.
- **Select Inspection Methods**: Choose appropriate inspection methods (visual, manual, automated testing, etc.), depending on the complexity of the items being inspected and the nature of potential defects.

Conducting:

- **Prepare Inspection Tools and Checklists**: Use detailed checklists based on the inspection criteria to ensure consistency and completeness in the inspection process.
- **Train Inspectors**: Ensure that inspectors are trained and competent to perform the inspections. They should understand the inspection criteria and how to use any tools or equipment involved in the process.
- **Perform Inspections**: Execute the inspections according to the plan. Inspectors check for conformity, identify defects, and document their findings.
- **Document Results**: Record the results of the inspections in a systematic manner. Documentation should include information about what was inspected, who performed the inspection, findings, and any actions taken.

Developing Inspection Criteria and Checklists

Key Considerations:

- **Clarity and Specificity**: Criteria should be specific and unambiguous to avoid interpretation errors during inspections. They should clearly describe the attributes being inspected and the standards they must meet.
- **Measurability**: Ensure that the criteria are measurable. Quantifiable measures facilitate objective inspections and make it easier to decide whether a criterion has been met.
- **Relevance**: Criteria should be relevant to the critical quality requirements of the project. Focus on aspects that directly affect functionality, performance, and regulatory compliance.
- **Checklist Design**: Design checklists to be user-friendly and systematic, covering all necessary inspection points in a logical order. Checklists should be easy to follow during inspections to ensure nothing is missed.

Conclusion

Inspections are a vital part of the Control Quality process, providing a mechanism to ensure that project deliverables meet predefined quality criteria. Effective planning and execution of inspections, along with well-developed criteria and checklists, are essential for maintaining quality control, minimizing risks, and ensuring project success. Through meticulous inspections, projects can achieve higher quality outputs, leading to greater customer satisfaction and fewer complications post-delivery. Change management and quality control are interlinked processes in project management. Approved change requests often necessitate alterations in project scope, schedule, or cost, which can, in turn, affect project quality. Ensuring that these changes do not negatively impact the quality is crucial for maintaining project integrity and stakeholder satisfaction.

Impact of Approved Change Requests on Quality Control

1. **Modification of Quality Baselines**: Approved change requests can alter the quality baselines, which are the standards against which project performance is measured. Changes in project scope or objectives might lead to new quality requirements and standards.

2. **Adjustment of Processes and Outputs**: Changes might require adjustments in work processes, methodologies, or materials used, which can influence the final quality of the project deliverables.

3. **Risks to Quality Consistency**: Without proper control, changes can introduce variability and inconsistency, potentially compromising the overall project quality.

Ensuring Quality Control with Approved Change Requests
1. Rigorous Change Control Process

- **Implementation**: Implement a structured change control process that evaluates every change request comprehensively before approval. This evaluation should include an analysis of the impact on project quality.
- **Documentation**: Document all changes and their impacts on the project, including how they affect quality metrics and standards.

2. Update Quality Management Plans

- **Adapt Quality Plans**: Once a change is approved, update quality management plans, quality metrics, and any associated documentation to align with the new project direction.
- **Communicate Changes**: Ensure that all stakeholders, including project team members and contractors, are aware of the changes and understand their roles in implementing them while maintaining quality.

3. Integration with Project Baselines

- **Rebaseline if Necessary**: Depending on the extent of the change, it may be necessary to rebaseline the project to integrate the changes fully into the project management plan.
- **Align Quality Standards**: Adjust the quality standards and practices to reflect the approved changes, ensuring they are still achievable and aligned with the project's objectives.

4. Quality Audits and Inspections

- **Conduct Audits**: Regular quality audits and inspections should be performed to ensure that the changes are implemented correctly and are meeting the modified quality standards.
- **Feedback Loops**: Establish feedback mechanisms to quickly identify and address any quality issues arising from the changes.

5. Training and Resources

- **Provide Training**: Offer training or briefings to the project team on the new requirements or processes introduced by the changes.
- **Allocate Resources**: Ensure that adequate resources are allocated to achieve the desired quality levels post-change.

Example of Managing Quality with Approved Changes

Suppose a project developing a new software application receives an approved change request to add additional features based on user feedback. Here's how quality control might be managed:

- **Update Quality Plans**: The Quality Management Plan is updated to include new testing procedures and quality metrics that accommodate the additional features.
- **Quality Training**: Developers and testers receive training on the new features and how to integrate these features without disrupting the existing system.
- **Quality Audits**: Conduct additional rounds of quality audits to ensure the new features do not introduce bugs or reduce the usability of the software.

Conclusion

Approved change requests have a significant impact on project quality, requiring careful management to ensure that quality standards are maintained or enhanced. By systematically integrating change management with quality control processes, and ensuring that changes are implemented correctly, project managers can minimize negative impacts on project quality, thus maintaining the integrity and value of the project outcomes. Root cause analysis (RCA) is a systematic process used to identify the underlying causes of problems or issues to prevent their recurrence. In the context of the Control Quality process in project management, RCA is crucial for uncovering the fundamental reasons behind quality defects or failures. By addressing these root causes, project teams can implement effective solutions that prevent future issues, thereby enhancing the quality and reliability of project deliverables.

Steps Involved in Conducting a Root Cause Analysis

1. **Identify the Problem**: Clearly define the specific problem or defect. Document what is observed, including the symptoms and the context in which the problem occurs.
2. **Collect Data**: Gather data related to the problem, which could include production data, process monitoring data, quality inspection reports, and any relevant observations about when and how the issue occurs.
3. **Analyze the Data**: Use RCA techniques to examine the data and trace the problem to its origin. The goal is to differentiate between the mere symptoms of the problem and its actual causes.
4. **Identify Possible Causal Factors**: Consider all the factors that might contribute to the problem. This can include human factors, methods, materials, machinery, and environmental conditions.
5. **Determine the Root Cause(s)**: Through iterative questioning and analysis, narrow down the list of potential causes to determine which is most likely responsible for the problem.
6. **Develop and Implement Solutions**: Propose and implement solutions that address the root causes. Solutions should be effective in preventing recurrence, feasible within project constraints, and acceptable to stakeholders.
7. **Monitor Effectiveness**: After solutions are implemented, monitor the situation to ensure the problem is resolved and does not recur. This monitoring might involve regular inspections or revisiting performance metrics.

Common Root Cause Analysis Techniques
1. **The 5 Whys Technique**:
- **Description**: This technique involves asking "Why?" multiple times (typically five) until the root cause of a problem is uncovered. Each answer forms the basis of the next question.
- **Example**: A project fails to meet its software deployment deadline.
  - **Why?** The final integration testing phase was delayed.
  - **Why?** The code modules were not ready for integration.

- **Why?** Several key developers were reassigned to another project.
- **Why?** The project scheduling did not account for overlapping project demands.
- **Why?** Project resource allocation practices were inadequate.
- **Application**: This method is straightforward and doesn't require statistical analysis, making it suitable for solving less complex problems.

2. Ishikawa (Fishbone) Diagram:

- **Description**: Also known as the cause-and-effect diagram, it helps teams systematically explore all potential or real causes that result in a particular problem. The diagram looks like a fish's skeleton, with the problem at the head and the causes extending to the left like fish bones.
- **Example**: Low customer satisfaction in a software project.
  - Causes branch out into categories such as People, Processes, Technology, and Materials. Under each category, specific potential causes are listed, like insufficient training (People), outdated software tools (Technology), or inadequate testing materials (Materials).
- **Application**: This method is useful for complex issues where multiple causes interlink and influence each other. It helps in visualizing the relationship between different causes of a problem.

Conclusion

Root cause analysis is an essential tool in the Control Quality process, enabling project teams to not only address symptoms but eliminate the underlying causes of problems. By using techniques such as the 5 Whys and Ishikawa diagrams, teams can ensure more durable and effective solutions, leading to higher quality outcomes and increased project success. Control charts are a vital statistical tool used in the Control Quality process within project management. These charts are used to monitor the performance of project processes over time, helping to ensure that process outputs remain within acceptable limits.

Purpose of Control Charts

Control charts primarily serve to:
1. **Monitor Process Stability**: They track the performance of processes to determine if these processes are stable (predictable) over time.
2. **Identify Variability**: Control charts help identify variations in process performance, distinguishing between common cause variability (inherent to the process) and special cause variability (resulting from specific circumstances).
3. **Facilitate Corrective Actions**: By providing a visual representation of process performance against defined upper and lower control limits, control charts indicate when processes are deviating from acceptable parameters, prompting necessary corrective actions.

How Control Charts Work

Control charts consist of points plotted on a time-ordered graph, with a central line (CL) representing the average value of all sampled data. The chart also displays an upper control limit (UCL) and a lower control limit (LCL), which define the boundaries of acceptable variation in the process. Here's how they function in project management:
1. **Setting Baselines**: The CL is calculated based on historical data from the process. This line serves as the baseline against which future data points are compared.
2. **Defining Control Limits**: UCL and LCL are typically set at ±3 standard deviations from the CL, based on the assumption that nearly all (99.73%) of the natural process variation is covered within this range.

3. **Real-Time Monitoring**: As new process data is collected, it is plotted in real-time against these predefined limits.

Using Control Charts to Monitor Process Performance

Detecting Variations: Regular plotting of process data helps in quickly detecting deviations beyond the control limits. Points outside these limits suggest the influence of special cause variations, which are unusual events that indicate potential process issues.

Trend Analysis: Control charts also help in identifying trends within the control limits, such as a series of consecutive points trending upwards or downwards. Such trends, even if within control limits, can indicate potential future issues that may require preemptive action.

Maintaining Process Consistency: By continuously monitoring process output, project managers can ensure a consistent quality of deliverables, essential for customer satisfaction and project success.

Examples of Control Chart Applications

1. **Software Development**: In a software project, a control chart could be used to monitor the number of defects identified per iteration. If the number of defects exceeds the UCL, this would signal a potential problem in the coding or testing processes that needs immediate investigation.
2. **Construction**: In construction, control charts might monitor the compressive strength of concrete batches. Measurements that fall outside the control limits could indicate issues with the mix components or process, prompting reviews and corrections to the mix procedure.

When to Take Corrective Action

Project managers should consider corrective actions when:

- Data points fall outside the UCL or LCL.
- There are runs or patterns within the control limits indicating non-random behavior (e.g., seven consecutive points on one side of the central line).

Conclusion

Control charts are an effective tool for maintaining quality control in projects. They provide a systematic approach to understanding process performance, detecting significant variations, and identifying the need for corrective actions. By enabling early detection of potential issues, control charts help project managers keep processes under control, thus ensuring project deliverables meet quality standards consistently. This proactive management tool is crucial for optimizing project outcomes and achieving operational excellence. Pareto diagrams, also known as Pareto charts, are a statistical tool based on the Pareto Principle, which asserts that roughly 80% of problems are caused by 20% of the causes. This principle is also commonly referred to as the "80/20 rule." In the context of project management and specifically within the Control Quality process, Pareto diagrams play a crucial role in identifying and prioritizing the issues that significantly impact project quality.

Role of Pareto Diagrams in Control Quality

Pareto diagrams help project managers and teams to:

1. **Visualize and Identify Problems**: By categorizing and displaying the frequency of occurrences or the magnitude of problems in descending order, Pareto diagrams highlight the most significant issues impacting project quality.
2. **Prioritize Issues**: This visualization allows teams to focus on the problems that will have the greatest effect if solved, facilitating efficient allocation of resources where they are most needed.

3. **Drive Effective Decision-Making**: The diagram provides a clear basis for making decisions about where to apply efforts to improve processes, fix issues, or implement corrective actions.
4. **Track Improvements**: Pareto diagrams can be used before and after improvement measures are implemented to visually assess how the landscape of quality issues has changed and whether the most significant issues have been effectively addressed.

Using Pareto Diagrams to Prioritize Quality Issues
Steps to Create and Use a Pareto Diagram:
1. **Data Collection**: Gather data on quality defects or issues. This data collection should be specific and quantifiable, detailing each type of defect and its frequency of occurrence.
2. **Categorization**: Classify the defects or problems into distinct categories. Each category should represent a type of defect or problem observed in the project.
3. **Sorting and Calculating**: Sort the categories from the most frequent to the least frequent. Calculate the cumulative impact of each category, typically focusing on how often each occurs or the cost associated with each.
4. **Chart Creation**: Create a bar graph where each category is represented by a bar. The bars are plotted in descending order of frequency or impact on the primary vertical axis. A cumulative percentage line is also plotted on a secondary vertical axis, helping to visualize the cumulative impact of addressing the defects in order.
5. **Analysis and Action**:
   - **Identify the "Vital Few"**: The first few categories that appear on the left side of the chart are typically the "vital few" that contribute to the majority of the problem.
   - **Focus on Critical Issues**: Prioritize corrective actions starting with these "vital few" categories. By solving these, the largest gains in quality improvement are typically achieved.
   - **Implement Solutions and Monitor Results**: Develop and implement strategies to address these key issues. Continuously monitor results and adjust actions as necessary to ensure that these primary problems are resolved.

Example
If a construction project is facing multiple quality issues, a Pareto diagram may reveal that 80% of the complaints are related to just 20% of the problem types – perhaps delays in material delivery and subcontractor errors. The project manager would then prioritize solving these two issues before focusing on less impactful problems, such as minor installation mistakes or administrative delays.

Conclusion
By applying Pareto diagrams, project managers can make informed decisions about addressing the most critical issues first, thus ensuring quality improvement efforts are both effective and efficient. This strategic approach not only optimizes resource utilization but also significantly enhances the overall quality of the project, leading to greater stakeholder satisfaction and project success. The project involved constructing a 50-story high-rise building in a major urban center, intended for mixed-use with both residential and commercial spaces. Given the complexity and the high visibility of the project, maintaining stringent quality standards was critical to ensure safety, compliance with regulations, and stakeholder satisfaction.

Quality Challenges Faced

1. **Complex Regulatory Requirements**: The project had to comply with numerous local and international building standards, which were often complex and required meticulous attention to detail.
2. **Supplier Quality Variability**: The quality of materials received from suppliers occasionally varied, affecting the consistency of the construction outputs.
3. **High Stakeholder Expectations**: The future residents and commercial tenants had high expectations regarding the building's quality and finish, which required exceptional quality management practices.
4. **Coordination Among Diverse Teams**: Multiple subcontractors and teams were involved in the project, making it challenging to maintain uniform quality standards across all aspects of construction.

Quality Management Strategies Employed
1. Implementation of a Comprehensive Quality Management Plan

- A detailed quality management plan was developed at the beginning of the project, outlining quality standards, procedures for managing and controlling quality, and specific quality metrics to be maintained.

2. Rigorous Quality Assurance Practices

- **Regular Inspections and Audits**: Scheduled and random inspections were conducted to ensure that all construction phases met the predefined quality standards.
- **Quality Training Sessions**: Regular training sessions were held for all team members, focusing on quality standards, new regulations, and best practices in construction quality.

3. Quality Control Measures

- **Control Charts**: Used to monitor critical parameters like concrete strength, curing times, and alignment precision, ensuring they remained within acceptable limits.
- **Checklists and Check Sheets**: Developed for every phase of the project to ensure all quality requirements were met before moving to the next phase.

4. Stakeholder Engagement and Communication

- Regular meetings with stakeholders were held to review the quality standards and gather feedback, ensuring alignment with their expectations and making adjustments as necessary.

5. Supplier Quality Management

- **Supplier Audits**: Conducted audits on key suppliers to ensure their materials met the project's quality requirements.
- **Performance Evaluations**: Suppliers were regularly evaluated based on the quality of their materials and timeliness of their deliveries.

Lessons Learned
1. Importance of Early and Continuous Planning

- The project manager noted that continuous adjustments and updates to the quality management plan were crucial, especially as new challenges emerged. Early planning helped in anticipating potential quality issues and mitigating them proactively.

2. Value of Integrative Tools and Techniques

- Employing various quality tools and techniques, such as control charts and Pareto diagrams, provided a multi-faceted approach to quality control, making it easier to pinpoint issues and focus efforts where they were most needed.

3. Critical Role of Communication

- Effective communication with all project stakeholders, including suppliers, contractors, and future tenants, was essential. It ensured that quality expectations were clearly understood and met, and it helped in managing expectations throughout the project lifecycle.

4. Training and Team Competence

- Continuous training and development of the project team played a significant role in maintaining high quality. It ensured that all team members were aware of the latest regulations and internal quality standards.

5. Proactive Supplier Management

- Regularly auditing suppliers and holding them to strict quality standards proved vital in ensuring the materials used in construction met the necessary quality levels.

Conclusion

The construction of the high-rise building demonstrated the effectiveness of proactive and comprehensive quality management in dealing with complex projects. The strategies employed not only addressed the initial quality challenges but also ensured that the project met all regulatory standards and stakeholder expectations. The lessons learned highlight the importance of planning, teamwork, and continuous improvement in achieving project quality objectives. Project quality management is critical for delivering successful project outcomes, yet it is often fraught with misunderstandings and oversights that can undermine its effectiveness. Understanding and addressing these common pitfalls and misconceptions is crucial for project managers aiming to maintain high standards of quality throughout the project lifecycle.

Common Pitfalls and Misconceptions

1. Quality Is Solely the Responsibility of the Quality Team:

- **Misconception**: Quality management is often seen as a task for the quality assurance team rather than a shared responsibility.
- **Pitfall**: This can lead to lack of engagement from other team members and a compartmentalized approach to quality.

2. Equating Quality with Compliance:

- **Misconception**: There is a belief that meeting the compliance standards is the same as achieving quality.
- **Pitfall**: Compliance with standards doesn't automatically ensure customer satisfaction or product usability.

3. Overlooking the Cost of Quality:

- **Misconception**: Investing in quality is seen as an increase in project costs rather than an investment.
- **Pitfall**: Failing to invest adequately in preventive measures can lead to higher costs later due to rework and defects.

4. Inadequate Planning for Quality:

- **Misconception**: Quality can be 'inspected in' at the end of the project rather than built into the process.
- **Pitfall**: This often results in higher defect rates and increased project costs and delays.

5. Ignoring Continuous Improvement:

- **Misconception**: Once quality levels are achieved, no further efforts are needed.
- **Pitfall**: This static approach can lead to deteriorations in quality over time and missed opportunities for process improvements.

Guidance for Avoiding Pitfalls

1. Integrate Quality Into All Aspects:

- Encourage every team member to take responsibility for quality, not just the quality assurance team. Foster a culture where quality is everyone's business.
- Use training sessions to raise awareness about the importance of quality in all phases of the project.

2. Define Quality Beyond Compliance:

- Clearly communicate that quality is about meeting customer needs and expectations, not just adhering to specifications.
- Engage stakeholders regularly to ensure that the project meets their requirements and adjust quality objectives as necessary.

3. Understand and Manage the Cost of Quality:

- Educate the team about the cost of quality, including the costs associated with prevention, appraisal, and failure.
- Conduct a cost-benefit analysis to justify investments in quality initiatives and demonstrate their value in reducing long-term costs.

4. Plan for Quality From the Start:

- Incorporate quality planning in the initial phases of the project. Define clear quality objectives, standards, and metrics in the project planning documents.
- Develop a comprehensive quality management plan that includes detailed processes for quality assurance and control.

5. Embrace Continuous Improvement:

- Implement a continuous improvement process that encourages feedback and learning from quality audits and control measures.
- Utilize tools like lessons learned and after-action reviews to integrate new insights into project processes continuously.

6. Leverage Quality Tools and Techniques:

- Use quality management tools (e.g., Pareto charts, Ishikawa diagrams) systematically to identify and address quality issues.

- Apply modern quality management methodologies such as Six Sigma, Lean, or Total Quality Management to enhance process efficiencies.

Conclusion

By recognizing and proactively addressing these pitfalls, project managers can ensure that quality is not merely an adjunct but a fundamental aspect of project management integrated throughout the project lifecycle. This proactive, prevention-oriented approach to quality helps in delivering projects that not only meet but exceed stakeholder expectations, thereby enhancing project success and customer satisfaction. Continuous improvement in project quality management refers to the ongoing efforts to enhance the quality of processes and outcomes within a project. This concept is rooted in various methodologies, including Total Quality Management (TQM), Lean, and Six Sigma, which emphasize incremental and breakthrough improvements.

Fostering a Culture of Continuous Improvement
Leadership Commitment:

Project managers must demonstrate a strong commitment to quality. This involves leading by example, ensuring that quality is a priority at all levels of the project team.

Open Communication:

Encourage open and transparent communication about quality issues and potential improvements. Regular meetings, feedback sessions, and open-door policies can help in fostering an environment where every team member feels valued and heard.

Training and Education:

Equip the team with the necessary skills and knowledge to identify and implement quality improvements. Training sessions, workshops, and seminars on quality management tools and techniques can be very effective.

Recognition and Rewards:

Recognize and reward team members who contribute to quality improvements. This not only motivates individuals but also sets a precedent for the importance of ongoing quality enhancement.

Empowerment:

Empower team members to identify issues and implement solutions. When team members are directly involved in quality improvement initiatives, they are more likely to buy into the continuous improvement culture.

Implementing Quality Improvements Across Projects

1. **Standardization of Processes**: Develop and use standardized processes that are known to produce quality outcomes. These standards can be continuously improved and applied across various projects to ensure consistency and efficiency.
2. **Lessons Learned**: Implement a robust system for capturing lessons learned from each project. These insights should be reviewed and used to refine project processes in future projects.
3. **Quality Audits**: Conduct regular quality audits across projects to identify best practices and areas for improvement. Audits help in maintaining standards and fostering a culture of accountability and excellence.

4. **Benchmarking**: Use benchmarking to compare project practices and performances against those of leaders in the industry. This can reveal gaps in processes and provide insights into areas for improvement.
5. **Integration of Quality Management Tools**: Use quality management tools such as PDCA (Plan-Do-Check-Act), control charts, and root cause analysis consistently across projects to monitor quality and facilitate continuous improvement.
6. **Collaborative Improvement Initiatives**: Encourage collaboration between project teams to share effective practices and improvements. This can be facilitated through regular inter-project meetings, shared digital platforms, or cross-project teams.

Example of Continuous Improvement in Practice

In a software development firm, project teams adopt Agile methodologies that inherently support continuous improvement through iterative processes and regular retrospectives. At the end of each sprint, teams discuss what went well and what didn't, providing a platform to plan and implement quality improvements in real-time. Over multiple sprints and projects, improvements such as more efficient code reviews, enhanced testing protocols, and better stakeholder communication protocols are standardized and shared across the firm, elevating the overall quality of software products.

Conclusion

Continuous improvement is vital in project quality management as it drives teams to constantly seek ways to enhance their work processes and outputs. By fostering a culture of continuous improvement, project managers can ensure that their teams are always looking for ways to improve, leading to higher quality outcomes and more successful projects. Implementing these practices requires commitment and coordination but results in significant benefits across the organization. Project Quality Management is deeply intertwined with other knowledge areas within project management, such as Project Scope Management and Project Risk Management. Understanding these interactions is crucial for effectively managing a project, as quality often influences and is influenced by various aspects of project management.

Interaction with Project Scope Management
Relationship:

The scope of a project defines what needs to be accomplished, and quality management ensures that the project's deliverables meet the required standards and stakeholder expectations.

Example:

- When defining the project scope, quality requirements for the deliverables must be clearly articulated to ensure they align with the client's expectations and regulatory standards.
- During scope verification, quality control processes are utilized to inspect and verify that the work products are complete and meet the predefined quality standards.
- If the scope needs to be adjusted, quality management processes ensure that the changes still align with quality requirements and do not compromise the overall project standards.

Dependency:

164

Effective scope management provides a clear baseline of what is to be delivered, which is essential for defining quality standards. Conversely, quality requirements might influence the scope by defining specific standards or practices that need to be included in the project deliverables.

Interaction with Project Risk Management

Relationship: Quality management and risk management are complementary disciplines; quality issues often pose significant risks to the project, impacting cost, time, and customer satisfaction.

Example:

- During the risk planning phase, potential quality risks, such as non-conformance to quality standards or the use of substandard materials, are identified and mitigation strategies are developed.
- Quality audits, a part of quality assurance, help in identifying new risks or changes to existing risks related to quality that may not have been apparent during the initial risk assessment.
- Implementing quality improvement processes as a part of continuous quality management can mitigate risks associated with process inefficiencies and prevent potential quality failures.

Dependency:

Effective risk management involves anticipating and mitigating risks that could impact quality, while robust quality management practices can reduce the occurrence and impact of project risks. For instance, by improving quality control processes, a project manager can reduce the risk of defects that would otherwise lead to rework, increased costs, and delays.

Broader Interactions

Quality management also interacts with other areas such as:

- **Project Integration Management**: Quality management must be integrated into the overall project plan, and changes in quality plans need to be coordinated with changes in other areas.
- **Project Cost Management**: There is a direct correlation between quality and cost. Poor quality can lead to higher costs due to rework, scrap, and penalties. Conversely, investing in preventive quality measures can reduce the total cost of the project.
- **Project Human Resource Management**: The level of training and expertise of the project team can directly impact project quality. Effective human resource management ensures that the right skills are available to meet the project's quality requirements.
- **Project Communications Management**: Effective communication of quality standards, policies, and procedures is vital. Quality metrics and performance reports need to be communicated to stakeholders regularly to ensure transparency and maintain stakeholder confidence.

Conclusion

The Project Quality Management processes are intricately linked with nearly every other knowledge area in project management. These relationships highlight the importance of a holistic view of project management, where quality is not treated in isolation but as an integral part of all project activities. By understanding and managing these interactions, project managers can better control project outcomes, ensuring high quality and meeting or exceeding stakeholder expectations. Here's a set of practice questions designed to test and reinforce understanding of Project Quality Management processes, quality tools and techniques, and their application in real-world scenarios. These questions are ideal for preparing for the CAPM exam or enhancing project management skills.

Question 1: What is the primary goal of Project Quality Management?

- A) To ensure that the project meets or exceeds stakeholder expectations
- B) To minimize the cost of the project
- C) To manage the project team effectively
- D) To ensure the project is completed on time

Correct Answer: A) To ensure that the project meets or exceeds stakeholder expectations

- **Explanation**: Project Quality Management focuses on ensuring that the project and its deliverables meet or exceed the stakeholders' expectations and requirements. It involves managing both the project management processes and the project outputs, emphasizing continuous improvement and customer satisfaction.

Question 2: Which tool is best used to identify the cause of defects in a manufacturing process?
- A) Histogram
- B) Scatter Diagram
- C) Pareto Chart
- D) Fishbone Diagram

Correct Answer: D) Fishbone Diagram

- **Explanation**: The Fishbone Diagram, also known as a Cause and Effect Diagram or Ishikawa Diagram, is specifically designed to help teams explore potential causes of a problem or quality defects. It is particularly useful in a manufacturing context to visually display the potential causes of defects and their root causes in a structured manner.

Question 3: What does a Control Chart primarily help to monitor?
- A) The sequence of project activities
- B) Project costs over time
- C) The relationship between variables
- D) Process variations over time

Correct Answer: D) Process variations over time

- **Explanation**: Control Charts are used to monitor process performance and stability over time. They help identify whether a process is in control by tracking data points against upper and lower control limits. This tool is essential in quality management for detecting variations that might require corrective actions.

Question 4: In quality management, what does a Pareto Chart effectively help to prioritize?
- A) Project tasks by duration
- B) Team members by performance
- C) Defects by frequency of occurrence
- D) Costs by budget allocation

Correct Answer: C) Defects by frequency of occurrence

- **Explanation**: A Pareto Chart is used to prioritize issues or defects based on their significance. It is built on the Pareto Principle (80/20 rule), which suggests that 80% of problems are often due to 20% of causes. This chart helps teams focus on the few causes that create the majority of problems.

Question 5: What is the significance of the Cost Performance Index (CPI) in quality management?
- A) It indicates the effectiveness of the project scheduling.
- B) It measures the cost efficiency of the work completed.

- C) It tracks the overall timeline of the project.
- D) It measures the quality of project deliverables.

Correct Answer: B) It measures the cost efficiency of the work completed

- **Explanation**: The Cost Performance Index (CPI) is a key performance index used in Earned Value Management (EVM) to measure the cost efficiency of the project work performed. A CPI value greater than 1 indicates that the project is under budget, reflecting good cost management that indirectly supports maintaining quality within financial constraints.

Question 6: How should project managers apply the lessons learned in quality management for continuous improvement?

- A) By documenting them at the end of the project only
- B) By sharing them only with top management
- C) By integrating them into the organization's best practices and training materials
- D) By ignoring them unless a major issue arises

Correct Answer: C) By integrating them into the organization's best practices and training materials

- **Explanation**: Lessons learned in quality management should be documented and shared across the organization. Integrating these insights into best practices and training materials ensures that improvements are continuous and that the same mistakes are not repeated in future projects.

These questions and detailed explanations will help readers deepen their understanding of Project Quality Management, equipping them with the knowledge necessary to manage projects effectively and prepare for the CAPM exam.

VIII. Project Resource Management:

The **Plan Resource Management** process is fundamental to project management, focusing on identifying, quantifying, and planning for the human, material, equipment, and supplies needed to complete project work successfully. This process establishes the framework and guidelines for how resources will be estimated, acquired, managed, and controlled throughout the project lifecycle.

Purpose and Importance of Plan Resource Management

1. **Efficient Resource Utilization**: Planning resource management ensures that the right resources are available at the right times, thereby optimizing their use and avoiding bottlenecks.
2. **Aligning Resources with Project Needs**: It aligns the project's resource allocation with its objectives and deliverables, ensuring that the project has adequate resources to meet its goals without over-resourcing or under-resourcing any aspects of the project.
3. **Cost Control**: Proper resource planning helps in budgeting by estimating the costs associated with resources, and it facilitates better financial management throughout the project.
4. **Enhancing Team Performance and Morale**: By clearly defining resource roles, responsibilities, and reporting relationships, the project can avoid conflicts and enhance team cooperation and morale.
5. **Risk Mitigation**: Effective resource management helps identify potential resource shortages and dependencies that could impact project timelines and costs, thus allowing for proactive risk mitigation.

Key Components of a Resource Management Plan

1. **Resource Requirements**: This component details the types and quantities of resources required for the project, broken down by project phase or activities. It includes human resources (skills, roles, responsibilities), as well as physical resources (materials, equipment, technology).
2. **Resource Acquisition**: Describes how resources will be acquired, whether hired internally, outsourced, or rented. This includes timelines for hiring and procurement processes.
3. **Resource Roles and Responsibilities**: Outlines the roles and responsibilities associated with each resource, providing clarity on who is responsible for what tasks. This helps in setting expectations and accountability.
4. **Resource Calendars**: Includes availability calendars for resources, noting when specific resources are available to work on the project. This is critical for scheduling and for identifying potential conflicts or periods of limited resource availability.
5. **Cost Estimates for Resources**: Provides an estimation of the cost associated with each resource type. This helps in budgeting and ensures that resource costs are tracked and managed against the project budget.
6. **Training Needs**: Identifies any gaps in skills or knowledge and outlines plans for training team members to ensure they have the necessary skills to complete their tasks effectively.
7. **Recognition and Rewards**: Describes the strategy for recognizing and rewarding team members, which is essential for maintaining motivation and morale throughout the project.
8. **Resource Control**: Details the methods and tools that will be used to monitor and control resource usage, ensuring that resources are used efficiently and effectively, and that deviations are addressed promptly.

Guiding Project Team in Managing Project Resources

The resource management plan serves as a comprehensive guide for the project team by:

- **Ensuring Clarity and Alignment**: Providing clear definitions of what resources are needed, when, and for what purpose helps align all team members and stakeholders with the project's objectives.
- **Optimizing Resource Allocation**: By clearly understanding resource availability and needs, project managers can schedule work more effectively, avoiding over-allocation or idle resources.
- **Enhancing Decision Making**: With a detailed resource management plan, project managers can make informed decisions about resource adjustments, procurements, and reallocations as project needs evolve.
- **Improving Team Dynamics**: Clear roles and responsibilities, along with recognition strategies, ensure that team members feel valued and understand their contributions to the project, leading to better performance and collaboration.

The Plan Resource Management process is vital for setting the foundation for efficient and effective resource utilization throughout the project. It ensures that the project team is well-prepared, adequately resourced, and aligned to achieve the project's goals within the specified constraints of budget and schedule. A project team charter is a crucial document developed at the beginning of the project during the Plan Resource Management process. It serves as a foundational tool that defines the team's roles, responsibilities, objectives, and operational boundaries. The charter helps establish clear expectations and guidelines for team conduct and interaction, which are vital for effective collaboration and project success.

Role of the Team Charter in Plan Resource Management

The team charter plays a significant role in resource management by:

1. **Clarifying Team Roles and Responsibilities**: It delineates the roles and responsibilities of each team member, reducing confusion and ensuring that all team members know what is expected of them.
2. **Setting Project Objectives and Goals**: The charter outlines the project's objectives and goals, aligning the team's efforts with the project's broader targets.
3. **Establishing Ground Rules**: It sets the ground rules for team interaction, decision-making processes, and conflict resolution, fostering a cooperative and productive work environment.
4. **Enhancing Communication**: By specifying communication protocols and expected interaction patterns, the charter helps optimize information flow among team members.
5. **Defining Authority Levels**: The document clarifies the authority levels within the team, detailing who has the power to make decisions and how those decisions should be communicated and documented.

Essential Elements of a Team Charter

1. **Purpose of the Project**: A brief description of the project, its significance, and expected outcomes to provide a clear understanding of why the team exists.
2. **Team Objectives**: Specific, measurable objectives that the team should achieve, which contribute to the project goals.
3. **Roles and Responsibilities**:
    - **Individual Roles**: Detailed descriptions of the responsibilities and duties of each team member, including the project manager.
    - **Team Responsibilities**: General responsibilities that the entire team shares.
4. **Project Authority Levels**:
    - A description of the decision-making authority of the project manager and other key team members.
    - Guidelines on how decisions are made and documented.
5. **Resources Available**: Information on the resources available to the team, including budget, tools, and technologies.
6. **Communication Plan**:
    - Preferred methods and frequency of communication among team members.
    - Contact information for all team members.
7. **Meeting Schedules**: Regularly scheduled meetings, their frequency, purpose, and expected attendees.
8. **Conflict Resolution Procedures**: Predefined methods for addressing and resolving disputes among team members.
9. **Performance Metrics**: Criteria and metrics used to measure team performance and individual contributions toward project goals.

Contributions to Project Success

The team charter contributes to project success by:

- **Enhancing Team Cohesion and Collaboration**: By setting clear guidelines and expectations, the charter helps in building a cohesive team that works collaboratively towards common goals.
- **Reducing Ambiguities**: It minimizes uncertainties regarding roles and responsibilities, which can lead to increased efficiency and effectiveness.
- **Improving Communication**: With established communication protocols, the team can avoid misunderstandings and ensure that information is shared timely and appropriately.

- **Facilitating Conflict Resolution**: Clear conflict resolution mechanisms help maintain a positive work environment and prevent disruptions.

Example

In a software development project, the team charter may specify roles such as the Project Manager, Software Developer, QA Analyst, and UI/UX Designer, with detailed responsibilities. It might establish bi-weekly sprint planning meetings, use email and Slack for daily communication, and utilize a specific process for logging and resolving conflicts regarding design decisions. Performance could be measured based on sprint deliverables, bug counts, and peer feedback.

Conclusion

A well-crafted team charter is a vital component in the Plan Resource Management process, serving as a roadmap for team operation throughout the project lifecycle. It ensures everyone is aligned from the start, which is crucial for maintaining harmony and efficiency in team activities, directly impacting the overall project performance. The **Plan Resource Management** process establishes the framework and approach for managing project resources effectively. Understanding the inputs, tools and techniques, and outputs (ITTOs) of this process is crucial for developing a comprehensive resource management strategy that aligns with project goals and objectives.

Inputs

1. **Project Charter**: Provides high-level project information, including project objectives, high-level risks, assumptions, and constraints which might influence resource planning.
2. **Project Management Plan**: Contains information about the project's scope, schedule, and cost baselines, which are crucial for defining the resource requirements and planning.
3. **Enterprise Environmental Factors (EEFs)**: Include organizational culture, existing human resources, market conditions, and available technologies which can influence resource management planning.
4. **Organizational Process Assets (OPAs)**: Encompass organizational policies, procedures, historical information, and lessons learned from previous projects which can provide insights into successful resource management practices.

Tools and Techniques

1. Expert Judgment:

Utilizing experience and knowledge from subject matter experts in resource planning, acquisition, and management to ensure that the resource management plan is realistic and feasible.

2. Organizational Theory:

Applying information about how humans, teams, and organizational units behave to ensure effective resource management. This may include motivational theories, team building theories, and human resource theories.

3. Data Representation Techniques:

- **Hierarchical Charts**: Such as Resource Breakdown Structures, which organize and categorize project resources by type or function.
- **Matrix-based Charts**: Such as the Responsibility Assignment Matrix (RAM), which shows the project resources assigned to each work package.

4. Meetings:

Planning meetings involving project team members and other stakeholders to discuss resource requirements, availability, assumptions, constraints, and to develop the resource management plan.

Outputs

1. **Resource Management Plan**: The primary output, this document outlines how project resources will be estimated, acquired, managed, and controlled. It includes:
   - **Resource Requirements**: Description of types and quantities of resources required for the project.
   - **Roles and Responsibilities**: Detailed information about the roles, responsibilities, required skills, and reporting relationships.
   - **Project Organization Charts**: Visual representations of the project's organizational structure.
   - **Training Needs**: Identification of training requirements to develop competencies and skills needed for project activities.
   - **Resource Control**: Techniques to be used for monitoring resource utilization, resolving resource conflicts, and ensuring resource availability.
2. **Team Charter**: Defines the norms, rules, and values by which the project team will operate. It may include team values, communication guidelines, and conflict resolution processes.

Significance in Developing a Comprehensive Resource Management Strategy
Expert Judgment and Organizational Theory:

- Leverage best practices and theoretical models to craft a resource management plan that is not only aligned with organizational policies but also enhances team performance and motivation.

Data Representation Techniques:

- Provide clarity and facilitate communication regarding resource allocation and responsibilities, thereby preventing misunderstandings and ensuring that everyone knows their roles and expectations.

Meetings:

- Engage stakeholders in the planning process, ensuring alignment and commitment to the project's resource management strategy.

Resource Management Plan and Team Charter:

- Serve as foundational documents that guide the project team through the acquisition, development, and management of resources, ensuring that the project has the necessary personnel and materials to achieve its objectives.

The inputs, tools and techniques, and outputs of the Plan Resource Management process collectively ensure that the project is well-equipped with the necessary resources and strategies to meet its deliverables efficiently and effectively. This comprehensive approach to resource management not only optimizes resource usage but also enhances team cohesion and project success. The Estimate Activity Resources process is a critical step in project management, focusing on determining the types, quantities, and characteristics of resources required to perform project activities. This process is foundational because it directly impacts the project's schedule and cost baselines, influencing the planning, execution, and budgeting phases of the project.

Role in Project Management

Estimate Activity Resources involves systematically identifying and quantifying the labor, equipment, materials, and supplies needed to complete each activity within the project's scope. The accuracy of these estimates significantly affects the project's overall schedule and cost efficiency.

Relationship to Project Schedule and Cost Baselines

1. Project Schedule Baseline:

- **Resource Availability and Allocation**: The availability and allocation of resources impact the duration and sequencing of activities. If resources are not available when needed, or if they are insufficient, activity start and end times may shift, affecting the project schedule.
- **Resource Optimization**: Optimizing resource allocation can compress or extend the project schedule. Techniques like resource leveling (adjusting the start and end of activities to balance resource use) and resource smoothing (adjusting activities within the constraints of a schedule to achieve a more uniform distribution of resource usage) are used.

2. Project Cost Baseline:

- **Resource Costs**: The cost of resources is a significant component of the project's budget. Accurate estimation of resource quantities and types ensures that the financial resources required are appropriately planned and controlled.
- **Budgeting**: Estimates of resources feed into the budgeting process, where costs are assigned to the identified resources, contributing to the overall cost baseline of the project.

Identifying and Documenting Resources

Steps to Estimate Resources:

1. **List Activities**: Start with a detailed list of all project activities from the work breakdown structure (WBS).
2. **Define Resource Requirements**:
   - **Expert Judgment**: Consult with team members and experts who have experience with similar projects to predict the resources needed for activities.
   - **Analogous Estimating**: Use historical data from previous projects to estimate resources for similar activities.
   - **Parametric Estimating**: Apply statistical models or metrics (e.g., hours per unit) to calculate resource needs based on the quantities of work.
3. **Identify Resource Types and Quantities**:
   - Specify skilled and unskilled labor, special equipment, materials specific to each activity, and any other supplies or services.
   - Determine the quantity of each resource type required, considering the duration and complexity of activities.
4. **Document Resource Attributes**:
   - Document specific characteristics, capabilities, or qualities required in resources, such as software version for technology tools or certifications for labor resources.
5. **Resource Aggregation**: Aggregate the resource needs over time to understand and document peak resource demands and to aid in resource leveling and smoothing.

6. **Tool Support**:
   - Utilize project management software tools that can assist in resource estimation and visualization, helping in the allocation and scheduling of resources across the project timeline.

Example of Resource Estimation

For a construction project, the project manager identifies the need for:

- **Labor**: Quantity and types, such as electricians, carpenters, and plumbers, including their skill levels and certifications.
- **Materials**: Specific types and quantities like cubic meters of concrete, tons of steel, number of bricks.
- **Equipment**: Cranes, drills, and other machinery, specifying operational capacity and availability.

Each resource type is then documented in a resource breakdown structure (RBS), which aligns with the project's activities listed in the WBS. This detailed documentation is critical for developing realistic schedule and cost baselines.

Conclusion

The Estimate Activity Resources process is integral to forming solid project foundations, directly impacting the schedule and cost baselines. By carefully identifying, quantifying, and documenting the resources needed for project activities, project managers can ensure that projects are well-planned, feasible, and set up for success from the outset. The Resource Breakdown Structure (RBS) is a hierarchical representation of resources categorized by resource type, which is used extensively in project management to organize and categorize the resources necessary for project execution. Similar to how a Work Breakdown Structure (WBS) breaks down a project into manageable sections based on project deliverables or phases, the RBS breaks down the resources into categories and subcategories, facilitating efficient resource management and planning.

Role of the RBS in Project Management

1. **Resource Organization**: The RBS systematically categorizes all types of resources required for the project, including human resources, equipment, materials, and supplies. This organization helps in identifying and grouping similar resources, making it easier to manage and deploy them.
2. **Resource Visibility**: It provides a clear overview of all resources involved in a project, helping project managers and team members understand the quantity and type of resources available and their allocation.
3. **Facilitates Planning and Control**: By having a structured view of resources, project managers can effectively plan resource usage, control costs, and avoid potential shortages or surpluses.
4. **Improves Communication**: The RBS serves as a reference point for discussions about resource requirements, allocations, and performance across the project team and with stakeholders.

Relationship Between RBS and WBS
Complementary Structures:

The RBS is often developed in conjunction with the WBS. While the WBS organizes project work into manageable tasks or deliverables, the RBS organizes the resources needed to complete these tasks. Each element in the WBS can be linked to specific resources defined in the RBS, ensuring that all project activities have the necessary resources allocated.

Integration for Comprehensive Planning:

Integrating the RBS with the WBS allows for detailed resource planning and allocation across all project activities. This integration helps in matching the resource capabilities and availability directly with the project needs, optimizing the use of resources throughout the project lifecycle.

Using the RBS for Resource Planning and Allocation
Resource Allocation:

The RBS allows project managers to allocate specific resources to specific tasks or phases of the project as delineated in the WBS. This helps in ensuring that resources are available when needed and are used efficiently.

Budgeting and Cost Management:

By categorizing resources, the RBS aids in estimating costs more accurately and managing the project budget. Each category of resources can be budgeted separately, and expenses can be tracked against these budgets.

Resource Leveling and Smoothing:

With a clear understanding of all resources involved in a project, project managers can perform resource leveling and smoothing to address the over-allocation or underutilization of resources. The RBS facilitates the identification of where resources can be adjusted to meet project demands without causing delays or increasing costs.

Performance Monitoring:

Monitoring the utilization and performance of resources against what was planned in the RBS helps in identifying inefficiencies and areas for improvement.

Example of an RBS in Use

Consider a software development project. The RBS might categorize resources as follows:

- **Human Resources**: Software Developers, Project Managers, QA Engineers
- **Technological Resources**: Servers, Software Licenses, Development Tools
- **Material Resources**: Office Supplies, Computer Hardware
- **Financial Resources**: Budget allocations for outsourcing, training

Each category is further broken down as needed. For instance, Software Developers can be categorized by specialty (Front-End, Back-End, Database).

Conclusion

The Resource Breakdown Structure (RBS) is an essential tool in project management that complements the WBS and enhances resource management efficiency. By providing a structured way to organize and categorize project resources, the RBS ensures thorough planning, effective allocation, and optimal utilization of resources, which are critical for successful project execution. **Estimate Activity Resources** is a crucial process in project management, aimed at determining what resources (people, equipment, and materials) and in what quantities are necessary to perform project activities. Effective resource estimation ensures that projects are well-equipped and planned to meet their objectives efficiently. Various techniques are used to estimate these resources, each suited to different situations and project needs.

1. Expert Judgment

Description: This technique involves consulting with and gathering input from individuals or groups with specialized knowledge or training in the specific area, often based on their experience with similar projects.

Example: Using expert judgment to determine the number of software developers needed to code a new application, based on a similar past project.

Appropriateness: Most suitable for projects where similar past activities can provide a reliable basis for estimates, or when specific technical or specialized knowledge is required.

Advantages:
- Quick and often cost-effective.
- Leverages real-world experience and historical insights.

Limitations:
- Dependent on the availability and reliability of experts.
- Subjective and potentially biased based on individual experiences.

2. Bottom-Up Estimating

Description: This method involves estimating resources for each individual activity at the lowest level of detail and then aggregating these to get a total quantity for the entire project.

Example: Estimating the number of bricks, bags of cement, and hours of labor needed for each part of a construction project, then summing these to determine the total resources required.

Appropriateness: Best for projects where detailed information about the tasks is available, and a high degree of accuracy is needed.

Advantages:
- Highly accurate when detailed information is available.
- Provides a detailed insight into resource needs, facilitating better management and scheduling.

Limitations:
- Time-consuming and potentially costly.
- Can be overly detailed, leading to information overload.

1. Parametric Estimating

Description: This method uses a statistical relationship between historical data and other variables to calculate an estimate. It involves the application of a unit cost or duration and the number of units required for the project.

Example: Estimating the amount of paint needed for a building by using a unit rate (gallons per square foot) multiplied by the total area to be painted.

Appropriateness: Useful when the project activities are quantifiable and the relationship between the units can be reliably established.

Advantages:
- Can be highly accurate if the underlying data is robust.
- Efficient for projects with standard repetitive elements.

Limitations:
- Requires accurate historical data for reliable estimates.
- Not suitable for unique or non-repetitive tasks where no statistical relationship exists.

Conclusion

Selecting the appropriate resource estimation technique largely depends on the nature of the project, the availability of data, the required accuracy of the estimates, and the complexity of the tasks. Expert judgment leverages experienced insights, bottom-up estimating provides detailed accuracy, and parametric estimating offers efficiency and speed. Often, a combination of these techniques is used to balance detail and efficiency, ensuring that resource estimates are comprehensive and reliable, setting the stage for successful project execution. A resource histogram is a graphical representation used in project management to illustrate the allocation and usage of specific resources over a period. It is particularly useful during the Estimate Activity Resources and Resource Leveling processes to visualize the demand against the availability of resources, allowing project managers to make informed decisions about resource allocation and scheduling.

Functionality of Resource Histograms

A resource histogram displays the amount of resource units required for project activities against a timeline. Each bar in the histogram represents the quantity of a specific resource needed at a given time interval (e.g., daily, weekly). This tool helps in identifying periods of over-allocation or under-utilization of resources, which is crucial for effective project planning and execution.

Usage in Estimate Activity Resources Process

1. **Visualizing Resource Demand**: The histogram allows project managers to see the total demand for each type of resource throughout the project's lifecycle. This visualization helps in assessing whether the current resource allocation is sufficient to meet project timelines.
2. **Identifying Resource Conflicts**: By plotting the resource requirements of all activities over time, the histogram can highlight when resources are over-allocated, indicating potential scheduling conflicts that could delay the project.
3. **Supporting Resource Leveling**: Resource histograms are instrumental in performing resource leveling—a technique used to resolve resource over-allocation by adjusting the start and end dates of activities. This ensures that the resource usage does not exceed the availability at any given time.
4. **Optimizing Resource Allocation**: The tool aids in adjusting the allocation of resources to match resource availability, thus avoiding delays and reducing idle times.

Example of a Resource Histogram

Scenario: Consider a construction project where the key resource in question is the number of construction workers needed over a three-month period. The project activities include foundation work, framing, and roofing, each requiring different numbers of workers.

- **Month 1 (Foundation)**: Requires 10 workers.
- **Month 2 (Framing)**: Requires 15 workers.
- **Month 3 (Roofing)**: Requires 8 workers.

Resource Histogram Representation:

- The x-axis represents the time (months), and the y-axis represents the number of workers.
- Three bars are plotted along the timeline:
  - **Bar for Month 1** rises to 10 on the y-axis.
  - **Bar for Month 2** rises to 15.
  - **Bar for Month 3** rises to 8.

This histogram visually communicates that the highest demand for workers is in Month 2 for framing. If only 12 workers are available at any time, the project manager can immediately see the shortfall in Month 2 and plan accordingly—either by extending the duration of framing or hiring additional workers temporarily.

Conclusion

Resource histograms are vital for effectively managing and planning resources in project management. They provide a clear visual representation of resource allocation over time, helping project managers identify potential issues in resource distribution. By using this tool, project managers can ensure that resource utilization is optimized, conflicts are minimized, and the project can progress according to schedule without unnecessary delays or cost overruns. The **Acquire Resources** process is pivotal in project management, as it involves securing the team members, equipment, materials, and other necessary resources to complete project activities. The effectiveness of this process directly impacts the project's ability to meet its deadlines, stay within budget, and achieve its objectives.

Significance of Acquire Resources Process

1. **Ensuring Availability**: Ensures that necessary resources are available when needed, which is critical for maintaining project schedule and momentum.
2. **Optimizing Resource Utilization**: Helps in aligning resource allocation with project needs, maximizing efficiency and productivity while minimizing resource-related delays or conflicts.
3. **Building the Project Team**: For human resources, this process is crucial in forming a capable project team with the necessary skills and competencies.
4. **Facilitating Project Success**: Adequate and timely resource acquisition is essential for project success, directly affecting the quality and timeliness of project deliverables.

Primary Methods for Acquiring Resources
1. Pre-Assignment

Description: Involves assigning specific resources that have been identified and selected prior to the detailed planning process, often during project initiation. These resources are usually critical and their early assignment is crucial for the project.

Example: A project manager who is chosen at the project's conception due to their unique expertise or a key engineer whose involvement is critical for the project's technical aspects.

Advantages:
- Ensures the availability of critical resources from the start.
- Helps in project planning with a clear view of key team members.

Limitations:
- May limit flexibility in resource selection.
- Depends heavily on the availability and commitment of pre-assigned resources.

2. Negotiation

Description: Often used to acquire resources in environments where resources are shared across projects or departments. Project managers may need to negotiate with other managers or departments to obtain the necessary personnel or resources.

Example: Negotiating with a department head to secure a part-time commitment from a subject matter expert who is involved in multiple projects.

Advantages:

- Allows for the effective use of organization-wide resources.
- Helps in fostering collaboration across different organizational units.

Limitations:
- Can be time-consuming.
- Success depends on the project manager's negotiation skills and organizational politics.

3. Procurement

Description: Involves acquiring external resources, services, or materials through a contractual arrangement. This is common for resources that are not available within the organization.

Example: Contracting with a vendor for the supply of specialized equipment or outsourcing part of the work to an external agency.

Advantages:
- Access to a wide range of resources and suppliers.
- Flexibility in scaling resources up or down based on project needs.

Limitations:
- Requires managing procurement processes and supplier relationships.
- Risks associated with vendor reliability and quality.

Conclusion

The Acquire Resources process is a cornerstone of successful project management. Whether through pre-assignment, negotiation, or procurement, effective resource acquisition ensures that projects are well-equipped and manned to meet their goals. Each method has its advantages and is suitable for different scenarios, and project managers may often find themselves using a combination of these strategies to meet the diverse needs of their projects. Virtual teams consist of individuals who work together from various geographical locations and rely on communication technology such as email, video conferencing, and collaboration tools to complete their projects. In the context of project resource management, virtual teams allow organizations to tap into a global talent pool and manage projects more flexibly.

Benefits of Virtual Teams

1. **Access to Global Talent**: Virtual teams enable organizations to hire the best talent without geographical constraints.
2. **Increased Flexibility**: Team members can work from anywhere, providing flexibility to manage their work and personal commitments more effectively.
3. **Cost Savings**: Organizations can save on overhead costs such as office space, utilities, and relocation expenses.
4. **Extended Work Hours**: Because team members can be in different time zones, work can potentially proceed around the clock.
5. **Diversity**: Virtual teams bring diverse perspectives that can lead to increased creativity and innovation.

Challenges of Virtual Teams

1. **Communication Barriers**: Without face-to-face interaction, miscommunications are more likely. Reliance on written communication can lead to misunderstandings.
2. **Cultural Differences**: Diverse teams can face challenges due to different cultural norms and work practices.

3. **Technology Dependency**: The effectiveness of virtual teams heavily depends on reliable technology, which can be disrupted.
4. **Isolation**: Team members may feel isolated from their peers, which can affect morale and productivity.
5. **Managing Performance**: It can be challenging to monitor and manage the performance of team members who work remotely.

Effective Leadership of Virtual Teams
1. Use of Technology
- Utilize robust project management and collaboration tools (like Asana, Slack, Microsoft Teams) that support video conferencing, real-time document sharing, and instant messaging.
- Ensure all team members have access to and training on these technologies.

2. Regular and Structured Communication
- Schedule regular check-ins and team meetings to foster a sense of belonging and keep everyone aligned with the project goals.
- Use video calls for more personal interaction and to build rapport.
- Establish clear communication protocols.

3. Clear Goals and Expectations
- Clearly define project goals, individual roles, and responsibilities to prevent ambiguity.
- Use project management tools to track progress and maintain visibility of each team member's contributions.

4. Building Trust and Inclusivity
- Create an inclusive team culture that values open communication and mutual respect.
- Encourage team members to share personal updates or professional challenges during team calls to build trust.

6. Performance Management
- Develop objective, results-oriented performance metrics that are aligned with project goals.
- Provide continuous feedback and support to ensure team members are motivated and aware of their performance levels.

6. Professional Development and Support
- Offer opportunities for skill enhancement to help team members stay competitive and engaged.
- Provide support for work-life balance and address any work-related stressors or issues.

7. Cultural Sensitivity
- Encourage cultural sensitivity by educating team members about different cultural practices and norms.
- Celebrate diversity by recognizing cultural holidays and facilitating cultural exchange within the team.

Example

Imagine a virtual team working on a software development project spanning three continents. The project manager uses Microsoft Teams for daily stand-ups, Slack for instant messaging, and GitHub for code sharing and version control. Regular virtual coffee meetings are scheduled to encourage informal interactions among team members. Performance is tracked through sprint reviews and retrospectives, ensuring that team members receive regular feedback on their work.

Conclusion

While virtual teams offer numerous benefits in terms of flexibility, cost savings, and access to a diverse talent pool, they also present unique challenges that require careful management. Effective leadership in virtual teams involves leveraging technology, fostering clear and open communication, and creating a supportive and inclusive environment. By addressing these challenges proactively, project managers can lead virtual teams to success in achieving their project objectives. A **resource calendar** is a tool used in project management to specify the working days, shifts, holidays, and availability of resources required for project activities. This calendar helps in planning and scheduling by detailing when resources are available to work on project tasks, thereby facilitating efficient allocation and utilization of resources throughout the life of the project.

Usage of Resource Calendar in the Acquire Resources Process

The resource calendar is instrumental during the Acquire Resources process as it:

- **Identifies Availability**: Helps determine when specific resources will be available to work on the project, taking into account their other commitments and time off.
- **Assists in Scheduling**: Integrates resource availability with the project schedule to ensure that work is planned for times when resources are available.
- **Prevents Overallocation**: Prevents scheduling more work for a resource than they can accomplish in their available time.
- **Coordinates Among Multiple Projects**: For resources shared across projects, a resource calendar helps in managing their time effectively among various assignments.

Example of a Resource Calendar

Imagine a project that involves both internal team members and external consultants. The resource calendar for each type of resource might look like this:

- **Internal Team Member (Software Developer)**:
- **Working Days**: Monday to Friday
- **Holidays**: All government-declared holidays plus the first Friday of every month for personal time off.
- **Availability**: 8 hours per day, except for Tuesdays when the team member attends training sessions from 1 PM to 5 PM.

- **External Consultant (Cybersecurity Specialist)**:
- **Working Days**: Agreed upon days are Tuesday and Thursday each week.
- **Holidays**: As per the consultant's contract agreement, aligned with their home company's holiday schedule.
- **Availability**: Consultant is available from 9 AM to 5 PM on their working days but is on a retainer for emergency consultations outside these hours.

Importance of Resource Calendars

- **Accurate Project Planning**: By having a clear view of when resources are available, project managers can create more realistic and achievable project schedules.
- **Efficiency Optimization**: Helps in maximizing the use of available time for project resources, thus enhancing productivity.
- **Conflict Avoidance**: Reduces the likelihood of scheduling conflicts that can arise from booking a resource who is not available, thus avoiding delays and frustrations.
- **Resource Leveling**: Enables resource leveling by allowing project managers to shift workloads appropriately to match resource availability, thus smoothing the demands on resources.

Conclusion

Resource calendars are vital for the effective planning and execution of projects. They provide essential information that helps project managers make informed decisions about resource allocation and scheduling. This tool ensures that resources are used efficiently and that project activities are aligned with resource availability, ultimately supporting the successful completion of the project. The Develop Team process is integral to project management, focusing on improving competencies, enhancing team interaction, and increasing the overall performance of the project team. This process is crucial for project success because it directly affects how effectively the team works together and achieves project objectives.

Role of the Develop Team Process

1. **Enhancing Competencies**: It aims to improve the knowledge, skills, and abilities of team members to ensure they can complete project tasks efficiently and effectively.
2. **Improving Interaction**: Facilitates better communication and collaboration among team members, which is vital for resolving conflicts, sharing information, and making collective decisions.
3. **Boosting Performance**: By improving skills and enhancing teamwork, the process helps elevate the overall performance of the team, leading to more successful project outcomes.

Key Strategies and Activities for Developing the Team
1. Training and Education

- **Purpose**: To close skill gaps and update the team on the latest trends, technologies, and methodologies relevant to the project.
- **Implementation**: This could include on-the-job training, formal educational courses, webinars, or workshops. Tailoring training programs to the specific needs of the team and project can significantly enhance their effectiveness.

2. Team-Building Activities

- **Purpose**: To improve trust and relationships among team members, which are crucial for fostering a collaborative team environment.
- **Implementation**: Organize activities that are not necessarily work-related but that can help build camaraderie, such as team outings, problem-solving challenges, or virtual meet-ups, especially in the case of remote teams.

3. Establishing Ground Rules

- **Purpose**: To create a clear understanding among team members about acceptable behavior and communication practices.
- **Implementation**: Engage the team in the development of these rules to ensure buy-in and compliance. This can include how meetings are conducted, how decisions are made, and how conflicts are resolved.

4. Recognition and Rewards

- **Purpose**: To motivate team members and acknowledge their contributions, enhancing morale and encouraging high performance.
- **Implementation**: Develop a system of rewards that can be tied to performance metrics, including both formal recognition such as bonuses or awards, and informal recognition like public acknowledgment in meetings.

5. Mentoring and Coaching

- **Purpose**: To provide ongoing support and development opportunities for team members, helping them to overcome challenges and grow professionally.
- **Implementation**: Pair less experienced team members with more experienced mentors who can provide guidance and feedback. Implement coaching sessions where team members can discuss career goals and receive advice.

6. Co-location

- **Purpose**: To enhance communication and interaction by placing all team members in the same physical location.
- **Implementation**: For projects where team interaction is critical, arrange for physical co-location or set up dedicated times for virtual co-working to simulate a shared environment.

7. Conflict Resolution Techniques

- **Purpose**: To address and manage conflicts constructively without allowing them to disrupt the team dynamics.
- **Implementation**: Train team members in conflict resolution techniques and establish a mediation process for when issues arise.

Example of Develop Team Implementation

Consider a project team working on a new software development project. The project manager arranges for specific technical training to update the team's skills in the latest programming languages. Team-building activities are scheduled regularly, focusing on both fun activities like a cooking class and project-related activities like hackathons. A recognition program is introduced to highlight individual and team achievements each month, fostering a sense of accomplishment and competitiveness.

Conclusion

The Develop Team process is crucial in building a capable and harmonious team that can effectively tackle project challenges. By strategically focusing on enhancing skills, fostering collaboration, and creating a supportive environment, project managers can significantly improve the productivity and satisfaction of their teams, directly impacting the success of the project. Interpersonal and team skills are vital components of project resource management. These skills are crucial for project managers and team members alike, as they facilitate effective communication, enhance collaboration, and ensure that team dynamics contribute positively to project outcomes. The integration of strong interpersonal skills in project management not only promotes a harmonious work environment but also drives the efficient and effective completion of project objectives.

Importance in Project Resource Management

1. **Fosters Collaboration**: Good interpersonal skills enable better collaboration among team members who may come from diverse backgrounds or have different areas of expertise.
2. **Enhances Communication**: Effective communication ensures that all team members are clear about project goals, their roles, and responsibilities, and are kept informed about project progress and changes.
3. **Resolves Conflicts**: Conflicts are inevitable in project teams. Effective conflict resolution ensures that these conflicts do not derail the project but are resolved in a way that potentially benefits project outcomes.
4. **Builds a Positive Team Environment**: Leadership and motivational skills contribute to building a positive team environment that boosts morale and increases productivity.

Examples of Essential Interpersonal and Team Skills
1. Communication

- **Example**: Regularly scheduled meetings, clear and concise email updates, and open lines of communication through project management tools.
- **Contribution**: Ensures everyone is aligned with the project's objectives, understands their tasks, and feels included in the project process, which is essential for timely and successful project delivery.

2. Conflict Resolution

- **Example**: When two team members have differing views on how to approach a project task, the project manager might use mediation techniques to understand both sides and guide them to a consensus or a constructive compromise.
- **Contribution**: Resolving conflicts quickly and effectively prevents disruptions in project workflow and helps maintain a cohesive and productive team environment.

2. Leadership

- **Example**: A project manager leading by example, setting clear expectations, being decisive, yet approachable, and showing recognition and appreciation for team members' efforts.
- **Contribution**: Strong leadership inspires and motivates the team, drives the project forward, and maintains team morale through the challenges of the project lifecycle.

4. Negotiation

- **Example**: Negotiating with resource providers to ensure resources are available when needed without exceeding the budget.
- **Contribution**: Helps in acquiring the best resources at optimal costs and scheduling them in a manner that does not interrupt the project flow.

5. Team Building

- **Example**: Organizing team-building activities that enhance camaraderie and help team members understand each other's strengths and weaknesses.
- **Contribution**: Builds a stronger, more cohesive team that can work effectively together, leveraging each member's strengths.

5. Decision Making

- **Example**: Making informed decisions about resource allocation based on the project's needs and team members' capabilities.
- **Contribution**: Ensures optimal use of resources, preventing burnout and overallocation, and contributing to the project's efficiency.

Conclusion

Interpersonal and team skills are not just complementary soft skills in project management—they are integral to managing the human aspects of projects effectively. By developing and utilizing these skills, project managers can enhance team performance, drive project success, and navigate the complexities of group dynamics in professional settings. These skills enable project leaders to create an environment where project goals are achieved collaboratively and efficiently, ensuring both project success and team satisfaction. Training and team-building activities are essential components of the Develop Team process in project management. These initiatives are designed to enhance the skills of team members and foster a collaborative and supportive team environment, which is crucial for achieving project goals efficiently and effectively.

Purpose of Training and Team-Building Activities

1. Training:

- **Skill Enhancement**: To update and enhance the professional skills of the team members, keeping them relevant and efficient in their roles.
- **Adaptability**: To equip the team with the necessary tools and knowledge to adapt to project changes and challenges effectively.

2. Team-Building:

- **Strengthen Relationships**: To build trust and good relationships among team members, which are vital for improving communication and collaboration.
- **Team Cohesion**: To create a sense of unity and alignment towards common project goals, reducing conflicts and misunderstandings.

Benefits of Training and Team-Building Activities

- **Increased Productivity**: Well-trained and cohesive teams can work more efficiently and manage project tasks more effectively.
- **Enhanced Communication**: These activities improve interpersonal relations and communication, which are critical for project success.
- **Higher Job Satisfaction**: Training and team-building can increase job satisfaction and morale, leading to lower turnover rates and fostering a positive work environment.
- **Innovation and Creativity**: A well-connected team is more likely to come up with innovative solutions to project challenges.

Designing and Implementing Effective Training Programs
1.   Assess Training Needs:

- Conduct a skills gap analysis to determine the specific training needs of the team members relative to the project's requirements.
- Consult with team members to understand their personal developmental needs and aspirations.

2.   Set Clear Objectives:

- Define clear, measurable objectives for the training program that align with both the project goals and team members' professional growth.

3.   Choose Appropriate Training Methods:

- Decide on the training format (e.g., workshops, e-learning, seminars) based on the content, availability of resources, and team preferences.
- Consider engaging external experts for specialized training topics.

4.   Implement the Program:

- Schedule training sessions at convenient times to ensure maximum participation.
- Provide necessary resources and support for the training activities.

5.   Evaluate Training Effectiveness:

- Gather feedback from participants to evaluate the training's impact and effectiveness.
- Measure the improvement in skills and performance to ensure the training objectives are met.

Organizing Effective Team-Building Events
1.   Identify Objectives:

- Clearly define the purpose of the team-building event (e.g., to improve communication, resolve conflicts, enhance collaboration).

2.   Plan Suitable Activities:

- Select activities that are fun, engaging, and relevant to the team-building objectives. Consider the team's demographics, interests, and physical limitations.
- Activities could range from problem-solving challenges to social outings or retreats.

3.   Facilitate Participation:

- Encourage full participation by making the activities inclusive and accessible to all team members.
- Foster an environment where all team members feel safe to express themselves and engage without fear of judgment.

4.   Debrief and Reflect:

- Conduct a debriefing session after the activity to discuss learnings and experiences.
- Encourage team members to share their insights and how they can apply them to their work.

5. **Follow-Up**:
   - Implement changes or strategies discussed during team-building activities.
   - Continuously monitor the team dynamics and schedule regular team-building events to maintain team cohesion.

Example

A project manager of a software development team organizes a two-day offsite retreat focusing on advanced Agile methodologies and interpersonal communication skills. Day one focuses on interactive workshops led by an Agile coach, and day two is dedicated to team-building activities, including a scavenger hunt to improve teamwork and problem-solving under pressure.

Conclusion

Effective training and team-building activities are critical for developing a skilled, cohesive, and high-performing project team. By carefully designing and implementing these programs, project managers can significantly enhance team capabilities and foster an environment conducive to project success. The Tuckman ladder model of team development, formulated by psychologist Bruce Tuckman in 1965, outlines a clear and structured progression of stages that teams typically go through as they develop and mature. This model is particularly relevant to the **Develop Team** process in project management, as it provides a framework that project managers can use to better understand and facilitate team dynamics and growth over the course of a project.

Five Stages of Team Development
1. Forming

Description: In the forming stage, team members are introduced. They start to learn about the project and their roles and responsibilities. Relationships are characterized by dependency on the leader for guidance and direction.

Strategies:
- Host kick-off meetings to set the project vision and objectives.
- Encourage team members to get to know each other on a personal and professional level.
- Clearly define roles and responsibilities to avoid confusion.

2. Storming

Description: This stage is marked by conflict and competition as team members start to push against established boundaries. Team dynamics can be contentious as personalities and working styles clash.

Strategies:
- Encourage open communication and constructive feedback.
- Mediate conflicts swiftly and fairly.
- Reaffirm team goals and roles to ensure alignment and focus.

3. Norming

Description: Teams begin to resolve their differences, appreciate colleagues' strengths, and respect the authority of the leader. Norms and processes are established, and the team starts to express more commitment to the project and each other.

Strategies:
- Promote team cohesion by organizing team-building activities.
- Develop and reinforce team norms and values.

- Encourage collaborative decision-making and shared ownership of the project.

4. Performing

Description: At this stage, the team is cohesive, highly motivated, and working efficiently towards the project goals. Team members are competent, autonomous, and able to handle decision-making processes without supervision.

Strategies:
- Delegate tasks and responsibilities to capitalize on team strengths.
- Encourage continuous improvement and innovation.
- Provide support and resources needed to achieve peak performance.

5. Adjourning

Description: Also known as "mourning," this stage occurs on projects that have a clear end. It involves completing the task and breaking up the team. Team members may experience uncertainty and sadness as they disengage and separate from the team.

Strategies:
- Conduct a closing meeting to celebrate the project's success and recognize individual and group contributions.
- Provide support for team members transitioning to new projects or roles.
- Encourage reflection on lessons learned and project experiences to enhance professional growth.

How It Relates to the Develop Team Process

The Tuckman model is integral to the **Develop Team** process because it provides a roadmap for understanding and managing the phases of team development. By recognizing which stage their team is in, project managers can effectively tailor their management approach, communication, conflict resolution, and team-building strategies to support the team's development and enhance its performance. This alignment is crucial for maintaining team morale, productivity, and ultimately, project success. The model emphasizes the dynamic and evolving nature of teams and highlights the importance of adaptive leadership throughout the life of a project. The Manage Team process is essential for ensuring that the project team operates efficiently and effectively. This process involves tracking team member performance, providing feedback, resolving issues, and making necessary adjustments to optimize team dynamics and project outcomes.

Significance of the Manage Team Process

1. **Performance Tracking**: Regular monitoring of team member performance against the project's requirements ensures that the project remains on track to meet its goals. It allows for early identification of areas where performance may be lagging.
2. **Feedback Provision**: Constructive feedback is crucial for personal and professional development of team members. It helps individuals understand their strengths and areas for improvement, aligning their efforts with project needs.
3. **Issue Resolution**: Proactively addressing and resolving interpersonal issues, conflicts, or other problems within the team is vital to maintaining a healthy working environment and ensuring team productivity.
4. **Adaptation and Improvement**: The Manage Team process facilitates necessary adjustments in team composition or individual roles based on evolving project requirements and team dynamics.

Tools and Techniques for Assessing and Improving Team Performance
1. Performance Assessments

- **Description**: Formal and informal evaluations of individual and team performance relative to the project's standards and objectives.
- **Application**: Regular performance reviews where project managers assess and discuss each team member's contributions and progress towards the project goals.

2. Observation and Conversation

- **Description**: Direct observation and informal conversations are used to gauge team morale, the effectiveness of communication, and the level of engagement among team members.
- **Application**: Daily or weekly informal check-ins to monitor workload levels, gather feedback, and identify any potential issues early.

3. Project Performance Appraisals

- **Description**: Structured evaluations focusing on how effectively team members are contributing to project objectives.
- **Application**: Semi-annual or annual performance appraisals that review a team member's achievements, challenges, and alignment with the project goals.

4. 360-Degree Feedback

- **Description**: A feedback mechanism where team members receive confidential, anonymous feedback from their peers, supervisors, and occasionally external stakeholders.
- **Application**: Implemented to provide a comprehensive view of individual performance and interpersonal skills, helping to identify hidden issues or opportunities for improvement.

5. Conflict Management Techniques

- **Description**: Strategies and methodologies used to resolve interpersonal tensions and disagreements in a constructive manner.
- **Application**: Techniques such as negotiation, mediation, or even arbitration to address and resolve conflicts that could impact team performance.

6. Training and Development Opportunities

- **Description**: Offering training sessions, workshops, or courses to help team members develop necessary skills and competencies.
- **Application**: Providing targeted training based on performance assessments that address specific skill gaps affecting project progress.

7. Reward and Recognition Systems

- **Description**: Mechanisms to acknowledge and reward excellent performance and significant contributions to the project.
- **Application**: Implementing a recognition program that rewards both individual achievements and team successes, which can enhance motivation and loyalty.

Example of Effective Team Management

Imagine a project manager leading a team on a large-scale software development project. Observations indicate that some team members are struggling with the new software tools introduced for the project.

The project manager decides to conduct a focused training session to enhance skills, followed by individual performance reviews to assess improvements and further refine skills where necessary. Additionally, recognizing the high stress levels within the team, the project manager organizes a team-building retreat aimed at improving morale and strengthening interpersonal relationships.

Conclusion

Effective management of the project team is crucial for achieving project objectives. By utilizing various tools and techniques to assess performance, provide feedback, resolve conflicts, and support team development, project managers can create a productive, harmonious, and highly effective project team. This proactive management not only drives project success but also fosters a positive and supportive work environment. Conflict management is a critical component of the **Manage Team** process in project management. Effective conflict management not only prevents disruptions and maintains a positive team dynamic but also leverages conflicts as opportunities for growth and improvement. Managing conflicts wisely helps to foster an environment of trust and open communication, essential for the success of any project.

Importance of Conflict Management

1. **Preserves Team Cohesion**: Properly managed conflict prevents disputes from escalating and causing divisions within the team, which can jeopardize project cohesion and productivity.
2. **Enhances Problem Solving**: Healthy conflict resolution can promote creativity and innovation by allowing different perspectives and ideas to surface and be considered.
3. **Improves Team Efficiency**: Resolving conflicts quickly and effectively prevents them from hindering the progress of the project, thus maintaining or improving team efficiency.
4. **Strengthens Relationships**: By addressing and resolving conflicts, relationships within the team can be strengthened, leading to better collaboration in the future.

Common Sources of Conflict in Project Teams

1. **Resource Allocation**: Disputes may arise over the distribution of resources, whether they are human resources, equipment, or time.
2. **Schedules and Priorities**: Conflicts often occur when team members or stakeholders have different priorities or disagree on scheduling.
3. **Technical Opinions and Performance Expectations**: Differing views on technical approaches or dissatisfaction with the performance of team members can lead to conflict.
4. **Personalities and Working Styles**: The diverse personalities and working styles within a team can sometimes clash, leading to interpersonal conflicts.
5. **Role Definitions**: Ambiguity in role definitions and job responsibilities can create conflict among team members who may feel that tasks are not fairly distributed or boundaries are being crossed.

Strategies for Effective Conflict Resolution
Encourage Open Communication:

Foster an environment where team members feel safe to express concerns and disagreements. This involves actively listening to all parties involved and understanding the root causes of the conflict.

Establish Clear Roles and Responsibilities:

Clearly defining each team member's role and responsibilities can minimize misunderstandings and conflicts related to task ownership and accountability.

Mediate and Facilitate Discussions:
As a neutral party, the project manager should facilitate discussions between conflicting parties to help them find common ground or a compromise that is acceptable to all involved.

Adopt Appropriate Conflict Resolution Techniques:
Problem Solving:
Address the issue directly with all parties involved to find a mutually beneficial solution.

Compromising:
Encourage conflicting parties to give up elements of their positions to establish an acceptable solution.

Smoothing:
Focus on areas of agreement, downplaying aspects of disagreement to reduce the emotional intensity of the conflict.

Forcing:
In a situation where a quick resolution is needed, enforce a decision that may not be fully agreed upon by all parties (used as a last resort).

Promote Team Building Activities:
Engage the team in activities that strengthen relationships and improve understanding among team members. This can help prevent conflicts or make them easier to resolve when they occur.

Establish Norms for Dealing with Conflicts:
Develop and implement team norms that outline how conflicts should be handled. This sets the expectation that conflicts are to be managed openly and constructively.

Use Third-Party Mediation:
In cases where internal resolution is ineffective, consider bringing in a neutral third party to mediate the conflict. Effective conflict management is essential for maintaining a harmonious and productive team environment. By implementing proactive strategies and fostering a culture of open communication and respect, project managers can ensure that conflicts are resolved in a manner that benefits both the team and the overall project. Team performance assessments are crucial in project management as they provide systematic evaluations of how well team members and the team as a whole are performing in relation to the project's objectives. These assessments help identify areas where the team is excelling and areas that require improvement, contributing to the overall effectiveness and efficiency of the project.

Purpose of Team Performance Assessments
1. **Identify Performance Gaps**: To pinpoint discrepancies between current performance levels and project goals or standards.
2. **Enhance Team Development**: To provide data-driven insights that can guide the development and training of team members, improving their competencies and productivity.
3. **Facilitate Effective Feedback**: To provide a basis for feedback sessions, helping team members understand how their contributions are perceived and valued.
4. **Drive Motivation and Engagement**: To motivate team members by recognizing their achievements and addressing their concerns, which can enhance their engagement and commitment to the project.

5. **Resolve Team Dynamics Issues**: To uncover underlying issues affecting team dynamics and address them proactively.

Key Components of Team Performance Assessments
360-Degree Feedback:
This comprehensive feedback tool involves collecting performance data about an individual from their supervisor, peers, subordinates, and sometimes clients. This method provides a well-rounded view of an individual's performance, highlighting strengths and areas for improvement.

Performance Appraisals:
Formal appraisals that occur at regular intervals (e.g., mid-year and year-end) where supervisors evaluate an individual's work performance against expected standards and objectives. These often inform decisions regarding promotions, bonuses, and other career development opportunities.

Team Satisfaction Surveys:
Surveys distributed to team members to gather opinions on various aspects of the project and team environment, such as communication effectiveness, workload management, and team spirit.

Self-Assessment:
Encouraging team members to conduct self-evaluations can provide insights into their perceptions of their own strengths and weaknesses.

Observation and Conversation:
Informal, ongoing monitoring and discussions provide real-time insights into team dynamics and individual performance, allowing for immediate adjustments if necessary.

Using Assessment Tools to Evaluate and Improve Team Performance
1. Implementing 360-Degree Feedback
- **Purpose**: To gather diverse perspectives on an individual's performance and behavior.
- **Use**: Analyze feedback to identify common themes and areas for development. Share results with each team member and discuss actionable steps in one-on-one feedback sessions.

2. Conducting Performance Appraisals
- **Purpose**: To formally assess and document performance and to plan future performance objectives.
- **Use**: Use appraisals to set specific, measurable, achievable, relevant, and time-bound (SMART) goals for team members, aligning their objectives with project needs.

3. Administering Team Satisfaction Surveys
- **Purpose**: To gauge the morale and satisfaction of the team with the project management, communication, and their roles.
- **Use**: Utilize survey results to make improvements in project management practices and team interactions. Address any specific areas of concern highlighted in the responses to improve the team environment.

4. Encouraging Self-Assessment

- **Purpose**: To promote self-reflection and personal growth.
- **Use**: Review self-assessments during performance discussions to understand team members' self-perceived strengths and weaknesses and to discuss ways to leverage or improve these areas.

5. Leveraging Observation and Conversation

- **Purpose**: To maintain an ongoing understanding of team dynamics and performance issues.
- **Use**: Regular informal interactions help build trust and open communication, making it easier to address issues promptly and keep the team aligned with project goals.

Example of Effective Use

A project manager leading a large IT project implements quarterly performance appraisals and biannual 360-degree feedback sessions to monitor and assess team performance. Additionally, monthly team satisfaction surveys are used to ensure that team concerns are quickly identified and addressed. The information gathered from these assessments is used to tailor individual development plans, resolve conflicts, and adjust project management strategies to better support team needs.

Conclusion

Team performance assessments are vital for understanding and improving the dynamics and outputs of a project team. By effectively using tools like 360-degree feedback, performance appraisals, and satisfaction surveys, project managers can ensure that their teams are not only meeting project objectives but are also motivated, engaged, and continuously developing their skills. The **Control Resources** process is vital in project management, focusing on ensuring that the physical and team resources are allocated properly, used efficiently, and are performing to expected levels throughout the project lifecycle. This process helps in identifying over-allocations, underutilizations, and resource conflicts, enabling adjustments to be made in a timely manner to keep the project on track.

Role of Control Resources Process

1. **Ensures Efficient Resource Use**: Monitors resource usage to confirm that resources are utilized efficiently without wastage or over-exertion, which can lead to burnout or decreased productivity.
2. **Maintains Budget Control**: By monitoring resource utilization, project managers can control costs associated with resource overuse or idle time, ensuring the project stays within budget.
3. **Optimizes Resource Allocation**: Adjusts resource allocation based on project demands and changes. This optimization ensures that the right resources are available at the right times to meet project deadlines and quality standards.
4. **Supports Project Performance**: By ensuring resources are correctly allocated and used, the process supports overall project performance, enhancing the likelihood of successful project completion.

Key Activities and Techniques
1. Resource Usage Monitoring

- **Activity**: Regular monitoring of how resources are being used versus the plan. This includes tracking the amount of resource allocated and used for each task or activity.

- **Technique**: Use of resource management software tools that provide real-time data on resource usage, enabling project managers to see at a glance where resources might be overcommitted or underutilized.

2. Performance Reviews

- **Activity**: Evaluating the performance of allocated resources to determine if they are meeting the expectations set out in the project plan.
- **Technique**: Performance metrics and KPIs designed to measure the effectiveness and efficiency of resource usage, such as actual cost versus budgeted cost, and actual timeline versus planned timeline.

3. Variance Analysis

- **Activity**: Comparing planned resource allocation and usage against actual figures to identify variances that might impact project timelines, costs, or quality.
- **Technique**: Statistical methods to analyze variance causes and decide whether corrective actions are needed.

4. Resource Leveling

- **Activity**: Adjusting the project schedule to resolve resource over-allocations or conflicts without affecting critical path tasks.
- **Technique**: Delaying or rescheduling non-critical tasks to balance the demand for resources with the supply.

5. Resource Reallocation

- **Activity**: Redistributing resources from lower priority or less urgent tasks to activities that are critical or behind schedule.
- **Technique**: Dynamic resource allocation strategies, often supported by decision-making models that prioritize tasks based on their urgency and impact on project objectives.

6. Forecasting

- **Activity**: Estimating future resource needs based on project progress and performance data.
- **Technique**: Trend analysis and predictive analytics to forecast future resource requirements and prevent potential shortages or bottlenecks.

Conclusion

Effective control of resources is crucial for project success. Through the systematic monitoring and adjustment of resource utilization, project managers can ensure that resources are not only available but are also being used in a way that maximizes efficiency and effectiveness. The **Control Resources** process is essential for maintaining control over project costs, schedule, and quality, ultimately ensuring that the project meets its objectives within the defined constraints. Resource leveling is a technique used in project management to address the problem of resource overallocation, which occurs when more tasks are assigned to a resource than can be accomplished within the available working hours. This technique is critical for ensuring that project demands do not exceed resource capacities, thereby preventing employee burnout and optimizing the allocation of resources throughout the project duration.

Purpose of Resource Leveling

1. **Resolve Resource Overallocation**: Resource leveling helps redistribute tasks to ensure that no resource is overextended, promoting a more manageable and equitable workload distribution.
2. **Minimize Schedule Conflicts**: By adjusting task schedules based on resource availability, resource leveling minimizes conflicts and ensures that resources are not double-booked.
3. **Maximize Resource Utilization**: It aims to use resources efficiently across the project timeline, reducing periods of underutilization and ensuring consistent project progress.
4. **Reduce Project Delays**: Adequate resource leveling can lead to fewer delays due to resource constraints, helping to maintain the project on schedule.

Application of Resource Leveling in Control Resources Process

Resource leveling can be employed during the Control Resources process, where the focus is on ensuring that resources are used as planned and adjustments are made as needed to respond to project changes or variances. Here's how project managers can apply resource leveling effectively:

1. Identify Resource Overallocation

- Use project management software tools to visually map out resource assignments and identify where resources are allocated more tasks than they can handle within their available hours.

2. Adjust Task Dependencies and Priorities

- Evaluate task dependencies to determine if any tasks can be rescheduled without affecting critical path tasks.
- Prioritize tasks based on their impact on project deliverables and milestones, adjusting schedules to align with resource availability.

3. Delay Non-Critical Activities

- Temporarily delay the start times of non-critical tasks to balance the workload more evenly across available resources.
- Ensure that these adjustments do not impact the project's critical path and overall timeline.

4. Reallocate Tasks Among Available Resources

- Shift tasks from overallocated resources to underutilized resources, maintaining balance and efficiency in resource utilization.
- Consider the skills and capacities of alternate resources to ensure they are suitable for the tasks reassigned to them.

5. Continuous Monitoring and Adjustment

- Regularly monitor resource utilization and workload distribution as the project progresses.
- Be prepared to make continual adjustments as new tasks emerge and as actual work might differ from the initial estimates.

6. Communication and Documentation

- Communicate any changes in task assignments and schedules to all affected project team members and stakeholders.
- Update project documentation and resource schedules to reflect the changes made through resource leveling.

Example of Resource Leveling

Consider a software development project where multiple key deliverables are due simultaneously, and the lead developers are scheduled to work more hours than available in a week. The project manager uses resource leveling by:

- Delaying the development of a non-critical module that does not impact the project's critical milestones.
- Reassigning some preparatory tasks (e.g., writing development documentation) to other team members who have available capacity.
- Continuously monitoring the progress and making adjustments to ensure all team members have a balanced workload and that project milestones are met on time.

Conclusion

Resource leveling is a vital technique in project management, particularly within the Control Resources process. By effectively using resource leveling, project managers can ensure that resources are not overallocated, thereby avoiding burnout and optimizing productivity. This strategic approach helps maintain a balanced resource allocation throughout the project, contributing to smoother project execution and enhanced overall performance. Performance reviews in the **Control Resources** process are critical for evaluating how effectively and efficiently resources are being used in a project and whether they are performing according to expectations. These reviews are instrumental in ensuring that resources are aligned properly with project needs throughout its lifecycle.

Primary Inputs of Performance Reviews

1. **Project Management Plan**: Includes resource management plans that outline expected resource utilization and performance metrics, serving as a benchmark for evaluating actual performance.
2. **Work Performance Data**: Detailed data collected from project activities that show the actual performance of resources. This data includes hours worked, costs incurred, and resources consumed for given tasks or during specified periods.
3. **Resource Calendars**: Provide information on the availability and scheduling of resources which is necessary for analyzing performance issues related to timing and allocation.
4. **Resource Breakdown Structure (RBS)**: Offers a hierarchical breakdown of resources by category and type, facilitating detailed analysis of resource usage and performance at different levels.

Primary Outputs of Performance Reviews

1. **Work Performance Information**: This is an analyzed and synthesized form of work performance data, converting raw data into actionable information about resource utilization and performance trends.
2. **Change Requests**: If the performance review identifies significant variances from the plan, or opportunities for improvement, change requests may be generated to reallocate resources, modify resource levels, or adjust strategies.
3. **Project Management Plan Updates**: Insights from performance reviews might necessitate updates to the resource management plan, reflecting changes in resource allocation strategies, adjustments in resource levels, or updated methods of resource management.
4. **Project Documents Updates**: Other project documents, such as resource calendars and RBS, may also be updated to reflect changes in resource availability, scheduling, or to incorporate new data about resource capabilities.

Using Performance Data to Assess Resource Performance and Make Decisions
Resource Utilization Metrics:

- **Metric Examples**: Percentage of resource capacity used, overtime hours, idle time, and cost variances.
- **Application**: Project managers use these metrics to assess whether resources are overworked or underutilized, which can impact both project costs and deadlines. For example, high overtime might indicate understaffing or inefficiencies, whereas significant idle time could signal overstaffing or poor allocation.

Earned Value Analysis (EVA):

- **Description**: EVA integrates scope, schedule, and resource metrics to assess project performance and progress in monetary terms.
- **Key Metrics**:
    - **Cost Performance Index (CPI)**: Indicates how efficiently the project team is utilizing the budget.
    - **Schedule Performance Index (SPI)**: Shows how efficiently the project team is using time.
- **Application**: By combining these metrics, project managers can get a comprehensive view of project health beyond simple budget or schedule adherence. For example, a CPI less than 1 indicates that the project is over budget, which could be due to inefficient resource use or unexpected resource costs.

Analysis Techniques:

- **Trend Analysis**: Examining performance data over time to identify patterns or trends that could indicate emerging issues or opportunities for improvement.
- **Variance Analysis**: Comparing planned resource attributes (like hours and costs) against actual figures to pinpoint deviations.

Conclusion

Performance reviews are essential in the Control Resources process, providing the necessary data and insights for making informed decisions about resource management. By effectively analyzing performance data and applying it in strategic decision making, project managers can optimize resource allocation, enhance efficiency, and improve the likelihood of project success. The project involved constructing a large-scale shopping center in a major metropolitan area. The project was scheduled to last 24 months and required a diverse mix of resources including skilled labor, construction machinery, and specialized materials. The complexity of the project stemmed from its scale, the need for coordination among various subcontractors, and the strict timelines imposed by stakeholders.

Resource Challenges Faced

1. **Skilled Labor Shortage**: There was a regional shortage of skilled labor such as electricians and carpenters, which posed a risk to the project timelines.
2. **Machinery Availability**: The availability of key construction machinery was limited due to concurrent construction projects in the area.
3. **Material Supply Delays**: Some specialized materials had long lead times, which could potentially delay certain phases of the construction.
4. **Subcontractor Coordination**: Managing multiple subcontractors and ensuring they met quality and timeline expectations was challenging.

Strategies Employed
1. Strategic Resource Planning and Acquisition

- Conducted a detailed resource assessment early in the project to identify the types and quantities of resources required throughout the project lifecycle.
- Established partnerships with local trade schools and labor unions to secure a steady supply of skilled workers.
- Entered into long-term rental agreements with equipment suppliers to ensure availability of machinery even during peak demand.

2. Developing the Project Team

- Implemented an onboarding program for all new team members to familiarize them with project objectives, processes, and safety protocols.
- Organized regular training workshops to enhance the skills of team members, focusing on areas critical to project success.
- Set up a mentorship program where experienced project members helped to quickly ramp up newer or less experienced team members.

3. Dynamic Resource Management

- Utilized advanced scheduling tools to manage the allocation and use of resources effectively, ensuring optimal utilization.
- Regularly reviewed resource allocations and project progress to make adjustments as needed, practicing resource leveling and smoothing to address any discrepancies.
- Established a responsive communication network among project managers, subcontractors, and suppliers to quickly address any issues that could impact resource availability.

4. Monitoring and Feedback Mechanisms

- Implemented a real-time feedback mechanism to continuously gather insights from the team on the ground, allowing for immediate adjustments.
- Conducted bi-weekly review meetings with subcontractors to monitor progress, address issues, and adjust plans as necessary.

Lessons Learned
1. Importance of Early Planning

- Early and thorough planning of resource requirements was crucial in mitigating the impact of resource shortages and ensuring the project remained on track.

2. Flexibility in Resource Management

- The ability to dynamically manage resources in response to project demands and external factors was key to navigating the challenges faced during the project.

3. Benefits of Strong Stakeholder Relationships

- Developing and maintaining strong relationships with subcontractors, suppliers, and local labor groups helped in ensuring resource availability and compliance with project standards.

4. Value of Team Development Initiatives

- Investing in team development significantly enhanced team performance. Training and mentorship programs helped maintain high levels of craftsmanship and reduced the learning curve for new team members.

5. Effective Subcontractor Management

- Establishing clear expectations and maintaining open lines of communication with subcontractors were essential for coordinating efforts and ensuring quality outcomes.

Conclusion

The construction of the shopping center was completed successfully, meeting the desired quality standards and project timelines. Effective project resource management, including strategic planning, proactive resource development, and dynamic management practices, played a crucial role in overcoming the challenges faced. This case study highlights the importance of comprehensive resource management in achieving project success, especially in complex, resource-intensive projects. Creating a set of practice questions and quizzes on Project Resource Management is an excellent way to assess and reinforce a reader's understanding of the key concepts and processes involved in managing project resources effectively. Below are practice questions designed to cover various aspects of Project Resource Management, suitable for preparation for the CAPM exam. Each question includes a detailed explanation to enhance understanding.

Practice Questions
Question 1:

What is the primary purpose of the Plan Resource Management process in project management?
A) To monitor the expenses associated with project resources
B) To ensure that project meets its performance objectives
C) To establish guidelines on how resources should be identified, acquired, and managed
D) To resolve conflicts among project team members
Answer: C
Explanation:
The primary purpose of the Plan Resource Management process is to establish guidelines on how project resources, including human resources, equipment, and materials, should be identified, acquired, and managed throughout the project. This helps ensure that the right resources are available at the right times and are used efficiently.

Question 2:

Which tool or technique is most effective for determining whether a project team is over-allocated or under-utilized?
A) Resource Histogram
B) Variance Analysis
C) Expert Judgment
D) Monte Carlo Simulation
Answer: A
Explanation:
A Resource Histogram is a bar chart that represents the amount of time a resource is scheduled to work over a specific period. It is especially useful for visualizing the distribution of resource allocations and identifying periods of over-allocation or under-utilization, making it an effective tool for this purpose.

Question 3:

What is a key output of the Acquire Resources process?
A) Change requests
B) Resource calendars
C) Project documents updates
D) Project charter updates

Answer: B

Explanation:

Resource calendars are a key output of the Acquire Resources process. These calendars detail the availability of each resource and are crucial for effective project scheduling and ensuring that resources are available when needed to meet project timelines.

Question 4:

In the context of project resource management, what does 'resource leveling' mean?
A) Reducing the amount of resources used on a project to cut costs
B) Adjusting the project schedule to spread the demand for resources more evenly
C) Increasing the efficiency of resource utilization without changing the project scope
D) Assigning additional resources to activities to decrease the time needed to complete them

Answer: B

Explanation:

Resource leveling involves adjusting the project schedule to spread the demand for resources more evenly over the course of the project. This is often necessary when resources are over-allocated or there is a desire to avoid having resources idle. It helps in managing limited resource availability without changing the project scope.

Question 5:

What role does the "Estimate Activity Resources" process play in project management?
A) Determines the amount and type of resources required for each project activity
B) Evaluates the performance of resources to determine if they are meeting project objectives
C) Assigns specific resources to project tasks and activities
D) Ensures that resources are released when they are no longer needed

Answer: A

Explanation:

The "Estimate Activity Resources" process involves determining the amount and type of resources required for each project activity. This estimation helps in planning resource allocation and ensuring that sufficient resources are available to complete each task effectively and efficiently.

Conclusion

These practice questions cover essential concepts of Project Resource Management and can help deepen understanding of how resources are planned, acquired, managed, and controlled in project management. Each explanation aids in connecting theoretical knowledge to practical applications, beneficial for preparing for the CAPM exam and enhancing overall project management skills.

IX. Project Communications Management:

Purpose and Importance of the Plan Communications Management Process

The Plan Communications Management process is a critical part of project management that involves developing an appropriate approach and plan for project communication based on stakeholders' information needs and requirements. This process ensures that timely and relevant information is delivered to all parties involved, facilitating effective decision-making and project execution.

Purpose of the Plan Communications Management Process

1. **Define Communication Needs**: To identify and define the communication requirements of the project stakeholders.
2. **Ensure Timely and Appropriate Information Flow**: To facilitate the flow of information among all project participants, ensuring that stakeholders have access to the information they need, when they need it, in a suitable format.
3. **Support Project Objectives**: To align communications with project objectives, ensuring that all communications help to advance the project towards its goals.
4. **Optimize Resource Use**: To plan communications efficiently, ensuring that resources are not wasted on unnecessary or ineffective communications.

Importance of the Process

- **Stakeholder Engagement and Satisfaction**: Effective communication is key to engaging stakeholders and maintaining their satisfaction throughout the project.
- **Mitigation of Risks**: Proper communications planning helps in anticipating and mitigating potential misunderstandings and conflicts.
- **Transparency**: It fosters transparency, building trust among project team members and stakeholders.
- **Project Success**: Strong communication practices are often correlated with the overall success of a project, as they enhance teamwork and facilitate smoother project execution.

Key Components of a Communications Management Plan
1. Stakeholder Communication Requirements:

- Details who needs what information, when they need it, and how it should be delivered.
- Considers the preferences of different stakeholders regarding communication formats, languages, and frequencies.

2. Information to be Communicated:

- Identifies the types of information that need to be communicated, including project status, changes, risks, and successes.
- Defines the level of detail required for different types of communications.

3. Communication Technology and Methods:

- Specifies the technology and methods for communication (e.g., emails, meetings, project management software, intranet portals).
- Includes considerations for remote and distributed teams, such as videoconferencing and collaborative tools.

4. Communication Roles and Responsibilities:

- Defines who is responsible for communicating specific information.
- Details the responsibilities of the project manager, team members, and other stakeholders in the communication process.

5. Frequency of Communication:

- Outlines how frequently each type of communication should occur, such as daily updates, weekly status meetings, or monthly reports.
- Adapts frequencies based on the phase of the project and the needs of stakeholders.

6. Escalation Processes:

- Provides a clear mechanism for escalating communications when issues arise that need higher-level attention.
- Defines the thresholds for escalation and the subsequent steps required.

7. Feedback Mechanisms:

- Establishes methods for receiving and incorporating feedback from stakeholders.
- Ensures that communications are effective and meet the needs of the audience.

8. Change Management Communications:

- Describes how communications will handle project changes, ensuring stakeholders are kept informed about decisions that affect the project scope, timeline, or resources.

9. Document Format and Access:

- Determines the standard formats for communication documents and how they are accessed by stakeholders.
- Ensures that information is secure yet accessible to authorized individuals.

Example of Effective Communication Management

In a large software development project, the project manager develops a communication plan that includes detailed weekly email updates to all stakeholders, monthly project review meetings with high-level executives, and daily stand-up meetings with the project team. The plan specifies using a project management tool for team updates and a secure online portal for stakeholders to access current project documentation. Feedback is collected through surveys after each major milestone to adjust the communication practices as needed.

Conclusion

The Plan Communications Management process is fundamental in setting up the project for success by ensuring efficient and effective communication among all stakeholders. By clearly defining communication requirements, methods, responsibilities, and protocols, the process helps in managing expectations, fostering stakeholder engagement, and driving project objectives forward. The **Communications Management Plan** and the **Project Stakeholder Register** are both crucial components of effective project management, serving interlinked roles that ensure all relevant parties are appropriately informed throughout the life of the project. Understanding the relationship between these two elements is key to developing a communications strategy that meets the needs and expectations of all stakeholders.

Relationship Between the Communications Management Plan and the Project Stakeholder Register

Foundation and Reference:

The stakeholder register serves as a foundational document in developing the communications management plan. It provides detailed information about all stakeholders involved in or affected by the project, including their roles, responsibilities, interests, influence, and communication requirements.

Tailored Communication Strategies:

Information from the stakeholder register is used to tailor communication strategies within the communications management plan. By understanding the needs, expectations, and impact of each stakeholder, the project manager can determine the most effective methods, frequency, and type of communication required for each group or individual.

Influence of Stakeholder Analysis on Communications Management Plan Development

Stakeholder analysis involves identifying stakeholders, assessing their needs and potential impact on the project, and categorizing them according to their interest, influence, and involvement. This analysis directly influences the communications management plan in several ways:

1. **Identifying Communication Needs**: Different stakeholders may require different levels of information and engagement based on their interest and influence over the project. For instance, high-influence stakeholders such as project sponsors may require more frequent and detailed updates than those with less influence or interest.
2. **Determining Communication Methods and Formats**: Stakeholder analysis helps in deciding the most effective communication methods (e.g., emails, meetings, reports) and formats (e.g., formal, informal, written, verbal) for different stakeholder groups.
3. **Setting Communication Frequency**: The analysis can determine how often stakeholders need to be updated. For example, active project team members might require daily updates, whereas external stakeholders might only need monthly or quarterly project summaries.

Key Considerations When Tailoring Communication Strategies

1. **Stakeholder Needs and Preferences**: Tailor communication methods to the preferences and requirements of stakeholders. Some may prefer detailed reports, while others might benefit more from summaries or visual presentations.
2. **Cultural and Organizational Factors**: Consider cultural and organizational norms that might influence how communication should be structured. Cultural sensitivity and respect for organizational hierarchies can play significant roles in how messages are perceived and received.
3. **Accessibility of Information**: Ensure that communication is accessible to all stakeholders, considering factors such as language, disability access, and technological availability.
4. **Feedback Mechanisms**: Include mechanisms for feedback in the communications management plan to ensure that stakeholders have the opportunity to respond to communications, provide input, and express concerns. This two-way communication fosters greater engagement and allows for adjustments in strategies as needed.
5. **Confidentiality and Transparency**: Balance the need for transparency with the necessity of confidentiality. Sensitive information must be carefully managed to avoid unauthorized or harmful disclosures, while still maintaining a transparent approach with those stakeholders who need access to information.

Conclusion

The communications management plan should be developed with a thorough understanding of the stakeholder register and the results of the stakeholder analysis. Effective communication is not a one-size-fits-all solution; it requires careful consideration of who the stakeholders are, what they need to know, and how best to provide them with that information. By aligning the communications management plan closely with stakeholder needs and preferences, project managers can ensure smoother interactions, more effective engagement, and ultimately, greater project success. The Plan Communications Management process is essential in establishing a structured approach to ensuring effective flow of project information among all stakeholders. Understanding the inputs, tools and techniques, and outputs (ITTOs) is crucial for developing a comprehensive communications management strategy.

Inputs

1. **Project Charter**:

Provides high-level project information and stakeholder details which are crucial in determining key communication requirements.

- **Example**: The project charter lists the project's major stakeholders, which helps the project manager identify who needs to receive project updates and critical decisions.

2. **Stakeholder Register**:

Contains detailed information about all stakeholders including their interests, influences, communication needs, and potential impact on the project.

- **Example**: The stakeholder register can highlight a stakeholder's preferred method of communication (e.g., email vs. face-to-face meetings), facilitating tailored communication strategies.

3. **Project Management Plan**:

Provides information on the project's objectives, baselines, and other management plans that influence communication needs.

- **Example**: The project scope and schedule from the management plan help define what details need to be communicated and when.

4. **Enterprise Environmental Factors (EEFs)**:

Include organizational culture and existing systems that can affect the communication approach.

- **Example**: If the organization has a robust intranet system, it may be used for project communications.

5. **Organizational Process Assets (OPAs)**:

Consist of historical information and lessons learned from previous projects, which can inform effective communication practices.

- **Example**: Previous project documentation might suggest regular briefings were effective in keeping stakeholders engaged.

Tools and Techniques

1. **Communication Requirements Analysis**:

Identifies and documents the information needs of the project stakeholders.

- **Example**: Analyzing who needs what information, when they will need it, and how it should be given to ensure all parties are adequately informed.

2. **Communication Technology**: The technology used for communications depending on factors like urgency, ease of use, and the project environment.

- **Example**: Choosing between email, instant messaging, video conferencing, or traditional mail based on the availability and effectiveness within the organization.

3. **Communication Models**: The process of creating, sending, receiving, and understanding messages.
   - **Example**: Applying sender-receiver models to enhance clarity and reduce the noise in project communications.
4. **Communication Methods**: Determining whether communication will be interactive, push, or pull.
   - **Example**: Deciding to use meetings (interactive), emails (push), or posting updates on a project portal (pull) based on the information and audience needs.
5. **Meetings**: Bringing stakeholders together to discuss project issues and updates.
   - **Example**: Regular status update meetings and review sessions with the project team and key stakeholders.

Outputs

1. **Communications Management Plan**: A document that outlines the communication objectives and strategies, including stakeholder communication requirements, information to be communicated, frequency of communication, and methods to be used.
   - **Example**: A detailed plan that includes a communication matrix specifying what information will be communicated, to whom, by whom, using what method, and how frequently.
2. **Project Management Plan Updates**: Any changes or updates needed in the project management plan as a result of planning communications.
   - **Example**: Adjusting the overall project management plan to integrate the newly developed communications management plan.
3. **Project Documents Updates**: Updates to project documents such as stakeholder engagement plans or risk registers based on the communication strategies developed.
   - **Example**: Updating the stakeholder register with information on stakeholder communication preferences and frequencies as decided during the communications planning process.

Conclusion

Effective communication is pivotal for project success. By systematically analyzing communication requirements and deploying appropriate tools and techniques, project managers can ensure that all project stakeholders are kept informed and engaged throughout the project lifecycle. The Communications Management Plan, developed from these ITTOs, serves as the blueprint for project communications, aligning stakeholder needs with project objectives to enhance overall project performance. Communication Requirements Analysis is a fundamental component of the Plan Communications Management process in project management. This analysis aims to determine and document the information needs of the project stakeholders, ensuring that the right messages are delivered to the right audiences at the right time and through the right channels. Proper execution of this analysis is critical for effective communication, which in turn drives project success by ensuring all parties are well-informed, engaged, and aligned.

Role in Plan Communications Management

The communication requirements analysis primarily serves to:

1. **Identify Stakeholders**: Recognize all individuals, groups, or organizations affected by the project or those who could influence its outcome.

2. **Determine Information Needs**: Ascertain what information needs to be shared with which stakeholders, including the level of detail required.
3. **Set Communication Preferences**: Understand the preferred communication format, frequency, and method for each stakeholder or stakeholder group.
4. **Align Communication Timing**: Schedule the distribution of information to coincide with project needs and stakeholder availability.
5. **Ensure Compliance**: Meet the information and reporting requirements dictated by organizational policies, legal obligations, or external regulatory bodies.

Factors to Consider in Communication Requirements Analysis

When performing communication requirements analysis, project managers should consider multiple factors to tailor the communication plan effectively:

1. **Stakeholder Roles and Responsibilities**:
   - Understand the role of each stakeholder in the project and their responsibilities, which influence the type and frequency of information they require.

2. **Interest and Influence**:
   - Assess how interested and influential each stakeholder is regarding the project's outcomes. High-interest, high-influence stakeholders might need more frequent and detailed communications compared to others.

3. **Information Sensitivity and Security**:
   - Consider the sensitivity of the information being communicated. Some information may require secure channels or might be restricted to certain audiences to protect confidentiality.

4. **Cultural and Organizational Norms**:
   - Take into account cultural and organizational factors that can affect communication styles and preferences. This includes understanding organizational hierarchies, cultural norms, and even local practices that might affect how information should be presented and shared.

5. **Communication Technology Access**:
   - Evaluate the availability and accessibility of different communication technologies among stakeholders. Some may prefer traditional methods like face-to-face meetings, while others might favor digital communications, such as emails or collaborative platforms.

6. **Language and Jargon**:
   - Be mindful of language barriers and the use of jargon. Communications should be clear and accessible, using language that is understandable to all stakeholders to avoid misinterpretations.

7. **Feedback Mechanisms**:
   - Plan for how stakeholders can provide feedback on the information received. Effective communications require a two-way flow, allowing stakeholders to ask questions, provide inputs, and express concerns.

Conclusion

Communication requirements analysis is crucial in the Plan Communications Management process as it ensures that all communications are effectively tailored to meet the needs of the project and its stakeholders. By carefully considering various factors affecting stakeholder communication needs, project managers can craft a comprehensive communications management plan that not only disseminates necessary information efficiently but also fosters stakeholder engagement and project success. This strategic approach minimizes misunderstandings, enhances collaboration, and drives better project outcomes. A communication matrix, also known as a communication plan or stakeholder communication matrix, is a vital tool used in project management to outline and organize the information needs of a project's stakeholders. This matrix helps ensure that all necessary parties receive the right information at the right time, through the most effective channels, thus facilitating efficient and effective communication throughout the project lifecycle.

Purpose of the Communication Matrix

The primary purpose of a communication matrix is to:
1. **Clarify Communication Responsibilities**: It specifies who is responsible for sending and receiving various types of information.
2. **Define Communication Channels and Tools**: It identifies the most appropriate communication methods and tools for each type of message and recipient.
3. **Schedule Communications**: It determines the timing and frequency of communications to meet the project and stakeholder needs.
4. **Ensure Alignment with Stakeholder Needs**: It aligns the communication strategy with the information needs and preferences of different stakeholder groups, ensuring that all parties are appropriately informed.

Components of a Communication Matrix

A typical communication matrix includes several key columns such as:
1. **Information Item**: What needs to be communicated? (e.g., project status updates, milestones achieved, changes in project scope)
2. **Purpose**: Why is this information being communicated? (e.g., to seek approval, provide updates, solicit feedback)
3. **Audience**: Who needs to receive this information? (e.g., project team, sponsors, clients)
4. **Frequency**: How often does this information need to be communicated? (e.g., daily, weekly, monthly)
5. **Method/Channel**: How will the information be communicated? (e.g., email, meetings, reports, project management software)
6. **Responsible**: Who is responsible for ensuring this information is communicated? (e.g., project manager, communications officer, team lead)
7. **Required Response**: Is a response required? By when? (This can help in tracking critical actions and decisions.)

Using the Communication Matrix in Project Management
1.   Development Stage:

- During the planning phase, develop a communication matrix as part of the communications management plan.
- Collaborate with key stakeholders to determine their information needs and preferences.

2. Documentation:

- Clearly document the communication requirements in the matrix format. This serves as a reference for the project team and ensures that all communication needs are considered and planned for.

3. Implementation:

- Use the matrix to guide the execution of communications throughout the project. It acts as a checklist to ensure all necessary communications are made as planned.

5.   Monitoring and Updating:

- Regularly review and update the communication matrix as the project progresses and as needs evolve. Changes in project scope, schedule, or stakeholder interest may necessitate adjustments to the communication plan.

6.   Ensuring Compliance:

- Ensure that all team members understand their roles in the communication process as outlined in the matrix. Regularly check that communications are made according to the plan and are achieving their intended purpose.

Example of Communication Matrix Usage

Imagine a project where the team is developing a new software system. The communication matrix might include:

- **Information Item**: Monthly project status.
- **Purpose**: To update stakeholders on progress and any issues.
- **Audience**: Project sponsors and key clients.
- **Frequency**: Monthly.
- **Method/Channel**: Email newsletter and a detailed report during a monthly steering committee meeting.
- **Responsible**: Project Manager.
- **Required Response**: Feedback required within one week.

Conclusion

The communication matrix is a fundamental tool in the Plan Communications Management process, helping project managers systematically plan, implement, and monitor communications. By effectively using this tool, project managers can ensure that all stakeholders are kept informed and engaged, thereby supporting the successful delivery of the project. The **Manage Communications** process is a critical component of project management, focusing on the timely and appropriate creation, collection, distribution, storage, and ultimate disposition of project information. This process ensures that project stakeholders have the necessary information to make informed decisions and remain engaged and aligned with the project goals.

Significance of Manage Communications Process

1. **Ensures Timely Information Flow**: Facilitates the efficient flow of information among project participants, which is essential for maintaining project momentum and making timely decisions.
2. **Promotes Stakeholder Engagement**: Keeps all stakeholders adequately informed and engaged, which is crucial for maintaining their support and addressing their concerns throughout the project lifecycle.
3. **Supports Project Transparency**: By effectively managing communications, the project remains transparent to stakeholders, enhancing trust and credibility.
4. **Aids in Risk Management**: Effective communication helps in identifying and addressing risks promptly by ensuring that crucial information reaches the right stakeholders at the right time.
5. **Enhances Project Documentation**: Ensures that all project information, including changes, decisions, and updates, is accurately documented and accessible, providing a valuable reference that aids in current and future project execution.

Primary Tools and Techniques for Effective Communication
1. Communication Technology

- **Description**: Involves using various software and electronic communication tools to share information, such as email, video conferencing, project management software, and social media tools.
- **Application**: Choosing the right technology based on the project environment, stakeholder locations, and the immediacy of the communication need.

2. Communication Models

- **Description**: Includes basic sender-receiver models, interactive communication models (which provide for feedback), and push/pull communication models (where information is either sent to recipients or made available for access at their discretion).
- **Application**: Understanding the strengths and limitations of each model helps tailor communications to ensure they are effective for different situations and stakeholder groups.

3. Communication Methods

- **Description**: Methods can be formal or informal, written or verbal, and official or unofficial. They include meetings, emails, reports, and dashboards.
- **Application**: Selecting the appropriate method depending on the complexity of information, the needs of the audience, and the formality required.

4. Performance Reporting

- **Description**: Involves the analysis and communication of project performance data regarding scope, schedule, cost, resources, and risks.
- **Application**: Regular performance reports keep stakeholders informed about the project's progress and deviations from the plan.

5. Information Management Systems

- **Description**: Systems used to collect, store, and disseminate information in a way that optimizes accessibility and usefulness across the project team and other stakeholders.
- **Application**: Implementing a centralized document management system or a project intranet that provides easy access to project information and documentation.

6. Feedback Mechanisms

- **Description**: Structured processes for receiving and processing feedback from stakeholders.
- **Application**: Surveys, comment forms, and review meetings can be used to gather feedback, which is essential for adjusting communication practices and addressing stakeholder concerns.

Conclusion

Effective communication management is pivotal in any project. By utilizing appropriate tools and techniques, project managers can ensure that communications are planned, executed, and adjusted as necessary to meet the project's needs and enhance stakeholder satisfaction. The **Manage Communications** process not only supports the operational aspects of project execution but also plays a strategic role in maintaining stakeholder relationships and project alignment. This holistic approach to communication fosters a collaborative project environment conducive to achieving project objectives. In project management, effective communication is crucial for ensuring that all team members and stakeholders are aligned with the project's goals and understand their roles. Various communication models can help project managers structure their communications to improve clarity, accuracy, and effectiveness. Among these, the sender-receiver model and the feedback loop are particularly significant.

1. Sender-Receiver Model

Description: The sender-receiver model is a basic concept where communication involves a sender who encodes and sends a message, and a receiver who decodes and processes that message. This model emphasizes the importance of clear encoding by the sender and effective decoding by the receiver to ensure the message is understood correctly.

Application:

- **Clarity and Encoding**: Project managers must ensure that the information is clear and unambiguous. This involves choosing simple, direct language and considering the receiver's background and knowledge level when crafting messages.
- **Effective Decoding**: Encourage receivers to ask questions if the message is unclear and to confirm understanding. This ensures that the information is interpreted as intended.

Improving Communications:

- Use visual aids and multiple communication channels to reinforce the message, ensuring that it is encoded in a manner that is accessible to all project stakeholders.

2. Feedback Loop

Description: The feedback loop is an extension of the sender-receiver model, adding a crucial step where the receiver sends a response back to the sender, indicating whether the message was understood and accepted. This loop allows for adjustments in the communication process based on the receiver's feedback, enhancing mutual understanding and effectiveness.

Application:

- **Continuous Improvement**: After delivering a message (e.g., during a project briefing), the project manager should solicit feedback to assess understanding and receptiveness.
- **Adaptation and Adjustment**: Based on the feedback received, the project manager can adjust the communication strategy, content, or delivery method to better suit the team's or stakeholders' needs.

Improving Communications:

- Implement regular check-ins and debrief sessions where team members can provide feedback on communications. This helps in refining future communications and addressing any ongoing issues.

Implementing Communication Models

Practical Steps for Project Managers:

1. **Understand Your Audience**: Analyze the audience's needs, preferences, and communication barriers. Tailor messages accordingly to ensure they are appropriate and effective.
2. **Choose the Right Medium**: Select the most effective medium for delivering your message, whether it be emails, meetings, reports, or instant messaging, based on the complexity of the information and the audience's preferences.
3. **Clarify and Simplify Messages**: Use clear, concise language and avoid jargon unless it is commonly understood by the audience. Simplify complex ideas using diagrams, charts, or examples.
4. **Encourage Open Dialogue**: Foster an environment where team members feel comfortable providing honest feedback. This can be facilitated through open-door policies, regular one-on-one meetings, and anonymous feedback tools.
5. **Monitor and Evaluate Communication Effectiveness**: Regularly assess how well communications are being received and understood. Use tools like surveys, questionnaires, and informal feedback to gauge the effectiveness of your communication strategies.

Example of Effective Use

In a large infrastructure project involving multiple contractors and stakeholders, the project manager uses the sender-receiver model to ensure all safety updates are communicated effectively. Each update is sent via email and discussed in subsequent safety briefings. The project manager then uses the feedback loop by asking for acknowledgments and questions to ensure all parties understand the safety protocols thoroughly.

Conclusion

Understanding and applying communication models like the sender-receiver model and the feedback loop can significantly enhance the manageability and success of a project. These models help project managers ensure that communications are clear, messages are understood, and any misunderstandings are quickly addressed, ultimately supporting the project's objectives and smooth execution. In the **Manage Communications** process, various communication methods and technologies are utilized to meet the diverse needs of project stakeholders effectively. The selection of these tools depends on factors like the urgency of the communication, the need for feedback, the geographical distribution of team members, and the formality required. Understanding the different types of communication methods and technologies, and their respective contexts, can significantly enhance the effectiveness of project communication.

Communication Methods
Formal Communication

- **Examples**: Official reports, project status updates, change requests, project charters, and contracts.
- **Advantages**: Provides a clear, structured, and official record of information; essential for documentation and accountability.

- **Limitations**: Can be time-consuming to prepare; may not be effective for urgent communication needs.

Informal Communication
- **Examples**: Emails, ad-hoc meetings, instant messaging, and informal discussions.
- **Advantages**: Faster and more flexible, allowing for quick problem-solving and updates; promotes a more open and collaborative environment.
- **Limitations**: Risk of miscommunication due to lack of structure; might not be adequately documented.

Communication Technologies
Synchronous Communication Technologies
- **Examples**: Video conferences, telephone calls, live chat, and face-to-face meetings.
- **Advantages**:
  - Immediate feedback, which is crucial for clarifying complex issues quickly.
  - More personal, helping to build better relationships and trust among team members.
- **Limitations**:
  - Requires all participants to be available at the same time, which can be challenging across different time zones.
  - Meetings can be time-consuming and may lead to productivity loss if not well-managed.

Asynchronous Communication Technologies
- **Examples**: Emails, discussion forums, shared document platforms (like Google Docs or SharePoint), and project management tools (like Asana or Trello).
- **Advantages**:
  - Provides participants the flexibility to respond at their convenience, enhancing convenience for globally distributed teams.
  - Useful for documenting discussions and decisions.
- **Limitations**:
  - Delayed feedback, which can slow down decision-making.
  - Risk of miscommunication if messages are not clearly written or if responses are delayed.

Considerations for Selecting Communication Methods and Technologies
- **Project Urgency and Information Sensitivity**: Urgent and sensitive information may require more direct and immediate communication methods, such as face-to-face meetings or synchronous calls.
- **Stakeholder Preferences and Requirements**: Understanding stakeholder preferences for receiving information can enhance engagement and ensure that communications are effective.
- **Documentation Needs**: Projects that require thorough documentation for compliance or auditing purposes may benefit more from formal communication methods.
- **Team Distribution**: For teams spread across different locations, asynchronous communication tools can bridge the gap and ensure continuous collaboration.

Conclusion

Choosing the right mix of communication methods and technologies is crucial for the success of any project. Project managers should carefully assess the project's needs, the nature of the information being communicated, and the characteristics of the project team and stakeholders to tailor their communication strategy effectively. This strategic approach not only ensures efficient and effective communication but also supports project alignment and stakeholder satisfaction. Effective communication skills are paramount in project management as they directly influence the success of the project. Communication bridges the gap between diverse stakeholders, ensures alignment with project goals, facilitates problem-solving, and helps manage expectations. Effective communication ensures that all parties involved are on the same page, reducing conflicts and enabling efficient decision-making processes.

Key Verbal Communication Skills
Clarity and Articulation:

Project managers must be able to articulate their thoughts and project needs clearly. This includes using precise language, avoiding jargon when communicating with non-expert stakeholders, and ensuring that instructions and expectations are explicitly stated.

Active Listening:

Effective verbal communication is not just about speaking but also listening. Active listening involves paying full attention to the speaker, understanding their message, and responding thoughtfully. This skill helps in building trust and validating the concerns of team members and stakeholders.

Questioning and Clarification:

The ability to ask the right questions and seek clarifications prevents misunderstandings. This includes open-ended questions that encourage discussion, as well as specific questions that drill down into the details of project tasks and responsibilities.

Persuasion and Influence:

A project manager often needs to persuade stakeholders and team members to accept decisions or changes in the project. Effective verbal persuasion involves presenting logical arguments, highlighting benefits, and understanding the perspectives of others to influence them positively.

Key Non-Verbal Communication Skills
1. **Body Language**: Non-verbal cues such as eye contact, gestures, posture, and facial expressions can significantly impact how messages are perceived. Positive body language (e.g., nodding, open gestures) can reinforce trust and openness.
2. **Tone of Voice**: The tone used in communication can convey confidence, urgency, empathy, or other emotions. It's crucial for project managers to be aware of their tone and adjust it according to the context to maintain a positive and professional atmosphere.
3. **Visual Aids**: Utilizing charts, graphs, timelines, and other visual aids to complement spoken or written communication can help clarify complex information and ensure that everyone understands project data and statuses.

Key Written Communication Skills
1. **Clarity and Precision**: Written communications such as emails, reports, and project documents should be clear and to the point. Avoiding ambiguity and ensuring that documents are easy to read and understand is critical.

2. **Consistency**: Maintaining a consistent format and style in project documents helps in setting a standard and expectations for project communication. This includes using standardized templates and terminologies across all project documentation.
3. **Attention to Detail**: Written communication should be accurate and detailed enough to convey the necessary information without room for misinterpretation. This includes thorough proofreading to avoid errors that could undermine the credibility of the communication.
4. **Adaptability**: Adapting writing styles to suit different audiences, such as technical write-ups for engineering teams or summary reports for executives, ensures that the information is accessible and understandable by all.

Effective Communication in Action

Imagine a project manager overseeing the development of a new software application. They utilize:

- **Verbal skills** during stakeholder meetings to articulate project needs, listen to stakeholder concerns, and negotiate resources.
- **Non-verbal skills** to show engagement and reassurance during team updates.
- **Written skills** to prepare clear, concise, and detailed project status reports that are tailored to the needs of both technical team members and non-technical stakeholders.

Conclusion

Effective communication is a cornerstone of successful project management. It involves more than just exchanging information; it's about ensuring that this information is completely understood and appropriately acted upon by all involved. By mastering verbal, non-verbal, and written communication skills, project managers can significantly enhance team collaboration, stakeholder satisfaction, and project success. Active listening is a critical skill in the **Manage Communications** process, particularly in the realms of project management where effective communication is essential for the success of any project. Active listening involves fully concentrating, understanding, responding, and then remembering what is being said. It goes beyond merely hearing the spoken words, encompassing attention to the speaker's body language and subtle cues that might indicate underlying concerns or ideas.

Role of Active Listening in Manage Communications

1. **Building Trust**: When project managers actively listen to team members and stakeholders, they demonstrate respect and value for their opinions and ideas. This validation helps to build and strengthen trust, which is foundational for effective teamwork and stakeholder engagement.
2. **Resolving Conflicts**: Active listening is particularly effective in conflict resolution as it ensures that all parties feel heard and understood. This understanding is critical for identifying the root causes of conflicts and developing effective solutions that are acceptable to all involved parties.
3. **Fostering Open Communication**: By practicing active listening, project managers encourage a more open and inclusive communication culture within the project team. Team members are more likely to share ideas, concerns, and feedback if they feel confident that they will be listened to attentively and respectfully.

How Project Managers Can Practice Active Listening
1. Pay Full Attention to the Speaker

- Avoid distractions and focus entirely on the person speaking. Put aside thoughts, phones, or other interruptions, and observe non-verbal cues and emotions to fully grasp the message being conveyed.

2. Show That You're Listening

- Use your own body language and gestures to convey your attention. Nod occasionally, smile at the person, and ensure your posture is open and inviting. These gestures show the speaker that you are genuinely engaged in the conversation.

3. Provide Feedback

- Reflect on what has been said by paraphrasing. "What I'm hearing is...", "Sounds like you are saying..." are great ways to reflect back the message to the speaker, confirming that you understand correctly, and also to correct any misunderstandings.

3. Defer Judgment

- Active listening requires an open mind. As a listener, you should avoid forming an opinion or interrupting with your solutions until the speaker has finished conveying their message. Interrupting disrupts the speaker's train of thought and can make them feel undermined.

5. Respond Appropriately

- Active listening is an interactive process. Offer appropriate responses to what has been said, not just with acknowledgment but also with thoughtful consideration of the speaker's message. Be candid, open, and honest in your response, and assert your opinions respectfully.

6. Ask Questions

- When appropriate, ask questions that promote discovery and insight. This shows that you are not only listening but also engaged and interested in understanding deeper.

7. Practice Empathy

- Try to empathize with the speaker's perspective, even if you don't agree. Understanding where they are coming from can help in resolving conflicts and finding common ground.

Conclusion

For project managers, active listening is not just a communication tool but a strategic asset that enhances interpersonal relationships, facilitates problem-solving, and fosters a positive project environment. It ensures that communication within the team and with stakeholders is effective, thereby supporting successful project outcomes. By mastering active listening, project managers can build stronger teams, navigate challenges more effectively, and lead projects to success with the full support and collaboration of all stakeholders involved. Effective communication is essential for successful project management, but several barriers can hinder this process. Recognizing and addressing these barriers is crucial to ensure clear and efficient communication among all project stakeholders.

Key Barriers to Communication

1. **Language Differences**: In globally distributed teams, language barriers can lead to misinterpretations and misunderstandings of important project information.
2. **Cultural Differences**: Cultural disparities can affect communication styles, decision-making processes, and conflict resolution methods, potentially leading to conflicts and miscommunications.
3. **Technological Issues**: Reliance on communication technology can introduce issues such as incompatibility of systems, connectivity problems, or data security concerns.

4. **Physical Barriers**: Remote teams may struggle with different time zones, which can delay responses and complicate the scheduling of meetings.
5. **Psychological Barriers**: These include personal biases, emotions, and perceptions that can distort the understanding of communications.

Strategies for Overcoming Communication Barriers
1. Addressing Language Differences

- **Use Simple Language**: Avoid jargon, slang, and complex vocabulary to make communication as clear as possible.
- **Employ Professional Translation Services**: For crucial documents or during significant meetings, use professional translators to avoid misinterpretations.
- **Language Training**: Offer language training options for team members where language barriers are a recurring issue.

2. Navigating Cultural Differences

- **Cultural Awareness Training**: Provide training for team members to increase awareness about different cultures, which can enhance mutual respect and understanding.
- **Diverse Teams**: Encourage diversity in project teams to foster a more inclusive atmosphere where various cultural perspectives are valued.
- **Adapt Communication Styles**: Recognize and adapt to different cultural communication styles and preferences, whether they are more direct or indirect.

3. Tackling Technological Issues

- **Standardize Tools**: Agree on standard communication tools and platforms across all team members to avoid compatibility issues.
- **Provide Training and Support**: Ensure all team members are trained on how to use the chosen communication technologies effectively.
- **Regularly Update and Maintain Systems**: Keep communication systems updated and maintain them regularly to avoid downtime or technical difficulties.

4. Overcoming Physical Barriers

- **Flexible Scheduling**: Be flexible in scheduling meetings to accommodate different time zones, possibly rotating meeting times to share inconvenience equitably.
- **Use Asynchronous Communication**: Utilize tools that allow asynchronous communication, such as emails, shared documents, and project management software, where immediate responses are not required.

5. Mitigating Psychological Barriers

- **Open Communication Culture**: Promote an open communication culture where team members feel safe to express their thoughts and feelings.
- **Conflict Resolution Mechanisms**: Implement effective conflict resolution mechanisms to manage and resolve personal conflicts within the team promptly.

Best Practices for Effective Communication

- **Regular Check-Ins**: Have regular one-on-one check-ins with team members to foster personal connections and address any concerns before they escalate.

- **Clear Communication Protocols**: Establish and communicate clear protocols regarding how, when, and what to communicate.
- **Feedback Mechanisms**: Implement mechanisms for feedback to continuously improve communication strategies based on what is or is not working.

Conclusion

Communication barriers can significantly impact project success but can be managed effectively with the right strategies. By addressing these barriers proactively, project managers can ensure that communication flows smoothly across all levels of the project, thereby enhancing team cohesion and project outcomes. The **Monitor Communications** process is crucial within project management as it ensures that the communication strategies in place effectively meet the project's needs and stakeholders' expectations. This process involves continuously evaluating and reviewing communication activities to verify their effectiveness and appropriateness, and to identify and address any areas needing improvement.

Role of Monitor Communications

1. **Assessment of Communication Effectiveness**: Ensures that all communications are appropriate, timely, clear, and understood by the intended audience. This ongoing assessment helps to maintain alignment between communication outputs and project objectives.
2. **Identification of Improvement Areas**: By monitoring the effectiveness of communications, project managers can identify shortcomings or gaps in the communication plan and strategize on how to address these issues.
3. **Adaptation to Project Needs**: Projects are dynamic, with needs that can change rapidly; the monitor communications process allows the communication strategies to be adapted in response to project evolution and stakeholder feedback.
4. **Ensuring Stakeholder Satisfaction**: Effective communication is key to stakeholder satisfaction. Monitoring communications helps in tweaking the communication plan to better serve stakeholder needs and enhance their engagement and satisfaction.

Key Activities and Techniques
2. Performance Measurements

- **Activity**: Utilize specific metrics to assess the effectiveness of communication efforts. These might include measures of stakeholder satisfaction, the timeliness of information delivery, and the accuracy of the information provided.
- **Technique**: Surveys and feedback forms can be used to gauge stakeholder satisfaction, while analytics tools can measure how often project communication tools (like newsletters, emails, project intranet) are accessed and utilized.

2. Feedback Collection

- **Activity**: Systematically collect feedback from team members and stakeholders regarding the clarity, timeliness, and effectiveness of project communications.
- **Technique**: Implement regular check-ins, feedback sessions, and use of digital feedback tools where stakeholders can comment on communication practices and suggest improvements.

3. Review Meetings

- **Activity**: Conduct regular review meetings with project teams and key stakeholders to discuss the communication strategies and their impact on project progress and morale.
- **Technique**: Use structured meeting agendas to focus on discussing communication effectiveness, challenges faced in communications, and potential areas for improvement.

4. Communication Audits

- **Activity**: Periodically audit all project communications to ensure they adhere to the project's communication plan and are achieving the intended goals.
- **Technique**: Review communication logs, emails, meeting minutes, and other communication documents to ensure compliance with the communication strategy and to identify discrepancies or failures.

5. Adjustments and Updates

- **Activity**: Based on the insights gained from performance measurements, feedback, and audits, make necessary adjustments to the communication plan.
- **Technique**: Update communication methods, tools, frequency, and even the communication plan itself to better align with project needs and stakeholder expectations.

Conclusion

Monitoring communications is a dynamic and continuous process that plays a vital role in maintaining the effectiveness of project communications. By regularly evaluating how communications are received and perceived, and by adapting strategies in response to feedback and changing project needs, project managers can ensure that communication remains effective throughout the project lifecycle. This proactive approach not only enhances stakeholder engagement but also supports the overall success of the project. Work performance reports are crucial tools in project management, utilized within the Monitor Communications process to assess and convey information regarding the progress, status, and overall performance of a project. These reports aggregate data from various sources to provide stakeholders with a comprehensive overview of how the project aligns with its planned objectives.

Purpose of Work Performance Reports

1. **Inform Decision Making**: Work performance reports provide essential data that stakeholders use to make informed decisions about the project's direction and management.
2. **Track Progress**: They help project managers and stakeholders track the progress of the project against its schedule, scope, and budget baselines.
3. **Identify Issues and Risks**: These reports highlight current and potential issues or risks, enabling proactive measures to mitigate them before they escalate.
4. **Enhance Communication**: They serve as a formal method of communication that ensures all stakeholders are uniformly informed about the project's status, fostering transparency and trust.

Key Components of Work Performance Reports

1. **Project Metrics**: Key performance indicators (KPIs) such as cost performance index (CPI), schedule performance index (SPI), and overall completion percentage. These metrics provide quantitative data on the project's health.
2. **Progress Updates**: Detailed accounts of what has been accomplished during the reporting period, including milestones reached and deliverables completed.

3. **Resource Utilization**: Information on resource allocation and usage, highlighting any over- or underutilization of project resources that could impact project timelines and costs.
4. **Risk and Issue Logs**: Updates on new and existing risks and issues, including how they are being managed and any changes in their status.
5. **Change Log**: Details of any changes made to the project scope, schedule, or resources, including the reason for the changes and their impact on the project.
6. **Future Outlook**: Projections for future project activities, potential challenges, and planned solutions or interventions to keep the project on track.
7. **Visual Aids**: Graphs, charts, and tables that make the data more accessible and easier to understand at a glance.

Using Work Performance Reports for Effective Communication
To Provide Project Updates:

- **Regular Scheduling**: Establish a regular schedule for distributing work performance reports (e.g., weekly, bi-weekly, or monthly), depending on the project's complexity and stakeholder needs.
- **Tailored Content**: Customize the content of the reports to meet the specific information needs of different stakeholder groups, ensuring that each report is relevant and useful.

To Facilitate Decision Making:

- **Data-Driven Insights**: Use the collected data to highlight trends, predict project trajectories, and provide actionable insights that can help stakeholders make informed decisions.
- **Scenario Analysis**: Include analysis of potential future scenarios and their implications on the project, advising on possible strategic decisions.

To Enhance Transparency and Trust:

- **Comprehensive and Accurate Reporting**: Ensure that all information is accurate and comprehensive, covering all aspects of the project necessary to provide a full picture of its status.
- **Prompt Communication**: Communicate important changes and updates as soon as they occur to maintain stakeholder trust and confidence.

Example of Application

Imagine a large-scale software development project where the project manager issues monthly work performance reports. These reports detail the progress of various development phases, use of budget versus actual spending, adherence to the project timeline, and any newly identified risks or necessary scope adjustments. The reports are distributed via email and also discussed in monthly stakeholder meetings to ensure that all parties are fully informed and able to provide feedback or request further information.

Conclusion

Work performance reports are a fundamental component of effective project communication, providing all stakeholders with critical information necessary to understand the project's status, make informed decisions, and identify areas that require attention or adjustment. By effectively using these reports, project managers can ensure that the project remains transparent, under control, and aligned with its goals. Information management systems are integral to the **Monitor Communications** process in project management, playing a pivotal role in organizing, storing, and retrieving project information efficiently.

These systems support the structured dissemination of information and enhance communication effectiveness, ultimately facilitating better decision-making and project governance.

Importance of Information Management Systems in Monitor Communications

1. **Centralized Information Access**: Information management systems provide a centralized platform where all project information is stored and can be accessed by stakeholders, ensuring that everyone has the latest, most accurate information.
2. **Enhances Transparency**: By maintaining a clear record of communications and decisions, these systems enhance the transparency of the project processes and outcomes.
3. **Improves Efficiency**: Automated tools within these systems can streamline communication processes, reducing the time and effort required to manage and disseminate information.
4. **Facilitates Decision Making**: The availability of real-time data and historical information helps project managers and stakeholders make informed decisions quickly.
5. **Ensures Consistency**: With standardized templates and communication practices embedded within these systems, the consistency of project communications is maintained, reducing errors and misunderstandings.

Common Types of Information Management Systems Used in Projects
1. Project Management Information Systems (PMIS)

- **Description**: A PMIS is a software system that is used to plan, execute, and close project management goals. It integrates information from various areas of the project such as scheduling, communications, resource allocation, and risk management.
- **Support for Communication and Decision-Making**:
  - **Centralized Communication Hub**: Serves as a single point for storing and sharing all communication documents, updates, and reports.
  - **Integrated Tools**: Often includes integrated email, chat functions, and forums to facilitate direct communication among team members and stakeholders.
  - **Real-Time Updates**: Enables real-time updates and alerts to ensure that all project members are aware of changes and new information as soon as they occur.

2. Document Management Systems

- **Description**: These systems manage and store documents, images, and other media files used during the project lifecycle. They support version control, access control, and efficient retrieval of documents.
- **Support for Communication and Decision-Making**:
  - **Document Version Control**: Ensures that all stakeholders are working with the most current versions of documents, preventing confusion and errors.
  - **Access Rights Management**: Controls who can view, edit, or delete documents, which is crucial for maintaining the integrity of project information.
  - **Searchable Archives**: Allows users to quickly find documents and information, significantly reducing the time spent searching for project files.

3. Collaboration Tools

- **Description**: Software tools like Slack, Microsoft Teams, or Asana that enable project teams to collaborate in real-time, share files, manage tasks, and organize discussions via integrated platforms.

- **Support for Communication and Decision-Making**:
  - **Task Tracking and Updates**: Allows for real-time tracking of tasks and project progress, facilitating immediate adjustments and updates.
  - **Integrated Communication Channels**: Provide integrated chat, video call functions, and discussion boards that keep all communications linked to specific tasks or project areas.
  - **Notification Systems**: Automated notifications keep team members informed about deadlines, changes, and new inputs, ensuring continuous alignment and responsiveness.

Conclusion

The integration of robust information management systems such as PMIS, document management systems, and collaboration tools into the Monitor Communications process is essential for maintaining efficient and effective communication across the project. These systems provide the necessary infrastructure to manage large volumes of information and ensure that this information is leveraged to support effective decision-making, ultimately contributing to project success. Effective communication is critical for the success of any project. To ensure that communication efforts are meeting the needs of the project and its stakeholders, it's important to utilize Key Performance Indicators (KPIs). These metrics provide a measurable way to assess the effectiveness of communication strategies and practices within the project.

Common Communication KPIs
1.   Response Time
- **Description**: Measures the speed at which communications are acknowledged or replied to by recipients.
- **Example**: Tracking how quickly project team members respond to emails or requests for information. A shorter response time generally indicates more efficient communications.
- **Measurement**: Calculate the average time taken from the sending of the message to the receipt of a response over a set period.

2.   Stakeholder Satisfaction
- **Description**: Assesses how satisfied stakeholders are with the communication they receive regarding clarity, frequency, relevance, and comprehensiveness.
- **Example**: Using surveys or feedback forms to gauge stakeholder satisfaction after meetings, reports, or updates.
- **Measurement**: Stakeholder satisfaction can be quantitatively measured through Likert scale questions in surveys, where stakeholders rate their satisfaction on various aspects of communication.

3.   Information Accessibility
- **Description**: Measures how easily stakeholders can access the information they need for the project.
- **Example**: Evaluating the effectiveness of the project's information repository, such as a project intranet or management software, in providing easy access to documents and reports.
- **Measurement**: Analyze usage logs of project management tools or document management systems to track access frequency, and conduct stakeholder surveys to ask about their experiences retrieving information.

4. Accuracy of Information

- **Description**: Measures the reliability of the information communicated in terms of correctness and up-to-dateness.
- **Example**: Reviewing the number of corrections or updates required after initial communications are sent out, such as project status updates or reports.
- **Measurement**: Track and analyze the number of issued corrections or clarifications over time as a proportion of total communications.

5. Engagement Levels

- **Description**: Tracks how engaged stakeholders are with communications, which can be an indicator of the communication's relevance and effectiveness.
- **Example**: Monitoring participation rates in meetings, feedback rates on surveys, or interaction levels on project communication platforms.
- **Measurement**: Calculate the percentage of active participation in scheduled communications and feedback mechanisms, or analyze interaction data from project communication tools.

6. Frequency of Communication

- **Description**: Measures whether the agreed-upon or expected frequency of communications is being met.
- **Example**: Checking if weekly updates, monthly newsletters, or daily briefs are occurring as planned.
- **Measurement**: Monitor and record each planned communication instance, noting any deviations from the schedule.

Using Communication KPIs Effectively

To effectively use these KPIs, project managers should:

- **Set Clear Benchmarks**: Establish clear, realistic targets for each KPI based on project requirements and stakeholder expectations.
- **Regular Review and Adjustment**: Regularly review KPI results and compare them against benchmarks. Adjust communication strategies and practices based on findings to continuously improve communication effectiveness.
- **Integrate Feedback into Practices**: Use feedback from stakeholders to refine communication strategies and practices, ensuring they remain aligned with stakeholder needs and project goals.

Conclusion

Communication KPIs are vital tools for assessing the effectiveness of communications within a project. By carefully selecting, measuring, and analyzing these KPIs, project managers can ensure that their communication strategies are effective, that stakeholders are well-informed and satisfied, and that the project has a robust foundation for success. The project involved implementing a new enterprise resource planning (ERP) system across multiple locations of a multinational corporation. The objective was to streamline operations, improve reporting accuracy, and enhance data accessibility across departments in North America, Europe, and Asia.

Communication Challenges Faced

1. **Cultural and Language Barriers**: With team members and stakeholders from various cultural and linguistic backgrounds, ensuring clear and effective communication was challenging.

2. **Time Zone Differences**: Coordinating meetings and updates across multiple time zones required meticulous planning.
3. **Diverse Technological Proficiencies**: Varying levels of comfort and familiarity with digital communication tools among team members affected the consistency of information flow.

Strategies Employed
1. Development of a Comprehensive Communications Management Plan:
- **Tailored Communication Approaches**: Developed a plan that respected cultural nuances and language preferences, including translation services and culturally sensitive communication materials.
- **Scheduled Overlapping Meetings**: Timed weekly meetings during hours that overlapped across time zones to maximize participation.

2. Utilization of Advanced Communication Technologies:
- **Centralized Communication Platform**: Implemented a project management information system (PMIS) like Microsoft Teams to serve as a one-stop-shop for all communications, document storage, and real-time collaboration.
- **Regular Virtual Check-Ins**: Used video conferencing tools to maintain a personal connection and ensure ongoing engagement.

3. Active Listening and Feedback Mechanisms:
- **Regular Surveys and Feedback Sessions**: Conducted to assess the effectiveness of communication strategies and gather input on potential improvements.
- **Open-Door Policy**: Encouraged team members to share concerns and suggestions directly with project management, promoting transparency and trust.

Monitoring and Controlling Communications
- **Performance Metrics**: Established specific communication metrics, such as response times to inquiries and the frequency of updates, to monitor the effectiveness of communications.
- **Audit and Adjustments**: Periodically audited communication practices, using findings to adjust strategies. For example, after noticing a drop in engagement during virtual meetings, interactive sessions with Q&A segments were introduced to boost participation.

Lessons Learned
1. **Flexibility is Key**: The project manager noted that adapting communication strategies in response to feedback and changing circumstances was crucial. What works at one stage of a project may not be effective in another.
2. **Importance of Cultural Sensitivity**: Acknowledging and respecting cultural differences in communication styles and preferences helped in building a more cohesive team.
3. **Proactive Conflict Management**: Early identification and management of communication issues prevented potential misunderstandings and conflicts, saving time and resources.
4. **Investment in Technology**: Investing in appropriate technologies facilitated smoother communication, but required initial and ongoing training to ensure all team members could utilize the tools effectively.
5. **Regular Reviews**: Continuously monitoring communication effectiveness and making necessary adjustments was vital for keeping the team aligned and motivated.

Conclusion

This case study illustrates the complexities involved in managing communications in a large, culturally diverse, multinational project. The strategic use of tailored communication plans, advanced technologies, and active listening led to successful project execution despite the initial challenges. The experiences and insights gained underscore the significance of adaptable, culturally aware, and technology-supported communication strategies in modern project management. Here's a set of practice questions designed to test and reinforce understanding of Project Communications Management processes, key concepts, and their application in real-world project scenarios. These questions are ideal for preparing for the CAPM exam or enhancing project management skills.

Question 1: What is the primary purpose of the Plan Communications Management process?

- A) To ensure all project communications are delivered in written form.
- B) To identify project risks through effective communication.
- C) To develop an appropriate approach and plan for project communications based on stakeholder's information needs.
- D) To document the project's budget constraints.

Correct Answer: C) To develop an appropriate approach and plan for project communications based on stakeholder's information needs.

- **Explanation**: The Plan Communications Management process aims to outline how project communications will be handled. This ensures that every stakeholder receives the right information at the right time and in the right form, facilitating effective decision-making and project execution.

Question 2: Which of the following best describes the use of a communication matrix in project management?

- A) It is used to track the costs associated with project communications.
- B) It outlines what information is communicated, to whom, when, and by which methods.
- C) It is a tool used exclusively for resolving conflicts in project teams.
- D) It schedules the project tasks in alignment with resource availability.

Correct Answer: B) It outlines what information is communicated, to whom, when, and by which methods.

- **Explanation**: A communication matrix is an essential tool for managing project communications. It specifies the communication requirements by detailing the information to be shared, the audience, the timing, and the methods of communication. This ensures that all stakeholders are appropriately informed throughout the project lifecycle.

Question 3: What role does feedback play in the Monitor Communications process?

- A) It is only used at the end of the project.
- B) It has no significant role in project communications.
- C) It is used to make adjustments in communication strategies and improve effectiveness.
- D) It is used to evaluate the project's final deliverables.

Correct Answer: C) It is used to make adjustments in communication strategies and improve effectiveness.

- **Explanation**: Feedback is crucial in the Monitor Communications process as it provides insights into how well communications are being received and understood by stakeholders. This feedback allows project managers to adjust their communication plans and strategies to enhance clarity, ensure stakeholder engagement, and improve the overall effectiveness of communications.

Question 4: Which factor is NOT typically considered when planning project communications?

- A) Cultural differences of stakeholders.
- B) Personal preferences of the project manager.
- C) Technological tools available for communication.
- D) Urgency and importance of the information to be communicated.

Correct Answer: B) Personal preferences of the project manager.

- **Explanation**: When planning project communications, the focus should be on stakeholder needs, the availability of technological tools, and the urgency and importance of the information. The personal preferences of the project manager are not typically a primary consideration, as communications should be designed to best serve the project and its stakeholders.

Question 5: How does effective communication impact project risk management?

- A) Effective communication has no impact on project risk management.
- B) It can increase the likelihood of risks occurring.
- C) It ensures that risk information is promptly shared, enabling proactive risk mitigation.
- D) It only matters when risks have already impacted the project budget.

Correct Answer: C) It ensures that risk information is promptly shared, enabling proactive risk mitigation.

- **Explanation**: Effective communication is essential in risk management because it ensures that all stakeholders, including the project team and management, are aware of potential risks and their impacts. Timely and clear communication about risks allows for quicker decision-making and more effective risk mitigation strategies, reducing the potential negative impacts on the project.

These practice questions and explanations will help enhance understanding of Project Communications Management, ensuring that learners are well-prepared for the CAPM exam and more effective in their project management roles. The concept of a **project communication rhythm** refers to the establishment of a consistent and predictable pattern or schedule of communication activities throughout the project lifecycle. This rhythm helps to ensure that all project stakeholders are regularly informed, engaged, and able to provide timely feedback, which is crucial for the success of the project.

Importance of Project Communication Rhythm

1. **Ensures Regular Updates**: Setting a communication rhythm ensures that information is shared on a regular and predictable basis, preventing information gaps or the buildup of unresolved issues.
2. **Enhances Stakeholder Engagement**: Regular, predictable communications help keep stakeholders engaged and informed about project progress, challenges, and successes.
3. **Builds Trust**: Consistency in communication fosters trust among project team members and stakeholders. They know when to expect updates and feel confident that the project management is transparent and proactive.
4. **Facilitates Better Planning and Response**: A set communication schedule allows stakeholders to plan their schedules to engage more effectively with the project. It also allows time for feedback to be gathered and acted upon in a timely manner.

Establishing an Effective Communication Rhythm
1. Define the Communication Needs

Start by understanding the information needs of various stakeholders. Assess how frequently each stakeholder group requires updates based on their level of involvement and interest in the project. High-impact stakeholders such as project sponsors may need weekly updates, while less directly involved stakeholders might only need monthly or quarterly updates.

2. Establish Regular Status Meetings

Schedule regular status meetings with the project team and key stakeholders. These meetings should occur with consistent frequency (e.g., weekly, bi-weekly) and at a regular time to ensure participants can plan their involvement. Use these meetings to discuss progress, address issues, and gather feedback.

- **Tip**: Always prepare an agenda in advance and circulate it to invitees. This helps ensure that meetings are focused and productive.

3. Develop a Schedule for Progress Reports

Create a timetable for distributing written progress reports that detail what has been achieved since the last report, current issues, and next steps. These reports provide a formal record of project progress and can be tailored to different audience needs.

- **Tip**: Utilize templates for progress reports to maintain consistency in the information provided and to reduce the time spent preparing them.

4. Utilize Dashboards for Real-Time Updates

Implement a project management dashboard that stakeholders can access to view real-time information on project metrics such as schedule adherence, budget status, and key performance indicators. This tool allows stakeholders to check in on project status at their convenience, complementing formal updates.

5. Schedule Stakeholder Updates

Plan regular updates specifically for stakeholders who are not involved in daily project operations but who need periodic assurance that the project is on track. This might include less frequent, but highly detailed, presentations or reports tailored to their specific interests and concerns.

- **Tip**: Always include time for questions and discussion in these updates to ensure that stakeholders have the opportunity to provide feedback or request additional information.

6. Adapt Communication Tools and Channels

Choose the most effective tools and channels for communication based on the preferences and locations of the stakeholders. This may include a mix of emails, project management tools, video conferences, and in-person meetings.

Conclusion

By establishing a regular and predictable project communication rhythm, project managers can maintain a steady flow of information that keeps all stakeholders appropriately informed and engaged. This rhythm not only ensures that stakeholders are up-to-date on project progress but also builds a foundation of trust and transparency critical for project success. Effective communication is critical in managing stakeholder expectations and engagement throughout the lifecycle of a project. It ensures that stakeholders are not only informed but also actively involved in the project, which enhances their commitment and support.

Key Aspects of Communication in Stakeholder Management
Aligning Expectations:

Communication helps to clarify and align the expectations of stakeholders with the project's objectives and deliverables. Regular updates enable stakeholders to understand the project's progress and any adjustments needed, reducing the risk of misalignments or misunderstandings.

Building and Maintaining Trust:

Open and transparent communication builds trust. By consistently sharing accurate and timely information, project managers can foster a trust-based relationship with stakeholders, crucial for project success.

Enhancing Engagement:

Effective communication strategies can increase stakeholder engagement by making them feel valued and part of the project process. Engaged stakeholders are more likely to contribute positively towards project outcomes.

Facilitating Decision Making:

Communication provides the necessary information that stakeholders need to make informed decisions regarding project scope, resource allocation, and strategic direction.

Strategies for Effective Communication with Different Stakeholder Groups
1. Sponsors

- **Tailored Communication**: Customize communication to focus on strategic outcomes, ROI, and project impacts that align with business objectives.
- **Formal Reporting**: Utilize formal communication methods like steering committee presentations and official status reports to provide detailed updates on project progress, risks, and decisions required.
- **Direct Access**: Maintain an open line for direct communication to quickly address any concerns or directives from sponsors.

2. Customers

- **Regular Updates**: Keep customers informed about project progress and developments, especially how these might impact them directly.
- **Feedback Mechanisms**: Implement structured processes for gathering customer feedback on deliverables and overall satisfaction, and use this feedback to tailor project outputs.
- **Customer-Centric Language**: Communicate in a way that focuses on how project outcomes will meet their needs and expectations.

3. Team Members

- **Open and Continuous Communication**: Foster an environment where team members can share information, express concerns, and contribute ideas freely.
- **Clarity on Roles and Responsibilities**: Clearly communicate what is expected from each team member, including how their contributions align with project goals.
- **Recognition and Encouragement**: Regularly acknowledge individual and team efforts and achievements, which motivates and maintains high morale.

4. All Stakeholders

- **Multi-Channel Approach**: Use various communication channels (meetings, emails, project management tools, etc.) to cater to different preferences and ensure the accessibility of information.
- **Inclusivity in Communication**: Ensure that communication practices respect cultural differences and language preferences, which is particularly important in diverse and global projects.
- **Proactive Conflict Resolution**: Address potential conflicts early through direct communication, seeking to understand different perspectives and finding mutually beneficial solutions.

Example of Communication Strategy in Practice

Consider a project to launch a new software product. The project manager might:

- **For Sponsors**: Deliver monthly executive dashboards that highlight key project metrics, upcoming milestones, and critical risks requiring decisions.
- **For Customers**: Host quarterly webinars to demonstrate product features and gather user feedback, supplemented by monthly newsletters detailing project advancements and expected release dates.
- **For Team Members**: Conduct weekly stand-up meetings to track progress, address impediments, and ensure team alignment. Use a project management platform for day-to-day updates and to facilitate collaborative problem-solving.

Conclusion

Effective communication is a cornerstone of successful stakeholder management. By employing strategic communication practices tailored to different stakeholder groups, project managers can effectively align expectations, foster engagement, and navigate the complexities of project dynamics. This proactive approach not only maintains stakeholder support but also significantly enhances the project's potential for success. Documenting and archiving project communications effectively is critical for ensuring that all project information is preserved, organized, and easily accessible for current and future needs. Proper documentation and archiving practices help in maintaining a historical record, assisting in dispute resolution, and providing valuable data for post-project reviews and future projects.

Best Practices for Documenting and Archiving Project Communications
1. Determine What Needs to Be Stored

Identify the types of documents and communications that need to be archived. Common items include:

- **Project Emails**: Correspondence related to project decisions, changes, and updates.
- **Meeting Minutes**: Records of discussions, decisions, and action items from project meetings.
- **Project Reports**: Progress, status, and financial reports.
- **Presentations**: Slides and notes from project presentations and stakeholder briefings.
- **Contractual Documents**: Contracts, agreements, and their amendments.
- **Change Requests**: Documentation of all changes requested, approved, or rejected.

2. Create a Standardized Naming Convention

Develop a consistent naming convention for documents to facilitate easy identification and retrieval. A good naming convention might include:

- **Date**: Place the date in a standard format (YYYY-MM-DD) at the beginning of the file name.
- **Document Type**: Specify the type of document (e.g., MeetingMinutes, ProgressReport, ChangeRequest).
- **Project Identifier**: Use a short code or name that identifies the project.
- **Version Number**: If documents are subject to revisions, include a version number (e.g., v1, v2).

Example: 2024-05-13_MeetingMinutes_ProjectX_v1.pdf

3. Implement an Organizational Structure

Organize the archive in a logical structure that reflects the phases of the project or functional categories. For example, folders could be organized by:

- **Project Phase**: Initiation, Planning, Execution, Monitoring, Closure.
- **Document Type**: Contracts, Communications, Reports, Change Logs.
- **Stakeholder Group**: Internal Team, External Clients, Suppliers.

4. Use Appropriate Storage Solutions

Choose a document management system or digital repository that suits the project's scale and complexity. Consider factors such as:

- **Security**: Ensure the platform is secure and complies with data protection regulations.
- **Accessibility**: Select a system that is accessible to all project stakeholders who need access, considering their geographic locations and devices.
- **Backup and Recovery**: Ensure the system has robust backup and recovery procedures to prevent data loss.

6.   Set Access Controls

Define who can access, modify, or delete documents. Implement access controls in the document management system to enforce these permissions. Consider the following levels:

- **Read-Only**: For stakeholders who need to view documents but should not alter them.
- **Read and Write**: For team members who contribute to document creation and editing.
- **Administrative Access**: For project managers and administrators who manage the repository.

6. Maintain a Document Register

Keep a register or log that tracks the existence and status of all documents, including a brief description, author, creation date, and version history. This register can be invaluable for audits and for ensuring document traceability.

7. Regularly Review and Update Archive Practices

Periodically review the effectiveness of the archiving strategy and make adjustments as needed. This could be triggered by changes in project scope, stakeholder feedback, or new technological solutions.

Conclusion

Effective documentation and archiving of project communications are foundational to good project management. By following these best practices, project managers can ensure that communications are preserved accurately, organized efficiently, and accessible when needed, supporting both current project success and future project endeavors.

X. Project Risk Management:

Plan Risk Management: Purpose and Importance
Purpose of Plan Risk Management

The Plan Risk Management process is fundamental in any project management framework as it prepares the project to handle uncertainties effectively. Its primary purpose is to ensure that the level, type, and visibility of risk management are commensurate with both the risks and the importance of the project to the organization. Essentially, it's about setting the ground rules for how risk management will be conducted throughout the project lifecycle.

Importance of Plan Risk Management

This process is crucial because it provides a structured approach to identifying, assessing, and managing risks, thereby reducing the likelihood and impact of negative events. It fosters a proactive rather than reactive culture within the project team, enhancing decision-making, improving project outcomes, and increasing the likelihood of achieving project objectives. It also ensures that risks are consistently identified, analyzed, and communicated, and that resources are appropriately allocated for risk mitigation.

Key Components of a Risk Management Plan

The risk management plan, a vital output of the Plan Risk Management process, contains several critical components that guide the project team. Let's get into each of these components:

Risk Management Strategy:

This outlines the general approach to managing risks on the project, including the methodologies and tools to be used, reflecting the organization's policies and the project's needs.

Risk Appetite and Thresholds:

Defines the levels of risk the organization is willing to accept before action is necessary. These thresholds help prioritize risk response strategies based on potential impact on the project's objectives.

Roles and Responsibilities:

Details who is responsible for managing specific risks, who makes decisions about risks, and the structure of the risk management team. This clarity helps streamline the risk management process and ensures accountability.

Budgeting for Risk Management Activities:

Allocates specific portions of the project budget for risk management activities, including contingency and management reserves. This ensures that funds are available to address risks as they arise.

Timing of Risk Management Activities:

Specifies when and how frequently risk management processes will be performed throughout the project lifecycle, aligning risk management activities with critical project milestones.

Risk Categories:

Organizes risks into categories (e.g., technical, organizational, external, etc.) to systematically identify and address risks across different areas of the project.

Risk Probability and Impact Scales:

Establishes how the probability and impact of risks will be assessed, often including a matrix to help quantify or qualify risks. This helps in prioritizing risks and determining where to focus management efforts.

Stakeholder Tolerances:

Recognizes the risk tolerances of key stakeholders to ensure that the risk management plan aligns with their expectations and needs.

Reporting Formats:

Determines how risk information will be documented, tracked, and reported to stakeholders, ensuring transparency and that informed decisions can be made throughout the project.

Tracking:

Defines how risks will be monitored and controlled throughout the project, including how changes in risk exposure are managed.

Guidance Provided by the Risk Management Plan

With these components in place, the risk management plan guides the project team in effectively identifying potential risks early on, analyzing their implications, and planning responses that align with the project's objectives and stakeholder expectations. This structured approach to risk management not only mitigates threats but also identifies opportunities, ultimately contributing to the project's success by ensuring that risks are understood and managed in a way that they do not derail critical project goals.

In project management, understanding risk appetite and risk tolerance is crucial for developing an effective risk management plan. These concepts help define how much risk a project or an organization is willing to accept as it pursues its goals, guiding the decision-making process regarding risk assessment, mitigation, and monitoring.

Risk Appetite

Definition: Risk appetite refers to the amount and type of risk that an organization is willing to pursue or retain in order to achieve its objectives. It is essentially a broad-based description of the acceptable level of risk that an organization is prepared to accept before action is deemed necessary.

Example: A technology startup may have a high risk appetite, willing to invest large sums in potentially disruptive but unproven technologies to gain a competitive advantage.

Risk Tolerance

Definition: Risk tolerance is the specific level of risk that an organization can cope with in the course of reaching its objectives. It quantifies the acceptable variation in outcomes related to specific risks. Essentially, it's the operationalization of risk appetite into specific thresholds or limits.

Example: The same technology startup might tolerate a 40% risk of project delays in the development of a new product, beyond which corrective actions must be initiated.

Influence on Risk Management Plan Development
Establishing Risk Management Policies:

Understanding the organization's risk appetite and tolerance helps project managers develop risk management policies that align with these preferences. This includes determining how risks will be identified, assessed, responded to, and monitored.

Risk Assessment Procedures:

Risk appetite and tolerance influence the procedures and tools used for risk assessments. They determine what levels of risk are acceptable and which require immediate attention, guiding the prioritization of risk responses.

Decision-Making Framework:
These concepts help establish a framework for decision-making throughout the project's lifecycle. For instance, if a particular risk exceeds the established tolerance levels but is within the appetite, it might still be accepted with plans for close monitoring.

Development of Risk Responses:
The risk responses—whether to avoid, mitigate, transfer, or accept risks—are developed based on the organization's tolerance and appetite. High-risk tolerance may lead to more aggressive risk responses, whereas low tolerance might push towards more conservative strategies.

Stakeholder Engagement:
Clearly defined risk appetite and tolerance levels ensure that stakeholders are on the same page, reducing conflicts and misunderstandings about risk handling. This helps in maintaining consistent communication and expectations around risk.

Resource Allocation:
They influence how resources are allocated for risk management. Projects with a lower risk tolerance might allocate more resources to risk mitigation practices than those with a higher tolerance.

Example of Application
Imagine a construction project where the company has a moderate risk appetite but a low tolerance for safety risks. The risk management plan would specifically emphasize safety risks, implementing stringent mitigation strategies and allocating substantial resources to safety training and equipment. Financial risks, however, might be managed with a different approach, accepting higher variability in project costs within the defined appetite.

Conclusion
Risk appetite and risk tolerance are foundational elements in the Plan Risk Management process. They provide critical guidelines for how risks are approached and managed throughout the project, ensuring that risk management efforts are aligned with organizational goals and capacities. By clearly understanding and defining these thresholds, project managers can tailor their risk management practices to effectively oversee and control project risks. The **Plan Risk Management** process is vital for establishing a systematic approach to identifying, analyzing, and responding to project risks. It sets the foundation for a risk management framework that guides the entire project team on how risks should be managed throughout the project lifecycle. Understanding the inputs, tools and techniques, and outputs (ITTOs) of this process is essential for effectively integrating risk management into the project planning and execution phases.

Inputs to Plan Risk Management
1. **Project Charter**: Provides high-level information about the project, including objectives, constraints, assumptions, and an initial description of possible risks based on the project's scope and objectives.
2. **Project Management Plan**: Elements of the project management plan, such as the schedule, cost, quality, and resource management plans, inform the risk management planning by providing information about planned approaches, resources, and processes that may influence risk planning.

3. **Stakeholder Register**: Contains information about project stakeholders, including their levels of influence, risk appetites, and particular interests related to risks, which could impact the risk management strategies.
4. **Enterprise Environmental Factors (EEFs)**: Include organizational culture and existing practices that influence risk management planning. This might involve risk attitudes, industry risk data, and risk databases.
5. **Organizational Process Assets (OPAs)**: Provide access to historical information and lessons learned from similar projects, which can guide the development of the risk management plan.

Tools and Techniques for Plan Risk Management

1. **Expert Judgment**: Utilizing the experience and knowledge of project team members, stakeholders, or other subject matter experts to develop the risk management plan. Expertise helps ensure that the plan is comprehensive and robust.
2. **Data Analysis Techniques**: Such as brainstorming, SWOT analysis (Strengths, Weaknesses, Opportunities, and Threats), and assumption analysis, which help in identifying and evaluating potential risks.
3. **Meetings**: Conducting risk management planning meetings involving project team members and stakeholders to discuss and develop the risk management approach, methodologies, and practices to be applied in the project.

Outputs of Plan Risk Management
1. Risk Management Plan:

The primary output of the Plan Risk Management process. This document describes how risk management activities will be structured and performed, covering aspects such as:

- **Risk Strategy**: Defines the general approach to manage risks, tailored to the project's complexity and stakeholders' needs.
- **Methodology**: Outlines the processes for identifying, analyzing, prioritizing, and responding to risks.
- **Roles and Responsibilities**: Details who is responsible for managing specific risks and who participates in the risk management processes.
- **Budgeting**: Allocates funds for risk management activities, including contingency and management reserves.
- **Timing**: Defines when and how often risk management processes will be performed throughout the project lifecycle.
- **Risk Categories**: Provides a structure for risk categorization, which helps in the identification and analysis of risks.
- **Stakeholder Engagement**: Plans for involving stakeholders in the risk management process.
- **Reporting Formats**: Describes how the outcomes of risk management processes will be recorded and communicated.

2. Project Documents Updates:

Various project documents may be updated as a result of the risk management planning, such as stakeholder register updates reflecting newly identified stakeholder information relevant to risk management.

Conclusion

The Plan Risk Management process establishes a critical framework for proactive risk identification, assessment, and response throughout the project. By carefully defining the inputs, employing effective tools and techniques, and generating comprehensive outputs like the Risk Management Plan, project managers can ensure that risks are managed systematically and effectively, enhancing the likelihood of project success. This structured approach not only mitigates potential threats but also capitalizes on opportunities, ultimately contributing to better project outcomes. The Identify Risks process is a continuous activity throughout the project's lifecycle. Its primary role is to determine which risks may impact the project's objectives and to document the characteristics of each risk. This process is crucial because early identification of risks provides the greatest opportunity for risk response planning and allocation of appropriate resources. It also helps in creating a comprehensive risk register, which serves as a fundamental tool in managing known and anticipated risks.

Tools and Techniques for Identifying Project Risks

Several tools and techniques are utilized in the Identify Risks process to ensure a thorough examination of all potential project uncertainties. Here are some of the primary methods:

Documentation Reviews:

This involves examining project documents, including plans, agreements, and communications, to identify inconsistencies or gaps that may indicate risks. Documentation reviews help ensure that all bases are covered and that no assumptions have been made without substantiation.

Brainstorming:

Often conducted with the project team and relevant stakeholders, brainstorming sessions encourage the generation of ideas and potential risks in an uninhibited, free-flowing environment. This technique leverages the collective experience and creativity of the group to identify risks that might not be evident through other methods.

SWOT Analysis:

This analytical tool helps in identifying strengths, weaknesses, opportunities, and threats related to the project. SWOT analysis is particularly useful in strategic risk identification because it encourages the team to view the project from multiple perspectives, thus uncovering potential internal and external risks.

Checklists:

Derived from historical data and lessons learned from previous projects, checklists can be an effective tool for risk identification. They provide a structured way to review common risk factors associated with similar projects.

Interviews:

Conducting interviews with stakeholders, experts, and experienced project participants can uncover risks derived from personal experience and professional expertise. This method provides deep insights and often reveals risks that are not immediately obvious.

Delphi Technique:

This technique involves a series of rounds of anonymous input from experts. Feedback is summarized and redistributed to the group until a consensus on potential risks is reached. The Delphi Technique helps mitigate bias and leverages expert judgment effectively.

Cause-and-Effect Diagrams:

Also known as fishbone or Ishikawa diagrams, these help in identifying the root causes of potential risks. By focusing on different categories such as methods, materials, equipment, and people, this technique can pinpoint specific areas of concern.

Failure Mode and Effect Analysis (FMEA):

This systematic, step-by-step approach helps in identifying possible failure modes in a process or product design and the effects of those failures. It is particularly useful in projects involving complex processes or where high reliability is crucial.

The Importance of Diverse Techniques

Each of these tools and techniques offers a unique angle from which to view the project, providing a comprehensive risk identification phase. By combining these approaches, the project team can ensure a robust and thorough identification process, capturing a wide range of potential risks. This diversity not only improves the quality of risk management but also enhances the project team's ability to respond effectively to unforeseen challenges, ultimately supporting the project's success. A risk register is a fundamental tool in project management, primarily used within the Identify Risks process. It serves as a comprehensive documentation of all potential risks identified throughout the project lifecycle, providing crucial information for risk analysis, response planning, and monitoring.

Purpose of the Risk Register

1. **Documentation of Identified Risks**: To record all identified risks associated with the project, providing a clear overview for project stakeholders and team members.
2. **Foundation for Risk Analysis**: To serve as the basis for subsequent risk analysis, prioritization, and response planning activities.
3. **Tracking and Monitoring**: To facilitate the ongoing tracking and monitoring of risks, their triggers, and the effectiveness of implemented responses.
4. **Communication Tool**: To act as a communication tool that informs all project participants about potential risks and the plans in place to manage them.

Components of a Risk Register

A comprehensive risk register typically includes the following key components:
1. **Risk ID**: A unique identifier for each risk for easy reference.
2. **Risk Description**: A detailed description of the risk to provide clarity on what the risk entails.
3. **Risk Category**: Classifies the risk into predefined categories such as operational, technical, environmental, financial, etc., to facilitate analysis and response strategies.
4. **Potential Causes**: Identifies potential causes or sources of the risk, helping in the development of more effective risk responses.
5. **Likelihood**: An assessment of how likely it is that the risk will occur.
6. **Impact**: An evaluation of the potential impact on the project if the risk materializes.
7. **Priority**: A ranking or prioritization of the risk based on its likelihood and impact, often used to determine the order of addressing risks.

8. **Proposed Responses**: Initial thoughts on how to respond to the risk, such as avoiding, transferring, mitigating, or accepting.
9. **Owner**: The designation of a person or team responsible for managing the risk, including monitoring triggers and implementing responses.
10. **Status**: Current status of the risk (active, monitoring, closed) and updates on the effectiveness of the response strategies.

Evolution of the Risk Register Throughout the Project Lifecycle

1. Initiation Phase: The risk register is initially created with known risks identified during the project charter development. It contains preliminary information mostly focused on high-level risks.

2. Planning Phase: As the project planning progresses, more detailed risk identification sessions (e.g., brainstorming, Delphi technique, SWOT analysis) are conducted, adding more risks to the register. This phase often involves more detailed assessments of likelihood, impact, and initial response planning.

3. Execution Phase: The risk register is continuously updated with new risks as they are identified. Existing risks are reassessed, and their management plans are revised based on actual project conditions and effectiveness of the initial responses.

4. Monitoring and Controlling Phase: Risks in the register are closely monitored, and their status is updated regularly. Information on risk triggers observed, the success of response strategies, and lessons learned are added.

5. Closing Phase: The risk register is reviewed to ensure all risks are closed or transferred. It is also used to document final risk outcomes and lessons learned for future projects.

Best Practices for Maintaining the Risk Register

- **Regular Reviews and Updates**: Ensure the risk register is a living document, regularly reviewed and updated throughout the project.
- **Stakeholder Involvement**: Engage various stakeholders in the risk identification and updating process to gain diverse perspectives and enhance the completeness of the risk register.
- **Clear Definitions**: Maintain clear and consistent definitions of risk likelihood, impact, and priority scales to ensure uniformity in risk assessment across the project team.

Conclusion

The risk register is an essential component of effective risk management in projects, providing a structured and systematic approach to identifying, analyzing, and responding to potential risks. Proper maintenance and continuous updating of the risk register are crucial for the dynamic environment of projects, ensuring that risks are managed proactively and effectively. The **Risk Breakdown Structure (RBS)** is a fundamental tool in project risk management, particularly useful during the **Identify Risks** process. An RBS is essentially a hierarchical decomposition of risks that could impact the project, organized by risk categories and subcategories. It is similar to the Work Breakdown Structure (WBS) used for project tasks but focuses specifically on potential risks.

Concept of Risk Breakdown Structure (RBS)

An RBS helps in structuring and categorizing risks into manageable and understandable groups. It usually starts with broad categories at the highest level and breaks down into more specific risks at lower levels. Common top-level categories might include:

- **Technical Risks**: Concerns related to technology implementation, design challenges, or technical performance.

- **Organizational Risks**: Relate to resource allocation, funding, prioritization, or organizational changes.
- **External Risks**: Include regulatory changes, market fluctuations, or environmental impacts.
- **Project Management Risks**: Associated with scheduling, planning, compliance, or communication.

Each of these categories is then further divided into subcategories to provide a detailed view of potential risks.

Application of RBS in the Identify Risks Process
Systematic Categorization and Organization of Risks

1. **Framework for Identification**: RBS provides a structured framework that ensures a systematic approach to identifying risks. By examining each category and subcategory, project managers and the team can comprehensively consider all possible areas of risk, reducing the chances of overlooking significant issues.
2. **Facilitates Brainstorming**: During risk identification meetings, the RBS can guide the brainstorming process, ensuring that discussions cover a wide range of areas. Teams can systematically go through each category and brainstorm potential risks, making the process thorough and structured.
3. **Improves Communication**: When discussing risks with stakeholders or team members, an RBS helps in communicating the types and areas of risk in a clear and organized manner. This aids in understanding and facilitates more targeted discussions.

Facilitating Comprehensive Risk Identification

1. **Complete Coverage**: By using an RBS, project managers are more likely to achieve complete coverage of all potential risks, from the most common to those that are less obvious but could have significant impacts.
2. **Prioritization and Assessment**: Once risks are identified and categorized within the RBS, they can be prioritized more easily. Risks within the same category can be compared and assessed in terms of their likelihood and impact, aiding in the efficient allocation of resources towards risk mitigation.
3. **Tracking and Monitoring**: RBS allows for better tracking and monitoring of risks throughout the project lifecycle. As the project progresses, the RBS can be updated to reflect new risks or changes in existing risk conditions.

Example of RBS Application

Consider a project to develop a new software product. The RBS might include categories such as:

- **Technical Risks**: Subcategories might include new technology integration, performance risks, or compatibility issues.
- **Project Management Risks**: Subcategories could cover scope creep, stakeholder engagement, or inaccurate effort estimation.
- **External Risks**: This could include competitive risks, market acceptance, or regulatory changes.

For each category and subcategory, specific risks are identified, such as "Integration of third-party services may lead to data privacy issues" under technical risks.

Conclusion

The Risk Breakdown Structure (RBS) is a powerful tool in the Identify Risks process of project management, ensuring a comprehensive, systematic approach to risk identification. By categorizing risks into a structured hierarchy, project managers can more effectively identify, assess, and manage risks, ultimately leading to better project outcomes and enhanced risk mitigation strategies. In project management, effectively identifying risks is critical for mitigating potential problems and seizing opportunities. Various information gathering techniques are employed to unearth these risks, each serving a unique purpose and providing different insights into potential project pitfalls or challenges. Let's explore three significant techniques: interviews, root cause analysis, and assumption analysis.

1. Interviews

Application: Interviews involve structured or semi-structured discussions with project stakeholders, including team members, project sponsors, clients, and experts. These discussions are aimed at gaining insights based on personal experience, expertise, and the stakeholder's unique perspective on the project.

Example: In a software development project, conducting interviews with the development team, project managers, and end-users can help identify risks related to technical challenges, user requirements not being met, or potential delays in delivery. For instance, developers might highlight potential integration issues with existing systems that non-technical stakeholders may overlook.

2. Root Cause Analysis

Application: Root cause analysis is used to explore the underlying reasons behind potential risks or problems. It involves identifying primary and secondary causes of risks and is often visualized through tools like fishbone diagrams or the '5 Whys' technique.

Example: In a construction project, if there is a risk of project delays, root cause analysis could be used to trace back to potential causes such as delayed material deliveries, inadequate manpower, or weather conditions. For instance, asking "why" repeatedly might reveal that the real threat is a single supplier's reliability, prompting the exploration of alternative suppliers or contingency plans.

3. Assumption Analysis

Application: Assumption analysis involves scrutinizing the assumptions made during the planning phase of the project. It's critical to identify and test these assumptions because they can be sources of major risks if proved incorrect.

Example: In an international expansion project for a retail chain, assumption analysis might involve questioning assumptions about customer behavior in a new market. For instance, assuming that customers in a new country will have the same preferences as those in the home market might be risky. Detailed market analysis and pilot testing could be used to validate or invalidate these assumptions, thus avoiding costly missteps in product offerings.

Combining Techniques for Comprehensive Risk Identification

These techniques should not be used in isolation but rather combined to provide a multi-faceted view of the project's risk landscape. Interviews can provide initial insights and personal opinions, root cause analysis can delve deeper into the identified issues to find underlying causes, and assumption analysis can challenge the foundational beliefs of the project plan, uncovering hidden risks.

By employing these techniques, project managers can ensure a more thorough and proactive approach to risk management. This approach not only helps in identifying risks early but also enriches the project planning and execution strategy, leading to higher chances of project success and sustainability. The Perform Qualitative Risk Analysis process is a critical step in project risk management, enabling project teams to prioritize risks based on their likelihood of occurrence and potential impact on project objectives. This process helps determine which risks require immediate attention, which can be monitored, and how resources should be allocated for risk mitigation.

Significance of the Process

1. **Prioritization of Risks**: By assessing risks qualitatively, project managers can prioritize them according to their potential impact and likelihood, focusing attention and resources on managing the most significant risks.
2. **Efficient Resource Allocation**: It helps in efficiently allocating limited resources by focusing on high-priority risks, thus optimizing the risk management efforts.
3. **Informs Decision Making**: The process provides crucial information that helps project managers make informed decisions about risk responses and contingency planning.
4. **Enhances Project Planning**: Understanding which risks pose the greatest threat to project objectives allows for better planning and can improve project outcomes.

Key Steps in Conducting a Qualitative Risk Analysis
1. Risk Identification

- **Description**: Compile a comprehensive list of potential risks using inputs from the risk register prepared during the Identify Risks process.
- **Tools**: Use documentation reviews, information gathering techniques (brainstorming, Delphi technique, interviews), and checklists.

2. Risk Categorization

- **Description**: Organize the identified risks into categories (e.g., operational, financial, technological) to help analyze related risks collectively and identify areas of the project most exposed to risk.
- **Tools**: Risk breakdown structure (RBS) or similar categorization tools.

3. Assessment of Probability and Impact

- **Description**: Evaluate each identified risk for its likelihood of occurrence and the extent of its potential impact on the project's objectives.
- **Tools**: Probability and impact matrix, where risks are rated on predefined scales (e.g., high, medium, low).

4. Risk Prioritization

- **Description**: Combine the probability and impact ratings to prioritize the risks. This helps in determining which risks need detailed quantitative analysis and immediate action.
- **Tools**: Risk Data Quality Assessment to evaluate the degree to which the data about risks is useful for risk management.

5. Documentation of Results

- **Description**: Document the outcomes of the qualitative risk analysis in the risk register update, including the probability, impact, and priority level of each risk.
- **Tools**: Updated risk register and reports that outline the findings from the analysis.

6. Development of Risk Urgency Assessment

- **Description**: Assess and document the urgency of each risk, considering how quickly the risk might affect the project, to determine the timing of risk responses.
- **Tools**: Risk urgency assessments which may consider time sensitivity of risk responses and windows of opportunity.

Example of Qualitative Risk Analysis Application

Consider a project to develop a new software application where risks include technological challenges, staffing issues, and budget constraints. Through qualitative risk analysis:

- **Technological risks** (e.g., integration difficulties) might be rated high probability and high impact because of potential significant delays and cost overruns.
- **Staffing risks** (e.g., difficulty hiring qualified developers) might be rated medium probability but high impact, affecting project quality and timelines.
- **Budget risks** (e.g., unexpected cost increases) could be low probability but high impact, potentially jeopardizing the project's financial viability.

These evaluations allow the project team to focus their efforts on developing strong response strategies for technological and staffing risks first, while monitoring budget risks for any changes in their probability or impact.

Conclusion

Perform Qualitative Risk Analysis is a foundational process in project risk management, providing the insights necessary to prioritize risks and plan effective mitigation strategies. By understanding the potential impact and likelihood of each risk, project teams can focus their efforts where they are most needed, enhancing the project's chance of success. The **Probability and Impact Matrix** is a fundamental tool used in the **Perform Qualitative Risk Analysis** process of project management. This matrix helps project teams evaluate and prioritize risks based on the likelihood of their occurrence and the potential impact on project objectives should they occur. This assessment is crucial for determining which risks require more immediate attention and resources, facilitating effective risk response planning.

Purpose of the Probability and Impact Matrix

1. **Risk Prioritization**: Helps in categorizing risks based on their severity, enabling project managers to focus attention and resources on the most critical risks.
2. **Facilitates Decision Making**: Provides a visual and systematic way to view the potential risks in terms of their probability and impact, aiding in more informed decision-making regarding risk responses.
3. **Enhances Risk Communication**: Offers a clear and concise format to communicate risks and their potential effects to stakeholders, improving understanding and support for mitigation strategies.

Use of the Probability and Impact Matrix
Constructing the Matrix

The matrix is typically structured with probability on one axis (e.g., from Low to High) and impact on the other axis (e.g., from Low to High). Each axis is often divided into three to five levels, depending on the desired granularity:

- **Probability**: Might be categorized as Rare, Unlikely, Possible, Likely, and Almost Certain.
- **Impact**: Could be rated as Negligible, Minor, Moderate, Major, and Catastrophic.

Each risk identified during the risk identification process is placed within this matrix according to its assessed probability and impact.

Mapping Likelihood and Consequence

1. **Assessing Each Risk**: Each identified risk is evaluated for how likely it is to occur and what the potential impact would be if it did occur. This assessment can be based on historical data, expert judgment, and available project information.
2. **Placing Risks on the Matrix**: Risks are plotted on the matrix according to their assessed probability and impact. This visual placement helps in immediately identifying which risks are the most severe (high probability and high impact).

Determining Attention and Resources

- **High Priority (High-High)**: Risks in this category have both a high probability of occurring and a high impact on project success. These are the top-priority risks for which immediate action plans are required.
- **Moderate Priority (High-Low or Low-High)**: Risks that have either a high probability of occurrence but low impact, or low probability but high impact. These require careful monitoring and may need proactive planning.
- **Lower Priority (Low-Low)**: Risks that are both unlikely to occur and would have minimal impact if they did. These risks may require minimal attention and are often accepted or monitored with no immediate action.

Example of Application

Consider a construction project where a risk identified is the potential delay in delivery of critical building materials. If assessed, the delay might be "Likely" to happen (due to ongoing supply chain issues) and could have a "Major" impact on the project schedule. This risk would be placed in the high-priority section of the matrix, signaling the need for urgent development of mitigation strategies, such as securing an alternative supplier or ordering materials well in advance.

Conclusion

The Probability and Impact Matrix is a key analytical tool in qualitative risk analysis, enabling project managers to systematically prioritize risks based on their potential impact on project objectives and their likelihood of occurrence. By effectively using this tool, project managers can ensure that resources and efforts are focused where they are most needed, thereby enhancing the project's ability to achieve its goals despite uncertainties. In the Perform Qualitative Risk Analysis process, assessing the quality and urgency of risk data is crucial. These assessments help project managers determine the reliability of the risk information and prioritize risks based on their immediacy. Let's delve into two primary techniques: risk data quality assessment and risk urgency assessment.

1. Risk Data Quality Assessment

Application: This technique evaluates the extent to which the data about risks is accurate, reliable, and complete. High-quality risk data is crucial for making informed decisions regarding which risks may require immediate attention and which may be monitored over time.

Example: In a large-scale infrastructure project, risk data quality assessment might involve evaluating the source of information about potential geological risks. If the data comes from a thorough geological survey conducted by experienced professionals, it would be considered reliable. However, if the data is based on outdated studies or second-hand information, its quality might be questioned, leading to further investigations or a new survey.

Key Criteria for Risk Data Quality Assessment:
- **Accuracy**: Is the information correct and reflective of the real situation?
- **Credibility**: How reliable is the source of the information?
- **Timeliness**: Is the information up-to-date?
- **Completeness**: Does the data cover all necessary aspects of the risk?

2. Risk Urgency Assessment

Application: This technique assesses how soon a risk may impact a project, considering factors that might accelerate its timing. This urgency assessment is crucial for prioritizing risks that require immediate response to prevent negative impacts on the project.

Example: In a technology upgrade project, if a key piece of software is scheduled to lose vendor support within the next six months, a risk urgency assessment would classify this as a high-priority risk due to the immediate need for action—either upgrading the software or securing extended support to mitigate potential disruptions.

Key Factors in Risk Urgency Assessment:
- **Time sensitivity**: Does the risk have a deadline or a window of occurrence?
- **Warning signs**: Are there early indicators that might signal the risk is becoming imminent?
- **Risk velocity**: How quickly can the risk impact the project once it occurs?

Impact of These Assessments on Project Management

By employing these assessments, project managers can enhance their understanding of the risks' nature and prepare more effectively. Risk data quality assessment ensures that the decisions are made based on solid, reliable data, while risk urgency assessment helps in prioritizing risks that could derail the project if not addressed promptly.

Together, these techniques allow project managers to allocate resources efficiently, focus on mitigating the most critical and immediate risks, and enhance overall project decision-making. This strategic approach to risk management not only helps in safeguarding the project outcomes but also contributes to the more effective use of time and resources, ensuring that the project remains on track and within its set goals. The Perform Quantitative Risk Analysis process is a crucial part of project risk management, focusing on numerically analyzing the potential effects of identified risks on overall project objectives. This process uses quantitative techniques to predict the likelihood and impact of risks, providing a more precise understanding of risks compared to qualitative methods.

Role of Quantitative Risk Analysis

1. **Objective Risk Assessment**: It quantifies the potential impact of risks on project objectives, particularly the project schedule, cost, and scope, enabling more informed decision-making.
2. **Improved Decision Making**: By providing a numerical basis for decision making, it helps project managers choose between different options with a clear understanding of their potential risk implications.
3. **Better Risk Response Planning**: Helps in planning more effective risk responses by predicting their potential effectiveness in mitigating risk impacts.
4. **Enhanced Stakeholder Confidence**: Quantitative data can improve stakeholders' confidence in the project's risk management approach by demonstrating a thorough analysis of potential risks.

Primary Tools and Techniques in Quantitative Risk Analysis
1. Sensitivity Analysis

- **Description**: Sensitivity analysis helps determine which risks have the most potential impact on project outcomes. It involves varying the values of uncertain project variables to see how these changes could impact the project's objectives.
- **Application**: Often represented visually through a tornado diagram, which shows the effect of changing one variable at a time while keeping others constant, highlighting which variables (risks) have the largest impact on project objectives.

2. Monte Carlo Simulation

- **Description**: This technique uses computerized modeling to simulate thousands of possible outcomes of the project based on the risks identified. Each variable (such as time, cost, or resource quantities) is assigned a probability distribution, and the simulation randomly selects different values to see how these affect the project.
- **Application**: Provides probability distributions of possible project outcomes (e.g., total project cost or completion date), allowing project managers to see the likelihood of meeting specific project objectives and to prepare for various scenarios.

3. Decision Tree Analysis

- **Description**: Decision tree analysis provides a graphical representation of decisions and their possible consequences, including chance event outcomes, resource costs, and utilities.
- **Application**: It is used to choose between several courses of action by factoring in the risks, rewards, and probabilities associated with each path, enabling a calculated decision-making process based on expected outcomes.

4. Expected Monetary Value Analysis (EMV)

- **Description**: EMV is calculated by multiplying the value of each possible outcome by its probability of occurrence and adding together all these values.
- **Application**: Useful in decision-making where outcomes carry financial risks and rewards, helping to quantify and compare different risk scenarios.

Example of Quantitative Risk Analysis Application

Consider a construction project with a tight deadline. A Monte Carlo simulation might be employed to assess the probability of meeting the deadline based on several risks such as weather delays, supply chain disruptions, or labor shortages. The output could show that there is only a 70% chance of meeting the deadline under current conditions. Based on this, sensitivity analysis might be conducted to determine which factors have the most significant impact on the schedule, leading to targeted risk mitigation strategies, such as contracting additional suppliers or increasing labor resources during critical phases.

Conclusion

Perform Quantitative Risk Analysis provides project managers and stakeholders with a numerical and probabilistic understanding of risks and their impacts. By employing sophisticated tools and techniques such as sensitivity analysis and Monte Carlo simulations, project teams can gain insights into the most significant risks, tailor their risk response strategies effectively, and enhance their ability to meet project objectives despite uncertainties. The concept of **Expected Monetary Value (EMV)** is a vital tool in the **Perform Quantitative Risk Analysis** process of project management. EMV is used to quantify the potential financial impact of risks on project outcomes. It helps project managers make informed decisions on whether the cost of implementing a risk response is justified by the potential benefit of avoiding the risk or mitigating its impact.

Understanding Expected Monetary Value (EMV)

EMV is a statistical technique used to calculate the average outcome when the future includes scenarios that may or may not happen (i.e., it incorporates the probability of various outcomes). This calculation helps in assessing the overall impact of risks on the project's budget and timeline.

Calculation of EMV

EMV is calculated using the following formula:

EMV=(Probability of the Risk Occurring)×(Monetary Impact of the Risk)EMV=(Probability of the Risk Occurring)×(Monetary Impact of the Risk)

Where:

- **Probability of the Risk Occurring** is a percentage that represents how likely it is that a given risk will occur.
- **Monetary Impact of the Risk** is the estimated financial impact if the risk does materialize.

The result gives a single monetary value that represents the expected financial impact of a risk adjusted for its likelihood of occurring.

Example of EMV Calculation

Suppose there is a risk that a key component delivery might be delayed, causing a project delay that could lead to a penalty of $10,000. If the probability of this delay is assessed at 20%, the EMV would be calculated as follows:

EMV=20%×$10,000=$2,000EMV=20%×$10,000=$2,000

This means that the expected cost to the project from this risk, considering the probability of occurrence, is $2,000.

Application of EMV in Project Management
Risk Assessment and Prioritization

EMV provides a quantitative method to compare risks and prioritize them based on their potential financial impacts. Risks with higher EMV values might require more attention or more robust response strategies compared to those with lower EMV values.

Informing Risk Response Decisions

By calculating the EMV of risks, project managers can make more informed decisions about where to allocate resources for risk responses. For example:

- If the cost of a risk response (e.g., paying for expedited shipping to avoid delays) is less than the EMV of the risk, it might be financially prudent to implement the response.
- Conversely, if the response costs more than the EMV, it might be more cost-effective to accept the risk or to choose a less expensive mitigation strategy.

Budgeting for Contingencies

EMV can also help in budgeting for contingencies. By summing the EMV of various project risks, project managers can estimate the total financial impact of potential risks and set aside a contingency reserve appropriately sized to cover these risks.

Conclusion

Expected Monetary Value (EMV) is a powerful tool in quantitative risk analysis, providing a clear, financially quantified perspective on the potential impacts of project risks. This method supports project managers in making data-driven decisions regarding risk responses and budget allocations, thereby enhancing the project's chances of success in the face of uncertainties. Through the effective use of EMV, projects can better manage financial exposures and ensure more accurate and effective planning and execution. Decision tree analysis is a potent tool employed in the Perform Quantitative Risk Analysis process of project management. This technique aids in making calculated decisions by systematically analyzing the various possible outcomes, their associated risks, probabilities, and impacts. Its core purpose is to assist project managers in visualizing and understanding the consequences of different decision paths in a structured and straightforward manner.

Use of Decision Tree Analysis

Decision trees are particularly useful for complex decisions that involve multiple stages and potential outcomes. They provide a graphical representation of choices, risks, outcomes, and their respective probabilities, making it easier to comprehend the risk-return trade-offs of each potential decision.

How Decision Trees Work

A decision tree is constructed from a root node (the initial decision point), branches (representing possible actions or outcomes), and leaf nodes (representing the final outcomes). Each branch of the decision tree has a probability and an outcome or payoff associated with it, allowing project managers to evaluate the expected values of different courses of action.

Application of Decision Trees in Project Management

Project managers can use decision tree analysis to weigh the costs, benefits, and likelihoods of various risk scenarios. Here's how they can apply this tool:

1. **Defining the Decision Points**: Start by identifying the key decisions that need to be made. This could involve choosing between different technological solutions, methods of project execution, or response strategies for identified risks.
2. **Identifying Possible Outcomes**: For each decision point, outline the possible outcomes. These might include successful implementation, partial success with some issues, failure, or encountering specific risks.
3. **Assigning Probabilities and Costs/Benefits**: Each outcome is assigned a probability based on past data, expert judgment, or statistical analysis. Additionally, costs or benefits associated with each outcome are estimated to calculate potential payoffs.
4. **Calculating Expected Monetary Value (EMV)**: For each branch of the decision tree, multiply the cost/benefit by the probability to derive the Expected Monetary Value. This calculation is pivotal as it provides a quantifiable measure to compare different decisions.

Example of Decision Tree Usage

Consider a project manager overseeing a new product development project. They might use a decision tree to decide whether to develop a new feature. The decision points would be to develop or not develop the feature. Outcomes might include high consumer acceptance or low acceptance, with associated probabilities and estimated financial returns. By calculating the EMV for each path, the project manager can visually and quantitatively assess which decision yields the highest expected return, taking into account the risk of low acceptance.

Optimizing Risk Response Strategy

Decision trees enable project managers to not just choose between risk responses but to strategically analyze the cascade of consequences that each decision might entail. This approach helps in mapping out a risk response strategy that optimizes the outcomes in terms of risk minimization and benefit maximization.

By providing a clear and structured way to evaluate complex decisions, decision tree analysis is invaluable in helping project managers navigate the uncertainty inherent in projects. It supports making informed, data-driven decisions that align with the project's objectives and risk appetite. The Plan Risk Responses process is a crucial stage in project risk management, where strategies are developed to address identified threats and opportunities. This process aims to minimize the potential impacts of risks on project objectives and capitalize on opportunities to enhance project outcomes.

Key Inputs

1. **Risk Register**: The primary input for this process, containing detailed information about all identified risks, including their descriptions, categories, root causes, likelihood, impacts, and other relevant details.
2. **Risk Management Plan**: This document provides the approaches, tools, and data sources that will be used to manage risk throughout the project. It includes methodologies, roles and responsibilities, budgeting for risk management activities, and timing of risk management activities.
3. **Project Management Plan**: Provides overall project context, including scope, schedule, cost baselines, and other management plans that could influence the risk response strategies.
4. **Results of Qualitative and Quantitative Risk Analysis**:
   - **Qualitative Risk Analysis Results**: Offer insights into the priority of risks based on their likelihood and impact, helping to determine which risks need focused response strategies.
   - **Quantitative Risk Analysis Results**: Provide probabilistic information about risks, including their potential cost and schedule impacts, which aids in understanding the severity of risks and the extent of responses required.

Key Outputs

1. Risk Response Plan:

The primary output, detailing specific strategies for dealing with each identified risk. Strategies might include:

- **Avoid**: Changing project plan elements to eliminate the threat or protect project objectives from its impact.
- **Mitigate**: Taking action to reduce the probability of occurrence or impact of the risk.
- **Transfer**: Outsourcing the risk to a third party who can manage the risk better.
- **Exploit**: Ensuring the opportunities are realized.
- **Enhance**: Increasing the probability of positive events.
- **Accept**: Acknowledging the risk and not taking any action unless the risk occurs.
- **Contingency Plans**: Plans that will be executed if certain identified risks occur.

2. Updated Risk Register:

The risk register is updated with the chosen risk response strategies, assigned risk owners, and any new risks identified during the risk response planning process.

3. **Project Management Plan Updates**: Changes required in the project management plan to accommodate the risk response strategies.
4. **Change Requests**: Proposals for changes to the project management plan, which might include requests for changes in schedule, budget allocations for risk responses, or changes in project scope.

Influence of Qualitative and Quantitative Risk Analysis on Risk Response Planning

The results from qualitative and quantitative risk analysis critically inform the development of risk response plans in several ways:

- **Prioritization**: Qualitative analysis helps prioritize risks, ensuring that resources and efforts are focused on the most significant risks. This helps in deciding which risks to address with detailed strategies.
- **Resource Allocation**: Quantitative analysis provides detailed data on the potential impacts of risks on project objectives, guiding how resources are allocated to risk responses. Higher impact risks might require more robust response strategies or more resources.
- **Strategy Development**: By understanding both the likelihood and potential impact of risks (from qualitative and quantitative analysis), project managers can develop more effective risk response strategies. For example, a risk with a high impact but low likelihood might be best managed with a contingency plan rather than immediate mitigation.

Example of Application

In a large infrastructure project, qualitative analysis identifies a critical risk of regulatory approval delays, while quantitative analysis shows a potential project delay of six months if this occurs. The project manager decides to mitigate this risk by hiring a consultant specializing in regulatory affairs to expedite the approval process. This response is documented in the Risk Response Plan, and the Risk Register is updated accordingly.

Conclusion

The Plan Risk Responses process is integral to project risk management, with inputs from risk analysis phases playing a pivotal role in shaping effective risk response strategies. By carefully analyzing these inputs, project managers can ensure that their response strategies are both effective and aligned with the project's needs and resources. Risk management involves identifying potential risks and implementing strategies to handle them effectively. These strategies vary depending on whether the risk poses a threat or presents an opportunity. Below are the four primary risk response strategies for threats and the corresponding strategies for opportunities, along with examples and considerations for their selection.

Risk Response Strategies for Threats
1. Avoid

- **Description**: Taking actions to remove the threat entirely, typically by eliminating its causes or changing aspects of the project where the risk occurs.
- **Example**: Changing a project supplier to avoid the risk of poor service delivery from a less reliable one.
- **Considerations**: Feasibility of completely avoiding the risk, potential impact on project scope or objectives.

2. Transfer

- **Description**: Shifting the impact of a risk to a third party, along with the ownership of the response.
- **Example**: Buying insurance to transfer the financial risk of project equipment damage or outsourcing complex tasks to reduce the risk of non-compliance with specialized regulations.
- **Considerations**: Cost of transferring the risk versus the cost of retaining it, reliability of the third party.

3. Mitigate

- **Description**: Reducing the probability or impact of the threat.
- **Example**: Conducting additional quality assurance checks to reduce the risk of software bugs in a new tech product.
- **Considerations**: Cost-effectiveness of mitigation activities, potential reduction in risk, and remaining residual risk.

4. Accept

- **Description**: Acknowledging the risk without taking any action to avoid, transfer, or mitigate it, often because the risk is deemed unlikely or its impact is minimal.
- **Example**: Accepting the risk that a low-cost material may be out of stock and having a minor impact on the project schedule.
- **Considerations**: Cost of responding to the risk versus the impact of the risk occurring, readiness to handle the consequences.

Risk Response Strategies for Opportunities
1. Exploit

- **Description**: Ensuring the opportunity is realized by adding resources or changing project aspects to make certain the opportunity is captured.
- **Example**: Adding more resources to a project task that is under budget and ahead of schedule to further accelerate project completion.
- **Considerations**: Availability of resources, potential benefits, and alignment with project objectives.

2. Enhance

- **Description**: Increasing the likelihood or the positive impacts of an opportunity.
- **Example**: Improving team training to enhance the likelihood of finishing ahead of schedule.
- **Considerations**: Cost and effort required to enhance the opportunity, probability of success.

3. Share

- **Description**: Allocating some or all of the ownership of an opportunity to a third party who is better positioned to capture the benefit, usually in exchange for sharing the gains.
- **Example**: Partnering with another organization to co-develop a new technology to market it more rapidly.
- **Considerations**: Trust and reliability of the partner, terms of sharing benefits.

4. Accept

- **Description**: Being willing to take advantage of the opportunity if it arises but not actively pursuing it.
- **Example**: Choosing not to alter project scope to integrate a new technology but being open to using it if it becomes easy to implement.
- **Considerations**: Impact of the opportunity, resource availability, other priorities.

Factors Influencing Strategy Selection

The selection of an appropriate risk response strategy depends on several factors:

- **Risk Impact and Probability**: The higher the impact and probability, the more aggressive the risk response strategy should be.
- **Resource Availability**: The availability of resources (budget, time, personnel) can limit or enable certain risk responses.
- **Project Objectives and Constraints**: The overall project objectives and existing constraints can determine which risk responses are viable.
- **Stakeholder Risk Appetite**: The willingness of stakeholders to tolerate risk influences whether risks should be avoided, mitigated, transferred, or accepted.
- **Cost vs. Benefit**: The cost of implementing a risk response should be justified by the expected benefit in terms of reduced risk or enhanced opportunities.

Understanding and applying these strategies effectively allows project managers to handle uncertainties proactively and strategically, enhancing the likelihood of project success. In project management, a risk owner is an individual who is assigned the responsibility for managing a specific risk throughout its lifecycle. The designation of a risk owner is a critical aspect of effective risk management because it ensures clear accountability and fosters prompt and precise actions toward risk mitigation. Risk owners are typically members of the project team with the appropriate skills, knowledge, and authority to take meaningful action on the risks they are assigned.

Responsibilities of Risk Owners

Risk owners play a pivotal role in the Implement Risk Responses process. Their responsibilities encompass a range of activities crucial for the effective management of risks:

1. **Planning Risk Responses**: Developing strategies and specific action plans to address the risks they own. This includes selecting and prioritizing risk response measures based on the severity and impact of the risk.
2. **Implementing Risk Responses**: Executing the risk response strategies according to plan. This involves coordinating with other team members and possibly external stakeholders to ensure the response is implemented effectively.
3. **Monitoring and Controlling Risks**: Continuously tracking the risk and the effectiveness of the response strategies. This includes updating risk assessments and response plans as project conditions change.
4. **Communicating Risk Status**: Keeping all relevant stakeholders informed about the status of risks and the outcomes of response strategies. Effective communication ensures that all parties are aware of risk impacts and are prepared to take additional actions if necessary.

Assignment of Risk Owners

Risk owners are typically assigned during the risk planning phase, often as a part of the risk analysis and risk response planning processes. Here's how risk owners are generally assigned:

Identifying Appropriate Personnel:

The assignment is based on an individual's specific expertise, role within the project, or influence over the risk area. For instance, a technical lead might be assigned to own a risk related to technological implementation, while a finance manager might own a financial risk.

Consideration of Authority and Responsibility:

It is crucial that the assigned risk owner has the authority to make decisions and access resources needed to manage the risk. This alignment ensures that the risk owner can implement response strategies effectively.

Approval by Project Management:

The assignment of risk owners is typically approved by the project manager or the project management team to ensure alignment with overall project objectives and resource allocation.

Key Activities Performed by Risk Owners

To ensure effective implementation of risk response plans, risk owners engage in several key activities:

- **Developing Detailed Response Plans**: Articulating specific steps, resources needed, and timelines for response actions.
- **Executing Response Actions**: Mobilizing resources, coordinating tasks, and adjusting plans in response to project dynamics and effectiveness of initial risk responses.
- **Regular Monitoring and Review**: Assessing the status of the risk and the effectiveness of the response over time, adjusting the response as needed.
- **Stakeholder Engagement**: Communicating regularly with other project stakeholders to ensure transparency and gather input that may refine risk response efforts.

By effectively fulfilling these roles, risk owners contribute significantly to reducing the negative impacts of risks on the project while maximizing potential opportunities. This level of dedicated focus helps maintain project stability and ensures that risk management remains a dynamic and integral part of the project management process. Residual risks are those risks that remain after planned risk responses have been implemented. They represent the exposure that still exists after all mitigative actions have been taken. Understanding and managing residual risks are crucial aspects of comprehensive risk management in projects.

Significance of Residual Risks

1. **Continued Risk Exposure**: Even after the best efforts to manage significant risks, residual risks may still pose threats to the project's objectives, necessitating ongoing monitoring and management.
2. **Informed Decision Making**: Awareness of residual risks helps project managers and stakeholders make informed decisions about whether further action is needed or if the remaining risk level is acceptable.
3. **Resource Allocation**: Understanding the magnitude and potential impact of residual risks helps in allocating resources efficiently for continued risk monitoring or additional mitigation strategies if necessary.
4. **Compliance and Reporting**: In many industries, documenting and reporting residual risks is a compliance requirement, ensuring transparency and systematic risk management.

Identifying and Managing Residual Risks
1.   Risk Assessment Review
- **Process**: After initial risk responses are implemented, review each risk again to assess the effectiveness of the response and identify any remaining risk exposure.
- **Tools**: Use updated risk assessments, including both qualitative and quantitative methods, to evaluate how much of the risk has been mitigated and what portion remains as residual risk.

2. Documentation
- **Process**: Update the risk register to document residual risks, including their revised probability and impact ratings after response strategies have been executed.
- **Importance**: This ensures that all project team members and stakeholders are aware of the ongoing risks and can access updated information for decision-making.

3. Development of Additional Risk Responses
- **Process**: If residual risks are still above the project's risk tolerance threshold, develop and implement additional risk responses. This could involve further mitigation, transferring the risk, or even accepting the risk if it falls within acceptable limits.
- **Tools**: Decision trees, further cost-benefit analysis, and scenario planning can aid in deciding the best course of action.

4. Continuous Monitoring
- **Process**: Implement a systematic approach to monitor residual risks throughout the project lifecycle. This involves regular check-ins and updates during project status meetings or through dedicated risk review sessions.
- **Tools**: Use dashboards and real-time monitoring tools to keep track of residual risks and their triggers.

5.   Contingency Planning
- **Process**: Prepare contingency plans for residual risks that are deemed acceptable but could still impact the project. This ensures readiness to act swiftly if the risk materializes.
- **Example**: If there is a residual risk of supply chain disruptions, maintain a list of alternative suppliers that can be engaged quickly.

6. Stakeholder Communication
- **Process**: Keep stakeholders informed about residual risks and the steps being taken to manage them. This communication should be clear, concise, and consistent, ensuring that stakeholders understand the risk landscape and the project's approach to managing it.
- **Tools**: Regular risk reports, updates in stakeholder meetings, and inclusion of residual risk information in project newsletters or bulletins.

Example of Managing Residual Risks
Consider a project to develop a new software system where initial risk responses have mitigated most security risks related to data breaches. However, a residual risk remains due to potential new vulnerabilities that might be discovered in the future. The project manager decides to:
- Continue with monthly security audits.
- Update the risk register to reflect the residual risk.

- Prepare a contingency plan that includes immediate response actions for any data breach.
- Inform stakeholders about the residual risk and the plans in place to manage it.

Conclusion

Residual risks are an inherent part of managing projects, and their proper identification, documentation, and management are crucial to ensuring project success. By effectively assessing and handling residual risks, project managers not only safeguard the project's objectives but also enhance stakeholders' confidence in the project's risk management processes. The **Monitor Risks** process in project management is essential for ensuring that identified risks are tracked, residual risks are monitored, and new risks are identified as the project progresses. This process involves continuous oversight to determine the effectiveness of risk responses and to adjust strategies as needed based on new information and changes in the project environment. Several tools and techniques are instrumental in performing these activities effectively.

Primary Tools and Techniques in Monitor Risks
1. Risk Reassessment

- **Description**: This involves periodically reviewing the identified risks to determine whether their probability, impact, or other characteristics have changed. It also includes identifying new risks that have emerged since the initial risk assessment.
- **Example**: Halfway through a construction project, a risk reassessment might be conducted to evaluate the impact of seasonal weather changes on the project schedule and cost.
- **Application**: Risk reassessments help ensure that the project's risk register remains up-to-date and relevant, reflecting the current risk landscape of the project.

2. Risk Audits

- **Description**: Conducting risk audits involves examining and evaluating the effectiveness of the risk management process and the accuracy of the risk analysis in predicting risk occurrences. It also assesses how well risk responses have been implemented and whether they are achieving their intended outcomes.
- **Example**: An external auditor might review a software development project's risk management practices to ensure that mitigation strategies for cybersecurity risks are in place and effective.
- **Application**: Risk audits provide an objective assessment of the risk management process, offering opportunities for improvement and ensuring compliance with organizational policies and standards.

3. Variance and Trend Analysis

- **Description**: These techniques involve analyzing performance data to detect variances from the planned baseline (variance analysis) and examining performance over time to identify trends that could indicate emerging risks (trend analysis).
- **Example**: In a project, variance analysis might reveal that the project is consistently spending over budget in certain areas, suggesting a risk of budget overrun. Trend analysis could show that the durations of certain critical activities are increasing over time, potentially indicating a risk to the project deadline.
- **Application**: Variance and trend analysis help project managers to proactively identify and address emerging risks before they have significant impacts on the project.

4. Technical Performance Measurement

- **Description**: This technique compares technical accomplishments during project execution against the project plan. It helps identify performance deviations that may be indicators of potential risks.
- **Example**: Measuring the performance parameters of a new software system against the specifications to detect any shortfalls that might indicate risks to final system quality or delivery timelines.
- **Application**: Technical performance measurements can serve as early warning signs of risks related to product quality and performance specifications.

5. Reserve Analysis

- **Description**: This technique involves analyzing the remaining contingency and management reserves to determine if they are adequate to address potential risks and uncertainties for the remainder of the project.
- **Example**: Regularly reviewing the contingency reserve to ensure it is sufficient to cover estimated risks based on current project performance and risk reassessments.
- **Application**: Reserve analysis ensures that funds are appropriately allocated to manage risks effectively throughout the project life cycle.

Conclusion

Effective monitoring of risks is crucial for managing project uncertainties proactively. By employing techniques like risk reassessment, risk audits, variance and trend analysis, technical performance measurement, and reserve analysis, project managers can keep a pulse on project risks, optimize risk responses, and ensure project objectives are achieved despite potential setbacks. These tools and techniques provide a dynamic approach to risk management, adapting to the project's changing conditions and ensuring that risk handling is both effective and efficient. Regular risk reviews and risk audits are essential components of the Monitor Risks process in project management. These activities are designed to evaluate the effectiveness of risk management practices and ensure that risk responses are appropriate and effective throughout the project lifecycle.

1. **Risk Reviews**: These are periodic assessments conducted to track the implementation of risk responses, to monitor residual risks, and to identify new risks as the project evolves. Risk reviews help maintain an up-to-date understanding of the project's risk landscape.
2. **Risk Audits**: These are more formal examinations of the risk management process itself, focusing on compliance, effectiveness, and efficiency. Risk audits aim to validate the accuracy of risk management practices and to ensure that risk responses are aligned with overall risk management policies.

Benefits of Risk Reviews and Risk Audits

- **Improved Risk Response Effectiveness**: Regular reviews and audits help ensure that risk responses are actively addressing identified risks and are adjusted appropriately as project conditions change.
- **Enhanced Decision-Making**: By providing ongoing feedback on risk management efforts, these activities support better-informed decisions regarding resource allocation and project planning.

- **Increased Project Alignment and Compliance**: Audits verify that risk management activities comply with organizational standards and project requirements, promoting alignment across the project's objectives.
- **Identification of New Risks**: Regular reviews help in detecting new risks early, allowing for timely responses before these risks can impact the project adversely.
- **Validation of Risk Assumptions**: These activities check whether the assumptions made during the initial risk analysis still hold true or if adjustments are needed based on project developments.

Using Risk Reviews and Risk Audits to Enhance Project Management
Evaluating the Effectiveness of Risk Responses

Project managers can use the insights gained from risk reviews to assess whether the risk responses have been effective in reducing or eliminating risks. For instance, if a risk response was to implement additional quality controls in a manufacturing process, a risk review might analyze defect rates before and after the control implementation to evaluate its effectiveness.

Assessing the Validity of Risk Assumptions

Risk assumptions are often made at the beginning of the project based on the information available at the time. Regular risk audits allow project managers to revisit these assumptions and validate them against current project realities. This might involve reassessing the likelihood of certain risks occurring or the expected impact of risk events based on new data.

Identifying Improvements to the Risk Management Process

Both risk reviews and audits provide opportunities for continuous improvement in risk management practices. They can highlight weaknesses in the existing risk management strategy, such as underestimation of risks, inadequate risk response strategies, or gaps in risk communication. Based on these findings, project managers can refine risk management plans, improve risk response techniques, and enhance overall risk governance.

Conclusion

Regular risk reviews and risk audits are crucial for maintaining a proactive risk management approach. They help ensure that the project remains responsive to new and evolving risks and that risk management strategies and practices are robust, effective, and aligned with the project's objectives. By integrating these activities into the regular project workflow, project managers not only safeguard the project against potential threats but also enhance its overall resilience and success. Here's a set of practice questions designed to test and reinforce understanding of Project Risk Management processes, key concepts, and their application in real-world project scenarios. These questions are ideal for preparing for the CAPM exam or enhancing project management skills.

Question 1: What is the primary purpose of the Perform Qualitative Risk Analysis process?
- A) To numerically analyze the impact of risks on project objectives.
- B) To prioritize risks based on their likelihood and impact.
- C) To transfer all identified risks to external parties.
- D) To mitigate all identified risks immediately.

Correct Answer: B) To prioritize risks based on their likelihood and impact.

- **Explanation**: The main goal of Perform Qualitative Risk Analysis is to prioritize risks by assessing and combining their probability of occurrence and potential impacts on project objectives. This helps in focusing efforts and resources on the most significant risks.

Question 2: Which tool or technique is typically used in the Perform Quantitative Risk Analysis process?
- A) Risk urgency assessment
- B) Monte Carlo simulation
- C) Expert judgment
- D) Risk categorization

Correct Answer: B) Monte Carlo simulation.
- **Explanation**: Monte Carlo simulations are used in Perform Quantitative Risk Analysis to model the probability of various outcomes in a process that cannot easily be predicted due to the intervention of random variables. It is a technique used to understand the impact of risk and uncertainty in prediction and forecasting models.

Question 3: What does a risk register typically include?
- A) List of team members only.
- B) Financial statements of the project.
- C) Detailed descriptions of identified risks, their causes, and responses.
- D) Contract agreements with suppliers.

Correct Answer: C) Detailed descriptions of identified risks, their causes, and responses.
- **Explanation**: A risk register is a tool used in risk management processes to detail each identified risk, its characteristics, and the measures that will be taken in response to the risk. It includes information about the probability, impact, response strategies, and ownership.

Question 4: In risk management, what is the purpose of a risk audit?
- A) To evaluate how effectively the risk management process is being implemented.
- B) To increase the project budget.
- C) To hire new project team members.
- D) To purchase insurance for the project.

Correct Answer: A) To evaluate how effectively the risk management process is being implemented.
- **Explanation**: A risk audit is conducted to review and evaluate the efficiency and effectiveness of the risk management process within a project. This audit checks if the identified risk responses are being executed as planned and are effective in reducing or eliminating the risks.

Question 5: What is meant by 'risk appetite' in project risk management?
- A) The specific outcomes of project risks.
- B) The amount of risk a company is financially able to handle.
- C) The level of risk that an organization is willing to accept while pursuing its objectives.
- D) The documentation needed for legal compliance.

Correct Answer: C) The level of risk that an organization is willing to accept while pursuing its objectives.
- **Explanation**: Risk appetite refers to the degree of uncertainty an organization is prepared to accept in anticipation of a reward. It reflects the organization's attitude towards risk-taking and is crucial for developing the risk management strategy.

These questions and explanations provide a clear understanding of various aspects of Project Risk Management, helping learners to deepen their knowledge and prepare effectively for the CAPM certification exam.

XI. Project Procurement Management:

The **Plan Procurement Management** process is critical in project management, especially for projects that require sourcing external goods, services, or resources to meet project objectives. This process involves documenting how procurement should be planned, executed, and controlled. It is essential for ensuring that procurement activities are well-organized, transparent, and aligned with the overall project goals.

Purpose and Importance of Plan Procurement Management

1. **Strategic Alignment**: Ensures that all procurement activities are aligned with the project objectives and project schedule, supporting the efficient and effective achievement of project goals.
2. **Risk Management**: Helps identify and manage risks associated with external procurements, such as delays, cost overruns, quality issues, or compliance problems.
3. **Cost Control**: Aids in controlling project costs by outlining standard procedures for vendor selection, contract management, and cost verification to ensure that expenditures stay within the approved budget.
4. **Quality Assurance**: Establishes criteria and processes for ensuring that procured goods and services meet the required standards and specifications, thereby maintaining the project's quality requirements.
5. **Efficiency**: Streamlines the procurement process by defining clear steps, responsibilities, and timeframes, which helps in avoiding delays and ensures timely project execution.

Key Components of a Procurement Management Plan

1. **Types of Contracts**: Identifies suitable contract types based on the project risks, complexity, and procurement needs (e.g., fixed-price, cost-reimbursable, time and materials). This section guides the project team on the best contractual approach to mitigate financial risks.
2. **Procurement Activities and Timeframes**: Outlines the steps involved in the procurement process, including planning, bidder conferences, selection criteria, contract awarding, and contract closure. It also includes timeframes for each of these activities to ensure they fit within the overall project schedule.
3. **Roles and Responsibilities**: Defines who within the project team or the wider organization is responsible for managing procurement activities. This includes roles related to authorizing purchases, managing vendors, and handling procurement documents.
4. **Selection Criteria**: Specifies the criteria for evaluating and selecting vendors or contractors. This may include factors such as price, capability, reliability, and past performance. Clear criteria help ensure fair and effective vendor selection.
5. **Vendor Management**: Describes how relationships with vendors will be managed. It covers the process for handling queries, resolving disputes, and managing contract changes. It also outlines the communication flow between the project team and the vendors.
6. **Performance Metrics**: Details the key performance indicators (KPIs) and metrics that will be used to assess vendor performance throughout the project lifecycle. This helps in ensuring vendors meet contractual obligations regarding timelines, budget, and quality.

7. **Risk Management Plan**: Includes specific strategies for managing procurement-related risks. This could involve plans for managing potential delays, ensuring quality, and addressing possible legal issues.
8. **Standard Documents and Templates**: Provides templates and standard documents that will be used in the procurement process. This may include RFP templates, contract templates, and procurement documentation guidelines.

How the Procurement Management Plan Guides the Project Team

- **Consistency and Standardization**: Provides a standardized approach to managing procurement across the project, ensuring that all team members follow the same procedures and guidelines.
- **Decision Support**: Offers a reference point for making informed decisions about procurement activities, helping to resolve issues and manage trade-offs between cost, schedule, and quality.
- **Communication Tool**: Acts as a communication tool both internally and with external vendors, ensuring that all parties have a clear understanding of expectations and requirements.

Conclusion

The Plan Procurement Management process is essential for any project involving external vendors or suppliers. By developing a comprehensive Procurement Management Plan, project managers can ensure that procurement activities are carried out effectively, efficiently, and in alignment with the project's strategic goals. This planning effort helps mitigate procurement risks, control costs, and ensure the quality and timeliness of external goods and services, contributing significantly to the project's success. Project baselines—specifically scope, schedule, and cost baselines—serve as the foundation for measuring project performance and guiding project execution. These baselines are crucial for setting expectations and maintaining control throughout the project lifecycle.

- **Scope Baseline**: Defines what is to be delivered by the project. It includes the project scope statement, the work breakdown structure (WBS), and the WBS dictionary.
- **Schedule Baseline**: Establishes when project tasks are to be completed, outlining the project timeline and key milestones.
- **Cost Baseline**: Sets the approved budget for the project, against which project expenditures are measured.

Influence on Procurement Management Plan

The procurement management plan outlines how the procurement processes will be managed from developing procurement documentation through contract closure. The relationship between the project baselines and the procurement management plan is both direct and influential, impacting how procurement activities are structured and executed.

1. Influencing Procurement Strategy

- **Scope Baseline Influence**: The scope baseline directly influences the procurement strategy by identifying what parts of the project work can be outsourced or need to be purchased. For example, if the project scope includes specialized work that cannot be completed in-house, the procurement management plan will need to address outsourcing these services.
- **Schedule Baseline Influence**: The schedule baseline impacts the procurement timeline, influencing when bids must be solicited, and contracts awarded to ensure that the procurement of goods and services aligns with project deadlines. If a project component critical to the

schedule is to be procured, delays in procurement could push back the project timeline, necessitating accelerated procurement processes.

- **Cost Baseline Influence**: The cost baseline helps determine the budget available for different procurements. It impacts how contracts are structured—whether fixed-price, cost-reimbursable, or time and materials—and influences negotiation strategies to ensure procurements stay within budget.

2. Identification of Goods and Services to Be Procured

- **Derived from Scope**: The scope baseline helps identify which components of the project will be procured externally. Detailed analysis of the WBS can pinpoint specific deliverables that need to be bought or contracted out, ensuring all required goods and services are planned for procurement.
- **Time Constraints from Schedule**: The timing of procurements is crucial to project success. The schedule baseline ensures that procurements are planned and executed at the right times during the project lifecycle to avoid bottlenecks or delays in project progress.
- **Budget Considerations from Cost**: The cost baseline provides a financial framework within which all procurements must be made. This helps in deciding the procurement methods (e.g., competitive bidding, direct selection) and the type of contracts that can be afforded under the project budget.

Conclusion

The interaction between the project baselines and the procurement management plan is a dynamic aspect of project management that requires careful coordination and integration. By aligning procurement activities with these baselines, project managers can ensure that procurement supports the project's objectives in terms of quality, timeliness, and cost-efficiency. This alignment is vital for the seamless integration of external resources and capabilities into the project's workflow, ultimately contributing to the project's overall success. The Plan Procurement Management process is essential in project management, especially for projects that involve external vendors or service providers. This process involves organizing and coordinating procurement activities to ensure that all necessary goods and services are acquired to meet project needs while adhering to the project timeline and budget.

Inputs

1. Project Management Plan:

- **Example**: Includes the scope baseline, schedule baseline, and cost baseline which help define what needs to be procured, when, and the budget constraints.
- **Significance**: Guides the procurement process to align with the overall project objectives and ensures that procurements support project plans.

2. Requirements Documentation:

- **Example**: Detailed descriptions of the project needs which might include specifications for materials, equipment, or services.
- **Significance**: Ensures that solicitations and contracts are comprehensive and meet the project's technical and functional requirements.

3. Risk Register:

- **Example**: Contains information about potential risks associated with procurement activities, such as delays from vendors or cost overruns.
- **Significance**: Helps in planning risk mitigation strategies in the procurement management plan.

4. Stakeholder Register:

- **Example**: Lists all stakeholders and their interests, influence, and impact on the project, including vendors and external partners.
- **Significance**: Aids in understanding stakeholder requirements and expectations from the procurement process.

5. Enterprise Environmental Factors (EEFs):

- **Example**: Market conditions, commercial databases, and regulatory requirements that affect procurement activities.
- **Significance**: Influences the choice of contracting methods, selection criteria, and procurement policies.

6. Organizational Process Assets (OPAs):

- **Example**: Standard procurement policies, templates for contracts, and historical information from previous projects.
- **Significance**: Provides a basis for developing the procurement management plan using proven templates and practices.

Tools and Techniques
1. Market Research:

- **Example**: Investigating potential suppliers, market trends, and technological developments.
- **Significance**: Ensures the project utilizes the best available resources and gets competitive rates.

2. Expert Judgment:

- **Example**: Consulting with procurement and contracting experts, legal counsel, and technical experts.
- **Significance**: Helps in making informed decisions regarding the procurement approach, contracts, and supplier evaluation.

3. Make-or-Buy Analysis:

- **Example**: Determining whether to procure a service externally or use internal capabilities.
- **Significance**: Critical for optimizing resource utilization and controlling project costs.

4. Cost-Benefit Analysis:

- **Example**: Comparing the costs of various procurement options against their expected benefits.
- **Significance**: Aids in selecting the most cost-effective procurement method.

Outputs

1. Procurement Management Plan:

- **Example**: A document that describes how procurement processes will be managed from developing procurement documentation through contract closure.
- **Significance**: Acts as a roadmap for procurement activities, ensuring all team members understand their roles and responsibilities.

2. Procurement Strategy:

- **Example**: Strategy outlining the approach for negotiating with suppliers, contract types to be used, and the timeline for key procurement activities.
- **Significance**: Aligns procurement actions with project objectives and stakeholder expectations.

3. Bid Documents:

- **Example**: Request for Proposal (RFP), Invitation for Bid (IFB), and other solicitation documents.
- **Significance**: Provides potential vendors with a clear and detailed statement of needs and selection criteria, ensuring fair and transparent vendor selection.

4. Source Selection Criteria:

- **Example**: Set of attributes desired in suppliers, such as delivery capabilities, cost, quality, and service.
- **Significance**: Ensures that the procurement decisions are made objectively and aligned with project needs.

5. Make-or-Buy Decisions:

- **Example**: Decisions documented regarding what products or services will be procured externally and what will be produced internally.
- **Significance**: Directly impacts the project's scope, budget, schedule, and risk management.

6. Change Requests:

- **Example**: Adjustments to the procurement management plan or other aspects of the project plan as needed based on insights gained during planning.
- **Significance**: Ensures that the project adapts to evolving project conditions and requirements.

Conclusion

The Plan Procurement Management process establishes a structured approach to procurement, ensuring that the project acquires the necessary goods and services in a timely and cost-effective manner. Properly executed, this process minimizes procurement risks, enhances vendor performance, and ensures a smooth supply chain flow critical for project success. The **make-or-buy analysis** is a critical decision-making tool used in the **Plan Procurement Management** process. It helps project managers and organizations decide whether it is more cost-effective or strategically sensible to produce a particular item or service internally (make) or to purchase it from an external source (buy). This analysis is essential for optimizing resource allocation, controlling costs, and aligning procurement activities with strategic business objectives.

Purpose of Make-or-Buy Analysis

1. **Cost Efficiency**: Determines the most cost-effective approach between making a product or service in-house or outsourcing it, considering both direct and indirect costs.
2. **Focus on Core Competencies**: Helps organizations focus on their core competencies by outsourcing non-core activities, potentially leading to improved efficiency and effectiveness.
3. **Resource Allocation**: Assists in optimal resource utilization by identifying activities that are cheaper or better performed by external suppliers, thus freeing up internal resources for other critical tasks.
4. **Risk Management**: Evaluates risks associated with both making and buying options, such as the risk of not meeting quality standards or the risk of supplier dependency.

Components of a Make-or-Buy Analysis
1. Cost Assessment

- **Description**: Compares the total costs associated with producing the item or service in-house versus the cost of purchasing it from an external provider.
- **Components**:
  - **Direct Costs**: Costs directly tied to production, such as labor, materials, and machinery.
  - **Indirect Costs**: Overhead, administrative costs, and any additional costs that may be incurred, such as training and maintenance.

2. Capability and Capacity Analysis

- **Description**: Evaluates whether the organization has the necessary skills, technology, and capacity to produce the item or service at the required quality and quantity.
- **Components**:
  - **Existing Capabilities**: Assessment of current skills and technologies.
  - **Capacity Constraints**: Analysis of whether the organization can meet production demands with the current workforce and facilities.

3. Quality Considerations

- **Description**: Considers whether the quality of the in-house production can meet the standards required versus the quality guaranteed by external suppliers.
- **Components**:
  - **Quality Standards**: Expected quality levels of the final product or service.
  - **Quality Assurance**: Measures to ensure that these quality standards are met, whether in-house or externally.

4. Strategic Alignment

- **Description**: Examines how the decision aligns with the organization's long-term strategic goals.
- **Components**:
  - **Long-term Impacts**: Effects on organizational strategy and goals.
  - **Supplier Relationships**: Potential for strategic relationships with suppliers and impact on the industry ecosystem.

5. Risk Evaluation

- **Description**: Analyzes potential risks associated with each option.
- **Components**:

- **Supply Chain Risks**: Risks associated with supplier reliability and supply chain disruptions.
- **Operational Risks**: Risks related to the internal execution of production tasks.

Application of Make-or-Buy Analysis

Project managers use this analysis by systematically evaluating each component for the specific item or service under consideration. They gather data on costs, assess internal capabilities and capacity, evaluate quality needs, and consider strategic and risk factors. Decision matrices or scoring systems can be used to weigh these factors and compare the total 'scores' for making versus buying.

Example

A project manager in a technology firm might perform a make-or-buy analysis for software development. If the analysis shows that external vendors offer advanced technology and innovation that the firm cannot economically replicate in-house, and if partnering with a tech vendor aligns with strategic goals like technological leadership, the decision might lean towards buying (outsourcing).

Conclusion

Make-or-buy analysis is a fundamental tool in procurement planning that ensures decisions are made based on thorough consideration of all relevant factors. By determining whether it is more viable to make a product or service internally or to buy it from outside, organizations can manage costs effectively, optimize resource use, focus on core competencies, and mitigate associated risks. The Procurement Statement of Work (SOW) is a detailed document that forms part of the procurement documents and is essential for clearly defining the procurement requirements. It describes the specific work to be performed by a vendor or contractor, the expected deliverables, and the performance criteria. The SOW is used to communicate to potential suppliers exactly what is required, how tasks should be performed, and the basis for evaluating vendor performance.

Role in the Plan Procurement Management Process

In the Plan Procurement Management process, the SOW plays a critical role in ensuring that the external vendor or contractor understands the project's needs and what they are expected to deliver. It sets the foundation for developing procurement contracts and helps in the selection of qualified suppliers. It also aids in defining the terms of engagement and the scope of work specific to each contracted entity, which is essential for the successful integration of external services into the project's main workflow.

Key Elements of a Well-Defined SOW

A well-defined SOW includes several critical elements that collectively ensure clarity and comprehensiveness:

1. **Scope of Work**: Detailed description of the work to be performed, processes to be followed, and the location of the work. This includes technical specifications, work conditions, and operational requirements.
2. **Deliverables**: Specifics of what is to be delivered, including formats and due dates. This section should clearly define physical or digital outputs, reporting requirements, and other tangible products expected from the contractor.
3. **Performance Standards**: Standards and benchmarks that will be used to assess the quality of work. These might include industry standards, time constraints, and specific quality metrics that the deliverables must meet.

4. **Acceptance Criteria**: Conditions under which the deliverables will be accepted or rejected. This includes the process for quality inspections, testing procedures, and validation methods to ensure the outputs meet the required standards.

5. **Work Timeline**: Detailed schedule including milestones, deadlines, and critical paths that align with the overall project schedule. This ensures that the vendor's work will integrate smoothly with the broader project timeline.

6. **Payment Terms**: Specifications of how and when the vendor will be compensated. This can include payment schedules tied to milestones, specific deliverables, or upon acceptance of the final work.

7. **Special Requirements**: Any additional legal, regulatory, or environmental requirements that must be adhered to during the project execution. This could also include safety protocols, intellectual property rights, and confidentiality agreements.

Differences Between SOW and Project Scope Statement

While both the SOW and the project scope statement define what needs to be accomplished, they serve different purposes and are used in different contexts:

- **Project Scope Statement**: This is a broader document that outlines the entire project's scope, including work breakdown, deliverables, and boundaries of the project. It is used internally to guide the project team and manage stakeholder expectations.

- **Procurement SOW**: Specifically focuses on the portion of the project work that is to be outsourced to external vendors. It is more detailed in terms of vendor responsibilities and focuses on contractual requirements, deliverables, and standards specific to external work.

The SOW for procurement is, therefore, a derivative of the project scope but tailored to external execution, ensuring that all external engagements are clearly defined, measurable, and aligned with the project's overall objectives. This distinction is crucial for effective project management and seamless integration of internal and external project activities. In project management, selecting the right contract type is crucial for managing risk, costs, and ensuring the quality of deliverables. The choice of contract can significantly impact the project's financial and operational performance. Here are the three most common types of contracts used in project procurement: fixed-price, cost-reimbursable, and time and materials.

1.   Fixed-Price Contracts

Description: A fixed-price contract sets a fixed total price for all project-related activities.
Examples:
- **Lump Sum Contract**: Used for well-defined projects with clear specifications and stable requirements.

Advantages:
- Predictability of costs for the buyer.
- The seller is incentivized to control costs and work efficiently.

Disadvantages:
- The risk for the seller if the project scope is not well-defined and costs exceed estimates.
- Changes or errors in scope definition can lead to disputes and claims for adjustments.

Appropriate Use Cases:
- When the scope and specifications of the project are clear and unlikely to change.
- Projects where the buyer wants to ensure the cost does not exceed a certain amount.

## 2.	Cost-Reimbursable Contracts

Description: Also known as cost-plus contracts, these agreements involve reimbursing the contractor for all legitimate actual costs incurred plus additional payment to allow for a profit margin.

Examples:

- **Cost Plus Fixed Fee (CPFF)**: The contractor is paid for all project costs plus a fixed fee percentage of the initial project cost.
- **Cost Plus Incentive Fee (CPIF)**: The contractor is paid for all project costs plus an incentive fee based upon achieving certain performance objectives.

Advantages:

- Flexibility to adjust scopes, such as for projects where exact specifications are not known in advance.
- Reduced risk for suppliers, encouraging them to focus on quality and innovation.

Disadvantages:

- Higher risk for the buyer as the total cost is not capped.
- Requires intensive oversight and audit mechanisms to ensure that only legitimate costs are paid.

Appropriate Use Cases:

- Complex projects where the exact scope and materials cannot be accurately estimated in advance.
- Research and development projects where innovation and finding unique solutions are more important than cost control.

3. Time and Materials (T&M) Contracts

Description: Under a time and materials contract, suppliers are paid for the number of labor hours at a fixed hourly rate and for materials at cost.

Examples:

- Used typically for small projects or for specialized services where the scope is not well-defined.

Advantages:

- Provides flexibility to modify the scope without renegotiating the price.
- Useful when it is difficult to estimate the extent or duration of the work.

Disadvantages:

- Potential lack of cost control as the duration and material usage are not capped.
- The buyer bears the risk of work taking longer than expected.

Appropriate Use Cases:

- Projects where labor and material costs are unpredictable or vary significantly.
- Short-term projects or tasks where a detailed scope is not known but immediate start is necessary.

Conclusion

Choosing the right contract type is pivotal in project procurement management. Each type of contract has its own set of advantages and risks, and the choice depends largely on the project specifics such as scope clarity, cost predictability, and risk tolerance. Project managers must carefully analyze the project requirements and external conditions to select the most appropriate contract type to align with project objectives and stakeholder needs. The **Conduct Procurements** process is essential in project management as it involves the complete set of activities required to identify, select, and contract with suppliers or vendors who will provide the goods or services necessary for the project. This process ensures that the project receives the best possible resources in terms of quality, cost, and timeliness, contributing significantly to the project's overall success.

Significance of Conduct Procurements

1. **Obtaining Seller Responses**: Enables the project to gather comprehensive proposals from potential vendors, which detail how they will meet the project requirements and at what cost.
2. **Selecting Sellers**: Facilitates the evaluation and comparison of these proposals to determine which vendors are most capable of fulfilling the project's needs effectively and efficiently.
3. **Awarding Contracts**: Involves finalizing and formalizing agreements with selected vendors, ensuring clear understanding and agreement on what is to be delivered, the timelines, costs, and terms and conditions of the engagement.

Primary Tools and Techniques
1. Bidder Conferences

- **Description**: Meetings with all potential bidders to discuss the procurement requirements, answer questions, and clarify any uncertainties regarding the request for proposal (RFP) or request for quote (RFQ).
- **Application**: Ensures that all potential bidders have a clear and uniform understanding of what the project requires, which helps in obtaining accurate and comparable proposals.

2. RFPs and RFQs

- **Description**: Documents that outline the project's requirements and criteria for the selection of vendors. An RFP (Request for Proposal) typically provides a detailed explanation of the project and asks for a solution approach, while an RFQ (Request for Quote) is used when the requirements are more straightforward and the project needs a simple price quote.
- **Application**: These are essential for communicating the project's needs to potential suppliers and form the basis for their proposals.

3. Proposal Evaluation Techniques

- **Description**: Structured evaluation methods to assess vendor proposals based on predefined criteria such as cost, technical capability, past performance, and financial stability.
- **Application**: Helps in objectively selecting the best vendor for the project. Techniques may include weighted scoring systems, vendor capability matrices, or compliance checks.

4.   Advertising

- **Description**: Publicizing the procurement needs through various channels to attract a wide range of potential suppliers.
- **Application**: Increases the pool of potential bidders, enhancing the chances of finding the right vendor at competitive prices.

5. Procurement Negotiations

- **Description**: Discussions held with potential suppliers to finalize the terms of the contract, including prices, key responsibilities, deadlines, and penalties for non-compliance.
- **Application**: Crucial for ensuring that the contract terms are favorable to the project and that any risks are appropriately mitigated through contractual agreements.

6. Analytical Techniques

- **Description**: Using methods such as cost-benefit analysis, market research, and vendor performance data to support the decision-making process.
- **Application**: These techniques help in understanding the market norms and the feasibility of the proposals, assisting in making informed procurement decisions.

Conclusion

The Conduct Procurements process is a cornerstone of successful project management, directly impacting the quality, cost, and timeliness of the project outputs. By effectively utilizing tools and techniques like bidder conferences, RFPs, proposal evaluation, and negotiations, project managers can ensure that they select the most suitable vendors and secure the best possible terms for their project procurements. This not only supports the immediate project needs but also sets the stage for long-term project success by establishing solid, reliable vendor relationships. Procurement documents are essential tools in the Plan Procurement Management process, used to solicit proposals, quotes, and bids from potential sellers. These documents ensure that the procurement requirements and expectations are clearly communicated to all parties, facilitating a transparent and fair procurement process. They also provide the means through which the project management team can evaluate and select the best vendor based on project needs.

Key Types of Procurement Documents
1. Request for Proposal (RFP)

- **Purpose**: RFPs are used when the project needs are complex and might require creative solutions or detailed methodology. The purpose is not just to ask for a price, but to understand what the vendor can offer in terms of solving a problem or delivering a service or product.
- **Components**:
    - **Background Information**: Provides context about the project and its objectives.
    - **Scope of Work/Statement of Work (SOW)**: Detailed description of the work to be performed.
    - **Submission Guidelines**: Instructions on how the proposals should be formatted and submitted.
    - **Evaluation Criteria**: Specific criteria that will be used to assess proposals.
    - **Contract Terms**: Outline of the contractual obligations and terms of engagement.

2. Request for Quotation (RFQ)

- **Purpose**: RFQs are typically used when the requirements are clear, specific, and quantifiable. This document is used to obtain pricing information under specified conditions.
- **Components**:
    - **Detailed Specifications**: Clear, detailed list of the specifications for the goods or services required.
    - **Quantity and Delivery Schedule**: Information on quantities needed and the schedule for delivery or execution.
    - **Price Breakdown**: Request for a detailed breakdown of prices, including unit costs.
    - **Quality Requirements**: Standards that the products or services must meet.

3. Invitation for Bid (IFB)

- **Purpose**: IFBs are used in situations where the cost is the primary or sole criterion for selection. This method is common in construction or large supply contracts where detailed specifications are available and the work does not vary much in complexity.

- **Components**:
  - **Project Specifications**: Detailed, unambiguous specifications of the work or products needed.
  - **Bid Submission Requirements**: Instructions on how bids should be prepared and submitted.
  - **Contractual Terms**: Specific terms that will govern the contract, including payment terms and legal obligations.
  - **Evaluation Process**: Details on how bids will be evaluated, typically focusing on price.

Communication of Procurement Requirements and Expectations

These procurement documents play a critical role in communicating project needs to potential sellers:

- **Clarity and Precision**: They provide clear and precise descriptions of what is being requested, which helps potential vendors understand the project's needs and align their proposals or bids accordingly.
- **Standardization**: By standardizing the information requested from all vendors, these documents ensure a fair and objective evaluation process based on predefined criteria.
- **Transparency**: The detailed criteria for evaluation and contractual terms laid out in these documents ensure transparency in the procurement process, building trust and encouraging competitive bids.
- **Legal and Regulatory Compliance**: They include necessary legal terms and conditions to ensure compliance with relevant laws and regulations, protecting both the project entity and the vendors.

Ultimately, RFPs, RFQs, and IFBs are vital for ensuring that the procurement process aligns with the project's strategic objectives, allowing for effective vendor selection and management. By effectively utilizing these documents, project managers can mitigate risks associated with procurement and ensure that they engage the best possible vendors for their project needs. Source selection criteria are the standards and requirements used to evaluate and compare bids or proposals from suppliers and contractors during the procurement process. These criteria are critical in ensuring that the selection of vendors aligns with the project's needs, quality standards, budget, and timelines.

Application in the Conduct Procurements Process

The application of source selection criteria is central to the Conduct Procurements process. It involves assessing vendor proposals based on predefined metrics to ensure fair and transparent vendor selection. This process includes receiving proposals, evaluating them against the criteria, and selecting the vendor that best meets the project's requirements.

Common Source Selection Criteria
1. Technical Capability:

- **Description**: Measures the vendor's ability to meet the technical and quality requirements specified in the project documentation.
- **Application**: Evaluated based on past project performance, technical skills, access to technology, and adherence to industry standards.

2. Management Approach:

- **Description**: Assesses the vendor's ability to manage the project effectively, considering their organizational structure, staffing, and management processes.
- **Application**: Evaluated through the vendor's proposed project management plan, organizational charts, and staff qualifications.

3. Price:

- **Description**: The cost of the vendor's proposal is always a significant criterion, especially in projects with tight budget constraints.
- **Application**: Evaluated based on the total cost of ownership, including initial costs, ongoing operational costs, and potential cost overruns.

4. Past Performance:

- **Description**: Examines the vendor's history with similar projects, focusing on their reliability, quality of work, and adherence to timelines.
- **Application**: Evaluated through references, performance data, and reviews from previous clients.

5. Financial Stability:

- **Description**: Assesses the vendor's financial health to ensure they have the resources to sustain the project over its duration.
- **Application**: Evaluated using financial statements, credit ratings, and market presence.

6. Sustainability and Compliance:

- **Description**: Considers the vendor's adherence to environmental, social, and corporate governance (ESG) standards.
- **Application**: Evaluated based on certifications, sustainability reports, and compliance with relevant laws and regulations.

Weighting and Scoring of Criteria

To effectively use source selection criteria, each criterion is typically weighted according to its importance to the project. For example, if technical capability is more critical than price for a specific project, it might be given a higher weight.

Steps in Weighting and Scoring:

1. **Assign Weights**: Each criterion is assigned a weight that reflects its relative importance in the vendor selection process. These weights are predetermined and documented in the procurement management plan.
2. **Score Proposals**: Each vendor's proposal is scored against each criterion. Scoring can be qualitative (e.g., excellent, good, fair, poor) or quantitative (using a numerical scale).
3. **Calculate Total Scores**: The scores for each criterion are multiplied by the weights, and these products are summed to derive a total score for each vendor.
4. **Rank Vendors**: Vendors are ranked based on their total scores, and the highest-ranking vendor is usually selected, provided they meet all mandatory criteria.

Example:

- Technical Capability (40% weight), Price (30% weight), Management Approach (20% weight), and Past Performance (10% weight).
- Vendor A scores 80 in Technical, 70 in Price, 90 in Management, and 85 in Performance, leading to a weighted score calculation and subsequent ranking.

Conclusion

Effective application of source selection criteria is vital for making informed decisions during the Conduct Procurements process. By meticulously defining, weighting, and scoring these criteria, project managers can select the vendor that offers the best balance of price, capability, and reliability, thus ensuring project success and aligning with the project's strategic goals. Effective procurement negotiations are critical in securing favorable contract terms, managing risks, and fostering good relationships with suppliers. These negotiations determine the cost, quality, and timing of the goods and services acquired for the project, directly impacting project success. To ensure effective negotiations, project managers must be well-prepared and adhere to certain best practices.

Key Considerations for Procurement Negotiations

1. **Understanding Project Needs and Priorities**: Know exactly what the project needs from the supplier, including the non-negotiable elements and areas where flexibility exists.
2. **Comprehensive Market Research**: Before entering negotiations, understand the market conditions, typical contract terms, and pricing structures. This knowledge prevents unfavorable terms and helps in achieving realistic agreements.
3. **Supplier Background and Performance**: Review the historical performance, financial stability, and reputation of the supplier to gauge their reliability and the quality of their goods or services.
4. **Risk Identification and Mitigation**: Identify potential risks associated with the procurement, such as delivery delays or quality issues, and discuss how these will be managed within the contract terms.

Best Practices for Conducting Effective Procurement Negotiations
1. Preparation and Planning

- **Detail**: Gather all necessary information about the project's requirements, the supplier's offerings, and standard industry practices.
- **Application**: Develop a negotiation plan that outlines key goals, desired pricing, terms, and conditions, and alternative options if negotiations stall.

2. Building Relationships

- **Detail**: Approach negotiations as an opportunity to build a long-term relationship with the supplier, rather than just a transaction.
- **Application**: Communicate openly and respectfully, seek to understand the supplier's constraints and objectives, and work towards solutions that offer mutual benefits.

2. Clearly Define Scope and Specifications

- **Detail**: Ensure that the scope of the procurement and the technical specifications are clearly defined and understood by both parties to avoid future conflicts.
- **Application**: Use precise language in discussions and in the contract to delineate exactly what is being procured, including quality standards and delivery expectations.

4. Leverage Competitive Bidding

- **Detail**: Use competitive bidding to your advantage, where possible, to get the best terms from negotiations.
- **Application**: Inform suppliers about the competitive nature of the procurement process to encourage better offers.

5. Effective Communication

- **Detail**: Maintain clear, open, and honest communication throughout the negotiation process.

- **Application**: Regularly update all stakeholders on negotiation progress and changes in terms that may affect project outcomes.

6. Focus on Total Cost of Ownership
- **Detail**: Consider all costs associated with procuring the good or service, not just the initial price. This includes maintenance, operational costs, and potential downtime costs.
- **Application**: Negotiate terms that minimize the total cost of ownership over the life of the product or service.

7. Document Agreements Thoroughly
- **Detail**: Ensure all agreed-upon terms are documented in detail in the contract to prevent misunderstandings.
- **Application**: Include detailed descriptions of the scope of work, delivery schedules, payment terms, and penalties for non-compliance.

8. Prepare for Concessions
- **Detail**: Know in advance what concessions you are prepared to make and understand the impact of these concessions on the project.
- **Application**: Use concessions strategically to close the deal without compromising key project objectives.

Conclusion

Effective procurement negotiations require thorough preparation, a clear understanding of project needs and market conditions, and skillful communication. By focusing on these areas, project managers can secure favorable contract terms that support project success while establishing and maintaining positive and productive relationships with suppliers. This approach not only achieves immediate project goals but also lays the groundwork for successful future collaborations. The Control Procurements process is integral to managing procurement relationships, monitoring contract performance, and administering contracts and changes throughout the project lifecycle. This process ensures that the buyer and seller both meet their contractual obligations, and the project's outcomes are aligned with the project management plan and procurement documents.

The key roles of the Control Procurements process include:

1. **Managing Procurement Relationships**: Ensures that the relationships between all parties involved in the procurement process are productive and collaborative. Effective management of these relationships helps in addressing issues, resolving conflicts, and facilitating communication to maintain project alignment.

2. **Monitoring Contract Performance**: Involves the regular review of vendor performance against the terms of the contract. This monitoring helps ensure timely delivery of goods and services, compliance with specifications, and the performance of the contract as expected.

3. **Making Changes and Corrections**: As projects evolve, changes to the procurement contracts may be necessary. This aspect of the process involves managing change requests, modifications, and ensuring that all adjustments are documented, approved, and communicated effectively.

Tools and Techniques for Controlling Project Procurement Activities

Several tools and techniques are used to effectively oversee and control project procurement activities. Here are the primary ones:

1. **Contract Audits**:
- **Purpose**: To ensure that both the buyer's and seller's performances meet contractual requirements.
- **Application**: Conducted periodically throughout the contract's lifecycle, these audits can identify compliance issues, areas for improvement, and risks associated with contract performance.

2. **Performance Reviews**:
- **Purpose**: To measure, monitor, and evaluate the seller's performance and compliance with the contract terms.
- **Application**: Involves the collection and analysis of KPIs, deliverable quality, adherence to timelines, and cost management against the contract stipulations.

3. **Inspections and Audits**:
- **Purpose**: To ensure that project deliverables meet the quality standards and are compliant with the specifications defined in the contract.
- **Application**: Typically involves regular scheduled inspections and systematic audits of the processes and products delivered by the seller.

4. **Procurement Performance Measurements**:
- **Purpose**: To quantitatively assess the efficiency and effectiveness of the procurement process.
- **Application**: Metrics might include cycle times for procurement processes, cost variances, and qualitative assessments of vendor responsiveness.

5. **Claims Administration**:
- **Purpose**: To manage claims related to changes or disputes within the procurement process.
- **Application**: This involves negotiation, resolution of claims, and ensuring any adjustments are legally documented and reflect mutual agreement.

6. **Records Management System**:
- **Purpose**: To ensure that all procurement documents and contract amendments are accurately recorded and easy to access.
- **Application**: This system helps in tracking the history of a procurement, from the contract award through to closure, including all correspondence and changes.

7. **Payment Systems**:
- **Purpose**: To manage the financial transactions associated with procurement.
- **Application**: Ensures payments are processed upon satisfactory delivery and performance, adhering to the terms of the contract, and providing financial controls.

Conclusion

The Control Procurements process is crucial for maintaining rigorous oversight of procurement activities, ensuring that vendor contributions align with project objectives, and managing the complexities of vendor relationships and contract performance. By applying these tools and techniques, project managers can effectively manage risks associated with procurements, ensure vendor performance is up to standard, and adapt to project changes fluidly and efficiently. This level of control is vital for the success of the project and the satisfaction of all stakeholders involved. The contract change control system is an integral component of the Control Procurements process in project management. It provides a structured approach for managing, documenting, and approving changes to the procurement contracts during the lifecycle of a project. This system is critical to maintaining contract integrity, compliance, and alignment with project goals.

Purpose of the Contract Change Control System

1. **Manage Changes Efficiently**: To systematically manage changes in procurement contracts that may arise due to project scope adjustments, schedule shifts, cost updates, or unforeseen circumstances.
2. **Maintain Contractual Alignment**: To ensure that any changes made to contracts are fully aligned with the overall project objectives and the interests of all parties involved.
3. **Document and Approve Changes**: To ensure all changes are appropriately documented, reviewed, and approved according to predefined processes before implementation.
4. **Minimize Scope Creep**: To control changes in a manner that minimizes scope creep and avoids unauthorized or uncontrolled growth in project scope.

Components of a Contract Change Control System

1. Change Control Procedures:

- **Description**: Detailed steps for how changes to contracts must be submitted, evaluated, approved, and communicated.
- **Example**: A procedure might require that all contract changes be submitted through a formal change request form, reviewed by a change control board, and approved by key stakeholders before implementation.

2. Change Authorization Levels:

- **Description**: Defines who has the authority to approve changes at various levels of impact and complexity.
- **Example**: Minor changes may be authorized by the project manager, while major changes requiring additional budget or significant extensions of the contract term may require approval from senior management or sponsors.

3. Change Documentation:

- **Description**: Systems for documenting changes, including the reasons for the changes, the impact on the project, and details of the approval process.
- **Example**: Maintaining a change log within the project management information system (PMIS) where all contract changes are recorded along with details such as the change requester, date of request, approval status, and approver comments.

4. Configuration Management:

- **Description**: Ensures that the current contract configuration and all approved changes are known, in place, and correctly applied.
- **Example**: Using software tools to track contract versions and ensure that the latest contract configuration is accessible and in use.

5. **Performance Measurement**:
- **Description**: Measures the effects of contract changes on project performance, helping to assess whether the changes are delivering the expected benefits.
- **Example**: Tracking metrics such as cost variance and schedule variance before and after the implementation of significant contract changes.

6. **Audit System**:
- **Description**: Regular reviews and audits to ensure compliance with change control procedures and to assess the effectiveness of the change management process.
- **Example**: Periodic audits by an external auditor to validate the accuracy of change documentation and the adherence to the change control procedures.

How the System Facilitates Change Management
- **Review and Approval**: The system ensures that every change undergoes a thorough review to assess its necessity, impact, and alignment with project objectives. It also ensures that changes are approved by the appropriate authority levels before implementation.
- **Documentation and Traceability**: By maintaining comprehensive documentation of all changes, the system provides a traceable audit trail that helps in future assessments and ensures all changes are recorded and retrievable.
- **Alignment with Objectives**: The structured approach to evaluating the impacts of changes helps ensure that modifications to contracts support the project's objectives and do not derail its goals.
- **Control Scope Creep**: By requiring formal documentation and approval for every change, the system helps prevent unauthorized changes and scope creep, ensuring project stability and integrity.

Conclusion
A contract change control system is essential for managing the dynamic nature of projects effectively. By ensuring that changes are made transparently, with approval and aligned to project goals, the system helps maintain contractual integrity and project alignment, ultimately contributing to project success. In the **Control Procurements** process, effectively monitoring and evaluating vendor performance is crucial to ensure that procurement activities align with project goals and deliver the expected value. Common procurement performance metrics and Key Performance Indicators (KPIs) provide quantitative ways to assess the efficiency, effectiveness, and compliance of suppliers and vendors throughout the project lifecycle. Here are some commonly used metrics:

Common Procurement Performance Metrics and KPIs
1. On-Time Delivery
- **Description**: Measures whether the vendor delivers goods or services by the agreed-upon date.
- **Measurement**: Calculated as the percentage of deliveries made on or before the promised delivery date over a specific period.
- **Application**: Regular tracking helps in identifying trends or issues with supplier reliability, which can impact project schedules and performance.

2. Quality Conformance
- **Description**: Assesses whether the delivered goods or services meet the quality standards and specifications agreed upon in the contract.

- **Measurement**: Often measured by the number of rejects or the acceptance rate of items inspected.
- **Application**: Critical for maintaining the project's quality requirements; poor quality conformance can lead to rework, increased costs, and delays.

3. Cost Variance

- **Description**: Compares the budgeted cost of goods and services procured against the actual cost paid.
- **Measurement**: Calculated as (Actual Cost - Budgeted Cost) / Budgeted Cost. A positive variance indicates overspending, whereas a negative variance indicates cost savings.
- **Application**: Provides insight into financial management effectiveness and helps in budget control.

4. Supplier Availability

- **Description**: Measures the availability of the supplier to meet requests for information, assistance, or problem resolution.
- **Measurement**: Can be quantified by response times to inquiries or the percentage of time the supplier was able to meet urgent demands.
- **Application**: Important for projects that require quick responses and high levels of interaction with the supplier.

5.   Contract Compliance

- **Description**: Evaluates how well the supplier adheres to the terms and conditions of the contract, including regulatory compliance and safety standards.
- **Measurement**: Monitored through regular audits and reviews of supplier deliverables and operations.
- **Application**: Ensures that all legal, safety, and project-specific requirements are met, minimizing the risk of penalties or legal issues.

6. Return Rate

- **Description**: Tracks the rate at which procured items are returned due to defects, non-conformance, or delivery errors.
- **Measurement**: Calculated as the number of returned items divided by the total items received.
- **Application**: A high return rate may indicate issues with product quality or shipment accuracy, impacting project efficiency and effectiveness.

How to Measure and Analyze These Metrics

- **Data Collection**: Systematically collect data through procurement systems, ERP systems, and direct reports from project teams and suppliers.
- **Regular Reviews**: Set regular intervals (monthly, quarterly) for reviewing these metrics against performance benchmarks or standards set in the contracts.
- **Performance Dashboards**: Utilize dashboards to visually monitor these KPIs, making it easier to identify trends and deviations in real-time.
- **Corrective Actions**: Based on the analysis, identify areas where suppliers are underperforming and collaborate with them to implement corrective actions. Regular feedback and discussions can help improve performance and resolve issues proactively.

Conclusion

Utilizing these procurement performance metrics and KPIs allows project managers and procurement officers to effectively monitor and control supplier performance, ensuring that all procured goods and services contribute positively to the project's success. By implementing rigorous measurement and analysis practices, organizations can enhance their procurement strategies, improve supplier relationships, and achieve better overall project outcomes. Regular procurement performance reviews are a systematic evaluation of a vendor's compliance with contract terms and conditions, their ability to meet agreed-upon standards and deadlines, and overall performance effectiveness in contributing to project objectives. These reviews are an integral component of the Control Procurements process, which ensures that the procurement activities align with the project's needs and expectations.

Benefits of Conducting Procurement Performance Reviews

1. **Ensures Contract Compliance**: Reviews help verify that the vendors are adhering to contractual obligations, including the scope, quality, and timelines specified in the contract.
2. **Enhances Vendor Management**: By regularly assessing vendor performance, project managers can manage vendor relationships more effectively, ensuring that communications are clear and productive.
3. **Improves Risk Management**: These reviews allow for early identification of potential risks and issues arising from vendor-related delays, quality issues, or non-compliance.
4. **Facilitates Timely Corrections**: Regular assessments provide opportunities to address issues before they escalate, helping to keep the project on track and within budget.
5. **Increases Project Success**: By continuously monitoring and adjusting vendor contributions, project managers can better ensure that all external efforts are contributing positively towards project deliverables.

Using Procurement Performance Reviews to Ensure Successful Project Delivery

Project managers can leverage procurement performance reviews in several strategic ways:

1. Evaluating Seller Progress:

- **Technique**: Utilize specific, measurable performance indicators such as delivery timeliness, quality of work, and adherence to budget.
- **Application**: Compare current performance data against the standards outlined in the SOW and contract. This comparison helps in identifying whether the vendor is on track or if there are deviations that need attention.

2. Identifying Issues and Risks:

- **Technique**: Analyze performance trends and feedback from project team members and stakeholders involved in the procurement process.
- **Application**: Use the insights from performance data and stakeholder feedback to pinpoint potential issues such as delays, substandard work, or escalating costs. Identify risks related to these issues, such as the impact of a delay on the project's critical path.

3. Implementing Corrective Actions:

- **Technique**: Develop a plan for corrective actions based on the severity and impact of the identified issues. This may involve renegotiating certain aspects of the contract, providing additional resources, or adjusting project schedules.

- **Application**: If a vendor is consistently missing deadlines, the project manager might negotiate expedited shipping for future deliveries or adjust project workflow to accommodate delays. They might also implement regular checkpoint meetings with the vendor to closely monitor progress and address issues in real-time.

4. Continuous Improvement:

- **Technique**: Gather lessons learned from each review cycle and apply these insights to improve future procurement activities.
- **Application**: After each review, document what was successful and what could be improved. Use this documentation to refine the procurement process for future phases of the project or for similar projects in the organization.

Conclusion

Regular procurement performance reviews are a critical tool for project managers to ensure that external vendors and suppliers contribute positively to project outcomes. These reviews not only help in maintaining rigorous control over the quality and timeliness of external work but also enhance the overall management of vendor relationships. By effectively using these reviews to evaluate, identify, and correct procurement-related issues, project managers can significantly boost the likelihood of project success. In the **Control Procurements** process, effectively monitoring and evaluating vendor performance is crucial to ensure that procurement activities align with project goals and deliver the expected value. Common procurement performance metrics and Key Performance Indicators (KPIs) provide quantitative ways to assess the efficiency, effectiveness, and compliance of suppliers and vendors throughout the project lifecycle. Here are some commonly used metrics:

Common Procurement Performance Metrics and KPIs
3. On-Time Delivery

- **Description**: Measures whether the vendor delivers goods or services by the agreed-upon date.
- **Measurement**: Calculated as the percentage of deliveries made on or before the promised delivery date over a specific period.
- **Application**: Regular tracking helps in identifying trends or issues with supplier reliability, which can impact project schedules and performance.

4. Quality Conformance

- **Description**: Assesses whether the delivered goods or services meet the quality standards and specifications agreed upon in the contract.
- **Measurement**: Often measured by the number of rejects or the acceptance rate of items inspected.
- **Application**: Critical for maintaining the project's quality requirements; poor quality conformance can lead to rework, increased costs, and delays.

3. Cost Variance

- **Description**: Compares the budgeted cost of goods and services procured against the actual cost paid.
- **Measurement**: Calculated as (Actual Cost - Budgeted Cost) / Budgeted Cost. A positive variance indicates overspending, whereas a negative variance indicates cost savings.
- **Application**: Provides insight into financial management effectiveness and helps in budget control.

4. Supplier Availability

- **Description**: Measures the availability of the supplier to meet requests for information, assistance, or problem resolution.
- **Measurement**: Can be quantified by response times to inquiries or the percentage of time the supplier was able to meet urgent demands.
- **Application**: Important for projects that require quick responses and high levels of interaction with the supplier.

5. Contract Compliance

- **Description**: Evaluates how well the supplier adheres to the terms and conditions of the contract, including regulatory compliance and safety standards.
- **Measurement**: Monitored through regular audits and reviews of supplier deliverables and operations.
- **Application**: Ensures that all legal, safety, and project-specific requirements are met, minimizing the risk of penalties or legal issues.

6. Return Rate

- **Description**: Tracks the rate at which procured items are returned due to defects, non-conformance, or delivery errors.
- **Measurement**: Calculated as the number of returned items divided by the total items received.
- **Application**: A high return rate may indicate issues with product quality or shipment accuracy, impacting project efficiency and effectiveness.

How to Measure and Analyze These Metrics

- **Data Collection**: Systematically collect data through procurement systems, ERP systems, and direct reports from project teams and suppliers.
- **Regular Reviews**: Set regular intervals (monthly, quarterly) for reviewing these metrics against performance benchmarks or standards set in the contracts.
- **Performance Dashboards**: Utilize dashboards to visually monitor these KPIs, making it easier to identify trends and deviations in real-time.
- **Corrective Actions**: Based on the analysis, identify areas where suppliers are underperforming and collaborate with them to implement corrective actions. Regular feedback and discussions can help improve performance and resolve issues proactively.

Conclusion

Utilizing these procurement performance metrics and KPIs allows project managers and procurement officers to effectively monitor and control supplier performance, ensuring that all procured goods and services contribute positively to the project's success. By implementing rigorous measurement and analysis practices, organizations can enhance their procurement strategies, improve supplier relationships, and achieve better overall project outcomes. The Project Procurement Management knowledge area is intricately linked with various other knowledge areas within project management, including Project Scope Management, Project Quality Management, and Project Risk Management. These interactions are crucial for ensuring that procurement activities are aligned with the overall project objectives and managed effectively throughout the project lifecycle.

1. Interaction with Project Scope Management

Example: In a construction project, the scope management plan outlines the work required to complete the project, including structural, electrical, and finishing work. The procurement management process uses this scope to develop a detailed Statement of Work (SOW) for contractors and suppliers. Decisions about what to procure, how much detail needs to be included in contracts, and how to integrate contractor work into the project schedule all depend on a clear understanding of the project scope.

Dependency: Procurement decisions are directly dependent on the scope baseline, as it provides the specifics of what needs to be procured from external sources. Any changes in the project scope directly impact procurement activities, potentially leading to contract amendments or the procurement of additional or different resources.

2. Interaction with Project Quality Management

Example: For a software development project, the quality management plan specifies performance benchmarks and testing procedures for the software. The procurement process must align with these quality requirements when selecting vendors, particularly in terms of their ability to meet these standards. For instance, if a vendor is required to supply a part of the code, their deliverables must be subjected to the same quality reviews and testing as in-house developed code.

Dependency: Procurement documents must include quality criteria that align with the project's quality management plan. The performance of vendors and suppliers is often monitored using quality metrics established in this plan. Non-conformance to these quality standards can lead to corrective actions, including rework by the vendor at their expense.

2. Interaction with Project Risk Management

Example: In an IT project, there could be significant risks associated with data security when outsourcing software development. The risk management plan would identify potential risks and propose mitigation strategies, such as requiring the vendor to adhere to strict data security protocols or having regular security audits.

Dependency: The procurement management process must consider these identified risks when selecting vendors and drafting contracts. The contracts might include clauses that address these risks, specifying penalties for security breaches and requiring vendors to carry insurance. The risk management process also needs to assess and respond to new risks that may arise from procurement activities, such as dependency on a single supplier or potential delays in delivery.

Integration Across Knowledge Areas

The integration of the Project Procurement Management processes with other knowledge areas ensures that procurement decisions support the project's objectives and comply with its requirements across all aspects:

- **Scope Management** ensures that procurement activities align with what needs to be achieved.
- **Quality Management** ensures that what is procured meets the necessary quality standards and contributes positively to the project outcome.
- **Risk Management** ensures that risks associated with procurement are identified, analyzed, and mitigated effectively.

These interactions highlight the importance of cohesive project management practices, where decisions in one area affect and are affected by decisions in other areas. Effective management of these interdependencies is critical for project success, ensuring that procurement supports the project holistically and helps achieve strategic objectives. The project involved constructing a new transportation network connecting three countries. Due to its scale and the involvement of multiple governments, the project required significant coordination and management of various procurement activities.

Procurement Challenges Faced

1. **Multiple Regulatory Environments**: Each country had different regulations governing construction and environmental protection, complicating the procurement of materials and services.
2. **Cultural and Language Barriers**: Working with suppliers and contractors from different cultural backgrounds and languages increased the complexity of negotiations and contract management.
3. **Logistical Complexities**: Coordinating the timely delivery of materials to various construction sites across international borders posed significant logistical challenges.
4. **Quality Assurance**: Ensuring that all procured materials met the project's high standards for quality and sustainability across different suppliers and countries.

Strategies Employed
Plan Procurements

- **Development of a Global Procurement Strategy**: The project team established a comprehensive procurement strategy that included detailed criteria for supplier selection, tailored to handle the complexities of international regulations and logistical challenges.
- **Risk Management Planning**: Specific strategies were implemented to manage potential procurement risks, including currency fluctuations, political instability, and supply chain disruptions.

Conduct Procurements

- **Utilization of International Tendering**: Open international tendering was used to attract a wide range of bidders, promoting competitive pricing and wide selection.
- **Multilingual Communication**: All procurement documents and communications were made available in multiple languages, facilitating clearer understanding and reducing miscommunications.
- **Technology Utilization**: Advanced procurement software was employed to manage bids and contracts efficiently, ensuring transparency and real-time updates across all locations.

Control Procurements

- **Regular Supplier Audits**: Conducted regular audits of suppliers to ensure compliance with the project's quality standards and contractual obligations.
- **Performance Reviews**: Regular performance reviews with key suppliers were held to discuss challenges and performance improvements, fostering a collaborative approach to achieving project goals.
- **Adaptive Contract Management**: Flexibility was built into contracts to allow for adjustments in response to unforeseen changes in project scope or external conditions.

Lessons Learned

1. **Importance of Early Planning**: Early and comprehensive planning in the procurement process was crucial in navigating the regulatory and logistical complexities of the project. This included detailed market research and risk analysis tailored to the project's multinational nature.

2. **Benefits of Technological Integration**: Employing advanced procurement and project management software provided a robust platform for managing international tenders, contracts, and supplier relationships effectively, underscoring the importance of technological integration in large-scale projects.
3. **Strategic Supplier Relationships**: Developing strategic relationships with suppliers was essential for managing the extensive requirements of the project. These relationships helped in mitigating risks associated with quality and supply chain disruptions.
4. **Adaptability and Communication**: The project highlighted the need for adaptability in contract management and the importance of clear, multilingual communication across all levels of procurement activities. This was critical not only for compliance with various international standards but also for maintaining good relationships with local and international stakeholders.

Conclusion

This case study illustrates the complexities of managing procurements in a large-scale, multinational infrastructure project. It demonstrates how effective planning, execution, and control of procurement activities, underpinned by robust strategies and advanced technologies, can lead to successful project outcomes. The lessons learned underscore the importance of adaptability, early and detailed planning, and the strategic use of technology in managing international procurements. Project procurement management encompasses a variety of ethical considerations and professional responsibilities that are critical for maintaining the integrity of both the procurement process and the project as a whole. Ethical conduct in procurement is essential not only for legal compliance but also for fostering trust among stakeholders, vendors, and project team members.

Common Ethical Considerations

1. **Conflicts of Interest**: It is crucial to avoid any personal or financial interests that might conflict with the role of a project manager or the goals of the project. Project managers should disclose any potential conflicts to relevant stakeholders to ensure transparency.
2. **Fairness and Impartiality**: All vendors and suppliers should be treated equally. Decisions should be based on objective criteria stated in the procurement documents, rather than on personal relationships or preferences.
3. **Confidentiality**: Sensitive information, particularly that shared by potential or chosen vendors during the procurement process, must be handled with confidentiality to protect the interests of all parties involved.
4. **Transparency**: Transparency involves clear communication about procurement processes, decision-making criteria, and the basis of awards. This helps in avoiding misunderstandings and disputes.
5. **Compliance with Laws and Regulations**: Adhering to all relevant local, national, and international laws is mandatory, including those governing contracts, labor, and trade.

Professional Responsibilities

- **Adherence to Organizational Policies**: Project managers must follow the policies and procedures established by their organizations. These might include specific guidelines on procurement ethics, vendor relations, and contract management.
- **Accurate Record Keeping**: Maintaining detailed and accurate records of all procurement activities is crucial for transparency and accountability. This includes documentation of all bids, communications, decisions, and contract changes.

- **Sustainable Procurement**: Increasingly, project managers also have a responsibility to consider environmental and social factors in their procurement decisions. This might involve choosing sustainable materials, considering the vendor's environmental policies, or the social impact of procurement decisions.

Importance of Ethical Practices in Procurement

1. **Building Trust**: Ethical behavior builds trust among project stakeholders, including sponsors, team members, and suppliers. Trust is fundamental to collaborative relationships and project success.
2. **Enhancing Reputation**: Maintaining high ethical standards can enhance the reputation of the organization and the project manager. This can lead to more competitive bids from suppliers and better cooperation from project stakeholders.
3. **Avoiding Legal Issues**: Adhering to laws and regulations helps avoid legal penalties and the costs associated with breaches of contract or non-compliance with regulatory requirements.
4. **Ensuring Fair Competition**: By ensuring a fair and transparent procurement process, project managers encourage competition, which can lead to better value and innovation in the solutions provided by vendors.
5. **Mitigating Risks**: Ethical procurement practices help mitigate risks related to fraud, corruption, and conflicts of interest, which can jeopardize project objectives and outcomes.

Conclusion

Ethical considerations and professional responsibilities are foundational to effective project procurement management. By adhering to principles of integrity, fairness, and transparency, and by ensuring compliance with all relevant laws and organizational policies, project managers can safeguard the interests of all stakeholders and contribute to the overall success and sustainability of their projects. Maintaining these ethical standards is not just about avoiding negative consequences; it is about fostering a positive, productive, and respectful working environment that promotes long-term success and stability. Here's a set of practice questions designed to assess and reinforce understanding of Project Procurement Management processes, key concepts, and their application in real-world scenarios. These questions can be particularly helpful for preparing for the CAPM exam or improving procurement management skills.

Question 1: What is the primary purpose of the Plan Procurement Management process?
- A) To complete all project procurements.
- B) To document how the project will procure goods and services.
- C) To pay vendors and contractors.
- D) To deliver project products or services.

Correct Answer: B) To document how the project will procure goods and services.
- **Explanation**: The Plan Procurement Management process is essential for defining the project's procurement strategy. It involves documenting how procurement should be performed from developing procurement documents through contract closure. This helps ensure that all procurement activities align with the project needs and management strategy.

Question 2: Which of the following is an output of the Conduct Procurements process?
- A) Procurement Management Plan
- B) Change Requests
- C) Seller Proposals
- D) Agreements

Correct Answer: D) Agreements

- **Explanation**: The primary outputs of the Conduct Procurements process include agreements (contracts) formed with sellers. These agreements define the formal relationship between the buyer and the seller, detailing the goods or services that the seller will provide.

Question 3: What role does a "bidder conference" play in procurement management?

- A) It is used to train project team members.
- B) It provides a means to discuss the project scope with potential sellers.
- C) It is where contracts are signed.
- D) It is used to finalize project deliverables.

Correct Answer: B) It provides a means to discuss the project scope with potential sellers.

- **Explanation**: Bidder conferences (also known as pre-bid meetings) are meetings with prospective sellers before they submit their bids. The purpose of these conferences is to clarify the project's procurement documents and requirements, ensuring that all potential bidders have a clear understanding of what is expected and can ask questions directly related to the procurement.

Question 4: What is the significance of the source selection criteria in the Plan Procurement Management process?

- A) They determine the project schedule.
- B) They specify the type of contract to be used.
- C) They establish the basis on which procurement decisions will be made.
- D) They are used to evaluate project team performance.

Correct Answer: C) They establish the basis on which procurement decisions will be made.

- **Explanation**: Source selection criteria are standards used to evaluate proposals from vendors and contractors. These criteria are critical as they guide the decision-making process in selecting the seller that best meets the project's requirements, ensuring fairness and transparency in the selection process.

Question 5: How can project managers effectively manage procurement risks?

- A) By avoiding all high-cost procurements.
- B) By transferring all procurement activities to external parties.
- C) By conducting thorough market research and including clear terms and conditions in contracts.
- D) By selecting only the lowest cost proposals.

Correct Answer: C) By conducting thorough market research and including clear terms and conditions in contracts.

- **Explanation**: Effective management of procurement risks involves understanding the market, potential suppliers, and the specific risks associated with each procurement. Conducting detailed market research helps in selecting reliable suppliers, while clear terms and conditions in contracts help manage and mitigate risks by specifying the obligations and rights of both parties.

These questions and detailed explanations not only help reinforce the fundamental concepts of Project Procurement Management but also prepare individuals for practical applications and certifications like the CAPM exam.

XII. Project Stakeholder Management:

The **Identify Stakeholders** process is a critical initial step in project management, forming the cornerstone of effective stakeholder engagement and communication. It involves systematically identifying all individuals, groups, or organizations that could impact or be impacted by the project, analyzing their expectations, and assessing how their participation could influence the project outcomes. This process is crucial for the success of any project as it directly influences the planning, execution, and conclusion phases.

Purpose and Importance of the Identify Stakeholders Process

1. **Early Identification of Influences**: Understanding who the stakeholders are from the beginning helps in anticipating their impact on project scope, objectives, and deliverables. Early identification helps in managing their expectations and in mitigating potential risks associated with their influences.
2. **Tailored Communication Strategies**: By knowing who the stakeholders are and what their needs and interests entail, project managers can develop tailored communication plans that address and engage each stakeholder or stakeholder group effectively throughout the project lifecycle.
3. **Enhanced Project Support and Acceptance**: Proper stakeholder identification and subsequent management foster greater project support and buy-in. Addressing stakeholders' concerns and expectations early and continuously can enhance project acceptance and reduce resistance.
4. **Resource Allocation**: Identifying stakeholders allows the project team to understand where to best allocate resources to ensure stakeholder requirements are met, thereby optimizing the chances of project success.

Key Activities in the Identify Stakeholders Process
1. Stakeholder Identification

- **Activity**: Compile a comprehensive list of individuals, groups, or organizations that are involved in or affected by the project. This can include the project team, suppliers, contractors, customers, end-users, and regulatory bodies.
- **Tools and Techniques**: Use project documents, organizational charts, procurement documents, and historical records. Engaging in discussions with project sponsors and team members can also reveal less obvious stakeholders.

2. Analysis of Stakeholder Characteristics

- **Activity**: Analyze each identified stakeholder's characteristics, including their interests, involvement, interdependencies, influence, and potential impact on project success.
- **Tools and Techniques**: Stakeholder analysis matrices and mapping tools like power/interest grids, influence/impact diagrams, and salience models are used to visualize and prioritize stakeholders based on these attributes.

3. Assessment of Stakeholder Impact

- **Activity**: Evaluate how stakeholders' participation and influence might affect the project. This includes understanding their potential to impact the project positively or negatively.
- **Tools and Techniques**: Techniques like SWOT analysis (Strengths, Weaknesses, Opportunities, Threats) can be useful in assessing how stakeholder interactions could impact project outcomes.

4. Development of Engagement Strategies

- **Activity**: Based on the analysis, develop strategies to effectively engage stakeholders by maximizing positive influences and mitigating potential negative impacts.
- **Tools and Techniques**: Engagement strategies are often documented in a stakeholder engagement plan, which details the methods and frequency of communication tailored to the needs of each stakeholder or stakeholder group.

How This Process Lays the Foundation for Stakeholder Management

- **Proactive Management**: By identifying stakeholders early, project managers can proactively address concerns, align expectations, and leverage stakeholder contributions throughout the project.
- **Continuous Process**: Stakeholder identification and analysis is not a one-time activity but a continuous process throughout the project lifecycle. As the project evolves, new stakeholders may emerge and the influence of existing stakeholders may change.
- **Risk Management**: Understanding stakeholder dynamics helps in anticipating and managing risks associated with stakeholder reactions and interactions.

Conclusion

The Identify Stakeholders process is vital for laying the groundwork for all subsequent project management activities, particularly those related to communication and risk management. By accurately identifying and analyzing stakeholders early in the project, managers can strategically plan and execute stakeholder engagement, enhancing the potential for project success and sustainability. The Identify Stakeholders process is a critical initial step in project management that involves the identification of people, groups, or organizations that could impact or be impacted by the project, analyzing their expectations and their influence, and developing appropriate strategies for engaging them effectively throughout the project. Understanding the inputs, tools and techniques, and outputs (ITTOs) of this process is essential for developing a comprehensive approach to stakeholder management.

Inputs
Project Charter:

The foundational document that formally authorizes a project, providing the project manager with the authority to apply organizational resources to project activities. The charter includes high-level project information and initial defined risks that help identify key stakeholders.

Business Documents:

These may include business case documents and benefits management plans, which contain information on the business need, business benefits, and potential influences on various stakeholder groups.

Project Management Plan and Project Documents:

Various elements of the project management plan and other project documents such as the communications management plan, can offer insights into planned communications and stakeholders already engaged in similar roles.

Agreements:

Contracts or agreements related to the project can define formal relationships and are critical for identifying external stakeholders like vendors or partners.

Enterprise Environmental Factors (EEFs):
These include organizational culture and structure, government or industry standards, and stakeholder risk tolerances that impact stakeholder identification and engagement strategies.

Organizational Process Assets (OPAs):
These are the organization's internal assets that can affect the Identify Stakeholders process. Examples include stakeholder registers from previous projects, lessons learned databases, and stakeholder engagement strategies.

Tools and Techniques

1. **Expert Judgment**: Consulting with individuals or groups with specialized knowledge or training in stakeholder analysis, project management, and industry specifics can help identify and classify stakeholders accurately.
2. **Data Gathering**:
   - **Brainstorming**: Team sessions to think freely and identify potential stakeholders from every possible angle.
   - **Interviews**: Conducting discussions with people who have experience or insight into the project's area to identify additional stakeholders.
3. **Data Analysis**:
   - **Stakeholder Analysis**: Analyzing potential stakeholders' possible impact or support, categorized by their interest, influence, and involvement needs in the project.
   - **Power/Interest Grid, Power/Influence Grid, Influence/Impact Grid**: Tools to categorize stakeholders and prioritize their engagement based on their attributes and potential impact on the project.
4. **Stakeholder Mapping/Representation**: Visualizing relationships among stakeholders and the project, such as stakeholder maps or matrices, to understand influence lines and communication channels.

Outputs

1. **Stakeholder Register**: The primary output of this process, which includes identification information, assessment information, and classification of all identified stakeholders. This register provides a comprehensive list of stakeholders, categorized by interest, influence, and potential impact, and serves as a dynamic tool that evolves throughout the project.
2. **Change Requests**: Identified stakeholder information might lead to changes in the project management plan or project documents.
3. **Project Management Plan Updates**: Particularly updates to the stakeholder engagement plan, which might be refined based on the stakeholder analysis.
4. **Project Documents Updates**: Other documents like the issue log might be updated based on stakeholder information and insights gained during the stakeholder identification process.

Significance in Stakeholder Landscape Development

Understanding the ITTOs of the Identify Stakeholders process is crucial for developing a comprehensive stakeholder landscape. By effectively identifying all relevant stakeholders and understanding their potential impact and influence, project managers can devise strategies that engage stakeholders appropriately, ensuring support and minimizing resistance throughout the project lifecycle. This not only helps in aligning project objectives with stakeholder expectations but also enhances communication, increases support, and facilitates smoother project execution. The stakeholder register is a crucial tool used in project management, specifically in the Identify Stakeholders process. Its primary purpose is to document detailed information about all identified stakeholders of a project. This documentation aids in managing stakeholder expectations, influences, and contributions throughout the project life cycle, ensuring that stakeholder needs are understood and considered effectively.

Purpose of the Stakeholder Register

1. **Documentation**: To capture and document comprehensive information about each stakeholder related to the project.
2. **Communication Planning**: To assist in developing an effective communication plan by understanding who needs what information, when they need it, and how it should be delivered.
3. **Stakeholder Engagement**: To facilitate strategies for engaging stakeholders in appropriate ways during different phases of the project, based on their interests and potential impact.
4. **Conflict Resolution**: To anticipate and mitigate potential conflicts by understanding the relationships, interests, and influence levels among various stakeholders.

Key Components of a Stakeholder Register

A comprehensive stakeholder register typically includes the following information for each stakeholder:

1. Stakeholder Identification:

- **Name and Organization**: Basic identification information including the stakeholder's name and affiliation.
- **Role on Project**: The role or function the stakeholder has in relation to the project (e.g., sponsor, client, team member, contractor).

2. Assessment Information:

- **Interests**: What the stakeholder hopes to gain or lose from the project. This includes understanding their vested interests in the project's success or failure.
- **Expectations**: The outcomes or conditions the stakeholder expects from the project. This can range from project deliverables to communication and reporting frequencies.
- **Influence**: The level of power or impact the stakeholder has on the project. This could be in terms of decision-making power, resource control, or their ability to influence other stakeholders.
- **Potential Impact**: How the stakeholder could positively or negatively affect the project. This involves understanding their capacity to alter project outcomes based on their actions or decisions.
- **Classification**: Categorization of stakeholders based on their interest, influence, or other relevant criteria such as internal/external, supporter/opponent, etc.

3. Communication Requirements:

- **Preferred Communication Methods**: How the stakeholder prefers to receive information (e.g., email, meetings, reports).
- **Frequency of Communication**: How often the stakeholder needs updates or engagements.
- **Key Messages**: Important messages that need to be communicated to the stakeholder to ensure their continued support and understanding of the project.

Using the Stakeholder Register

The information captured in the stakeholder register is used throughout the project to:

- **Plan and implement stakeholder engagement strategies**: Tailoring approaches based on the specific needs, interests, and influence of stakeholders.
- **Develop and maintain a communication plan**: Ensuring all stakeholders are kept informed and engaged according to their needs and potential impact on the project.
- **Monitor and adjust strategies**: Continually updating the stakeholder register as relationships evolve and new stakeholders are identified.

Example: In a large construction project, the project manager uses the stakeholder register to differentiate between local government officials who need regular legal and compliance updates, investors who are interested in financial updates and progress reports, and contractors who require detailed technical communication.

Conclusion

The stakeholder register is an essential document in the Identify Stakeholders process, enabling effective stakeholder management by providing a structured approach to understanding and addressing the diverse needs and influences of all project stakeholders. Proper maintenance and utilization of this register are fundamental to achieving project objectives and ensuring stakeholder satisfaction. Stakeholder analysis is a systematic technique used in project management to identify, evaluate, and prioritize individuals or groups that have an interest in or influence over the project. This analysis is crucial during the Identify Stakeholders process as it helps the project team understand who the stakeholders are, what their needs and expectations might be, and how best to engage them.

Role of Stakeholder Analysis

1. **Identification**: Distinguishes who the stakeholders are, both internal and external to the organization, ensuring that all potential influences or impacts on the project are considered.
2. **Assessment**: Evaluates the extent of each stakeholder's interest in and influence on the project, which is vital for effective management and communication.
3. **Prioritization**: Helps prioritize stakeholders by their level of interest and influence, which facilitates efficient allocation of resources and effort in managing stakeholder engagement.

Tools for Stakeholder Analysis
1. Power/Interest Grid

- **Description**: This grid classifies stakeholders based on their level of authority (power) and their level of concern (interest) regarding the project outcomes.
- **Application**:
    - **High Power, High Interest**: These stakeholders are key players and must be fully engaged and frequently communicated with to ensure their needs are met and their influence is utilized positively.
    - **High Power, Low Interest**: Keep these stakeholders satisfied, but not overwhelmed with information to avoid unnecessary attention or interference.
    - **Low Power, High Interest**: Keep these stakeholders adequately informed, and ensure that their high interest is used positively to support the project's objectives.
    - **Low Power, Low Interest**: Monitor these stakeholders, but minimal effort is needed to keep them informed.

- **Example**: A government body may have high power and high interest in a public infrastructure project due to regulatory concerns, requiring close engagement.

2. Influence/Impact Matrix

- **Description**: Similar to the Power/Interest Grid, this matrix helps to assess stakeholders based on their influence over project execution and the impact they can have on the project's success.
- **Application**:
  - **High Influence, High Impact**: Stakeholders who can significantly affect project outcomes and are heavily affected by the project. They require active efforts to engage and manage.
  - **High Influence, Low Impact**: Important to keep these stakeholders informed and onside even though the project may not significantly impact them.
  - **Low Influence, High Impact**: Stakeholders who are greatly affected by the project but have little control over it. They should be kept informed and supported.
  - **Low Influence, Low Impact**: Stakeholders with minimal effect on or from the project. Less frequent communication is typically adequate.
- **Example**: Employees may have low influence but high impact if a project outcome significantly alters their work processes, requiring careful change management communication.

Using Stakeholder Analysis Effectively

Project managers can utilize these tools to develop tailored strategies for stakeholder engagement. By understanding where stakeholders fall on these grids or matrices, project managers can allocate their time and resources more effectively, focusing on stakeholders who require more attention due to their ability to influence project outcomes or their high interest in the project. Regular reviews and updates to these classifications are crucial as stakeholders' levels of interest and influence can change as the project progresses.

Conclusion

Stakeholder analysis, facilitated by tools such as the power/interest grid and the influence/impact matrix, is vital for understanding the complex landscape of project influences. By classifying and prioritizing stakeholders based on these analyses, project managers can strategically plan how to engage each stakeholder group effectively, ensuring project support and minimizing resistance or negative impacts. The

Plan Stakeholder Engagement

process is pivotal in project management, designed to outline strategies for effectively engaging stakeholders throughout the duration of the project. This process focuses on understanding the needs, expectations, and potential impact of stakeholders, and creating a systematic approach to fostering positive relationships, promoting efficient communication, and ensuring their active involvement in project decisions and execution.

Significance of Plan Stakeholder Engagement

1. **Ensures Effective Communication**: Establishes a clear plan for how and when stakeholders will be informed about project progress, changes, and decisions that may affect them. This helps in managing expectations and maintaining transparency.

2. **Enhances Stakeholder Support**: By actively engaging stakeholders and addressing their concerns and expectations, the project is more likely to receive continuous support and less resistance, contributing to smoother project execution.
3. **Improves Project Outcomes**: Engaged stakeholders can provide valuable insights, resources, and support, leading to improved problem-solving, decision-making, and innovation in project processes and outcomes.
4. **Mitigates Risks**: Understanding stakeholder concerns and expectations allows for early identification and mitigation of potential risks associated with stakeholder interactions and impacts on the project.

Key Considerations in Creating a Stakeholder Engagement Plan
1. Stakeholder Identification and Analysis

- **Consideration**: Accurate identification and comprehensive analysis are crucial. It's important to know who the stakeholders are, what their interests and levels of influence are, and how the project impacts them.
- **Tool**: Use stakeholder analysis tools like power/interest grids or influence/impact matrices to classify stakeholders based on their importance and impact on the project.

2. Assessment of Engagement Levels

- **Consideration**: Determine the current level of engagement of each stakeholder (e.g., unaware, resistant, neutral, supportive, leading) and the desired level of engagement needed to achieve project objectives.
- **Tool**: Engagement assessment matrices can help visualize and plan the necessary actions to move stakeholders from their current level of engagement to the desired level.

3. Communication Requirements

- **Consideration**: Different stakeholders may require different frequencies, formats, and details in communications. Tailoring communication strategies to fit the stakeholder's needs and preferences is essential.
- **Tool**: Develop a communication plan that details what will be communicated, through which medium, how often, and by whom, ensuring alignment with stakeholders' information needs and preferences.

4. Cultural and Social Considerations

- **Consideration**: Be aware of and sensitive to the cultural, social, and personal backgrounds of stakeholders, which can influence their perceptions, behaviors, and reactions to project activities.
- **Tool**: Cultural awareness training for the project team and the use of culturally appropriate communication and engagement tactics.

5. Monitoring and Feedback Mechanisms

- **Consideration**: Regular monitoring of stakeholder engagement and openness to feedback are important for making necessary adjustments in engagement strategies and addressing issues promptly.
- **Tool**: Implement feedback mechanisms like surveys, focus groups, or informal check-ins, and use tools like stakeholder engagement dashboards to monitor engagement activities and stakeholder responses.

6. Resource Allocation

- **Consideration**: Ensure that sufficient resources (time, budget, personnel) are allocated to stakeholder engagement activities to support effective implementation.
- **Tool**: Resource allocation plans that specify what resources are needed for engagement activities, ensuring they are included in the overall project budget and schedule.

Conclusion

The Plan Stakeholder Engagement process is critical for building and maintaining robust relationships with all project stakeholders. By developing a thoughtful and strategic stakeholder engagement plan, project managers can ensure that stakeholders are not only informed and consulted but actively involved in the project where appropriate. This leads to enhanced project cooperation, reduced risks, and greater overall project success. In the Plan Stakeholder Engagement process, understanding stakeholder needs, expectations, and potential concerns is crucial for developing an effective stakeholder engagement strategy. Various techniques can be employed to assess how stakeholders can best be engaged throughout the project lifecycle. Here's a look at some common stakeholder engagement assessment techniques: stakeholder interviews, focus groups, and surveys.

Stakeholder Interviews

Application: Stakeholder interviews involve one-on-one conversations with key project stakeholders to gain an in-depth understanding of their views, expectations, needs, and concerns regarding the project.

Benefits:
- Provides deep insights into individual stakeholder perspectives.
- Allows for a confidential setting where stakeholders might be more willing to share honest feedback and concerns.
- Helps in building relationships and trust between the project team and stakeholders.

Usage by Project Managers: Project managers can use these interviews to tailor communication and engagement strategies to individual needs, ensuring that stakeholders feel heard and valued, which can increase their support for the project.

Focus Groups

Application: Focus groups consist of facilitated discussions with a group of stakeholders who are brought together to discuss specific aspects of the project. This setting allows for interaction between different stakeholders, providing a diverse range of insights.

Benefits:
- Enables the project team to gather a broad range of views and opinions in a single session.
- Facilitates understanding of the dynamics between different stakeholder groups.
- Can highlight areas of consensus or disagreement that might need special attention.

Usage by Project Managers: By facilitating focus group discussions, project managers can identify alignment or gaps in stakeholder expectations and perceptions. This understanding can help in crafting strategies that address collective concerns and leverage common interests.

Surveys

Application: Surveys are structured questionnaires that are distributed to a larger group of stakeholders. They are designed to gather quantitative and qualitative data about stakeholders' views and expectations regarding the project.

Benefits:

- Allows for data collection from a large number of stakeholders quickly and efficiently.
- Provides quantifiable data that can be analyzed to identify trends and commonalities among stakeholder groups.
- Ensures anonymity, which may encourage more honest and critical responses.

Usage by Project Managers: Surveys can be used to gauge the overall sentiment about the project across a wide stakeholder base. This data can help project managers to prioritize areas of concern, measure stakeholder engagement levels over time, and adjust engagement strategies as needed.

Integrating These Techniques for Comprehensive Assessment

To maximize insights from these techniques, project managers can employ a mixed-methods approach by integrating various techniques to balance the depth and breadth of stakeholder feedback. For instance, initial surveys can identify key areas of concern that might be explored in more detail through follow-up interviews or focus groups. This integrative approach ensures that engagement strategies are robust, data-driven, and tailored to meet the needs and expectations of all stakeholder groups effectively.

Conclusion

Employing these stakeholder engagement assessment techniques provides project managers with valuable insights into how best to engage each stakeholder group throughout the project. By understanding stakeholders' needs, expectations, and concerns, project managers can devise engagement plans that not only foster positive relationships but also enhance cooperation and project support, ultimately contributing to a more successful project outcome. The Plan Stakeholder Engagement process is a crucial element of project management, involving the development of approaches to effectively engage stakeholders throughout the project lifecycle. This process ensures that stakeholders are appropriately involved in a manner that aligns with their interests, influence, and impact on the project, ultimately contributing to project success.

Importance of Stakeholder Engagement Strategies

1. **Aligns Stakeholder Expectations**: Ensures that stakeholders have a clear understanding of the project objectives, the benefits they will gain, and the role they play, helping to align their expectations with the project goals.
2. **Enhances Cooperation and Support**: Effective engagement increases stakeholder support, reduces resistance, fosters positive relationships, and facilitates smoother project execution.
3. **Improves Decision-Making**: By involving key stakeholders in decision-making processes, the project can benefit from diverse perspectives, leading to more informed and robust decisions.
4. **Increases Project Success Rate**: Active and positive stakeholder involvement can significantly increase the chances of project success by ensuring that stakeholder needs are met and that they actively support the project's direction.

Types of Stakeholder Engagement Strategies
1. Inform:
- **Purpose**: To keep stakeholders apprised of progress and developments without soliciting their input in decision-making.
- **When to Use**: Appropriate for stakeholders with low influence and low impact, where the primary need is to ensure they are aware of project progress and developments.
- **Example**: Sending regular newsletters or updates to a wider community or minor suppliers.
2. Consult:

- **Purpose**: To seek advice or feedback from stakeholders on specific issues, allowing them to contribute to the decision-making process without giving them decision-making authority.
- **When to Use**: Suitable for stakeholders with moderate influence and/or impact who can provide valuable insights but whose approval is not critical for decisions.
- **Example**: Conducting surveys, focus groups, or review sessions with customers or user groups to gather feedback on project plans or prototypes.

3. Involve:

- **Purpose**: To work directly with stakeholders throughout the decision-making process to ensure that their concerns and aspirations are consistently understood and considered.
- **When to Use**: Effective for stakeholders with moderate to high impact, particularly when their contribution can significantly drive project success.
- **Example**: Regular workshop sessions with end-users to co-design a system or product features.

4. Collaborate:

- **Purpose**: To partner with stakeholders in each aspect of the decision-making process, including the development of alternatives and the identification of the preferred solution.
- **When to Use**: Best for stakeholders with high influence and high impact, where their active cooperation is crucial for project success.
- **Example**: Jointly planning project activities with contractors or partnering NGOs in community development projects.

5. Empower:

- **Purpose**: To place final decision-making in the hands of stakeholders, allowing them full control over certain decisions.
- **When to Use**: Applicable when stakeholders are the ones primarily affected by the outcomes, such as department heads in an organizational project, or when their commitment is crucial.
- **Example**: Allowing a local community council to make key decisions regarding the project components that directly affect their community.

Selecting Engagement Strategies

The selection of these strategies is based on a thorough analysis of each stakeholder's interests, influence, needs, and potential impact on the project. This involves:

- **Assessing Stakeholder Attributes**: Understanding the level of interest, influence, expectations, and needs of each stakeholder or stakeholder group.
- **Matching Strategy to Stakeholder Needs**: Aligning the engagement strategy with the stakeholders' attributes and how critically they can impact or are impacted by the project.
- **Adapting to Stakeholder Changes**: Continuously updating and adapting strategies based on changes in stakeholder characteristics or project requirements.

Conclusion

Developing and implementing appropriate stakeholder engagement strategies is essential for managing stakeholder relationships effectively. By understanding the different levels of engagement and applying them judiciously based on stakeholder characteristics, project managers can enhance stakeholder satisfaction, reduce risks associated with poor stakeholder management, and improve overall project performance. The **Manage Stakeholder Engagement** process is pivotal for maintaining productive relationships with stakeholders throughout the project lifecycle. This process involves actively involving stakeholders in project decisions and activities, ensuring their needs and expectations are met, and addressing any issues that arise. Effective stakeholder engagement not only enhances project cooperation and support but also minimizes risks associated with stakeholder dissatisfaction.

Role of Manage Stakeholder Engagement

1. **Meeting Needs and Expectations**: Ensures that stakeholder expectations are clearly understood and managed proactively. Regular engagement helps in aligning the project outcomes with stakeholder expectations.
2. **Issue Resolution**: Provides a structured approach to identify, address, and resolve issues raised by stakeholders promptly, which helps in maintaining their support and reducing the likelihood of opposition.
3. **Fostering Involvement**: Encourages stakeholders to participate actively in the project, leveraging their expertise, insights, and influence to facilitate smoother project execution and acceptance.
4. **Continuous Communication**: Maintains an ongoing dialogue with stakeholders to keep them informed of project progress and developments. This transparency builds trust and helps in managing perceptions and attitudes toward the project.

Primary Tools and Techniques Used in Manage Stakeholder Engagement
1. Communication Methods

- **Description**: Various methods of communication such as meetings, emails, newsletters, reports, and presentations are used to ensure stakeholders are kept informed and engaged according to their preferences and needs.
- **Application**: Tailoring communication methods to the specific requirements of different stakeholder groups ensures that the information is effective and engaging.

2. Interpersonal and Team Skills

- **Description**: Skills such as active listening, conflict resolution, negotiation, and facilitation are crucial in managing interactions with and between stakeholders.
- **Application**: These skills are used to understand stakeholder concerns fully, resolve disputes, facilitate discussions, and negotiate solutions that align with project goals.

3. Engagement Assessment Tools

- **Description**: Tools like stakeholder engagement assessment matrices help in monitoring the level of stakeholder engagement and satisfaction throughout the project.
- **Application**: These tools are used to measure the effectiveness of engagement strategies and identify areas where changes may be needed to enhance stakeholder involvement.

4. Management Systems

- **Description**: Project management software and systems that include features for tracking communications, feedback, and updates related to stakeholders.
- **Application**: These systems help in organizing, documenting, and retrieving interactions with stakeholders, ensuring that all engagement activities are recorded and traceable.

5. Feedback Mechanisms
- **Description**: Mechanisms such as surveys, comment forms, and feedback sessions are integrated into the engagement strategy to gather stakeholder opinions and responses to project developments.
- **Application**: Feedback collected is analyzed to adjust project approaches, address stakeholder concerns, and improve future engagement practices.

6. Change Management Techniques
- **Description**: Techniques that prepare, support, and help individuals, teams, and organizations in making organizational change.
- **Application**: Used to manage changes within the project that affect stakeholders, ensuring that transitions are smooth and that stakeholders remain supportive of the project direction.

Conclusion
The Manage Stakeholder Engagement process is essential for ensuring that stakeholders are not just informed but are actively involved and supportive of the project. By using a combination of effective communication methods, interpersonal In the Manage Stakeholder Engagement process, interpersonal and communication skills are vital for fostering positive relationships, ensuring stakeholders are effectively engaged, and achieving project objectives. Effective engagement involves not just sharing information but also actively managing relationships to garner support and mitigate opposition.

Key Interpersonal and Communication Skills for Project Managers
1. Active Listening
- **Importance**: Active listening is crucial for understanding stakeholders' perspectives, concerns, and suggestions. It ensures that stakeholders feel heard and valued, which can strengthen their commitment to the project.
- **Application**: Project managers should practice active listening by focusing intently on the speaker, asking clarifying questions, and paraphrasing their understanding of the message. This skill is especially important during stakeholder meetings and one-on-one conversations.

2. Emotional Intelligence (EI)
- **Importance**: Emotional intelligence refers to the ability to perceive, control, and evaluate emotions—both one's own and those of others. High EI helps project managers handle interpersonal relationships judiciously and empathetically.
- **Application**: By recognizing their own emotional states and those of others, project managers can better manage their responses and interactions, adapting communication and engagement strategies to suit different emotional contexts and personalities.

3. Conflict Resolution
- **Importance**: Conflict is almost inevitable in projects, especially as different stakeholders often have competing interests. Effective conflict resolution ensures that conflicts are resolved constructively, without damaging relationships.
- **Application**: Project managers can employ techniques such as mediation, negotiation, and compromise to resolve conflicts. They should aim to address conflicts early and openly, ensuring that all parties feel they are part of the solution.

4. Persuasion and Influence

- **Importance**: The ability to persuade and influence stakeholders is crucial for gaining buy-in and encouraging stakeholders to support project decisions.
- **Application**: Project managers should use rational persuasion, appealing to stakeholders' logical reasoning, and inspirational appeals, connecting project goals with stakeholders' values and emotions.

5. Communication Clarity and Precision

- **Importance**: Clear and precise communication helps prevent misunderstandings and misinterpretations that could derail stakeholder relationships and project outcomes.
- **Application**: Project managers should ensure that all communication is straightforward and unambiguous, tailoring the message to the audience's level of understanding and cultural context.

6. Cultural Sensitivity

- **Importance**: Projects often involve stakeholders from diverse cultural backgrounds. Being sensitive to cultural differences is essential for respectful and effective engagement.
- **Application**: Project managers should educate themselves about the cultural norms and communication styles of the stakeholders involved, adapting their engagement methods to be culturally appropriate.

Integrating Skills for Effective Stakeholder Engagement

The integration of these skills enables project managers to create a positive project environment where all stakeholders feel involved and respected. By effectively managing stakeholder engagement, project managers can harness the strengths and insights of all stakeholders, leading to better decision-making, enhanced project cooperation, and increased likelihood of project success.

Conclusion

Interpersonal and communication skills are not just beneficial but essential for the successful management of stakeholder engagement. These skills empower project managers to navigate the complexities of human interactions, foster positive relationships, and facilitate a collaborative project atmosphere. Mastery of these skills translates into better project outcomes and more robust, effective stakeholder management. Issue management is a systematic process within the Manage Stakeholder Engagement phase of project management. It involves identifying, documenting, and resolving issues that arise during the project lifecycle and could potentially impact stakeholder engagement and project success.

Significance of Issue Management

1. **Ensures Continuous Engagement**: Effective issue management helps maintain and enhance stakeholder engagement by addressing concerns and challenges proactively, ensuring stakeholders feel valued and heard.
2. **Prevents Escalation**: By managing issues promptly, project managers can prevent them from escalating into more significant problems that could derail the project.

3. **Improves Project Performance**: Resolving issues efficiently contributes to smoother project execution, reducing delays and avoiding potential conflicts.
4. **Builds Trust**: Demonstrating the ability to effectively handle issues enhances stakeholders' trust in the project management team, fostering a cooperative and supportive project environment.

Steps in Issue Management
1. Issue Identification

- **Process**: Continuously monitor project activities and communications with stakeholders to identify any concerns, complaints, or problems that arise.
- **Tools**: Use regular meetings, stakeholder surveys, and informal feedback channels to gather insights into potential issues.

2. Issue Documentation

- **Process**: Document each identified issue in an issue log, detailing the nature of the issue, the stakeholders affected, the impact on the project, and any other relevant details.
- **Example**: An issue log entry might include a description of a delay in delivering critical project materials, noting which aspects of the project are impacted and which stakeholders have raised concerns.

3. Issue Analysis

- **Process**: Analyze each issue to understand its causes, the stakeholders involved, and the potential impact on the project.
- **Tools**: Root cause analysis or the "5 Whys" technique can be effective in identifying underlying causes of issues.

4. Issue Resolution Planning

- **Process**: Develop a plan to resolve each issue, identifying specific actions, responsible individuals, and timelines.
- **Example**: If a key stakeholder is dissatisfied with a project deliverable, the resolution plan might involve revising the deliverable based on their feedback and scheduling extra review sessions with them.

5. Issue Resolution Implementation

- **Process**: Implement the resolution plan, involving the relevant stakeholders in the process to ensure the issue is resolved to their satisfaction.
- **Tools**: Project management software can be used to track the progress of issue resolution actions and communicate updates to stakeholders.

6. Issue Monitoring and Closure

- **Process**: Monitor the effectiveness of the issue resolution, ensuring the issue does not reoccur and that stakeholders are satisfied with the outcome. Once resolved, formally close the issue in the issue log.
- **Example**: Follow up with all stakeholders involved in an issue to confirm that the resolution has been effective and that no further action is needed.

Proactive Issue Management Practices

- **Regular Stakeholder Communication**: Maintain open lines of communication with all stakeholders to identify issues early.
- **Stakeholder Meetings**: Conduct regular meetings with key stakeholders to discuss the project's progress and any concerns they may have.
- **Feedback Mechanisms**: Implement and encourage the use of feedback mechanisms such as suggestion boxes, surveys, and interactive sessions.
- **Early Warning Systems**: Develop and utilize early warning systems that can alert the project team to potential issues based on project performance data.

Conclusion

Effective issue management is critical in managing stakeholder engagement and ensuring the overall success of a project. By proactively identifying, documenting, and resolving issues, project managers can maintain positive relationships with stakeholders, address concerns promptly, and prevent minor issues from becoming major obstacles. This proactive approach not only keeps the project on track but also fosters a supportive and collaborative project environment. Project managers often face various challenges in stakeholder engagement, which can significantly impact project success if not managed effectively. These challenges include conflicting stakeholder interests, resistance to change, and limited resources. Addressing these challenges requires strategic planning, adept communication, and proactive stakeholder management.

Common Stakeholder Engagement Challenges
1. Conflicting Stakeholder Interests

- **Description**: Stakeholders often have diverse or conflicting interests related to the project's outcomes, priorities, or processes.
- **Challenge**: Balancing these interests without compromising the project's objectives can be difficult, potentially leading to delays or dissatisfaction.

2. Resistance to Change

- **Description**: Stakeholders may resist changes introduced by the project, especially if the changes affect their current processes or benefits.
- **Challenge**: Overcoming resistance requires effective change management strategies to ensure stakeholder buy-in and support.

3. Limited Resources

- **Description**: Resource constraints can affect how well stakeholder engagement activities are planned and executed.
- **Challenge**: Limited time, budget, or personnel can hinder effective communication and engagement efforts.

Strategies and Best Practices for Overcoming These Challenges
Addressing Conflicting Interests

1. **Stakeholder Analysis and Prioritization**
   - **Strategy**: Conduct thorough stakeholder analysis to understand the needs, interests, and influence of each stakeholder.

- **Best Practice**: Use tools like power/interest grids to prioritize stakeholders and tailor engagement strategies accordingly.

2. **Facilitated Workshops and Mediation**
   - **Strategy**: Organize workshops or mediation sessions to address conflicts and find common ground.
   - **Best Practice**: Engage a neutral facilitator to help navigate discussions and ensure that all voices are heard.

Overcoming Resistance to Change

1. **Effective Communication**
   - **Strategy**: Communicate changes clearly and frequently, explaining the reasons behind changes and their expected benefits.
   - **Best Practice**: Use multiple communication channels to ensure messages are received and understood by all stakeholders.

2. **Involvement in Change Process**
   - **Strategy**: Involve stakeholders in the change process from the beginning to increase their sense of ownership and acceptance.
   - **Best Practice**: Include stakeholders in planning sessions and decision-making processes related to changes.

Managing Limited Resources

1. **Efficient Use of Resources**
   - **Strategy**: Plan and allocate resources efficiently to maximize the impact of stakeholder engagement activities.
   - **Best Practice**: Develop a clear stakeholder engagement plan that outlines resource needs and schedules activities based on available resources.

2. **Leveraging Technology**
   - **Strategy**: Use technology to facilitate communication and engagement with stakeholders efficiently.
   - **Best Practice**: Implement project management and communication tools that allow virtual meetings, real-time updates, and centralized information sharing.

General Best Practices for Maintaining Positive Relationships

1. **Regular Updates and Transparency**
   - Keep stakeholders informed about project progress and any issues that arise. Transparency builds trust and reduces uncertainties.

2. **Recognize and Address Concerns Promptly**
   - Actively seek out stakeholder concerns and address them promptly. Being responsive demonstrates respect for their input and dedication to their satisfaction.

3. **Build Trust through Consistency**
   - Be consistent in your interactions and follow through on commitments. Consistency builds reliability and trust over time.

Conclusion

Managing stakeholder engagement effectively requires a thoughtful approach that considers the unique dynamics and challenges of each project. By understanding and addressing the specific concerns related to conflicting interests, resistance to change, and resource limitations, project managers can foster stronger, more productive relationships with stakeholders. These relationships are critical for navigating project challenges and achieving successful outcomes. The Monitor Stakeholder Engagement process is pivotal in ensuring that stakeholder relationships are actively managed and optimized throughout the project lifecycle. This process involves regularly evaluating the effectiveness of the stakeholder engagement strategies and making necessary adjustments to enhance communication, understanding, and cooperation between the project team and its stakeholders.

Purpose of Monitoring Stakeholder Engagement

1. **Assess Engagement Levels**: Determine if stakeholders are as engaged as planned and identify any shifts in their engagement levels that might impact the project.
2. **Adjust Engagement Strategies**: Refine or update strategies to address and adapt to stakeholder feedback, changing expectations, or project evolution.
3. **Enhance Communication**: Improve methods of communication based on stakeholder preferences and feedback to ensure clarity and effective information sharing.
4. **Ensure Stakeholder Satisfaction**: Continuously gauge stakeholder satisfaction and address any concerns promptly to maintain supportive and constructive relationships.

Key Activities in the Monitor Stakeholder Engagement Process

1. **Collecting Feedback**: Regularly collecting feedback through various means such as meetings, surveys, and informal conversations helps understand stakeholders' perceptions and experiences related to the project.
2. **Analyzing Stakeholder Engagement**: Using tools to analyze the collected data to determine the effectiveness of the current engagement efforts. This analysis helps identify areas where stakeholder needs are not being met.
3. **Reviewing and Updating the Stakeholder Engagement Plan**: Based on the feedback and analysis, the stakeholder engagement plan may need to be updated to address new issues or shifts in stakeholder attitudes.
4. **Reporting**: Documenting and reporting on stakeholder engagement activities and their outcomes for transparency and for informing decision-making processes.

Techniques Used to Assess Effectiveness of Engagement Efforts

1. **Surveys and Questionnaires**: Distributing surveys and questionnaires to stakeholders to gather quantitative and qualitative data on their satisfaction and engagement levels.
2. **Stakeholder Interviews**: Conducting one-on-one interviews to collect in-depth insights into the stakeholders' views and experiences.
3. **Focus Groups**: Bringing together various stakeholders to discuss their views and perceptions in a structured setting, which can provide diverse perspectives and deeper understanding.
4. **Observation**: Observing stakeholder behavior and participation in project activities can provide non-verbal cues about their engagement and satisfaction levels.
5. **Stakeholder Engagement Metrics**: Developing and tracking specific metrics like participation rates, feedback timeliness, and the nature of the feedback (positive/negative/neutral) to measure engagement.
6. **Stakeholder Engagement Assessment Tools**: Tools such as the Stakeholder Engagement Assessment Matrix which helps in mapping out the current versus desired engagement levels to visually identify gaps and areas needing attention.

Conclusion

The Monitor Stakeholder Engagement process is essential for ensuring that the strategies and plans for stakeholder interaction remain effective and responsive to the project's and stakeholders' evolving needs. By continuously monitoring and adjusting the approach to stakeholder engagement, project managers can maintain strong, supportive relationships that contribute positively to project success. This proactive approach helps in anticipating and mitigating issues that could affect project outcomes and ensures that stakeholders feel valued and understood throughout the project duration.

Issue Log: Purpose and Components

The issue log is a fundamental tool in the Monitor Stakeholder Engagement process, serving as a dynamic document where issues, concerns, disputes, and action items related to stakeholders are recorded and tracked throughout the project lifecycle. This tool is essential for effective project management, ensuring that all stakeholder-related issues are addressed in a timely and systematic manner.

Purpose of the Issue Log

1. **Documentation**: The issue log provides a formal record of issues raised by stakeholders. This documentation is crucial for transparency and accountability in how issues are handled.
2. **Tracking**: It allows for the systematic tracking of the status of each issue from identification through resolution, ensuring that no concerns are overlooked.
3. **Communication**: The log serves as a communication tool, informing the project team and relevant stakeholders about the issues at hand and the actions taken to resolve them.
4. **Resolution**: It aids in the timely resolution of issues by assigning responsibility and deadlines for action items, thereby minimizing potential impacts on project progress.
5. **Learning**: Over time, the issue log can be a valuable source of lessons learned, helping improve the management of stakeholder engagement and issue resolution in future projects.

Components of an Issue Log

An effective issue log typically includes several key components:

1. **Issue Identification Number**: A unique identifier for each issue logged. This helps in easily referencing and tracking specific issues.
2. **Date Reported**: The date on which the issue was first identified or reported. This helps in tracking the duration an issue remains open and in prioritizing issues based on their reporting dates.
3. **Reporter**: The name or identification of the stakeholder who reported the issue. This is important for follow-up and for understanding the perspective of different stakeholders.
4. **Description**: A clear and concise description of the issue. This should include any relevant details that will help in understanding the context and specifics of the problem.
5. **Impact**: An assessment of the issue's potential impact on the project if it is not resolved. This helps in prioritizing issues based on their severity and urgency.
6. **Priority**: The priority level of the issue, typically categorized as high, medium, or low. This prioritization helps manage resources effectively and address the most critical issues first.
7. **Assigned To**: The person or team responsible for resolving the issue. Assigning responsibility is crucial for accountability and ensures that each issue is addressed.
8. **Status**: The current status of the issue (e.g., open, in progress, resolved, closed). This helps the project team monitor progress in issue resolution and communicate updates to stakeholders.
9. **Resolution Date**: The date by which the issue was resolved. Tracking resolution times can provide insights into the efficiency of the issue resolution process.

10. **Resolution Description**: Details on how the issue was resolved, including any actions taken and decisions made. This component is essential for closing out issues and for recording outcomes that may inform future decisions.

How the Issue Log Helps Project Managers

The issue log is instrumental in helping project managers effectively manage stakeholder concerns and maintain the health of the project. By providing a structured way to document, track, and manage issues, project managers can ensure that:

- Stakeholder concerns are addressed promptly and efficiently.
- Communication regarding issues is clear and consistent across the project team and stakeholders.
- Project risks associated with unresolved issues are minimized.
- Stakeholder satisfaction is maintained through transparent and responsive handling of concerns.

Issue Log: Purpose and Components

The issue log is an essential tool within the Monitor Stakeholder Engagement process, primarily serving to document, track, and manage issues that affect stakeholders throughout the duration of a project. This tool is critical for maintaining clear and open lines of communication, ensuring that all stakeholder concerns and issues are addressed in a timely and effective manner.

Purpose of the Issue Log

Documentation: The issue log provides a formal record of all issues identified by stakeholders or affecting stakeholders. This documentation is crucial for transparency and accountability.

Tracking: It allows for the systematic tracking of each issue from the point of identification to resolution. This helps ensure that no issues are overlooked and that they are resolved in a timely manner.

Communication: The log serves as a communication tool, informing the project team and stakeholders about current issues, actions taken, and the status of resolutions.

Prioritization: By documenting the severity and impact of issues, the issue log helps in prioritizing them based on their potential impact on the project. This aids in efficient resource allocation.

Resolution and Follow-up: The log facilitates the resolution of issues by assigning responsibilities and tracking progress toward resolution. It ensures that every issue is followed up until it is resolved.

Components of an Issue Log

An effective issue log typically includes several key components to ensure comprehensive tracking and management:

Issue Identification Number: A unique identifier for each issue for easy reference.

Date Reported: The date on which the issue was identified or reported, which helps in tracking the duration the issue has been open and prioritizing action.

Issue Description: A detailed description of the issue, providing enough context to understand the problem and its implications.

Identified By: The person or group who reported the issue, which can be critical for follow-up questions and clarifications.

Assigned To: The individual or team responsible for addressing the issue, ensuring accountability.

Priority: An indication of the issue's urgency and importance, helping to manage and allocate resources effectively.

Status: The current status of the issue (e.g., open, in progress, resolved, closed), which is essential for tracking progress over time.

Expected Resolution Date: The target date by which the issue should be resolved.

Actual Resolution Date: The date on which the issue was actually resolved.

Outcome/Resolution: A summary of how the issue was resolved, including any decisions made or actions taken.

How the Issue Log Helps Project Managers

Tracking and Management: The issue log allows project managers to keep a finger on the pulse of all stakeholder-related concerns, ensuring they are managed before escalating into more significant problems.

Documentation and Communication: It provides a historical record of issues and their resolutions, which is invaluable for current problem-solving and future project planning. It also ensures that all team members and stakeholders are informed of issues and their status, promoting transparency.

Efficient Resolution: By clearly assigning responsibility and tracking progress, the issue log helps ensure efficient resolution of issues. It also helps project managers evaluate the effectiveness of solutions, providing insights into process improvements for future projects.

Stakeholder Satisfaction: Effective use of the issue log contributes to higher stakeholder satisfaction by demonstrating that their concerns are taken seriously and addressed promptly. This can lead to better stakeholder relations and smoother project execution.

The issue log is a critical tool in project management, particularly in stakeholder engagement, where the ability to quickly address and resolve issues is directly tied to project success. By maintaining a well-structured issue log, project managers can ensure better project outcomes and more robust stakeholder relationships.

The **Stakeholder Engagement Assessment Matrix** is an essential tool used in the **Monitor Stakeholder Engagement** process. It serves as a strategic instrument for project managers to evaluate and visualize the level of engagement of each stakeholder or stakeholder group relative to the project. This matrix helps in assessing whether stakeholders are as engaged as they need to be for the project's success and identifies where improvements in engagement strategies might be required.

Purpose of the Stakeholder Engagement Assessment Matrix

The matrix is designed to assess the current engagement levels of stakeholders and compare these levels against where they ideally should be (desired levels). This assessment allows project managers to strategically focus their efforts on stakeholders who require more attention or different strategies to enhance their engagement and support for the project.

Components of the Stakeholder Engagement Assessment Matrix

The matrix typically involves a simple framework categorizing stakeholder engagement into several levels, such as:

- **Unaware**: Stakeholders are unaware of the project and its potential impacts.
- **Resistant**: Stakeholders are aware of the project but resistant to change.
- **Neutral**: Stakeholders are aware of the project but neither supportive nor resistant.
- **Supportive**: Stakeholders are supportive of the project and its outcomes.
- **Leading**: Stakeholders actively engage with the project and take actions to ensure its success.

Each stakeholder is plotted on the matrix based on their current and desired levels of engagement.

Application in Monitor Stakeholder Engagement
1. Evaluating Current Engagement Levels

- **Activity**: Project managers assess each stakeholder's current level of engagement based on observations, feedback, and interactions. This evaluation considers stakeholders' awareness, support, participation, and influence regarding the project.
- **Tool Usage**: By placing each stakeholder in the matrix according to their current engagement level, managers get a visual representation of overall stakeholder engagement.

2. Determining Desired Engagement Levels

- **Activity**: Define the optimal level of engagement for each stakeholder, considering their influence and interest in the project. Desired levels are typically based on the stakeholder's potential to impact the project.
- **Tool Usage**: This allows for a comparison between current and desired states, highlighting gaps that need strategic interventions.

3. Identifying Gaps and Planning Interventions

- **Activity**: Identify gaps between current and desired engagement levels. These gaps help pinpoint stakeholders who are not sufficiently engaged according to their capacity to affect project outcomes.
- **Tool Usage**: Project managers can develop targeted strategies to move stakeholders from their current to desired engagement levels. For example, increasing communication with a resistant stakeholder or providing more detailed information to an unaware stakeholder.

4. Implementing and Adjusting Strategies

- **Activity**: Implement specific actions designed to shift stakeholders to their desired engagement level. Monitor the effectiveness of these strategies and make adjustments as needed.
- **Tool Usage**: Reassessment using the matrix at regular intervals or after significant project milestones can track changes in engagement levels, providing empirical evidence of strategy effectiveness.

Conclusion

The Stakeholder Engagement Assessment Matrix is a dynamic tool that helps project managers monitor and adjust their engagement strategies throughout the project lifecycle. By regularly assessing the engagement levels of stakeholders and comparing these to desired states, project managers can effectively allocate their efforts and resources. This proactive approach ensures that all stakeholders are appropriately involved and committed, which is crucial for navigating the complexities of project management and achieving successful project outcomes.

In the **Monitor Stakeholder Engagement** process, measuring and analyzing the effectiveness of stakeholder engagement strategies is crucial. This is done through various metrics and Key Performance Indicators (KPIs), which provide insights into the health of stakeholder relationships and the success of engagement efforts. These metrics help project managers identify areas where engagement strategies may need adjustment and validate the approaches that are working well.

Common Stakeholder Engagement Metrics and KPIs
1. Stakeholder Satisfaction

- **Description**: Measures how satisfied stakeholders are with the project's progress, communication, and outcomes.
- **Measurement**: Typically gauged through surveys or feedback forms where stakeholders rate their satisfaction on various aspects of the project.
- **Application**: Regularly measuring stakeholder satisfaction helps in understanding how well the project meets or exceeds stakeholder expectations. It also highlights areas needing improvement.

2. Participation Rates

- **Description**: Tracks the level of active participation or involvement of stakeholders in project activities, meetings, and decision-making processes.
- **Measurement**: Measured by attendance records at meetings, contributions to discussions, and responsiveness to project communications.
- **Application**: High participation rates generally indicate good stakeholder engagement and support. Monitoring these rates can help identify stakeholders who might be disengaging from the project, allowing timely intervention.

3. Issue Resolution Time

- **Description**: Measures the time taken to address and resolve issues raised by stakeholders.
- **Measurement**: The time from when an issue is first reported until it is resolved.
- **Application**: Faster resolution times are often associated with better stakeholder satisfaction and trust. Tracking this metric helps ensure that stakeholder concerns are addressed efficiently.

4. Change Requests Initiated by Stakeholders

- **Description**: The number of changes or adjustments requested by stakeholders, which can indicate their level of engagement and investment in the project.
- **Measurement**: Count of change requests submitted by stakeholders during a specific period.
- **Application**: A high number of change requests might indicate strong engagement but can also suggest issues with project alignment or communication. Analyzing these requests can provide insights into stakeholder expectations and project performance.

5. Feedback Quality and Frequency

- **Description**: Evaluates the quality and frequency of feedback provided by stakeholders on project deliverables, processes, and management practices.
- **Measurement**: Analyzed through content analysis of feedback received and counting the instances of feedback over time.
- **Application**: Quality feedback from stakeholders can drive continuous improvement and innovation in the project. Tracking this metric helps assess the effectiveness of communication strategies and stakeholder understanding of project goals.

Analyzing Stakeholder Engagement Metrics

- **Data Collection**: Systematic collection of data through surveys, digital tracking tools, and direct feedback during stakeholder interactions.
- **Trend Analysis**: Look for trends over time in each metric to understand whether stakeholder engagement is improving, declining, or remaining stable. This can help identify patterns that predict project challenges or successes.

- **Comparative Analysis**: Compare current data with past data or benchmarks to assess performance against project goals or industry standards.
- **Actionable Insights**: Use insights gained from the analysis to make informed decisions about modifying engagement strategies, improving communication methods, or addressing specific stakeholder concerns.

Conclusion

Monitoring stakeholder engagement through specific metrics and KPIs is essential for maintaining healthy relationships and ensuring project success. These measurements provide valuable insights that help project managers adapt their strategies to better meet stakeholder needs, enhance communication, and proactively manage project challenges. By regularly analyzing these metrics, project teams can ensure that stakeholder engagement remains strong throughout the project lifecycle, contributing to a more collaborative and supportive project environment.

The **Project Stakeholder Management** knowledge area interacts extensively with other knowledge areas, particularly **Project Communications Management** and **Project Risk Management**. These interactions are crucial as they ensure that stakeholder needs and expectations are adequately addressed throughout the project lifecycle, that communication is effective, and that risks associated with stakeholders are properly managed.

Interaction with Project Communications Management

Project Stakeholder Management and **Project Communications Management** are inherently intertwined, as effective communication is a cornerstone of stakeholder engagement.

- **Plan Communications Management**: This process involves determining the information and communications needs of the project stakeholders. For instance, the stakeholder engagement plan developed in **Plan Stakeholder Engagement** directly influences the communication plan. It dictates the frequency, format, and level of detail of the information to be shared with different stakeholder groups based on their interest, influence, and impact on the project.
- **Manage Communications**: Effective implementation of communication strategies relies on a solid understanding of stakeholder preferences and requirements, which are identified in the **Identify Stakeholders** process. For example, if key stakeholders prefer detailed reports, the manage communications process must adapt to meet this preference to keep these stakeholders effectively engaged.
- **Monitor Communications**: This process ensures that information needs of stakeholders are met as per the communication management plan. Feedback and reactions from stakeholders during this monitoring phase can lead to adjustments in stakeholder engagement strategies if communication is found to be ineffective.

Interaction with Project Risk Management

Stakeholders can pose risks to the project but can also help in identifying and mitigating other risks. Hence, stakeholder management should be integrated with risk management practices.

- **Identify Risks**:

Stakeholders are a vital source of information on potential risks due to their different perspectives and expertise. In the **Identify Stakeholders** process, understanding who the stakeholders are and what their interests and potential points of influence are can provide insights into potential risks. For instance, a stakeholder with environmental concerns may highlight potential compliance risks related to environmental regulations.

- **Perform Qualitative Risk Analysis** and **Perform Quantitative Risk Analysis**: Stakeholder attitudes and their potential reactions to project decisions can significantly impact the project's risk profile. For example, stakeholder resistance can be identified as a risk, and the probability and impact of this risk can be analyzed to determine how it might affect the project timeline and cost.
  - **Plan Risk Responses**: Stakeholder preferences and involvement can directly influence the risk response strategies. Engaging stakeholders who are resistant to certain project aspects by addressing their concerns proactively can be an effective risk mitigation strategy.
  - **Monitor Risks**: Regularly reviewing and reassessing the stakeholder engagement plan can reveal new risks or changes in existing risks, which must be communicated back to the risk management processes.

Conclusion

The Project Stakeholder Management processes interact dynamically with those in Project Communications Management and Project Risk Management. These interactions are essential for the successful integration of stakeholder needs into project planning and execution, ensuring that all communications are tailored to stakeholder requirements, and that risks related to stakeholders are effectively managed. Understanding and leveraging these interactions enhance the project's ability to meet its objectives while maintaining strong and constructive relationships with all stakeholders.

Case Study: The Greenway Urban Renewal Project
Project Overview

The Greenway Urban Renewal Project was a large-scale initiative undertaken by the city to revitalize an old industrial area into a vibrant mixed-use development that included residential units, parks, a shopping district, and community spaces. The project's complexity was heightened by the diverse group of stakeholders involved, which included local government, investors, residents, businesses, environmental groups, and historical preservation societies.

Stakeholder Management Challenges

1. **Diverse Stakeholder Interests**: The project faced significant challenges in balancing the different and often conflicting interests of stakeholders, such as development goals versus environmental and historical preservation concerns.
2. **Community Resistance**: Initial plans met with resistance from local residents and small businesses concerned about displacement and loss of the area's historical character.
3. **Communication Barriers**: Effective communication was initially hindered by the stakeholders' diverse backgrounds and interests, leading to misunderstandings and delays.

Stakeholder Management Strategies

1. **Identify Stakeholders**: The project team used a combination of tools such as stakeholder interviews, surveys, and public meetings to identify and categorize stakeholders based on their influence and interest. This helped in creating a comprehensive stakeholder register, which was critical for the subsequent engagement strategies.
2. **Plan Stakeholder Engagement**: The team developed a stakeholder engagement plan that detailed tailored communication strategies for different stakeholder groups. For example, regular town

hall meetings were scheduled to engage local residents and businesses, while private meetings and presentations were arranged for government officials and investors.

3. **Engage Stakeholders**: The project manager prioritized open, transparent communication to build trust among stakeholders. This included:
   - **Interactive Workshops**: Conducted with residents to gather input on project design elements that directly affected the community.
   - **Regular Updates**: Distributed through newsletters, a dedicated project website, and social media to keep all stakeholders informed of progress and decisions.
   - **Conflict Resolution Sessions**: Facilitated by a third-party mediator to address specific disputes that arose, particularly regarding environmental concerns and historical preservation.

4. **Monitor Stakeholder Engagement**: The project team implemented a dynamic system to monitor stakeholder engagement through feedback mechanisms embedded in all communication channels. They maintained an updated issue log to track and manage concerns and adapted their strategies based on ongoing feedback.

Lessons Learned

1. **Early and Continuous Engagement is Key**: One of the critical lessons learned was the importance of engaging stakeholders as early as possible and maintaining that engagement throughout the project lifecycle. Early engagement helped in identifying potential issues and addressing them before they escalated.

2. **Flexibility in Engagement Plans**: The project manager noted that stakeholder dynamics could change as the project progresses. Being flexible and ready to adapt engagement strategies in response to new information or changing stakeholder needs was crucial for maintaining support and cooperation.

3. **Value of Transparency**: Maintaining a high level of transparency was essential in building and retaining trust, particularly in a project with significant community impact. Transparent processes minimized rumors and misinformation that could derail the project.

4. **Importance of Documenting Lessons Learned**: The project underscored the importance of documenting strategies and outcomes throughout the project, which proved invaluable for continuous improvement and for guiding future projects.

Conclusion

The Greenway Urban Renewal Project showcased the complexities of managing a diverse stakeholder group in a dynamic project environment. Through careful planning, continuous engagement, and adaptive strategies, the project was successfully completed, meeting most stakeholder expectations and delivering substantial community and economic benefits. The lessons learned from this project emphasize the critical role of effective stakeholder management in achieving project success.

Stakeholder Trust in Project Management

The Importance of Stakeholder Trust Stakeholder trust is pivotal in the realm of project management. It serves as the foundational element that can significantly dictate the success or failure of a project. Stakeholder trust is essentially the confidence that stakeholders place in the project team to deliver on promises, meet deadlines, stay within budget, and uphold the quality and scope of the work. When trust is established, stakeholders are more likely to support the project and provide necessary resources, which facilitates smoother project execution and enhances the likelihood of achieving project objectives.

Key Factors in Building and Maintaining Trust

1. **Transparency:** Open communication is crucial. This means keeping stakeholders informed about project progress, decisions, changes, and any issues that arise. Transparency involves sharing both good and bad news promptly, ensuring that there are no unpleasant surprises. By doing so, project managers reinforce the perception that they are honest and forthcoming, which builds stakeholder confidence.

2. **Reliability:** Stakeholders trust a project team that consistently meets its commitments. This includes delivering outputs on time, within budget, and at the required quality. Reliability can be fostered through effective project planning, resource management, and by setting realistic expectations from the outset of the project.

3. **Responsiveness:** Being responsive to stakeholder concerns and queries is another critical trust-building factor. This means acknowledging communications promptly and addressing issues swiftly. Responsiveness shows stakeholders that their input and concerns are valued, which not only strengthens trust but also encourages more open and constructive feedback.

Cultivating a Trust-Based Relationship

To cultivate and maintain a trust-based relationship, project managers can employ several strategies:

- **Regular Updates and Meetings:** Regularly scheduled meetings and updates help keep stakeholders in the loop. Utilizing project management tools that allow stakeholders to see real-time progress can also enhance transparency.
- **Stakeholder Engagement:** Engaging stakeholders in the decision-making process can significantly enhance their trust in the project team. This includes soliciting their input on key decisions and genuinely considering their feedback.
- **Clear Roles and Responsibilities:** Clearly defining roles and responsibilities for all team members helps in managing expectations and avoiding conflicts. This clarity supports the project manager's efforts to delegate effectively and ensure accountability.
- **Ethical Conduct:** Upholding a high standard of ethics, such as fairness, honesty, and respect towards all stakeholders, lays a strong foundation for trust. Ethical dilemmas should be handled with care, prioritizing transparency and the welfare of the project over short-term gains.
- **Conflict Resolution:** Efficiently managing and resolving conflicts among stakeholders is crucial. Project managers should strive to address conflicts fairly and transparently, fostering an environment where all parties feel heard and respected.

Now, let's look into the practical applications. Imagine you're overseeing a complex project with multiple stakeholders. By integrating these trust-building strategies into your project management approach—being transparent about challenges, reliable in your commitments, responsive to feedback, and proactive in stakeholder engagement—you create a robust framework for collaboration. This approach not only smooths the path to project success but also solidifies your reputation as a trustworthy leader.

Stakeholder trust is not just about managing a project effectively; it's about fostering relationships that empower every participant, driving collective success through shared goals and mutual respect. By focusing on transparency, reliability, and responsiveness, project managers can create an environment where trust thrives, paving the way for successful project outcomes and long-term benefits for all involved.

Project Stakeholder Management: Practice Questions and Quizzes
Question 1: Understanding Stakeholder Identification

Which of the following best describes the purpose of stakeholder identification in project management?
A) To determine the project schedule B) To identify all people or organizations affected by the project and

document relevant information regarding their interests, involvement, and impact on project success C) To develop a project budget D) To communicate project progress

Correct Answer: B Explanation: The process of stakeholder identification is crucial as it involves recognizing all entities (individuals, groups, or organizations) affected by the project. It allows project managers to gather essential information about these stakeholders, including their interests, the degree of their potential impact on the project, and the level of influence they wield. This information is foundational for developing effective engagement strategies, ensuring that the needs and expectations of the most influential stakeholders are met, and thus supporting the project's overall success.

Question 2: Stakeholder Engagement Assessment Matrix

What is the primary function of the Stakeholder Engagement Assessment Matrix in project stakeholder management? A) To prioritize tasks in the project schedule B) To track project costs C) To understand the level of engagement of various stakeholders D) To assign project roles

Correct Answer: C Explanation: The Stakeholder Engagement Assessment Matrix is a tool used to identify and assess the current level of stakeholder engagement and compare it to the level of engagement required for successful project completion. It helps project managers visualize which stakeholders are not as engaged as they need to be and allows for strategic planning to improve their involvement through targeted communication and engagement strategies.

Question 3: Effective Communication in Stakeholder Engagement

Which strategy is LEAST effective in fostering stakeholder engagement? A) Regular, transparent communication B) Tailoring the communication style to each stakeholder C) Using technical jargon to impress stakeholders D) Ensuring timely updates about project changes

Correct Answer: C Explanation: Using technical jargon is often counterproductive in stakeholder communications. It can create barriers to understanding and alienate stakeholders who may not be familiar with the terminology. Effective communication should be clear, accessible, and adapted to the audience's level of expertise. This ensures that all stakeholders understand the project's details and their roles within it, thereby facilitating better engagement and support.

Question 4: Managing Stakeholder Expectations

In project management, why is it important to manage stakeholder expectations? A) To ensure the project is completed without any changes to the scope B) To ensure stakeholders do not interact with the project team C) To align project objectives with stakeholder expectations, thus minimizing resistance and enhancing cooperation D) Only to meet budget constraints

Correct Answer: C Explanation: Managing stakeholder expectations is vital for aligning their vision and hopes with the project's planned objectives and deliverables. By clearly defining and agreeing upon what is achievable and realistic, project managers can minimize the likelihood of resistance and maximize stakeholder satisfaction and cooperation throughout the project lifecycle. This alignment helps in smooth project execution and achieving the desired outcomes.

Question 5: Real-World Application of Stakeholder Analysis

Imagine you are managing a project that involves constructing a new public park. Which of the following stakeholders would likely have high influence and high interest, and should therefore be managed closely? A) Local government bodies B) A supplier providing low-cost park benches C) Tourists visiting the city D) Local small businesses that do not face the park

Correct Answer: A Explanation: Local government bodies usually have high influence and high interest in public infrastructure projects such as the construction of a new park. They are key stakeholders because their approval, support, and regulations will significantly impact project progress and success. Managing this relationship closely is crucial for ensuring that the project meets regulatory requirements, secures necessary funding, and aligns with community development goals.

Reflective Exercise:

Think about a project you have been involved in. Identify a key stakeholder and reflect on how their level of engagement could have impacted the project outcome. What strategies could have been used to improve their engagement? This exercise will help you understand the practical implications of stakeholder engagement in real-world scenarios.

XIII. Professional Responsibility:

A. PMI Code of Ethics and Professional Conduct
PMI Code of Ethics and Professional Conduct

Purpose and Importance The PMI Code of Ethics and Professional Conduct outlines the standards of honesty, integrity, professionalism, and fairness that those in the project management profession are expected to meet. Its primary purpose is to instill confidence in the project management profession by ensuring that practitioners adhere to high ethical standards in their professional activities. This code is not just a set of rules but a guide that helps project managers navigate the complex ethical dilemmas they may face in their professional lives.

The importance of this code is manifold. First, it provides project managers with a clear framework for ethical decision-making, reducing ambiguity in professional conduct. It also serves to protect the public, stakeholders, colleagues, and the environments in which projects operate by demanding respect, fairness, and care from practitioners. Furthermore, the PMI Code enhances the profession's reputation and credibility, fostering trust among clients, team members, and other stakeholders.

Framework for Ethical Behavior and Decision-Making

The PMI Code of Ethics and Professional Conduct establishes its framework around four key values:

1. **Responsibility:** Project managers are urged to take ownership of their decisions and the consequences that follow. This value encourages them to make decisions based on the best interests of society, public safety, and the environment, and to meet their commitments faithfully.
2. **Respect:** This value underscores the importance of treating others with dignity and respect. Project managers are expected to listen to different opinions, recognize the contributions of others, and approach situations with fairness and understanding. This not only helps in managing diverse teams but also in negotiating and resolving conflicts ethically.
3. **Fairness:** The code calls for impartiality, justice, and equality. By being fair, project managers ensure equal opportunities for all, making decisions that are free from discrimination or favoritism. This value is crucial in stakeholder engagement and resource allocation.
4. **Honesty:** Transparency and truthfulness in all project dealings are vital. Honesty in communicating with stakeholders, reporting on project status, and conducting negotiations reinforces the trust that stakeholders place in project managers and the project management profession.

Now, let's look into how this framework is applied in practice. Consider a scenario where a project manager discovers a significant error in a project report that, if corrected, could delay the project and increase costs. Following the PMI Code of Ethics, the project manager would choose to report the error honestly, take responsibility for correcting it, treat all affected stakeholders with respect by communicating the issue clearly and fairly, and managing the resulting changes with impartiality.

The PMI Code of Ethics and Professional Conduct is a cornerstone of professional project management, providing a robust framework that not only guides project managers in making ethical decisions but also builds a foundation of trust and respect that is crucial for the success of any project. This framework ensures that ethical practices are maintained, thereby enhancing the overall integrity and effectiveness of the project management profession.

PMI Code of Ethics: Core Values
Responsibility

Responsibility is about being accountable for one's actions and their outcomes. It involves making decisions that are not only effective but also ethical. In the daily grind, project managers can demonstrate responsibility by owning up to mistakes instead of shifting the blame. For instance, if a deadline is missed, a responsible project manager would analyze the reasons, communicate the setback to stakeholders honestly, and devise a plan to mitigate any impact. Additionally, taking responsibility includes proactively addressing potential risks and ensuring the project complies with all applicable laws and standards.

Respect

Respect in project management translates to acknowledging and valuing the perspectives and interests of all stakeholders. It involves actively listening, giving thoughtful consideration to differing viewpoints, and engaging with others in a manner that builds trust and mutual respect. For example, during team meetings, a project manager could ensure that all members have an opportunity to express their ideas and concerns, facilitating a respectful dialogue. When conflicts arise, showing respect means handling them with diplomacy and fairness, seeking solutions that acknowledge each party's contributions and needs.

Fairness

Fairness is about making decisions impartially and objectively. Project managers can embody this value by ensuring that resources, recognition, and opportunities are distributed based on merit and necessity rather than favoritism or bias. This could involve transparent criteria for allocating tasks or rewards and being open about the processes behind these decisions. Moreover, fairness means applying the project rules consistently to all team members, regardless of their role or relationship with the project manager.

Honesty

Honesty involves being truthful and transparent in communications and actions. This means providing accurate information about project progress, challenges, and outcomes. An honest project manager does not manipulate facts or withhold information that stakeholders need to make informed decisions. For instance, if budget overruns are projected, it is important to alert stakeholders as soon as this is known rather than concealing the issue to avoid immediate conflict. Honesty also encompasses integrity in dealings, such as avoiding conflicts of interest and ensuring that all project transactions are conducted ethically.

Practical Applications in Day-to-Day Activities

Demonstrating these values in everyday project management activities fosters a positive and productive work environment that can lead to more successful outcomes. Here's how a project manager might integrate these values into daily interactions:

- **During Planning:** Clearly define the roles, responsibilities, and expectations for all team members. Use an open and fair process to assign tasks based on skills and project needs, and be responsible for providing the necessary resources to accomplish these tasks.

- **In Execution:** Maintain honest and frequent communication with stakeholders about project status, challenges, and successes. Ensure that all project decisions and changes are documented and communicated in a timely and clear manner.
- **In Monitoring:** Regularly check the project's progress against its goals and the team's adherence to ethical standards. Respectfully address any issues or deviations and adjust plans responsibly to stay on track.
- **In Closing:** Conduct a fair and thorough project review that acknowledges all contributions, learns from the project's successes and challenges, and shares these insights honestly with stakeholders.

By actively practicing these core values, project managers not only uphold the standards set by the PMI but also enhance their leadership and the performance of their teams, ultimately driving project success and advancing the reputation of the project management profession.

Overview of the PMI Code of Ethics and Professional Conduct Sections

The PMI Code of Ethics and Professional Conduct is structured to provide a comprehensive framework for ethical decision-making and actions in the project management profession. It is divided into four main sections: Introduction, Values, Responsibility, and Enforcement. Each section plays a crucial role in guiding project managers toward ethical practices.

1. Introduction

The Introduction sets the stage for the Code's purpose and scope. It emphasizes the importance of ethics in project management and outlines the objectives of the Code. The Introduction explains that the Code applies to anyone who is a part of PMI or holds a PMI certification, underlining the universal relevance and applicability of the ethical standards across the global project management community. This section is crucial as it helps project managers understand the significance of their commitment to ethical behavior and the impact of their actions on the profession and stakeholders.

Key Points:

- Purpose of the Code: To ensure professionalism and ethical conduct in all project management activities.
- Scope and Applicability: Applies to all PMI members and credential holders.
- Objective: To foster trust and respect among practitioners and stakeholders through ethical conduct.

2. Values

The Values section outlines the core values that are fundamental to the Code: responsibility, respect, fairness, and honesty. This section provides a detailed explanation of each value and how it should be reflected in the conduct of project managers. By defining these values clearly, the Code helps project managers internalize these principles and use them as a guiding light in their decision-making processes.

Key Points:
- Responsibility: Encourages accountability and owning the consequences of one's actions.
- Respect: Stresses the importance of treating everyone with dignity and consideration.
- Fairness: Advocates for impartiality and equity in all decisions and actions.
- Honesty: Emphasizes the necessity of transparency and truthfulness.

3. Responsibility

This section delves deeper into the ethical responsibilities of project managers. It covers the obligations practitioners have towards themselves, their profession, their peers, and the broader community. This includes adhering to laws and regulations, continuously improving their competence, and contributing to the knowledge base of project management. This section reinforces the idea that ethical behavior extends beyond personal conduct to include professional and societal responsibilities.

Key Points:

- Personal and Professional Growth: Commit to ongoing learning and skill development.
- Contribution to the Profession: Engage in activities that advance the knowledge and practice of project management.
- Compliance with Laws: Adhere to applicable laws and regulations governing their professional activities.

4. Enforcement

The Enforcement section describes the mechanisms in place to uphold the Code. It details the processes for handling allegations of unethical conduct, including the investigation, determination, and resolution of such issues. This section is vital as it ensures that there are clear repercussions for ethical violations, which underscores the seriousness with which PMI views ethical adherence.

Key Points:

- Procedures for Reporting and Handling Ethical Violations: Outline of how members can report ethical issues and how these reports will be processed.
- Consequences of Code Violations: Description of potential disciplinary actions for breaches of the Code.

Contribution to a Culture of Ethics Together, these sections create a robust framework for ethical practice in project management. They not only provide the principles and expectations but also the means to enforce them, which collectively contributes to a culture of high ethical standards within the project management community. By adhering to this Code, project managers can ensure that their projects are managed not only effectively but also ethically, which ultimately contributes to the credibility and success of the entire profession. This ethical foundation is essential for building trust with stakeholders and achieving sustainable results that align with both organizational goals and societal norms.

B. Ethical decision-making
Importance of Ethical Decision-Making in Project Management

Ethical decision-making is paramount in project management due to its significant impact on project outcomes, stakeholder trust, and the project manager's professional reputation. Making ethical choices ensures that a project not only achieves its goals but does so in a way that is fair, transparent, and respectful to all parties involved.

Impact on Project Outcomes

Ethical decision-making directly influences the success of a project. Decisions that adhere to ethical standards help ensure that projects are completed within their scope, budget, and timelines while meeting or exceeding stakeholder expectations. Conversely, unethical behaviors such as cutting corners, misreporting progress, or misallocating resources can lead to project failure. Such practices might initially seem to save time or money, but they often result in rework, financial losses, legal penalties, and damage to the organization's credibility.

Stakeholder Relationships

The relationship between stakeholders and the project team is built on trust. Ethical decision-making fosters trust and strengthens stakeholder relationships by demonstrating respect, fairness, and honesty. Stakeholders who feel they are treated ethically are more likely to remain engaged, provide necessary support, and champion the project within and outside the organization. On the other hand, unethical behavior can damage trust irreparably, leading to conflict, withdrawal of stakeholder support, or active opposition to the project.

Professional Reputation of the Project Manager

A project manager's professional reputation is a critical asset. Ethical behavior enhances this reputation, positioning the manager as a trustworthy and competent leader. This reputation opens doors to future opportunities and professional growth. In contrast, unethical behavior can tarnish a project manager's reputation, potentially leading to career stagnation or termination. In severe cases, legal action might ensue, professional certifications could be revoked, and the individual could be blacklisted within the professional community.

Long-Term Consequences

The long-term consequences of unethical behavior extend beyond immediate project outcomes. They can affect the organization's culture and ethical climate. A single instance of unethical behavior can set a precedent, potentially normalizing such conduct for other employees. This erosion of ethical standards can lead to widespread organizational issues, making it difficult to attract and retain top talent and possibly leading to greater scrutiny from regulators and the public.

Cultivating Ethical Practices

To avoid these detrimental effects, project managers should strive to embed ethical considerations into every aspect of project planning and execution. This involves:

- **Clear Communication**: Ensuring all team members understand the importance of ethics via training and clear guidelines.
- **Transparency**: Openly sharing information about project progress, challenges, and decisions.
- **Accountability**: Holding oneself and team members accountable for ethical practices.
- **Stakeholder Engagement**: Regularly involving stakeholders in discussions about project issues and decisions, ensuring their needs and concerns are addressed ethically.

Ethical decision-making in project management is not merely about adhering to moral principles; it is a strategic imperative that impacts project success, stakeholder trust, and the project manager's career. By prioritizing ethics, project managers can ensure sustainable success and maintain a positive professional standing.

Ethical Decision-Making Framework in Project Management

The ethical decision-making framework provides a structured approach for addressing and resolving ethical dilemmas. This methodical process helps project managers navigate complex situations where competing interests and values can make the right course of action unclear. Here's an overview of the key steps involved:

Recognizing the Ethical Issue

The first step is to identify and clearly define the ethical issue. This involves discerning whether a situation involves conflicting values, rights, duties, or professional guidelines. For project managers, this might mean recognizing when a decision impacts stakeholder interests unequally or when there is pressure to compromise on quality or safety to meet deadlines or budget constraints.

Considering the Alternatives

Once the ethical issue is identified, the next step is to think through all possible courses of action. This involves brainstorming different ways to handle the situation, considering various perspectives, and involving relevant stakeholders in the decision-making process if appropriate. Project managers should think creatively about how to solve the problem while adhering to ethical standards and aligning with the project's goals.

Evaluating the Consequences

After listing the alternatives, the next step is to evaluate the potential consequences of each option. This involves analyzing the implications of each choice on the project, stakeholders, the organization, and oneself. Project managers should consider both short-term and long-term consequences, weighing the benefits and risks associated with each alternative. This step also involves assessing which options align with the core ethical values of responsibility, respect, fairness, and honesty.

Making and Implementing the Decision

Once the options have been evaluated, the project manager must make a decision. This choice should be based on which alternative best aligns with ethical principles and the overall goals of the project. After deciding, the project manager must then implement the decision effectively. This includes communicating the decision to all impacted stakeholders, explaining the rationale behind it, and preparing to manage any fallout or repercussions.

Reflecting on the Outcome

After the decision has been implemented, it is important to reflect on the outcome. This reflection should assess whether the decision effectively addressed the ethical issue and what could be learned from the situation to improve future ethical decision-making. This step ensures continuous improvement in ethical standards and decision-making processes.

Application in Navigating Complex Ethical Dilemmas

To illustrate the application of this framework, consider a scenario where a project manager discovers that a project is likely to exceed its budget significantly. The manager faces pressure to conceal this overrun from stakeholders to secure a bonus for on-time and on-budget delivery. Using the ethical decision-making framework, the manager would:

- **Recognize the Ethical Issue**: Acknowledge the conflict between personal gain and transparency.
- **Consider Alternatives**: Options might include disclosing the overrun immediately, seeking additional budget quietly, or delaying the disclosure until more information is available.
- **Evaluate Consequences**: Assess the impact of each option on stakeholder trust, project success, and personal integrity.
- **Make and Implement the Decision**: Choose to disclose the budget overrun promptly, as it aligns with honesty and responsibility, even if it risks personal loss.

- **Reflect on the Outcome**: Review the decision's impact on the project and personal reputation to learn and improve future ethical decision-making.

By following these steps, project managers can ensure that they handle ethical dilemmas systematically and transparently, leading to decisions that uphold ethical standards and enhance trust and integrity in project management practices.

Common Ethical Challenges in Project Management

Project managers often encounter a range of ethical challenges that can test their integrity and decision-making skills. Common issues include conflicts of interest, breaches of confidentiality, and misuse of resources. Each of these challenges can have significant implications for the success of a project and the reputation of all involved parties.

1. **Conflicts of Interest** A conflict of interest occurs when a project manager's personal interests potentially interfere with their professional duties or decision-making.

Example: A project manager might have a financial interest in a vendor company that is bidding for a project contract.

Strategies for Addressing Conflicts of Interest:

- **Disclosure**: Immediately disclose any potential conflicts of interest to relevant stakeholders or the organization's ethics board.
- **Recusal**: Step back from decision-making processes where the conflict of interest may influence outcomes.
- **Consultation**: Seek guidance from superiors or an ethics advisor to ensure decisions are made impartially.

2. Breaches of Confidentiality Confidentiality involves maintaining privacy regarding sensitive information related to the project and its stakeholders.

Example: A project manager inadvertently shares sensitive financial data about the project with a vendor who is not cleared to receive this information.

Strategies for Addressing Breaches of Confidentiality:

- **Training and Awareness**: Regularly train all team members on what constitutes confidential information and the importance of maintaining confidentiality.
- **Secure Communication Channels**: Use secure systems for storing and sharing sensitive information.
- **Immediate Remediation**: If a breach occurs, take immediate action to secure the information and mitigate any damage. Inform affected parties and investigate the cause to prevent future breaches.

3. Misuse of Resources This involves using organizational resources for non-project or unauthorized purposes, which can range from budget misallocation to inappropriate use of staff time.

Example: A project manager uses project funds to purchase equipment that is more luxurious than necessary, or allocates excessive work hours to a preferred contractor.

Strategies for Addressing Misuse of Resources:

- **Clear Guidelines and Monitoring**: Establish and enforce clear guidelines for resource allocation and usage. Regular audits and monitoring can help ensure resources are used appropriately.
- **Transparency**: Make all resource-related decisions transparent to stakeholders and team members, providing justifications for allocations and expenditures.

- **Accountability**: Hold all team members, including oneself, accountable for their use of resources. Any discrepancies or misuses should be addressed immediately and rectified.

Integrating PMI Code of Ethics and Professional Conduct

To address these challenges effectively and ethically, project managers should integrate the principles outlined in the PMI Code of Ethics and Professional Conduct into every aspect of their decision-making and leadership:

- **Responsibility**: Accept the responsibility to act in the broad public interest and faithfully meet the obligations of the role.
- **Respect**: Treat all individuals with respect, valuing their input and acknowledging their contributions.
- **Fairness**: Ensure decisions are made fairly and impartially, providing equal opportunities for all stakeholders.
- **Honesty**: Uphold the truth and avoid actions that are false or misleading. Transparency in actions and decisions builds trust among team members and stakeholders.

By consistently applying these strategies and adhering to the PMI Code, project managers can navigate ethical challenges effectively, maintaining both their integrity and the integrity of the project. This proactive approach to ethics ensures that projects are not only successful in terms of deliverables but are also exemplary in their ethical execution.

C. Conflict of interest and cultural differences
Conflict of Interest in Project Management

Definition A conflict of interest in project management occurs when a project manager or team member has competing interests or loyalties that could potentially influence their judgment and objectivity in project decisions. This situation can compromise the individual's ability to act in the best interests of the project or uphold the integrity of their role due to personal gain or advantage.

Types of Conflicts of Interest

1. **Personal Conflicts**: These arise when personal relationships influence or appear to influence a project manager's decisions. For example, if a project manager hires or favors a family member or friend for a contract or position within the project, despite there being more qualified candidates.
2. **Financial Conflicts**: Financial conflicts occur when a project manager or team member stands to gain financially from their decisions within the project's context. This might include owning stock in a supplier company, receiving kickbacks from a contractor, or having a financial stake in a project outcome.
3. **Organizational Conflicts**: These conflicts emerge when a project manager's obligations to different organizations or departments with diverging interests might compromise their decision-making. For instance, a project manager working for a consultancy might prioritize that employer's interests over those of a client if both are not aligned.

Impact on Project Decision-Making and Stakeholder Trust

Influence on Decision-Making: Conflicts of interest can severely impair a project manager's ability to make impartial decisions. They might make choices that benefit their interests at the expense of the project's objectives. This could lead to poor project planning, resource allocation, and overall project management, which can ultimately jeopardize the project's success.

Erosion of Stakeholder Trust: The presence of a conflict of interest, whether real or perceived, can erode stakeholder trust. Stakeholders need to feel confident that decisions are made based on the project's best interests rather than personal gain. When conflicts of interest are not managed properly, it can lead to skepticism and a lack of confidence among stakeholders, which can make it difficult to secure their cooperation and support throughout the project lifecycle.

Strategies for Managing Conflicts of Interest

1. **Disclosure**: The most critical step is to disclose any potential conflicts of interest to the relevant parties or authorities within the organization. Full transparency allows stakeholders to understand the situation and helps mitigate any negative perceptions or impacts.
2. **Recusal**: In cases where a significant conflict of interest is identified, it may be necessary for the project manager or involved individual to recuse themselves from decision-making processes where their interests conflict with those of the project.
3. **Policies and Procedures**: Organizations should have clear policies and procedures for identifying, disclosing, and managing conflicts of interest. Training and regular communication on these policies can help maintain ethical standards and awareness among team members.
4. **Monitoring and Enforcement**: Regular audits and monitoring can help detect and address conflicts of interest early. An enforcement mechanism should be in place to handle violations effectively.

Managing conflicts of interest is crucial for maintaining ethical standards and operational integrity in project management. By effectively identifying, disclosing, and addressing conflicts of interest, project managers can preserve stakeholder trust and ensure that project decisions are made impartially and in the best interests of the project outcomes.

Importance of Recognizing and Disclosing Potential Conflicts of Interest

Recognizing and disclosing potential conflicts of interest is crucial in project management as it directly impacts the integrity and success of a project. This practice ensures that all decisions made during the course of a project are based on objective criteria and the best interests of the project, rather than being influenced by personal gain. Transparency in disclosing conflicts helps maintain stakeholder trust and confidence, which are vital for collaborative and effective project execution.

Steps to Proactively Identify, Report, and Manage Conflicts of Interest
1. Education and Awareness

Training: Project managers and their teams should undergo regular training on what constitutes a conflict of interest. This training should cover examples specific to the industry and the nature of their projects.
Resources: Provide team members with easy access to information and resources about conflicts of interest, including policies and procedures for handling such situations.

2. Establishing Clear Policies

Policy Development: Develop a comprehensive policy that defines conflicts of interest, outlines procedures for disclosure, and describes the steps to be taken when a conflict is identified.
Accessibility and Enforcement: Ensure that the policy is accessible to all team members and that it is enforced consistently to maintain a standard of integrity across the organization.

3. Routine Disclosure Procedures

Initial Disclosure: At the start of a project, and at regular intervals throughout its lifecycle, require team members to disclose any potential conflicts of interest. This could be part of the project kickoff activities or integrated into regular project status meetings.

Continuous Disclosure: Encourage an ongoing dialogue about conflicts of interest. Make it easy and non-punitive for team members to update their disclosure should their circumstances change during the project.

4. Active Monitoring and Review

Regular Audits: Conduct regular audits of project activities and decisions to ensure compliance with ethical standards and to detect any potential conflicts of interest.

Conflict Resolution Mechanisms: Establish clear mechanisms for resolving situations where a conflict of interest has been identified. This may include reviewing the decisions made, reassigning roles, or other actions to mitigate any adverse effects.

5. Recusal When Necessary

Recusal Process: If a significant conflict of interest is disclosed, the project manager or the affected team member should recuse themselves from related decision-making processes. Clearly define what this recusal entails and ensure that other qualified personnel can step in to fill the gap.

6. Transparent Communication

Stakeholder Engagement: Keep all stakeholders informed about how conflicts of interest are managed. When a conflict is disclosed that may impact project decisions, communicate what steps are being taken to manage it, thus preserving trust and transparency.

7. Documenting and Reporting

Documentation: Maintain thorough documentation of all disclosed conflicts of interest and the actions taken to manage them. This documentation will be critical for audits and for resolving any disputes that might arise.

Reporting Mechanisms: Implement a straightforward and confidential mechanism for reporting undisclosed conflicts of interest, which might be observed by other team members.

By proactively identifying, reporting, and managing conflicts of interest, project managers can uphold the ethical standards expected in project management. This proactive approach not only ensures that project decisions are made impartially but also enhances stakeholder confidence and trust, which are essential for the project's overall success and the organization's reputation.

Cultural Differences in Project Management

Concept and Significance Cultural differences refer to the diverse values, beliefs, norms, and practices that people from different backgrounds bring to a project. In the context of project management, understanding and appreciating these differences is crucial, especially in global projects involving team members, stakeholders, and suppliers from various cultural backgrounds. Recognizing cultural diversity can significantly enhance team collaboration, decision-making, and the overall success of a project.

The significance of cultural differences In project management extends beyond merely avoiding misunderstandings. It involves leveraging the diverse perspectives and approaches to improve problem-solving, innovation, and adaptation to changing project environments. Effective management of cultural differences helps in building a more inclusive and productive project atmosphere.

Impact on Ethical Expectations and Decision-Making

1. **Values and Norms**
   - Different cultures have different perceptions of what is considered ethical, which can influence project ethics. For example, what is deemed an acceptable business practice in one culture might be viewed as bribery in another. These differences can impact the ethical standards that are expected and practiced within the project team.
   - Decision-making processes can also be affected. Some cultures value collective decision-making, while others prefer a more individualistic approach. This can influence how decisions are made within the project, who is involved in making them, and how conflicts are resolved.

2. **Communication Styles**
   - Communication is key in any project, and cultural differences in communication styles can lead to misunderstandings and misinterpretations. For instance, in some cultures, direct communication is valued and expected, while in others, more indirect and subtle forms of communication are the norm.
   - These differences can impact how information is shared and understood among team members, affecting project coordination and the execution of tasks. Miscommunication can lead to errors, delays, and frustrations within the team, which might compromise ethical practices and decision-making.

Strategies for Managing Cultural Differences in Project Teams

1. **Cultural Awareness Training**
   - Conduct training sessions to educate all team members about cultural differences and their implications for project work. This training should cover aspects such as communication styles, negotiation techniques, conflict resolution, and ethical practices across cultures.

2. **Inclusive Leadership**
   - Project leaders should demonstrate cultural sensitivity and inclusiveness in their leadership style. This involves being aware of and respectful toward the cultural backgrounds of team members and adapting leadership practices to accommodate these differences.

3. **Clear Communication Protocols**
   - Establish clear communication protocols that consider cultural nuances. This might include specifying the medium of communication preferred, the level of formality required, and the clarity and directness expected in communications.

4. **Ethical Guidelines and Standards**
   - Develop a set of shared ethical guidelines that align with universal principles but also respect cultural differences. Ensure these guidelines are clearly communicated to all team members and that there is a mutual understanding of what is expected.

5. **Regular Feedback and Adaptation**
   - Encourage regular feedback from team members about what is working well and what needs adjustment. Be prepared to adapt management and communication strategies based on feedback to better align with the cultural needs of the team.

By effectively managing cultural differences, project managers can create a more ethically conscious and decision-efficient environment. This not only enhances project performance but also builds a stronger, more cohesive team that can navigate the complexities of global project demands with greater agility and understanding.

Strategies for Fostering a Culture of Respect, Inclusivity, and Sensitivity to Cultural Differences

Project managers play a critical role in shaping the team culture, especially in environments that are culturally diverse. The following strategies can help foster an atmosphere of respect, inclusivity, and sensitivity, thereby enhancing team collaboration and ethical behavior:

1. Cultural Competence Training

- **Implementation**: Integrate cultural competence training into the project lifecycle. This training should focus on understanding cultural differences, communication styles, and working practices across different cultures.
- **Example**: Organize workshops that simulate project scenarios involving cultural conflicts or misunderstandings to teach team members how to respond effectively.

2. Establish Clear Communication Guidelines

- **Implementation**: Develop and implement communication guidelines that address language barriers, non-verbal communication, and cultural nuances in communication styles.
- **Example**: Use simple and clear language for project documentation and communication. Encourage the use of visuals or diagrams where possible to ensure that non-native speakers fully understand project materials and discussions.

3. Create an Inclusive Leadership Style

- **Implementation**: Adopt a leadership approach that values and seeks input from all team members, regardless of their cultural background.
- **Example**: Rotate meeting times to accommodate different time zones and ensure that team members in remote locations feel equally involved and valued.

4. Diverse Team Building Activities

- **Implementation**: Organize team-building activities that not only foster teamwork but also celebrate cultural diversity.
- **Example**: Host virtual "cultural days" where team members share insights about their culture, traditions, or local business practices. This can include presentations, storytelling, or sharing of traditional music or food recipes.

5. Ethical Standards and Universal Respect

- **Implementation**: Clearly communicate the project's ethical guidelines, ensuring they align with universal principles of respect, fairness, and honesty, while being sensitive to cultural variations.
- **Example**: Develop a project charter that includes a code of conduct specifically addressing respect for cultural diversity and ethical behavior. Have all team members sign this charter to demonstrate their commitment.

6. Encourage Open Dialogue and Feedback

- **Implementation**: Foster an environment where team members feel safe to express concerns about cultural misunderstandings or ethical issues without fear of reprisal.

- **Example**: Set up regular check-ins or feedback sessions where team members can discuss cultural or ethical challenges in an open, non-judgmental forum.

7. Conflict Resolution Mechanisms

- **Implementation**: Implement effective conflict resolution mechanisms that consider cultural sensitivities and provide a fair process for all parties involved.
- **Example**: Train project managers and leaders in culturally sensitive conflict resolution techniques. Ensure that mediators or facilitators are aware of cultural backgrounds and potential biases.

8. Monitor and Adapt Policies

- **Implementation**: Regularly review and adapt policies and practices to ensure they remain effective and relevant to a culturally diverse team.
- **Example**: Conduct annual reviews of communication policies, training programs, and team feedback to identify areas for improvement or adjustments that better support the cultural dynamics of the team.

9. Role Modeling Ethical Behavior

- **Implementation**: As a project manager, consistently demonstrate ethical behavior and decision-making that respects cultural differences. Lead by example in every aspect of project management.
- **Example**: Publicly acknowledge and rectify any cultural misunderstandings or missteps in your own behavior. This shows the team that cultural sensitivity and ethical integrity are taken seriously at all levels.

10. Celebrate Multicultural Achievements

- **Implementation**: Recognize and celebrate the achievements of team members from different cultural backgrounds. Highlight how their unique perspectives contribute to the project's success.
- **Example**: During project meetings or in newsletters, feature 'success stories' that illustrate how cultural diversity has positively impacted the project, such as innovative solutions derived from different cultural approaches to problem-solving.

11. Provide Support Systems

- **Implementation**: Offer support systems that cater to the specific needs of culturally diverse teams, such as translation services, access to cultural advisors, or resources that help team members understand and navigate different cultural landscapes.
- **Example**: Establish a buddy system where team members from different cultural backgrounds pair up to offer mutual support, share knowledge about their cultures, and help each other navigate the project environment.

By employing these strategies, project managers can create a work environment that not only respects and embraces cultural differences but also promotes an ethical framework where inclusivity is a norm. This approach not only enhances team cohesion and project success but also builds a positive reputation for the organization in a globalized business environment. The integration of these practices into everyday project management ensures that cultural diversity is seen as an asset rather than a challenge, fostering innovation, ethical behavior, and a truly collaborative project team.

D. Practice questions and quizzes

Practice Questions on PMI Code of Ethics and Professional Conduct, Ethical Decision-Making, Conflicts of Interest, and Cultural Differences

Question 1: PMI Code of Ethics and Professional Conduct Which core value in the PMI Code of Ethics and Professional Conduct emphasizes transparency and truthfulness in all project dealings?

A) Responsibility
B) Respect
C) Fairness
D) Honesty

Correct Answer: D) Honesty

Explanation: Honesty involves being truthful and transparent in communications and actions, which means providing accurate information about project progress, challenges, and outcomes. This core value ensures that all stakeholders are fully informed and that there is no manipulation of information, which builds trust and integrity within the project environment.

Question 2: Ethical Decision-Making In the ethical decision-making process, what is the first step that should be taken when faced with an ethical dilemma?

A) Evaluating the consequences of possible actions
B) Identifying and considering all possible alternatives
C) Recognizing that an ethical issue exists
D) Consulting the project stakeholders

Correct Answer: C) Recognizing that an ethical issue exists

Explanation: The first step in ethical decision-making is recognizing that an ethical issue exists. Identifying the issue is crucial as it sets the stage for thoughtful consideration of the ethical dimensions involved and guides the subsequent steps in the decision-making process.

Question 3: Conflicts of Interest Which action is most appropriate for a project manager to take when they identify a potential conflict of interest involving a close friend bidding on a project contract?

A) Allow the friend to adjust their bid based on insider information
B) Disclose the conflict of interest to the appropriate organizational body and recuse themselves from the decision-making process
C) Continue with the bidding process as the personal relationship does not necessarily imply bias
D) Handle the situation discreetly without involving other project team members

Correct Answer: B) Disclose the conflict of interest to the appropriate organizational body and recuse themselves from the decision-making process

Explanation: Disclosing the conflict and recusing oneself from the decision-making process is the ethical action to take. This ensures transparency and maintains the integrity of the bidding process by eliminating any bias that might arise from personal relationships.

Question 4: Cultural Differences How can cultural differences impact the communication within a project team?

A) They have no significant impact as long as the project goals are clearly defined
B) They can lead to misunderstandings and misinterpretations if not effectively managed
C) They enhance communication as everyone brings the same expectations to the project
D) They decrease the overall efficiency of the project

Correct Answer: B) They can lead to misunderstandings and misinterpretations if not effectively managed

Explanation: Cultural differences can significantly impact communication styles, leading to potential misunderstandings and misinterpretations. Effective management of these differences, such as through cultural competence training or establishing clear communication guidelines, is essential to ensure clear and effective communication across culturally diverse teams.

Reflective Exercise: Reflect on a time when you faced an ethical dilemma in any team environment. How did you resolve it? Could the PMI Code of Ethics and Professional Conduct have guided a different approach? This exercise encourages you to think about practical applications of ethical principles in real-life situations, enhancing your understanding and preparation for ethical decision-making in your professional life.

These questions and exercises not only test your knowledge of the PMI Code of Ethics and ethical practices in project management but also prepare you for practical scenarios you might encounter in your project management career, particularly if aiming for certifications like CAPM.

Scenario-Based Ethical Dilemma Questions for Project Managers
Scenario 1: Budget Pressure and Quality Compromise

You are a project manager working on a critical infrastructure project. Due to unforeseen circumstances, the project is running over budget. A senior executive suggests using cheaper, sub-standard materials to stay within budget, arguing that the likelihood of future issues is minimal. You know that using inferior materials could potentially compromise the safety and durability of the infrastructure.

Question:

What is the most appropriate course of action according to the PMI Code of Ethics and Professional Conduct? A) Follow the executive's suggestion to use cheaper materials to maintain the budget. B) Refuse the executive's suggestion and report the situation to the project's governance board. C) Use the cheaper materials but document the decision thoroughly to avoid personal liability. D) Negotiate with the executive to find other areas to cut costs without compromising on quality.

Correct Answer: B) Refuse the executive's suggestion and report the situation to the project's governance board

Explanation: According to the PMI Code of Ethics, it is essential to prioritize honesty, responsibility, and the welfare of the public. Using sub-standard materials could jeopardize the safety of the infrastructure, posing risks to the public. Reporting the situation to the governance board aligns with the principles of integrity and responsibility, ensuring that ethical standards are upheld and safety is not compromised.

Scenario 2: Conflict of Interest in Hiring

You are leading a project that requires hiring an external consultant. One of the leading candidates is your sibling, who is highly qualified for the role. Hiring your sibling could raise questions about nepotism and conflict of interest.

Question:

How should you handle this situation to adhere to the PMI Code of Ethics and Professional Conduct? A) Hire your sibling since their qualifications are superior to other candidates. B) Exclude yourself from the hiring process and disclose your relationship to the decision-making panel. C) Do not disclose the relationship but ensure that your sibling offers the best terms for the project. D) Avoid hiring your sibling to eliminate any perception of bias.

Correct Answer: B) Exclude yourself from the hiring process and disclose your relationship to the decision-making panel

Explanation: The ethical approach involves avoiding any potential conflict of interest. By recusing yourself from the hiring process and disclosing your personal connection, you maintain transparency and fairness, as stipulated by the PMI Code of Ethics. This action helps preserve trust and integrity in the hiring process.

Scenario 3: Handling Confidential Information

During a meeting, a colleague accidentally shares confidential information about another company's project that could potentially benefit your project. The information was not intended to be shared publicly.

Question:

What should you do in this situation based on the PMI Code of Ethics and Professional Conduct? A) Use the information to gain a competitive advantage in your project. B) Discuss the information with your team but do not use it directly. C) Report the incident to your superior and ensure the information is not used. D) Ignore the information since it was not obtained through official channels.

Correct Answer: C) Report the incident to your superior and ensure the information is not used

Explanation: Ethical handling of confidential information is a key component of professional integrity. Reporting the incident aligns with the values of honesty and responsibility. Ensuring that the information is not used upholds the ethical standards of respecting the confidentiality and proprietary rights of others, as outlined in the PMI Code of Ethics.

These scenario-based questions challenge project managers to apply ethical principles in realistic situations, reinforcing the importance of ethical decision-making in maintaining professional integrity and stakeholder trust.

XIV. Test-Taking Strategies and Final Review:

Importance of Effective Time Management During the CAPM Exam

Effective time management is crucial during the Certified Associate in Project Management (CAPM) exam. This exam, designed by the Project Management Institute (PMI), tests candidates on their understanding of fundamental project management principles and practices. Proper time management not only ensures that candidates can answer all the questions within the allotted time but also improves the quality of answers by reducing the rush that can lead to careless mistakes.

Key Strategies for Pacing During the CAPM Exam
Reading Questions Carefully:

Strategy: Take the time to read each question thoroughly before answering. This prevents misunderstandings that could lead to incorrect answers.

Benefit: Understanding the question fully from the beginning saves time by reducing the need to reread the question multiple times or having to correct answers later.

Marking Difficult Questions for Review:

Strategy: Use the exam's feature to mark questions you find difficult or are unsure about. This allows you to move on and return to these questions later, ensuring that they do not consume disproportionate amounts of your time.

Benefit: This approach prevents difficult questions from interrupting your exam flow and helps maintain a steady pace throughout, allowing more time to focus on questions you can answer confidently.

Prioritizing Questions Based on Ease or Difficulty:

Strategy: Quickly scan through the questions at the start or as you go, and answer the ones you find easiest first. This builds confidence and ensures you secure all the points you readily can before tackling more challenging questions.

Benefit: This strategy maximizes the number of questions answered correctly within the limited time and reduces the pressure as the exam progresses, as you will have already completed a substantial part of the test.

Time Allocation:

Strategy: Allocate your time based on the total number of questions and the total time available. For example, if the CAPM exam consists of 150 questions to be completed in 3 hours, aim to spend about one minute per question, reserving extra time for review.

Benefit: Systematic time allocation ensures that you are on track throughout the exam and prevents any last-minute rush that could lead to mistakes or unanswered questions.

Practice with Timed Quizzes:

Strategy: While preparing for the exam, regularly practice with timed quizzes that mimic the actual exam environment. This helps you gauge how much time to spend on different types of questions.

Benefit: Familiarity with the pressure of a timed exam reduces anxiety on the actual test day and improves your ability to manage time effectively under exam conditions.

Using Breaks Wisely:

Strategy: If breaks are allowed during the exam, use them strategically to refresh yourself without losing focus. Plan quick breaks to stretch or clear your mind, but keep them brief to maintain momentum.

Benefit: A short break can help rejuvenate your mental energy, improving concentration and efficiency when you return to the test. By integrating these strategies into your exam preparation and execution, you can effectively manage your time, which is a critical component of success on the CAPM exam. Time management not only affects your ability to complete the exam but also significantly influences the overall quality of your performance, ultimately enhancing your chances of achieving a high score.

Managing Time Pressure on the CAPM Exam

Time pressure can be one of the most challenging aspects of taking the CAPM exam. Managing this pressure effectively is crucial for maximizing performance. Here are practical tips for handling time constraints and avoiding common pitfalls:

1. Understand the Format and Timing of the Exam

- **Tip**: Before the exam, be fully aware of the format—number of questions and total time allotted. This familiarity helps in creating a realistic plan for time management.
- **Benefit**: Knowing the exam structure reduces anxiety and allows for strategic planning on how to approach each section based on your strengths and weaknesses.

2. Set Time Limits for Each Question

- **Tip**: Decide in advance approximately how much time you will spend on each question. For instance, if you have 180 minutes for 150 questions, aim to spend about one minute per question, leaving extra time for review.
- **Benefit**: Setting time limits prevents spending too much time on any single question and helps ensure that enough time is left to attempt all questions.

3. First Pass for Easy Questions

- **Tip**: On your first pass through the exam, quickly answer all the questions you find easy or are certain about. Skip questions that you find difficult or are unsure about.
- **Benefit**: This approach secures all the easy points early on and builds confidence. It also leaves more time to focus on harder questions later without the pressure of unanswered easy questions lingering.

4. Use a Systematic Approach to Marking Questions

- **Tip**: Utilize the exam software's marking feature to flag questions you are unsure about. This allows you to easily return to them after the first pass.
- **Benefit**: Marking questions for review helps manage your exam time by keeping track of which questions need more attention, ensuring that you revisit them as time allows.

5. Avoid Overthinking and Second-Guessing

- **Tip**: If you find yourself stuck on a question, make the best choice based on your initial instinct, mark it for review, and move on. Avoid dwelling too long on any single question.
- **Benefit**: This prevents wasting time on second-guessing and overthinking, which can consume valuable minutes and increase exam stress.

6. Review Marked Questions Strategically

- **Tip**: Once you've answered all the questions to the best of your ability, use any remaining time to go back to the ones you marked. Focus on those you can realistically solve with a bit more thought rather than ones that you found completely baffling.
- **Benefit**: This selective approach in reviewing questions maximizes the use of remaining time by focusing on questions where you are most likely to gain additional points.

7. Practice with Timed Mock Exams

- **Tip**: Regularly practice with timed mock exams to build your speed and accuracy under time constraints. Adjust your timing strategy based on these practice sessions.
- **Benefit**: Practicing under timed conditions helps you get accustomed to the pressure of the actual exam and improves your time management skills.

8. Stay Calm and Maintain Focus

- **Tip**: Develop techniques to maintain calm and focus during the exam, such as deep breathing or positive affirmations.
- **Benefit**: Keeping calm under pressure allows for clearer thinking and better decision-making, which are crucial for effective time management and performance on the exam.

By implementing these strategies, test-takers can strike an optimal balance between thoroughness and efficiency, enabling them to maximize their performance within the allotted time. Managing time effectively not only helps in covering all the exam questions but also reduces the stress associated with time pressure, leading to a more composed and successful exam experience.

Tackling Common Types of Multiple-Choice Questions

Multiple-choice questions can vary in structure and complexity. Understanding how to approach different types can significantly improve your test-taking strategy, especially in a context like the CAPM exam where time management and accuracy are key. Here are some common types of multiple-choice questions and strategies for tackling them effectively:

1. "All of the Above" Questions

- **Strategy**: Evaluate each option individually before selecting "all of the above." If even one option is clearly incorrect, then "all of the above" cannot be the right answer. Conversely, if you are certain that most of the listed options are correct, this can be a strong choice.
- **Tip**: Be thorough in your evaluation of each statement. This question type tests your knowledge comprehensively on the topic at hand.

2. "None of the Above" Questions

- **Strategy**: Treat these questions with caution. Review each option carefully and decide if any could be correct. Choose "none of the above" only when you are confident that all other options are incorrect based on your knowledge.
- **Tip**: This option requires you to be confident in your ability to eliminate all other possible answers as incorrect, which can be challenging if you are less familiar with the topic.

3. "Except" Questions (e.g., Which of the following is NOT...?)

- **Strategy**: These questions require you to identify the item that does not fit with the others. It's essential to understand each option's relationship to the question's topic. Mark options that are clearly related, and the one that remains, which seems out of context or contradictory, is likely the correct answer.
- **Tip**: Focus on keywords and project management concepts that are supposed to link the options together. Understanding the foundational concepts of project management can be particularly useful here.

Leveraging Project Management Knowledge for Informed Guessing

When unsure of the correct answer, leveraging your understanding of project management principles can guide you toward a more informed guess:

- **Utilize Process of Elimination**: Based on your knowledge, start by eliminating any options that are obviously incorrect. Often, removing just one or two incorrect answers can significantly improve your odds of selecting the right one.
- **Look for Keywords**: Certain keywords related to project management processes, phases, or principles can provide clues about the correct answer. For instance, terms like "initiation" or "closure" might help align the question with a specific phase of project management.
- **Consistency with PMBOK® Guide**: The PMBOK® Guide outlines standardized guidelines, rules, and characteristics that are common in the field of project management. Answers that align with these standards are more likely to be correct.
- **Common Sense and Logical Reasoning**: Sometimes, simple logic or common sense can help deduce the right answer, especially in questions dealing with basic project management practices or ethical considerations.
- **Educated Guesses Based on Patterns**: If you've noticed patterns in the answers from previous questions (although this can be risky and less reliable), it might help in cases where you are completely unsure.

By combining these strategies with solid preparation and a good understanding of project management concepts, test-takers can effectively navigate the complexities of multiple-choice questions on the CAPM exam. This approach not only helps in answering questions where the answer is known but also provides a methodology for tackling questions where you may be less certain, thereby enhancing overall performance on the exam.

Impact of Stress and Anxiety on Exam Performance

Stress and anxiety, particularly in the context of exams, can have a profound impact on performance. High levels of stress can lead to physical symptoms such as headaches, nausea, and excessive sweating, as well as psychological effects like difficulty concentrating, blanking out, and negative thoughts. This state not only impairs recall and cognitive functions necessary for answering questions accurately but can also affect time management and overall test-taking strategy.

Practical Techniques for Managing Stress Before and During the Exam

To mitigate these effects and enhance performance, consider these effective stress management techniques:

1. Deep Breathing Exercises

- **Technique**: Practice deep breathing exercises to calm your nervous system. This involves taking slow, deep breaths, inhaling through your nose and exhaling through your mouth. The goal is to breathe deeply enough to fill your lungs completely, which can help reduce tension and anxiety.
- **Application**: Before the exam begins and during breaks, take a few minutes to focus on your breathing. This can also be done discreetly during the exam if you start feeling overwhelmed.

2. Positive Self-Talk

- **Technique**: Engage in positive self-talk to combat negative thoughts that often accompany exam stress. This involves consciously replacing negative thoughts with positive affirmations or encouraging statements.
- **Application**: Prepare a set of affirmations such as "I am well-prepared and can handle this exam," or "I am capable of solving these problems." Repeat these affirmations quietly to yourself before and during the exam to maintain a positive mindset.

3. Visualization

- **Technique**: Use visualization techniques to imagine a positive exam experience. This involves closing your eyes and vividly imagining yourself successfully completing the exam, feeling confident and calm throughout the process.
- **Application**: Spend several minutes the night before and on the morning of the exam visualizing a successful exam performance. Picture yourself reading questions, understanding them easily, and recalling the answers effortlessly.

4. Adequate Preparation and Practice

- **Technique**: One of the most effective ways to reduce exam stress is thorough preparation. This includes not only studying the material well but also practicing under exam conditions.
- **Application**: Take timed practice exams in the weeks leading up to your test date. This will help build familiarity with the format and timing of the exam, reducing anxiety and boosting confidence.

5. Physical Activity and Sleep

- **Technique**: Engage in regular physical activity and ensure you get enough sleep during the exam preparation period. Exercise is known to reduce stress and improve mood, while adequate sleep is crucial for cognitive function and memory.
- **Application**: Maintain a regular exercise routine and aim for 7-9 hours of sleep each night, especially in the days leading up to the exam.

6. Structured Exam-Day Routine

- **Technique**: Develop a structured routine for the day of the exam. This can help reduce anxiety by making the day feel more predictable and under your control.
- **Application**: Plan out the entire day from when you wake up, including what you will eat, when you will leave for the exam, what you will bring with you, and even when you will take breaks during the exam.

By employing these techniques, candidates can effectively manage stress and anxiety, paving the way for enhanced focus, better recall, and improved overall performance on the exam. Remember, the goal is to enter the exam room feeling calm, prepared, and confident in your ability to succeed.

Importance of a Structured Study Schedule

Creating and adhering to a structured study schedule is crucial for effective exam preparation, particularly for comprehensive assessments like the CAPM exam. A well-planned study schedule helps ensure that all necessary material is covered in a systematic way, allowing for better retention and understanding of complex project management concepts.

Benefits of a Structured Study Schedule:

1. **Efficient Use of Time**: A study schedule breaks down the vast amount of material into manageable segments, ensuring that time is allocated efficiently across different topics. This approach prevents overwhelming last-minute cramming and promotes a more in-depth understanding of the subject matter.
2. **Consistent Study Habits**: Regular study intervals help establish a routine, making studying a habitual part of daily life. This consistency is key to long-term retention of information.
3. **Goal Setting and Tracking**: A schedule allows for setting specific, measurable goals (e.g., mastering a PMBOK® Guide knowledge area each week) and provides a mechanism to track progress against these goals, which can be highly motivating and reassuring.

Integrating Self-Care Practices into Study Plans

Incorporating self-care practices such as regular exercise, healthy eating, and sufficient sleep into your study plan is vital for maintaining both physical and mental health during intense exam preparation periods.

Contribution of Self-Care to Mental Readiness and Resilience:

1. **Exercise**: Regular physical activity is known to reduce stress, anxiety, and symptoms of depression while boosting mood and overall energy levels. Exercise can also improve cognition, enhancing memory and critical thinking skills, which are essential for understanding and applying project management principles.
2. **Healthy Eating**: A balanced diet provides the necessary nutrients to fuel the brain and body. Foods rich in omega-3 fatty acids, antioxidants, and vitamins have been shown to enhance

cognitive function and mental clarity, while a poor diet can lead to fatigue and impaired concentration.
3. **Sufficient Sleep**: Adequate sleep is crucial for cognitive functions such as memory, problem-solving, and decision-making. During sleep, the brain consolidates new knowledge into long-term memory, making it critical for learning. Lack of sleep, on the other hand, can significantly impair these functions and reduce exam performance.

Mental Readiness and Resilience on Exam Day

By combining a well-structured study schedule with regular self-care practices, candidates can build not just their knowledge base but also their mental endurance and resilience. Here's how these elements work together:

- **Reduced Burnout**: Balancing study with self-care helps prevent burnout, which can occur from excessive mental strain without adequate rest or relaxation.
- **Increased Stamina**: Regular exercise and good nutrition build physical stamina that translates into mental stamina, enabling longer and more productive study sessions as well as sustained focus during the exam.
- **Enhanced Focus and Concentration**: A rested, well-nourished brain performs at its peak, with improved concentration and alertness, both critical for performing well under the pressures of a timed exam.
- **Emotional Equilibrium**: Managing stress through regular self-care practices helps maintain emotional stability, allowing candidates to approach the exam with confidence and calm.

A balanced approach that includes both rigorous academic preparation and dedicated self-care leads to optimal performance on exam day. Candidates are thus advised to see their preparation as a holistic process, where mastering the material and taking care of their mental and physical health are both essential components of success.

Creating a full-length practice exam that mirrors the CAPM exam format and difficulty is a fantastic way to prepare for the actual test. Below, you'll find a sample set of 50 questions designed to cover the various knowledge areas and processes as outlined in the PMBOK® Guide. While a real CAPM exam would include 150 questions, this condensed version will still provide a comprehensive assessment of exam readiness.

Practice Exam for CAPM Certification
Project Integration Management
1. What is the primary purpose of the Develop Project Charter process?
2. During which process would a project manager integrate all aspects of a project?
3. How does a project manager ensure changes are properly managed?

Project Scope Management
4. What tool or technique is most effective in defining the project scope?
5. What is the key benefit of the Collect Requirements process?
6. Describe a situation where a project scope statement would be used to communicate with stakeholders.

Project Schedule Management
7. Which process involves determining the resources needed for each project activity?
8. Identify the technique most commonly used for establishing the sequence of activities.
9. What is a critical path in project management?

Project Cost Management

10. Which document would you refer to estimate costs in the project?
11. What is earned value management and how is it used in monitoring project performance?
12. Differentiate between cost baseline and budget.

Project Quality Management

13. What is the main objective of the Manage Quality process?
14. How does quality management affect project outcomes?
15. Explain the difference between quality assurance and quality control.

Project Resource Management

16. What are the primary functions of resource management in a project?
17. How would a project manager address resource overallocation?
18. What is the purpose of a team charter?

Project Communication Management

19. What factors would you consider when planning project communications?
20. Describe a communication tool that facilitates project status reporting.
21. How can project managers ensure that communication is effective among international teams?

Project Risk Management

22. How is qualitative risk analysis different from quantitative risk analysis?
23. What is a risk response strategy for an opportunity?
24. Describe the process of identifying project risks.

Project Procurement Management

25. What is the significance of the Conduct Procurements process?
26. How would a project manager manage relationships with vendors?
27. What types of contracts are most commonly used in project management?

Project Stakeholder Management

28. Describe the key steps involved in managing stakeholder engagement.
29. How does the project manager monitor stakeholder relationships?
30. Why is it important to identify all stakeholders early in the project?

Professional and Social Responsibility

31. Explain the importance of ethics in project management.
32. How would you handle a situation where a project team member acts unethically?
33. What are some key responsibilities of a project manager to promote professional conduct?

Mixed Questions Across All Domains

34. What is a project life cycle?
35. How do project management processes interact with project phases?
36. Define a project management office (PMO) and its function.
37. What tools would a project manager use for project integration?
38. Describe a scenario where stakeholder influence is detrimental to the project.
39. How are project baselines used during the Control Scope process?

40. What role does change management play in project success?
41. Identify a scenario where conflict resolution is necessary.
42. How do environmental factors influence project outcomes?
43. Explain the process groups of the project management life cycle.
44. What is a work breakdown structure (WBS) and how is it used?
45. Discuss the importance of risk management plans.
46. What techniques are used for scope verification?
47. How would you apply the PMI Code of Ethics in a real-world project?
48. Explain how to manage project knowledge effectively.
49. Describe how project scheduling tools can impact project timelines.
50. What is a stakeholder engagement plan and how is it developed?

Instructions for Test-Takers:

- Allow 3 hours to complete this practice exam.
- Answer each question to the best of your ability.
- Review your answers and ensure you understand why certain answers are correct.
- Focus on areas where your answers were incorrect or unsure.

This practice exam should serve as a tool to assess your readiness for the actual CAPM exam, identifying areas where further study may be needed and helping you become comfortable with the exam format and types of questions asked.

Given the length and depth of the task, I'll provide detailed explanations for a selected set of 5 questions from the practice exam provided earlier. These explanations will highlight key concepts from the PMBOK® Guide, rationale for correct and incorrect answers, and guide further study.

Question 7: Which process involves determining the resources needed for each project activity?

Correct Answer: Estimate Activity Resources **Explanation:** Estimate Activity Resources is a process within the Project Resource Management knowledge area. This process is critical for ensuring that each project activity has the necessary resources (human resources, equipment, materials) allocated to it, which enables realistic scheduling and budgeting. The correct identification and allocation of resources help in executing the project efficiently and effectively.

PMBOK® Guide Reference:

Section 9.2 – "Estimate Activity Resources involves estimating the team resources (human resources) and the physical resources (materials, equipment) needed to perform any scheduled activities."

Question 19: What factors would you consider when planning project communications?

Correct Answer: Communication technology, stakeholder requirements, and information security requirements. **Explanation:** Effective communication planning involves understanding and incorporating several critical factors to ensure that all project stakeholders receive the right information at the right time. These factors include:

- **Communication technology**: The technology or methods used for communication, which should suit the project environment and stakeholder accessibility.
- **Stakeholder requirements**: Different stakeholders may have different needs regarding the frequency, detail, and method of communications.
- **Information security requirements**: Ensuring that sensitive information is protected according to the information security policies of the organization.

Section 10.1 – "Plan Communications Management process includes the collection of techniques, methods, and technologies that will be used to transfer information among project stakeholders."

Question 23: How is qualitative risk analysis different from quantitative risk analysis?
Correct Answer: Qualitative risk analysis assesses the impact and likelihood of risks occurring in a subjective manner, while quantitative risk analysis numerically analyzes the effect of identified risks on overall project objectives. **Explanation:** Qualitative risk analysis involves prioritizing risks based on their probability of occurrence and impact on project objectives using a relative or descriptive scale (e.g., high, medium, low). It is usually a faster and less costly method of risk assessment. On the other hand, quantitative risk analysis seeks to numerically estimate the probability of achieving specific project goals and quantifies the effect of risks by using data and statistical techniques.

PMBOK® Guide Reference:
Section 11.3 – "Perform Qualitative Risk Analysis is the process of prioritizing risks for further analysis or action by assessing their probability of occurrence and impact."

Question 33: What are some key responsibilities of a project manager to promote professional conduct?
Correct Answer: Upholding the PMI Code of Ethics, ensuring team adherence to legal and organizational standards, and fostering an ethical work environment. **Explanation:** A project manager has several responsibilities to promote professionalism and ethical conduct within a project team. Upholding the PMI Code of Ethics and Professional Conduct is crucial, as it sets the standards for making decisions and interacting with others. Ensuring that all team members understand and comply with legal and organizational standards prevents legal issues and promotes trust. Additionally, creating an ethical work environment encourages team members to behave responsibly and respectfully.

PMBOK® Guide Reference:
Section 2.4 – "The Role of the Project Manager emphasizes the importance of the project manager in leading the team and stakeholders, adhering to ethical norms, and fostering a positive environment."

Question 44: What is a work breakdown structure (WBS) and how is it used? Correct Answer:
A WBS is a hierarchical decomposition of the total scope of work to be carried out by the project team to accomplish the project objectives and create the required deliverables. **Explanation:** The Work Breakdown Structure (WBS) is a fundamental project management tool that breaks down the project's scope into manageable sections. Each level of the WBS represents a more detailed definition of the project work. The WBS helps in organizing team responsibilities, estimating costs and timelines, and controlling the project scope.

PMBOK® Guide Reference:
Section 5.4 – "Create WBS is the process of subdividing project deliverables and project work into smaller, more manageable components."
These detailed explanations provide insights into the rationale behind each correct answer and help in clarifying common misconceptions. They also guide where to find more detailed information in the PMBOK® Guide, aiding in further study and improving understanding of complex project management concepts.
Given the expansive nature of a full-length practice exam for the CAPM certification, here we'll focus on detailed explanations for a selected set of questions from various knowledge areas. These will include

insights into why particular answers are correct, point out the incorrect options, and reference relevant sections of the PMBOK Guide. This approach is aimed to deepen understanding, clarify misconceptions, and indicate areas for further study.

Question 1: What is the primary purpose of the Develop Project Charter process?

Correct Answer: To formally authorize a project or a phase and document initial requirements which satisfy the stakeholder's needs and expectations. **Explanation:** The Develop Project Charter process is crucial as it marks the official start of the project and provides the project manager with the authority to apply organizational resources to project activities. This process is outlined in the initiation phase and is essential for setting the project's direction aligned with the business's strategic objectives. **PMBOK Guide Reference:** Section 4.1 – Develop Project Charter

Question 6: What is the key benefit of the Collect Requirements process?

Correct Answer: Ensuring that stakeholders' needs are understood and managed throughout the project. **Explanation:** The Collect Requirements process is foundational for successful project scope management. By gathering requirements from stakeholders, project managers can ensure that the project deliverables will satisfy stakeholder needs and expectations, thus avoiding scope creep and increasing customer satisfaction. **PMBOK Guide Reference:** Section 5.2 – Collect Requirements

Question 17: How would a project manager address resource overallocation?

Correct Answer: By leveling the resources, which might involve delaying tasks to resolve the overallocation. **Explanation:** Resource leveling is a technique used in project management to address the issue of overallocation. When resources are stretched too thin across multiple tasks, project managers can adjust schedules and delay non-critical tasks to ensure that workloads are manageable and do not exceed the available resource capacity. **PMBOK Guide Reference:** Section 9.3 – Acquire Resources

Question 34: What is a project life cycle?

Correct Answer: The series of phases that a project passes through from its initiation to its closure. **Explanation:** Understanding the project life cycle is crucial for effective project management. It provides a structured approach from the start to the end of a project, helping managers ensure that deliverables are achieved at each phase before moving on to the next. The life cycle approach aids in managing the progression of a project systematically. **PMBOK Guide Reference:** Section 1.2 – The Project Life Cycle

Question 50: What is a stakeholder engagement plan and how is it developed?

Correct Answer: A plan that identifies strategies for engaging stakeholders based on their needs, expectations, interests, and potential impact on the project. **Explanation:** The stakeholder engagement plan is critical for effective communication and continuous engagement with stakeholders throughout the project. By understanding and addressing the various requirements and influences of stakeholders, project managers can enhance cooperation and mitigate potential risks related to stakeholder satisfaction. **PMBOK Guide Reference:** Section 13.2 – Plan Stakeholder Engagement

These explanations not only provide the rationale behind each correct answer but also incorporate references to the PMBOK Guide for detailed study. They help test-takers understand the broader context of each question, reinforcing learning and highlighting how project management practices are applied in real scenarios. This approach will also assist in identifying any gaps in knowledge and focusing revision efforts more effectively.

PRACTICE TEST QUESTIONS

Welcome to the Practice Test section of the Certified Associate in Project Management (CAPM) Exam Prep Study Guide. This section is designed to enhance your preparation by providing you with a series of practice questions that simulate the type of questions you might encounter on the actual CAPM exam. Each question has been carefully crafted to test your understanding of key project management concepts and methodologies, ensuring you are well-prepared for the exam.

To maximize the effectiveness of your study time, the answers and detailed explanations are provided directly after each question. Here's why this approach can be particularly beneficial:

Instant Feedback: Immediate access to the answer and its explanation allows you to quickly gauge your grasp of the material. This setup helps reinforce what you already know and promptly addresses any areas where you may have gaps in your understanding.

Efficient Learning: By eliminating the need to flip back and forth between questions and an answer key, this format enables you to concentrate more fully on the content, streamlining your study sessions and maintaining your focus and momentum.

Enhanced Retention: Studies have indicated that immediate feedback can significantly boost both learning and retention rates. By reviewing the explanation right after answering, you're more likely to solidify the information in your memory, improving your ability to recall and apply these concepts on the exam and in professional scenarios.

Practical Advice: To avoid inadvertently viewing the answers, we recommend using a piece of paper or a card to cover the answers as you work through the questions. This will ensure that you can test your knowledge effectively before reviewing the solution.

In this section, some important topics might be covered several times to reinforce critical concepts and ensure you are thoroughly versed in various aspects of project management.

With these practices in place, you're all set to begin your test prep. Good luck, and remember that each question is a step towards becoming a Certified Associate in Project Management!

1. Which of the following is not a characteristic of a project?
a. temporary endeavor
b. creates a unique product, service, or result
c. has a defined beginning and end
d. involves ongoing, repetitive tasks

Answer: d. involves ongoing, repetitive tasks. Explanation: Projects are temporary endeavors with a defined beginning and end, creating unique outcomes. Ongoing, repetitive tasks are typically part of operational work, not projects.

2. Which project life cycle phase involves developing the project charter?
a. initiating
b. planning
c. executing
d. closing

Answer: a. initiating. Explanation: The project charter is developed during the initiating phase. It formally authorizes the project and documents the initial requirements that satisfy the stakeholder's needs and expectations.

3. Which organizational structure has a project manager with full authority over the project and assigned project resources?
a. functional
b. weak matrix
c. balanced matrix
d. projectized

Answer: d. projectized. Explanation: In a projectized structure, the project manager has full authority over the project and resources are assigned to work on projects full-time. Functional and matrix structures involve varying levels of shared authority between functional managers and project managers.

4. What is the primary benefit of using a project management information system (PMIS)?
a. automatically resolving project issues
b. eliminating the need for a project manager
c. facilitating communication and decision-making
d. replacing the project management plan

Answer: c. facilitating communication and decision-making. Explanation: A PMIS is a set of tools and techniques used to gather, integrate, and disseminate the outputs of project management processes. It supports communication and decision-making but does not replace the project manager, automatically resolve issues, or replace the project management plan.

5. Which project management process group focuses on defining the total scope of the project?
a. initiating
b. planning
c. executing
d. monitoring and controlling

Answer: b. planning. Explanation: The planning process group establishes the total scope of the project and defines the objectives and the courses of action required to attain them. Initiating formally authorizes the project, executing performs the work, and monitoring and controlling tracks progress.

6. Which project management knowledge area involves identifying, analyzing, and responding to project risks?
a. project scope management
b. project quality management
c. project resource management
d. project risk management

Answer: d. project risk management. Explanation: Project risk management includes the processes of conducting risk management planning, identification, analysis, response planning, response implementation, and monitoring on a project. The other options relate to managing the project's scope, quality, and resources.

7. What is the purpose of a project kickoff meeting?
a. to assign project tasks to team members
b. to mark the end of the project planning phase
c. to introduce stakeholders and establish a common understanding of the project
d. to review and approve the project management plan

Answer: c. to introduce stakeholders and establish a common understanding of the project. Explanation: A project kickoff meeting brings key stakeholders together to introduce the project team, review project objectives, and establish a shared understanding of the project. Task assignments, plan approvals, and phase transitions are handled separately.

8. Which document describes the work that must be performed to deliver a product, service, or result with specified features and functions?
a. project charter
b. scope management plan
c. requirements management plan
d. project scope statement

Answer: d. project scope statement. Explanation: The project scope statement provides a detailed description of the project and product scope, including the project's deliverables, assumptions, and constraints. The other documents serve different purposes related to authorizing, planning, and managing the project scope.

9. What is the main purpose of the work breakdown structure (WBS)?
a. to identify the critical path of the project
b. to assign resources to project tasks
c. to decompose project deliverables into smaller, more manageable components
d. to determine the project budget

Answer: c. to decompose project deliverables into smaller, more manageable components. Explanation: The WBS is a hierarchical decomposition of the total scope of work to be carried out by the project team to accomplish the project objectives and create the required deliverables. It organizes and defines the total scope of the project but does not identify the critical path, assign resources, or determine the budget.

10. What is the correct order of the project management process groups?
a. initiating, planning, executing, monitoring and controlling, closing
b. initiating, executing, planning, monitoring and controlling, closing
c. planning, initiating, executing, monitoring and controlling, closing

d. planning, initiating, monitoring and controlling, executing, closing

Answer: a. initiating, planning, executing, monitoring and controlling, closing. Explanation: The project management process groups are performed in the order of initiating (defining a new project), planning (establishing the scope and objectives), executing (completing the work), monitoring and controlling (tracking, reviewing, and regulating progress), and closing (formally finishing the project).

11. Which of the following is not a characteristic of a project?
a. it has a unique purpose
b. it is temporary in nature
c. it involves a series of routine, repetitive tasks
d. it requires resources from various sources

Answer: c. it involves a series of routine, repetitive tasks. Explanation: Projects are non-routine, non-repetitive undertakings. They involve unique activities designed to accomplish a singular goal, unlike operational work, which involves ongoing, repetitive tasks.

12. A project manager is assigned to a project with a defined beginning and end. What other characteristic must be present for this endeavor to be considered a project?
a. it must be complex
b. it must have a budget greater than $100,000
c. it must have a project charter
d. it must create a unique product, service, or result

Answer: d. it must create a unique product, service, or result. Explanation: Projects are temporary endeavors undertaken to create a unique product, service, or result. Having a defined beginning and end is not sufficient; the outcome must also be unique. Complexity, budget size, and the presence of a project charter are not defining characteristics of a project.

13. Which of the following scenarios best describes a project?
a. developing a new software application for a client
b. conducting routine maintenance on a fleet of company vehicles
c. processing weekly payroll for an organization
d. monitoring and controlling a project's progress against the project management plan

Answer: a. developing a new software application for a client. Explanation: Developing a new software application is a unique, temporary endeavor that results in a distinct product, making it a project. Routine maintenance, payroll processing, and project monitoring and controlling are ongoing, repetitive operational activities, not projects.

14.What distinguishes a project from ongoing operations?
a. the presence of a project manager
b. the use of a project management methodology

c. its temporary nature and unique outcomes
d. the involvement of cross-functional teams

Answer: c. its temporary nature and unique outcomes. Explanation: Projects are distinguished from operations by their temporary nature (defined beginning and end) and the creation of unique deliverables. The presence of a project manager, use of a methodology, and involvement of cross-functional teams can apply to both projects and operations.

15. Which of the following is an example of a project?
a. performing regular software updates on company computers
b. constructing a new office building for a client
c. providing ongoing technical support to customers
d. conducting annual performance reviews for employees

Answer: b. constructing a new office building for a client. Explanation: Constructing a new office building is a temporary endeavor that results in a unique deliverable, making it a project. Regular software updates, ongoing technical support, and annual performance reviews are examples of operational activities that are ongoing and repetitive.

16. Which statement best describes the relationship between projects and organizational strategy?
a. projects are always independent of organizational strategy
b. projects are used to achieve organizational strategies and objectives
c. organizational strategy is always developed after projects are completed
d. there is no direct relationship between projects and organizational strategy

Answer: b. projects are used to achieve organizational strategies and objectives. Explanation: Projects are often the means by which organizations implement their strategic initiatives and achieve their objectives. Projects are not independent of strategy; rather, they are typically aligned with and driven by the organization's strategic goals.

17. What term is used to describe the application of knowledge, skills, tools, and techniques to project activities to meet project requirements?
a. project management
b. program management
c. portfolio management
d. operations management

Answer: a. project management. Explanation: Project management is the application of knowledge, skills, tools, and techniques to project activities to meet project requirements. Program management involves managing a group of related projects, while portfolio management deals with selecting and managing projects to meet strategic objectives. Operations management focuses on ongoing, repetitive activities.

18. Which of the following is not an essential characteristic of a project?

a. a defined beginning and end
b. the creation of a unique product, service, or result
c. progressive elaboration throughout the project life cycle
d. a guarantee of success

Answer: d. a guarantee of success. Explanation: While projects are planned and executed with the intent to succeed, there is no guarantee of success. Projects inherently involve uncertainty and risk. The essential characteristics of a project include a defined beginning and end, the creation of unique deliverables, and progressive elaboration (iterative refinement of plans as more information becomes available).

19. What term describes the gradual development and refinement of project details as more information becomes available over time?
a. rolling wave planning
b. project integration management
c. plan-do-check-act cycle
d. progressive elaboration

Answer: d. progressive elaboration. Explanation: Progressive elaboration is the iterative process of increasing the level of detail in a project management plan as more specific information and accurate estimates become available over time. Rolling wave planning, project integration management, and the plan-do-check-act cycle are related concepts but do not specifically describe this gradual refinement process.

20. Which of the following is an example of a project constraint?
a. the project's budget
b. the project manager's leadership style
c. the organization's project management methodology
d. the availability of skilled team members

Answer: a. the project's budget. Explanation: Project constraints are limiting factors that can affect the execution or performance of a project. The triple constraint of project management includes scope, schedule, and cost (budget). The project manager's leadership style, the chosen methodology, and the availability of skilled resources are factors that can influence a project but are not typically considered constraints.

21. A project manager is leading an initiative to implement a new customer relationship management (CRM) system. Which characteristic of a project is most evident in this scenario?
a. it is a temporary endeavor
b. it requires a cross-functional team
c. it has a defined beginning and end
d. it creates a unique product, service, or result

Answer: d. it creates a unique product, service, or result. Explanation: Implementing a new CRM system results in a unique outcome tailored to the organization's specific needs. While the project is also temporary with a defined beginning and end and may require a cross-functional team, the creation of a unique deliverable is the most prominent characteristic in this scenario.

22. Which of the following is not a characteristic of a project?
a. it is temporary
b. it is unique
c. it is ongoing
d. it has a specific goal

Answer: c. it is ongoing. Explanation: Projects are temporary endeavors with a defined beginning and end, unlike ongoing operations. They are unique, meaning they create distinct products, services, or results, and have specific goals or objectives to be met within the given constraints.

23. A company is upgrading its existing software to improve efficiency. This initiative can be considered a project because:
a. it involves routine maintenance
b. it is a repetitive task performed by the IT department
c. it results in a unique outcome
d. it has no defined end date

Answer: c. it results in a unique outcome. Explanation: Upgrading software to improve efficiency creates a unique result tailored to the company's needs, making it a project. It is not routine maintenance or a repetitive task, and it should have a defined end date, as projects are temporary endeavors.

24. Which of the following scenarios best exemplifies the temporary nature of a project?
a. developing a new mobile app for a client
b. providing ongoing technical support to software users
c. conducting regular performance reviews for employees
d. monitoring and controlling a project's progress

Answer: a. developing a new mobile app for a client. Explanation: Developing a new mobile app has a clear beginning and end, demonstrating the temporary nature of a project. Providing ongoing support, conducting regular reviews, and monitoring project progress are continuous, operational activities rather than temporary endeavors.

25. A project is initiated to construct a new highway bridge. Which characteristic of a project is most prominent in this example?
a. it is performed by a cross-functional team
b. it involves a series of repetitive tasks
c. it has a well-defined objectives and constraints
d. it requires progressive elaboration

Answer: c. it has a well-defined objectives and constraints. Explanation: Constructing a highway bridge has specific objectives (purpose, location, design) and constraints (budget, schedule, resources) that must be met. While it may involve a cross-functional team and progressive elaboration, these characteristics are less prominent than the well-defined objectives and constraints in this example. The tasks involved are unique to this project and not repetitive.

26. What term best describes the characteristic of a project that involves gradual development and refinement of project details over time?
a. rolling wave planning
b. project integration management
c. progressive elaboration
d. project lifecycle

Answer: c. progressive elaboration. Explanation: Progressive elaboration is the iterative process of gradually developing and refining project details as more specific information becomes available over time. Rolling wave planning is a related concept, while project integration management and project lifecycle are broader terms that do not specifically describe this characteristic.

27. Which of the following is not an essential element of a project charter?
a. project purpose and justification
b. high-level project description and boundaries
c. detailed project schedule and resource assignments
d. high-level risks, assumptions, and constraints

Answer: c. detailed project schedule and resource assignments. Explanation: A project charter provides a high-level overview of the project and does not typically include detailed schedules or resource assignments, which are developed later in the planning process. The charter should include the project purpose, high-level description, and high-level risks, assumptions, and constraints.

28. A project is considered successful when it:
a. meets or exceeds stakeholder expectations
b. is completed within the approved budget
c. is delivered on or before the scheduled completion date
d. all of the above

Answer: d. all of the above. Explanation: Project success is determined by meeting or exceeding stakeholder expectations, completing the project within the approved budget, and delivering the project deliverables on or before the scheduled completion date. All three factors (expectations, budget, and schedule) must be met for a project to be considered truly successful.

29. Which characteristic of a project is most closely related to the concept of "monitoring and controlling"?
a. uniqueness of the project deliverables
b. interdependencies among project activities

c. uncertainty and risk inherent in projects
d. temporary nature of projects

Answer: c. uncertainty and risk inherent in projects. Explanation: Monitoring and controlling processes are used to track project progress, identify potential problems, and take corrective action when necessary. These processes are most closely related to managing the uncertainty and risk inherent in projects. While monitoring and controlling are important throughout the project lifecycle (temporary nature), they are not directly related to the uniqueness of deliverables or interdependencies among activities.

30. A project manager is assigned to a project with several interrelated activities. Which project characteristic is most relevant to this scenario?
a. progressive elaboration
b. project constraints
c. interdependencies among project activities
d. project lifecycle phases

Answer: c. interdependencies among project activities. Explanation: Interrelated activities within a project exemplify the characteristic of interdependencies among project activities. These interdependencies require careful planning and coordination to ensure the project progresses smoothly. Progressive elaboration, project constraints, and lifecycle phases are other important characteristics but are not directly related to the scenario of interrelated activities.

31. Which of the following is not considered one of the primary project constraints?
a. scope
b. cost
c. quality
d. stakeholder satisfaction

Answer: d. stakeholder satisfaction. Explanation: The primary project constraints, often referred to as the "triple constraint" or "iron triangle," are scope, time, cost, quality, resources, and risks. Stakeholder satisfaction, while an important consideration, is not typically included as one of the primary constraints. It is more of an outcome or measure of project success.

32. A project manager is faced with a situation where the project scope needs to be increased to meet stakeholder expectations. Which of the following is most likely to be affected by this change?
a. project schedule
b. project budget
c. project risks
d. all of the above

Answer: d. all of the above. Explanation: When the project scope is increased, it often impacts other project constraints. Adding more scope typically requires more time (affecting the schedule), additional resources (impacting the budget), and introduces new risks that need to be managed. This scenario demonstrates the interrelated nature of project constraints.

33. Which project constraint is most likely to be impacted by a change in project requirements?
a. project schedule
b. project scope
c. project budget
d. project quality

Answer: b. project scope. Explanation: A change in project requirements directly affects the project scope, which defines the boundaries and deliverables of the project. While a scope change may also impact the schedule, budget, and quality, the most direct and immediate impact is on the project scope itself.

34. A project sponsor requests that the project be completed two weeks earlier than originally planned. Which project constraint is being challenged in this scenario?
a. scope
b. time
c. cost
d. quality

Answer: b. time. Explanation: The project sponsor's request to complete the project two weeks earlier is directly challenging the time constraint, which refers to the project schedule or duration. Compressing the schedule may also affect other constraints like cost (overtime pay) or quality (less time for testing), but the primary constraint being challenged is time.

35. In the context of project constraints, what does the term "scope creep" refer to?
a. uncontrolled changes to the project schedule
b. unexpected increases in project costs
c. gradual expansion of project boundaries without formal approval
d. progressive elaboration of project requirements

Answer: c. gradual expansion of project boundaries without formal approval. Explanation: Scope creep refers to the uncontrolled expansion of project scope without formal approval or corresponding adjustments to time, cost, and other constraints. It is not directly related to changes in schedule, cost increases, or the progressive elaboration of requirements, which is a planned and controlled process.

36. A project manager is allocating resources to various project activities. Which project constraint is being directly managed in this scenario?
a. project scope
b. project quality
c. project resources
d. project risks

Answer: c. project resources. Explanation: Allocating resources to project activities is a direct management of the resource constraint, which includes the people, materials, equipment, and facilities needed to complete the project. While resource allocation may indirectly affect scope, quality, and risks, the primary constraint being managed is resources.

37. Which of the following statements best describes the relationship between project constraints?
a. each constraint is managed independently of the others
b. changes to one constraint have no impact on the other constraints
c. constraints are interconnected, and a change in one often affects the others
d. the project manager must prioritize one constraint above all others

Answer: c. constraints are interconnected, and a change in one often affects the others. Explanation: Project constraints are interrelated, and a change in one constraint often has a ripple effect on the others. For example, increasing scope may require more time and resources, affecting the schedule and budget. Constraints cannot be managed independently, and the project manager must strive to balance them rather than prioritizing one above all others.

38. A project stakeholder suggests using higher-quality materials in the construction of a new building. Which project constraint is most likely to be affected by this suggestion?
a. project scope
b. project schedule
c. project budget
d. project risks

Answer: c. project budget. Explanation: Using higher-quality materials will likely increase the project costs, directly impacting the budget constraint. While it may also affect other constraints like scope (additional work) or schedule (longer lead times), the most immediate and significant impact is on the project budget.

39. In a software development project, the team discovers a critical security vulnerability that must be addressed. Which project constraint is most likely to be impacted by this discovery?
a. project scope
b. project schedule
c. project quality
d. project risks

Answer: a. project scope. Explanation: Addressing a critical security vulnerability will likely require additional work, such as designing and implementing a solution, which expands the project scope. This change in scope may also affect the schedule, quality, and risks, but the most direct impact is on the project scope.

40. Which of the following scenarios best illustrates the concept of balancing project constraints?
a. reducing project scope to meet a tight deadline
b. increasing the project budget to accommodate additional resources
c. accepting higher project risks to deliver the project on time and within budget

d. all of the above

Answer: d. all of the above. Explanation: Balancing project constraints involves making trade-offs between scope, time, cost, quality, resources, and risks to meet project objectives. Reducing scope to meet a deadline, increasing budget to add resources, and accepting higher risks to deliver on time and budget are all examples of balancing constraints. The project manager must carefully consider the impact of changes on all constraints and make decisions that best serve the overall project goals.

41. Which of the following is the correct sequence of project life cycle phases?
a. initiating, executing, planning, closing, monitoring and controlling
b. initiating, planning, executing, monitoring and controlling, closing
c. planning, initiating, executing, monitoring and controlling, closing
d. planning, initiating, monitoring and controlling, executing, closing

Answer: b. initiating, planning, executing, monitoring and controlling, closing. Explanation: The correct sequence of project life cycle phases is initiating (defining the project), planning (establishing the roadmap), executing (performing the work), monitoring and controlling (tracking progress and making adjustments), and closing (finalizing deliverables and documentation). The monitoring and controlling phase occurs in parallel with the executing phase.

42. Which project life cycle phase involves developing the project management plan?
a. initiating
b. planning
c. executing
d. closing

Answer: b. planning. Explanation: The project management plan, which defines how the project will be executed, monitored, controlled, and closed, is developed during the planning phase. The initiating phase involves authorizing the project, the executing phase involves performing the planned work, and the closing phase involves finalizing all activities and documenting lessons learned.

43. What is the main focus of the monitoring and controlling phase of the project life cycle?
a. defining project goals and objectives
b. developing detailed project plans
c. performing the work defined in the project management plan
d. measuring project performance and taking corrective action

Answer: d. measuring project performance and taking corrective action. Explanation: The monitoring and controlling phase involves tracking, reviewing, and regulating project progress and performance. This includes measuring performance against the project management plan, identifying deviations, and taking corrective actions to realign the project with the plan. Defining goals, developing plans, and performing work are the focus of other project life cycle phases.

44. Which project document is finalized during the closing phase of the project life cycle?
a. project charter
b. project management plan
c. lessons learned register
d. risk register

Answer: c. lessons learned register. Explanation: The lessons learned register, which captures the project team's experiences, insights, and recommendations for future projects, is finalized during the closing phase. The project charter is developed in the initiating phase, the project management plan is created in the planning phase, and the risk register is maintained throughout the project life cycle.

45. In which project life cycle phase are the project deliverables verified and accepted by the customer or sponsor?
a. initiating
b. planning
c. executing
d. closing

Answer: d. closing. Explanation: The closing phase involves obtaining final acceptance of the project deliverables by the customer or sponsor. This phase also includes completing project documentation, releasing resources, and transitioning the project to operations. Verifying deliverables is not the primary focus of the initiating (defining), planning (developing plans), or executing (performing work) phases.

46. Which of the following activities is performed during the initiating phase of the project life cycle?
a. developing the project schedule
b. identifying project risks
c. executing project tasks
d. defining the project scope

Answer: d. defining the project scope. Explanation: The initiating phase involves defining the project scope, which includes identifying the project's goals, objectives, and high-level requirements. Developing the project schedule and identifying risks are typically done during the planning phase, while executing tasks occurs in the executing phase.

47. What is the purpose of a phase gate or stage gate in the project life cycle?
a. to mark the beginning of a new project phase
b. to identify project risks and plan risk responses
c. to review project progress and make go/no-go decisions
d. to assign project tasks to team members

Answer: c. to review project progress and make go/no-go decisions. Explanation: Phase gates or stage gates are decision points at the end of each project phase where the project's progress, performance, and continued viability are evaluated. The project sponsor or steering committee uses these gates to make go/no-go decisions about whether the project should proceed to the next phase. Phase gates do not mark the beginning of phases, identify risks, or assign tasks.

48. Which project life cycle model is most appropriate for a project with evolving requirements and a high degree of stakeholder involvement?
a. predictive (waterfall) life cycle
b. iterative life cycle
c. incremental life cycle
d. agile life cycle

Answer: d. agile life cycle. Explanation: Agile life cycle models, such as Scrum and Kanban, are designed for projects with evolving requirements and a high degree of stakeholder involvement. These models use short iterations and frequent feedback loops to accommodate changing needs and priorities. Predictive (waterfall) models are better suited for projects with well-defined requirements, while iterative and incremental models involve repeated cycles of development and delivery.

49. In a multi-phase project, what is the relationship between project phases and the overall project life cycle?
a. project phases are the same as project life cycle phases
b. each project phase contains all five project life cycle phases
c. the project life cycle is repeated within each project phase
d. the project life cycle encompasses all project phases

Answer: d. the project life cycle encompasses all project phases. Explanation: In a multi-phase project, the project life cycle encompasses all the project phases, from the initiation of the first phase to the closure of the last phase. Each project phase represents a distinct stage of the project, such as design, development, or implementation, but is not equivalent to a project life cycle phase (initiating, planning, executing, monitoring and controlling, closing). The project life cycle phases are applied across all project phases.

50. Which of the following statements best describes the relationship between the project life cycle and the product life cycle?
a. the project life cycle and product life cycle are the same
b. the project life cycle is a subset of the product life cycle
c. the product life cycle is a subset of the project life cycle
d. the project life cycle and product life cycle are independent of each other

Answer: b. the project life cycle is a subset of the product life cycle. Explanation: The project life cycle, which encompasses the phases of a project from initiation to closure, is typically a subset of the product life cycle. The product life cycle includes additional phases such as operations, maintenance, and retirement, which occur after the project is completed. The project delivers the product, but the product's life extends beyond the project's boundaries.

51. Which of the following documents formally authorizes the project and grants the project manager authority to use organizational resources for project activities?

a. project management plan
b. project charter
c. project scope statement
d. business case

Answer: b. project charter. Explanation: The project charter is the document that formally authorizes the project and grants the project manager the authority to apply organizational resources to project activities. It is developed during the initiating phase and is approved by the project sponsor or a higher level of management. The project management plan, project scope statement, and business case serve different purposes and do not formally authorize the project.

52. In the initiating phase, what is the primary purpose of conducting a stakeholder analysis?
a. to develop a detailed project schedule
b. to identify and document project risks
c. to determine the project's budget and resource requirements
d. to understand stakeholder interests, expectations, and influence

Answer: d. to understand stakeholder interests, expectations, and influence. Explanation: Stakeholder analysis, performed during the initiating phase, aims to identify project stakeholders and understand their interests, expectations, and potential impact on the project. This information helps the project manager develop strategies for engaging and managing stakeholders throughout the project life cycle. Developing schedules, identifying risks, and determining budgets and resources are typically done during the planning phase.

53. Which of the following is not typically included in the project charter?
a. project purpose and justification
b. high-level project description and deliverables
c. detailed project schedule and resource assignments
d. project approval requirements and key stakeholders

Answer: c. detailed project schedule and resource assignments. Explanation: The project charter is a high-level document that authorizes the project and provides an overview of the project's purpose, objectives, and key stakeholders. It does not typically include detailed project schedules or resource assignments, which are developed later in the planning phase. The charter should include the project purpose, high-level description, and project approval requirements.

54. What is the main objective of the initiating phase in the project life cycle?
a. to develop detailed project plans and schedules
b. to define the project scope, objectives, and success criteria
c. to execute project tasks and create project deliverables
d. to monitor project progress and take corrective actions

Answer: b. to define the project scope, objectives, and success criteria. Explanation: The primary objective of the initiating phase is to define the project scope, objectives, and success criteria. This involves identifying project stakeholders, developing the project charter, and establishing a high-level understanding of what the project aims to achieve. Developing detailed plans, executing tasks, and monitoring progress are the focus of later project life cycle phases.

55. Which of the following is an input to the develop project charter process?
a. project management plan
b. work performance data
c. project statement of work
d. change requests

Answer: c. project statement of work. Explanation: The project statement of work (SOW) is an input to the develop project charter process. The SOW is a narrative description of the products, services, or results to be delivered by the project and is used to create the project charter. The project management plan is an output of the planning phase, work performance data is collected during the executing and monitoring and controlling phases, and change requests are processed during the monitoring and controlling phase.

56. During the initiating phase, which of the following tools and techniques is used to assess project alignment with organizational strategy?
a. project selection criteria
b. stakeholder analysis
c. expert judgment
d. project management information system (PMIS)

Answer: a. project selection criteria. Explanation: Project selection criteria, which may include strategic fit, financial benefits, risk profile, and resource availability, are used during the initiating phase to assess project alignment with organizational strategy and determine whether a project should be pursued. Stakeholder analysis focuses on identifying and understanding stakeholders, expert judgment relies on the expertise of individuals, and the PMIS is used to manage and share project information throughout the project life cycle.

57. In the context of project integration management, what is the purpose of the business case document?
a. to authorize the project manager to start the project
b. to provide a detailed description of the project scope
c. to justify the project in terms of costs, benefits, and risks
d. to outline the project team's roles and responsibilities

Answer: c. to justify the project in terms of costs, benefits, and risks. Explanation: The business case is a document that justifies the project in terms of costs, benefits, and risks. It is used to determine whether the project is worth the required investment and aligns with the organization's strategic objectives. The project charter, not the business case, authorizes the project manager to start the project. The project scope statement, not the business case, provides a detailed description of the project scope. The project management plan, not the business case, outlines the project team's roles and responsibilities.

58. What is the main benefit of involving stakeholders in the initiating phase of the project?
a. to ensure stakeholders are aware of their roles and responsibilities
b. to gain stakeholder support and buy-in for the project
c. to assign project tasks to stakeholders
d. to provide stakeholders with a detailed project schedule

Answer: b. to gain stakeholder support and buy-in for the project. Explanation: Involving stakeholders in the initiating phase helps gain their support and buy-in for the project. By engaging stakeholders early, the project manager can understand their needs, expectations, and potential concerns, and develop strategies to keep them engaged and supportive throughout the project. Assigning roles and responsibilities, distributing tasks, and providing detailed schedules are typically addressed in the planning phase and do not necessarily require stakeholder involvement in the initiating phase.

59. Which of the following is not a key output of the initiating phase?
a. project charter
b. stakeholder register
c. project scope statement
d. risk register

Answer: d. risk register. Explanation: The risk register, which documents identified project risks, their characteristics, and risk response plans, is typically developed during the planning phase, not the initiating phase. Key outputs of the initiating phase include the project charter (authorizing the project), the stakeholder register (identifying and documenting project stakeholders), and the project scope statement (providing a high-level description of the project scope). The project management plan, which includes the scope statement, is also developed during the planning phase.

60. Which of the following best describes the relationship between the project charter and the project scope statement?
a. the project charter and project scope statement are the same document
b. the project charter is a subset of the project scope statement
c. the project scope statement is a subset of the project charter
d. the project charter authorizes the project, while the project scope statement details the project scope

Answer: d. the project charter authorizes the project, while the project scope statement details the project scope. Explanation: The project charter and project scope statement are separate documents with different purposes. The project charter formally authorizes the project and grants the project manager authority to use organizational resources, while the project scope statement provides a detailed description of the project scope, including deliverables, assumptions, and constraints. The project charter is developed in the initiating phase, while the project scope statement is created during the planning phase.

61. Which of the following is the primary output of the planning process group?
a. project charter
b. project management plan
c. work performance data
d. change requests

Answer: b. project management plan. Explanation: The project management plan is the primary output of the planning process group. It integrates and consolidates all of the subsidiary plans and baselines from the planning processes, describing how the project will be executed, monitored, controlled, and closed. The project charter is an output of the initiating process group, work performance data is collected during the executing and monitoring and controlling process groups, and change requests are processed during the monitoring and controlling process group.

62. Which of the following is not typically included in the project scope statement?
a. project deliverables
b. project assumptions and constraints
c. project cost estimates and budget
d. acceptance criteria

Answer: c. project cost estimates and budget. Explanation: The project scope statement is a detailed description of the project and product scope. It includes the project deliverables, assumptions, constraints, and acceptance criteria but does not typically include cost estimates or the project budget. Cost estimates and the budget are part of the project cost management plan, which is a separate component of the overall project management plan.

63. What is the main purpose of the work breakdown structure (WBS) in project planning?
a. to identify project risks and plan risk responses
b. to decompose project deliverables into manageable work packages
c. to develop the project schedule and assign resources to tasks
d. to establish the project's quality standards and metrics

Answer: b. to decompose project deliverables into manageable work packages. Explanation: The work breakdown structure (WBS) is a hierarchical decomposition of the total scope of work to be carried out by the project team to accomplish the project objectives and create the required deliverables. It organizes and defines the total scope of the project by breaking it down into increasingly detailed levels of work packages. The WBS does not directly address risks, schedules, resource assignments, or quality standards, which are managed through other project management processes and plans.

64. During the planning phase, what is the primary purpose of the communications management plan?
a. to identify project stakeholders and their communication needs
b. to determine the project's communication channels and technologies
c. to establish the frequency, format, and content of project communications
d. all of the above

Answer: d. all of the above. Explanation: The communications management plan, developed during the planning phase, comprehensively addresses project communication. It involves identifying stakeholders and their communication needs, determining the most appropriate communication channels and technologies, and establishing the frequency, format, and content of project communications. The plan ensures that project information is effectively generated, collected, distributed, stored, retrieved, and ultimately disposed of.

65. In the context of project risk management, what is the purpose of a risk register?
a. to identify and prioritize project risks
b. to analyze the impact and probability of identified risks
c. to document risk response strategies and risk owners
d. all of the above

Answer: d. all of the above. Explanation: The risk register is a comprehensive document used throughout the project risk management processes. It is used to identify and prioritize project risks, analyze their potential impact and probability, document planned risk response strategies, and assign risk owners responsible for managing each risk. The risk register is initiated during the planning phase and is continuously updated throughout the project life cycle as new risks are identified and existing risks are managed.

66. Which of the following project management plans is concerned with defining the processes for verifying and controlling changes to the project deliverables?
a. scope management plan
b. schedule management plan
c. quality management plan
d. change management plan

Answer: a. scope management plan. Explanation: The scope management plan is a component of the project management plan that describes how the project and product scope will be defined, validated, and controlled. It includes the processes for verifying and controlling changes to the project deliverables, ensuring that only approved changes are implemented. The schedule management plan focuses on developing and managing the project schedule, the quality management plan addresses quality standards and control processes, and the change management plan deals with the overall process for managing changes to the project.

67. During the planning phase, what is the primary purpose of a responsibility assignment matrix (RAM)?
a. to identify project risks and assign risk owners
b. to map project roles and responsibilities to project tasks
c. to establish the project's communication channels and frequencies
d. to determine the project's quality standards and acceptance criteria

Answer: b. to map project roles and responsibilities to project tasks. Explanation: A responsibility assignment matrix (RAM), also known as a RACI (Responsible, Accountable, Consulted, Informed) matrix, is used to map project roles and responsibilities to specific project tasks or deliverables. It clarifies who is responsible for executing each task, who is accountable for the task's completion, who needs to be consulted for input or feedback, and who needs to be kept informed of progress or decisions. The RAM is developed during the planning phase as part of the human resource management plan. It does not directly address risks, communication, or quality management, which are covered in other project management plans.

68. What is the purpose of the critical path method (CPM) in project schedule development?
a. to identify the sequence of activities that represents the longest path through the project
b. to determine the minimum project duration and identify schedule flexibility
c. to calculate the early start, early finish, late start, and late finish dates for project activities
d. all of the above

Answer: d. all of the above. Explanation: The critical path method (CPM) is a technique used in project schedule development to analyze the sequence of activities and determine the minimum project duration. It identifies the critical path, which is the sequence of activities that represents the longest path through the project and determines the shortest possible project duration. CPM also calculates the early start, early finish, late start, and late finish dates for each activity, helping to identify schedule flexibility (float or slack) for non-critical activities. By focusing on the critical path and managing schedule float, project managers can more effectively control the project schedule.

69. Which of the following is not an input to the estimate costs process?
a. project schedule
b. risk register
c. resource requirements
d. cost baseline

Answer: d. cost baseline. Explanation: The cost baseline is not an input to the estimate costs process; rather, it is an output of the determine budget process, which uses the cost estimates as an input. The project schedule, risk register, and resource requirements are all inputs to the estimate costs process. The project schedule provides information about the timing and duration of project activities, the risk register identifies potential risks that may impact project costs, and the resource requirements document the types and quantities of resources needed for each project activity.

70. Which of the following is a key benefit of developing a project management plan during the planning phase?
a. it helps the project manager identify and plan for project risks
b. it ensures that project stakeholders understand their roles and responsibilities
c. it provides a comprehensive roadmap for executing, monitoring, and controlling the project
d. all of the above

Answer: d. all of the above. Explanation: Developing a comprehensive project management plan during the planning phase offers multiple benefits. It helps the project manager identify and plan for project risks by incorporating risk management strategies into the overall plan. It ensures that project stakeholders understand their roles and responsibilities by clearly defining and communicating them in the human resource management plan. Most importantly, the project management plan provides a comprehensive roadmap for executing, monitoring, and controlling the project by integrating all the subsidiary plans and baselines into a cohesive document that guides the project team throughout the project life cycle.

71. In the executing process group, what is the primary role of the project manager?
a. to develop detailed project plans and schedules
b. to monitor project progress and identify deviations from the plan
c. to direct and manage the work defined in the project management plan
d. to close the project or phase and obtain final acceptance of deliverables

Answer: c. to direct and manage the work defined in the project management plan. Explanation: During the executing process group, the project manager's primary role is to lead and manage the project team in performing the work defined in the project management plan. This involves coordinating resources, managing stakeholder expectations, and ensuring that project activities are executed according to the plan. Developing detailed plans is the focus of the planning process group, monitoring progress is the main concern of the monitoring and controlling process group, and closing the project or phase is the responsibility of the closing process group.

72. Which of the following is not a key activity performed during the executing process group?
a. acquiring and managing project resources
b. implementing approved changes and corrective actions
c. developing the project team and managing team performance
d. creating the project charter and obtaining project authorization

Answer: d. creating the project charter and obtaining project authorization. Explanation: Creating the project charter and obtaining project authorization are activities performed during the initiating process group, not the executing process group. Key activities in the executing process group include acquiring and managing project resources, implementing approved changes and corrective actions, and developing the project team and managing team performance. These activities focus on carrying out the work defined in the project management plan and ensuring that project objectives are met.

73. During project execution, what is the main purpose of the manage project knowledge process?
a. to capture, distribute, and archive project documents and deliverables
b. to identify, create, and share project knowledge and lessons learned
c. to ensure that project team members have access to project management tools
d. to monitor project progress and report status to stakeholders

Answer: b. to identify, create, and share project knowledge and lessons learned. Explanation: The manage project knowledge process, performed during project execution, aims to identify, create, and share project knowledge and lessons learned. This involves capturing insights, experiences, and best practices from the project team and stakeholders, and making this knowledge available for use in the current project and future projects. While managing project knowledge may involve archiving documents and deliverables, providing access to tools, and communicating with stakeholders, these are not the main focus of this specific process.

74. Which of the following tools and techniques is used to assess and improve team interactions and enhance project performance?
a. project management information system (PMIS)
b. interpersonal and team skills
c. meetings and communication technology
d. project management plan updates

Answer: b. interpersonal and team skills. Explanation: Interpersonal and team skills, such as conflict management, emotional intelligence, and team building, are used during project execution to assess and improve team interactions and enhance project performance. These skills help the project manager motivate, influence, and guide the project team, resolve conflicts, and create a collaborative and productive working environment. The PMIS is used to manage and share project information, meetings and communication technology facilitate team interactions, and project management plan updates document changes to the project approach or scope.

75. What is the primary purpose of the direct and manage project work process in the executing process group?
a. to define the project scope and create the work breakdown structure (WBS)
b. to implement the project management plan and perform the work defined in it
c. to monitor project progress and take corrective action when necessary
d. to close the project or phase and transition the deliverables to operations

Answer: b. to implement the project management plan and perform the work defined in it. Explanation: The direct and manage project work process, part of the executing process group, is focused on implementing the project management plan and performing the work defined in it. This involves leading and managing the project team, executing project activities according to the plan, and delivering project outputs. Defining the project scope and creating the WBS are planning activities, monitoring progress and taking corrective action are part of the monitoring and controlling process group, and closing the project or phase is the responsibility of the closing process group.

76. Which of the following is a key output of the manage project team process?
a. project staff assignments
b. team performance assessments
c. resource breakdown structure
d. project schedule updates

Answer: b. team performance assessments. Explanation: Team performance assessments are a key output of the manage project team process in the executing process group. These assessments evaluate the effectiveness of the project team, identify areas for improvement, and measure individual and team performance against project goals and expectations. Project staff assignments are an output of the acquire resources process, the resource breakdown structure is a tool used in resource planning, and project schedule updates are an output of the monitor and control project work process.

77. During project execution, what is the main focus of the manage communications process?

a. to identify project stakeholders and plan their engagement
b. to create, collect, distribute, and store project information
c. to monitor and control project risks and implement risk responses
d. to measure project performance and report status to stakeholders

Answer: b. to create, collect, distribute, and store project information. Explanation: The manage communications process, part of the executing process group, focuses on creating, collecting, distributing, and storing project information according to the communications management plan. This involves generating project reports, facilitating information sharing among stakeholders, and managing project communications throughout the project life cycle. Identifying stakeholders and planning their engagement are part of the planning process group, monitoring and controlling risks is a monitoring and controlling activity, and measuring project performance and reporting status are also part of the monitoring and controlling process group.

78. What is the primary goal of the implement risk responses process in the executing process group?
a. to identify project risks and analyze their potential impact
b. to plan risk response strategies for identified risks
c. to execute the planned risk response strategies and modify them as needed
d. to monitor the effectiveness of risk response strategies and control risks

Answer: c. to execute the planned risk response strategies and modify them as needed. Explanation: The implement risk responses process, performed during project execution, aims to execute the risk response strategies planned during the risk management planning process. This involves implementing risk mitigation, avoidance, transfer, or acceptance strategies, and modifying these strategies as needed based on project performance and changing risk conditions. Identifying and analyzing risks, planning risk responses, and monitoring the effectiveness of risk strategies are all activities performed in other project risk management processes.

79. Which of the following is a key interpersonal skill for project managers during project execution?
a. active listening and effective communication
b. technical expertise in project management software
c. proficiency in financial management and budgeting
d. knowledge of quality control tools and techniques

Answer: a. active listening and effective communication. Explanation: Active listening and effective communication are critical interpersonal skills for project managers during project execution. These skills enable project managers to build trust, resolve conflicts, motivate team members, and ensure that project information is clearly understood by all stakeholders. Technical expertise in project management software, financial management proficiency, and knowledge of quality control tools are all valuable skills but are not specifically interpersonal in nature.

80. Which of the following is not typically an input to the direct and manage project work process?
a. project management plan
b. approved change requests

c. enterprise environmental factors
d. project funding requirements

Answer: d. project funding requirements. Explanation: Project funding requirements are not typically a direct input to the direct and manage project work process. Funding requirements are usually established during the planning process group and are an input to the determine budget process. The key inputs to the direct and manage project work process include the project management plan, which guides project execution, approved change requests, which authorize modifications to the project scope or plan, and enterprise environmental factors, which can influence project execution and decision-making.

81. What is the primary purpose of the monitoring and controlling process group?
a. to define the project scope and create the project management plan
b. to perform the work defined in the project management plan
c. to track project progress, identify deviations, and take corrective action
d. to finalize project activities and transfer deliverables to operations

Answer: c. to track project progress, identify deviations, and take corrective action. Explanation: The monitoring and controlling process group focuses on tracking project progress, comparing actual performance to planned performance, identifying deviations or variances, and taking corrective action to bring the project back on track. Defining the project scope and creating the project management plan are activities in the planning process group, performing the work is part of the executing process group, and finalizing activities and transferring deliverables are part of the closing process group.

82. Which of the following is not a key activity performed during the monitoring and controlling process group?
a. measuring project performance using appropriate tools and techniques
b. managing changes to the project scope, schedule, and budget
c. identifying, analyzing, and responding to new project risks
d. acquiring and developing the project team and resources

Answer: d. acquiring and developing the project team and resources. Explanation: Acquiring and developing the project team and resources are activities performed during the executing process group, not the monitoring and controlling process group. Key activities in the monitoring and controlling process group include measuring project performance using tools like earned value management, managing changes to the project scope, schedule, and budget through the integrated change control process, and identifying, analyzing, and responding to new risks that emerge during project execution.

83. What is the main purpose of the monitor and control project work process?
a. to authorize the project and secure funding for project activities
b. to define the project scope and create the work breakdown structure (WBS)
c. to track project progress, monitor deviations, and take corrective actions
d. to close the project or phase and obtain final acceptance of deliverables

Answer: c. to track project progress, monitor deviations, and take corrective actions. Explanation: The monitor and control project work process, part of the monitoring and controlling process group, aims to track project progress, monitor deviations from the project management plan, and take corrective actions to realign the project with the plan. This involves collecting project performance data, measuring progress against baselines, and identifying areas that require preventive or corrective action. Authorizing the project and securing funding are initiating activities, defining scope and creating the WBS are planning activities, and closing the project is part of the closing process group.

84. In the context of project quality management, what is the purpose of the control quality process?
a. to identify quality standards and define quality management activities
b. to execute quality assurance activities and implement process improvements
c. to monitor and record results of quality control activities
d. to continuously improve the quality of project deliverables and processes

Answer: c. to monitor and record results of quality control activities. Explanation: The control quality process, performed during the monitoring and controlling process group, focuses on monitoring and recording the results of quality control activities to assess performance and ensure that project deliverables meet the established quality standards. This involves performing quality inspections, identifying defects or nonconformities, and recommending necessary changes or corrective actions. Identifying quality standards is part of the plan quality management process, executing quality assurance activities is part of the manage quality process, and continuously improving quality is an overarching goal of project quality management.

85. Which of the following tools and techniques is used to measure project performance and identify variances from the project management plan?
a. earned value management
b. risk probability and impact assessment
c. quality audits and inspections
d. stakeholder engagement and communication

Answer: a. earned value management. Explanation: Earned value management (EVM) is a tool used to measure project performance and identify variances from the project management plan. EVM integrates scope, schedule, and resource measurements to assess project progress and performance, comparing the planned value of work to the actual value of work completed. It helps project managers detect deviations from the plan and make informed decisions about corrective actions. Risk probability and impact assessments are used in risk management, quality audits and inspections are quality management tools, and stakeholder engagement and communication are part of project communications management.

86. What is the primary purpose of the perform integrated change control process?
a. to identify and plan for potential project changes and their impacts
b. to review, approve, and manage changes to the project and project baselines
c. to communicate approved changes to project stakeholders
d. to implement approved changes and update project documents accordingly

Answer: b. to review, approve, and manage changes to the project and project baselines. Explanation: The perform integrated change control process, part of the monitoring and controlling process group, aims to review, approve, and manage changes to the project and project baselines in a comprehensive and integrated manner. This involves evaluating the impact of proposed changes on project scope, schedule, cost, quality, risk, and other factors, and ensuring that changes are properly documented, approved, and communicated to stakeholders. Identifying and planning for potential changes is part of risk management and change management planning, communicating approved changes and implementing them are separate activities that follow the integrated change control process.

87. During the monitoring and controlling process group, what is the main focus of the monitor risks process?
a. to identify new project risks and update the risk register
b. to perform qualitative and quantitative risk analysis on identified risks
c. to implement planned risk responses and monitor their effectiveness
d. to track identified risks, monitor residual risks, and identify new risks

Answer: d. to track identified risks, monitor residual risks, and identify new risks. Explanation: The monitor risks process, performed during the monitoring and controlling process group, focuses on tracking identified risks, monitoring residual risks, and identifying new risks that may emerge throughout the project life cycle. This involves reviewing the risk register, assessing the effectiveness of risk response strategies, and updating the risk management plan as needed. Identifying new risks and updating the risk register is part of the identify risks process, performing qualitative and quantitative risk analysis is done in separate risk management processes, and implementing risk responses is part of the implement risk responses process in the executing process group.

88. Which of the following is a key output of the validate scope process?
a. accepted deliverables
b. work performance information
c. change requests
d. project document updates

Answer: a. accepted deliverables. Explanation: Accepted deliverables are a key output of the validate scope process, which is part of the monitoring and controlling process group. This process involves formalizing the acceptance of completed project deliverables that meet the established acceptance criteria. Work performance information, change requests, and project document updates are all outputs of the monitor and control project work process, which is a separate process within the monitoring and controlling process group.

89. What is the main purpose of the monitor communications process in the monitoring and controlling process group?
a. to identify project stakeholders and plan their engagement
b. to create, collect, distribute, and store project information
c. to assess the effectiveness of communication activities and make adjustments
d. to measure project performance and report status to stakeholders

Answer: c. to assess the effectiveness of communication activities and make adjustments. Explanation: The monitor communications process, part of the monitoring and controlling process group, aims to assess the effectiveness of communication activities throughout the project life cycle and make adjustments as needed to ensure that project information is effectively shared and understood by stakeholders. This involves monitoring the implementation of the communications management plan, evaluating the impact of communication activities on stakeholder engagement, and identifying areas for improvement. Identifying stakeholders and planning their engagement are part of the planning process group, creating and distributing project information is part of the manage communications process in the executing process group, and measuring project performance and reporting status are separate activities within the monitoring and controlling process group.

90. Which of the following is not typically an input to the control procurements process?
a. project management plan
b. procurement documents
c. seller performance reports
d. project funding requirements

Answer: d. project funding requirements. Explanation: Project funding requirements are not typically a direct input to the control procurements process. Funding requirements are usually established during the planning process group and are an input to the plan procurement management process. The key inputs to the control procurements process include the project management plan, which guides procurement management activities, procurement documents, which define the terms and conditions of procurement contracts, and seller performance reports, which provide information on the performance of sellers and the status of procurements.

91. What is the primary focus of the closing process group?
a. to define the project scope and objectives
b. to perform the work defined in the project management plan
c. to monitor and control project performance and manage changes
d. to finalize project activities, complete documentation, and transfer deliverables

Answer: d. to finalize project activities, complete documentation, and transfer deliverables. Explanation: The closing process group focuses on finalizing all project activities, completing project documentation, and transferring the project deliverables to the appropriate stakeholders or operational teams. This involves obtaining final acceptance of deliverables, archiving project information, releasing resources, and conducting post-project reviews. Defining scope and objectives is part of the planning process group, performing work is part of the executing process group, and monitoring and controlling performance is part of the monitoring and controlling process group.

92. Which of the following is not a key activity performed during the closing process group?
a. obtaining final acceptance of project deliverables
b. documenting lessons learned and archiving project information
c. releasing project resources and closing procurement contracts
d. identifying and analyzing new project risks and opportunities

Answer: d. identifying and analyzing new project risks and opportunities. Explanation: Identifying and analyzing new project risks and opportunities is an activity typically performed during the planning and executing process groups, not the closing process group. Key activities in the closing process group include obtaining final acceptance of project deliverables from stakeholders, documenting lessons learned and archiving project information for future reference, releasing project resources and closing procurement contracts, and transitioning the project deliverables to the appropriate operational or maintenance teams.

93. What is the main purpose of the close project or phase process?
a. to authorize the project and secure funding for project activities
b. to define the project scope and create the work breakdown structure (WBS)
c. to track project progress, monitor deviations, and take corrective actions
d. to finalize project activities, transfer deliverables, and close the project or phase

Answer: d. to finalize project activities, transfer deliverables, and close the project or phase. Explanation: The close project or phase process, part of the closing process group, aims to finalize all project activities, transfer the completed deliverables to the appropriate stakeholders, and formally close the project or a specific project phase. This involves obtaining final acceptance of deliverables, documenting lessons learned, updating project records, and communicating project closure to stakeholders. Authorizing the project and securing funding are initiating activities, defining scope and creating the WBS are planning activities, and tracking progress and taking corrective actions are monitoring and controlling activities.

94. Which of the following documents is typically updated and finalized during the closing process group?
a. project charter
b. project management plan
c. lessons learned register
d. risk register

Answer: c. lessons learned register. Explanation: The lessons learned register is typically updated and finalized during the closing process group. This document captures the knowledge gained throughout the project, including successes, challenges, and recommendations for future projects. The project charter is created during the initiating process group, the project management plan is developed and updated throughout the project life cycle, and the risk register is primarily used during the planning, executing, and monitoring and controlling process groups.

95. What is the primary purpose of conducting a post-project review during the closing process group?
a. to identify and document the causes of project failures
b. to celebrate project successes and reward team performance
c. to evaluate project outcomes, document lessons learned, and identify improvements
d. to plan for future projects and allocate resources accordingly

Answer: c. to evaluate project outcomes, document lessons learned, and identify improvements. Explanation: The primary purpose of conducting a post-project review during the closing process group is to evaluate the project outcomes, document lessons learned, and identify areas for improvement in future projects. This review involves analyzing project performance, assessing the effectiveness of project management processes, and gathering feedback from stakeholders. While the review may also acknowledge project successes and team performance, its main focus is on learning and continuous improvement rather than celebration or future project planning.

96. Which of the following is not a key input to the close project or phase process?
a. project management plan
b. accepted deliverables
c. project documents
d. procurement strategy

Answer: d. procurement strategy. Explanation: The procurement strategy is not typically a direct input to the close project or phase process. The procurement strategy is usually developed during the planning process group as part of the plan procurement management process. The key inputs to the close project or phase process include the project management plan, which guides the closing activities, accepted deliverables, which are the final project outcomes, and project documents, such as the lessons learned register and final performance reports.

97. What is the main purpose of the final product, service, or result transition in the closing process group?
a. to transfer ownership of project deliverables to the appropriate stakeholders
b. to release project resources and reassign them to other projects or activities
c. to archive project documents and store them for future reference
d. to evaluate the project team's performance and provide feedback

Answer: a. to transfer ownership of project deliverables to the appropriate stakeholders. Explanation: The main purpose of the final product, service, or result transition in the closing process group is to transfer ownership and responsibility for the project deliverables to the appropriate stakeholders, such as the client, end-users, or operational teams. This transition ensures that the deliverables are properly handed over and that the necessary knowledge and support are provided for their ongoing use and maintenance. Releasing project resources, archiving documents, and evaluating team performance are separate activities within the closing process group.

98. Which of the following is a key output of the close project or phase process?
a. project charter
b. project management plan updates
c. final product, service, or result transition
d. change requests

Answer: c. final product, service, or result transition. Explanation: The final product, service, or result transition is a key output of the close project or phase process. This output represents the formal transfer of ownership and responsibility for the project deliverables to the appropriate stakeholders. The project charter is an output of the initiating process group, project management plan updates are typically associated with the monitoring and controlling process group, and change requests are processed during the integrated change control process.

99. What is the purpose of the administrative closure procedure in the closing process group?
a. to ensure that all project activities are completed and deliverables are accepted
b. to document the reasons for project termination and the impact on stakeholders
c. to evaluate the project team's performance and provide feedback for improvement
d. to archive project documents, close contracts, and release project resources

Answer: d. to archive project documents, close contracts, and release project resources. Explanation: The administrative closure procedure in the closing process group focuses on archiving project documents, closing out contracts, and releasing project resources. This procedure ensures that all project-related documentation is properly organized, stored, and accessible for future reference. It also involves finalizing and closing any outstanding contracts or agreements with suppliers, contractors, or other stakeholders, and releasing project resources, such as team members and equipment, for reallocation to other projects or activities.

100. What is the significance of obtaining formal acceptance of project deliverables during the closing process group?
a. to ensure that the project has met all scope requirements and quality standards
b. to transfer ownership and responsibility for the deliverables to the appropriate stakeholders
c. to document the project team's performance and identify areas for improvement
d. to celebrate the successful completion of the project and recognize team achievements

Answer: b. to transfer ownership and responsibility for the deliverables to the appropriate stakeholders. Explanation: Obtaining formal acceptance of project deliverables during the closing process group is significant because it marks the transfer of ownership and responsibility for the deliverables from the project team to the appropriate stakeholders, such as the client, end-users, or operational teams. This acceptance indicates that the deliverables meet the agreed-upon requirements and quality standards and that the stakeholders are satisfied with the project outcomes. While the acceptance process may also acknowledge the project team's performance and the successful completion of the project, its primary purpose is to ensure a smooth transition of the deliverables to the stakeholders who will use, maintain, and benefit from them.

101. In a functional organizational structure, the project manager has:
a. full authority over the project and project resources
b. limited authority and must negotiate with functional managers for resources
c. no authority and acts solely as a coordinator between functional departments
d. authority only over the project budget, but not the project team

Answer: b. limited authority and must negotiate with functional managers for resources. Explanation: In a functional organization, the project manager has limited authority and must coordinate with functional managers to secure resources for the project. The functional managers maintain control over their resources and assign them to projects based on their availability and expertise. The project manager does not have full authority over the project team and must negotiate with functional managers to obtain the necessary resources.

102. Which organizational structure is characterized by a strong project manager who has full authority over the project and project resources?
a. functional
b. weak matrix
c. balanced matrix
d. projectized

Answer: d. projectized. Explanation: In a projectized organizational structure, the project manager has full authority over the project and project resources. The project team members are assigned to the project full-time and report directly to the project manager. This structure is best suited for large, complex, or strategically important projects that require a dedicated team and a high level of project management control.

103. In a matrix organizational structure, the project manager and functional manager share responsibility for:
a. assigning project tasks to team members
b. conducting performance reviews of project team members
c. making decisions about project scope changes
d. allocating the project budget

Answer: b. conducting performance reviews of project team members. Explanation: In a matrix organizational structure, the project manager and functional manager share responsibility for conducting performance reviews of project team members. The functional manager is responsible for the technical performance and career development of team members, while the project manager assesses their performance on the project. The project manager is primarily responsible for assigning tasks, making scope change decisions, and managing the project budget, while the functional manager ensures the overall performance and development of their staff.

104. Which organizational structure is most suitable for an organization that executes projects infrequently and has a strong functional department focus?
a. functional
b. weak matrix
c. balanced matrix
d. projectized

Answer: a. functional. Explanation: A functional organizational structure is most suitable for organizations that execute projects infrequently and have a strong focus on functional departments. In this structure, projects are typically managed within the existing functional hierarchy, with functional managers overseeing project work as part of their regular responsibilities. This structure works well when projects are small, simple, and do not require extensive cross-functional collaboration.

105. In a projectized structure, project team members are:
a. assigned to the project full-time and report to the project manager
b. assigned to the project part-time and report to their functional manager

c. assigned to the project full-time but report to their functional manager
d. assigned to the project part-time and report to both the project manager and functional manager

Answer: a. assigned to the project full-time and report to the project manager. Explanation: In a projectized organizational structure, project team members are assigned to the project full-time and report directly to the project manager. This structure creates a dedicated project team that is focused solely on the project objectives and is not distracted by other functional responsibilities. The project manager has full authority over the team and is responsible for their performance and career development within the context of the project.

106. Which organizational structure is most likely to experience resource allocation conflicts between project managers and functional managers?
a. functional
b. weak matrix
c. balanced matrix
d. projectized

Answer: c. balanced matrix. Explanation: A balanced matrix organizational structure is most likely to experience resource allocation conflicts between project managers and functional managers. In this structure, the project manager and functional manager have roughly equal authority and influence over project resources. This shared responsibility can lead to conflicts when both managers have competing priorities or disagree on the allocation of resources to projects. Effective communication and negotiation skills are essential for managing these conflicts and ensuring the success of projects in a balanced matrix environment.

107. In which organizational structure does the project manager have the least amount of authority and influence over the project and project resources?
a. functional
b. weak matrix
c. balanced matrix
d. projectized

Answer: a. functional. Explanation: In a functional organizational structure, the project manager has the least amount of authority and influence over the project and project resources. Projects are typically managed within the existing functional hierarchy, with functional managers maintaining control over their resources and assigning them to projects as needed. The project manager acts more as a coordinator or facilitator, with limited authority to make decisions or direct the work of the project team.

108. Which of the following is a key advantage of a projectized organizational structure?
a. improved communication and coordination between functional departments
b. increased resource flexibility and utilization across multiple projects
c. clear lines of authority and dedicated project teams for improved project focus
d. reduced project management overhead and administrative costs

Answer: c. clear lines of authority and dedicated project teams for improved project focus. Explanation: A key advantage of a projectized organizational structure is the clear lines of authority and dedicated project teams, which allow for improved project focus and performance. In this structure, the project manager has full authority over the project and the team members are assigned to the project full-time. This enables the team to concentrate on the project objectives without the distractions of other functional responsibilities, leading to better project outcomes and faster decision-making.

109. What is the primary disadvantage of a functional organizational structure for managing projects?
a. lack of project management expertise and standardized processes
b. difficulty in coordinating and integrating project work across functional departments
c. increased project management overhead and administrative costs
d. limited career development opportunities for project managers

Answer: b. difficulty in coordinating and integrating project work across functional departments. Explanation: The primary disadvantage of a functional organizational structure for managing projects is the difficulty in coordinating and integrating project work across functional departments. In this structure, projects are managed within the existing functional hierarchy, with each department focused on its own specialized area of work. This can lead to silos and communication breakdowns, making it challenging to coordinate project activities and ensure seamless integration of project deliverables.

110. Which of the following is a key benefit of a matrix organizational structure for project management?
a. clear lines of authority and single point of accountability for project success
b. reduced project management overhead and administrative costs
c. improved resource utilization and flexibility across multiple projects
d. stronger team cohesion and loyalty to the project manager

Answer: c. improved resource utilization and flexibility across multiple projects. Explanation: A key benefit of a matrix organizational structure for project management is the improved resource utilization and flexibility across multiple projects. In a matrix structure, resources are shared between functional departments and projects, allowing for more efficient allocation of skills and expertise. This flexibility enables the organization to respond quickly to changing project needs and optimize the use of resources across the project portfolio. However, this structure may also lead to conflicts between project managers and functional managers over resource priorities and allocation.

111. In a functional organizational structure, project team members are typically:
a. assigned to the project full-time and report to the project manager
b. assigned to the project part-time and report to their functional manager
c. assigned to the project full-time but report to their functional manager
d. assigned to the project part-time and report to both the project manager and functional manager

Answer: b. assigned to the project part-time and report to their functional manager. Explanation: In a functional organizational structure, project team members are typically assigned to the project on a part-time basis while continuing to report to their functional manager. They perform project work in addition to their regular functional duties and remain under the authority of their functional department. This structure can lead to challenges in coordinating project work and ensuring team members' commitment to the project.

112. Which of the following is a key advantage of a functional organizational structure?
a. improved project focus and dedicated resources
b. enhanced career development opportunities for project managers
c. increased resource flexibility and utilization across multiple projects
d. specialized expertise and skill development within functional areas

Answer: d. specialized expertise and skill development within functional areas. Explanation: A key advantage of a functional organizational structure is the development of specialized expertise and skills within each functional area. In this structure, employees are grouped by their specific functions (e.g., marketing, finance, engineering) and report to a functional manager who is an expert in that area. This allows for deep skill development, knowledge sharing, and process optimization within each function, but may create challenges for cross-functional collaboration and project integration.

113. In a functional organization, the role of the project manager is often:
a. a full-time, dedicated position with complete authority over the project
b. a part-time role with limited authority, acting as a coordinator between functional departments
c. a temporary role assigned to a functional manager for the duration of the project
d. a shared responsibility among the functional managers involved in the project

Answer: b. a part-time role with limited authority, acting as a coordinator between functional departments. Explanation: In a functional organizational structure, the role of the project manager is often a part-time position with limited authority. The project manager acts primarily as a coordinator, facilitating communication and collaboration between the various functional departments involved in the project. They do not have direct control over project resources, which remain under the authority of the functional managers. This can create challenges in terms of project prioritization and resource allocation.

114. Which of the following best describes the flow of communication in a functional organizational structure?
a. communication flows horizontally between project team members and the project manager
b. communication flows vertically within each functional department and horizontally between departments
c. communication flows diagonally between the project manager and functional managers
d. communication flows in all directions, with equal emphasis on vertical and horizontal channels

Answer: b. communication flows vertically within each functional department and horizontally between departments. Explanation: In a functional organizational structure, communication typically flows vertically within each functional department, following the chain of command from employees to their functional managers. Cross-functional communication flows horizontally between departments, often through the coordination efforts of the project manager or designated liaisons. This structure can sometimes result in communication silos and challenges in ensuring effective project-wide communication.

115. What is a potential drawback of a functional organizational structure for managing projects?
a. duplication of resources and expertise across functional departments
b. lack of a centralized project management office to provide support and guidance
c. difficulty in prioritizing and allocating resources across multiple projects
d. increased project management overhead and administrative costs

Answer: c. difficulty in prioritizing and allocating resources across multiple projects. Explanation: A potential drawback of a functional organizational structure for managing projects is the difficulty in prioritizing and allocating resources across multiple projects. In this structure, functional managers are responsible for assigning their staff to projects based on functional priorities and resource availability. This can lead to conflicts and resource constraints when multiple projects require the same expertise or when functional managers prioritize their departmental work over project needs.

116. In a functional organization, how are project priorities typically determined?
a. by the project manager, based on the project's strategic importance
b. by the functional managers, based on their departmental priorities
c. by the project sponsor, based on the project's alignment with organizational goals
d. by a project prioritization committee, representing all functional areas

Answer: b. by the functional managers, based on their departmental priorities. Explanation: In a functional organizational structure, project priorities are typically determined by the functional managers based on their departmental priorities and resource availability. Each functional department focuses on its own goals and objectives, which may not always align with project needs. The project manager has limited authority to influence project prioritization and must negotiate with functional managers to secure resources and ensure project progress.

117. Which of the following is a key challenge for project managers in a functional organization?
a. managing a dedicated project team with clear lines of authority
b. securing adequate project funding and resources from the project sponsor
c. coordinating project work across multiple functional departments with competing priorities
d. ensuring compliance with project management methodologies and best practices

Answer: c. coordinating project work across multiple functional departments with competing priorities. Explanation: A key challenge for project managers in a functional organization is coordinating project work across multiple functional departments with competing priorities. The project manager must navigate the different goals, schedules, and resource constraints of each department to ensure project deliverables are completed on time and within budget. This requires strong communication, negotiation, and conflict resolution skills to align functional efforts with project objectives.

118. How does a functional organizational structure impact project team dynamics and performance?
a. enhances team cohesion and collaboration due to clear lines of authority and dedicated resources
b. improves team adaptability and responsiveness to change due to flexible resource allocation
c. fosters a strong sense of project ownership and accountability among team members
d. may limit team integration and performance due to competing functional priorities and loyalties

Answer: d. may limit team integration and performance due to competing functional priorities and loyalties. Explanation: A functional organizational structure can limit project team integration and performance due to competing functional priorities and loyalties. In this structure, team members are assigned to projects on a part-time basis while continuing to report to their functional managers. This divided focus and allegiance can result in conflicts, communication breakdowns, and reduced commitment to project goals. The lack of a dedicated project team and clear lines of authority can also hinder team cohesion and collaboration.

119. What is a common strategy for mitigating the challenges of managing projects in a functional organization?
a. establishing a project management office (PMO) to provide centralized support and guidance
b. implementing a matrix organizational structure to balance functional and project priorities
c. assigning project managers as full-time, dedicated resources with complete authority over projects
d. adopting agile project management methodologies to improve team flexibility and responsiveness

Answer: a. establishing a project management office (PMO) to provide centralized support and guidance. Explanation: A common strategy for mitigating the challenges of managing projects in a functional organization is establishing a project management office (PMO). A PMO is a centralized unit that provides support, guidance, and oversight for project management activities across the organization. It can help standardize project management processes, facilitate resource allocation, and improve communication and coordination between functional departments. By acting as a liaison between the project manager and functional managers, the PMO can help align project priorities with organizational goals and ensure the successful delivery of projects within the constraints of a functional structure.

120. How can project managers build effective relationships with functional managers in a functional organization?
a. by emphasizing the project manager's authority and decision-making power over functional resources
b. by focusing solely on project goals and objectives, regardless of functional priorities
c. by engaging functional managers early, communicating regularly, and addressing their concerns
d. by escalating resource conflicts to senior management for resolution

Answer: c. by engaging functional managers early, communicating regularly, and addressing their concerns. Explanation: Project managers can build effective relationships with functional managers in a functional organization by engaging them early in the project lifecycle, communicating regularly, and addressing their concerns. This proactive approach involves understanding the functional managers' priorities, constraints, and expectations, and working collaboratively to align project needs with departmental goals. Regular communication helps build trust, facilitate problem-solving, and ensure a shared understanding of project status and resource requirements. By demonstrating respect for functional expertise and a willingness to find mutually beneficial solutions, project managers can foster positive relationships and secure the support needed for project success.

121. In a weak matrix organization, the balance of power and influence favors:
a. the project manager
b. the functional manager

c. equally shared between the project manager and functional manager
d. the project sponsor

Answer: b. the functional manager. Explanation: In a weak matrix organizational structure, the balance of power and influence favors the functional manager over the project manager. Functional managers maintain primary control over project resources and have the authority to prioritize functional work over project needs. The project manager has limited authority and acts more as a coordinator or expediter, relying on the goodwill and cooperation of the functional managers to secure resources and complete project tasks.

122. Which of the following best describes the role of the project manager in a strong matrix organization?
a. a part-time coordinator with limited authority over the project
b. a full-time manager with complete authority over the project and project resources
c. a facilitator who supports the functional managers in achieving project goals
d. a team member who reports to the functional manager and contributes to the project

Answer: b. a full-time manager with complete authority over the project and project resources. Explanation: In a strong matrix organizational structure, the project manager is a full-time role with complete authority over the project and project resources. The project manager has the power to make project decisions, assign tasks, and manage the project budget. Project team members are assigned to the project full-time and report directly to the project manager, who is responsible for their performance and career development within the context of the project.

123. In a balanced matrix organization, the project manager and functional manager share:
a. equal authority and responsibility for project success
b. control over the project budget and resource allocation
c. responsibility for assigning project tasks and monitoring progress
d. accountability for project team members' performance and career development

Answer: a. equal authority and responsibility for project success. Explanation: In a balanced matrix organizational structure, the project manager and functional manager share equal authority and responsibility for project success. They collaborate and make joint decisions regarding project priorities, resource allocation, and task assignments. The project manager focuses on project-specific goals and deliverables, while the functional manager ensures the overall development and performance of their staff. This shared responsibility can lead to conflicts and requires effective communication and negotiation skills to maintain a balance between project and functional needs.

124. Which matrix structure is most likely to experience power struggles and conflicts between the project manager and functional managers?
a. weak matrix
b. balanced matrix
c. strong matrix
d. all matrix structures are equally prone to power struggles and conflicts

Answer: b. balanced matrix. Explanation: A balanced matrix organizational structure is most likely to experience power struggles and conflicts between the project manager and functional managers. In this structure, the project manager and functional managers have equal authority and influence over project resources and decisions. This shared power can lead to disagreements and conflicts when priorities, resources, or expectations are not aligned. The lack of a clear hierarchy and decision-making authority can result in power struggles and the need for constant negotiation and conflict resolution.

125. In which matrix structure does the project manager have the least amount of authority and influence over the project?
a. weak matrix
b. balanced matrix
c. strong matrix
d. all matrix structures grant the project manager equal authority and influence

Answer: a. weak matrix. Explanation: In a weak matrix organizational structure, the project manager has the least amount of authority and influence over the project compared to other matrix structures. The functional managers retain primary control over resources and project decisions, while the project manager acts as a coordinator or expediter with limited power. The project manager must rely on the cooperation and support of the functional managers to secure resources, assign tasks, and ensure project progress.

126. What is a key advantage of a strong matrix organizational structure for project management?
a. improved coordination and collaboration between functional departments
b. increased flexibility and adaptability to changing project requirements
c. clear lines of authority and dedicated project resources for improved project focus
d. balanced distribution of power and influence between project and functional managers

Answer: c. clear lines of authority and dedicated project resources for improved project focus. Explanation: A key advantage of a strong matrix organizational structure for project management is the clear lines of authority and dedicated project resources, which allow for improved project focus and performance. In this structure, the project manager has complete authority over the project and the project team members are assigned to the project full-time. This enables the team to concentrate on project goals and deliverables without the distractions of other functional responsibilities, leading to better project outcomes and faster decision-making.

127. Which matrix structure is best suited for organizations that execute a high volume of complex projects?
a. weak matrix
b. balanced matrix
c. strong matrix
d. functional matrix

Answer: c. strong matrix. Explanation: A strong matrix organizational structure is best suited for organizations that execute a high volume of complex projects. In this structure, project managers have full authority over project resources and decisions, allowing them to effectively manage the unique challenges and demands of complex projects. The dedicated project teams and clear lines of authority enable faster decision-making, improved communication, and better alignment with project goals. This structure prioritizes project needs and allows for the efficient allocation of resources across multiple complex projects.

128. In a matrix organization, how can project managers and functional managers work together effectively?
a. by clearly defining and communicating roles, responsibilities, and expectations
b. by prioritizing functional goals over project objectives to maintain departmental efficiency
c. by avoiding direct communication and relying on senior management to resolve conflicts
d. by focusing solely on their respective areas of authority and minimizing collaboration

Answer: a. by clearly defining and communicating roles, responsibilities, and expectations. Explanation: In a matrix organization, project managers and functional managers can work together effectively by clearly defining and communicating roles, responsibilities, and expectations. This involves establishing a shared understanding of project goals, resource requirements, and performance metrics, as well as agreeing on decision-making protocols and communication channels. By openly discussing and documenting these aspects, project managers and functional managers can minimize confusion, duplication of effort, and conflicts. Regular communication, joint problem-solving, and a willingness to compromise are essential for maintaining a collaborative and productive working relationship in a matrix environment.

129. What is a common pitfall of matrix organizational structures?
a. lack of flexibility and adaptability to changing project needs
b. under-utilization of functional expertise and resources across projects
c. unclear reporting lines and conflicting loyalties for project team members
d. excessive bureaucracy and slow decision-making processes

Answer: c. unclear reporting lines and conflicting loyalties for project team members. Explanation: A common pitfall of matrix organizational structures is the presence of unclear reporting lines and conflicting loyalties for project team members. In a matrix structure, team members often report to both a project manager and a functional manager, which can create confusion and conflicting priorities. This dual reporting structure can lead to team members feeling torn between their commitment to the project and their allegiance to their functional department. The lack of a single, clear line of authority can result in communication breakdowns, delays, and reduced team morale.

130. How can organizations mitigate the challenges associated with a balanced matrix structure?
a. by establishing clear guidelines and protocols for decision-making and conflict resolution
b. by eliminating the role of the functional manager and granting full authority to the project manager
c. by assigning project team members to multiple projects simultaneously to maximize resource utilization
d. by discouraging cross-functional collaboration and focusing on departmental goals

Answer: a. by establishing clear guidelines and protocols for decision-making and conflict resolution. Explanation: Organizations can mitigate the challenges associated with a balanced matrix structure by establishing clear guidelines and protocols for decision-making and conflict resolution. This involves defining the roles, responsibilities, and authority of project managers and functional managers, as well as outlining the processes for escalating and resolving conflicts. By providing a framework for collaborative decision-making and problem-solving, organizations can reduce power struggles and ensure that project and functional interests are balanced. Additionally, investing in training and development programs that foster effective communication, negotiation, and conflict management skills can help project managers and functional managers navigate the complexities of a balanced matrix structure.

131. A project manager in a projectized organization:
a. reports to the functional manager and coordinates with the project sponsor
b. has little authority over the project and acts as a part-time coordinator
c. has full authority over the project and reports directly to senior management
d. shares authority with the functional manager and reports to a matrix manager

Answer: c. has full authority over the project and reports directly to senior management. Explanation: In a projectized organization, the project manager has complete authority over the project and reports directly to senior management, such as a director or vice president. The project manager is responsible for all aspects of the project, including planning, execution, and delivery, and has the power to make decisions and allocate resources as needed to meet project goals.

132. In a projectized structure, project team members are:
a. part-time resources who report to their functional managers
b. part-time resources who report to the project manager
c. full-time resources who are assigned to the project for its duration
d. full-time resources who are shared across multiple projects

Answer: c. full-time resources who are assigned to the project for its duration. Explanation: In a projectized organization, project team members are assigned to the project on a full-time basis for the duration of the project. They report directly to the project manager and are dedicated solely to the project's activities. This allows for a high level of focus, cohesion, and alignment among team members, as they are not distracted by other functional responsibilities or competing priorities.

133. What is a key benefit of a projectized organizational structure?
a. improved resource utilization across multiple projects
b. enhanced functional expertise and skill development
c. clear lines of authority and accountability for project success
d. reduced project management overhead and administrative costs

Answer: c. clear lines of authority and accountability for project success. Explanation: A key benefit of a projectized organizational structure is the clear lines of authority and accountability for project success. In this structure, the project manager has complete control over the project resources and is solely responsible for project outcomes. This eliminates ambiguity and conflicts that may arise in other structures, such as matrix organizations, where authority is shared between project managers and functional managers. The clear chain of command and single point of accountability in a projectized structure can lead to faster decision-making, improved communication, and a stronger focus on project goals.

134. Which of the following is a potential drawback of a projectized structure?
a. lack of standardization and consistency across projects
b. limited opportunities for knowledge sharing and learning between projects
c. reduced flexibility to respond to changing project needs and priorities
d. all of the above

Answer: d. all of the above. Explanation: A projectized organizational structure can have several potential drawbacks, including a lack of standardization and consistency across projects, limited opportunities for knowledge sharing and learning between projects, and reduced flexibility to respond to changing project needs and priorities. Because each project operates as a separate entity with its own dedicated resources, there may be duplication of efforts, inconsistent practices, and a siloed approach to problem-solving. Additionally, the strong focus on individual projects can hinder the organization's ability to adapt quickly to new opportunities or shifting strategic objectives.

135. In a projectized organization, how are resources allocated to projects?
a. resources are permanently assigned to functional departments and loaned to projects as needed
b. resources are temporarily assigned to projects based on functional manager approval
c. resources are dedicated to projects full-time and report directly to the project manager
d. resources are shared across multiple projects based on priority and availability

Answer: c. resources are dedicated to projects full-time and report directly to the project manager. Explanation: In a projectized organization, resources are allocated to projects on a full-time basis for the duration of the project. Project team members are assigned directly to the project and report to the project manager, who has complete authority over their work assignments and performance evaluations. This dedicated resource allocation allows for a strong focus on project deliverables and minimizes conflicts or competing demands from other projects or functional departments.

136. What is the primary focus of a projectized organization?
a. maintaining functional excellence and expertise
b. optimizing resource utilization across the organization
c. delivering successful projects and achieving project objectives
d. balancing project and operational work for maximum efficiency

Answer: c. delivering successful projects and achieving project objectives. Explanation: The primary focus of a projectized organization is delivering successful projects and achieving project objectives. In this structure, projects are the primary means of achieving organizational goals, and the entire organization is structured around project delivery. Functional departments, if they exist, play a supporting role and are subordinate to project needs. The success of the organization is largely measured by the success of its projects, making project management a core competency and strategic priority.

137. In a projectized structure, how is project performance evaluated?

a. based on the project manager's ability to coordinate with functional managers
b. based on the project team's contribution to functional department goals
c. based on the project's adherence to organizational standards and processes
d. based on the project's success in achieving its objectives within constraints

Answer: d. based on the project's success in achieving its objectives within constraints. Explanation: In a projectized organization, project performance is evaluated based on the project's success in achieving its specific objectives within the given constraints of time, cost, scope, and quality. The project manager is held accountable for project outcomes and is assessed on their ability to lead the team, manage resources, and deliver results that align with project goals. Project performance is not typically measured by the project's contribution to functional department goals or adherence to organizational standards, as these are secondary to the primary focus on project success.

138. How does communication typically flow in a projectized organization?
a. vertically within functional departments and horizontally between departments
b. horizontally among project team members and vertically to senior management
c. diagonally between project managers and functional managers
d. informally based on personal relationships and social networks

Answer: b. horizontally among project team members and vertically to senior management. Explanation: In a projectized organization, communication typically flows horizontally among project team members and vertically to senior management. Project team members communicate directly with each other to coordinate tasks, share information, and solve problems, with the project manager facilitating and overseeing these interactions. The project manager, in turn, communicates vertically with senior management to provide updates, escalate issues, and ensure alignment with organizational goals. There is minimal communication between projects or with functional departments, as each project operates as a self-contained unit.

139. What is a common challenge faced by project managers in a projectized structure?
a. securing resources and support from functional managers
b. maintaining team members' connection to their functional expertise
c. aligning project goals with overall organizational strategy
d. managing conflicts and competing priorities between projects

Answer: c. aligning project goals with overall organizational strategy. Explanation: A common challenge faced by project managers in a projectized structure is aligning project goals with the overall organizational strategy. Because projects operate as separate entities with dedicated resources and a strong focus on project-specific objectives, there is a risk of project managers becoming disconnected from the broader organizational context. Project managers must actively work to understand and align project goals with the organization's strategic priorities, ensure that project outcomes contribute to the organization's long-term vision, and communicate the project's strategic value to senior management and other stakeholders.

140. Which of the following is a key skill for project managers in a projectized organization?

a. negotiating with functional managers for resource allocation
b. balancing the needs of multiple projects and stakeholders
c. building and leading high-performing project teams
d. maintaining technical expertise in the project's functional area

Answer: c. building and leading high-performing project teams. Explanation: A key skill for project managers in a projectized organization is building and leading high-performing project teams. In this structure, project managers have full authority over their team members and are responsible for all aspects of team performance, from selection and development to motivation and conflict resolution. Effective project managers must be able to create a cohesive team culture, foster collaboration and communication, and ensure that team members have the skills, resources, and support needed to deliver project results. While negotiation, stakeholder management, and technical expertise are important, the ability to build and lead a strong project team is critical for success in a projectized environment.

141. Which process group involves defining and authorizing a new project or project phase?
a. planning process group
b. executing process group
c. initiating process group
d. monitoring and controlling process group

Answer: c. initiating process group. Explanation: The initiating process group involves defining and authorizing a new project or project phase. This process group includes the processes necessary to define a new project or project phase, obtain authorization to start the project or phase, and identify the project's stakeholders. The primary output of the initiating process group is the project charter, which formally authorizes the project and documents the initial requirements that satisfy the stakeholder's needs and expectations.

142. Which process group involves defining the scope, refining the objectives, and developing the course of action required to achieve the project objectives?
a. planning process group
b. executing process group
c. closing process group
d. monitoring and controlling process group

Answer: a. planning process group. Explanation: The planning process group involves defining the project scope, refining the objectives, and developing the course of action required to achieve the project objectives. This process group consists of the processes necessary to establish the total scope of the project, define and refine the objectives, and develop the project management plan that will guide project execution. The primary output of the planning process group is the project management plan, which integrates and consolidates all of the subsidiary plans and baselines from the planning processes.

143. Which process group involves coordinating people and resources to carry out the project management plan?
a. initiating process group

b. planning process group
c. executing process group
d. closing process group

Answer: c. executing process group. Explanation: The executing process group involves coordinating people and resources to carry out the project management plan and create the project deliverables. This process group consists of the processes necessary to complete the work defined in the project management plan to satisfy the project requirements. The executing process group involves directing, managing, and performing the planned project activities, managing stakeholder engagement, and implementing approved changes to achieve project objectives.

144. Which process group involves tracking, reviewing, and regulating the progress and performance of the project?
a. planning process group
b. executing process group
c. initiating process group
d. monitoring and controlling process group

Answer: d. monitoring and controlling process group. Explanation: The monitoring and controlling process group involves tracking, reviewing, and regulating the progress and performance of the project. This process group consists of the processes necessary to monitor project progress, identify deviations from the plan, and take corrective action to ensure that the project objectives are met. The monitoring and controlling process group includes processes such as monitor and control project work, perform integrated change control, and control scope, schedule, cost, quality, and risks.

145. Which process group formalizes the acceptance of the project deliverables and brings the project or project phase to an orderly end?
a. initiating process group
b. planning process group
c. executing process group
d. closing process group

Answer: d. closing process group. Explanation: The closing process group formalizes the acceptance of the project deliverables and brings the project or project phase to an orderly end. This process group consists of the processes necessary to finalize all project activities, transfer the completed deliverables to the appropriate parties, obtain formal acceptance of the project outcomes, and document lessons learned. The primary outputs of the closing process group include the final product, service, or result transition, as well as the final project report and updates to organizational process assets.

146. Which of the following is not one of the five project management process groups?
a. initiating
b. planning
c. executing
d. controlling

Answer: d. controlling. Explanation: The five project management process groups are initiating, planning, executing, monitoring and controlling, and closing. Controlling is not a separate process group but is part of the monitoring and controlling process group. The monitoring and controlling process group involves tracking project progress, identifying deviations, and taking corrective action, which encompasses the concept of controlling project performance and outcomes.

147. Which process group is an iterative process that occurs throughout the project life cycle?
a. planning process group
b. executing process group
c. monitoring and controlling process group
d. closing process group

Answer: c. monitoring and controlling process group. Explanation: The monitoring and controlling process group is an iterative process that occurs throughout the project life cycle. Unlike the other process groups, which are typically performed in a sequential manner, the monitoring and controlling processes are conducted continuously from project initiation through project closure. This ongoing process group involves regularly tracking project progress, measuring performance against the project management plan, identifying variances, and implementing corrective actions as needed to keep the project on track.

148. Which of the following statements best describes the relationship between the project management process groups?
a. the process groups are performed sequentially, with no overlap between them
b. the process groups are independent of each other and can be performed in any order
c. the process groups are iterative and may overlap, with the outputs of one group becoming the inputs to another
d. the process groups are only performed once during the project life cycle, at the beginning of the project

Answer: c. the process groups are iterative and may overlap, with the outputs of one group becoming the inputs to another. Explanation: The project management process groups are iterative and may overlap, with the outputs of one group becoming the inputs to another. While the process groups are often presented as discrete, sequential steps, in practice they are interrelated and can be performed concurrently. For example, the outputs of the planning process group, such as the project management plan, become inputs to the executing and monitoring and controlling process groups. Similarly, the outputs of the monitoring and controlling process group, such as change requests and performance reports, can trigger updates to the project plans and require a return to the planning processes.

149. What is the purpose of the Develop Project Charter process?
a. to create a document that authorizes the project manager to use organizational resources for project activities
b. to define the project scope, objectives, and success criteria
c. to develop a comprehensive project schedule and budget
d. to identify and analyze project risks and plan risk responses

Answer: a. to create a document that authorizes the project manager to use organizational resources for project activities. Explanation: The purpose of the Develop Project Charter process, which is part of the initiating process group, is to create a document that formally authorizes the existence of the project and grants the project manager the authority to apply organizational resources to project activities. The project charter establishes a partnership between the performing and requesting organizations, identifies the high-level project requirements and boundaries, and documents the business needs, assumptions, constraints, and stakeholder expectations. It serves as a reference of authority for the future of the project and is a crucial output of the initiating process group.

150. Which of the following is not an input to the Close Project or Phase process?
a. project management plan
b. accepted deliverables
c. organizational process assets
d. project charter

Answer: d. project charter. Explanation: The project charter is not an input to the Close Project or Phase process. The project charter is an output of the initiating process group and serves to authorize the project and document initial requirements. The key inputs to the Close Project or Phase process, which is part of the closing process group, include the project management plan, accepted deliverables, and organizational process assets. The project management plan guides the project closure activities, the accepted deliverables are the final project outcomes that are transferred to the appropriate stakeholders, and the organizational process assets, such as lessons learned and historical information, are reviewed and updated as part of the project closure process.

151. What is the main purpose of the initiating process group?
a. to develop a detailed project plan and schedule
b. to define the project scope and objectives
c. to execute the project work and deliver the project outcomes
d. to authorize the project and identify key stakeholders

Answer: d. to authorize the project and identify key stakeholders. Explanation: The main purpose of the initiating process group is to formally authorize the project and identify the project's key stakeholders. This process group includes the processes necessary to define a new project, obtain authorization to start the project, and identify the stakeholders who will be impacted by or have an influence on the project. The primary output of the initiating process group is the project charter, which formally authorizes the project and documents the initial requirements that satisfy the stakeholder's needs and expectations.

152. Which of the following is not a key process in the initiating process group?
a. develop project charter
b. identify stakeholders
c. collect requirements
d. select project manager

Answer: c. collect requirements. Explanation: Collecting requirements is not a key process in the initiating process group but rather part of the planning process group. The key processes in the initiating process group are develop project charter and identify stakeholders. The develop project charter process involves creating a document that formally authorizes the project and grants the project manager the authority to apply organizational resources to project activities. The identify stakeholders process involves identifying the people, groups, or organizations that could impact or be impacted by the project and documenting their interests, involvement, and impact on project success.

153. What is the primary output of the develop project charter process?
a. project scope statement
b. project management plan
c. project charter
d. stakeholder register

Answer: c. project charter. Explanation: The primary output of the develop project charter process is the project charter. The project charter is a document that formally authorizes the existence of the project and grants the project manager the authority to apply organizational resources to project activities. It establishes a partnership between the performing and requesting organizations, identifies the high-level project requirements and boundaries, and documents the business needs, assumptions, constraints, and stakeholder expectations. The project scope statement and project management plan are outputs of the planning process group, while the stakeholder register is an output of the identify stakeholders process.

154. Which of the following best describes the purpose of the identify stakeholders process?
a. to determine the project's objectives and success criteria
b. to identify and document the project's stakeholders and their interests
c. to select the project manager and define their authority
d. to develop a detailed project budget and resource plan

Answer: b. to identify and document the project's stakeholders and their interests. Explanation: The purpose of the identify stakeholders process is to identify the people, groups, or organizations that could impact or be impacted by the project and to document relevant information regarding their interests, involvement, and impact on project success. This process involves analyzing stakeholder expectations and their impact on the project, and developing appropriate management strategies for effectively engaging stakeholders throughout the project life cycle. The output of this process is the stakeholder register, which documents the identified stakeholders and their relevant information.

155. Which document is used to formally authorize a project and document initial requirements?
a. project scope statement
b. project management plan
c. project charter
d. business case

Answer: c. project charter. Explanation: The project charter is the document used to formally authorize a project and document initial requirements. It is developed during the initiating process group and is the primary output of the develop project charter process. The project charter establishes a partnership between the performing and requesting organizations, identifies the high-level project requirements and boundaries, and documents the business needs, assumptions, constraints, and stakeholder expectations. It serves as a reference of authority for the future of the project and provides the project manager with the authority to apply organizational resources to project activities.

156. What is the main difference between the project charter and the project scope statement?
a. the project charter authorizes the project, while the project scope statement defines the project deliverables
b. the project charter is developed in the initiating process group, while the project scope statement is created in the planning process group
c. the project charter is a high-level document, while the project scope statement provides a detailed description of the project scope
d. all of the above

Answer: d. all of the above. Explanation: The main differences between the project charter and the project scope statement are: (1) The project charter formally authorizes the project and grants the project manager authority to use organizational resources, while the project scope statement provides a detailed description of the project deliverables and boundaries. (2) The project charter is developed in the initiating process group, while the project scope statement is created during the planning process group. (3) The project charter is a high-level document that provides an overview of the project, while the project scope statement offers a more detailed and comprehensive description of the project scope.

157. Which of the following is not an input to the develop project charter process?
a. business case
b. project statement of work
c. enterprise environmental factors
d. project management plan

Answer: d. project management plan. Explanation: The project management plan is not an input to the develop project charter process. The project management plan is an output of the planning process group and is created after the project charter has been developed and approved. The key inputs to the develop project charter process include the business case, which provides the necessary information from a business standpoint to determine whether the project is worth the required investment; the project statement of work, which is a narrative description of the products, services, or results to be delivered by the project; and enterprise environmental factors, which refer to the conditions outside of the project that influence, constrain, or direct the project.

158. Who is responsible for approving the project charter?
a. the project manager
b. the project team
c. the project sponsor or initiator
d. the stakeholders

Answer: c. the project sponsor or initiator. Explanation: The project sponsor or initiator is responsible for approving the project charter. The project sponsor is the person or group who provides the financial resources and support for the project, and has the authority to authorize the project. The project charter is typically approved and signed off by the project sponsor to formally initiate the project and grant the project manager the authority to apply organizational resources to project activities. The project manager is responsible for developing the project charter, but does not have the authority to approve it. The project team and stakeholders may provide input and feedback on the project charter, but the final approval rests with the project sponsor.

159. What is the main benefit of identifying stakeholders early in the project life cycle?
a. to ensure that all stakeholders agree with the project objectives
b. to develop a detailed project budget and resource plan
c. to understand stakeholder expectations and manage their influence on the project
d. to select the project manager and define their authority

Answer: c. to understand stakeholder expectations and manage their influence on the project. Explanation: The main benefit of identifying stakeholders early in the project life cycle is to understand their expectations and manage their influence on the project. By identifying stakeholders during the initiating process group, the project manager can engage with them early, understand their needs and expectations, and develop strategies for effectively communicating and managing their involvement throughout the project. This proactive approach to stakeholder management helps to build trust, minimize potential conflicts, and ensure that stakeholder interests are aligned with project objectives. Early stakeholder identification also allows for the incorporation of stakeholder feedback into the project planning processes.

160. What is the primary tool or technique used in the identify stakeholders process?
a. stakeholder analysis
b. expert judgment
c. meetings
d. documentation reviews

Answer: a. stakeholder analysis. Explanation: The primary tool or technique used in the identify stakeholders process is stakeholder analysis. Stakeholder analysis involves systematically gathering and analyzing information to determine whose interests should be taken into account throughout the project. This includes identifying potential stakeholders, understanding their interests, expectations, and influence on the project, and determining how they should be involved in the project. Common stakeholder analysis techniques include stakeholder mapping, which plots stakeholders based on their power and interest in the project, and the power/influence grid, which categorizes stakeholders based on their level of authority and active involvement in the project. Expert judgment, meetings, and documentation reviews are also used in this process, but stakeholder analysis is the key technique for identifying and understanding project stakeholders.

161. What is the primary focus of the planning process group?
a. authorizing the project and identifying stakeholders
b. defining the project scope, schedule, and budget
c. executing the project work and delivering the project outcomes
d. monitoring project progress and controlling changes

Answer: b. defining the project scope, schedule, and budget. Explanation: The primary focus of the planning process group is to establish the total scope of the project, refine the objectives, and define the course of action required to attain the objectives that the project was undertaken to achieve. This process group involves developing the project management plan and the documents that will be used to carry out the project. The key processes in this group include defining the project scope, creating the work breakdown structure (WBS), defining and sequencing activities, estimating resources and durations, developing the schedule, estimating costs, and determining the budget.

162. Which of the following is not an output of the planning process group?
a. project management plan
b. project documents
c. project funding requirements
d. deliverables

Answer: d. deliverables. Explanation: Deliverables are not an output of the planning process group but rather an output of the executing process group. Deliverables are the unique and verifiable products, results, or capabilities that must be produced to complete a project or part of a project. The key outputs of the planning process group include the project management plan, which defines how the project is executed, monitored and controlled, and closed; project documents, such as the scope statement, WBS, schedule, cost estimates, and risk register; and project funding requirements, which determine the financial resources needed to complete the project.

163. What is the purpose of the project management plan?
a. to authorize the project and identify key stakeholders
b. to define how the project will be executed, monitored, controlled, and closed
c. to provide a detailed description of the project deliverables
d. to track project progress and performance

Answer: b. to define how the project will be executed, monitored, controlled, and closed. Explanation: The purpose of the project management plan is to define how the project will be executed, monitored, controlled, and closed. It integrates and consolidates all of the subsidiary plans and baselines from the planning processes, and provides a comprehensive roadmap for the project. The project management plan covers all aspects of the project, including scope, schedule, cost, quality, resources, communications, risks, and procurement. It is a living document that is updated and revised throughout the project life cycle as more detailed information becomes available.

164. Which process in the planning process group involves subdividing project deliverables into smaller, more manageable components?
a. define activities
b. sequence activities
c. create WBS
d. develop schedule

Answer: c. create WBS. Explanation: The create WBS (Work Breakdown Structure) process involves subdividing project deliverables and project work into smaller, more manageable components. The WBS is a hierarchical decomposition of the total scope of work to be carried out by the project team to accomplish the project objectives and create the required deliverables. It organizes and defines the total scope of the project and represents the work specified in the current approved project scope statement. The other processes mentioned (define activities, sequence activities, and develop schedule) are part of the project time management knowledge area and focus on defining and sequencing specific activities and creating the project schedule.

165. What is the main difference between the project scope statement and the WBS?
a. the project scope statement is a detailed document, while the WBS is a high-level summary
b. the project scope statement defines the project deliverables, while the WBS decomposes the deliverables into work packages
c. the project scope statement is created in the initiating process group, while the WBS is developed in the planning process group
d. the project scope statement is mandatory for all projects, while the WBS is optional

Answer: b. the project scope statement defines the project deliverables, while the WBS decomposes the deliverables into work packages. Explanation: The main difference between the project scope statement and the WBS is that the project scope statement provides a detailed description of the project deliverables, while the WBS decomposes those deliverables into smaller, manageable work packages. The project scope statement describes the project's scope, including the product scope and the project boundaries, while the WBS is a hierarchical structure that organizes the project work into logical groupings and defines the total scope of the project. Both the project scope statement and the WBS are created during the planning process group and are required for effective project scope management.

166. Which of the following is not an input to the estimate activity durations process?
a. project scope statement
b. activity list
c. resource calendars
d. risk register

Answer: a. project scope statement. Explanation: The project scope statement is not a direct input to the estimate activity durations process. The key inputs to this process are the activity list, which identifies the specific schedule activities that need to be performed to produce the project deliverables; the activity attributes, which provide the detailed information about each activity; the resource calendars, which specify when project resources are available; the project schedule network diagrams, which show the logical relationships between project activities; the resource requirements, which specify the types and quantities of resources required for each activity; the enterprise environmental factors, such as productivity metrics and published estimating data; and the organizational process assets, such as historical duration information and lessons learned.

167. What is the purpose of the critical path method (CPM) in project scheduling?
a. to identify the activities with the least amount of scheduling flexibility
b. to determine the shortest possible project duration

c. to optimize resource allocation across project activities

d. to calculate the amount of schedule contingency needed

Answer: b. to determine the shortest possible project duration. Explanation: The purpose of the critical path method (CPM) in project scheduling is to determine the shortest possible project duration by identifying the sequence of activities that represents the longest path through the project (the critical path). CPM calculates the early start, early finish, late start, and late finish dates for all project activities and determines the critical activities that have no scheduling flexibility (i.e., they have zero float). By focusing on managing the critical path activities, project managers can ensure that the project is completed on time. CPM does not directly address resource optimization, contingency planning, or the identification of non-critical activities.

168. What is the main output of the plan quality management process?

a. quality management plan

b. quality metrics

c. quality checklists

d. process improvement plan

Answer: a. quality management plan. Explanation: The main output of the plan quality management process is the quality management plan. The quality management plan is a component of the project management plan that describes how applicable policies, procedures, and guidelines will be implemented to achieve the project's quality objectives. It outlines the quality standards, roles and responsibilities, quality control and assurance activities, and the tools and techniques that will be used to ensure that the project meets the required quality specifications. Quality metrics, checklists, and process improvement plans are also outputs of this process, but they are considered subsidiary components or tools that support the implementation of the quality management plan.

169. Which of the following is not a key benefit of the plan risk management process?

a. providing resources and time for risk management activities

b. agreeing on a common approach to managing project risks

c. ensuring that the level, type, and visibility of risk management are commensurate with the risk and importance of the project

d. eliminating all project risks

Answer: d. eliminating all project risks. Explanation: Eliminating all project risks is not a realistic or achievable benefit of the plan risk management process. The purpose of risk management is to identify potential risks, assess their impact and probability, and develop strategies to mitigate or respond to them, not to eliminate them entirely. Some degree of risk is inherent in all projects, and attempting to eliminate all risks is often counterproductive and can lead to missed opportunities. The key benefits of the plan risk management process include providing resources and time for risk management activities, agreeing on a common approach to managing risks, and ensuring that the level of risk management is appropriate for the specific project context.

170. What is the primary technique used for estimating project costs in the estimate costs process?

a. bottom-up estimating
b. parametric estimating
c. three-point estimating
d. reserve analysis

Answer: a. bottom-up estimating. Explanation: The primary technique used for estimating project costs in the estimate costs process is bottom-up estimating. Bottom-up estimating involves estimating the cost of individual work packages or activities and then aggregating these estimates to determine the overall project budget. This approach provides a detailed and accurate cost estimate, as it considers the specific resources, materials, and tasks required for each work package. Other techniques, such as parametric estimating (using statistical relationships between historical data and other variables), three-point estimating (using optimistic, pessimistic, and most likely estimates), and reserve analysis (determining contingency reserves) can also be used in this process, but bottom-up estimating is considered the most comprehensive and reliable method for project cost estimation.

171. What is the primary focus of the executing process group?
a. defining the project scope, schedule, and budget
b. monitoring project progress and controlling changes
c. carrying out the work defined in the project management plan
d. closing the project and obtaining final acceptance

Answer: c. carrying out the work defined in the project management plan. Explanation: The primary focus of the executing process group is to carry out the work defined in the project management plan to achieve the project's objectives. This process group involves coordinating people and resources, managing stakeholder expectations, and performing the activities necessary to create the project deliverables. The key processes in this group include direct and manage project work, manage project knowledge, manage quality, acquire and manage project team, manage communications, conduct procurements, and manage stakeholder engagement.

172. Which of the following is not a key process in the executing process group?
a. direct and manage project work
b. manage project knowledge
c. control quality
d. manage communications

Answer: c. control quality. Explanation: Control quality is not a key process in the executing process group but rather part of the monitoring and controlling process group. The control quality process involves monitoring and recording the results of quality management activities to assess performance and ensure that the project outputs are complete, correct, and meet customer expectations. The key processes in the executing process group focus on performing the planned work, managing project knowledge, acquiring and managing the project team, managing communications, conducting procurements, and managing stakeholder engagement.

173. What is the main purpose of the direct and manage project work process?

a. to define the project scope and create the project management plan
b. to monitor project progress and take corrective action as needed
c. to lead and perform the work defined in the project management plan
d. to close the project or phase and obtain final approval

Answer: c. to lead and perform the work defined in the project management plan. Explanation: The main purpose of the direct and manage project work process is to lead and perform the work defined in the project management plan to achieve the project's objectives. This process involves managing and performing the activities necessary to create the project deliverables, implementing approved changes, and managing project knowledge. The project manager coordinates and directs the work of the project team, manages vendor and supplier relationships, and communicates with stakeholders to ensure that the project work is executed as planned.

174. Which of the following is a key output of the manage project knowledge process?
a. project management plan updates
b. deliverables
c. lessons learned register
d. change requests

Answer: c. lessons learned register. Explanation: The lessons learned register is a key output of the manage project knowledge process. This process involves using existing knowledge and creating new knowledge to achieve the project's objectives and contribute to organizational learning. The lessons learned register captures the knowledge gained during the project, including best practices, challenges, and recommendations for future projects. Other outputs of this process may include project management plan updates, project document updates, and organizational process assets updates, but the lessons learned register is the primary tool for documenting and sharing project knowledge.

175. What is the main difference between the manage quality and control quality processes?
a. manage quality is performed during executing, while control quality is performed during monitoring and controlling
b. manage quality focuses on preventing defects, while control quality focuses on identifying and correcting defects
c. manage quality applies to the project deliverables, while control quality applies to the project management processes
d. manage quality is the responsibility of the project manager, while control quality is the responsibility of the quality assurance team

Answer: a. manage quality is performed during executing, while control quality is performed during monitoring and controlling. Explanation: The main difference between the manage quality and control quality processes is that manage quality is performed during the executing process group, while control quality is performed during the monitoring and controlling process group. Manage quality focuses on implementing the quality management plan, ensuring that project activities adhere to quality standards, and identifying opportunities for process improvement. Control quality, on the other hand, involves monitoring specific project results to determine if they comply with relevant quality standards and identifying ways to eliminate causes of unsatisfactory performance.

176. Which process in the executing process group involves obtaining and managing the human resources needed for the project?
a. develop project team
b. manage project team
c. acquire resources
d. manage communications

Answer: c. acquire resources. Explanation: The acquire resources process in the executing process group involves obtaining and managing the human resources needed for the project. This process includes confirming human resource availability, acquiring the necessary team members, and providing resources as needed. The develop project team and manage project team processes focus on improving team competencies, interaction, and performance, while the manage communications process ensures the timely and appropriate collection, distribution, and storage of project information.

177. What is the primary tool used in the manage communications process?
a. communication management plan
b. project management information system (PMIS)
c. performance reports
d. project communications

Answer: b. project management information system (PMIS). Explanation: The primary tool used in the manage communications process is the project management information system (PMIS). The PMIS is a comprehensive set of tools, techniques, methodologies, resources, and procedures used to collect, integrate, and disseminate project information. It supports all aspects of the project, from initiating through closing, and enables effective communication and decision-making. The communication management plan, performance reports, and project communications are also important elements of the manage communications process, but they are considered inputs, outputs, or communication methods rather than the primary tool.

178. Which process in the executing process group involves obtaining seller responses, selecting sellers, and awarding contracts?
a. plan procurement management
b. conduct procurements
c. control procurements
d. close procurements

Answer: b. conduct procurements. Explanation: The conduct procurements process in the executing process group involves obtaining seller responses, selecting sellers, and awarding contracts. This process includes activities such as advertising procurement opportunities, holding bidder conferences, evaluating proposals, negotiating contracts, and finalizing the procurement agreement. The plan procurement management process is part of the planning process group, while the control procurements and close procurements processes are part of the monitoring and controlling process group.

179. What is the main purpose of the manage stakeholder engagement process?
a. to identify project stakeholders and plan their engagement
b. to communicate and work with stakeholders to meet their needs and expectations
c. to monitor stakeholder relationships and adjust engagement strategies
d. to close out stakeholder communications and obtain final acceptance

Answer: b. to communicate and work with stakeholders to meet their needs and expectations. Explanation: The main purpose of the manage stakeholder engagement process is to communicate and work with stakeholders to meet their needs and expectations, address issues as they occur, and foster appropriate stakeholder engagement in project activities. This process involves implementing the stakeholder engagement plan, managing stakeholder communications, and collaborating with stakeholders to ensure their continued support and satisfaction. Identifying stakeholders and planning their engagement occurs in the initiating and planning process groups, while monitoring stakeholder relationships and adjusting engagement strategies is part of the monitor stakeholder engagement process in the monitoring and controlling process group.

180. Which of the following is not an input to the direct and manage project work process?
a. project management plan
b. approved change requests
c. enterprise environmental factors
d. organizational process assets

Answer: d. organizational process assets. Explanation: Organizational process assets are not a direct input to the direct and manage project work process. While organizational process assets, such as policies, procedures, and historical information, may influence how the project work is executed, they are not a required input for this specific process. The key inputs to the direct and manage project work process are the project management plan, which guides the execution of the project work; approved change requests, which modify the project scope, schedule, or budget; and enterprise environmental factors, which may impact the execution of the project work, such as organizational culture, infrastructure, and market conditions.

181. What is the primary purpose of the monitoring and controlling process group?
a. to define the project scope, schedule, and budget
b. to perform the work defined in the project management plan
c. to track, review, and regulate the progress and performance of the project
d. to finalize all project activities and formally close the project

Answer: c. to track, review, and regulate the progress and performance of the project. Explanation: The primary purpose of the monitoring and controlling process group is to track, review, and regulate the progress and performance of the project. This process group involves monitoring project execution, identifying deviations from the plan, and taking corrective action to ensure that the project objectives are met. The key processes in this group include monitor and control project work, perform integrated change control, validate scope, control scope, control schedule, control costs, control quality, control resources, monitor communications, monitor risks, control procurements, and monitor stakeholder engagement.

182. Which of the following is not a key process in the monitoring and controlling process group?
a. monitor and control project work
b. perform integrated change control
c. manage project knowledge
d. monitor risks

Answer: c. manage project knowledge. Explanation: Manage project knowledge is not a key process in the monitoring and controlling process group but rather part of the executing process group. The manage project knowledge process involves using existing knowledge and creating new knowledge to achieve the project's objectives and contribute to organizational learning. The key processes in the monitoring and controlling process group focus on tracking project progress, managing changes, controlling project scope, schedule, costs, quality, resources, communications, risks, procurements, and stakeholder engagement.

183. What is the main purpose of the monitor and control project work process?
a. to authorize the project and assign the project manager
b. to define the project deliverables and acceptance criteria
c. to track project progress and identify areas requiring attention
d. to obtain final acceptance and close the project

Answer: c. to track project progress and identify areas requiring attention. Explanation: The main purpose of the monitor and control project work process is to track project progress and identify areas that may require special attention. This process involves comparing actual performance with planned performance, assessing variances, and taking corrective action as needed to ensure that the project objectives are met. The monitor and control project work process is an overarching process that coordinates the other monitoring and controlling processes, such as control scope, control schedule, and control costs.

184. What is the primary tool used in the perform integrated change control process?
a. change log
b. change control board (CCB)
c. project management plan
d. work performance reports

Answer: b. change control board (CCB). Explanation: The primary tool used in the perform integrated change control process is the change control board (CCB). The CCB is a formally chartered group responsible for reviewing, evaluating, approving, deferring, or rejecting changes to the project. It includes representatives from various stakeholder groups and ensures that changes are assessed and managed in an integrated manner, considering the overall impact on the project. The change log, project management plan, and work performance reports are also important elements of the change control process, but they are considered inputs or outputs rather than the primary tool.

185. Which process in the monitoring and controlling process group involves formalizing the acceptance of the completed project deliverables?
a. validate scope
b. control quality
c. control procurements
d. monitor stakeholder engagement

Answer: a. validate scope. Explanation: The validate scope process in the monitoring and controlling process group involves formalizing the acceptance of the completed project deliverables. This process includes reviewing the deliverables with the customer or sponsor to ensure that they are complete and satisfactory and obtaining formal sign-off. The control quality process focuses on monitoring and recording the results of quality control activities, while the control procurements process manages procurement relationships and monitors contract performance. The monitor stakeholder engagement process tracks overall stakeholder relationships and adjusts engagement strategies as needed.

186. What is the main difference between the validate scope and control scope processes?
a. validate scope is performed during executing, while control scope is performed during monitoring and controlling
b. validate scope focuses on accepting deliverables, while control scope focuses on managing scope changes
c. validate scope applies to the project management processes, while control scope applies to the project deliverables
d. validate scope is the responsibility of the project manager, while control scope is the responsibility of the project team

Answer: b. validate scope focuses on accepting deliverables, while control scope focuses on managing scope changes. Explanation: The main difference between the validate scope and control scope processes is that validate scope focuses on formalizing the acceptance of completed deliverables, while control scope focuses on monitoring the status of the project and product scope and managing changes to the scope baseline. Validate scope ensures that the completed deliverables meet the specified acceptance criteria and obtains formal sign-off from the customer or sponsor. Control scope, on the other hand, involves monitoring the scope performance, identifying and controlling scope changes, and ensuring that all requested changes and recommended corrective or preventive actions are processed through the perform integrated change control process.

187. Which of the following is a key output of the control schedule process?
a. schedule baseline
b. schedule forecasts
c. resource calendars
d. schedule management plan

Answer: b. schedule forecasts. Explanation: Schedule forecasts are a key output of the control schedule process. Schedule forecasts are estimates or predictions of conditions and events in the project's future, based on information and knowledge available at the time of the forecast. They are used to update the project schedule and to inform stakeholders about the current status and expected future performance of the project. The schedule baseline, resource calendars, and schedule management plan are inputs to the control schedule process, rather than outputs.

188. What is the primary technique used in the control costs process?
a. earned value management (EVM)
b. forecasting
c. to-complete performance index (TCPI)
d. reserve analysis

Answer: a. earned value management (EVM). Explanation: The primary technique used in the control costs process is earned value management (EVM). EVM is a methodology that combines scope, schedule, and resource measurements to assess project performance and progress. It compares the amount of work that was planned with what was actually earned and what was actually spent to determine if cost and schedule performance are as planned. EVM helps to forecast future performance and allows for early identification of issues that may impact project objectives. Forecasting, TCPI, and reserve analysis are also techniques used in the control costs process, but EVM is considered the most comprehensive and widely used approach.

189. Which process in the monitoring and controlling process group involves monitoring the status of identified risks and evaluating the effectiveness of risk response plans?
a. plan risk management
b. identify risks
c. perform qualitative risk analysis
d. monitor risks

Answer: d. monitor risks. Explanation: The monitor risks process in the monitoring and controlling process group involves monitoring the status of identified risks, identifying new risks, evaluating the effectiveness of risk response plans, and updating the risk register accordingly. This process ensures that project risks are continuously monitored and that appropriate risk responses are implemented and adjusted as needed. The plan risk management, identify risks, and perform qualitative risk analysis processes are part of the planning process group and focus on establishing the risk management strategy, identifying individual project risks, and prioritizing risks for further analysis and action.

190. Which of the following is not an input to the control quality process?
a. project management plan
b. quality control measurements
c. approved change requests
d. quality audits

Answer: d. quality audits. Explanation: Quality audits are not an input to the control quality process but rather a tool and technique used in this process. Quality audits are structured, independent reviews to determine whether project activities comply with organizational and project policies, processes, and procedures. They are used to identify ineffective and inefficient processes and to recommend improvements. The key inputs to the control quality process are the project management plan, which includes the quality management plan; quality control measurements, which are the results of control quality activities; approved change requests, which can impact the quality of the project deliverables; and work performance data, which includes information about project progress and quality control measurements.

191. What is the primary focus of the closing process group?
a. to define the project scope, objectives, and success criteria
b. to develop detailed project plans and obtain necessary approvals
c. to execute the project work and deliver the project outcomes
d. to finalize project activities, complete documentation, and transfer deliverables

Answer: d. to finalize project activities, complete documentation, and transfer deliverables. Explanation: The primary focus of the closing process group is to finalize all project activities, complete project documentation, and formally transfer the project deliverables to the appropriate stakeholders. This process group ensures that the project or project phase is properly concluded, and that all necessary closure activities are performed. The key processes in this group are close project or phase, which includes finalizing all project activities, archiving project information, releasing resources, and communicating project closure to stakeholders.

192. Which of the following is not a key activity performed during the closing process group?
a. obtaining final acceptance of project deliverables
b. documenting lessons learned and archiving project documents
c. releasing project resources and closing procurement contracts
d. monitoring and controlling project work to ensure successful completion

Answer: d. monitoring and controlling project work to ensure successful completion. Explanation: Monitoring and controlling project work is not a key activity performed during the closing process group, but rather an ongoing activity throughout the executing and monitoring and controlling process groups. The closing process group focuses on finalizing project activities, completing documentation, and transferring deliverables. Key activities in this group include obtaining final acceptance of project deliverables, documenting lessons learned, archiving project documents, releasing project resources, and closing procurement contracts.

193. What is the main purpose of the close project or phase process?
a. to authorize the project and allocate necessary resources
b. to define the project scope and create the project management plan
c. to monitor and control project performance and manage changes
d. to finalize all project activities and transfer the project deliverables

Answer: d. to finalize all project activities and transfer the project deliverables. Explanation: The main purpose of the close project or phase process is to finalize all project or phase activities and formally transfer the project deliverables to the appropriate stakeholders. This process involves obtaining final acceptance of the deliverables, documenting lessons learned, updating organizational process assets, closing procurement contracts, and communicating project closure to all stakeholders. The close project or phase process ensures that the project or phase is properly concluded and that all necessary closure activities are performed.

194. Which of the following documents is not a key input to the close project or phase process?
a. project charter
b. project management plan
c. accepted deliverables
d. organizational process assets

Answer: a. project charter. Explanation: The project charter is not a key input to the close project or phase process, as it is primarily used during the initiating process group to authorize the project and identify key stakeholders. The main inputs to the close project or phase process are the project management plan, which guides the closure activities; accepted deliverables, which are the final project outcomes that need to be transferred to the stakeholders; and organizational process assets, such as lessons learned and historical information, which are reviewed and updated during project closure.

195. What is the purpose of the final product, service, or result transition in the closing process group?
a. to transfer ownership of the project deliverables to the appropriate stakeholders
b. to release project resources and reassign them to other projects or operations
c. to archive project documents and store them for future reference
d. to evaluate the project team's performance and provide feedback

Answer: a. to transfer ownership of the project deliverables to the appropriate stakeholders. Explanation: The purpose of the final product, service, or result transition in the closing process group is to formally transfer ownership of the project deliverables to the appropriate stakeholders, such as the client, sponsor, or end-users. This transition ensures that the deliverables are accepted, and that the necessary knowledge and support are provided for their ongoing maintenance and use. The final product, service, or result transition is a key output of the close project or phase process and is essential for ensuring a smooth handover and realizing the intended benefits of the project.

196. What is the main benefit of documenting lessons learned during the closing process group?
a. to assign blame for project failures and identify underperforming team members
b. to celebrate project successes and reward high-performing team members
c. to capture knowledge gained during the project for future use and continuous improvement
d. to justify project decisions and defend against potential legal claims or disputes

Answer: c. to capture knowledge gained during the project for future use and continuous improvement. Explanation: The main benefit of documenting lessons learned during the closing process group is to capture the knowledge and insights gained throughout the project lifecycle, including successes, challenges, and recommendations for improvement. This information is valuable for future projects and can help organizations continuously improve their project management practices. Lessons learned should be documented objectively and focus on the project processes, tools, and techniques, rather than on individual performance or assigning blame. They are not intended to justify decisions or defend against legal claims, but rather to support organizational learning and knowledge sharing.

197. Which of the following is a key activity of the administrative closure procedure in the closing process group?
a. obtaining formal acceptance of project deliverables
b. documenting lessons learned and updating the lessons learned repository
c. releasing project resources and closing procurement contracts
d. all of the above

Answer: d. all of the above. Explanation: The administrative closure procedure in the closing process group includes all of the mentioned activities: obtaining formal acceptance of project deliverables, documenting lessons learned and updating the lessons learned repository, and releasing project resources and closing procurement contracts. Administrative closure ensures that all project information is properly documented, archived, and disseminated, and that all project resources, including team members, equipment, and facilities, are released and reassigned. It also involves finalizing and closing any outstanding contracts or agreements with suppliers, vendors, or other stakeholders.

198. What is the purpose of the final project report in the closing process group?
a. to document the project's objectives, scope, and deliverables
b. to summarize the project's performance, outcomes, and lessons learned
c. to provide a detailed description of the project's technical specifications and design
d. to outline the project's budget, resource allocation, and cost performance

Answer: b. to summarize the project's performance, outcomes, and lessons learned. Explanation: The purpose of the final project report in the closing process group is to provide a comprehensive summary of the project's performance, outcomes, and lessons learned. This report includes information on the project's objectives, scope, schedule, budget, quality, and stakeholder management, as well as an assessment of the project's success in meeting its goals and delivering the intended benefits. The final project report serves as a historical record of the project and a reference for future projects, helping organizations to continuously improve their project management practices.

199. Which of the following is not a key output of the close project or phase process?
a. final product, service, or result transition
b. organizational process assets updates
c. project management plan updates
d. project documents updates

Answer: c. project management plan updates. Explanation: Project management plan updates are not a key output of the close project or phase process, as the project management plan is primarily used during the planning, executing, and monitoring and controlling process groups to guide project activities and decision-making. The main outputs of the close project or phase process are the final product, service, or result transition, which transfers ownership of the project deliverables to the appropriate stakeholders; organizational process assets updates, which include documenting lessons learned and updating the lessons learned repository; and project documents updates, which involve finalizing and archiving all project documentation.

200. What is the significance of obtaining formal acceptance of project deliverables during the closing process group?
a. to ensure that the project scope has been fully met and all requirements have been satisfied
b. to transfer ownership and responsibility for the deliverables to the appropriate stakeholders
c. to confirm that the project has been completed within the approved budget and schedule
d. to verify that the project team has followed all necessary organizational policies and procedures

Answer: b. to transfer ownership and responsibility for the deliverables to the appropriate stakeholders. Explanation: The significance of obtaining formal acceptance of project deliverables during the closing process group is to formally transfer ownership and responsibility for the deliverables from the project team to the appropriate stakeholders, such as the client, sponsor, or end-users. This acceptance confirms that the deliverables meet the agreed-upon requirements and quality standards and that the stakeholders are satisfied with the project outcomes. While formal acceptance also helps to ensure that the project scope has been met, it is primarily focused on the handover and transition of the deliverables to the stakeholders who will use, maintain, and benefit from them.

201. What is the primary focus of the closing process group?
a. to define the project scope, objectives, and success criteria
b. to develop detailed project plans and obtain necessary approvals
c. to execute the project work and deliver the project outcomes
d. to finalize project activities, complete documentation, and transfer deliverables

Answer: d. to finalize project activities, complete documentation, and transfer deliverables. Explanation: The primary focus of the closing process group is to finalize all project activities, complete project documentation, and formally transfer the project deliverables to the appropriate stakeholders. This process group ensures that the project or project phase is properly concluded, and that all necessary closure activities are performed. The key processes in this group are close project or phase, which includes finalizing all project activities, archiving project information, releasing resources, and communicating project closure to stakeholders.

202. Which of the following is not a key activity performed during the closing process group?
a. obtaining final acceptance of project deliverables
b. documenting lessons learned and archiving project documents
c. releasing project resources and closing procurement contracts
d. monitoring and controlling project work to ensure successful completion

Answer: d. monitoring and controlling project work to ensure successful completion. Explanation: Monitoring and controlling project work is not a key activity performed during the closing process group, but rather an ongoing activity throughout the executing and monitoring and controlling process groups. The closing process group focuses on finalizing project activities, completing documentation, and transferring deliverables. Key activities in this group include obtaining final acceptance of project deliverables, documenting lessons learned, archiving project documents, releasing project resources, and closing procurement contracts.

203. What is the main purpose of the close project or phase process?
a. to authorize the project and allocate necessary resources
b. to define the project scope and create the project management plan
c. to monitor and control project performance and manage changes
d. to finalize all project activities and transfer the project deliverables

Answer: d. to finalize all project activities and transfer the project deliverables. Explanation: The main purpose of the close project or phase process is to finalize all project or phase activities and formally transfer the project deliverables to the appropriate stakeholders. This process involves obtaining final acceptance of the deliverables, documenting lessons learned, updating organizational process assets, closing procurement contracts, and communicating project closure to all stakeholders. The close project or phase process ensures that the project or phase is properly concluded and that all necessary closure activities are performed.

204. Which of the following documents is not a key input to the close project or phase process?
a. project charter
b. project management plan
c. accepted deliverables
d. organizational process assets

Answer: a. project charter. Explanation: The project charter is not a key input to the close project or phase process, as it is primarily used during the initiating process group to authorize the project and identify key stakeholders. The main inputs to the close project or phase process are the project management plan, which guides the closure activities; accepted deliverables, which are the final project outcomes that need to be transferred to the stakeholders; and organizational process assets, such as lessons learned and historical information, which are reviewed and updated during project closure.

205. What is the purpose of the final product, service, or result transition in the closing process group?
a. to transfer ownership of the project deliverables to the appropriate stakeholders
b. to release project resources and reassign them to other projects or operations
c. to archive project documents and store them for future reference
d. to evaluate the project team's performance and provide feedback

Answer: a. to transfer ownership of the project deliverables to the appropriate stakeholders. Explanation: The purpose of the final product, service, or result transition in the closing process group is to formally transfer ownership of the project deliverables to the appropriate stakeholders, such as the client, sponsor, or end-users. This transition ensures that the deliverables are accepted, and that the necessary knowledge and support are provided for their ongoing maintenance and use. The final product, service, or result transition is a key output of the close project or phase process and is essential for ensuring a smooth handover and realizing the intended benefits of the project.

206. What is the main benefit of documenting lessons learned during the closing process group?
a. to assign blame for project failures and identify underperforming team members
b. to celebrate project successes and reward high-performing team members
c. to capture knowledge gained during the project for future use and continuous improvement
d. to justify project decisions and defend against potential legal claims or disputes

Answer: c. to capture knowledge gained during the project for future use and continuous improvement. Explanation: The main benefit of documenting lessons learned during the closing process group is to capture the knowledge and insights gained throughout the project lifecycle, including successes, challenges, and recommendations for improvement. This information is valuable for future projects and can help organizations continuously improve their project management practices. Lessons learned should be documented objectively and focus on the project processes, tools, and techniques, rather than on individual performance or assigning blame. They are not intended to justify decisions or defend against legal claims, but rather to support organizational learning and knowledge sharing.

207. Which of the following is a key activity of the administrative closure procedure in the closing process group?
a. obtaining formal acceptance of project deliverables
b. documenting lessons learned and updating the lessons learned repository
c. releasing project resources and closing procurement contracts
d. all of the above

Answer: d. all of the above. Explanation: The administrative closure procedure in the closing process group includes all of the mentioned activities: obtaining formal acceptance of project deliverables, documenting lessons learned and updating the lessons learned repository, and releasing project resources and closing procurement contracts. Administrative closure ensures that all project information is properly documented, archived, and disseminated, and that all project resources, including team members, equipment, and facilities, are released and reassigned. It also involves finalizing and closing any outstanding contracts or agreements with suppliers, vendors, or other stakeholders.

208. What is the purpose of the final project report in the closing process group?
a. to document the project's objectives, scope, and deliverables
b. to summarize the project's performance, outcomes, and lessons learned
c. to provide a detailed description of the project's technical specifications and design
d. to outline the project's budget, resource allocation, and cost performance

Answer: b. to summarize the project's performance, outcomes, and lessons learned. Explanation: The purpose of the final project report in the closing process group is to provide a comprehensive summary of the project's performance, outcomes, and lessons learned. This report includes information on the project's objectives, scope, schedule, budget, quality, and stakeholder management, as well as an assessment of the project's success in meeting its goals and delivering the intended benefits. The final project report serves as a historical record of the project and a reference for future projects, helping organizations to continuously improve their project management practices.

209. Which of the following is not a key output of the close project or phase process?
a. final product, service, or result transition
b. organizational process assets updates
c. project management plan updates
d. project documents updates

Answer: c. project management plan updates. Explanation: Project management plan updates are not a key output of the close project or phase process, as the project management plan is primarily used during the planning, executing, and monitoring and controlling process groups to guide project activities and decision-making. The main outputs of the close project or phase process are the final product, service, or result transition, which transfers ownership of the project deliverables to the appropriate stakeholders; organizational process assets updates, which include documenting lessons learned and updating the lessons learned repository; and project documents updates, which involve finalizing and archiving all project documentation.

210. What is the significance of obtaining formal acceptance of project deliverables during the closing process group?
a. to ensure that the project scope has been fully met and all requirements have been satisfied
b. to transfer ownership and responsibility for the deliverables to the appropriate stakeholders
c. to confirm that the project has been completed within the approved budget and schedule
d. to verify that the project team has followed all necessary organizational policies and procedures

Answer: b. to transfer ownership and responsibility for the deliverables to the appropriate stakeholders. Explanation: The significance of obtaining formal acceptance of project deliverables during the closing process group is to formally transfer ownership and responsibility for the deliverables from the project team to the appropriate stakeholders, such as the client, sponsor, or end-users. This acceptance confirms that the deliverables meet the agreed-upon requirements and quality standards and that the stakeholders are satisfied with the project outcomes. While formal acceptance also helps to ensure that the project scope has been met, it is primarily focused on the handover and transition of the deliverables to the stakeholders who will use, maintain, and benefit from them.

211. What is the primary goal of project integration management?
a. to ensure that the project deliverables meet the required quality standards
b. to coordinate the various project elements and ensure that they are properly integrated
c. to manage the project budget and control project costs
d. to identify, analyze, and respond to project risks

Answer: b. to coordinate the various project elements and ensure that they are properly integrated. Explanation: The primary goal of project integration management is to coordinate the various elements of a project, such as scope, schedule, cost, quality, resources, communications, risk, and procurement, and ensure that they are properly integrated and aligned. This knowledge area focuses on the processes and activities needed to identify, define, combine, unify, and coordinate the various project management processes and activities within the project management process groups.

212. Which of the following is not one of the subsidiary plans that make up the project management plan?
a. scope management plan
b. requirements management plan
c. project charter
d. cost management plan

Answer: c. project charter. Explanation: The project charter is not a subsidiary plan that makes up the project management plan. The project charter is a document that formally authorizes the existence of a project and provides the project manager with the authority to apply organizational resources to project activities. It is an output of the develop project charter process in the initiating process group. The subsidiary plans that make up the project management plan include the scope management plan, requirements management plan, schedule management plan, cost management plan, quality management plan, resource management plan, communications management plan, risk management plan, procurement management plan, and stakeholder engagement plan.

213. What is the main purpose of the collect requirements process in project scope management?
a. to define the project scope and create the work breakdown structure (WBS)
b. to develop a detailed project schedule and allocate resources to project activities
c. to determine the project budget and establish the cost baseline
d. to identify, document, and manage project and product requirements

Answer: d. to identify, document, and manage project and product requirements. Explanation: The main purpose of the collect requirements process in project scope management is to identify, document, and manage the project and product requirements that define the project scope. This process involves eliciting, analyzing, and recording the needs, wants, and expectations of the project stakeholders, and translating them into clear, actionable, and measurable requirements. The collect requirements process is critical for ensuring that the project scope is well-defined and aligned with stakeholder expectations, and for establishing a basis for project planning, execution, and validation.

214. Which project management knowledge area focuses on ensuring that the project includes all the work required, and only the work required, to complete the project successfully?
a. project integration management
b. project scope management
c. project schedule management
d. project quality management

Answer: b. project scope management. Explanation: Project scope management is the project management knowledge area that focuses on ensuring that the project includes all the work required, and only the work required, to complete the project successfully. This knowledge area involves defining and controlling what is and is not included in the project, and creating a detailed description of the project deliverables, requirements, and boundaries. The key processes in project scope management include plan scope management, collect requirements, define scope, create WBS, validate scope, and control scope.

215. What is the purpose of the define activities process in project schedule management?

a. to identify the specific actions to be performed to produce the project deliverables
b. to sequence the project activities in the order in which they will be executed
c. to estimate the resources needed to complete each project activity
d. to develop the project schedule and determine the project duration

Answer: a. to identify the specific actions to be performed to produce the project deliverables. Explanation: The purpose of the define activities process in project schedule management is to identify the specific actions that need to be performed to produce the project deliverables. This process involves breaking down the work packages from the work breakdown structure (WBS) into smaller, more manageable components called activities. Activities are the fundamental units of work in a project schedule, and they represent the work that needs to be done to complete the project deliverables. The define activities process is a prerequisite for the other project schedule management processes, such as sequence activities, estimate activity durations, and develop schedule.

216. Which of the following is not a key benefit of project cost management?
a. determining the project budget and establishing the cost baseline
b. monitoring project spending and identifying deviations from the cost baseline
c. improving project quality and ensuring that deliverables meet requirements
d. evaluating the cost impact of project changes and making informed decisions

Answer: c. improving project quality and ensuring that deliverables meet requirements. Explanation: Improving project quality and ensuring that deliverables meet requirements is not a key benefit of project cost management. While cost management is closely related to other project management knowledge areas, such as scope and quality, its primary focus is on planning, estimating, budgeting, financing, funding, managing, and controlling project costs. The key benefits of project cost management include determining the project budget, establishing the cost baseline, monitoring project spending, identifying cost variances, and evaluating the cost impact of project changes to support decision-making.

217. What is the main difference between quality assurance and quality control in project quality management?
a. quality assurance focuses on the project deliverables, while quality control focuses on the project processes
b. quality assurance is performed during project planning, while quality control is performed during project execution
c. quality assurance aims to prevent defects, while quality control aims to identify and correct defects
d. quality assurance is the responsibility of the project manager, while quality control is the responsibility of the project team

Answer: c. quality assurance aims to prevent defects, while quality control aims to identify and correct defects. Explanation: The main difference between quality assurance and quality control in project quality management is that quality assurance focuses on preventing defects, while quality control focuses on identifying and correcting defects. Quality assurance is a proactive approach that involves planning, designing, and implementing processes, procedures, and standards to ensure that the project deliverables will meet the required quality specifications. Quality control, on the other hand, is a reactive approach that involves monitoring, measuring, and testing project outputs to detect and correct defects or non-conformities. Both quality assurance and quality control are performed throughout the project lifecycle and are the responsibility of the entire project team, with the project manager playing a key role in leading and coordinating quality management efforts.

218. Which project management knowledge area is concerned with identifying, analyzing, and responding to project risks?
a. project scope management
b. project schedule management
c. project cost management
d. project risk management

Answer: d. project risk management. Explanation: Project risk management is the project management knowledge area that is concerned with identifying, analyzing, and responding to project risks. This knowledge area involves the processes of conducting risk management planning, identification, analysis, response planning, response implementation, and monitoring risk on a project. The main objectives of project risk management are to increase the likelihood and impact of positive events and decrease the likelihood and impact of negative events in the project. By effectively managing project risks, organizations can improve the chances of project success, minimize potential threats, and maximize potential opportunities.

219. What is the primary focus of project resource management?
a. acquiring and managing the financial resources needed to complete the project
b. identifying, acquiring, and managing the human and physical resources needed to complete the project
c. planning and managing project communications to ensure effective information exchange
d. identifying and engaging project stakeholders to understand their needs and expectations

Answer: b. identifying, acquiring, and managing the human and physical resources needed to complete the project. Explanation: The primary focus of project resource management is on identifying, acquiring, and managing the human and physical resources needed to complete the project successfully. This knowledge area involves the processes necessary to ensure that the project team has the appropriate skills, knowledge, and experience, and that the necessary equipment, materials, and facilities are available when needed. The key processes in project resource management include plan resource management, estimate activity resources, acquire resources, develop team, manage team, and control resources.

220. What is the main purpose of the project communications management knowledge area?
a. to ensure that project information is collected, stored, and disseminated effectively
b. to identify, prioritize, and engage project stakeholders throughout the project lifecycle
c. to plan, execute, and control the procurement of goods and services for the project
d. to define and manage the overall scope of the project and its deliverables

Answer: a. to ensure that project information is collected, stored, and disseminated effectively.
Explanation: The main purpose of the project communications management knowledge area is to ensure that project information is collected, stored, and disseminated in an effective and timely manner. This

knowledge area involves the processes necessary to plan, manage, and control the flow of project information among stakeholders, and to ensure that the right information reaches the right people at the right time. The key processes in project communications management include plan communications management, manage communications, and monitor communications. Effective project communications management is critical for keeping stakeholders informed, engaged, and aligned with project objectives, and for fostering trust, collaboration, and decision-making.

221. What is the primary purpose of the develop project charter process?
a. to identify the project stakeholders and their requirements
b. to formally authorize the project and define high-level project objectives
c. to develop a detailed project schedule and budget
d. to establish the project team and assign roles and responsibilities

Answer: b. to formally authorize the project and define high-level project objectives. Explanation: The primary purpose of the develop project charter process is to create a document that formally authorizes the existence of a project and provides the project manager with the authority to apply organizational resources to project activities. The project charter establishes a partnership between the performing and requesting organizations, identifies high-level project objectives, and documents key stakeholder needs and expectations. It serves as a reference of authority for the future of the project and is a crucial output of the initiating process group.

222. Which of the following is not an input to the develop project management plan process?
a. project charter
b. outputs from other processes
c. enterprise environmental factors
d. work performance data

Answer: d. work performance data. Explanation: Work performance data is not an input to the develop project management plan process. Work performance data, which includes information about project progress, deliverables status, and resource utilization, is generated during the executing process group and is an input to various monitoring and controlling processes. The key inputs to the develop project management plan process are the project charter, which provides the high-level project description and requirements; outputs from other processes, such as the scope statement, WBS, and risk register; enterprise environmental factors, such as organizational culture and infrastructure; and organizational process assets, such as policies, procedures, and templates.

223. What is the main purpose of the direct and manage project work process?
a. to define the project scope and create the project management plan
b. to monitor project progress and take corrective action as needed
c. to lead and perform the work defined in the project management plan
d. to close the project or phase and obtain final approval

Answer: c. to lead and perform the work defined in the project management plan. Explanation: The main purpose of the direct and manage project work process is to lead and perform the work defined in the project management plan to achieve the project's objectives. This process involves managing and performing the activities needed to create the project deliverables, implementing approved changes, and managing project knowledge. The project manager coordinates and directs the work of the project team, manages vendor and supplier relationships, and communicates with stakeholders to ensure that the project work is executed as planned.

224. Which of the following is not a key benefit of the monitor and control project work process?
a. understanding the current state of the project and identifying corrective actions
b. ensuring that only authorized changes are implemented and documented
c. providing feedback to stakeholders on project progress and performance
d. minimizing the impact of project risks and uncertainties

Answer: d. minimizing the impact of project risks and uncertainties. Explanation: Minimizing the impact of project risks and uncertainties is not a key benefit of the monitor and control project work process. While this process does involve monitoring project risks and identifying potential issues, its primary focus is on tracking project progress, comparing actual performance to planned performance, and taking corrective action as needed. The key benefits of the monitor and control project work process include understanding the current state of the project, identifying areas requiring attention, ensuring that only authorized changes are implemented, and providing feedback to stakeholders on project progress and performance. Risk management is primarily addressed through the project risk management processes, such as plan risk management, identify risks, and monitor risks.

225. What is the main difference between the perform integrated change control process and the monitor and control project work process?
a. perform integrated change control is focused on managing changes to the project, while monitor and control project work is focused on tracking project progress
b. perform integrated change control is performed during the executing process group, while monitor and control project work is performed during the monitoring and controlling process group
c. perform integrated change control is the responsibility of the project manager, while monitor and control project work is the responsibility of the project team
d. perform integrated change control applies to all project management knowledge areas, while monitor and control project work applies only to project integration management

Answer: a. perform integrated change control is focused on managing changes to the project, while monitor and control project work is focused on tracking project progress. Explanation: The main difference between the perform integrated change control process and the monitor and control project work process is their focus. Perform integrated change control is primarily concerned with reviewing, approving, and managing changes to the project and project baselines in a comprehensive and integrated manner. This process ensures that changes are properly assessed, approved, and communicated and that the project remains aligned with its objectives. Monitor and control project work, on the other hand, is focused on tracking project progress, identifying deviations from the plan, and taking corrective action to ensure that the project objectives are met. Both processes are part of the monitoring and controlling process group and are the responsibility of the project manager, with support from the project team.

226. Which of the following is the primary output of the close project or phase process?

a. project charter
b. project management plan
c. final product, service, or result transition
d. lessons learned register

Answer: c. final product, service, or result transition. Explanation: The primary output of the close project or phase process is the final product, service, or result transition. This output involves transferring the completed project deliverables to the appropriate stakeholders, such as the client, sponsor, or end-users, and ensuring that they accept and approve the project outcomes. The final product, service, or result transition marks the formal completion of the project or phase and the handover of the deliverables to the groups responsible for their ongoing maintenance and support. Other important outputs of the close project or phase process include the final project report, lessons learned register, and updates to organizational process assets.

227. What is the purpose of the project management plan in project integration management?
a. to formally authorize the project and define high-level project objectives
b. to provide a comprehensive roadmap for executing, monitoring, and controlling the project
c. to identify and document the project stakeholders and their requirements
d. to establish the project budget and allocate resources to project activities

Answer: b. to provide a comprehensive roadmap for executing, monitoring, and controlling the project. Explanation: The purpose of the project management plan in project integration management is to provide a comprehensive roadmap for executing, monitoring, and controlling the project. The project management plan integrates and consolidates all of the subsidiary plans and baselines from the other project management knowledge areas, such as scope, schedule, cost, quality, resources, communications, risk, procurement, and stakeholder management. It describes how the project will be executed, monitored, controlled, and closed, and serves as the primary source of information for how the project will be managed. The project management plan is a living document that is updated and refined throughout the project lifecycle as more detailed information becomes available.

228. What is the main benefit of the manage project knowledge process in project integration management?
a. to ensure that project information is properly documented and archived
b. to facilitate knowledge sharing and continuous improvement within the organization
c. to identify and resolve project issues and conflicts in a timely manner
d. to ensure that project deliverables meet the required quality standards

Answer: b. to facilitate knowledge sharing and continuous improvement within the organization. Explanation: The main benefit of the manage project knowledge process in project integration management is to facilitate knowledge sharing and continuous improvement within the organization. This process involves using existing knowledge and creating new knowledge to achieve the project's objectives and contribute to organizational learning. By capturing, sharing, and applying project knowledge, organizations can improve their project management practices, avoid repeating mistakes, and leverage best practices and lessons learned across projects. The manage project knowledge process helps to build a culture of learning and innovation, where project teams are encouraged to share their experiences and insights and to continuously improve their skills and performance.

229. Which of the following is not a key input to the develop project charter process?
a. project statement of work
b. business case
c. agreements
d. project management plan

Answer: d. project management plan. Explanation: The project management plan is not a key input to the develop project charter process. The project charter is developed during the initiating process group, before the project management plan is created. The key inputs to the develop project charter process are the project statement of work, which provides a narrative description of the products, services, or results to be delivered by the project; the business case, which provides the necessary information from a business standpoint to determine whether the project is worth the required investment; agreements, which define the initial intentions for the project, such as MOUs or contracts; enterprise environmental factors, such as government or industry standards; and organizational process assets, such as policies, procedures, and templates.

230. What is the main purpose of the project integration management knowledge area?
a. to ensure that project stakeholders are identified and engaged throughout the project lifecycle
b. to define and manage the project scope and its requirements
c. to coordinate project activities and ensure alignment with project objectives
d. to plan, execute, and control project communications

Answer: c. to coordinate project activities and ensure alignment with project objectives. Explanation: The main purpose of the project integration management knowledge area is to coordinate project activities across all project management process groups and ensure alignment with project objectives. This knowledge area involves unifying, consolidating, and integrating the various processes and activities within the project management process groups to ensure that the project is executed effectively and efficiently. Project integration management is an overarching function that affects and is affected by all other project management knowledge areas. It involves making trade-offs among competing objectives and alternatives to meet or exceed stakeholder needs and expectations. The key processes in project integration management include develop project charter, develop project management plan, direct and manage project work, manage project knowledge, monitor and control project work, perform integrated change control, and close project or phase.

231. What is the primary purpose of the project scope management knowledge area?
a. to ensure that the project includes all the required work and only the required work
b. to develop a detailed project schedule and allocate resources to project activities
c. to determine the project budget and establish the cost baseline
d. to identify, assess, and control project risks throughout the project lifecycle

Answer: a. to ensure that the project includes all the required work and only the required work.
Explanation: The primary purpose of the project scope management knowledge area is to ensure that the project includes all the work required, and only the work required, to complete the project successfully. This knowledge area involves defining and controlling what is and is not included in the project, and creating a detailed description of the project and product scope, deliverables, requirements, boundaries, and acceptance criteria.

232. Which of the following processes is not part of the project scope management knowledge area?
a. plan scope management
b. collect requirements
c. estimate activity durations
d. define scope

Answer: c. estimate activity durations. Explanation: The estimate activity durations process is not part of the project scope management knowledge area. It belongs to the project schedule management knowledge area and involves estimating the number of work periods needed to complete individual activities with estimated resources. The processes in the project scope management knowledge area include plan scope management, collect requirements, define scope, create WBS, validate scope, and control scope.

233.What is the main difference between the project scope and the product scope?
a. project scope includes the work required to deliver the product, while product scope refers to the features and functions of the product itself
b. project scope is defined in the project charter, while product scope is defined in the project management plan
c. project scope is managed by the project manager, while product scope is managed by the product owner
d. project scope is measured in terms of time and cost, while product scope is measured in terms of quality and performance

Answer: a. project scope includes the work required to deliver the product, while product scope refers to the features and functions of the product itself. Explanation: The main difference between the project scope and the product scope is that the project scope encompasses all the work required to deliver a product, service, or result with the specified features and functions, while the product scope refers to the features and functions that characterize the product, service, or result itself. The project scope is typically broader than the product scope and includes project management activities, quality assurance, testing, and other supporting work.

234. Which of the following is not an input to the collect requirements process?
a. project charter
b. stakeholder register
c. requirements documentation
d. requirements traceability matrix

Answer: d. requirements traceability matrix. Explanation: The requirements traceability matrix is not an input to the collect requirements process, but rather an output of this process. The key inputs to collect requirements are the project charter, which provides the high-level project description and stakeholder requirements; the stakeholder register, which identifies the stakeholders who have requirements for the project; the project management plan, which provides the scope baseline and other relevant information; and enterprise environmental factors and organizational process assets, which may influence requirements collection.

235. What is the purpose of the scope baseline in project scope management?
a. to provide a snapshot of the approved project scope at a given point in time
b. to document the procedures for validating and controlling the project scope
c. to describe how the project scope will be defined, developed, and verified
d. to define the work that needs to be performed to deliver a product, service, or result

Answer: a. to provide a snapshot of the approved project scope at a given point in time. Explanation: The purpose of the scope baseline in project scope management is to provide a snapshot of the approved project scope, including the scope statement, work breakdown structure (WBS), and WBS dictionary, at a given point in time. The scope baseline serves as a reference for managing project scope and assessing change requests throughout the project lifecycle. It is a component of the project management plan and is used to measure and control the project scope.

236. Which tool is used to decompose the total project scope into smaller, more manageable components?
a. scope statement
b. work breakdown structure (WBS)
c. product breakdown structure (PBS)
d. requirements traceability matrix

Answer: b. work breakdown structure (WBS). Explanation: The work breakdown structure (WBS) is a hierarchical decomposition of the total project scope into smaller, more manageable components called work packages. The WBS organizes and defines the total scope of the project and represents the work specified in the current approved project scope statement. It arranges the project deliverables and work into a hierarchy of increasing detail, with each descending level representing an increasingly detailed definition of the project work.

237. What is the main purpose of the validate scope process in project scope management?
a. to monitor the status of the project scope and manage changes to the scope baseline
b. to subdivide project deliverables into smaller, more manageable components
c. to formalize the acceptance of the completed project deliverables by the stakeholders
d. to define how the project and product scope will be defined, validated, and controlled

Answer: c. to formalize the acceptance of the completed project deliverables by the stakeholders. Explanation: The main purpose of the validate scope process in project scope management is to formalize the acceptance of the completed project deliverables by the stakeholders. This process involves reviewing the deliverables with the customer or sponsor to ensure that they are completed satisfactorily and have achieved the required acceptance criteria. The validate scope process provides an objective assessment of the project deliverables and results in either formal acceptance by the stakeholders or a request for rework or corrective action.

238. Which of the following is not an output of the define scope process?
a. project scope statement
b. scope baseline
c. project document updates
d. requirements traceability matrix

Answer: d. requirements traceability matrix. Explanation: The requirements traceability matrix is not an output of the define scope process. It is an output of the collect requirements process and is used to track requirements throughout the project lifecycle. The key outputs of the define scope process are the project scope statement, which provides a detailed description of the project and product scope, deliverables, and acceptance criteria; the project document updates, which may include updates to the stakeholder register, requirements documentation, and risk register based on the defined scope; and the scope baseline, which is used to measure and control project scope.

239. What is the difference between gold plating and scope creep in project scope management?
a. gold plating adds unnecessary features to the project scope, while scope creep adds necessary features that were not originally planned
b. gold plating is initiated by the project team, while scope creep is initiated by the project stakeholders
c. gold plating occurs during project execution, while scope creep occurs during project planning
d. gold plating is a positive aspect of project management, while scope creep is a negative aspect

Answer: a. gold plating adds unnecessary features to the project scope, while scope creep adds necessary features that were not originally planned. Explanation: The main difference between gold plating and scope creep in project scope management is that gold plating involves adding unnecessary features or enhancements to the project scope that were not originally agreed upon, while scope creep refers to the uncontrolled expansion of the project scope by adding necessary features or requirements that were not part of the original scope baseline. Both gold plating and scope creep can negatively impact project performance, leading to schedule delays, cost overruns, and decreased customer satisfaction. However, while gold plating is often initiated by the project team in an attempt to impress the stakeholders or exceed expectations, scope creep is typically driven by stakeholder requests or changing requirements that were not adequately defined or controlled.

240. What is the main purpose of the control scope process in project scope management?
a. to formalize the acceptance of the completed project deliverables by the stakeholders
b. to define and document the stakeholders' needs and requirements for the project
c. to create a detailed description of the project and product scope, deliverables, and acceptance criteria
d. to monitor the status of the project scope and manage changes to the scope baseline

Answer: d. to monitor the status of the project scope and manage changes to the scope baseline.
Explanation: The main purpose of the control scope process in project scope management is to monitor the status of the project and product scope and manage changes to the scope baseline. This process involves assessing the status of the project and product scope at regular intervals, identifying any deviations from the scope baseline, and taking corrective or preventive actions as needed. The control scope process also includes managing actual changes to the scope baseline through the integrated change control process, which involves reviewing all change requests, approving or rejecting changes, and managing the implementation of approved changes. By effectively controlling project scope, project managers can ensure that the project remains aligned with the agreed-upon scope and delivers the expected results.

241. What is the primary goal of project schedule management?
a. to ensure that the project is completed within the approved budget
b. to define the project scope and create the work breakdown structure (WBS)
c. to develop a detailed project schedule and manage timely completion of project activities
d. to identify, assess, and control project risks throughout the project lifecycle

Answer: c. to develop a detailed project schedule and manage timely completion of project activities.
Explanation: The primary goal of project schedule management is to develop a detailed project schedule and manage the timely completion of project activities. This knowledge area involves defining the activities, sequence, duration, resources, and constraints required to create a project schedule, and managing changes to the schedule as the project progresses. Project schedule management focuses on ensuring that the project is completed on time and within the agreed-upon timeframe.

242. What is the correct order of the following project schedule management processes?
a. define activities, sequence activities, estimate activity durations, develop schedule
b. develop schedule, define activities, estimate activity durations, sequence activities
c. sequence activities, estimate activity durations, develop schedule, define activities
d. estimate activity durations, develop schedule, define activities, sequence activities

Answer: a. define activities, sequence activities, estimate activity durations, develop schedule.
Explanation: The correct order of the project schedule management processes is as follows: define activities (identifying the specific actions to be performed), sequence activities (arranging the activities in a logical order), estimate activity durations (estimating the time required for each activity), and develop schedule (creating the schedule model by analyzing activity sequences, durations, resource requirements, and schedule constraints).

243. Which of the following tools and techniques is used in the sequence activities process?
a. expert judgment
b. leads and lags
c. bottom-up estimating
d. three-point estimating

411

Answer: b. leads and lags. Explanation: Leads and lags are a tool and technique used in the sequence activities process. A lead is the amount of time by which a successor activity can start before a predecessor activity has finished, while a lag is the amount of time by which a successor activity must wait after a predecessor activity has finished before it can start. Leads and lags allow for overlapping activities or waiting periods between activities, influencing the overall project schedule. Expert judgment, bottom-up estimating, and three-point estimating are tools and techniques used in other project schedule management processes.

244. What is the critical path in a project schedule?
a. the sequence of activities with the highest risk
b. the longest sequence of activities that determines the minimum project duration
c. the shortest sequence of activities that determines the maximum project duration
d. the sequence of activities with the most allocated resources

Answer: b. the longest sequence of activities that determines the minimum project duration. Explanation: The critical path in a project schedule is the longest sequence of activities that determines the minimum project duration. It represents the series of activities that must be completed on time for the project to finish on schedule. Any delay in a critical path activity will delay the entire project. The critical path is calculated using the critical path method (CPM), which analyzes activity sequences, durations, and dependencies to determine the minimum project duration and identify schedule flexibility.

245. What is the purpose of the schedule baseline in project schedule management?
a. to provide a snapshot of the approved project schedule at a given point in time
b. to document the procedures for validating and controlling the project schedule
c. to define the work that needs to be performed to deliver a product, service, or result
d. to identify the specific resources required to complete project activities

Answer: a. to provide a snapshot of the approved project schedule at a given point in time. Explanation: The purpose of the schedule baseline in project schedule management is to provide a snapshot of the approved version of the project schedule at a given point in time. The schedule baseline includes the planned start and finish dates for activities and milestones, resource assignments, and schedule reserves. It serves as a reference for measuring schedule performance and monitoring progress throughout the project lifecycle. The schedule baseline is used in the control schedule process to identify and manage schedule variances and changes.

246. Which of the following is not an input to the estimate activity durations process?
a. activity list
b. activity attributes
c. resource breakdown structure (RBS)
d. resource calendars

Answer: c. resource breakdown structure (RBS). Explanation: The resource breakdown structure (RBS) is not an input to the estimate activity durations process. The RBS is a hierarchical representation of the project's resources, but it does not directly influence the estimation of activity durations. The key inputs to the estimate activity durations process are the activity list (a comprehensive list of project activities), activity attributes (detailed information about each activity), resource calendars (information on resource availability), project scope statement (the description of the project scope, including assumptions and constraints), enterprise environmental factors (external factors that may influence duration estimates), and organizational process assets (historical information, policies, and templates).

247. What is the difference between effort and duration in project schedule management?
a. effort is the amount of time required to complete an activity, while duration is the total number of work periods required to complete an activity
b. effort is the number of work periods required to complete an activity, while duration is the actual calendar time required to complete an activity
c. effort is the number of resources assigned to an activity, while duration is the amount of time required to complete an activity
d. effort is the cost of completing an activity, while duration is the amount of time required to complete an activity

Answer: b. effort is the number of work periods required to complete an activity, while duration is the actual calendar time required to complete an activity. Explanation: The main difference between effort and duration in project schedule management is that effort represents the number of work periods (e.g., person-hours, machine-hours) required to complete an activity, while duration represents the actual calendar time (e.g., days, weeks) required to complete an activity. Effort is typically used to estimate resource requirements and costs, while duration is used to develop the project schedule and determine the overall project timeline. The relationship between effort and duration can be influenced by factors such as resource availability, productivity, and calendar constraints.

248. What is the purpose of the schedule compression technique in project schedule management?
a. to reduce the project schedule by adding more resources to critical path activities
b. to reduce the project schedule by overlapping or paralleling activities
c. to reduce the project schedule by removing unnecessary activities from the schedule
d. to reduce the project schedule by increasing the efficiency of project team members

Answer: b. to reduce the project schedule by overlapping or paralleling activities. Explanation: The purpose of the schedule compression technique in project schedule management is to reduce the project schedule by overlapping or paralleling activities, without changing the project scope. Schedule compression can be achieved through two main techniques: crashing (adding more resources to critical path activities to decrease duration) and fast-tracking (performing activities in parallel that would normally be done sequentially). Both techniques involve accepting increased risk and potentially increased costs to achieve a shorter project duration. Schedule compression is often used when the project is behind schedule or when there is a need to accelerate the project timeline.

249. Which of the following is not a valid reason for creating a milestone list in project schedule management?
a. to identify significant points or events in the project schedule
b. to monitor progress towards project completion
c. to communicate key dates to project stakeholders

d. to determine the project budget and allocate resources

Answer: d. to determine the project budget and allocate resources. Explanation: Determining the project budget and allocating resources is not a valid reason for creating a milestone list in project schedule management. A milestone is a significant point or event in a project, such as the completion of a major deliverable or a key decision point. The main reasons for creating a milestone list are to identify these significant points in the project schedule, monitor progress towards project completion, and communicate key dates to project stakeholders. Milestones are often used as checkpoints for measuring project performance and making strategic decisions. Project budgeting and resource allocation are separate processes that are not directly related to the creation of a milestone list.

250. What is the main purpose of the control schedule process in project schedule management?
a. to identify the specific activities required to produce the project deliverables
b. to estimate the time required to complete each project activity
c. to develop a detailed project schedule based on activity sequences, durations, and resource requirements
d. to monitor the status of the project schedule and manage changes to the schedule baseline

Answer: d. to monitor the status of the project schedule and manage changes to the schedule baseline. Explanation: The main purpose of the control schedule process in project schedule management is to monitor the status of the project schedule and manage changes to the schedule baseline. This process involves monitoring the actual progress of project activities, comparing it to the planned progress, and identifying any schedule variances or deviations. The control schedule process also includes managing changes to the schedule baseline through the integrated change control process, which involves reviewing change requests, assessing their impact on the project schedule, and updating the schedule baseline as needed. Other important activities in this process include determining corrective actions to address schedule variances, updating the project schedule and schedule data, and communicating schedule information to stakeholders.

251. What is the primary goal of project cost management?
a. to ensure that the project is completed within the approved budget
b. to define the project scope and create the work breakdown structure (WBS)
c. to identify, assess, and control project risks throughout the project lifecycle
d. to develop a detailed project schedule and manage timely completion of project activities

Answer: a. to ensure that the project is completed within the approved budget. Explanation: The primary goal of project cost management is to ensure that the project is completed within the approved budget. This knowledge area involves estimating, budgeting, financing, funding, managing, and controlling project costs to keep the project within the approved budget. Project cost management focuses on managing the costs required to complete project activities and delivering the project's scope while adhering to the budget constraints.

252. Which of the following is not an input to the estimate costs process?
a. project management plan

b. project schedule
c. risk register
d. cost baseline

Answer: d. cost baseline. Explanation: The cost baseline is not an input to the estimate costs process. The cost baseline is an output of the determine budget process and represents the approved version of the project budget. The key inputs to the estimate costs process are the project management plan (which includes the scope baseline, schedule baseline, and other information), the project schedule (which provides information about the timing and duration of project activities), the risk register (which identifies potential risks that may impact project costs), the enterprise environmental factors (such as market conditions and currency exchange rates), and organizational process assets (such as historical cost data and templates).

253. What is the main difference between bottom-up estimating and analogous estimating?
a. bottom-up estimating is more accurate, while analogous estimating is faster
b. bottom-up estimating is based on historical data, while analogous estimating is based on expert judgment
c. bottom-up estimating involves estimating the cost of individual work packages, while analogous estimating involves estimating the cost of the entire project based on similar projects
d. bottom-up estimating is used for small projects, while analogous estimating is used for large projects

Answer: c. bottom-up estimating involves estimating the cost of individual work packages, while analogous estimating involves estimating the cost of the entire project based on similar projects. Explanation: The main difference between bottom-up estimating and analogous estimating is that bottom-up estimating involves estimating the cost of individual work packages and then aggregating these estimates to determine the overall project cost, while analogous estimating involves estimating the cost of the entire project based on the costs of similar projects. Bottom-up estimating is generally more accurate but time-consuming, as it requires detailed analysis of each work package. Analogous estimating is faster but less accurate, as it relies on historical data from similar projects.

254. What is the purpose of the cost baseline in project cost management?
a. to provide a snapshot of the approved project budget at a given point in time
b. to document the procedures for estimating and controlling project costs
c. to define the resources required to complete project activities
d. to establish the cost performance measurements for the project

Answer: a. to provide a snapshot of the approved project budget at a given point in time. Explanation: The purpose of the cost baseline in project cost management is to provide a snapshot of the approved version of the project budget at a given point in time. The cost baseline is the sum of the approved budgets for all project activities and is used as a reference for measuring and monitoring cost performance throughout the project. It is a component of the project management plan and is used in the control costs process to identify and manage cost variances and changes.

255. Which of the following is not a valid technique for determining the budget in project cost management?
a. cost aggregation
b. reserve analysis
c. funding limit reconciliation
d. parametric estimating

Answer: d. parametric estimating. Explanation: Parametric estimating is not a valid technique for determining the budget in project cost management. Parametric estimating is a technique used in the estimate costs process, where a statistical relationship between historical data and other variables is used to calculate an estimate for project costs. The valid techniques for determining the budget are cost aggregation (summing up the estimated costs of individual activities or work packages), reserve analysis (determining the contingency and management reserves for the project), and funding limit reconciliation (adjusting the budget to account for funding limits and constraints).

256. What is the main purpose of the control costs process in project cost management?
a. to establish the policies, procedures, and documentation for planning and controlling project costs
b. to develop an approximation of the monetary resources needed to complete project activities
c. to monitor the status of the project to update the project costs and manage changes to the cost baseline
d. to aggregate the estimated costs of individual activities or work packages to establish a cost baseline

Answer: c. to monitor the status of the project to update the project costs and manage changes to the cost baseline. Explanation: The main purpose of the control costs process in project cost management is to monitor the status of the project to update the project costs and manage changes to the cost baseline. This process involves monitoring cost performance, identifying and analyzing cost variances, and implementing appropriate corrective actions. The control costs process also includes managing changes to the cost baseline through the integrated change control process, updating the project budget and cost documents, and informing stakeholders of the project's cost performance.

257. What is the primary tool used in the control costs process?
a. cost of quality (COQ)
b. earned value management (EVM)
c. reserve analysis
d. to-complete performance index (TCPI)

Answer: b. earned value management (EVM). Explanation: The primary tool used in the control costs process is earned value management (EVM). EVM is a methodology that integrates scope, schedule, and resource measurements to assess project performance and progress. It compares the amount of work that was planned with what was actually earned and what was actually spent to determine if the project is on track in terms of cost and schedule. EVM uses key metrics such as planned value (PV), earned value (EV), and actual cost (AC) to calculate cost and schedule variances and performance indices. These metrics help project managers identify potential cost overruns or underruns and take corrective actions as needed.

258. What is the difference between the cost variance (CV) and the schedule variance (SV) in earned value management?
a. CV measures the difference between the planned cost and the actual cost, while SV measures the difference between the planned schedule and the actual schedule
b. CV measures the difference between the earned value and the actual cost, while SV measures the difference between the earned value and the planned value
c. CV measures the difference between the budget at completion and the actual cost, while SV measures the difference between the budget at completion and the earned value
d. CV measures the difference between the estimate to complete and the actual cost, while SV measures the difference between the estimate to complete and the earned value

Answer: b. CV measures the difference between the earned value and the actual cost, while SV measures the difference between the earned value and the planned value. Explanation: The main difference between the cost variance (CV) and the schedule variance (SV) in earned value management is that CV measures the difference between the earned value (EV) and the actual cost (AC), while SV measures the difference between the earned value (EV) and the planned value (PV). A positive CV indicates that the project is under budget, while a negative CV indicates that the project is over budget. A positive SV indicates that the project is ahead of schedule, while a negative SV indicates that the project is behind schedule. These variances help project managers assess the project's cost and schedule performance and identify areas that may require corrective action.

259. What is the difference between the cost performance index (CPI) and the schedule performance index (SPI) in earned value management?
a. CPI measures the cost efficiency of the project, while SPI measures the schedule efficiency of the project
b. CPI measures the schedule efficiency of the project, while SPI measures the cost efficiency of the project
c. CPI measures the overall efficiency of the project, while SPI measures the cost efficiency of the project
d. CPI measures the overall efficiency of the project, while SPI measures the schedule efficiency of the project

Answer: a. CPI measures the cost efficiency of the project, while SPI measures the schedule efficiency of the project. Explanation: The main difference between the cost performance index (CPI) and the schedule performance index (SPI) in earned value management is that CPI measures the cost efficiency of the project, while SPI measures the schedule efficiency of the project. CPI is calculated by dividing the earned value (EV) by the actual cost (AC), while SPI is calculated by dividing the earned value (EV) by the planned value (PV). A CPI value greater than 1 indicates that the project is under budget, while a CPI value less than 1 indicates that the project is over budget. An SPI value greater than 1 indicates that the project is ahead of schedule, while an SPI value less than 1 indicates that the project is behind schedule. These indices provide a measure of the project's efficiency in terms of cost and schedule performance.

260. What is the formula for calculating the estimate at completion (EAC) in earned value management?
a. EAC = BAC / CPI
b. EAC = AC + ETC
c. EAC = BAC / SPI

d. EAC = AC + BAC - EV

Answer: b. EAC = AC + ETC. Explanation: The formula for calculating the estimate at completion (EAC) in earned value management is EAC = AC + ETC, where AC is the actual cost incurred to date and ETC is the estimate to complete the remaining work. The EAC represents the expected total cost of the project at completion, based on the project's current performance and the estimated cost of the remaining work. The EAC can be compared to the budget at completion (BAC) to determine if the project is likely to be completed within budget. If the EAC is greater than the BAC, the project is expected to be over budget at completion, while if the EAC is less than the BAC, the project is expected to be under budget at completion.

261. What is the main purpose of project quality management?
a. to ensure that the project deliverables meet the required quality standards
b. to develop a detailed project schedule and manage timely completion of project activities
c. to identify, assess, and control project risks throughout the project lifecycle
d. to ensure that the project is completed within the approved budget

Answer: a. to ensure that the project deliverables meet the required quality standards. Explanation: The main purpose of project quality management is to ensure that the project deliverables meet the required quality standards and satisfy the needs for which they were undertaken. This knowledge area involves defining quality standards, planning quality management activities, performing quality assurance and control, and continuously improving the quality of project processes and deliverables.

262. Which of the following is not a key process in project quality management?
a. plan quality management
b. manage quality
c. control quality
d. perform quality audits

Answer: d. perform quality audits. Explanation: Performing quality audits is not a separate process in project quality management, but rather a tool and technique used in the manage quality and control quality processes. The three key processes in project quality management are plan quality management (identifying quality requirements and standards), manage quality (executing the planned quality activities to ensure that the project deliverables meet the quality standards), and control quality (monitoring and recording the results of quality control activities to assess performance and recommend necessary changes).

263. What is the difference between quality assurance and quality control?
a. quality assurance focuses on the project deliverables, while quality control focuses on the project processes
b. quality assurance aims to prevent defects, while quality control aims to identify and correct defects
c. quality assurance is performed during project planning, while quality control is performed during project execution

d. quality assurance is the responsibility of the project manager, while quality control is the responsibility of the project team

Answer: b. quality assurance aims to prevent defects, while quality control aims to identify and correct defects. Explanation: The main difference between quality assurance and quality control is that quality assurance focuses on preventing defects and ensuring that the project processes are followed, while quality control focuses on identifying and correcting defects in the project deliverables. Quality assurance involves proactive activities such as process planning, documentation, and auditing to ensure that the project adheres to the defined quality standards. Quality control involves reactive activities such as inspection, testing, and defect repair to ensure that the project deliverables meet the required quality criteria.

264. Which of the following is not an input to the plan quality management process?
a. project management plan
b. stakeholder register
c. risk register
d. quality control measurements

Answer: d. quality control measurements. Explanation: Quality control measurements are not an input to the plan quality management process, but rather an output of the control quality process. The key inputs to the plan quality management process are the project management plan (which includes the scope baseline, schedule baseline, and other information), the stakeholder register (which identifies the project stakeholders and their expectations), the risk register (which identifies potential risks that may impact project quality), the requirements documentation (which defines the quality requirements for the project deliverables), and the enterprise environmental factors and organizational process assets (which may influence quality planning).

265. What is the purpose of a quality management plan?
a. to define the quality standards and requirements for the project deliverables
b. to identify the quality control activities and tools to be used in the project
c. to establish the roles and responsibilities for quality management in the project
d. all of the above

Answer: d. all of the above. Explanation: The purpose of a quality management plan is to define the quality standards and requirements for the project deliverables, identify the quality control activities and tools to be used in the project, and establish the roles and responsibilities for quality management in the project. The quality management plan is a component of the project management plan and describes how the project team will implement the organization's quality policy. It includes the quality objectives, standards, and metrics for the project, as well as the tools, techniques, and processes that will be used to ensure and control the quality of the project deliverables.

266. Which of the following is not one of the seven basic quality tools?
a. cause-and-effect diagram
b. control chart

c. scatter diagram
d. force field analysis

Answer: d. force field analysis. Explanation: Force field analysis is not one of the seven basic quality tools. The seven basic quality tools, also known as the 7 QC tools, are a set of graphical and statistical techniques used to analyze and solve quality problems. They include cause-and-effect diagrams (also known as fishbone or Ishikawa diagrams), control charts, scatter diagrams, check sheets, histograms, Pareto charts, and flowcharts. Force field analysis is a different technique used to analyze the forces that drive or hinder change in a situation, but it is not specifically related to quality management.

267. What is the purpose of a Pareto chart in project quality management?
a. to identify the root causes of quality problems
b. to monitor the performance of a process over time
c. to prioritize quality issues based on their frequency or impact
d. to illustrate the relationship between two variables

Answer: c. to prioritize quality issues based on their frequency or impact. Explanation: The purpose of a Pareto chart in project quality management is to prioritize quality issues based on their frequency or impact. A Pareto chart is a type of bar graph that displays the relative importance of quality problems or causes, with the most significant issues represented by the tallest bars. The chart is based on the Pareto principle, also known as the 80/20 rule, which states that approximately 80% of the effects come from 20% of the causes. By using a Pareto chart, project teams can focus their quality improvement efforts on the most critical issues that have the greatest impact on project quality.

268. What is the main difference between prevention costs and appraisal costs in cost of quality (COQ) analysis?
a. prevention costs are incurred to avoid quality problems, while appraisal costs are incurred to identify quality problems
b. prevention costs are incurred during project planning, while appraisal costs are incurred during project execution
c. prevention costs are variable costs, while appraisal costs are fixed costs
d. prevention costs are the responsibility of the project manager, while appraisal costs are the responsibility of the quality assurance team

Answer: a. prevention costs are incurred to avoid quality problems, while appraisal costs are incurred to identify quality problems. Explanation: The main difference between prevention costs and appraisal costs in cost of quality (COQ) analysis is that prevention costs are incurred to avoid quality problems before they occur, while appraisal costs are incurred to identify quality problems during or after project execution. Prevention costs include activities such as quality planning, training, process design, and supplier evaluation, which aim to prevent defects and ensure that the project deliverables meet the required quality standards. Appraisal costs include activities such as inspection, testing, and auditing, which aim to detect and measure the level of conformance to the quality standards.

269. What is the purpose of a control chart in project quality management?

a. to identify the root causes of quality problems
b. to prioritize quality issues based on their frequency or impact
c. to monitor the performance of a process over time and detect variations
d. to illustrate the relationship between two variables

Answer: c. to monitor the performance of a process over time and detect variations. Explanation: The purpose of a control chart in project quality management is to monitor the performance of a process over time and detect variations that may indicate quality problems. A control chart is a graphical tool that plots the results of process measurements over time, with upper and lower control limits that define the acceptable range of variation. By comparing the actual process measurements to the control limits, project teams can identify when a process is out of control and take corrective action to bring it back within the acceptable range. Control charts can help to distinguish between common cause variation (inherent in the process) and special cause variation (caused by external factors), and to assess the stability and capability of the process.

270. What is the main objective of the control quality process in project quality management?
a. to define the quality standards and requirements for the project deliverables
b. to ensure that the project processes are followed and that quality problems are prevented
c. to monitor and record the results of quality control activities and recommend necessary changes
d. to continuously improve the quality of project processes and deliverables

Answer: c. to monitor and record the results of quality control activities and recommend necessary changes. Explanation: The main objective of the control quality process in project quality management is to monitor and record the results of quality control activities and recommend necessary changes to ensure that the project deliverables meet the required quality standards. This process involves measuring the quality characteristics of the project deliverables, comparing them to the quality standards and metrics defined in the quality management plan, identifying any defects or nonconformities, and recommending corrective actions to address the quality issues. The control quality process also includes updating the project documents and organizational process assets based on the results of quality control activities, and communicating the quality status to project stakeholders.

271. What is the primary focus of project resource management?
a. managing the financial resources required to complete the project
b. acquiring, developing, and managing the project team and physical resources
c. identifying and engaging project stakeholders to ensure their needs are met
d. planning and managing project communications to ensure effective information exchange

Answer: b. acquiring, developing, and managing the project team and physical resources. Explanation: The primary focus of project resource management is on acquiring, developing, and managing the project team and physical resources needed to successfully complete the project. This knowledge area involves identifying resource requirements, obtaining resources, developing team skills and competencies, managing team performance, and ensuring the efficient and effective use of resources throughout the project lifecycle.

272. Which of the following is not a key process in project resource management?
a. plan resource management
b. estimate activity resources
c. acquire resources
d. control stakeholder engagement

Answer: d. control stakeholder engagement. Explanation: Control stakeholder engagement is not a key process in project resource management but rather a process in the project stakeholder management knowledge area. The key processes in project resource management are plan resource management (defining how to estimate, acquire, manage, and utilize resources), estimate activity resources (estimating the type and quantity of resources needed for each project activity), acquire resources (obtaining team members, facilities, equipment, materials, supplies, and other resources), develop team (improving the competencies, team member interaction, and overall team environment), manage team (tracking team member performance, providing feedback, resolving issues, and managing changes), and control resources (ensuring that the physical resources are available as planned and monitoring the planned versus actual resource utilization).

273. What is the main difference between a resource breakdown structure (RBS) and a work breakdown structure (WBS)?
a. an RBS focuses on the project deliverables, while a WBS focuses on the project activities
b. an RBS is a hierarchical representation of the project resources, while a WBS is a hierarchical representation of the project scope
c. an RBS is used to estimate activity durations, while a WBS is used to estimate activity resources
d. an RBS is created during project execution, while a WBS is created during project planning

Answer: b. an RBS is a hierarchical representation of the project resources, while a WBS is a hierarchical representation of the project scope. Explanation: The main difference between a resource breakdown structure (RBS) and a work breakdown structure (WBS) is their focus and purpose. An RBS is a hierarchical representation of the project resources, organized by category and type, used to facilitate resource planning and management. A WBS, on the other hand, is a hierarchical decomposition of the total scope of work to be carried out by the project team, used to organize and define the total project scope. Both the RBS and WBS are typically created during project planning, but they serve different functions in project management.

274. Which of the following is not an input to the acquire resources process?
a. project management plan
b. enterprise environmental factors
c. organizational process assets
d. resource calendars

Answer: d. resource calendars. Explanation: Resource calendars are not an input to the acquire resources process, but rather an output of the estimate activity resources process. Resource calendars document the working days, shifts, start and end times of the resource availability periods, and any known non-working periods, such as holidays or planned team training. The key inputs to the acquire resources process are the project management plan (which includes the resource management plan and other relevant information), the project documents (such as the project schedule and resource requirements), enterprise environmental factors (such as market conditions and resource availability), and organizational process assets (such as policies, procedures, and templates related to resource acquisition).

275. What is the purpose of a responsibility assignment matrix (RAM) in project resource management?
a. to identify the project stakeholders and their communication requirements
b. to map the project roles and responsibilities to the project scope
c. to define the skills and competencies required for each project role
d. to illustrate the relationship between the project activities and the resources assigned to them

Answer: b. to map the project roles and responsibilities to the project scope. Explanation: The purpose of a responsibility assignment matrix (RAM) in project resource management is to map the project roles and responsibilities to the project scope, deliverables, or activities. A RAM, also known as a RACI (Responsible, Accountable, Consulted, Informed) matrix, is a grid that shows the project team members' participation in completing project deliverables or activities. It clarifies the roles and responsibilities of the team members and helps to ensure that each deliverable or activity has a clear owner and that all team members understand their involvement in the project.

276. Which of the following is not one of the five stages of team development according to Tuckman's model?
a. forming
b. storming
c. norming
d. performing
e. adjourning
f. transforming

Answer: f. transforming. Explanation: Transforming is not one of the five stages of team development according to Tuckman's model. The five stages are forming (the team comes together and starts to understand the project goals and their roles), storming (team members compete for position and have different opinions on how to approach the project), norming (the team begins to work together, agree on rules and values, and make progress towards the goals), performing (the team is highly functional, autonomous, and able to handle complex tasks), and adjourning (the team completes the work and disbands). Some variations of the model include a fifth stage called "mourning" or "termination," but transforming is not a commonly recognized stage.

277. What is the main objective of the develop team process in project resource management?
a. to identify the skills and competencies required for the project
b. to obtain the human resources needed to complete the project work
c. to improve the competencies and interaction of team members to enhance project performance
d. to monitor team member performance and provide feedback

Answer: c. to improve the competencies and interaction of team members to enhance project performance. Explanation: The main objective of the develop team process in project resource management is to improve the competencies, interaction, and overall team environment to enhance project performance. This process involves conducting training, team-building activities, and other initiatives to develop the technical, interpersonal, and contextual skills of the team members, foster a collaborative and supportive team culture, and create an environment that enables high team performance. Identifying skill requirements and obtaining human resources are part of the plan resource management and acquire resources processes, while monitoring performance and providing feedback are part of the manage team process.

278. What is the purpose of a team charter in project resource management?
a. to define the project scope, objectives, and deliverables
b. to identify the project stakeholders and their expectations
c. to establish the rules, norms, and operating principles for the project team
d. to assess the skills and competencies of the project team members

Answer: c. to establish the rules, norms, and operating principles for the project team. Explanation: The purpose of a team charter in project resource management is to establish the rules, norms, and operating principles that guide the behavior and performance of the project team. A team charter is a document that defines the team's purpose, goals, roles and responsibilities, communication protocols, decision-making processes, conflict resolution methods, and other ground rules that help the team work together effectively. It serves as a "social contract" among the team members and helps to create a shared understanding and commitment to the project objectives and team norms.

279. What is the main difference between resource leveling and resource smoothing?
a. resource leveling adjusts the project schedule to address resource overallocation, while resource smoothing adjusts the resource allocation to fit the project schedule
b. resource leveling is used to optimize resource utilization, while resource smoothing is used to minimize resource fluctuations
c. resource leveling is performed during project planning, while resource smoothing is performed during project execution
d. resource leveling is the responsibility of the project manager, while resource smoothing is the responsibility of the functional managers

Answer: a. resource leveling adjusts the project schedule to address resource overallocation, while resource smoothing adjusts the resource allocation to fit the project schedule. Explanation: The main difference between resource leveling and resource smoothing is how they address resource constraints in project scheduling. Resource leveling is a technique that adjusts the project schedule by delaying or splitting activities to resolve resource overallocation, where the demand for a resource exceeds its available capacity. This may result in an extended project duration but ensures that the resource limits are not exceeded. Resource smoothing, on the other hand, is a technique that adjusts the resource allocation within the available float or slack to minimize resource fluctuations and maintain a stable resource profile, without changing the project duration. Both techniques aim to optimize resource utilization and balance the supply and demand of resources, but they use different approaches to achieve this goal.

280. What is the main objective of the control resources process in project resource management?
a. to identify the types and quantities of resources required for the project
b. to obtain the resources needed to complete the project work
c. to develop the skills and competencies of the project team members
d. to monitor and manage the allocation and utilization of physical and team resources

Answer: d. to monitor and manage the allocation and utilization of physical and team resources.
Explanation: The main objective of the control resources process in project resource management is to monitor and manage the allocation and utilization of physical and team resources to ensure that the project objectives are met. This process involves comparing the planned versus actual resource utilization, identifying and correcting any deviations or issues, and making adjustments to the resource allocation as needed. The control resources process helps to optimize resource use, minimize waste, and ensure that the project team has the necessary resources to complete the work efficiently and effectively. Identifying resource requirements, obtaining resources, and developing team skills are addressed in other processes, such as estimate activity resources, acquire resources, and develop team.

281. During a project's execution phase, the project manager identifies significant gaps between stakeholder expectations and project deliverables. What is the most appropriate first action for the project manager to address this issue?
a. Redefine the project scope to meet stakeholder expectations.
b. Arrange a meeting to realign stakeholder expectations with the current project deliverables.
c. Update the project management plan without consulting stakeholders.
d. Ignore the gaps as long as the project is within the approved budget.

Answer: b. Arrange a meeting to realign stakeholder expectations with the current project deliverables.
Explanation: Effective communication and engagement with stakeholders are critical in project management to ensure that all parties have a clear and common understanding of the project's deliverables. Option b is the best approach as it involves discussing the discrepancies and working towards a consensus, which is vital for maintaining project alignment and support. Options a and c fail to address the need for stakeholder involvement and consensus, while d ignores potential issues that could escalate and affect project success.

282. A project team is struggling to meet communication expectations outlined in the stakeholder engagement plan. Which tool should they prioritize to enhance efficiency and effectiveness of communications?
a. Work breakdown structure
b. Lessons learned register
c. Communication technology
d. Risk management plan

Answer: c. Communication technology. Explanation: The use of appropriate communication technology is essential for effective project communication management, especially in projects involving diverse or remote teams. Communication technology tools can significantly enhance the efficiency and effectiveness of communications by ensuring timely and precise information exchange. The work breakdown structure (option a) and risk management plan (option d) are critical for project planning and control but do not directly facilitate communication. The lessons learned register (option b) is valuable for capturing insights and improvements but is not a tool for active communication enhancement.

283. In an ongoing project, the project manager wants to ensure that communication is as effective as possible. What is the most crucial element to consider when planning communications?
a. The cost of communication
b. The physical means of communication
c. The communication preferences of the team members
d. The frequency of communication

Answer: c. The communication preferences of the team members. Explanation: Understanding and accommodating the communication preferences of team members are vital for effective communication. This approach ensures that information is received and understood as intended, thereby enhancing collaboration and productivity. While costs (option a), means (option b), and frequency (option d) are also important, they are secondary to ensuring that the communication style aligns with team preferences to maximize understanding and engagement.

284. A project manager discovers that the weekly project status reports are not being read by several key stakeholders. What should the project manager do first to address this issue?
a. Switch to a more detailed monthly report format.
b. Investigate the reasons why the reports are not being read.
c. Discontinue the reports and update only in meetings.
d. Send reminders to stakeholders to read the reports.

Answer: b. Investigate the reasons why the reports are not being read. Explanation: Investigating why the reports are not engaging or reaching stakeholders can provide insights necessary to adjust the method or content of the communications effectively. Understanding the root cause is essential before making decisions about changing the communication strategy. Options a, c, and d assume actions without understanding the underlying issues, which might not resolve the communication problem.

285. During a project meeting, a key stakeholder expresses concerns that not all voices are being heard in project decisions. What is the best method for the project manager to ensure more inclusive communication?
a. Hold smaller, more frequent meetings with various subgroups.
b. Limit the meeting attendance to senior project members only.
c. Increase the frequency of the status updates via email.
d. Provide a suggestion box for anonymous feedback.

Answer: a. Hold smaller, more frequent meetings with various subgroups. Explanation: Holding smaller meetings can foster a more comfortable environment where more stakeholders feel encouraged to participate and express their opinions. This approach helps in capturing a diverse range of inputs, essential for inclusive decision-making. Limiting meeting attendance (option b) could exacerbate the issue by reducing inclusivity, while increasing email frequency (option c) and anonymous feedback (option d) do not directly address the need for active and open dialogue during decision-making.

286. A project manager notices that the project's intended outcomes are not well understood among the team members. Which communication tool is most effective to clarify these outcomes?
a. A project charter
b. A Gantt chart
c. A stakeholder map
d. A risk register

Answer: a. A project charter. Explanation: The project charter is a critical document that outlines the project's objectives, scope, and participants. It serves as an essential tool for communicating the project's goals and expected outcomes to all project members, ensuring everyone is aligned from the start. While a Gantt chart (option b) helps with scheduling, a stakeholder map (option c) identifies project influences, and a risk register (option d) focuses on potential issues, none are as directly relevant to defining and communicating project outcomes as the project charter.

287. A project communication plan fails to mention any protocols for informal communications. What risk does this omission most likely introduce to the project?
a. Misinterpretations of formal communications
b. Delays in decision-making
c. Misunderstandings and misinformation
d. Over-reliance on formal reports

Answer: c. Misunderstandings and misinformation. Explanation: Without clear guidelines for informal communications, there is a high risk of misunderstandings and the spread of misinformation among project team members and stakeholders. Informal communications are frequent in projects, and guidelines help ensure that these interactions are constructive and aligned with project objectives. Misinterpretations of formal communications (option a) and delays in decision-making (option b) are also potential issues, but they are less directly impacted by the lack of informal communication protocols.

288. In a complex project involving multiple stakeholders, which technique would best ensure that all necessary information is conveyed effectively during communications?
a. Utilizing a single communication method for simplicity
b. Tailoring the communication style to each stakeholder group
c. Sending mass emails for efficiency
d. Limiting communication to key stakeholders only

Answer: b. Tailoring the communication style to each stakeholder group. Explanation: Different stakeholders may have different needs, priorities, and preferences in how they receive information. Tailoring the communication style, medium, and frequency to match each group ensures that the message is effectively conveyed and understood. This approach helps in managing stakeholder engagement more effectively than a one-size-fits-all method (option a), mass emails (option c), or restricted communications (option d), which might overlook or alienate important participants.

289. After receiving feedback that project updates are not clear, what should the project manager do to improve the clarity of the communications?
a. Use more technical jargon to enhance precision.
b. Include more detailed statistical data in updates.
c. Simplify the language and focus on key points.
d. Increase the length of the written updates for completeness.

Answer: c. Simplify the language and focus on key points. Explanation: Clarity in communication is often best achieved by simplifying the language and focusing on essential information, making it easier for all stakeholders to understand the updates without unnecessary complexity. Using technical jargon (option a) may confuse non-specialist stakeholders, while more detailed data (option b) and longer updates (option d) could potentially overwhelm recipients and detract from the clarity of the message.

290. When planning project communications, which factor should be prioritized to adapt communications to the needs of international stakeholders?
a. The preferred language of the project manager
b. The technological capabilities of the project team
c. The cultural and linguistic preferences of the stakeholders
d. The time zone of the project headquarters

Answer: c. The cultural and linguistic preferences of the stakeholders. Explanation: Effective international communication must consider the cultural and linguistic preferences of the stakeholders to ensure messages are both understood and respectfully received. This consideration helps in building trust and enhancing cooperation among culturally diverse teams. While technology (option b) and time zones (option d) are also important, they do not directly address the fundamental need for culturally sensitive communication that respects the stakeholders' backgrounds.

291. A project manager is evaluating risks for a new infrastructure project. Which of the following would be considered a secondary risk?
a. The discovery of archaeological artifacts during excavation, halting progress.
b. Delays in project schedule due to sudden unavailability of key staff.
c. Increase in material costs due to new tariffs imposed on imported steel.
d. Development of a risk response plan that inadvertently creates new risks.

Answer: d. Development of a risk response plan that inadvertently creates new risks. Explanation: Secondary risks arise as a direct outcome of implementing a risk response. The other options, such as archaeological finds (option a), staff unavailability (option b), and increased material costs (option c), are primary risks that trigger directly from identified project uncertainties.

292. During the quantitative risk analysis phase, what is the primary purpose of using Monte Carlo simulations?
a. To identify the risks associated with the project.
b. To determine the probability of meeting the project deadlines.
c. To allocate the necessary resources for risk mitigation.

d. To assess the impact of risks on project scheduling and budgeting.

Answer: b. To determine the probability of meeting the project deadlines. Explanation: Monte Carlo simulations are used in project management to model the probability of different outcomes in processes that are uncertain, helping project managers understand the likelihood of completing the project on time and within budget. This tool does not identify new risks (option a) nor specifically allocate resources (option c), although it helps in understanding impacts on scheduling and budgeting (option d) which is broader than just assessing impacts.

293. Which risk response strategy should a project manager use when there is a high impact but low probability of risk occurrence?
a. Mitigate
b. Accept
c. Transfer
d. Avoid

Answer: b. Accept. Explanation: Acceptance is a risk response strategy appropriate for risks that have low probability and high impact where it may not be cost-effective or possible to respond actively (mitigate, transfer, or avoid). Acceptance means being prepared to deal with the consequences should the risk occur. Mitigation (option a) involves reducing the probability or impact of the risk, which isn't always feasible for high-impact, low-probability risks. Transfer (option c) involves shifting the impact to a third party and is typically used for high-probability or high-cost risks. Avoidance (option d) completely eliminates the risk but may not be possible or practical for all risks, especially those with low probability.

294. A project in its early stages has identified a significant risk of legal challenges due to a newly enacted regulation. Which strategy would be most effective in managing this risk?
a. Ignoring the risk until it becomes unavoidable.
b. Seeking expert legal advice to understand compliance requirements.
c. Transferring the risk to a contractor.
d. Accepting the risk as part of the business environment.

Answer: b. Seeking expert legal advice to understand compliance requirements. Explanation: Proactively seeking expert advice to fully understand and comply with new regulations is the best strategy for managing legal risks. This enables the project to mitigate potential legal challenges effectively. Transferring the risk (option c) might not eliminate the legal obligations of the original project team, while ignoring (option a) or accepting (option d) the risk does not actively manage or mitigate the identified risk.

295. A project has several risk management strategies in place. Which tool or technique will most effectively monitor these risks?
a. SWOT analysis
b. Risk audits
c. Earned value analysis
d. Stakeholder analysis

Answer: b. Risk audits. Explanation: Risk audits are used to examine and review the effectiveness of risk responses in dealing with identified risks and ensuring that the risk management process remains effective throughout the project lifecycle. SWOT analysis (option a) is more generally used for strategic assessment, not ongoing monitoring. Earned value analysis (option c) monitors project performance against the plan but is not specific to risks. Stakeholder analysis (option d) helps understand stakeholder perspectives and does not monitor risk responses.

296. When prioritizing risks for further analysis and action, what should a project manager consider first?
a. The cost of potential risk responses.
b. The risk's proximity to the critical path.
c. The overall impact of the risk on project objectives.
d. The ease of implementing risk responses.

Answer: c. The overall impact of the risk on project objectives. Explanation: The primary consideration in prioritizing risks should be their potential impact on project objectives, as this directly relates to the project's success. Factors such as cost (option a), proximity to the critical path (option b), and ease of response (option d) are secondary to understanding the risk's potential effect on the project's goals.

297. In managing project risks, which approach is best for a risk with high probability and high impact?
a. Avoidance
b. Transfer
c. Acceptance
d. Exploitation

Answer: a. Avoidance. Explanation: For risks with both high probability and high impact, avoidance is typically the most prudent strategy. This approach involves changing the project plan to eliminate the risk or condition. Transfer (option b) shifts the impact but does not eliminate the risk. Acceptance (option c) is generally not advisable for high-impact risks, and exploitation (option d) is used for positive risks (opportunities).

298. If a project manager decides to use the 'exploit' strategy for a risk, what is their objective?
a. To eliminate the risk entirely.
b. To reduce the probability of the risk occurring.
c. To ensure the opportunity associated with the risk is realized.
d. To pass the impact of the risk to another party.

Answer: c. To ensure the opportunity associated with the risk is realized. Explanation: Exploit strategy is used for opportunities (positive risks) where the objective is to ensure that the opportunity is realized to the project's benefit. It involves actively seeking to make the opportunity happen. This is different from eliminating a risk (option a), reducing its probability (option b), or transferring it (option d).

299. A risk response plan for an IT project includes provisions for both mitigation and contingency measures. What is the primary difference between these two types of responses?

a. Mitigation strategies are implemented before the risk occurs, while contingency measures are used only if the risk occurs.
b. Mitigation strategies are more costly than contingency measures.
c. Contingency measures are documented in the risk management plan, while mitigation strategies are not.
d. Contingency measures address only identified risks, while mitigation can address both identified and unidentified risks.

Answer: a. Mitigation strategies are implemented before the risk occurs, while contingency measures are used only if the risk occurs. Explanation: Mitigation involves actions taken to reduce the probability and impact of a risk before it occurs, whereas contingency measures are planned strategies that are executed in response to the risk if it occurs. This distinction focuses on the timing and condition of the response's implementation.

300. When integrating risk management processes with quality management processes, what is the primary benefit for the project?
a. Reduced documentation
b. Enhanced stakeholder satisfaction
c. Lowered direct costs
d. Improved risk identification and response strategies

Answer: d. Improved risk identification and response strategies. Explanation: Integrating risk management with quality management processes allows for a more thorough approach to identifying potential risks and crafting more effective responses, as quality issues can often signal or constitute project risks. This integration helps in preventing quality issues from becoming larger risks and vice versa, enhancing the project's overall management approach.

301. During the procurement planning process, a project manager decides to use a fixed-price contract. What is a primary risk associated with this type of contract from the buyer's perspective?
a. The seller may experience financial loss if the costs exceed the agreed price.
b. The buyer may face quality issues as the seller might cut corners to control costs.
c. The contract will be too flexible, allowing scope creep without proper adjustments.
d. The seller might frequently request changes to the contract terms to cover costs.

Answer: b. The buyer may face quality issues as the seller might cut corners to control costs. Explanation: In fixed-price contracts, the seller bears the cost risk because they are committed to completing the project within an agreed price. This scenario might incentivize the seller to reduce costs in ways that could compromise the quality of the deliverables. Option a describes a risk for the seller, not the buyer. Option c is incorrect because fixed-price contracts are typically stringent about scope, reducing the likelihood of scope creep. Option d is less likely because fixed-price contracts limit the feasibility of renegotiating terms once the contract is finalized.

302. A project requires specialized equipment that only a few suppliers can provide. To manage this risk, what procurement document should the project manager prioritize to obtain detailed proposals from potential sellers?
a. Request for Information (RFI)
b. Request for Quotation (RFQ)
c. Request for Proposal (RFP)
d. Invitation for Bid (IFB)

Answer: c. Request for Proposal (RFP). Explanation: An RFP is suitable when the project requirements are complex and may require detailed proposals on how the project needs will be met, including how the specialized equipment will be provided and at what cost. RFIs are generally used for gathering information, RFQs are used when cost is the primary concern with standard goods, and IFBs are typically used for more straightforward bidding processes where the requirements are clear and the cost is the decisive factor.

303. When negotiating a contract with a new software vendor, what aspect should a project manager emphasize to ensure clarity and prevent disputes during project execution?
a. Penalties for early termination
b. Specifics of the project scope and deliverables
c. Incentives for early completion
d. Flexibility in payment terms

Answer: b. Specifics of the project scope and deliverables. Explanation: Clear definitions of scope and deliverables in a contract are crucial to avoid misunderstandings and disputes about what is expected of each party. This clarity helps ensure that all participants are aligned with the project's objectives and requirements. While penalties (option a), incentives (option c), and payment terms (option d) are important, they do not directly impact the mutual understanding of project expectations as significantly as the clear articulation of scope and deliverables.

304. Which type of contract provides the greatest incentive for the seller to control costs and operate efficiently?
a. Cost Plus Fixed Fee (CPFF)
b. Cost Plus Incentive Fee (CPIF)
c. Fixed Price Incentive Fee (FPIF)
d. Time and Materials (T&M)

Answer: c. Fixed Price Incentive Fee (FPIF). Explanation: FPIF contracts combine the cost-controlling incentives of a fixed-price contract with the flexibility of incentive fees based on performance. This structure encourages the seller to control costs and complete the work efficiently to meet defined performance targets. CPFF and CPIF (options a and b) reimburse the seller for all legitimate costs, which reduces their motivation to lower costs. T&M (option d) might lead to inefficiencies as payment is based on time and materials used, not on cost efficiency.

305. In a project characterized by a high degree of uncertainty, what procurement contract would be least appropriate?
a. Cost Plus Award Fee (CPAF)
b. Fixed Price with Economic Price Adjustment (FP-EPA)
c. Firm Fixed Price (FFP)
d. Cost Plus Incentive Fee (CPIF)

Answer: c. Firm Fixed Price (FFP). Explanation: FFP contracts are least suitable for projects with high uncertainty because they do not allow for adjusting the contract price based on actual costs incurred, which can be unpredictable in uncertain environments. CPAF, FP-EPA, and CPIF (options a, b, and d) provide mechanisms to adjust costs or fees based on different criteria like performance or economic conditions, making them more adaptable to changing project conditions.

306. When drafting a contract for the acquisition of IT services, what is the most critical element to specify to avoid scope creep?
a. Detailed service level agreements (SLAs)
b. General terms and conditions
c. Supplier's annual turnover
d. Penalties for non-compliance

Answer: a. Detailed service level agreements (SLAs). Explanation: SLAs are critical in IT service contracts as they clearly define what services will be provided, the expected level of service, and the metrics by which services will be measured. This level of detail helps prevent scope creep by clearly defining the boundaries of the contract's coverage. General terms and conditions (option b) are important but not as specifically geared toward controlling scope. Supplier's financial details (option c) and penalties (option d) do not directly prevent scope expansion.

307. In a project with significant environmental risks, what type of contract would best protect the buyer from potential increases in costs due to regulatory changes?
a. Firm Fixed Price (FFP)
b. Cost Plus Fixed Fee (CPFF)
c. Cost Plus Incentive Fee (CPIF)
d. Fixed Price with Economic Price Adjustment (FP-EPA)

Answer: d. Fixed Price with Economic Price Adjustment (FP-EPA). Explanation: FP-EPA contracts are designed to protect both parties from financial risks associated with economic changes, including regulatory adjustments. This contract type allows for price adjustments based on defined economic conditions, which could include changes in regulations affecting environmental factors. FFP (option a) offers no flexibility for economic changes, while CPFF and CPIF (options b and c) place the cost risk more on the buyer.

308. For a long-term project sensitive to market price fluctuations, which contractual method is best suited to mitigate financial risk for the buyer?
a. Firm Fixed Price (FFP)

b. Cost Plus Award Fee (CPAF)
c. Fixed Price with Economic Price Adjustment (FP-EPA)
d. Cost Plus Incentive Fee (CPIF)

Answer: c. Fixed Price with Economic Price Adjustment (FP-EPA). Explanation: FP-EPA contracts are particularly beneficial for long-term projects where cost predictability is necessary, but there is also a need to accommodate financial risks arising from significant market fluctuations. This type of contract allows adjustments to the agreed price based on predefined economic indicators, providing a balance between cost certainty and flexibility.

309. If a project manager needs to procure custom software development services, which evaluation criterion is most critical?
a. The lowest bid price
b. The technical capability of the vendor
c. The vendor's geographical location
d. The length of time the vendor has been in business

Answer: b. The technical capability of the vendor. Explanation: For custom software development, the vendor's technical expertise and capability to deliver as per the project's specific requirements are paramount. While cost (option a), location (option c), and experience (option d) are significant, none outweigh the importance of having the necessary technical skills to meet the unique demands of the project.

310. A project manager is planning to outsource part of a construction project. What should be a key consideration when selecting a contract type?
a. The degree of project scope clarity
b. The preference for multi-year contracts
c. The nationality of the subcontractor
d. The current economic conditions

Answer: a. The degree of project scope clarity. Explanation: The clarity of the project scope is crucial in determining the most appropriate contract type. Clear, well-defined scopes are suitable for fixed-price contracts, while more ambiguous scopes might require a cost-reimbursable contract to accommodate changes more flexibly. Other factors like contract duration (option b), subcontractor nationality (option c), and economic conditions (option d) are also important but secondary to the impact of scope definition on contract selection.

311. A project manager is conducting a stakeholder analysis for a new urban development project. What is the most critical information to determine about each stakeholder?
a. The financial contribution of each stakeholder to the project
b. The potential for each stakeholder to impact the project's objectives
c. The number of stakeholders involved in similar projects
d. The geographical location of each stakeholder's headquarters

Answer: b. The potential for each stakeholder to impact the project's objectives. Explanation: Understanding the influence and potential impact of each stakeholder on the project's objectives is crucial for effective stakeholder management. This knowledge helps prioritize stakeholder engagement strategies to ensure project success. Financial contributions (option a) and geographical locations (option d) are less critical than the influence they may wield, and the number of similar projects (option c) does not directly relate to their impact on the current project.

312. A project in a highly regulated industry is about to launch. Which stakeholder's interests should most influence the project management plan?
a. Local government bodies
b. The project management team
c. Future users of the project's outputs
d. Media organizations

Answer: a. Local government bodies. Explanation: In a regulated industry, compliance with local government regulations is critical to project success. Their requirements often have significant implications for project scope, budget, schedule, and quality. While future users (option c) and the project team (option b) are important, non-compliance with governmental regulations can halt a project, making these stakeholders paramount. Media (option d) has an influence on public perception but does not impact the regulatory aspects of the project management plan.

313. During a project lifecycle, a new stakeholder group is identified that is crucial to the project's continuation. What is the first action the project manager should take?
a. Inform the project sponsor about the need for additional budget.
b. Update the stakeholder register to include the new group.
c. Reassess the project's risk management plan.
d. Organize a press release to acknowledge the new stakeholder group.

Answer: b. Update the stakeholder register to include the new group. Explanation: When a new stakeholder group is identified, it is essential to first update the stakeholder register. This ensures that they are formally recognized within the project's communication and management plans, allowing for appropriate engagement strategies. Adjusting the budget (option a), reassessing risks (option c), or public announcements (option d) may follow but only after formally recognizing and understanding the stakeholder's influence and needs.

314. A project team is dealing with conflicting stakeholder demands that are impacting project progress. What technique should the project manager employ to resolve these conflicts effectively?
a. Increase the frequency of project team meetings.
b. Deploy a stakeholder engagement assessment matrix.
c. Conduct a benefit-cost analysis for the requested changes.
d. Limit communication to only major stakeholders.

Answer: b. Deploy a stakeholder engagement assessment matrix. Explanation: Using a stakeholder engagement assessment matrix allows the project manager to systematically evaluate and manage stakeholder needs and expectations, and address conflicts by understanding their current engagement levels versus desired levels. This tool helps in prioritizing stakeholder issues based on their impact and influence. Simply increasing meetings (option a) or restricting communication (option d) does not address the root causes of conflicts, and a cost-benefit analysis (option c) is more suitable for evaluating project changes rather than resolving stakeholder conflicts.

315. In the execution phase, it is discovered that an influential stakeholder's expectations are not aligned with the project's deliverables. What should the project manager do next?
a. Redefine the project scope to meet the stakeholder's expectations.
b. Arrange a meeting to discuss the discrepancies with the stakeholder.
c. Document the issue in the project risk register.
d. Proceed with the project as planned and address discrepancies later.

Answer: b. Arrange a meeting to discuss the discrepancies with the stakeholder. Explanation: Directly engaging with the stakeholder to discuss and clarify any discrepancies between their expectations and the project's deliverables is critical. This proactive approach helps to realign expectations or adjust project plans as needed, maintaining stakeholder satisfaction and project integrity. Redefining the project scope (option a) prematurely or documenting as a risk (option c) without engagement might not resolve the underlying issues. Ignoring the discrepancy (option d) could lead to greater issues down the line.

316. How should a project manager handle a situation where stakeholder interests conflict with the ethical standards of the profession?
a. Prioritize stakeholder interests to maintain good relations.
b. Follow professional ethical standards strictly.
c. Seek a compromise between ethical standards and stakeholder interests.
d. Resign from the project to avoid ethical dilemmas.

Answer: b. Follow professional ethical standards strictly. Explanation: Adhering to professional ethical standards is non-negotiable, even when stakeholder interests conflict with these standards. The integrity of the project and the profession must be upheld. Seeking compromises (option c) or prioritizing stakeholder interests (option a) could potentially harm the project's ethical standing and the project manager's professional integrity. Resigning from the project (option d) is an extreme measure that does not actively resolve the ethical conflict.

317. During project planning, which stakeholder analysis output can best guide the development of communication plans?
a. Stakeholder engagement levels
b. Stakeholder influence/power matrix
c. List of stakeholder names and positions
d. Historical information on stakeholder behaviors

Answer: b. Stakeholder influence/power matrix. Explanation: The stakeholder influence/power matrix is a vital tool for understanding the levels of influence and interest of each stakeholder. This information is crucial for developing effective communication plans that cater to the needs and expectations of the most influential stakeholders, ensuring project support and successful management. While engagement levels (option a) and historical behaviors (option d) are useful, they do not provide the strategic insight required for communication planning as directly as the influence/power matrix.

318. What is the most effective strategy for maintaining long-term stakeholder engagement throughout a project?
a. Regular updates via mass email communications.
b. Personalized updates and targeted communications.
c. Periodic rewards and recognition for stakeholder contributions.
d. Exclusive meetings with high-power, high-interest stakeholders only.

Answer: b. Personalized updates and targeted communications. Explanation: Personalized and targeted communications are critical for maintaining long-term stakeholder engagement. This approach ensures that communications are relevant and meaningful to each stakeholder, respecting their specific interests and levels of influence within the project. Mass emails (option a) may be perceived as impersonal, rewards (option c) might not address communication needs effectively, and exclusive meetings (option d) could alienate other important stakeholders.

319. A new stakeholder is added midway through a project, which could potentially alter the project timeline. What should the project manager do first?
a. Re-baseline the project schedule immediately.
b. Assess the new stakeholder's potential impact on the project.
c. Request additional budget to accommodate the new stakeholder.
d. Introduce the new stakeholder in the next project meeting.

Answer: b. Assess the new stakeholder's potential impact on the project. Explanation: Before making any changes to the project, it is crucial to assess the potential impact of the new stakeholder. This assessment helps determine the necessary adjustments to the project plan, schedule, or budget. Immediate re-baselining (option a) or budget adjustments (option c) without this understanding may lead to inappropriate or inefficient changes. While introduction in a meeting (option d) is important, it should follow an initial impact assessment.

320. When a project impacts multiple external stakeholders, which approach should a project manager take to manage the potential increase in scope due to their varied requirements?
a. Adopt an open scope policy to accommodate all stakeholder requests.
b. Implement strict change control procedures to manage scope changes.
c. Focus only on the requirements of the most influential external stakeholders.
d. Increase the project budget to cover potential scope expansions.

Answer: b. Implement strict change control procedures to manage scope changes. Explanation: Implementing strict change control procedures is essential when dealing with multiple external stakeholders to effectively manage and control scope changes. This approach ensures that all changes are evaluated and approved systematically, preventing scope creep and maintaining project integrity. An open scope policy (option a) could lead to unmanageable increases in scope, focusing solely on influential stakeholders (option c) may ignore less influential but still important needs, and increasing the budget (option d) does not address the root issue of scope control.

321. During the execution phase of a project, the project manager notices that the integration of various project elements is not proceeding as planned. What should the project manager do first?
a. Adjust the project baseline to reflect current progress.
b. Conduct an integrated change control process.
c. Reassign project team members to new tasks.
d. Consult the project sponsor for advice.

Answer: b. Conduct an integrated change control process. Explanation: When integration issues arise, the first step should be to engage the integrated change control process, which assesses the impact of changes and adjusts the project plan, scope, and resources accordingly. This ensures all changes are reviewed and approved systematically, maintaining project alignment. Adjusting the baseline (option a) without a formal review, reassigning team members (option c) prematurely, and consulting the sponsor (option d) before assessing changes might not effectively address integration issues.

322. A project manager is about to initiate a project but realizes there is a significant misalignment between stakeholder expectations and the project's objectives. What should be done to address this before proceeding?
a. Redefine the project scope to align with stakeholder expectations.
b. Initiate a stakeholder engagement strategy to realign expectations.
c. Proceed with the project as planned and manage expectations through status meetings.
d. Cancel the project due to conflicting objectives.

Answer: b. Initiate a stakeholder engagement strategy to realign expectations. Explanation: Before altering project plans or scope, it is crucial to engage stakeholders to realign their expectations with the project's objectives through targeted communication and negotiation. This helps in establishing a clear understanding and support, preventing potential conflicts during execution. Redefining the scope (option a) or canceling the project (option d) may be premature without first attempting to address the misalignment through dialogue.

323. A project is in its planning phase when a new regulatory requirement is introduced that impacts the project scope. What is the project manager's best course of action?
a. Ignore the regulation until the execution phase.
b. Update the project management plan to reflect the new requirement.
c. Consult the project team for opinions on whether to adhere to the regulation.
d. Apply for an exemption from the regulation.

Answer: b. Update the project management plan to reflect the new requirement. Explanation: When new regulatory requirements arise that impact the project scope, the project management plan should be updated to ensure compliance. This includes adjusting the scope, schedule, and cost baselines as necessary. Consulting the team (option c) or applying for an exemption (option d) might not ensure compliance, and ignoring the regulation (option a) could lead to significant risks and penalties.

324. In the context of Project Integration Management, what is the primary purpose of the Direct and Manage Project Work process?
a. To track project performance and make necessary adjustments.
b. To handle the complete integration of all project work.
c. To develop the project charter and define initial scope.
d. To ensure all project deliverables are produced as planned.

Answer: d. To ensure all project deliverables are produced as planned. Explanation: The Direct and Manage Project Work process is primarily concerned with carrying out the project management plan and ensuring that project deliverables are produced according to specifications, on time, and within budget. While integration (option b) and adjustments (option a) are part of this process, its core focus is on the execution of planned activities to produce project outputs.

325. When a project manager is integrating project plans, which element should be prioritized for a successful Project Integration Management?
a. Risk management plans
b. Cost management plans
c. Change management plans
d. Quality management plans

Answer: c. Change management plans. Explanation: Effective integration of project plans must prioritize change management plans because these plans provide the framework for managing, approving, and documenting changes across all aspects of the project. This ensures project objectives remain aligned with organizational goals despite alterations. While risk, cost, and quality plans (options a, b, and d) are important, they are all impacted by how changes are managed.

326. How should a project manager ensure that project integration is maintained when multiple departments and external contractors are involved?
a. By holding frequent project status meetings with all parties.
b. By using a project management software tool.
c. By establishing a project integration management team.
d. By documenting all project decisions and changes.

Answer: c. By establishing a project integration management team. Explanation: Establishing a dedicated integration management team ensures that there is a focused effort on maintaining the cohesive management of project elements, especially when multiple departments and external contractors are involved. This team can address integration challenges that arise and keep the project aligned with its objectives. While documentation (option d), software tools (option b), and meetings (option a) support integration, a dedicated team provides continuous oversight and proactive management.

327. What is the main advantage of performing the Integrated Change Control process in project management?
a. It speeds up the decision-making process.
b. It helps in reallocating the project budget.

c. It ensures changes are agreed upon by all stakeholders.

d. It avoids the need for a formal project closure phase.

Answer: c. It ensures changes are agreed upon by all stakeholders. Explanation: The Integrated Change Control process is crucial as it ensures that all proposed changes are reviewed, approved, and documented across all stakeholders, maintaining project coherence and alignment. This process prevents unilateral decisions that could disrupt project harmony and objectives, ensuring collaborative decision-making.

328. Which tool or technique is most effective in assisting with the integration of different aspects of a project plan?

a. Expert judgment

b. Project management information system (PMIS)

c. Analytical techniques

d. Benchmarking

Answer: b. Project management information system (PMIS). Explanation: A PMIS is an effective tool for integrating various aspects of a project plan as it provides a central repository for information and supports the coordination of scheduling, budgeting, and resource allocation. It facilitates communication among project team members and stakeholders, thereby enhancing overall project integration.

329. What is a critical factor for maintaining integration throughout the project lifecycle?

a. Regular risk audits

b. Continuous stakeholder engagement

c. Frequent scope reviews

d. Ongoing project documentation

Answer: b. Continuous stakeholder engagement. Explanation: Continuous stakeholder engagement is critical for maintaining project integration as it ensures that stakeholder expectations and needs are continuously aligned with the project's progress and changes. This alignment helps in managing expectations and securing ongoing support, which is vital for project success.

330. When should a project manager establish a baseline for measuring project integration performance?

a. During the project closing phase

b. After the first project deliverable is completed

c. At the beginning of the project planning phase

d. Once the project scope is fully defined

Answer: d. Once the project scope is fully defined. Explanation: Establishing a baseline for integration performance should occur once the project scope is fully defined. This provides a clear framework against which all project activities, changes, and outcomes can be measured and managed effectively, ensuring that the project remains aligned with its defined objectives.

331. A project manager is tasked with developing a project charter for a new client service implementation. What is the most critical element to include in the project charter to ensure project governance?
a. Detailed project budget
b. High-level project risks
c. Project scope statement
d. List of project milestones

Answer: c. Project scope statement. Explanation: The project scope statement is critical for the project charter as it defines the boundaries of the project, what it will and will not include, providing a basis for making future project decisions and for project governance. It establishes clear expectations and deliverables. While risks (option b) and milestones (option d) are important, they do not provide the governance framework that a scope statement does. A detailed budget (option a) is usually developed after the charter during the planning phase.

332. In the initial stage of a project, which stakeholder is primarily responsible for authorizing the project charter?
a. Project manager
b. Project sponsor
c. Chief Financial Officer
d. Lead consultant

Answer: b. Project sponsor. Explanation: The project sponsor is primarily responsible for authorizing the project charter, which signifies formal approval to commence the project and allocates the necessary resources. The project manager (option a) typically develops the charter but does not authorize it. The CFO (option c) and lead consultant (option d) may contribute insights or approvals but are not primarily responsible for the charter's authorization.

333. When preparing a project charter, what is essential to clarify the project's purpose and objectives?
a. A detailed project timeline
b. A comprehensive risk assessment
c. A concise statement of work
d. An extensive stakeholder list

Answer: c. A concise statement of work. Explanation: A concise statement of work (SOW) in the project charter clearly outlines the purpose, objectives, and key deliverables of the project. It provides a high-level overview of what the project intends to achieve, essential for guiding subsequent project planning and execution. A timeline (option a) is too detailed for this stage, a risk assessment (option b) supports planning but does not define purpose, and while stakeholders (option d) are important, they do not clarify the project's objectives as directly as the SOW.

334. Which aspect of the project charter assists most in defining the authority level of the project manager?
a. The preliminary budget

b. The project timeline

c. The project's high-level milestones

d. The roles and responsibilities section

Answer: d. The roles and responsibilities section. Explanation: The roles and responsibilities section of the project charter explicitly outlines the authority granted to the project manager, including what decisions they can make and resources they can allocate. This clarity is crucial for empowering the project manager to lead effectively. Other sections like the budget (option a), timeline (option b), and milestones (option c) are informative but do not directly define authority levels.

335. What should be included in a project charter to help manage stakeholder expectations?

a. A detailed Gantt chart

b. High-level project requirements

c. An exhaustive list of potential risks

d. A comprehensive communication plan

Answer: b. High-level project requirements. Explanation: Including high-level project requirements in the project charter helps manage stakeholder expectations by clearly stating what the project will deliver. This clarity helps prevent misunderstandings and misaligned expectations as the project progresses. Gantt charts (option a) and detailed communication plans (option d) are too detailed for the charter stage, and while risk lists (option c) are important, they do not directly set expectations about project outcomes.

336. During the drafting of a project charter, what element is critical to establish the project's alignment with the organization's strategic objectives?

a. An analysis of competitive market trends

b. A linkage statement to organizational goals

c. Endorsements from all project stakeholders

d. A legal review by the organization's attorneys

Answer: b. A linkage statement to organizational goals. Explanation: Including a statement that links the project to the organization's strategic goals in the charter is critical to demonstrating how the project aligns with and supports broader organizational objectives. This ensures that the project is seen as relevant and contributing to the strategic direction of the company. Market trends (option a) and legal reviews (option d) are supportive but secondary, and while stakeholder endorsements (option c) are valuable, they do not demonstrate strategic alignment.

337. What is the primary benefit of having a well-defined project charter in place before project execution begins?

a. It allows for the detailed scheduling of project tasks.

b. It provides a basis for making future project decisions.

c. It guarantees the project will stay within its budget.

d. It ensures that all project risks are identified early.

Answer: b. It provides a basis for making future project decisions. Explanation: A well-defined project charter provides a foundational document from which all project decisions can be guided and justified. It sets project boundaries and defines key objectives and deliverables, serving as a reference throughout the project lifecycle. While it helps with scheduling (option a) and risk identification (option d), its primary role is not to guarantee budget adherence (option c) but to guide decision-making.

338. How does defining a clear escalation path in the project charter support project success?
a. It speeds up the project delivery by bypassing standard procedures.
b. It provides a structured method for resolving issues and decision-making.
c. It eliminates the need for regular project status meetings.
d. It reduces the project's dependence on the project manager.

Answer: b. It provides a structured method for resolving issues and decision-making. Explanation: A clear escalation path in the project charter outlines how and when to escalate unresolved project issues or critical decisions, ensuring they are addressed at the correct level of authority promptly. This structure supports effective problem-solving and governance, contributing to project success. It doesn't bypass procedures (option a), eliminate meetings (option c), or reduce dependence on the project manager (option d) but rather enhances governance.

339. Why is it important for a project charter to be formally approved by senior management?
a. It legally binds senior management to provide necessary resources.
b. It formalizes the initiation of the project and secures funding.
c. It allows the project team to begin recruiting additional staff.
d. It ensures that the project will not require any further changes.

Answer: b. It formalizes the initiation of the project and secures funding. Explanation: Formal approval of the project charter by senior management is crucial as it signifies organizational commitment to the project, formalizes its initiation, and typically secures the necessary funding and resources. This endorsement is key to moving forward with planning and execution. It doesn't legally bind management (option a), necessarily allow for staff recruitment (option c), nor ensure no further changes (option d), but rather legitimizes and empowers the project within the organization.

340. In project charter development, why is it crucial to identify and document major project assumptions?
a. To ensure that the project is completed without delays
b. To facilitate the project scope definition process
c. To provide a baseline for future project audits
d. To guide the strategic planning of the organization

Answer: b. To facilitate the project scope definition process. Explanation: Documenting major project assumptions in the project charter is crucial because assumptions influence the definition of project scope and planning. They provide a context in which the project is expected to operate, affecting estimations, resource allocations, and risk assessments. They are not primarily about preventing delays (option a), serving as audit baselines (option c), or guiding organizational strategy (option d), but about ensuring clarity and realistic planning frameworks.

341. In the process of developing a project schedule, which input is essential for defining activities?
a. Activity resource requirements
b. Work performance data
c. Scope baseline
d. Risk register

Answer: c. Scope baseline. Explanation: The scope baseline is essential for defining activities as it includes the project scope statement, the Work Breakdown Structure (WBS), and the WBS dictionary, which together provide detailed deliverables, work packages, and requirements. Activity resource requirements (option a) and risk register (option d) are inputs for later planning steps like estimating resources and assessing risks, respectively. Work performance data (option b) is an output from project execution used for monitoring and controlling the project, not for defining activities.

342. Which tool or technique is most effective in developing the project team to enhance their ability to complete project deliverables?
a. Interpersonal and team skills
b. Performance assessments
c. Project management software
d. Work performance reports

Answer: a. Interpersonal and team skills. Explanation: Interpersonal and team skills are crucial in developing the project team as they include motivation, conflict management, and communication skills, which are essential for improving team interaction, cohesion, and overall performance. Performance assessments (option b) evaluate team effectiveness but do not directly enhance skills. Project management software (option c) facilitates project scheduling and tracking but does not develop team capabilities. Work performance reports (option d) provide information on team performance but again do not facilitate development.

343. What is a key output of the Perform Integrated Change Control process?
a. Change request status updates
b. Project management plan updates
c. Approved change requests
d. Enterprise environmental factors

Answer: c. Approved change requests. Explanation: Approved change requests are a key output of the Perform Integrated Change Control process. This process reviews all change requests, approves changes that are necessary, and manages the changes to deliverables, organizational process assets, project documents, or the project management plan. Change request status updates (option a) are part of the communication during the process but are not an output. Project management plan updates (option b) can result from approved change requests but are themselves separate outputs. Enterprise environmental factors (option d) influence the project but are not an output of this process.

344. When identifying risks, which tool or technique allows for a comprehensive and systematic identification of risks based on categories?
a. SWOT analysis
b. Expert judgment
c. Risk data quality assessment
d. Risk categorization

Answer: d. Risk categorization. Explanation: Risk categorization, often done using a risk breakdown structure (RBS), helps organize identified risks into categories that relate to their source or area affected, facilitating a more comprehensive and systematic approach to identifying potential risks across the project. SWOT analysis (option a) helps identify strengths, weaknesses, opportunities, and threats but does not categorize risks systematically. Expert judgment (option b) is used to identify risks based on experience but without a structured categorization. Risk data quality assessment (option c) evaluates the reliability and integrity of risk data.

345. Which input is crucial for the Manage Stakeholder Engagement process?
a. Stakeholder engagement plan
b. Cost management plan
c. Quality metrics
d. Scope statement

Answer: a. Stakeholder engagement plan. Explanation: The stakeholder engagement plan is a crucial input for the Manage Stakeholder Engagement process as it outlines the approach to engaging stakeholders, including communication methods and strategies to gain support or mitigate resistance. The cost management plan (option b), quality metrics (option c), and scope statement (option d) are important for other processes but do not directly influence stakeholder engagement strategies.

346. What is an essential output of the Control Quality process?
a. Quality metrics
b. Change requests
c. Quality control measurements
d. Project management plan updates

Answer: c. Quality control measurements. Explanation: Quality control measurements are critical outputs of the Control Quality process. These measurements document the results of quality activities to assess performance and ensure the project outputs meet the necessary quality standards and requirements. Quality metrics (option a) are tools used within the process, change requests (option b) may arise from the findings, and project management plan updates (option d) might result from actions taken in response to quality issues identified.

347. For the Collect Requirements process, which tool or technique is best suited for ensuring that the stakeholders have a clear and shared understanding of the requirements?
a. Benchmarking
b. Prototyping

c. Focus groups
d. Surveys

Answer: b. Prototyping. Explanation: Prototyping is an effective tool in the Collect Requirements process for facilitating a clear and shared understanding among stakeholders by providing a working model of the expected product before final production. It allows for adjustments based on feedback and ensures the final deliverables meet stakeholder expectations. Benchmarking (option a) is used for comparing actual project practices against those of other projects. Focus groups (option c) gather expectations and attitudes from specific user groups, and surveys (option d) collect broad feedback but might not ensure a shared understanding.

348. In the process of Monitor and Control Project Work, what is an indispensable tool or technique?
a. Earned value analysis
b. Decomposition
c. Precedence diagramming method
d. Variance analysis

Answer: d. Variance analysis. Explanation: Variance analysis is a critical tool in the Monitor and Control Project Work process, used to assess the magnitude of variation from the original project management plan. This analysis helps in identifying the need for corrective or preventive actions in the project. Earned value analysis (option a) is part of performance review techniques, decomposition (option b) is used in creating work breakdown structures, and the precedence diagramming method (option c) is used for scheduling.

349. What output from the Direct and Manage Project Work process provides updates to reflect the current project environment?
a. Work performance data
b. Project documents updates
c. Change requests
d. Project calendars

Answer: b. Project documents updates. Explanation: Project documents updates are key outputs from the Direct and Manage Project Work process, reflecting revisions due to changes occurring during project execution. These updates ensure that project documents remain relevant and accurate as the project environment changes. Work performance data (option a) represents raw observations and measurements of project work, change requests (option c) are formal suggestions for modifications, and project calendars (option d) schedule the project work.

350. Which technique in the Estimate Costs process is most effective for a project that has performed similar tasks in past projects?
a. Parametric estimating
b. Bottom-up estimating
c. Analogous estimating
d. Three-point estimating

Answer: c. Analogous estimating. Explanation: Analogous estimating is most effective when the project can leverage actual cost data from similar past projects, providing a quicker and often sufficiently accurate cost estimate. This technique uses historical data to estimate project costs based on similar projects. Parametric (option a) uses statistical relationships, bottom-up (option b) involves estimating individual work items and summing them, and three-point (option d) uses optimistic, pessimistic, and most likely costs to estimate work package costs.

351. When initiating a project, why is a business case important?
a. It outlines the project schedule and resource allocation.
b. It provides the justification for undertaking the project.
c. It lists the technical specifications of the project deliverables.
d. It details the project's communication plan to stakeholders.

Answer: b. It provides the justification for undertaking the project. Explanation: The business case is crucial as it outlines the rationale for why the project should be undertaken, including an analysis of feasible alternatives, alignment with business objectives, cost-benefit analysis, and potential return on investment. This helps stakeholders and decision-makers assess the viability and strategic importance of the project. Schedules and resource allocations (option a) are part of project planning, technical specifications (option c) are typically detailed in project specifications documents, and communication plans (option d) are outlined in the stakeholder management plan.

352. Which component should be included in a project's statement of work (SOW) to ensure all teams understand their tasks?
a. Project timeline
b. Scope of work
c. Financial audit requirements
d. Stakeholder list

Answer: b. Scope of work. Explanation: The scope of work in the statement of work is essential as it clearly defines what tasks the project will include, the deliverables to be provided, and the work that will be performed. This clarity ensures all teams involved understand their responsibilities and the project's requirements. While a project timeline (option a) is important for scheduling, it doesn't provide detail on individual tasks. Financial audit requirements (option c) and a stakeholder list (option d) are typically not included in the SOW.

353. What is the primary purpose of including success criteria in a project statement of work?
a. To define what the project should achieve to be considered successful.
b. To outline the project budget constraints.
c. To specify the software tools required for project management.
d. To document the project team members' responsibilities.

Answer: a. To define what the project should achieve to be considered successful. Explanation: Including success criteria in the statement of work is crucial for clearly defining the standards and conditions under which the project will be considered successful. These criteria help measure project performance and ensure alignment with the project objectives and stakeholders' expectations. Budget constraints (option b), software tools (option c), and team responsibilities (option d) are important but serve different purposes in project documentation.

354. In a business case, what analysis is crucial to determine the feasibility of the project?
a. Stakeholder analysis
b. Cost-benefit analysis
c. Risk management analysis
d. Competitor analysis

Answer: b. Cost-benefit analysis. Explanation: Cost-benefit analysis is crucial in a business case as it helps quantify and compare the expected costs and benefits associated with a project. This analysis provides a basis for determining the economic feasibility of the project and justifying the investment, supporting decision-making processes about project initiation. Stakeholder analysis (option a) and risk management analysis (option c) are also important but focus more on identifying influences and potential issues rather than economic feasibility. Competitor analysis (option d) is more relevant to strategic positioning than project feasibility.

355. How does the statement of work (SOW) for a project relate to the business case?
a. The SOW describes how the business case will be communicated to stakeholders.
b. The SOW is derived from the project requirements stated in the business case.
c. The SOW outlines the financial implications detailed in the business case.
d. The SOW lists the stakeholders identified in the business case.

Answer: b. The SOW is derived from the project requirements stated in the business case. Explanation: The statement of work (SOW) is directly derived from the project requirements and objectives outlined in the business case. It takes the high-level project justification and requirements from the business case and translates them into detailed descriptions of the work to be performed. Communication plans (option a), financial implications (option c), and stakeholder lists (option d) are not direct derivations but separate components of project documentation and planning.

356. What should be included in a business case to assess project alignment with organizational goals?
a. A detailed project schedule
b. A strategic alignment matrix
c. A list of project milestones
d. A Gantt chart

Answer: b. A strategic alignment matrix. Explanation: A strategic alignment matrix in a business case helps demonstrate how the project aligns with the organization's strategic goals. This matrix maps project objectives against strategic priorities to justify the project's initiation, ensuring that it supports broader organizational aims. Project schedules (option a), milestones (option c), and Gantt charts (option d) are tools for planning and tracking but do not inherently assess strategic alignment.

357. When developing a business case, which element is essential to justify project initiation?

448

a. Historical data from similar projects
b. Project team preferences
c. Vendor contracts
d. Detailed task assignments

Answer: a. Historical data from similar projects. Explanation: Including historical data from similar projects in a business case is essential as it provides empirical evidence to support the feasibility, cost estimates, and success likelihood of the new project. This data can help justify project initiation by showing past successes or lessons learned under similar circumstances. Team preferences (option b), vendor contracts (option c), and task assignments (option d) do not primarily serve to justify project initiation but rather pertain to project execution details.

358. What role does the statement of work play in project procurement management?
a. It specifies the criteria for vendor selection.
b. It defines the procurement budget.
c. It details the work for which the vendor is contracted.
d. It outlines the payment schedule for vendors.

Answer: c. It details the work for which the vendor is contracted. Explanation: In project procurement management, the statement of work is critical as it specifies in detail the work, deliverables, and quality expectations for which the vendor is contracted. This ensures clarity and mutual understanding between the buyer and the seller about what is expected. Selection criteria (option a), budget definitions (option b), and payment schedules (option d) are related to other aspects of procurement management but are not the primary role of the SOW.

359.In a business case, why is it important to identify and document key assumptions?
a. To outline the project's communication channels
b. To ensure that all project risks are mitigated
c. To provide a realistic context for project decisions
d. To specify the software tools used in project management

Answer: c. To provide a realistic context for project decisions. Explanation: Documenting key assumptions in a business case is important because assumptions provide a realistic context that influences project decisions, planning, and strategy. These assumptions are based on current knowledge and conditions expected during the project, helping stakeholders understand the basis for forecasts and projections. While communication channels (option a), risk mitigation (option b), and tools (option d) are important, they do not directly relate to the foundational context provided by key assumptions.

360. Which of the following is a primary reason for documenting the project scope in the statement of work?
a. To facilitate change management processes during the project
b. To define what is included and excluded from the project
c. To establish the project schedule and timeline
d. To allocate the project budget and resources

Answer: b. To define what is included and excluded from the project. Explanation: Documenting the project scope in the statement of work is crucial as it clearly defines the boundaries of the project, specifying what will and will not be included. This clarity helps prevent scope creep and ensures that all parties have a common understanding of the project limits. Change management (option a), scheduling (option c), and budgeting (option d) are managed through other documents and processes.

361. When developing the Project Management Plan, which document provides the foundational baseline from which all project work should align?
a. Project funding requirements
b. Project scope statement
c. Change management plan
d. Stakeholder register

Answer: b. Project scope statement. Explanation: The project scope statement is essential as it defines the project's objectives, deliverables, boundaries, and methods of acceptance, providing the foundation from which the entire project management plan is developed. It ensures all project activities are aligned with the defined scope. Funding requirements (option a) relate to budget management, the change management plan (option c) addresses how changes are handled, and the stakeholder register (option d) identifies project stakeholders but does not serve as a foundational baseline.

362. In the integration of a project management plan, which tool is most effective for ensuring consistency across all knowledge areas?
a. Expert judgment
b. Facilitation techniques
c. Project management information systems (PMIS)
d. Dependency determination

Answer: c. Project management information systems (PMIS). Explanation: PMIS is highly effective in ensuring consistency across all project management knowledge areas by integrating processes and allowing for the management, monitoring, and controlling of various aspects of the project centrally. Expert judgment (option a) and facilitation techniques (option b) are valuable in the planning phases but do not provide a systemized approach to integration. Dependency determination (option d) is more related to schedule management.

363. What is a primary output of the Develop Project Management Plan process?
a. Project charter
b. Deliverable status reports
c. Approved project management plan
d. Resource calendars

Answer: c. Approved project management plan. Explanation: The primary output of the Develop Project Management Plan process is the approved project management plan itself, which includes all subsidiary plans and baselines. This document guides the project execution, monitoring, and control phases. The project charter (option a) is an input to this process, deliverable status reports (option b) are outputs of monitoring and controlling processes, and resource calendars (option d) are developed in the resource management processes.

364. How should changes to the project management plan be managed?
a. By informal negotiations and agreements
b. Through the Perform Integrated Change Control process
c. By direct updates from the project sponsor
d. Through ad hoc team meetings

Answer: b. Through the Perform Integrated Change Control process. Explanation: Changes to the project management plan should be managed formally through the Perform Integrated Change Control process. This ensures that all changes are reviewed, approved, or rejected by a responsible authority, maintaining control over the project's scope, schedule, and cost. Informal agreements (option a), direct sponsor updates (option c), and ad hoc meetings (option d) lack the formal control and documentation needed for effective project management.

365. Which of the following best describes the purpose of developing a project management plan?
a. To outline the project deliverables and schedule only
b. To define how the project is executed, monitored, controlled, and closed
c. To specify the communication methods to be used in the project
d. To provide a detailed budget and expense tracking system

Answer: b. To define how the project is executed, monitored, controlled, and closed. Explanation: The project management plan outlines the processes and procedures that will be followed to ensure the project is executed, monitored, controlled, and closed systematically and according to the project's defined scope and objectives. While communication methods (option c) and budgeting details (option d) are included, they are part of the broader scope of the plan, which encompasses all aspects of project execution.

366. What should be included in the project management plan to address potential risks identified during the planning phase?
a. A list of approved project vendors and suppliers
b. Detailed risk management plan
c. An exclusive focus on high-impact risks
d. A generic contingency plan applicable to any project

Answer: b. Detailed risk management plan. Explanation: A detailed risk management plan should be included within the project management plan to outline how identified risks will be managed and mitigated. This plan includes processes for risk identification, analysis, response planning, and monitoring, ensuring that risks do not derail the project's objectives. Focusing only on high-impact risks (option c) ignores other potential threats, while a generic plan (option d) may not adequately address specific project risks.

367. In creating a project management plan, which process ensures that earlier planning efforts are refined and integrated into a cohesive plan?
a. Scope definition
b. Plan development
c. Progressive elaboration
d. Preliminary scoping

Answer: c. Progressive elaboration. Explanation: Progressive elaboration involves continuously improving and detailing a plan as more detailed and specific information and more accurate estimates become available. This process ensures that the project management plan evolves to meet the project's needs as they are more clearly understood over time. Scope definition (option a) and preliminary scoping (option d) are initial steps, while plan development (option b) is a broad term not specific to integration and refinement.

368. Which component is essential for ensuring the project management plan's alignment with the project's strategic objectives?
a. Stakeholder influence diagram
b. Organizational process assets
c. Business case linkage
d. Resource leveling tools

Answer: c. Business case linkage. Explanation: Including a clear linkage to the business case in the project management plan ensures that the project aligns with the organization's strategic objectives. This linkage helps justify the project's goals and ensures consistency with broader business goals. Organizational process assets (option b) provide support but not strategic alignment, stakeholder diagrams (option a) map influences and not strategic objectives, and resource leveling tools (option d) are technical aspects of resource management.

369. During project planning, what role does the project management plan serve in terms of stakeholder communication?
a. It specifies only the frequency of communication
b. It details the project's approach to managing stakeholder engagement
c. It limits communication to key stakeholders
d. It prescribes specific technologies for communication

Answer: b. It details the project's approach to managing stakeholder engagement. Explanation: The project management plan includes a stakeholder engagement plan, which details how the project will manage and engage stakeholders, including methods, frequency, and the type of information to be communicated. This ensures that stakeholder expectations are managed and that communication is effective and appropriate. Limiting communication (option c) or prescribing technologies (option d) are too specific, and focusing only on frequency (option a) does not comprehensively address engagement.

370. What is the significance of the baseline in the project management plan?
a. It provides a standard for vendor assessment.

b. It serves as the standard for measuring project performance.

c. It dictates the project's compliance with industry standards.

d. It offers a flexible approach to manage project changes.

Answer: b. It serves as the standard for measuring project performance. Explanation: The baseline in a project management plan is crucial as it serves as the standard against which project performance is measured. This includes scope, schedule, and cost baselines, which help determine how variations from the plan are handled and whether the project is on track to meet its objectives. While compliance with standards (option c) is important, it is not the primary role of the baseline. Vendor assessment (option a) and managing changes flexibly (option d) are not directly related to the baseline's purpose in performance measurement.

371. When managing a complex software development project, which input is crucial for performing the Sequence Activities process?

a. Schedule management plan

b. Risk management plan

c. Milestone list

d. Activity list

Answer: d. Activity list. Explanation: The activity list is crucial for the Sequence Activities process as it includes all the schedule activities required on the project, which need to be sequenced to understand the logical order of work. The schedule management plan (option a) provides guidance on how schedule development will be managed, not the specific activities themselves. The risk management plan (option b) is used for identifying and addressing risks, while the milestone list (option c) indicates significant points or events in the project timeline but does not detail the activities between milestones.

372. In the Cost Estimating process, what tool or technique is most effective for a project that requires an estimation of the statistical relationship between historical data and other variables?

a. Parametric estimating

b. Analogous estimating

c. Bottom-up estimating

d. Three-point estimating

Answer: a. Parametric estimating. Explanation: Parametric estimating uses a statistical relationship between historical data and other variables to estimate costs, making it ideal for projects where quantifiable data is available. Analogous estimating (option b) uses data from a similar, previous project and is less precise. Bottom-up estimating (option c) involves estimating individual elements and summing them, suitable for detailed or unique projects. Three-point estimating (option d) provides a range but lacks the statistical basis provided by parametric methods.

373. Which output from the Develop Schedule process serves as a key status and progress reporting tool during project execution?

a. Project schedule

b. Schedule baseline

c. Change requests
d. Schedule data

Answer: b. Schedule baseline. Explanation: The schedule baseline, once approved, serves as a standard for comparing actual project progress against the planned schedule, making it a fundamental tool for status and progress reporting. The project schedule (option a) is a detailed plan that includes this baseline. Change requests (option c) may arise if deviations occur, and schedule data (option d) provides supporting details but isn't a tool for reporting like the baseline.

374. What is the primary output of the Plan Procurement Management process that guides how procurement activities will be monitored and controlled?
a. Procurement management plan
b. Procurement strategy
c. Bid documents
d. Seller proposals

Answer: a. Procurement management plan. Explanation: The procurement management plan is the primary output of the Plan Procurement Management process and includes guidelines on how procurement processes will be managed from developing procurement documents through contract closure. This plan is vital for monitoring and controlling procurement activities. The procurement strategy (option b) is part of this plan, while bid documents (option c) and seller proposals (option d) are inputs and outputs of subsequent processes in procurement.

375. During the Perform Quality Assurance process, what tool or technique involves the selection of a representative subset of a population of project results to draw conclusions about the quality of the entire project?
a. Quality audits
b. Statistical sampling
c. Quality control measurements
d. Process analysis

Answer: b. Statistical sampling. Explanation: Statistical sampling is a tool or technique used in Perform Quality Assurance to select a part of a population of project results to test or review for quality assurance purposes. This method allows for cost-effective quality checks that are representative of the entire project. Quality audits (option a) review processes, quality control measurements (option c) assess specific project outputs, and process analysis (option d) identifies needed improvements in processes.

376. What is an essential input needed to perform the Identify Stakeholders process effectively in any project?
a. Stakeholder register
b. Project charter
c. Communications management plan
d. Change log

Answer: b. Project charter. Explanation: The project charter is a key input to the Identify Stakeholders process as it contains information about the project and its potential impacts, which are essential for identifying all relevant stakeholders. The stakeholder register (option a) is an output of this process, not an input. The communications management plan (option c) and the change log (option d) are used later in the project lifecycle.

377. For the Control Scope process, which tool or technique is crucial for determining if the project scope has deviated from the scope baseline?
a. Scope audits
b. Variance analysis
c. Change control tools
d. Configuration management systems

Answer: b. Variance analysis. Explanation: Variance analysis is crucial in the Control Scope process to compare the actual project performance against the scope baseline, helping to identify any deviations that need to be addressed. Scope audits (option a) are not a standard tool or technique in this context, while change control tools (option c) manage changes once variance is detected, and configuration management systems (option d) are used for tracking changes to product characteristics.

378. Which output of the Manage Communications process ensures that stakeholders have access to timely and relevant information about the project?
a. Communications management plan
b. Work performance reports
c. Information distribution
d. Project documents updates

Answer: c. Information distribution. Explanation: Information distribution is a key output of the Manage Communications process and involves making necessary information available to project stakeholders in a timely manner. The communications management plan (option a) guides how this process is executed, work performance reports (option b) are one type of information distributed, and project documents updates (option d) may also be distributed but are not solely related to communications.

379. What is the main purpose of the Validate Scope process in project management?
a. To integrate the project scope with the project plan
b. To formally accept completed project deliverables
c. To update the project scope documentation
d. To align project scope with stakeholders' expectations

Answer: b. To formally accept completed project deliverables. Explanation: The main purpose of the Validate Scope process is to obtain formal acceptance of the completed project deliverables from the customer or sponsor. This ensures that deliverables meet the agreed-upon project and product scope. Integrating scope with the project plan (option a) is part of scope planning, updating documentation (option c) happens in scope control, and aligning scope with expectations (option d) is ongoing throughout project planning and execution.

380. In project management, why is it crucial to perform the Collect Requirements process thoroughly?
a. To ensure the project's schedule is adhered to
b. To set the baseline for project costs
c. To define and manage stakeholders' needs and expectations
d. To streamline the project closure phase

Answer: c. To define and manage stakeholders' needs and expectations. Explanation: Performing the Collect Requirements process thoroughly is essential to accurately define and manage stakeholders' needs and expectations, ensuring the project deliverables will satisfy those requirements. This process lays the groundwork for all subsequent project planning activities. Adherence to schedule (option a), setting cost baselines (option b), and streamlining closure (option d) are important but secondary to the fundamental goal of meeting stakeholder requirements.

381. Which component of the project management plan specifies the actions required to identify the people, groups, or organizations that could impact or be impacted by the project?
a. Stakeholder management plan
b. Scope management plan
c. Cost management plan
d. Quality management plan

Answer: a. Stakeholder management plan. Explanation: The stakeholder management plan is a critical component of the project management plan that outlines strategies and actions for identifying stakeholders and managing their engagement throughout the project lifecycle. The scope management plan (option b) deals with how the project scope will be defined, validated, and controlled. The cost management plan (option c) outlines how project costs will be planned, structured, and controlled, while the quality management plan (option d) describes how the project will validate that it meets the required standards and stakeholder expectations.

382. In the development of a project management plan, what is the primary purpose of the communications management plan?
a. To document how project communications will be planned, structured, and monitored
b. To provide a detailed list of project milestones and deliverables
c. To outline the project's risk assessment processes
d. To specify the project's cost estimation procedures

Answer: a. To document how project communications will be planned, structured, and monitored. Explanation: The communications management plan is a vital part of the project management plan that details how project communications will be handled. This includes the planning, structuring, monitoring, and controlling of communications to ensure effective internal and external flows of project information. Options b, c, and d refer to different aspects of the project management plan not specifically related to communication processes.

383. What does the resource management plan primarily include within the project management plan?
a. Details on risk mitigation strategies for resource availability

b. Guidelines on how project resources are to be identified, acquired, and managed
c. The communication preferences of project stakeholders
d. The legal implications of the project's procurement contracts

Answer: b. Guidelines on how project resources are to be identified, acquired, and managed. Explanation: The resource management plan is a crucial component of the project management plan that provides detailed guidelines on the identification, acquisition, and management of project resources, which includes human resources, materials, equipment, and supplies. It specifies how resources will be allocated, managed, and released. Option a deals with risk management aspects, option c relates to communications management, and option d pertains to procurement management.

384. Which component of the project management plan defines the processes that will be used to ensure that the project includes all the work required—and only the work required—to complete the project successfully?
a. Scope management plan
b. Integration management plan
c. Quality management plan
d. Configuration management plan

Answer: a. Scope management plan. Explanation: The scope management plan is a component of the project management plan that defines how the project scope will be defined, validated, and controlled. It ensures that the project includes all necessary work to complete the project successfully and helps prevent scope creep. The integration management plan (option b) oversees project plan development and integration, the quality management plan (option c) addresses meeting the quality requirements, and the configuration management plan (option d) pertains to handling changes in project deliverables.

385. What role does the cost management plan play within the overall project management plan?
a. To outline the schedule for project deliverables
b. To describe how project costs will be planned, structured, and controlled
c. To establish methods for improving team performance
d. To detail the standards for ethical conduct within the project

Answer: b. To describe how project costs will be planned, structured, and controlled. Explanation: The cost management plan is a fundamental component of the project management plan that describes how costs will be estimated, budgeted, managed, and controlled throughout the project. Unlike option a, which is concerned with scheduling, or option c and d, which deal with team performance and ethical standards, respectively, the cost management plan specifically addresses financial aspects of project management.

386. For managing changes in project documents, deliverables, and baseline, which component of the project management plan is utilized?
a. Change management plan
b. Communications management plan
c. Stakeholder engagement plan
d. Procurement management plan

Answer: a. Change management plan. Explanation: The change management plan is a part of the project management plan that outlines how changes to the project scope, deliverables, and documentation will be managed and controlled. It includes procedures for submitting, evaluating, and approving changes to ensure project objectives remain aligned with business goals. It is not primarily concerned with communications (option b), stakeholder engagement (option c), or procurement activities (option d).

387. How does the schedule management plan contribute to the project management plan?
a. By providing strategies for potential financial investments
b. By detailing the project timeline, including start and end dates for project tasks
c. By documenting the process for quality control testing
d. By outlining the communication channels for stakeholder interaction

Answer: b. By detailing the project timeline, including start and end dates for project tasks. Explanation: The schedule management plan, a component of the project management plan, outlines how the project schedule will be managed. It details the timeline, including the start and end dates for tasks, milestones, and control accounts. It helps ensure timely project execution and is distinct from financial strategies (option a), quality control processes (option c), and communication plans (option d).

388. What is the purpose of including a procurement management plan in the project management plan?
a. To specify how project purchases and acquisitions will be managed
b. To ensure all project communications are archived
c. To manage the project team's performance reviews
d. To track changes to the project scope

Answer: a. To specify how project purchases and acquisitions will be managed. Explanation: The procurement management plan is integral to the project management plan and details how the procurement processes from planning purchases to contract closure will be managed. It outlines how resources and services from external vendors will be acquired, addressing aspects such as contract types, suppliers' selection, and contract administration processes. Options b, c, and d describe the roles of other plans.

389. In what way does the risk management plan impact the project management plan?
a. It provides a methodology for identifying, analyzing, and responding to project risks.
b. It outlines the frequency of project meetings.
c. It describes the software tools used for project scheduling.
d. It lists the project team members and their roles.

Answer: a. It provides a methodology for identifying, analyzing, and responding to project risks. Explanation: The risk management plan is crucial for preparing the project management plan as it provides structured methods for risk identification, analysis, response planning, and monitoring. This ensures that risks are proactively managed to minimize their impact on the project. It does not concern meeting frequencies (option b), software tools (option c), or team member roles (option d).

390. Which part of the project management plan outlines the approach for how project performance will be monitored and reported?
a. Performance measurement plan
b. Scope verification plan
c. Cost baseline
d. Quality metrics

Answer: a. Performance measurement plan. Explanation: The performance measurement plan, often part of the project management plan, outlines the approach for monitoring and measuring project performance. It includes specific metrics and tools that will be used to assess performance against the project plan. This is essential for tracking progress and making necessary adjustments. The scope verification plan (option b) deals with confirming project scope, the cost baseline (option c) establishes financial benchmarks, and quality metrics (option d) define specific criteria for measuring project quality.

391. A project manager is overseeing the construction of a new office building. During the execution phase, what should the project manager prioritize to ensure the Direct and Manage Project Work process is effective?
a. Updating the risk management plan
b. Managing stakeholders' expectations
c. Performing quality assurance on project deliverables
d. Ensuring work performance data are collected and disseminated

Answer: d. Ensuring work performance data are collected and disseminated. Explanation: During the execution phase, it's crucial for the project manager to ensure that work performance data related to scope, schedule, cost, and resources are accurately collected and disseminated. This data helps in monitoring project progress and making informed decisions, which is central to effectively directing and managing project work. While managing stakeholders' expectations (option b) and performing quality assurance (option c) are important, they support rather than drive the process. Updating the risk management plan (option a) is also critical but secondary to the immediate need to manage work performance during project execution.

392. In the Direct and Manage Project Work process, which output is essential for documenting changes that occur during project execution?
a. Change requests
b. Project management plan updates
c. Deliverables
d. Work performance reports

Answer: a. Change requests. Explanation: Change requests are an essential output of the Direct and Manage Project Work process. They are used to propose alterations to the scope, schedule, cost, or quality of a project and are crucial for documenting and formalizing changes that occur during project execution. While project management plan updates (option b) and work performance reports (option d) are also outputs, they deal with documenting the overall plan and reporting on performance, respectively. Deliverables (option c) refer to the tangible or intangible products completed during the project.

393. What tool or technique is critical when a project manager needs to integrate non-cohesive project team activities during the Direct and Manage Project Work process?
a. Performance assessments
b. Project management information system (PMIS)
c. Expert judgment
d. Interpersonal and team skills

Answer: b. Project management information system (PMIS). Explanation: A PMIS is critical for integrating diverse project activities, providing a centralized communication and documentation platform to track, manage, and align project efforts. This system helps ensure consistency and coordination across project teams. While expert judgment (option c) and interpersonal and team skills (option d) play significant roles in handling team dynamics and decision-making, a PMIS directly facilitates the integration of activities on a broader scale. Performance assessments (option a) are used to evaluate team efficiency and effectiveness post-integration.

394. During a software development project, if a key component fails testing, what should the project manager do under the Direct and Manage Project Work process?
a. Request additional funding to address the issue
b. Issue a change request for the necessary modifications
c. Adjust the project scope to exclude the faulty component
d. Document the failure as a risk for future projects

Answer: b. Issue a change request for the necessary modifications. Explanation: If a component fails testing, the project manager should issue a change request to formally propose the necessary modifications to address the failure. This process is critical to ensuring that changes are approved and documented properly within the project's governance framework. Requesting additional funding (option a) may be necessary but follows the approval of a change request. Adjusting the project scope to exclude the component (option c) is not addressing the problem, while documenting the failure as a risk (option d) is important but doesn't solve the immediate issue.

395. How does the implementation of approved change requests impact the Direct and Manage Project Work process?
a. It initiates the process of project closure.
b. It can alter the project scope, schedule, or costs.
c. It reduces the need for further project documentation.
d. It decreases the frequency of communication with stakeholders.

Answer: b. It can alter the project scope, schedule, or costs. Explanation: The implementation of approved change requests during the Direct and Manage Project Work process can significantly alter the project scope, schedule, or costs depending on the nature of the change. This is a direct consequence of incorporating approved modifications into the project work. Initiating project closure (option a) is incorrect as this occurs at the end of the project. Reducing documentation (option c) and decreasing communication (option d) are not effects of implementing change requests; in fact, they typically increase due to these changes.

396. What is the primary reason for generating work performance data during the Direct and Manage Project Work process?
a. To provide a basis for creating the final project report
b. To support project billing and accounting practices
c. To provide insights into project progress and performance
d. To fulfill compliance requirements with external regulations

Answer: c. To provide insights into project progress and performance. Explanation: The primary reason for generating work performance data during the Direct and Manage Project Work process is to track and provide insights into the project's progress and performance against the project management plan. This data helps in making informed decisions and taking corrective actions as needed. While it may also support billing and accounting practices (option b) and help in creating the final project report (option a), these are secondary to its role in performance assessment. Fulfilling external regulations (option d) might require work performance data but is not the primary purpose.

397. Which factor should a project manager consider most when allocating resources during the Direct and Manage Project Work process?
a. Historical information from past projects
b. The phase of the moon and its potential impact on team morale
c. Current resource availability and project schedule requirements
d. The personal preferences of the project team members

Answer: c. Current resource availability and project schedule requirements. Explanation: When allocating resources during the Direct and Manage Project Work process, the most critical factors to consider are current resource availability and the requirements of the project schedule. This ensures that resources are assigned efficiently and can meet the demands of the project at the right times. Historical information (option a) can provide useful insights but is less immediate than current availability. Personal preferences (option d) and external factors like the phase of the moon (option b) are generally irrelevant and unprofessional considerations in resource allocation.

398. In the context of Direct and Manage Project Work, what is the significance of deliverable status updates?
a. They indicate the project's compliance with industry standards.
b. They provide stakeholders with information on the progress toward meeting project objectives.
c. They are used exclusively for external auditing purposes.
d. They dictate the strategic direction of the parent organization.

Answer: b. They provide stakeholders with information on the progress toward meeting project objectives. Explanation: Deliverable status updates are crucial during the Direct and Manage Project Work process as they provide stakeholders with timely and accurate information regarding the progress of project deliverables toward meeting the defined project objectives. This helps in managing expectations and facilitating decision-making. Compliance with standards (option a) may be part of the updates but is not their primary purpose, nor are they used exclusively for auditing (option c) or to dictate organizational strategy (option d).

399. What should a project manager do if they discover that project work is not aligning with the project management plan during the Direct and Manage Project Work process?
a. Ignore the discrepancies as minor variances are expected.
b. Adjust the project management plan unilaterally without consultation.
c. Perform integrated change control to realign the project work.
d. Immediately halt all project work and reassess the project objectives.

Answer: c. Perform integrated change control to realign the project work. Explanation: If project work is not aligning with the project management plan, the project manager should engage in integrated change control to assess and realign the project work with the plan. This involves reviewing the discrepancies, proposing changes, and seeking approval through formal change control processes. Ignoring discrepancies (option a) can lead to larger issues, unilateral adjustments (option b) may bypass necessary stakeholder input and approval, and halting all project work (option d) is an extreme response that should be reserved for severe issues.

400. What is the primary input required for the process of defining the project scope?
a. Scope management plan
b. Project charter
c. Stakeholder register
d. Cost management plan

Answer: b. Project charter. Explanation: The project charter serves as a primary input for defining the project scope because it contains the initial project purpose, objectives, and constraints that form the foundation for developing a detailed project scope statement. The scope management plan (option a) guides how the scope is defined, not an input. The stakeholder register (option c) lists individuals and groups impacted by the project, and the cost management plan (option d) addresses financial aspects, neither directly influencing scope definition.

401. In the Estimate Costs process, what tool or technique might a project manager use to improve estimation accuracy based on project parameters and historical data?
a. Analogous estimating
b. Parametric estimating
c. Expert judgment
d. Cost aggregation

Answer: b. Parametric estimating. Explanation: Parametric estimating uses statistical relationships between historical data and other variables (like project parameters) to estimate costs, making it highly effective for improving estimation accuracy. Analogous estimating (option a) is less precise and uses data from a similar project. Expert judgment (option c) relies on experience rather than statistical methods, and cost aggregation (option d) sums costs from individual activities to form a total estimate, not improving the accuracy of individual estimates.

402. Which output from the Monitor and Control Risks process provides updates on potential challenges that might impact the project timeline or budget?

a. Risk register updates
b. Change requests
c. Risk audits
d. Work performance reports

Answer: a. Risk register updates. Explanation: Risk register updates are a critical output from the Monitor and Control Risks process as they provide current information on identified risks, their status, and actions taken to mitigate them, affecting both project timelines and budgets. Change requests (option b) are formal proposals to modify any aspect of the project, while risk audits (option c) are reviews of how risks are being managed. Work performance reports (option d) focus on overall project performance.

403. During the Plan Quality Management process, what tool or technique could be specifically used to identify the cause of defects in project deliverables?
a. Quality metrics
b. Benchmarking
c. Cause and effect diagrams
d. Quality audits

Answer: c. Cause and effect diagrams. Explanation: Cause and effect diagrams, also known as fishbone or Ishikawa diagrams, are used in the Plan Quality Management process to visually identify potential causes of defects, aiding in the prevention of these defects. Quality metrics (option a) define how results are measured, benchmarking (option b) compares actual project practices against those of other projects, and quality audits (option d) evaluate how well the project adheres to organizational standards and processes.

404. What input is essential for performing the Develop Project Team process to ensure the team's skills are aligned with project needs?
a. Resource calendars
b. Project staff assignments
c. Team performance assessments
d. Human resource management plan

Answer: b. Project staff assignments. Explanation: Project staff assignments are essential inputs for the Develop Project Team process because they detail which resources (human resources) are assigned to the project, allowing the project manager to tailor development activities to enhance team competencies aligned with project requirements. Resource calendars (option a) show when resources are available, team performance assessments (option c) review team effectiveness after development, and the human resource management plan (option d) provides strategies and planning details but does not detail specific assignments.

405. In the Collect Requirements process, which tool or technique would be most effective for ensuring that all project stakeholders agree on the project deliverables?
a. Surveys
b. Focus groups
c. Facilitated workshops

d. Questionnaires

Answer: c. Facilitated workshops. Explanation: Facilitated workshops involve direct interaction among project stakeholders, making them highly effective for achieving consensus quickly on project requirements and deliverables. Surveys (option a) and questionnaires (option d) can gather information but lack the interactive element to resolve differences and ensure agreement. Focus groups (option b) are useful for obtaining feedback from specific groups but are less comprehensive in facilitating broad agreement.

406. Which tool or technique in the Control Schedule process allows for a graphical representation of scheduled tasks in order to identify the effects of changes to the project timeline?
a. Gantt charts
b. Critical path method
c. Schedule network analysis
d. Variance analysis

Answer: a. Gantt charts. Explanation: Gantt charts provide a visual timeline for all project activities and are useful in the Control Schedule process for illustrating how changes to one task may impact other tasks or the overall project schedule. The critical path method (option b) and schedule network analysis (option c) help identify the longest path of planned activities to the end of the project but are more analytical tools, while variance analysis (option d) compares planned to actual performance.

407. When developing the Process Improvement Plan, what output from the quality management processes is utilized to identify potential areas for improvement?
a. Quality metrics
b. Process analysis results
c. Quality control measurements
d. Quality audit findings

Answer: d. Quality audit findings. Explanation: Quality audit findings, an output from the Perform Quality Assurance process, provide critical insights into process effectiveness and reveal areas needing improvement, making them invaluable for developing the Process Improvement Plan. Quality metrics (option a) describe specific quality criteria that should be met, process analysis results (option b) identify needed improvements, and quality control measurements (option c) reflect the operational aspects of quality control.

408. What is a key output of the Perform Integrated Change Control process that directly impacts the project scope, schedule, and cost?
a. Change log
b. Approved change requests
c. Project management plan updates
d. Project document updates

Answer: b. Approved change requests. Explanation: Approved change requests are a key output of the Perform Integrated Change Control process. They authorize alterations to the project scope, schedule, or cost after review and approval, directly influencing the project's trajectory. The change log (option a) records all requests, approved or not, while project management plan updates (option c) and project document updates (option d) are subsequent adjustments made in response to approved changes.

409. In managing project knowledge, which input is critical to capture and share knowledge and learning throughout the project?
a. Lessons learned register
b. Project team assignments
c. Resource breakdown structure
d. Stakeholder engagement plan

Answer: a. Lessons learned register. Explanation: The lessons learned register is an essential input in the Manage Knowledge process as it captures and documents knowledge and experiences gained throughout the project, facilitating continuous learning and improvement. It serves as a repository for both positive and negative experiences to be used by current and future projects. Project team assignments (option b), resource breakdown structure (option c), and stakeholder engagement plan (option d) are unrelated to the systematic capture and sharing of project knowledge.

410. What is the primary purpose of the Manage Project Knowledge process?
a. to define how project knowledge will be identified, captured, and disseminated
b. to ensure that project information is properly stored and archived
c. to facilitate knowledge sharing and continuous improvement within the project and organization
d. to protect confidential project information from unauthorized access

Answer: c. to facilitate knowledge sharing and continuous improvement within the project and organization. Explanation: The primary purpose of the Manage Project Knowledge process is to leverage existing knowledge and create new knowledge to achieve project objectives and contribute to organizational learning. This process promotes a culture of knowledge sharing, enables the project team to learn from experiences, and supports continuous improvement in project management practices.

411. Which of the following is not an example of explicit knowledge in project management?
a. project documents and templates
b. lessons learned databases
c. project management methodologies and standards
d. team members' skills and expertise

Answer: d. team members' skills and expertise. Explanation: Team members' skills and expertise are examples of tacit knowledge, which is the personal and experiential knowledge that resides within individuals' minds. Explicit knowledge, on the other hand, refers to the codified and documented knowledge that can be easily shared and transferred, such as project documents, templates, lessons learned databases, and project management methodologies and standards.

412. What is the main benefit of conducting lessons learned sessions throughout the project lifecycle?
a. to assign blame for project failures and identify underperforming team members
b. to celebrate project successes and reward high-performing team members
c. to capture and apply knowledge gained during the project to improve future performance
d. to demonstrate the project manager's competence and expertise to stakeholders

Answer: c. to capture and apply knowledge gained during the project to improve future performance.
Explanation: The main benefit of conducting lessons learned sessions throughout the project lifecycle is to identify, document, and share the knowledge gained from project experiences, including successes, challenges, and recommendations for improvement. By capturing and applying these lessons, project teams can avoid repeating mistakes, leverage best practices, and continuously enhance their project management capabilities. Lessons learned should focus on objective learning and improvement rather than assigning blame or celebrating successes.

413. Which of the following is a key tool or technique used in the Manage Project Knowledge process?
a. knowledge management plan
b. knowledge elicitation techniques
c. information management systems
d. all of the above

Answer: d. all of the above. Explanation: The Manage Project Knowledge process employs various tools and techniques to capture, share, and apply project knowledge effectively. These include knowledge management plans (defining how knowledge will be managed throughout the project), knowledge elicitation techniques (such as interviews, workshops, and storytelling to extract tacit knowledge), and information management systems (such as databases, document repositories, and collaboration platforms to store, retrieve, and share explicit knowledge).

414. What is the purpose of a knowledge repository in project management?
a. to store and organize project documents and deliverables
b. to capture and share best practices and lessons learned
c. to provide a centralized platform for project communication and collaboration
d. all of the above

Answer: d. all of the above. Explanation: A knowledge repository serves multiple purposes in project management. It acts as a centralized store for project documents and deliverables, making it easier for team members to access and retrieve relevant information. It also captures and shares best practices, lessons learned, and other forms of knowledge assets, promoting knowledge reuse and continuous improvement. Additionally, a knowledge repository can facilitate project communication and collaboration by providing a common platform for team members to exchange ideas, discuss issues, and work together on project tasks.

415. Which of the following is a critical success factor for effective project knowledge management?
a. implementing the latest technology tools and platforms
b. enforcing strict security measures to protect project information

c. fostering a culture of trust, openness, and collaboration within the team
d. dedicating a full-time knowledge management specialist to the project

Answer: c. fostering a culture of trust, openness, and collaboration within the team. Explanation: While technology, security, and dedicated resources can support project knowledge management, the most critical success factor is fostering a culture that encourages trust, openness, and collaboration among team members. When team members feel psychologically safe to share their knowledge, experiences, and ideas without fear of criticism or retribution, they are more likely to engage in knowledge exchange and learning. A collaborative culture also promotes knowledge flow, innovation, and problem-solving, leading to better project outcomes.

416. What is the role of the project manager in facilitating knowledge sharing within the project team?
a. to create and enforce policies and procedures for knowledge management
b. to identify and document the knowledge gaps within the team
c. to lead by example and create opportunities for knowledge exchange and learning
d. to monitor and report on the team's knowledge management performance

Answer: c. to lead by example and create opportunities for knowledge exchange and learning. Explanation: The project manager plays a crucial role in facilitating knowledge sharing within the project team by leading by example and creating a supportive environment for knowledge exchange and learning. This involves modeling knowledge-sharing behaviors, such as openly sharing lessons learned, admitting mistakes, and seeking feedback. The project manager should also create opportunities for team members to interact, collaborate, and learn from each other, such as through team-building activities, cross-functional assignments, and knowledge-sharing sessions. While policies, procedures, and performance monitoring can support knowledge management, the project manager's leadership and actions have the greatest impact on the team's knowledge-sharing culture.

417. How can project teams leverage knowledge from external sources to enhance project performance?
a. by conducting benchmarking studies with similar projects in other organizations
b. by attending industry conferences and training programs
c. by engaging subject matter experts and consultants
d. all of the above

Answer: d. all of the above. Explanation: Project teams can leverage knowledge from various external sources to bring in new perspectives, best practices, and expertise that can enhance project performance. Conducting benchmarking studies with similar projects in other organizations can provide insights into successful strategies, common challenges, and performance metrics. Attending industry conferences and training programs can expose team members to the latest trends, techniques, and innovations in project management. Engaging subject matter experts and consultants can bring specialized knowledge and experience to address specific project challenges or opportunities. By actively seeking and applying external knowledge, project teams can expand their capabilities and deliver better results.

418. What is the relationship between the Manage Project Knowledge process and the Close Project or Phase process?

a. the Manage Project Knowledge process is a subset of the Close Project or Phase process
b. the Close Project or Phase process is a subset of the Manage Project Knowledge process
c. the two processes are independent and have no direct relationship
d. the Manage Project Knowledge process provides inputs to the Close Project or Phase process

Answer: d. the Manage Project Knowledge process provides inputs to the Close Project or Phase process. Explanation: The Manage Project Knowledge process and the Close Project or Phase process are distinct but interconnected processes within the Project Integration Management knowledge area. The Manage Project Knowledge process is performed throughout the project lifecycle, focusing on capturing, sharing, and applying knowledge to support project objectives and organizational learning. The Close Project or Phase process, on the other hand, is performed at the end of the project or a specific phase to finalize all activities, transfer deliverables, and document lessons learned. The knowledge assets created and managed through the Manage Project Knowledge process, such as lessons learned documentation and knowledge repositories, serve as important inputs to the Close Project or Phase process, ensuring that valuable knowledge is preserved and made available for future projects.

419. What is the main challenge in capturing and transferring tacit knowledge within a project team?
a. the lack of appropriate technology tools and platforms
b. the difficulty in codifying and documenting personal experiences and insights
c. the resistance of team members to share their knowledge with others
d. the time and effort required to capture and transfer knowledge

Answer: b. the difficulty in codifying and documenting personal experiences and insights. Explanation: The main challenge in capturing and transferring tacit knowledge within a project team lies in the nature of tacit knowledge itself. Unlike explicit knowledge, which can be easily codified, stored, and transferred through documents and databases, tacit knowledge is deeply rooted in individuals' experiences, insights, and intuition. It is often difficult to articulate, document, and share tacit knowledge, as it requires converting personal know-how into a form that others can understand and apply. While factors such as technology, team culture, and resources can influence knowledge transfer, the inherent complexity of capturing and conveying tacit knowledge remains the primary challenge. Strategies such as storytelling, mentoring, and hands-on collaboration can help facilitate the transfer of tacit knowledge within project teams.

420. What does the acronym "ITTO" stand for in project management?
a. Inputs, Tools, Techniques, and Outputs
b. Inputs, Tasks, Techniques, and Outcomes
c. Initiating, Tracking, Tailoring, and Optimizing
d. Integration, Timing, Tailoring, and Oversight

Answer: a. Inputs, Tools, Techniques, and Outputs. Explanation: In project management, ITTO stands for Inputs, Tools, Techniques, and Outputs. ITTOs are the elements that guide the project manager in carrying out project management processes effectively. Inputs are the items required to start a process, tools and techniques are the methods used to process the inputs, and outputs are the resulting items from the process.

421. Which of the following is not an example of an input in the context of ITTOs?
a. project charter
b. stakeholder register
c. project management plan
d. work performance data

Answer: d. work performance data. Explanation: Work performance data is an example of an output, not an input. Inputs are the documents, plans, designs, or other items that are required to start a project management process. Examples of inputs include the project charter, stakeholder register, and project management plan. Work performance data, on the other hand, is information and documentation generated during the execution of project activities, making it an output.

422. In the ITTO framework, what is the purpose of tools and techniques?
a. to initiate a project management process
b. to process inputs and generate outputs
c. to monitor and control project progress
d. to close a project or phase

Answer: b. to process inputs and generate outputs. Explanation: In the ITTO framework, tools and techniques are the methods, skills, and mechanisms used to process inputs and generate outputs. They are the means by which project managers and teams transform the inputs into the desired outputs. Examples of tools and techniques include data gathering techniques, data analysis techniques, decision-making techniques, and project management methodologies.

423. Which of the following is an example of an output in the context of ITTOs?
a. project scope statement
b. requirements documentation
c. enterprise environmental factors
d. organizational process assets

Answer: a. project scope statement. Explanation: A project scope statement is an example of an output in the context of ITTOs. Outputs are the results, deliverables, or work products that are generated by processing inputs using tools and techniques. Other examples of outputs include project management plan updates, change requests, and project documents. Requirements documentation is an input, while enterprise environmental factors and organizational process assets are considered as inputs or constraints that influence the project management processes.

424. What is the relationship between ITTOs and project management process groups?
a. each process group has its own unique set of ITTOs
b. ITTOs are only relevant to the planning process group
c. ITTOs are used to transition from one process group to another
d. ITTOs are applied throughout all process groups to manage the project effectively

Answer: d. ITTOs are applied throughout all process groups to manage the project effectively. Explanation: ITTOs are not limited to a specific process group but are applied throughout all project management process groups (initiating, planning, executing, monitoring and controlling, and closing) to effectively manage the project. Each process within these groups has its own set of inputs, tools and techniques, and outputs that are tailored to the specific needs and objectives of that process. The outputs of one process often serve as the inputs for the next process, creating a continuous flow of information and deliverables throughout the project lifecycle.

425. Which of the following is not a common tool and technique used in the Direct and Manage Project Work process?
a. expert judgment
b. project management information system (PMIS)
c. meetings
d. procurement management plan

Answer: d. procurement management plan. Explanation: The procurement management plan is not a common tool and technique used in the Direct and Manage Project Work process. This process, which is part of the executing process group, utilizes tools and techniques such as expert judgment (to provide insights and inform decision-making), project management information system (to manage and share project information), and meetings (to discuss project status, issues, and actions). The procurement management plan, on the other hand, is an input to the Direct and Manage Project Work process, providing guidance on how project procurement activities will be managed.

426. What is the primary input to the Develop Project Charter process?
a. project management plan
b. business documents
c. agreements
d. enterprise environmental factors

Answer: b. business documents. Explanation: Business documents are the primary input to the Develop Project Charter process. These documents, which include the project statement of work, business case, and benefits management plan, provide the necessary information to justify the project and define its high-level objectives and requirements. The project charter, which is the main output of this process, formally authorizes the project and documents the initial requirements that satisfy the stakeholders' needs and expectations. Other inputs, such as agreements and enterprise environmental factors, provide additional context and constraints for the project.

427. Which of the following is an output of the Plan Scope Management process?
a. requirements management plan
b. scope baseline
c. project scope statement
d. WBS dictionary

Answer: a. requirements management plan. Explanation: The requirements management plan is an output of the Plan Scope Management process. This plan describes how project requirements will be analyzed, documented, and managed throughout the project lifecycle. It is a component of the project management plan and helps ensure that the project scope is well-defined and aligned with stakeholder expectations. The scope baseline, project scope statement, and WBS dictionary are outputs of other processes within the project scope management knowledge area, such as Define Scope and Create WBS.

428. In the Estimate Costs process, what is the main difference between analogous estimating and parametric estimating?
a. analogous estimating relies on historical data, while parametric estimating uses statistical modeling
b. analogous estimating is a bottom-up approach, while parametric estimating is a top-down approach
c. analogous estimating is more accurate than parametric estimating
d. analogous estimating is used for small projects, while parametric estimating is used for large projects

Answer: a. analogous estimating relies on historical data, while parametric estimating uses statistical modeling. Explanation: The main difference between analogous estimating and parametric estimating in the Estimate Costs process is the approach used to develop cost estimates. Analogous estimating, also known as top-down estimating, uses historical data from similar past projects to estimate the cost of the current project. It relies on expert judgment to identify similarities and adjust for differences. Parametric estimating, on the other hand, uses statistical modeling to estimate project costs based on historical data and project-specific parameters. It involves developing a mathematical model that relates cost to one or more project variables, such as size, complexity, or duration.

429. Which of the following is an example of an organizational process asset that can be used as an input to the Identify Risks process?
a. risk management plan
b. risk register template
c. stakeholder register
d. project schedule

Answer: b. risk register template. Explanation: A risk register template is an example of an organizational process asset that can be used as an input to the Identify Risks process. Organizational process assets are plans, processes, policies, procedures, and knowledge bases that are specific to and maintained by the performing organization. They can be used to influence and support project management activities. In the context of risk management, a risk register template provides a standardized format and structure for documenting and tracking identified risks, their characteristics, and risk response strategies. Other examples of organizational process assets relevant to risk identification include lessons learned databases, risk breakdown structures, and risk category frameworks.

430. In the context of project management, what is the primary purpose of capturing lessons learned?
a. to assign blame for project failures and mistakes
b. to celebrate project successes and recognize high-performing team members
c. to identify areas for improvement and inform future project planning and execution
d. to provide a historical record of the project for legal and compliance purposes

Answer: c. to identify areas for improvement and inform future project planning and execution.
Explanation: The primary purpose of capturing lessons learned in project management is to identify areas for improvement and inform future project planning and execution. Lessons learned are the knowledge gained during a project, including successes, challenges, and recommendations for improvement. By documenting and sharing these lessons, project teams can avoid repeating past mistakes, leverage best practices, and continuously enhance their project management capabilities. Lessons learned should focus on objective learning and improvement rather than assigning blame or celebrating successes, although recognizing high-performing team members can be a part of the process. While lessons learned can serve as a historical record, their main purpose is to drive organizational learning and performance improvement.

431. Which of the following is the most effective way to capture lessons learned throughout the project lifecycle?
a. conducting a single lessons learned review at the end of the project
b. encouraging team members to document lessons learned individually
c. holding regular lessons learned sessions at key project milestones
d. relying on informal conversations and team meetings to discuss lessons learned

Answer: c. holding regular lessons learned sessions at key project milestones. Explanation: Holding regular lessons learned sessions at key project milestones is the most effective way to capture lessons learned throughout the project lifecycle. By conducting lessons learned reviews at regular intervals, such as at the end of each project phase or after significant deliverables, project teams can capture fresh insights while the experiences are still recent. This approach allows for timely identification and application of lessons learned, rather than waiting until the end of the project when details may be forgotten or the opportunity to apply the lessons has passed. Documenting lessons learned individually or relying on informal conversations can be helpful but may lack the structure and consistency of dedicated lessons learned sessions. Conducting a single review at the end of the project can provide valuable insights but misses the opportunity to apply lessons learned during the project itself.

432. What is the main benefit of using a knowledge management system in project management?
a. to reduce the need for project documentation and record-keeping
b. to automate project planning and scheduling activities
c. to facilitate the capture, storage, and retrieval of project knowledge assets
d. to eliminate the need for lessons learned sessions and debriefings

Answer: c. to facilitate the capture, storage, and retrieval of project knowledge assets. Explanation: The main benefit of using a knowledge management system in project management is to facilitate the capture, storage, and retrieval of project knowledge assets. A knowledge management system is a combination of processes, tools, and techniques used to identify, create, represent, distribute, and enable the adoption of knowledge across an organization. In the context of project management, a knowledge management system can help project teams to document and share lessons learned, best practices, templates, and other forms of project knowledge. By providing a centralized repository and effective search and retrieval capabilities, a knowledge management system makes it easier for project teams to access and reuse relevant knowledge, improving efficiency and decision-making. It complements, rather than replaces, other project management activities such as documentation, planning, and lessons learned sessions.

433. Which of the following is a key barrier to effective knowledge sharing in project teams?
a. lack of time and resources dedicated to knowledge management activities
b. over-reliance on formal documentation and reports
c. use of specialized project management software and tools
d. emphasis on individual rather than team performance metrics

Answer: a. lack of time and resources dedicated to knowledge management activities. Explanation: A key barrier to effective knowledge sharing in project teams is the lack of time and resources dedicated to knowledge management activities. In many organizations, project teams are under pressure to deliver results quickly and may view knowledge management as a lower priority compared to other project activities. Without sufficient time, resources, and support for knowledge capture, storage, and sharing, valuable lessons learned and best practices may be lost or forgotten. Over-reliance on formal documentation, use of specialized software, or emphasis on individual performance can also hinder knowledge sharing to some extent, but the lack of dedicated resources is often the most significant barrier. To overcome this challenge, organizations should recognize the value of knowledge management and allocate appropriate time, budget, and personnel to support knowledge-sharing activities within and across project teams.

434. How can project managers encourage a culture of knowledge sharing within their teams?
a. by emphasizing the importance of individual expertise and specialization
b. by relying primarily on formal reports and documentation to capture knowledge
c. by leading by example and creating opportunities for collaboration and learning
d. by implementing strict controls and approval processes for knowledge sharing

Answer: c. by leading by example and creating opportunities for collaboration and learning. Explanation: Project managers can encourage a culture of knowledge sharing within their teams by leading by example and creating opportunities for collaboration and learning. As leaders, project managers set the tone for the team and can model knowledge-sharing behaviors, such as openly discussing lessons learned, seeking feedback, and encouraging open communication. They can create a psychologically safe environment where team members feel comfortable sharing their ideas, experiences, and challenges without fear of criticism or retribution. Project managers can also facilitate knowledge sharing by creating opportunities for collaboration, such as cross-functional team assignments, peer review sessions, and knowledge-sharing workshops. By prioritizing and actively promoting knowledge sharing, project managers can foster a culture of continuous learning and improvement within their teams. Relying on individual expertise, formal documentation, or strict controls may have their place in project management but are less effective in encouraging a culture of knowledge sharing compared to leadership and collaboration.

435. What is the relationship between lessons learned and the project closure process?
a. lessons learned are not relevant to the project closure process
b. the project closure process is a prerequisite for capturing lessons learned
c. capturing and documenting lessons learned is a key activity in the project closure process
d. lessons learned should only be captured and documented after the project is formally closed

Answer: c. capturing and documenting lessons learned is a key activity in the project closure process. Explanation: Capturing and documenting lessons learned is a key activity in the project closure process. The project closure process involves finalizing all project activities, transitioning deliverables to the customer or sponsor, and documenting the project's performance and lessons learned. Capturing lessons learned during project closure helps to ensure that the knowledge gained during the project is not lost and can be applied to future projects. It involves conducting a final lessons learned review, documenting the lessons in a lessons learned report or database, and communicating the lessons to relevant stakeholders. While lessons learned should be captured throughout the project lifecycle, the project closure process provides a formal opportunity to consolidate and summarize the lessons learned from the entire project. Lessons learned are highly relevant to project closure, and the closure process is not a prerequisite for capturing lessons learned, as they should be documented throughout the project.

436. How can organizations effectively disseminate lessons learned across projects and teams?
a. by storing lessons learned documents in a centralized database or repository
b. by conducting post-project reviews and distributing the findings to all employees
c. by incorporating lessons learned into project management methodologies and templates
d. all of the above

Answer: d. all of the above. Explanation: Organizations can effectively disseminate lessons learned across projects and teams by using a combination of approaches, including storing lessons learned documents in a centralized database or repository, conducting post-project reviews and distributing the findings, and incorporating lessons learned into project management methodologies and templates. A centralized lessons learned database provides a single source of truth and makes it easy for project teams to access and search for relevant lessons. Post-project reviews help to validate and prioritize the lessons learned and communicate them to a wider audience. Incorporating lessons learned into project management methodologies and templates ensures that best practices and proven approaches are consistently applied across projects. By using multiple dissemination channels and embedding lessons learned into standard processes, organizations can promote a culture of continuous learning and improvement.

437. What is the role of storytelling in capturing and sharing lessons learned?
a. to provide a more engaging and memorable way to convey lessons learned
b. to replace formal documentation and reporting of lessons learned
c. to assign blame or credit for project successes and failures
d. to entertain project stakeholders and improve team morale

Answer: a. to provide a more engaging and memorable way to convey lessons learned. Explanation: Storytelling plays a valuable role in capturing and sharing lessons learned by providing a more engaging and memorable way to convey the lessons. Stories are a powerful tool for communicating complex ideas and experiences in a relatable and impactful way. When used to share lessons learned, stories can help to provide context, convey emotions, and illustrate the real-world application of the lessons. Stories can make the lessons learned more vivid and easier to remember compared to dry, factual reports. They can also help to break down silos and facilitate knowledge sharing across different projects and teams. However, storytelling should complement, rather than replace, formal documentation and reporting of lessons learned. It is not an appropriate vehicle for assigning blame or credit or merely entertaining stakeholders. When used effectively, storytelling can enhance the impact and retention of lessons learned and contribute to a culture of learning and knowledge sharing.

438. What is the purpose of a lessons learned register or database?
a. to provide a formal record of project successes and failures for performance evaluations
b. to assign responsibility for implementing lessons learned on future projects
c. to serve as a searchable repository of lessons learned for future reference and application
d. to replace the need for conducting lessons learned sessions and reviews

Answer: c. to serve as a searchable repository of lessons learned for future reference and application. Explanation: The purpose of a lessons learned register or database is to serve as a searchable repository of lessons learned for future reference and application. A lessons learned register is a centralized document or database that captures and organizes the lessons learned from various projects across an organization. It provides a structured way to document, categorize, and store lessons learned, making it easier for project teams to find and apply relevant lessons to their own projects. The register typically includes fields such as project name, date, lesson learned description, category, and keywords to facilitate searching and retrieval. By maintaining a lessons learned register, organizations can promote knowledge sharing, prevent the repetition of past mistakes, and continuously improve their project management practices. The register is not intended to replace lessons learned sessions, assign responsibility, or provide a formal record for performance evaluations, but rather to support the ongoing capture, dissemination, and application of lessons learned.

439. In the context of knowledge management, what is the difference between explicit and tacit knowledge?
a. explicit knowledge is easy to articulate and share, while tacit knowledge is difficult to express and transfer
b. explicit knowledge is specific to a particular project, while tacit knowledge applies to all projects
c. explicit knowledge is more valuable than tacit knowledge for project success
d. explicit knowledge is owned by the organization, while tacit knowledge belongs to individuals

Answer: a. explicit knowledge is easy to articulate and share, while tacit knowledge is difficult to express and transfer. Explanation: In the context of knowledge management, the main difference between explicit and tacit knowledge is that explicit knowledge is easy to articulate, codify, and share, while tacit knowledge is difficult to express and transfer. Explicit knowledge refers to knowledge that can be readily documented, stored, and communicated through written or digital means, such as reports, manuals, or databases. It is often structured, formal, and can be easily shared across an organization. In contrast, tacit knowledge is the personal, experiential, and intuitive knowledge that resides within individuals' minds. It is often difficult to articulate, document, and transfer to others, as it is deeply rooted in an individual's experiences, insights, and expertise. Both explicit and tacit knowledge are valuable for project success, and effective knowledge management involves strategies to capture, share, and apply both types of knowledge. The ownership and applicability of knowledge are not necessarily determined by its explicit or tacit nature.

440. What is the primary purpose of the Monitor and Control Project Work process?
a. to authorize the project and assign the project manager

b. to develop a detailed project schedule and budget

c. to track project progress, identify deviations, and take corrective action

d. to formally close the project and obtain final acceptance of deliverables

Answer: c. to track project progress, identify deviations, and take corrective action. Explanation: The primary purpose of the Monitor and Control Project Work process is to track project progress, identify deviations from the project management plan, and take corrective action to bring the project back on track. This process involves collecting, measuring, and analyzing project performance data, comparing actual results to planned results, and implementing necessary changes to ensure that project objectives are met. Monitoring and controlling project work is an ongoing process that occurs throughout the project lifecycle, from initiation to closure.

441. Which of the following is not a key input to the Monitor and Control Project Work process?

a. project management plan

b. project documents

c. work performance data

d. change requests

Answer: d. change requests. Explanation: Change requests are not a key input to the Monitor and Control Project Work process, but rather an output of this process. The key inputs to Monitor and Control Project Work are the project management plan (which provides the baseline for measuring project performance), project documents (such as the issue log and risk register, which help to identify potential problems), and work performance data (which includes information on project progress, resource utilization, and quality metrics). Change requests, on the other hand, are generated as an output of this process when deviations or issues are identified that require modifications to the project scope, schedule, or budget.

442. What is the main difference between the Monitor and Control Project Work process and the Perform Integrated Change Control process?

a. Monitor and Control Project Work focuses on identifying deviations, while Perform Integrated Change Control focuses on implementing corrective actions

b. Monitor and Control Project Work is performed throughout the project, while Perform Integrated Change Control is only performed at the end of the project

c. Monitor and Control Project Work is the responsibility of the project manager, while Perform Integrated Change Control is the responsibility of the change control board

d. Monitor and Control Project Work is a process within the monitoring and controlling process group, while Perform Integrated Change Control is a process within the executing process group

Answer: a. Monitor and Control Project Work focuses on identifying deviations, while Perform Integrated Change Control focuses on implementing corrective actions. Explanation: The main difference between the Monitor and Control Project Work process and the Perform Integrated Change Control process is their focus. Monitor and Control Project Work is primarily concerned with tracking project progress, comparing actual performance to planned performance, and identifying deviations or issues that may require corrective action. Perform Integrated Change Control, on the other hand, is focused on reviewing, approving, and managing changes to the project baseline in a comprehensive and integrated manner. Both processes are part of the monitoring and controlling process group and are performed throughout the project lifecycle, with the project manager and the change control board playing key roles in their respective processes.

443. Which of the following is a key tool or technique used in the Monitor and Control Project Work process?
a. expert judgment
b. data analysis
c. meetings
d. all of the above

Answer: d. all of the above. Explanation: Expert judgment, data analysis, and meetings are all key tools and techniques used in the Monitor and Control Project Work process. Expert judgment involves drawing upon the expertise and experience of individuals or groups to assess project performance, identify issues, and recommend corrective actions. Data analysis techniques, such as earned value analysis, trend analysis, and forecasting, are used to analyze project performance data and predict future outcomes. Meetings, such as status reviews and progress meetings, provide a forum for discussing project performance, identifying issues, and making decisions. Other tools and techniques used in this process may include project management information systems, work performance reports, and project management software.

444. In the context of the Monitor and Control Project Work process, what is the purpose of work performance information?
a. to provide data on project progress, status, and performance
b. to identify the specific deliverables and activities required to complete the project
c. to estimate the time and resources needed to complete project activities
d. to document the processes and procedures for managing project work

Answer: a. to provide data on project progress, status, and performance. Explanation: In the context of the Monitor and Control Project Work process, the purpose of work performance information is to provide data on project progress, status, and performance. Work performance information includes data on project scope, schedule, cost, resource utilization, quality, and other performance metrics. This information is collected through various tools and techniques, such as status reports, progress meetings, and project management software. Work performance information is a key input to the Monitor and Control Project Work process, as it provides the basis for comparing actual performance to planned performance and identifying deviations or issues that may require corrective action.

445. What is the main purpose of a project status report in the Monitor and Control Project Work process?
a. to provide a detailed description of the project scope and deliverables
b. to communicate project progress, issues, and risks to project stakeholders
c. to document the project team's roles, responsibilities, and performance
d. to provide a formal record of project changes and their impact on the project baseline

Answer: b. to communicate project progress, issues, and risks to project stakeholders. Explanation: The main purpose of a project status report in the Monitor and Control Project Work process is to communicate project progress, issues, and risks to project stakeholders. A project status report is a document that provides a snapshot of the project's current state, including information on project scope, schedule, budget, quality, and risk. It is typically prepared by the project manager and distributed to key stakeholders, such as the project sponsor, team members, and clients, on a regular basis (e.g., weekly or monthly). The status report helps to keep stakeholders informed about the project's performance, highlights any issues or risks that may impact the project, and facilitates decision-making and communication among the project team and stakeholders.

446. What is the role of the project management information system (PMIS) in the Monitor and Control Project Work process?
a. to provide a centralized repository for storing and accessing project data and documents
b. to automate the creation of project schedules and resource allocation plans
c. to facilitate communication and collaboration among project team members
d. to analyze project performance data and generate performance reports

Answer: a. to provide a centralized repository for storing and accessing project data and documents. Explanation: The primary role of the project management information system (PMIS) in the Monitor and Control Project Work process is to provide a centralized repository for storing and accessing project data and documents. A PMIS is a set of tools, techniques, and processes used to collect, integrate, and disseminate project information. It serves as a single source of truth for project data, including project plans, schedules, budgets, performance metrics, and status reports. By providing a centralized location for storing and accessing project information, a PMIS enables project managers and team members to easily retrieve and analyze data, track project progress, and make informed decisions. While a PMIS may also facilitate communication, collaboration, and reporting, its main purpose in the context of monitoring and controlling project work is to serve as a comprehensive and reliable source of project data.

447. What is the purpose of earned value analysis in the Monitor and Control Project Work process?
a. to compare actual project costs to planned project costs
b. to measure project progress and performance against the project baseline
c. to identify the critical path and optimize the project schedule
d. to assess the quality of project deliverables and processes

Answer: b. to measure project progress and performance against the project baseline. Explanation: The purpose of earned value analysis in the Monitor and Control Project Work process is to measure project progress and performance against the project baseline. Earned value analysis is a technique that integrates scope, schedule, and resource data to assess project performance and progress. It compares the amount of work that was planned to be completed with what has actually been completed and what has been spent, providing a more accurate and comprehensive picture of project performance than simply comparing actual costs to planned costs. By calculating metrics such as planned value (PV), earned value (EV), and actual cost (AC), earned value analysis helps project managers to identify schedule and cost variances, forecast future performance, and make informed decisions about corrective actions.

448. What is the main benefit of using trend analysis in the Monitor and Control Project Work process?
a. to identify the root causes of project issues and problems
b. to predict future project performance based on historical data

c. to optimize resource allocation and utilization across the project

d. to assess the impact of project changes on the project baseline

Answer: b. to predict future project performance based on historical data. Explanation: The main benefit of using trend analysis in the Monitor and Control Project Work process is to predict future project performance based on historical data. Trend analysis involves using mathematical techniques to analyze project performance data over time and identify patterns or trends that can be used to forecast future outcomes. By examining trends in project metrics such as schedule variance, cost variance, and resource utilization, project managers can anticipate potential issues or opportunities and take proactive measures to keep the project on track. Trend analysis can also help to identify areas of the project that may require additional attention or resources, and to assess the effectiveness of corrective actions taken in response to performance issues.

449. What is the relationship between the Monitor and Control Project Work process and the project management plan?

a. the project management plan is an input to the Monitor and Control Project Work process

b. the project management plan is an output of the Monitor and Control Project Work process

c. the Monitor and Control Project Work process is not related to the project management plan

d. the project management plan is created during the Monitor and Control Project Work process

Answer: a. the project management plan is an input to the Monitor and Control Project Work process. Explanation: The relationship between the Monitor and Control Project Work process and the project management plan is that the project management plan is a key input to the Monitor and Control Project Work process. The project management plan is a comprehensive document that describes how the project will be executed, monitored, controlled, and closed. It integrates and consolidates all of the subsidiary plans and baselines, such as the scope management plan, schedule management plan, cost management plan, and quality management plan. The Monitor and Control Project Work process uses the project management plan as a baseline for measuring project performance and progress, identifying deviations, and taking corrective actions. Any changes to the project management plan resulting from the Monitor and Control Project Work process are managed through the Perform Integrated Change Control process.

450. Which of the following is not an input to the Develop Project Charter process?

a. project statement of work

b. business case

c. agreements

d. enterprise environmental factors

Answer: d. enterprise environmental factors. Explanation: Enterprise environmental factors, such as organizational culture, infrastructure, and market conditions, are not a direct input to the Develop Project Charter process. They are considered as general inputs that may influence the project, but they are not specifically required to create the project charter. The key inputs to this process are the project statement of work (describing the product, service, or result to be delivered), the business case (providing the reasoning for initiating the project), and agreements (relevant contracts or documents defining initial intentions).

451. What is the main output of the Plan Scope Management process?
a. project scope statement
b. work breakdown structure (WBS)
c. scope management plan
d. requirements documentation

Answer: c. scope management plan. Explanation: The main output of the Plan Scope Management process is the scope management plan. This plan is a component of the project management plan that describes how the project scope will be defined, validated, and controlled. It outlines the processes, tools, and techniques to be used in managing project scope and serves as a guide for scope-related decision-making throughout the project. The project scope statement, work breakdown structure (WBS), and requirements documentation are outputs of other processes within the Scope Management knowledge area.

452. Which of the following is a tool and technique used in the Estimate Activity Durations process?
a. parametric estimating
b. bottom-up estimating
c. three-point estimating
d. all of the above

Answer: d. all of the above. Explanation: Parametric estimating, bottom-up estimating, and three-point estimating are all tools and techniques used in the Estimate Activity Durations process. Parametric estimating uses historical data and project parameters to calculate durations, while bottom-up estimating involves estimating the duration of individual activities and rolling them up to obtain the total duration. Three-point estimating considers the optimistic, pessimistic, and most likely durations to create a more accurate estimate. Other tools and techniques used in this process include analogous estimating, reserve analysis, and expert judgment.

453. In the Determine Budget process, what is the main difference between the cost baseline and the project funding requirements?
a. the cost baseline includes management reserves, while the project funding requirements do not
b. the cost baseline is time-phased, while the project funding requirements are not
c. the cost baseline is an output, while the project funding requirements are an input
d. the cost baseline and the project funding requirements are the same thing

Answer: b. the cost baseline is time-phased, while the project funding requirements are not. Explanation: The main difference between the cost baseline and the project funding requirements in the Determine Budget process is that the cost baseline is time-phased, while the project funding requirements are not. The cost baseline is a time-phased budget that is used as a basis against which to measure, monitor, and control overall cost performance on the project. It includes all the authorized budgets for the project, including management reserves. The project funding requirements, on the other hand, represent the projected funding requirements over time, which are derived from the cost baseline and can be used to determine periodic funding requirements for the project.

454. What is the primary technique used in the Estimate Costs process?

a. analogous estimating
b. parametric estimating
c. three-point estimating
d. bottom-up estimating

Answer: d. bottom-up estimating. Explanation: The primary technique used in the Estimate Costs process is bottom-up estimating. Bottom-up estimating involves estimating the cost of individual work packages or activities and then aggregating these estimates to obtain the total project cost. This technique provides a more accurate and detailed cost estimate than other techniques like analogous estimating (using historical data from similar projects) or parametric estimating (using statistical modeling). Three-point estimating is also used in this process, but it is more commonly associated with the Estimate Activity Durations process.

455. Which of the following is not an output of the Plan Quality Management process?
a. quality management plan
b. process improvement plan
c. quality metrics
d. quality checklists

Answer: d. quality checklists. Explanation: Quality checklists are not an output of the Plan Quality Management process. The key outputs of this process are the quality management plan (describing how quality will be managed and validated), the process improvement plan (identifying steps for analyzing processes to generate improvements), and quality metrics (defining the attributes of the project or product that will be measured to ensure compliance with quality standards). Quality checklists, which are structured tools used to verify that a set of required steps has been performed, are an output of the Manage Quality process.

456. What is the main purpose of the Manage Communications process?
a. to determine the information and communication needs of the project stakeholders
b. to create, collect, distribute, store, retrieve, and dispose of project information
c. to monitor and control communications throughout the project life cycle
d. to identify, prioritize, and engage project stakeholders

Answer: b. to create, collect, distribute, store, retrieve, and dispose of project information. Explanation: The main purpose of the Manage Communications process is to create, collect, distribute, store, retrieve, and dispose of project information in accordance with the communications management plan. This process involves managing project communications throughout the project life cycle to ensure that the information needs of the project stakeholders are met. Determining the information and communication needs of stakeholders is part of the Plan Communications Management process, while monitoring and controlling communications is the focus of the Monitor Communications process. Identifying, prioritizing, and engaging stakeholders is part of the Manage Stakeholder Engagement process.

457. Which of the following is a key input to the Identify Risks process?
a. risk management plan
b. cost management plan

c. quality management plan
d. procurement management plan

Answer: a. risk management plan. Explanation: The risk management plan is a key input to the Identify Risks process. This plan defines how risk management activities will be structured and performed on the project. It includes the methodology, roles and responsibilities, budgeting, timing, risk categories, definitions of risk probability and impact, and other relevant information needed for effective risk management. The cost management plan, quality management plan, and procurement management plan are inputs to other processes within their respective knowledge areas, but they are not directly used in the Identify Risks process.

458. What is the main purpose of the Control Procurements process?
a. to plan and document project purchasing decisions
b. to obtain seller responses, select sellers, and award contracts
c. to manage procurement relationships, monitor contract performance, and make changes as needed
d. to close out project procurements and verify that all work and deliverables are acceptable

Answer: c. to manage procurement relationships, monitor contract performance, and make changes as needed. Explanation: The main purpose of the Control Procurements process is to manage procurement relationships, monitor contract performance, and make changes and corrections as needed. This process ensures that the performance of both the buyer and seller meets the project's requirements according to the terms of the legal agreements. It involves managing procurement relationships, monitoring contract performance against established requirements, inspecting and verifying the conformance of procured products or services, and making payments. Planning and documenting purchasing decisions is part of the Plan Procurement Management process, while obtaining seller responses and awarding contracts is the focus of the Conduct Procurements process. Closing out procurements is handled in the Close Project or Phase process.

459. Which of the following is an output of the Close Project or Phase process?
a. project charter
b. project management plan
c. accepted deliverables
d. final product, service, or result transition

Answer: d. final product, service, or result transition. Explanation: The final product, service, or result transition is an output of the Close Project or Phase process. This output involves transferring the completed product, service, or result to the next phase or to production and/or operations as defined in the project management plan. It includes obtaining formal acceptance from the relevant stakeholders and documenting the transition. The project charter and project management plan are inputs to this process, not outputs. Accepted deliverables, which are verified and accepted by the customer or sponsor, are an input to the Close Project or Phase process.

460. Which of the following is not an input to the Develop Project Charter process?
a. project statement of work

b. business case

c. agreements

d. enterprise environmental factors

Answer: d. enterprise environmental factors. Explanation: Enterprise environmental factors, such as organizational culture, infrastructure, and market conditions, are not a direct input to the Develop Project Charter process. They are considered as general inputs that may influence the project, but they are not specifically required to create the project charter. The key inputs to this process are the project statement of work (describing the product, service, or result to be delivered), the business case (providing the reasoning for initiating the project), and agreements (relevant contracts or documents defining initial intentions).

461. What is the main output of the Plan Scope Management process?

a. project scope statement

b. work breakdown structure (WBS)

c. scope management plan

d. requirements documentation

Answer: c. scope management plan. Explanation: The main output of the Plan Scope Management process is the scope management plan. This plan is a component of the project management plan that describes how the project scope will be defined, validated, and controlled. It outlines the processes, tools, and techniques to be used in managing project scope and serves as a guide for scope-related decision-making throughout the project. The project scope statement, work breakdown structure (WBS), and requirements documentation are outputs of other processes within the Scope Management knowledge area.

462. Which of the following is a tool and technique used in the Estimate Activity Durations process?

a. parametric estimating

b. bottom-up estimating

c. three-point estimating

d. all of the above

Answer: d. all of the above. Explanation: Parametric estimating, bottom-up estimating, and three-point estimating are all tools and techniques used in the Estimate Activity Durations process. Parametric estimating uses historical data and project parameters to calculate durations, while bottom-up estimating involves estimating the duration of individual activities and rolling them up to obtain the total duration. Three-point estimating considers the optimistic, pessimistic, and most likely durations to create a more accurate estimate. Other tools and techniques used in this process include analogous estimating, reserve analysis, and expert judgment.

463. In the Determine Budget process, what is the main difference between the cost baseline and the project funding requirements?

a. the cost baseline includes management reserves, while the project funding requirements do not

b. the cost baseline is time-phased, while the project funding requirements are not

c. the cost baseline is an output, while the project funding requirements are an input

d. the cost baseline and the project funding requirements are the same thing

Answer: b. the cost baseline is time-phased, while the project funding requirements are not. Explanation: The main difference between the cost baseline and the project funding requirements in the Determine Budget process is that the cost baseline is time-phased, while the project funding requirements are not. The cost baseline is a time-phased budget that is used as a basis against which to measure, monitor, and control overall cost performance on the project. It includes all the authorized budgets for the project, including management reserves. The project funding requirements, on the other hand, represent the projected funding requirements over time, which are derived from the cost baseline and can be used to determine periodic funding requirements for the project.

464. What is the primary technique used in the Estimate Costs process?
a. analogous estimating
b. parametric estimating
c. three-point estimating
d. bottom-up estimating

Answer: d. bottom-up estimating. Explanation: The primary technique used in the Estimate Costs process is bottom-up estimating. Bottom-up estimating involves estimating the cost of individual work packages or activities and then aggregating these estimates to obtain the total project cost. This technique provides a more accurate and detailed cost estimate than other techniques like analogous estimating (using historical data from similar projects) or parametric estimating (using statistical modeling). Three-point estimating is also used in this process, but it is more commonly associated with the Estimate Activity Durations process.

465. Which of the following is not an output of the Plan Quality Management process?
a. quality management plan
b. process improvement plan
c. quality metrics
d. quality checklists

Answer: d. quality checklists. Explanation: Quality checklists are not an output of the Plan Quality Management process. The key outputs of this process are the quality management plan (describing how quality will be managed and validated), the process improvement plan (identifying steps for analyzing processes to generate improvements), and quality metrics (defining the attributes of the project or product that will be measured to ensure compliance with quality standards). Quality checklists, which are structured tools used to verify that a set of required steps has been performed, are an output of the Manage Quality process.

466. What is the main purpose of the Manage Communications process?
a. to determine the information and communication needs of the project stakeholders
b. to create, collect, distribute, store, retrieve, and dispose of project information
c. to monitor and control communications throughout the project life cycle
d. to identify, prioritize, and engage project stakeholders

Answer: b. to create, collect, distribute, store, retrieve, and dispose of project information. Explanation: The main purpose of the Manage Communications process is to create, collect, distribute, store, retrieve, and dispose of project information in accordance with the communications management plan. This process involves managing project communications throughout the project life cycle to ensure that the information needs of the project stakeholders are met. Determining the information and communication needs of stakeholders is part of the Plan Communications Management process, while monitoring and controlling communications is the focus of the Monitor Communications process. Identifying, prioritizing, and engaging stakeholders is part of the Manage Stakeholder Engagement process.

467. Which of the following is a key input to the Identify Risks process?
a. risk management plan
b. cost management plan
c. quality management plan
d. procurement management plan

Answer: a. risk management plan. Explanation: The risk management plan is a key input to the Identify Risks process. This plan defines how risk management activities will be structured and performed on the project. It includes the methodology, roles and responsibilities, budgeting, timing, risk categories, definitions of risk probability and impact, and other relevant information needed for effective risk management. The cost management plan, quality management plan, and procurement management plan are inputs to other processes within their respective knowledge areas, but they are not directly used in the Identify Risks process.

468. What is the main purpose of the Control Procurements process?
a. to plan and document project purchasing decisions
b. to obtain seller responses, select sellers, and award contracts
c. to manage procurement relationships, monitor contract performance, and make changes as needed
d. to close out project procurements and verify that all work and deliverables are acceptable

Answer: c. to manage procurement relationships, monitor contract performance, and make changes as needed. Explanation: The main purpose of the Control Procurements process is to manage procurement relationships, monitor contract performance, and make changes and corrections as needed. This process ensures that the performance of both the buyer and seller meets the project's requirements according to the terms of the legal agreements. It involves managing procurement relationships, monitoring contract performance against established requirements, inspecting and verifying the conformance of procured products or services, and making payments. Planning and documenting purchasing decisions is part of the Plan Procurement Management process, while obtaining seller responses and awarding contracts is the focus of the Conduct Procurements process. Closing out procurements is handled in the Close Project or Phase process.

469. Which of the following is an output of the Close Project or Phase process?
a. project charter
b. project management plan
c. accepted deliverables
d. final product, service, or result transition

Answer: d. final product, service, or result transition. Explanation: The final product, service, or result transition is an output of the Close Project or Phase process. This output involves transferring the completed product, service, or result to the next phase or to production and/or operations as defined in the project management plan. It includes obtaining formal acceptance from the relevant stakeholders and documenting the transition. The project charter and project management plan are inputs to this process, not outputs. Accepted deliverables, which are verified and accepted by the customer or sponsor, are an input to the Close Project or Phase process.

470. What is the primary purpose of the Perform Integrated Change Control process?
a. to identify potential changes to the project and assess their impact
b. to review, approve, and manage changes to the project in a comprehensive manner
c. to implement approved changes and update project documents accordingly
d. to prevent changes from occurring during the project lifecycle

Answer: b. to review, approve, and manage changes to the project in a comprehensive manner. Explanation: The primary purpose of the Perform Integrated Change Control process is to review, approve, and manage changes to the project in a comprehensive and integrated manner. This process ensures that all changes are carefully evaluated, their impact on the project is assessed, and they are approved or rejected based on their alignment with project objectives. It involves coordinating changes across all project knowledge areas and ensuring that they are communicated to relevant stakeholders. Identifying potential changes and assessing their impact is part of the process, but not its primary focus. Implementing approved changes is a separate activity that follows the Perform Integrated Change Control process, and preventing changes altogether is not realistic or desirable in most projects.

471. Which of the following is not an input to the Perform Integrated Change Control process?
a. project management plan
b. work performance reports
c. change requests
d. project funding requirements

Answer: d. project funding requirements. Explanation: Project funding requirements are not a direct input to the Perform Integrated Change Control process. The key inputs to this process are the project management plan (which provides the baseline against which changes are evaluated), work performance reports (which provide information on project progress and performance that may trigger change requests), change requests (which are formal proposals to modify any aspect of the project), and enterprise environmental factors and organizational process assets (which may influence how changes are managed). Project funding requirements are an input to the Determine Budget process in the Cost Management knowledge area.

472. What is the main tool or technique used in the Perform Integrated Change Control process?
a. expert judgment
b. change control tools
c. meetings
d. data analysis

Answer: b. change control tools. Explanation: The main tool or technique used in the Perform Integrated Change Control process is change control tools. These are manual or automated tools used to manage, control, and communicate changes throughout the project lifecycle. Examples include change request forms, change logs, and configuration management systems. These tools help to capture, document, and track changes, as well as facilitate the change review and approval process. Expert judgment, meetings, and data analysis are also used in this process, but they are not as central as the change control tools.

473. Which of the following is not a valid reason for initiating a change request?
a. to correct errors or defects in project deliverables
b. to respond to external factors affecting the project, such as market changes or new regulations
c. to accommodate stakeholder preferences or expectations
d. to improve the project manager's reputation and visibility within the organization

Answer: d. to improve the project manager's reputation and visibility within the organization. Explanation: Improving the project manager's reputation and visibility within the organization is not a valid reason for initiating a change request. Change requests should be based on legitimate project needs or opportunities, such as correcting errors or defects, responding to external factors, or accommodating stakeholder preferences (within reason). They should not be driven by personal or political motivations. Valid reasons for initiating change requests include addressing issues or risks, optimizing project performance, aligning the project with changing business objectives, or incorporating lessons learned. The Perform Integrated Change Control process ensures that all change requests are carefully evaluated and approved only if they are justified and beneficial to the project.

474. What is the role of the change control board (CCB) in the Perform Integrated Change Control process?
a. to identify and prioritize potential changes to the project
b. to evaluate the impact of change requests and make approval decisions
c. to implement approved changes and update project documents
d. to communicate the status of change requests to project stakeholders

Answer: b. to evaluate the impact of change requests and make approval decisions. Explanation: The role of the change control board (CCB) in the Perform Integrated Change Control process is to evaluate the impact of change requests and make approval decisions. The CCB is a formally chartered group responsible for reviewing, approving, deferring, or rejecting changes to the project. It typically includes representatives from key stakeholder groups, such as the project sponsor, client, and functional managers. The CCB assesses the impact of change requests on project scope, schedule, cost, quality, risk, and other relevant factors, and makes decisions based on the project's overall objectives and priorities. Identifying and prioritizing changes, implementing approved changes, and communicating change status are typically the responsibility of the project manager and team, not the CCB.

475. Which of the following is a key output of the Perform Integrated Change Control process?
a. change requests
b. project management plan updates
c. project documents updates
d. all of the above

Answer: d. all of the above. Explanation: Change requests, project management plan updates, and project documents updates are all key outputs of the Perform Integrated Change Control process. Change requests are an input to this process, representing proposed modifications to the project. As part of the change control process, these requests are reviewed, evaluated, and either approved, deferred, or rejected. Approved changes result in updates to the project management plan and project documents, such as the scope statement, WBS, schedule, budget, and risk register. These updates ensure that the project baseline and documentation reflect the approved changes and remain aligned with the current project scope and objectives.

476. What is the relationship between the Perform Integrated Change Control process and the Monitor and Control Project Work process?
a. they are the same process with different names
b. Perform Integrated Change Control is a subprocess of Monitor and Control Project Work
c. Monitor and Control Project Work is a subprocess of Perform Integrated Change Control
d. they are separate but interrelated processes within the Monitoring and Controlling process group

Answer: d. they are separate but interrelated processes within the Monitoring and Controlling process group. Explanation: The Perform Integrated Change Control process and the Monitor and Control Project Work process are separate but interrelated processes within the Monitoring and Controlling process group. Monitor and Control Project Work is focused on tracking project progress, comparing actual performance to planned performance, and identifying areas that may require preventive or corrective action. When issues or opportunities are identified that require changes to the project, change requests are generated as an output of Monitor and Control Project Work. These change requests then become an input to the Perform Integrated Change Control process, which is responsible for reviewing, approving, and managing changes in a comprehensive and integrated manner. The two processes work together to ensure that the project remains on track and aligned with its objectives, while also allowing for necessary changes to be made in a controlled and coordinated way.

477. How does the Perform Integrated Change Control process relate to the Project Integration Management knowledge area?
a. it is one of the processes within the Project Integration Management knowledge area
b. it ensures that changes are integrated across all project knowledge areas
c. it is not directly related to Project Integration Management
d. it is the only process in Project Integration Management that deals with changes

Answer: a. it is one of the processes within the Project Integration Management knowledge area. Explanation: The Perform Integrated Change Control process is one of the key processes within the Project Integration Management knowledge area. Project Integration Management is focused on coordinating and unifying all aspects of the project, including managing changes in a comprehensive and integrated manner. The Perform Integrated Change Control process is a critical component of this integration, as it ensures that changes are evaluated, approved, and implemented in a way that considers their impact on all project knowledge areas and maintains the integrity of the project baseline and objectives. While this process does help to integrate changes across knowledge areas, it is not the only process in Project Integration Management, which also includes processes such as Develop Project Charter, Develop Project Management Plan, Direct and Manage Project Work, and Close Project or Phase.

478. What is the main benefit of having a formal change control process in place?
a. to eliminate the need for changes during the project lifecycle
b. to empower the project manager to make unilateral decisions about changes
c. to ensure that changes are evaluated, approved, and implemented in a controlled and transparent manner
d. to increase the number of changes that can be made to the project

Answer: c. to ensure that changes are evaluated, approved, and implemented in a controlled and transparent manner. Explanation: The main benefit of having a formal change control process, such as the Perform Integrated Change Control process, is to ensure that changes are evaluated, approved, and implemented in a controlled and transparent manner. A well-defined change control process helps to minimize the risk of uncontrolled or unauthorized changes, which can have negative impacts on project scope, schedule, cost, and quality. It provides a structured framework for reviewing and assessing the impact of changes, making informed decisions about their approval, and communicating the status and implications of changes to relevant stakeholders. This transparency and control helps to maintain project alignment, manage stakeholder expectations, and prevent scope creep. The goal is not to eliminate changes altogether or to increase the number of changes, but rather to ensure that changes are made in a thoughtful, deliberate, and transparent way that supports the project's overall objectives.

479. What is the potential consequence of not having an effective Perform Integrated Change Control process in place?
a. increased efficiency and agility in project execution
b. improved stakeholder satisfaction and engagement
c. enhanced project team morale and motivation
d. uncontrolled scope creep and project delays

Answer: d. uncontrolled scope creep and project delays. Explanation: The potential consequence of not having an effective Perform Integrated Change Control process in place is uncontrolled scope creep and project delays. Without a formal change control process, changes may be made to the project without proper evaluation, approval, or communication. This can lead to uncontrolled expansion of project scope (scope creep), as stakeholders may request additional features or modifications without considering the impact on project schedule, budget, or resources. Unmanaged changes can also cause project delays, as the project team may struggle to accommodate the additional work or rework required. This can result in missed deadlines, cost overruns, and reduced project quality. Effective change control helps to prevent these negative consequences by ensuring that changes are carefully evaluated, approved only if they are justified and feasible, and implemented in a coordinated and communicated manner.

480. What is the main output of the Validate Scope process?
a. accepted deliverables
b. work performance information
c. change requests
d. project documents updates

Answer: a. accepted deliverables. Explanation: The main output of the Validate Scope process is accepted deliverables. This process involves formalizing the acceptance of completed project deliverables by reviewing them with the customer or sponsor to ensure they are satisfactory and meet the specified acceptance criteria. Work performance information, change requests, and project documents updates are outputs of other monitoring and controlling processes, such as Monitor and Control Project Work and Perform Integrated Change Control.

481. Which of the following is not a tool or technique used in the Estimate Activity Resources process?
a. bottom-up estimating
b. parametric estimating
c. analogous estimating
d. three-point estimating

Answer: d. three-point estimating. Explanation: Three-point estimating is not a tool or technique used in the Estimate Activity Resources process. It is a technique used in the Estimate Activity Durations process to improve the accuracy of duration estimates by considering the optimistic, pessimistic, and most likely durations. The tools and techniques used in the Estimate Activity Resources process include expert judgment, bottom-up estimating (estimating resources for individual activities and aggregating them), parametric estimating (using historical data and project parameters), analogous estimating (using data from similar past projects), and alternatives analysis (considering different resource options).

482. What is the primary input to the Plan Risk Responses process?
a. risk register
b. risk management plan
c. project management plan
d. project documents

Answer: a. risk register. Explanation: The primary input to the Plan Risk Responses process is the risk register. The risk register is a document that contains the results of risk identification, risk analysis, and risk response planning. It includes details about identified risks, their causes, potential impacts, probability, and priority, as well as initial response strategies. The Plan Risk Responses process uses this information to develop detailed risk response plans for the highest-priority risks. The risk management plan, project management plan, and project documents are also inputs to this process but are not as central as the risk register.

483. Which of the following is not an output of the Define Scope process?
a. project scope statement
b. project documents updates
c. requirement documentation
d. scope baseline

Answer: d. scope baseline. Explanation: The scope baseline is not an output of the Define Scope process. The scope baseline is created in a separate process, Create WBS, which decomposes the project scope into smaller, more manageable components. The key outputs of the Define Scope process are the project scope statement (a detailed description of the project and product scope), requirement documentation (a list of requirements that the project must meet), and project documents updates (such as the stakeholder register and risk register, which may be updated based on the defined scope).

484. What are the two primary inputs to the Estimate Costs process?
a. project management plan and project documents
b. cost management plan and risk register
c. scope baseline and risk register
d. project schedule and resource requirements

Answer: a. project management plan and project documents. Explanation: The two primary inputs to the Estimate Costs process are the project management plan and project documents. The project management plan includes the scope baseline, schedule baseline, resource management plan, and other information needed to estimate costs. The project documents include the risk register, assumptions log, and lessons learned register, which can also influence cost estimates. The cost management plan, risk register, scope baseline, project schedule, and resource requirements are all important but are not the primary inputs to this process.

485. Which of the following is a key tool or technique used in the Manage Team process?
a. project management information system (PMIS)
b. interpersonal and team skills
c. organizational theory
d. co-location

Answer: b. interpersonal and team skills. Explanation: Interpersonal and team skills are a key tool and technique used in the Manage Team process. This process involves tracking team member performance, providing feedback, resolving issues, and managing changes to optimize project performance. Interpersonal and team skills, such as conflict management, influencing, leadership, and team building, are essential for effectively managing and motivating the project team. The project management information system (PMIS) is a tool used across many processes to manage project information. Organizational theory and co-location can influence team dynamics but are not specific tools and techniques of the Manage Team process.

486. What is the main purpose of the Monitor Risks process?
a. to identify new risks that may affect the project
b. to analyze the probability and impact of identified risks
c. to track identified risks and evaluate the effectiveness of risk responses
d. to plan and implement risk responses for high-priority risks

Answer: c. to track identified risks and evaluate the effectiveness of risk responses. Explanation: The main purpose of the Monitor Risks process is to track identified risks, monitor residual risks, identify new risks, and evaluate the effectiveness of risk response plans throughout the project life cycle. This process involves continuously monitoring the project environment for changes that may affect risk priorities or trigger new risks, and ensuring that risk responses are effectively implemented and achieving the desired results. Identifying new risks, analyzing risk probability and impact, and planning risk responses are the focus of other risk management processes, such as Identify Risks, Perform Qualitative Risk Analysis, and Plan Risk Responses.

487. Which of the following is an input to the Plan Procurement Management process?
a. procurement strategy
b. source selection criteria
c. project schedule
d. make-or-buy decisions

Answer: d. make-or-buy decisions. Explanation: Make-or-buy decisions are an input to the Plan Procurement Management process. These decisions determine whether project work or components will be produced internally by the project team or procured from external sources. They are based on factors such as cost, capability, risk, and strategic priorities. The Plan Procurement Management process uses these decisions, along with other inputs such as the project management plan, requirements documentation, and risk register, to develop the procurement management plan and procurement statement of work. The procurement strategy, source selection criteria, and project schedule are outputs of this process or other procurement management processes.

488. What is the main difference between the Manage Quality and Control Quality processes?
a. Manage Quality is performed during project planning, while Control Quality is performed during project execution
b. Manage Quality focuses on the project deliverables, while Control Quality focuses on the project management processes
c. Manage Quality involves quality assurance activities, while Control Quality involves quality control activities
d. Manage Quality is the responsibility of the project manager, while Control Quality is the responsibility of the project team

Answer: c. Manage Quality involves quality assurance activities, while Control Quality involves quality control activities. Explanation: The main difference between the Manage Quality and Control Quality processes is that Manage Quality focuses on quality assurance, while Control Quality focuses on quality control. Quality assurance involves proactively auditing the quality requirements and results of quality control measurements to ensure that appropriate quality standards and definitions are used. Quality control involves monitoring and recording the results of executing the quality management activities to assess performance and recommend necessary changes. Both processes are performed throughout the project, involve the project manager and team, and cover both project deliverables and processes. The distinction is in their focus on preventing defects (quality assurance) versus identifying and correcting defects (quality control).

489. Which of the following is not an output of the Close Project or Phase process?
a. final product, service, or result transition
b. organizational process assets updates
c. project documents updates
d. project charter

Answer: d. project charter. Explanation: The project charter is not an output of the Close Project or Phase process. The project charter is created during the Initiating process group and formally authorizes the project and the project manager. The key outputs of the Close Project or Phase process include the final product, service, or result transition (transferring the completed deliverables to the customer or sponsor), organizational process assets updates (such as lessons learned and knowledge base entries), and project documents updates (finalizing and archiving project documents). This process focuses on finalizing all project activities, not on initiating the project.

490. What is the primary role of the change control board (CCB) in project management?
a. to identify and prioritize potential changes to the project
b. to evaluate change requests and make decisions on their approval or rejection
c. to implement approved changes and update project documents accordingly
d. to communicate the status of change requests to project stakeholders

Answer: b. to evaluate change requests and make decisions on their approval or rejection. Explanation: The primary role of the change control board (CCB) is to evaluate change requests and make decisions on their approval or rejection. The CCB is a formally chartered group of stakeholders responsible for reviewing, evaluating, and approving or rejecting changes to the project baselines. They assess the impact of proposed changes on project scope, schedule, cost, quality, risk, and other factors, and make decisions based on the project's overall objectives and constraints. Identifying and prioritizing changes, implementing approved changes, and communicating change status are typically the responsibility of the project manager and team, not the CCB.

491. Who typically chairs the change control board (CCB) meetings?
a. the project manager
b. the project sponsor
c. a designated CCB chairperson
d. the client representative

Answer: a. the project manager. Explanation: The project manager typically chairs the change control board (CCB) meetings. As the person responsible for overall project execution and integration management, the project manager is best positioned to facilitate the CCB meetings, present the change requests, and guide the decision-making process. The project manager ensures that the CCB has all the necessary information to evaluate the impact of changes and make informed decisions. The project sponsor, a designated CCB chairperson, or a client representative may also participate in the CCB meetings, but the project manager usually takes the lead role in managing the change control process.

492. What is the purpose of a change log in project management?
a. to document the initial project scope and objectives
b. to track the status and history of change requests throughout the project
c. to assign responsibility for implementing approved changes
d. to estimate the impact of proposed changes on project schedule and budget

Answer: b. to track the status and history of change requests throughout the project. Explanation: The purpose of a change log in project management is to track the status and history of change requests throughout the project. A change log is a document that records all change requests submitted for a project, along with their status, priority, impact assessment, and final disposition (approved, deferred, or rejected). It serves as a central repository for change-related information and helps the project manager and team to monitor and control changes in a structured and transparent manner. The change log does not document initial project scope, assign responsibilities, or estimate change impact, as these activities are handled through other project management processes and tools.

493. Which of the following is not a typical status for a change request in the change log?
a. submitted
b. approved
c. rejected
d. implemented

Answer: d. implemented. Explanation: "Implemented" is not a typical status for a change request in the change log. The change log tracks the lifecycle of change requests from submission to final disposition, but it does not usually include the implementation status of approved changes. Common statuses for change requests in the change log include "submitted" (the change request has been formally submitted for review), "approved" (the change request has been approved by the CCB), "rejected" (the change request has been rejected by the CCB), and "deferred" (the change request has been postponed for later consideration). Once a change request is approved, its implementation is managed through the Perform Integrated Change Control and Direct and Manage Project Work processes.

494. What is the main benefit of using a formal change control process with a CCB and change log?
a. to reduce the number of changes proposed during the project
b. to ensure that changes are evaluated and managed in a consistent and transparent manner
c. to eliminate the need for stakeholder involvement in change decisions
d. to accelerate the implementation of changes without impacting project baselines

Answer: b. to ensure that changes are evaluated and managed in a consistent and transparent manner. Explanation: The main benefit of using a formal change control process with a CCB and change log is to ensure that changes are evaluated and managed in a consistent and transparent manner. The CCB provides a structured forum for reviewing and deciding on change requests based on their potential impact and alignment with project objectives. The change log documents the status and history of all change requests, providing transparency and accountability. Together, the CCB and change log help to minimize the risk of uncontrolled changes, manage stakeholder expectations, and maintain project baselines. The goal is not to reduce the number of changes, eliminate stakeholder involvement, or accelerate change implementation without regard for project impacts, but rather to ensure that changes are handled in a disciplined and transparent way.

495. How often should the change control board (CCB) meet during a project?
a. daily
b. weekly
c. monthly

d. as needed, based on the volume and urgency of change requests

Answer: d. as needed, based on the volume and urgency of change requests. Explanation: The frequency of change control board (CCB) meetings should be based on the volume and urgency of change requests received during the project. The CCB should meet as often as necessary to review and make timely decisions on pending change requests, but not so frequently that it becomes a burden or delays other project work. For some projects, weekly or bi-weekly CCB meetings may be sufficient, while others may require more frequent meetings during peak change periods. The project manager should work with the CCB members to establish an appropriate meeting schedule that balances the need for timely change decisions with the availability and workload of the CCB members.

496. What is the role of the project sponsor in the change control process?
a. to submit change requests for CCB review
b. to approve or reject change requests on behalf of the CCB
c. to provide input and support for change request evaluation and decision-making
d. to implement approved changes and update project documents

Answer: c. to provide input and support for change request evaluation and decision-making. Explanation: The role of the project sponsor in the change control process is to provide input and support for change request evaluation and decision-making. As a key project stakeholder and decision-maker, the project sponsor should be involved in the change control process, either as a member of the CCB or as an escalation point for high-impact or controversial changes. The project sponsor can provide strategic guidance, ensure alignment with organizational objectives, and help to resolve conflicts or issues that arise during the change control process. However, the project sponsor does not typically submit change requests, unilaterally approve or reject changes, or implement approved changes, as these responsibilities belong to other project team members and the CCB.

497. What should the project manager do if the CCB is unable to reach a consensus on a change request?
a. reject the change request outright
b. approve the change request and proceed with implementation
c. escalate the decision to a higher-level authority, such as the project sponsor or steering committee
d. postpone the decision until more information is available or the change request is modified

Answer: c. escalate the decision to a higher-level authority, such as the project sponsor or steering committee. Explanation: If the CCB is unable to reach a consensus on a change request, the project manager should escalate the decision to a higher-level authority, such as the project sponsor or steering committee. This situation may arise if the change request is particularly complex, controversial, or high-impact, or if the CCB members have conflicting opinions or priorities. By escalating the decision, the project manager can seek guidance and support from stakeholders with the appropriate level of authority and perspective to make a final determination. Rejecting or approving the change request without consensus, or postponing the decision indefinitely, can lead to project delays, stakeholder dissatisfaction, or uncontrolled changes.

498. What should be included in the change log for each change request?

a. the name and contact information of the person who submitted the request
b. a detailed implementation plan and timeline for the change
c. a description of the change, its justification, and its potential impact on the project
d. the estimated cost and resource requirements for implementing the change

Answer: c. a description of the change, its justification, and its potential impact on the project. Explanation: For each change request, the change log should include a description of the proposed change, its justification or rationale, and its potential impact on the project scope, schedule, cost, quality, risk, and other relevant factors. This information is essential for the CCB to evaluate the merits and feasibility of the change request and make an informed decision on whether to approve, reject, or defer it. The change log may also include other details such as the date of submission, the name of the requester, and the priority or urgency of the change, but these are less critical than the description, justification, and impact assessment. Detailed implementation plans, cost estimates, and resource requirements are typically developed after a change request is approved, not as part of the initial change log entry.

499. How can project managers ensure that the change control process is followed consistently throughout the project?
a. by personally reviewing and approving all change requests before they are submitted to the CCB
b. by delegating change control responsibilities to a team member or subcommittee
c. by establishing clear change control policies, procedures, and templates, and communicating them to all project stakeholders
d. by minimizing the number of stakeholders involved in the change control process to streamline decision-making

Answer: c. by establishing clear change control policies, procedures, and templates, and communicating them to all project stakeholders. Explanation: To ensure that the change control process is followed consistently throughout the project, project managers should establish clear change control policies, procedures, and templates, and communicate them to all project stakeholders. This includes defining the roles and responsibilities of the CCB, the criteria and process for submitting and evaluating change requests, the format and content of the change log, and the expectations for implementing and communicating approved changes. By documenting and sharing these standards, the project manager can create a common understanding and commitment to the change control process among all stakeholders. Personally reviewing all change requests, delegating change control responsibilities, or minimizing stakeholder involvement may be counterproductive and undermine the consistency and transparency of the process.

500. What is the primary focus of the Close Project or Phase process?
a. to finalize all project activities and transfer the completed product, service, or result to the appropriate stakeholders
b. to obtain authorization to start a new project phase or iteration
c. to plan and execute the project closing activities and celebrate team achievements
d. to evaluate the project's success and document lessons learned for future projects

Answer: a. to finalize all project activities and transfer the completed product, service, or result to the appropriate stakeholders. Explanation: The primary focus of the Close Project or Phase process is to finalize all project activities and transfer the completed product, service, or result to the appropriate stakeholders, such as the client, end-users, or operations team. This process ensures that all project or phase activities are completed, deliverables are accepted, and project documentation is archived. Obtaining authorization for a new phase, planning and executing closing activities, and documenting lessons learned are secondary objectives that support the main goal of formally closing the project or phase.

501. Which of the following is not a key input to the Close Project or Phase process?
a. project charter
b. project management plan
c. accepted deliverables
d. organizational process assets

Answer: a. project charter. Explanation: The project charter is not a key input to the Close Project or Phase process. The project charter is an output of the Develop Project Charter process in the initiating stage and serves to formally authorize the project and document initial requirements and stakeholder expectations. The key inputs to the Close Project or Phase process include the project management plan (which guides the closing activities), the accepted deliverables (which are verified and transferred to the client or end-users), and organizational process assets (such as closure guidelines and templates).

502. What is the main purpose of the Final Report document in the Close Project or Phase process?
a. to provide a detailed technical description of the project deliverables and their specifications
b. to summarize the project's performance, key achievements, challenges, and lessons learned
c. to outline the remaining project activities and resources needed to complete the project
d. to formally accept the project deliverables and authorize the release of project resources

Answer: b. to summarize the project's performance, key achievements, challenges, and lessons learned. Explanation: The main purpose of the Final Report document in the Close Project or Phase process is to provide a comprehensive summary of the project's performance, key achievements, challenges faced, and lessons learned. The Final Report is a key output of the closing process and serves as a historical record of the project that can be referenced by stakeholders and future projects. It typically includes information on the project objectives, scope, schedule, budget, quality, and stakeholder management, as well as an assessment of the project's success in achieving its goals and delivering the intended benefits.

503. Which of the following is a key activity of the Close Project or Phase process?
a. updating the project management plan with final project information
b. obtaining formal acceptance and sign-off from the project sponsor or client
c. releasing project team members and reassigning them to new projects or operational roles
d. all of the above

Answer: d. all of the above. Explanation: Updating the project management plan, obtaining formal acceptance and sign-off, and releasing project team members are all key activities of the Close Project or

Phase process. Updating the project management plan involves documenting the final project scope, schedule, cost, and performance information, as well as archiving project documents and deliverables. Obtaining formal acceptance and sign-off from the project sponsor or client is crucial for verifying that project objectives have been met and deliverables are complete and satisfactory. Releasing project team members and resources is necessary for ensuring an orderly transition and reallocation of resources to new projects or operational roles.

504. What is the purpose of the administrative closure procedure in the Close Project or Phase process?
a. to plan and execute the project closing activities and celebrate team achievements
b. to evaluate the project team's performance and provide individual feedback and recognition
c. to update and archive project records, close contracts, and transition project resources
d. to obtain formal acceptance of project deliverables and handover the product to the client

Answer: c. to update and archive project records, close contracts, and transition project resources. Explanation: The purpose of the administrative closure procedure in the Close Project or Phase process is to ensure that all project records and documentation are updated, archived, and stored for future reference, that project-related contracts and agreements are formally closed out, and that project resources (such as equipment, facilities, and materials) are transitioned and redeployed as appropriate. This procedure is essential for maintaining accurate historical records, fulfilling contractual obligations, and optimizing resource utilization across the organization. Planning closing activities, evaluating team performance, and obtaining formal acceptance are related activities but are not the primary focus of administrative closure.

505. What is the main benefit of conducting a post-project review or retrospective during the Close Project or Phase process?
a. to assign blame for project failures and identify underperforming team members
b. to celebrate project successes and reward high-performing team members
c. to capture lessons learned and identify opportunities for process improvement
d. to plan and prioritize future projects based on the results of the current project

Answer: c. to capture lessons learned and identify opportunities for process improvement. Explanation: The main benefit of conducting a post-project review or retrospective during the Close Project or Phase process is to capture lessons learned and identify opportunities for continuous improvement in project management processes, tools, and practices. A post-project review brings together the project team, stakeholders, and other relevant parties to discuss and document what worked well, what could have been done better, and what insights and recommendations can be applied to future projects. The focus is on learning and improvement, not on assigning blame or celebrating successes (although recognition and celebration can be part of the process). The lessons learned from the post-project review are typically documented and shared with the organization to support knowledge management and process enhancement initiatives.

506. What is the difference between the Close Project or Phase process and the Closeout or Termination process in project procurement management?
a. Close Project or Phase focuses on finalizing project activities, while Closeout or Termination focuses on closing project contracts and agreements

b. Close Project or Phase is performed at the end of each project phase, while Closeout or Termination is performed only at the end of the project

c. Close Project or Phase is the responsibility of the project manager, while Closeout or Termination is the responsibility of the procurement manager

d. Close Project or Phase and Closeout or Termination are different names for the same process

Answer: a. Close Project or Phase focuses on finalizing project activities, while Closeout or Termination focuses on closing project contracts and agreements. Explanation: The main difference between the Close Project or Phase process and the Closeout or Termination process is their focus and scope. Close Project or Phase is a comprehensive process that involves finalizing all project activities, transferring deliverables, documenting lessons learned, and releasing project resources. Closeout or Termination, on the other hand, is a specific process within project procurement management that focuses on closing out project-related contracts and agreements, ensuring that all contractual obligations have been met, and resolving any outstanding claims or disputes. Closeout or Termination is typically performed as part of, or in parallel with, the Close Project or Phase process, but it has a narrower scope and is primarily concerned with the legal and administrative aspects of closing project procurements.

507. Which of the following is not a typical output of the Close Project or Phase process?
a. final product, service, or result transition
b. project documents updates
c. final report
d. procurement statement of work

Answer: d. procurement statement of work. Explanation: A procurement statement of work (SOW) is not a typical output of the Close Project or Phase process. The procurement SOW is a document that describes the work to be performed by a vendor or supplier as part of a project procurement, and it is typically an output of the Plan Procurement Management process in the planning stage. The key outputs of the Close Project or Phase process include the final product, service, or result transition (transferring the completed deliverables to the client or end-users), project documents updates (updating and archiving all project documentation), final report (summarizing project performance and lessons learned), and organizational process assets updates (reflecting project knowledge and experience in the organization's policies, procedures, and knowledge repositories).

508. What is the role of the project manager in ensuring a smooth transition of project deliverables to the client or end-users during the Close Project or Phase process?
a. to personally deliver and install the project deliverables at the client's site
b. to obtain formal acceptance and sign-off from the project sponsor or steering committee
c. to coordinate the handover activities, provide necessary training and documentation, and ensure a seamless transfer of ownership and knowledge
d. to negotiate the terms and conditions of the deliverable acceptance criteria and warranty period with the client

Answer: c. to coordinate the handover activities, provide necessary training and documentation, and ensure a seamless transfer of ownership and knowledge. Explanation: The role of the project manager in ensuring a smooth transition of project deliverables to the client or end-users during the Close Project or Phase process is to coordinate the handover activities, provide necessary training and documentation, and ensure a seamless transfer of ownership and knowledge. This includes working closely with the client or end-users to plan and execute the transition, verifying that the deliverables meet the acceptance criteria and are fit for purpose, providing user manuals, guides, and other supporting documentation, and conducting training sessions or workshops to ensure that the client or end-users have the knowledge and skills needed to operate and maintain the delivered product, service, or result. The project manager may also assist in setting up support and maintenance arrangements, but the primary focus is on facilitating a smooth and successful transition that meets the client's needs and expectations.

509. What is the purpose of the lessons-learned review in the Close Project or Phase process?
a. to identify and document the root causes of project failures and assign blame to responsible parties
b. to celebrate project successes, reward high-performing team members, and boost morale for future projects
c. to capture and share the knowledge gained during the project, including best practices, challenges, and recommendations for improvement
d. to evaluate the project team's adherence to organizational policies, procedures, and quality standards

Answer: c. to capture and share the knowledge gained during the project, including best practices, challenges, and recommendations for improvement. Explanation: The purpose of the lessons-learned review in the Close Project or Phase process is to capture and share the knowledge gained during the project, including best practices, challenges faced, and recommendations for improvement. The lessons-learned review is a structured activity that brings together the project team, stakeholders, and other relevant parties to discuss and document the key learnings from the project, both positive and negative. The focus is on identifying what worked well, what could have been done better, and what insights and recommendations can be applied to future projects to enhance project performance and outcomes. The lessons learned are typically documented in a lessons-learned report or database and shared with the wider organization to support knowledge management, continuous improvement, and organizational learning. The purpose is not to assign blame, celebrate successes, or evaluate compliance, but rather to promote a culture of learning and knowledge sharing that benefits the entire organization.

510. When is a formal change request required during a project?
a. When the project team requires confirmation on a previously decided scope detail
b. When there is a need to update the project's schedule due to resource reallocation
c. When modifications to the project's scope, schedule, or cost baselines are needed
d. When the project manager decides to update the risk management approach

Answer: c. When modifications to the project's scope, schedule, or cost baselines are needed. Explanation: Formal change requests are necessary when there are proposed alterations to the agreed-upon project scope, schedule, or cost baselines, as these changes can impact the project's overall delivery and must be formally reviewed and approved through the change control process. Confirmations of scope details (option a) typically do not require a change request unless altering the baseline. Resource reallocations (option b) might not require a change request unless they impact the baseline. Changing the risk management approach (option d) internally may not require a formal change request unless it impacts the baselines.

511. What type of performance report provides stakeholders with a snapshot of project status at a particular point in time?
a. Status report
b. Forecast report
c. Trend report
d. Variance report

Answer: a. Status report. Explanation: Status reports offer a snapshot of the project's current status at a specific point in time, detailing the current state of the project, what has been accomplished, and what tasks are pending, making it crucial for regular stakeholder updates. Forecast reports (option b) predict future project status based on current performance. Trend reports (option c) analyze performance over time to identify patterns. Variance reports (option d) compare planned performance against actual performance.

512. Which tool or technique is most effective for integrating change requests into the overall project management plan?
a. Change control tools
b. Project management information system (PMIS)
c. Expert judgment
d. Performance reviews

Answer: a. Change control tools. Explanation: Change control tools are designed specifically to facilitate the assessment, processing, and approval or rejection of change requests within the project. These tools ensure that any changes are consistently integrated into the project management plan if approved. A PMIS (option b) supports project management but is broader and not specific to change integration. Expert judgment (option c) can aid in evaluating changes but is not a tool for integration. Performance reviews (option d) assess team and project performance but are not directly involved in integrating changes.

513. When should change requests be submitted for evaluation and approval?
a. Immediately after any project stakeholder suggests a change
b. As part of the scheduled performance review meetings
c. When project deviations exceed predefined thresholds
d. At any point when a deviation from the project plan is identified

Answer: c. When project deviations exceed predefined thresholds. Explanation: Change requests should be formally submitted for evaluation and approval when project deviations exceed predefined thresholds that impact the project's scope, schedule, or cost baselines. This ensures that all significant changes are controlled and processed effectively. While suggestions for changes (option a) can arise at any time, not all require formal submission. Scheduled meetings (option b) and identification of deviations (option d) are relevant but change requests need specific reasons related to project impact.

514. What is a primary function of performance reports in project management?
a. To document the decision-making process for changes
b. To provide stakeholders with information on project progress and performance

c. To serve as a contract between the project team and external vendors

d. To finalize the project during the closing phase

Answer: b. To provide stakeholders with information on project progress and performance. Explanation: The primary function of performance reports in project management is to inform stakeholders about how the project is performing against its objectives, including status updates, progress, and current issues or risks. These reports help stakeholders make informed decisions regarding the project's direction. Documenting decision-making (option a) is part of change management, not specifically performance reporting. Serving as a contract (option c) or finalizing the project (option d) are not functions of performance reports.

515. In which scenario would a change request be considered unnecessary?

a. The project has experienced unforeseen external events that will delay deliverables.

b. The project's budget needs a minor adjustment due to an error in the original estimation.

c. A stakeholder requests additional features that align with the project's goals.

d. Team members decide to switch to a more efficient software tool that doesn't impact cost or schedule.

Answer: d. Team members decide to switch to a more efficient software tool that doesn't impact cost or schedule. Explanation: Change requests are unnecessary when changes within the project do not impact the baseline elements (scope, schedule, cost) or project quality. Switching to a more efficient tool that doesn't affect the project's baseline or deliverables typically does not require a formal change request. In other scenarios mentioned, changes impact key project elements or stakeholder expectations, necessitating formal change control.

516. What should a project manager do if a change request is approved?

a. Update all project baseline documents immediately without team consultation.

b. Communicate the change to all stakeholders and integrate it into the project plan.

c. Ignore the change if it is deemed too minor to affect the project's trajectory.

d. Wait for additional changes before updating any project documentation.

Answer: b. Communicate the change to all stakeholders and integrate it into the project plan. Explanation: Once a change request is approved, the project manager should communicate the change to all relevant stakeholders and ensure the change is integrated into the project management plan and any affected project baselines or documents. This maintains project alignment and ensures all team members are informed. Ignoring the change (option c) or waiting for additional changes (option d) could lead to mismanagement and project failure.

517. How can performance reports aid in the change control process?

a. By eliminating the need for change requests

b. By providing data that justify or support the need for changes

c. By documenting stakeholder approval of changes

d. By automatically updating project baselines

Answer: b. By providing data that justify or support the need for changes. Explanation: Performance reports can aid in the change control process by providing data and insights that justify or highlight the need for changes in the project. This includes trends, variances, and performance issues that might necessitate adjustments to scope, schedule, or cost. They do not eliminate the need for change requests (option a), document approvals (option c), or automatically update baselines (option d).

518. What is an example of a corrective action resulting from a change request in project management?
a. Revising the project schedule to accommodate a new compliance requirement
b. Reducing the project scope to meet budget constraints
c. Increasing resource allocation to accelerate a delayed task
d. All of the above

Answer: d. All of the above. Explanation: Corrective actions in project management may involve revising the project schedule, reducing scope, or adjusting resources to address deviations from the project plan or to integrate new requirements. Each example given represents a potential corrective action that could arise from issues identified during the project lifecycle, necessitating a formal change request and subsequent approval.

519. In what circumstance might a change request lead to a project scope reduction?
a. Stakeholders demand additional features that are outside of the initial budget.
b. Project analysis reveals that certain features are no longer feasible within the current constraints.
c. Team members identify an opportunity to add value through technological innovation.
d. External vendors offer a discount on key materials, increasing the project budget.

Answer: b. Project analysis reveals that certain features are no longer feasible within the current constraints. Explanation: A change request might lead to a reduction in project scope if analysis indicates that some features are no longer feasible due to budgetary, temporal, or resource constraints, necessitating a focus on essential deliverables only. Requests for additional features (option a) or opportunities for innovation (option c) typically expand scope, while a discount from vendors (option d) would more likely increase scope or enhance project deliverables within existing constraints.

520. What is the primary purpose of the final product, service, or result transition in a project?
a. To initiate the project closure phase.
b. To transfer the final product, service, or result to the next phase or operations.
c. To begin the process of stakeholder sign-off on project deliverables.
d. To revise the project scope to reflect the final product.

Answer: b. To transfer the final product, service, or result to the next phase or operations. Explanation: The primary purpose of the final product, service, or result transition is to ensure that the deliverables created by the project are successfully handed over to the next phase or operations, ensuring continuity and functionality within the customer's environment or the next stage of the project lifecycle. Initiating the closure phase (option a) and revising project scope (option d) are part of project closure activities, not transition, and stakeholder sign-off (option c) may be a part of this process but is not its primary purpose.

521. What critical activity should be performed during the final product transition to ensure seamless integration into the customer's existing systems?
a. Conducting a post-implementation review.
b. Delivering training sessions to the customer.
c. Performing final quality assurance tests.
d. Revising the project budget.

Answer: b. Delivering training sessions to the customer. Explanation: Delivering training sessions to the customer is crucial during the final product transition to ensure that the customer's team can effectively use and maintain the new system or product. This activity supports seamless integration by addressing potential knowledge gaps and ensuring that the user base is competent and confident in utilizing the new solution. Post-implementation review (option a) is valuable but follows integration, quality assurance tests (option c) should occur before transition, and revising the project budget (option d) does not directly impact integration.

522. Which documentation should be updated as part of the final product, service, or result transition?
a. Stakeholder register
b. Project management plan
c. Lessons learned database
d. Work performance data

Answer: c. Lessons learned database. Explanation: Updating the lessons learned database is essential during the final product, service, or result transition to capture valuable insights and experiences that occurred during the project, especially during the transition phase. This ensures that both successes and issues are documented for future projects to learn from. The stakeholder register (option a) and project management plan (option b) are not typically updated during transition, and work performance data (option d) is not documentation but data collected throughout the project execution.

523. In transitioning the final product to operations, which process ensures that the product meets the operational needs and is ready for release?
a. Scope verification
b. Operational readiness review
c. Quality control
d. Scope management

Answer: b. Operational readiness review. Explanation: An operational readiness review is crucial in transitioning the final product to operations, as it assesses whether all aspects of the project and product are in place and ready for operational deployment. This review ensures that the product meets the operational needs and is ready for release, aligning operational capabilities with project outputs. Scope verification (option a) and scope management (option d) focus more on confirming and managing project scope, not operational transition, while quality control (option c) is typically performed before the transition phase.

524. How should project management ensure that a new software tool integrates smoothly into an existing suite of tools during the transition phase?
a. By revising the initial project scope to include additional features.
b. By performing comprehensive integration testing.
c. By updating the risk management plan to include new risks.
d. By initiating a new project to handle integration.

Answer: b. By performing comprehensive integration testing. Explanation: Comprehensive integration testing during the transition phase is essential for ensuring that a new software tool integrates smoothly with existing tools. This type of testing checks compatibility, functionality, and performance within the existing software environment, addressing potential issues before full-scale deployment. Revising the project scope (option a) or updating the risk management plan (option c) are important but secondary to actual testing, while initiating a new project (option d) may not be necessary if integration is planned as part of the original project.

525. What is the primary goal of administrative closure in a project management process?
a. To allocate remaining project resources to other projects
b. To complete and settle each contract associated with the project
c. To ensure all project deliverables have been formally accepted
d. To document lessons learned and integrate them into organizational process assets

Answer: d. To document lessons learned and integrate them into organizational process assets. Explanation: The primary goal of administrative closure is to document lessons learned and integrate them into the organization's process assets for future reference and improvement. While ensuring deliverables are accepted (option c) and completing contracts (option b) are part of project closeout, they are not specific to administrative closure. Resource reallocation (option a) happens after administrative tasks are completed.

526. During the administrative closure, what is the significance of obtaining formal acceptance of the final deliverable?
a. It releases the project team from further obligations.
b. It initiates the disbursement of final payments to contractors.
c. It indicates stakeholder satisfaction with project outcomes.
d. It legally transfers ownership of deliverables to the client.

Answer: c. It indicates stakeholder satisfaction with project outcomes. Explanation: Obtaining formal acceptance of the final deliverable during administrative closure is critical as it indicates that stakeholders are satisfied with the project outcomes and that the deliverables meet the agreed-upon requirements. While it may lead to legal transfer of ownership (option d) and initiate final payments (option b), and release the team (option a), the direct significance is the affirmation of satisfaction and project success.

527. What document is essential to complete during the administrative closure to ensure compliance with financial auditing requirements?
a. Project charter

b. Cost management plan
c. Project closure report
d. Financial closure document

Answer: d. Financial closure document. Explanation: Completing a financial closure document during administrative closure is essential for ensuring all financial transactions related to the project are accurately recorded, reviewed, and closed. This document is critical for compliance with auditing requirements as it provides a transparent, detailed account of financial management throughout the project. While the project closure report (option c) summarizes all aspects of the project, the financial closure document specifically addresses the financial audit compliance.

528. How does the completion of a procurement audit contribute to administrative closure?
a. It ensures that all project resources are returned to the organization.
b. It assesses vendor performance and project procurement processes.
c. It verifies that all legal requirements have been met in the procurement process.
d. It facilitates the release of final payments to all vendors.

Answer: b. It assesses vendor performance and project procurement processes. Explanation: A procurement audit during administrative closure assesses vendor performance and the effectiveness of the project procurement processes.

529. What is the primary objective of the Define Scope process in project management?
a. To identify the work required to complete the project deliverables.
b. To formalize the acceptance of the project deliverables.
c. To track project progress against the performance baseline.
d. To evaluate the project's success upon completion.

Answer: a. To identify the work required to complete the project deliverables. Explanation: The primary objective of the Define Scope process is to develop a detailed description of the project and its boundaries by identifying the work required to complete the project deliverables. This includes specifying what is included and what is excluded from the project, ensuring that the project team and stakeholders have a clear understanding of what needs to be accomplished. Formalizing deliverable acceptance (option b) is part of the Validate Scope process, tracking progress (option c) occurs in the Monitor and Control Project Work process, and evaluating project success (option d) is part of the Closing process.

530. Which document is most critical when creating the Project Scope Statement?
a. Project Charter
b. Stakeholder Register
c. Risk Management Plan
d. Change Management Plan

Answer: a. Project Charter. Explanation: The Project Charter is crucial when creating the Project Scope Statement as it provides the project's purpose, objectives, and the preliminary defined scope. It acts as a reference point for further detailed planning, helping to ensure that the scope statement aligns with the project's initial goals and intentions. While the Stakeholder Register (option b) is important for understanding influences and requirements, and the Risk (option c) and Change Management Plans (option d) are vital for project planning, they are not as directly relevant to defining the scope as the Project Charter.

531. In Scope Management, what tool or technique is used to subdivide project deliverables into smaller, more manageable components?
a. Decomposition
b. Variance Analysis
c. Expert Judgment
d. Change Requests

Answer: a. Decomposition. Explanation: Decomposition is a technique used in scope management to break down project deliverables and work into smaller, more manageable components, forming the Work Breakdown Structure (WBS). This method helps in organizing and defining the total scope of the project. Variance Analysis (option b) is used for measuring project performance against the scope baseline, Expert Judgment (option c) is used to assess the details of project activities, and Change Requests (option d) are used to propose alterations to the project scope.

532. How does the creation of a Work Breakdown Structure (WBS) contribute to project success?
a. It provides a timeline for project delivery.
b. It outlines the project's budget constraints.
c. It helps in the accurate estimation of cost, time, and resources.
d. It documents the project's communication channels.

Answer: c. It helps in the accurate estimation of cost, time, and resources. Explanation: A Work Breakdown Structure (WBS) contributes to project success by providing a clear and detailed map of what needs to be done in the project. This breakdown helps in the accurate estimation of cost, time, and resources, essential for planning, scheduling, budgeting, and resource allocation. The WBS does not provide a timeline (option a), outline budget constraints (option b), nor document communication channels (option d) directly; it primarily facilitates detailed project planning and control.

533. What is the main purpose of the Scope Baseline in project scope management?
a. To serve as a standard for project changes.
b. To manage the project team's performance.
c. To outline the project's contractual obligations.
d. To integrate the project's schedules and cost baselines.

Answer: a. To serve as a standard for project changes. Explanation: The Scope Baseline in project scope management includes the approved version of the scope statement, WBS, and WBS dictionary, serving as the standard against which project performance is measured and controlled. It provides a basis for comparing actual results to what was planned and is crucial for managing changes effectively. It does not manage team performance (option b), outline contractual obligations (option c), nor integrate schedules and cost baselines (option d).

534. When should the Validate Scope process be performed?
a. Before the project planning phase begins.
b. During the project execution, to formalize acceptance of completed deliverables.
c. After the project is closed to assess customer satisfaction.
d. At the beginning of each phase to define scope boundaries.

Answer: b. During the project execution, to formalize acceptance of completed deliverables. Explanation: The Validate Scope process is typically performed during the project execution phase, where completed project deliverables are formally reviewed and accepted by the customer or sponsor. This ensures that deliverables meet the agreed-upon project requirements and are completed satisfactorily before moving forward. It is not used before planning (option a), after project closure (option c), nor at the beginning of each phase (option d) specifically for defining scope boundaries.

535. What role does the Collect Requirements process play in Project Scope Management?
a. It determines how requirements will be analyzed, documented, and managed.
b. It ensures that all required resources are available for project execution.
c. It assesses the impact of scope changes on the project schedule.
d. It tracks the project's performance against its objectives.

Answer: a. It determines how requirements will be analyzed, documented, and managed. Explanation: In Project Scope Management, the Collect Requirements process is crucial as it involves determining, documenting, and managing stakeholder needs and requirements to meet the project objectives. This process sets the foundation for defining and managing the project scope effectively. It is not directly concerned with resource availability (option b), assessing the impact of scope changes on the schedule (option c), nor tracking performance against objectives (option d), which are part of other management processes.

536. What is the consequence of poor scope definition in the early stages of a project?
a. Increased risk of project delays and cost overruns.
b. Improved flexibility in handling project changes.
c. Enhanced stakeholder engagement and satisfaction.
d. Reduced complexity in project execution.

Answer: a. Increased risk of project delays and cost overruns. Explanation: Poor scope definition at the early stages of a project often leads to misunderstandings and misalignments on project deliverables and requirements, significantly increasing the risk of project delays and cost overruns as changes and clarifications become necessary later in the project. It does not lead to improved flexibility (option b), enhanced stakeholder satisfaction (option c), nor reduced complexity (option d); rather, it complicates project management and stakeholder relations.

537. During project execution, which document should be referred to when a stakeholder requests an addition to the project scope?
a. Project Charter
b. Scope management plan
c. Stakeholder register
d. Change management plan

Answer: b. Scope management plan. Explanation: When a stakeholder requests an addition to the project scope during execution, the project manager should refer to the scope management plan. This plan outlines how scope changes are managed and controlled, providing guidance on procedures for scope modification, including how to handle requests, assess impacts, and integrate changes. The project charter (option a) initiates the project, the stakeholder register (option c) lists stakeholders and their information, and the change management plan (option d) deals with managing all types of changes, not specifically scope changes.

538. What is the final step in the Project Scope Management process?
a. Developing the project management plan.
b. Conducting the project kick-off meeting.
c. Closing the project.
d. Updating the project scope statement.

Answer: c. Closing the project. Explanation: The final step in the Project Scope Management process involves closing the project, which includes confirming that all project work complies with the scope baseline and that all deliverables have been accepted. This step ensures that the project has met its objectives and that all scope-related work is completed and documented before formally closing the project. Developing the project management plan (option a) and conducting the kick-off meeting (option b) occur earlier in the project lifecycle, and updating the scope statement (option d) is part of ongoing scope control, not a final step.

539. During the initial phase of a project, the project manager decides to employ the Delphi Technique to ensure an unbiased and comprehensive identification of potential risks in the project scope. What is the primary advantage of using the Delphi Technique in this context?
a. it allows for face-to-face team discussions and immediate consensus
b. it facilitates anonymous input that can reduce the influence of dominant personalities
c. it offers a structured sequence of information gathering via direct observation
d. it relies heavily on historical data from past projects of a similar nature

Answer: b. it facilitates anonymous input that can reduce the influence of dominant personalities. Explanation: The Delphi Technique is used to gather data from respondents within their domain of expertise. It is done anonymously to avoid the influence of others in the group, allowing for free expression of opinions and converging towards a true or consensus opinion without being dominated by a single opinion leader. Options a, c, and d are incorrect because the Delphi Technique does not require face-to-face meetings, is not observational, and does not primarily rely on historical data.

540. A project manager is developing the Scope Management Plan for a new project. Which document should primarily guide the development of the Scope Management Plan?
a. Project charter
b. Work breakdown structure
c. Project schedule
d. Risk management plan

Answer: a. Project charter. Explanation: The Project Charter officially authorizes a project and provides the project manager with the objectives and constraints of the project. It forms the primary basis for defining the scope in the Scope Management Plan. The Work breakdown structure (option b) is an output derived from the Scope Management Plan, not a guiding document for its creation. The project schedule (option c) and the risk management plan (option d) are also outputs of other planning processes and do not guide the development of the Scope Management Plan.

541. In a project's scope planning stage, a project manager opts to use a mind mapping technique. What is the primary purpose of this approach during this stage?
a. To quantify the resources needed for each task
b. To establish a timeline for project milestones
c. To facilitate brainstorming and visualization of scope components
d. To assign tasks to project team members

Answer: c. To facilitate brainstorming and visualization of scope components. Explanation: Mind mapping is a visual thinking tool that aids in structuring information, helping to better analyze, comprehend, synthesize, recall, and generate new ideas. Its visual form makes it a powerful tool for brainstorming and exploring key components of the project scope. It is not typically used for quantifying resources, scheduling, or assigning tasks.

542. A project team is utilizing product analysis to define the project scope. Which of the following best describes an activity involved in product analysis?
a. Identifying quality metrics for the product deliverables
b. Developing a detailed project schedule
c. Translating product characteristics into project deliverables
d. Assigning roles and responsibilities to project team members

Answer: c. Translating product characteristics into project deliverables. Explanation: Product analysis involves understanding a product's components, assembly, and environment to better define the scope of the project by translating these product characteristics into specific project deliverables. It does not directly involve developing project schedules, identifying quality metrics, or assigning team roles.

543. The project scope statement for a new software development project includes detailed descriptions of both the project and product deliverables. What is the primary purpose of including detailed product deliverables in the project scope statement?
a. To define the functional and non-functional requirements of the product
b. To specify the budget allocated for each deliverable

c. To outline the project's communication plan

d. To describe the project's change control process

Answer: a. To define the functional and non-functional requirements of the product. Explanation: The project scope statement should include a detailed description of both project and product deliverables to clearly define what the project will and will not include. This description particularly helps in defining the functional (what the product will do) and non-functional (how the product will perform) requirements, which are critical for project planning and execution. The budget allocation, communication plan, and change control process are addressed in other parts of the project management plan.

544. When establishing the scope baseline, which of the following components are typically included?

a. Project scope statement, WBS, and WBS dictionary

b. Project charter, project schedule, and risk register

c. Cost management plan, quality management plan, and scope management plan

d. Stakeholder register, requirements documentation, and project team assignments

Answer: a. Project scope statement, WBS, and WBS dictionary. Explanation: The scope baseline is primarily composed of the project scope statement, the Work Breakdown Structure (WBS), and the WBS dictionary. These components collectively define and document the total scope of work for the project. Options b, c, and d include elements that are crucial for project management but are not part of the scope baseline.

545. During scope verification, a stakeholder disputes some completed deliverables based on her interpretation of the scope description. What document should primarily be consulted to resolve this dispute?

a. Scope management plan

b. Project scope statement

c. Quality management plan

d. Project management plan

Answer: b. Project scope statement. Explanation: The project scope statement provides a detailed description of the project scope, including boundaries and deliverables, and is the key document used during scope verification to determine if deliverables have met the documented standards and requirements. The scope management plan (option a) outlines how the scope will be managed and controlled, rather than details of the deliverables themselves.

546. A new project manager is unsure about the difference between the Scope Management Plan and the Project Management Plan. Which statement best clarifies this for them?

a. The Scope Management Plan is a subset of the Project Management Plan that outlines how scope will be defined, validated, and controlled

b. The Project Management Plan is tailored to comply with the requirements outlined in the Scope Management Plan

c. Both plans are interchangeable in smaller projects where scope is not a major concern

d. The Scope Management Plan should be developed after the Project Management Plan to adjust the scope according to available resources

Answer: a. The Scope Management Plan is a subset of the Project Management Plan that outlines how scope will be defined, validated, and controlled. Explanation: The Scope Management Plan is indeed a component of the broader Project Management Plan and focuses specifically on the processes and activities related to managing the project's scope. It is not developed after but rather as a part of the overall Project Management Plan.

547. In developing a Scope Management Plan, which technique could be effectively used to ensure all project and product deliverables are accounted for and clearly understood by the project team?
a. Critical Path Method
b. Earned Value Management
c. Decomposition
d. Monte Carlo simulation

Answer: c. Decomposition. Explanation: Decomposition involves breaking down project deliverables into smaller, more manageable components, which can help ensure that all aspects of the project's scope are clearly understood and properly managed. It is a key technique used in creating the Work Breakdown Structure (WBS), a fundamental part of scope planning. The Critical Path Method and Earned Value Management are used for schedule and cost management respectively, while Monte Carlo simulations are used for risk assessment.

548. The project manager is reviewing the detailed scope of work included in the contract and notices discrepancies between what is outlined in the project documentation and the client's expectations discussed in meetings. What is the best first step to address these discrepancies?
a. Update the project documentation to reflect what was discussed in the meetings
b. Organize a meeting with the client to clarify the discrepancies and realign expectations
c. Proceed with the work as outlined in the project documentation assuming it is more accurate
d. Request a legal review of the contract to determine binding terms

Answer: b. Organize a meeting with the client to clarify the discrepancies and realign expectations. Explanation: The best first step is to clarify any discrepancies directly with the client to ensure that both the project team and the client have a mutual understanding of the project scope. This helps prevent future conflicts and misalignments between the project deliverables and the client's expectations. Proceeding without this clarification or assuming the documentation is correct without verification can lead to issues later in the project lifecycle.

549. During the project initiation phase, the project manager decides to develop a detailed Scope Management Plan. Which document must first be referenced to guide this process?
a. Project schedule
b. Project charter
c. Stakeholder register
d. Risk register

Answer: b. Project charter. Explanation: The Project Charter is the document that formally authorizes a project and provides the project manager with the objectives and high-level requirements. It acts as a primary reference for developing the Scope Management Plan by outlining the project's purpose and boundaries, which is critical before further detailed planning can occur. The project schedule (a), stakeholder register (c), and risk register (d) are important documents, but they do not provide the foundational authorization or high-level scope needed at the initiation phase.

550. A project team decides to implement the MoSCoW method during the scope definition phase. What is the primary purpose of using this technique in scope management?
a. To identify and prioritize stakeholders' needs based on their importance and contribution to project success
b. To sequence project activities efficiently
c. To assess and integrate risk management with scope definitions
d. To prioritize requirements by distinguishing what must be done from what should or could be done

Answer: d. To prioritize requirements by distinguishing what must be done from what should or could be done. Explanation: The MoSCoW method is a prioritization technique used in project management to categorize requirements into "Must have," "Should have," "Could have," and "Won't have." This method helps teams focus on delivering the most critical functionalities within scope limitations, ensuring efficient resource allocation and scope containment. The other options, while relevant to project management, are not the primary purpose of the MoSCoW method in scope management.

551. When creating a WBS (Work Breakdown Structure), a project manager ensures each level of the WBS is detailed enough to support which aspect of scope management?
a. Risk identification
b. Cost estimation
c. Scheduling
d. All of the above

Answer: d. All of the above. Explanation: A well-constructed WBS helps in various aspects of project management, including risk identification by breaking down the deliverables into manageable segments where specific risks can be identified, cost estimation by providing detailed deliverable-based cost forecasting, and scheduling by defining deliverable timelines at each breakdown level. Hence, a detailed WBS supports comprehensive scope management.

552. The project scope statement is being drafted. Which element is essential to include for effective scope management?
a. Detailed resource allocation for each team member
b. Acceptance criteria for project deliverables
c. A list of potential vendors for project procurement
d. Detailed cost estimates for each phase of the project

Answer: b. Acceptance criteria for project deliverables. Explanation: Acceptance criteria are essential as they define the conditions under which project deliverables are accepted, clarifying the project scope by detailing what must be done to satisfy project stakeholders. This element is crucial for effective scope management as it ensures all parties have a mutual understanding of what constitutes project success.

Resource allocation, vendor lists, and detailed cost estimates are important but not specifically part of the scope statement.

553. In developing the Scope Management Plan, which tool or technique is essential for defining project scope?
a. Earned Value Management (EVM)
b. Expert judgment
c. Monte Carlo simulation
d. Critical Path Method (CPM)

Answer: b. Expert judgment. Explanation: Expert judgment involves consulting with experienced individuals or groups to make decisions and estimations regarding project scope based on their expertise in similar projects. This technique is crucial in scope definition as it helps to leverage historical insights and industry knowledge to accurately define the scope. EVM, Monte Carlo simulation, and CPM are valuable in other aspects of project management but not primarily used for defining scope.

554. During a scope review meeting, a stakeholder suggests adding new features to the project deliverables. What should be the project manager's first step according to the Scope Management Plan?
a. Approve the changes as the stakeholder is very important
b. Review the impact of the suggested changes on project constraints
c. Immediately update the project documentation to include the new features
d. Reject the changes to avoid scope creep

Answer: b. Review the impact of the suggested changes on project constraints. Explanation: According to best practices in scope management, the project manager should first assess the impact of any suggested changes on the project's scope, budget, schedule, and resources before making any decisions. This ensures that decisions are made with a clear understanding of how changes will affect overall project deliverables and success.

555. The Scope Management Plan is being updated. Which change would typically require an update to this plan?
a. A new technology is adopted that affects how information is documented
b. The project budget is reduced by 10%
c. A key project deliverable is completed ahead of schedule
d. The project sponsor requests a weekly progress report

Answer: a. A new technology is adopted that affects how information is documented. Explanation: An update to the Scope Management Plan is necessary when changes occur that affect how project scope is defined, controlled, or verified. Adopting new technology that changes documentation processes may impact how project deliverables are scoped and managed. Budget changes, scheduling advancements, and reporting requirements typically do not require updates to the Scope Management Plan itself but rather to the overall Project Management Plan.

557. When a project manager is facilitating a scope definition session, which technique might they use to ensure comprehensive coverage of all project aspects?
a. Brainstorming
b. Benchmarking
c. Parametric estimating
d. Variance analysis

Answer: a. Brainstorming. Explanation: Brainstorming is an effective technique during scope definition sessions to generate ideas and requirements from various stakeholders. This technique ensures that diverse perspectives are considered, enhancing the comprehensiveness and completeness of the project scope. Benchmarking, parametric estimating, and variance analysis are more aligned with performance measurement and cost estimation.

558. A project manager is considering the integration of scope management practices with sustainability objectives. Which action best aligns with this integration?
a. Including environmental impact assessments in the project scope statement
b. Requiring all project documentation to be printed on recycled paper
c. Implementing strict penalties for non-compliance with sustainability practices
d. Ensuring all project meetings are held virtually to reduce carbon footprint

Answer: a. Including environmental impact assessments in the project scope statement. Explanation: Integrating sustainability objectives into scope management effectively involves considering the environmental impacts associated with project deliverables. Including such assessments in the project scope statement ensures that sustainability is considered throughout the project lifecycle, aligning project outcomes with broader environmental sustainability goals.

559. A project scope statement has been created, and the client requests an addition that would significantly alter project deliverables. According to best practices, what is the appropriate next step?
a. Modify the project scope statement to accommodate the client's request
b. Conduct a feasibility study to assess the impact of the addition
c. Initiate the change management process to evaluate the request
d. Inform the client that no changes can be made at this stage

Answer: c. Initiate the change management process to evaluate the request. Explanation: The appropriate next step is to initiate the change management process, which includes documenting the change request, assessing the impacts on scope, cost, and time, and obtaining the necessary approvals before any changes are made. This process ensures that all changes are controlled and integrated into the project management plan systematically.

560. A project team is initiating the Collect Requirements process for a complex software development project. What tool or technique is most effective for ensuring that both functional and non-functional requirements are clearly understood and recorded?
a. Benchmarking
b. Focus groups

c. Prototyping

d. Questionnaires

Answer: c. Prototyping. Explanation: Prototyping is an effective tool in requirements collection, especially for complex projects like software development, as it allows stakeholders to interact with a working model of the product. This interaction helps in clarifying both functional (what the software should do) and non-functional (how the software performs) requirements by providing a tangible representation of the product. Benchmarking (a) is used for comparing against industry standards, focus groups (b) are ideal for discussions but less specific in terms of technical requirements, and questionnaires (d) are more rigid and less interactive, potentially missing nuanced requirements.

561. During the requirements collection phase, a project manager decides to use observation as a technique. What scenario best justifies the use of this method?

a. The project aims to improve the efficiency of an existing manufacturing line.

b. The project involves developing a new technology unfamiliar to the end-users.

c. The project is short on time, and quick feedback is needed on the requirements.

d. The project stakeholders are spread across different geographical locations.

Answer: a. The project aims to improve the efficiency of an existing manufacturing line. Explanation: Observation, also known as job shadowing, is particularly useful when the project's goal is to enhance current processes, such as improving a manufacturing line. It allows the observer to gain a deep understanding of the process flows and identify inefficiencies firsthand. In scenarios b, c, and d, other techniques like prototyping, surveys, or virtual meetings might be more effective due to the nature of technology, time constraints, or geographical spread.

562. A project manager is using interviews to collect requirements for a new client portal. What is the primary advantage of using this technique?

a. It allows for detailed, personalized feedback and the exploration of ideas that may not emerge in group settings.

b. It is the most cost-effective method for gathering large amounts of data.

c. It minimizes the risk of scope creep as responses are limited and structured.

d. It provides quantitative data that can be easily analyzed statistically.

Answer: a. It allows for detailed, personalized feedback and the exploration of ideas that may not emerge in group settings. Explanation: Interviews offer a unique advantage in collecting deep, qualitative data from stakeholders, particularly when exploring complex or innovative ideas for new projects like a client portal. They allow for in-depth discussions and the emergence of unique requirements that might not surface in group settings or through impersonal surveys. The other options are incorrect as interviews are not necessarily cost-effective (b), do not inherently minimize scope creep (c), and do not typically provide quantitative data (d).

563. For a project focused on developing a new educational app, the project manager opts to use questionnaires to gather requirements from a large group of teachers. What is the major limitation of this method?

a. It may not provide insights into the specific educational contexts of different classrooms.
b. It always requires a follow-up interview to verify responses.
c. It is less useful when the respondent group is homogeneous.
d. It cannot be used to collect demographic data.

Answer: a. It may not provide insights into the specific educational contexts of different classrooms. Explanation: While questionnaires allow for broad data collection from a large number of respondents efficiently, they may lack the depth to capture context-specific details, such as varying classroom environments or specific educational needs, which are critical in designing an educational app. They do not necessarily require follow-up interviews (b), are actually more useful in homogeneous groups (c), and can certainly be used to collect demographic data (d).

564. A project requires gathering complex user requirements for a new public transportation system. Which technique would be most appropriate to ensure comprehensive stakeholder input and buy-in?
a. Surveys
b. Workshops
c. Delphi Technique
d. Statistical sampling

Answer: b. Workshops. Explanation: Workshops are highly effective for projects that need comprehensive requirement gathering from various stakeholders, such as a new public transportation system. They facilitate interactive discussion, immediate clarification, and consensus-building, crucial for complex and multifaceted projects. Surveys (a) might not capture complex discussions, the Delphi Technique (c) is better for reaching consensus among experts on specific issues rather than broad input, and statistical sampling (d) is more about predicting trends than collecting detailed system requirements.

565. When applying the requirement gathering technique of user stories to a software development project, what is the primary benefit?
a. They provide a legal framework for requirement documentation.
b. They encourage the formalization of software specifications early in the project.
c. They facilitate communication and understanding of requirements between developers and stakeholders.
d. They eliminate the need for further requirements validation.

Answer: c. They facilitate communication and understanding of requirements between developers and stakeholders. Explanation: User stories are an informal technique that captures requirements from the end-user perspective, helping bridge communication gaps between developers and non-technical stakeholders. They make it easier for developers to understand what users truly need from the software, enhancing the development process. They do not provide a legal framework (a), do not necessarily formalize specifications early (b), and do not eliminate the need for validation (d).

566. In an international project, the project manager opts to use the Delphi Technique for collecting requirements related to environmental compliance. What is the key reason for choosing this method?

a. It provides anonymity, reducing the influence of dominant individuals and helping to gather unbiased data.
b. It is faster than other techniques due to its iterative rounds of questioning.
c. It allows for direct confrontation of conflicting opinions, speeding up consensus.
d. It is the only method suitable for dealing with international regulations.

Answer: a. It provides anonymity, reducing the influence of dominant individuals and helping to gather unbiased data. Explanation: The Delphi Technique is particularly useful in scenarios involving diverse and potentially conflicting international perspectives because it offers anonymity, reducing biases from dominant personalities or political influences, which is crucial for sensitive topics like environmental compliance. It's not necessarily faster (b), does not involve direct confrontation (c), and is not the only method for handling international issues (d).

567. For a project involving the upgrade of a hospital management system, the project manager utilizes focus groups to collect requirements from doctors and nurses. What is a significant challenge of using this technique?
a. It does not allow for anonymous feedback, which can inhibit honest responses.
b. It can be deployed online with minimal effort.
c. It requires a less diverse group to be effective.
d. It focuses only on quantitative data collection.

Answer: a. It does not allow for anonymous feedback, which can inhibit honest responses. Explanation: Focus groups involve direct interaction among participants and a facilitator, which can deter participants from sharing honest feedback due to peer pressure or hierarchical influences, especially in structured environments like hospitals. They are not typically easy to deploy online (b), benefit from diversity (c), and primarily collect qualitative, not quantitative, data (d).

568. When determining which requirements collection techniques to use for a new infrastructure project, the project manager must consider several factors. What should be the primary consideration?
a. The geographical distribution of stakeholders
b. The preference of the project manager
c. The cost of deploying high-tech tools
d. The industry standard for requirements gathering

Answer: a. The geographical distribution of stakeholders. Explanation: The primary consideration for choosing requirement gathering techniques should be the geographical distribution of stakeholders, as this affects the feasibility and effectiveness of different methods. For infrastructure projects, stakeholders may be spread across wide areas, influencing the choice between virtual and in-person techniques. The project manager's preference (b) is less relevant than practical logistics, the cost of tools (c) is a factor but not the primary one, and industry standards (d) should be adapted to the specific context of the project.

569. In a software development project, the project manager plans to use the requirements traceability matrix extensively. What is the most significant benefit of implementing this tool during the Collect Requirements process?

a. It ensures that all requirements are approved by the legal department.
b. It provides a historical record for future projects.
c. It links requirements to their origin and tracks changes throughout the project lifecycle.
d. It automatically updates requirements as project scopes evolve.

Answer: c. It links requirements to their origin and tracks changes throughout the project lifecycle.
Explanation: The requirements traceability matrix is a crucial tool in managing project requirements as it not only links each requirement to its origin (such as business needs, project objectives, or stakeholder interviews) but also tracks its progress and any changes throughout the project lifecycle. This ensures clear accountability and visibility, which is vital for maintaining project alignment and quality. It does not involve legal approvals (a), although it can serve as a historical record (b), its primary function is not automatic updates (d).

570. A project manager is reviewing the requirements documentation for a new project. Which section of the documentation is critical for aligning stakeholder expectations and project deliverables?
a. Project scope statement
b. Assumptions and constraints
c. High-level project timeline
d. Stakeholder communication plan

Answer: a. Project scope statement. Explanation: The project scope statement is a critical component of requirements documentation because it clearly defines what the project will and will not include, thus aligning stakeholder expectations with the planned deliverables. Assumptions and constraints (b) detail other important project facets but do not directly align deliverables and expectations. A high-level project timeline (c) and stakeholder communication plan (d) are also important but do not specifically serve to align expectations with deliverables.

571. When establishing a Requirements Traceability Matrix (RTM), what is the primary purpose of linking requirements to project objectives?
a. To ensure each requirement is justifiable and directly contributes to the project's goals
b. To facilitate the creation of the work breakdown structure
c. To prioritize project risks according to their impact on requirements
d. To streamline the change management process

Answer: a. To ensure each requirement is justifiable and directly contributes to the project's goals.
Explanation: The main purpose of linking requirements to project objectives in an RTM is to ensure that each requirement contributes directly to the project's overall goals, enhancing justifiability and relevance. This traceability helps maintain focus on the project's objectives, ensuring that all requirements are necessary and aligned with the intended outcomes. Options b, c, and d, while relevant to project management, are not directly related to the fundamental purpose of linking requirements to objectives in an RTM.

572. A project manager needs to update the requirements documentation after a major project scope change. What is the most important reason for keeping this documentation up to date?

a. To support the project's communication plan
b. To ensure project requirements remain aligned with business objectives
c. To comply with industry standards for documentation
d. To facilitate the project's closure process

Answer: b. To ensure project requirements remain aligned with business objectives. Explanation: The primary reason for keeping requirements documentation updated, particularly after significant scope changes, is to ensure that the project's requirements continue to align with the evolving business objectives. This alignment is crucial for the project's success and relevance. While compliance with standards (c) and support for communication (a) and closure processes (d) are important, they are secondary to the fundamental goal of maintaining alignment with business objectives.

573. In the context of software development, how can the Requirements Traceability Matrix (RTM) assist in managing changes during the project lifecycle?
a. By providing a framework for approval of all changes by the project sponsor
b. By linking specific requirements to test cases and project deliverables to track adjustments
c. By automatically updating the project budget and timeline when requirements change
d. By documenting all stakeholder meetings and decisions regarding requirements

Answer: b. By linking specific requirements to test cases and project deliverables to track adjustments. Explanation: An RTM is invaluable in software development for linking requirements to their corresponding test cases and deliverables, which facilitates the tracking and management of changes throughout the project. This linkage ensures that any modifications to the requirements are reflected in the deliverables and tested appropriately. Options a, c, and d, though potentially useful, do not capture the primary function of an RTM in change management.

574. For a project focused on constructing a new hospital wing, why is it essential to include operational requirements in the requirements documentation?
a. To ensure compliance with healthcare regulations
b. To define the scope of construction accurately
c. To facilitate the integration of the new wing with existing hospital operations
d. To manage the expectations of hospital donors and stakeholders

Answer: c. To facilitate the integration of the new wing with existing hospital operations. Explanation: Including operational requirements in the requirements documentation for a construction project like a new hospital wing is essential for ensuring that the new facilities will integrate seamlessly with existing operations. This includes considerations for patient flow, staff requirements, and interfacing with current systems. While compliance with regulations (a) and managing stakeholder expectations (d) are important, they are broader considerations that do not specifically address the operational integration as directly as option c.

575. What role does the Requirements Traceability Matrix play in the quality management process of a project?
a. It ensures that all project outcomes meet the required standards of quality

b. It provides a basis for identifying quality metrics for project deliverables
c. It tracks the fulfillment of quality requirements throughout the project lifecycle
d. It defines the quality standards and testing procedures for project requirements

Answer: c. It tracks the fulfillment of quality requirements throughout the project lifecycle. Explanation: The RTM plays a critical role in quality management by tracking how each requirement, including those related to quality, is being met throughout the project's lifecycle. This ensures that all quality requirements are fulfilled as the project progresses from initiation to closure.
Options a, b, and d, while related to quality management, do not specifically describe the tracking function of an RTM.

576. How does incorporating feedback mechanisms in the requirements documentation process enhance project outcomes?
a. By ensuring that all project decisions are documented and traceable
b. By providing continuous input to refine project requirements based on stakeholder and user feedback
c. By facilitating the legal auditing of project activities
d. By guaranteeing faster project delivery

Answer: b. By providing continuous input to refine project requirements based on stakeholder and user feedback. Explanation: Incorporating feedback mechanisms into the requirements documentation process allows for continuous refinement of the project requirements based on real-time input from stakeholders and users. This adaptability enhances the relevance and effectiveness of the project outcomes by ensuring that the project evolves in alignment with user needs and expectations. Options a, c, and d do not directly relate to the enhancement of project outcomes through the refinement of requirements.

577. What is the primary benefit of using a dynamic documentation tool for maintaining requirements documentation in a fast-paced project environment?
a. It decreases the dependency on project managers for information dissemination
b. It allows for real-time updates and accessibility by all project stakeholders
c. It reduces the need for formal project status meetings
d. It eliminates the risk of data breaches in project documentation

Answer: b. It allows for real-time updates and accessibility by all project stakeholders. Explanation: In fast-paced project environments, using dynamic documentation tools that allow for real-time updates and access is crucial. This ensures that all stakeholders have the latest information on project requirements, facilitating timely decisions and adaptations. This benefit is central to maintaining project agility and stakeholder engagement. Options a, c, and d, while potentially beneficial, do not directly impact the effectiveness of requirement management as significantly as real-time updates do.

578. In a large-scale IT project, the Requirements Traceability Matrix is found to be incomplete. What is the most likely consequence of this during the project execution phase?
a. Increased risk of project delays and budget overruns
b. Decreased effectiveness in stakeholder communication
c. Reduced accuracy in the project's risk management plan

d. Lower overall satisfaction with the project deliverables

Answer: a. Increased risk of project delays and budget overruns. Explanation: An incomplete RTM during project execution can lead to misalignment between project requirements and their corresponding deliverables and test cases, increasing the risk of delays and budget overruns due to unmet or misunderstood requirements. This misalignment can necessitate rework and adjustments late in the project, impacting the schedule and costs. Options b, c, and d, although possible, are not direct consequences of an incomplete RTM.

579. For a project upgrading an enterprise resource planning (ERP) system, why is it crucial to have a well-maintained and accessible Requirements Traceability Matrix?
a. It ensures that all system requirements are aligned with business goals and are met by the end of the project
b. It provides a competitive advantage over other businesses in the industry
c. It simplifies the process for system maintenance and future upgrades
d. It ensures that the project can be completed without any further stakeholder input

Answer: a. It ensures that all system requirements are aligned with business goals and are met by the end of the project. Explanation: For complex projects like an ERP system upgrade, having a well-maintained RTM is crucial for ensuring that all system requirements are clearly linked to business objectives and are fulfilled by the project's conclusion. This alignment is vital for maximizing the system's effectiveness and ensuring it supports the business's strategic goals. Options b, c, and d, while potentially beneficial, do not capture the fundamental purpose of an RTM in ensuring requirement fulfillment and alignment.

580. During the Define Scope process in a software development project, which ITTO (Inputs, Tools, Techniques, and Outputs) ensures that the project and product objectives are fully aligned and documented?
a. Scope baseline
b. Project scope statement
c. Stakeholder register
d. Change log

Answer: b. Project scope statement. Explanation: The project scope statement is crucial in the Define Scope process as it provides a detailed description of the project and product objectives, deliverables, boundaries, and acceptance criteria. It ensures all project efforts are aligned toward achieving the defined goals. The scope baseline (a) includes the project scope statement but is established later, the stakeholder register (c) identifies project stakeholders but does not align objectives, and the change log (d) tracks changes and is not used for defining scope.

581. Which technique is most effective for ensuring the scope of a project is fully inclusive of the necessary functionalities when defining the scope for a new customer relationship management (CRM) system?
a. Alternatives analysis
b. Product breakdown

c. Product analysis
d. Facilitated workshops

Answer: d. Facilitated workshops. Explanation: Facilitated workshops involving key stakeholders are particularly effective in defining the scope for systems like a CRM because they allow for real-time exchange of ideas, consensus-building, and immediate clarification of requirements. Product analysis (c) is useful for understanding product requirements but less so for scope inclusivity, alternatives analysis (a) explores different approaches, and product breakdown (b) helps in understanding product structure but not in gathering comprehensive requirements.

582. In the Define Scope process, what is the primary role of expert judgment?
a. To provide a quantitative assessment of the scope's impact on the budget
b. To leverage specialized knowledge in refining the project scope
c. To document the decisions made during the scope definition
d. To predict potential future changes in project scope

Answer: b. To leverage specialized knowledge in refining the project scope. Explanation: Expert judgment involves consulting with individuals or groups with specialized knowledge in the project's industry or subject matter to refine and define the project scope accurately. This ensures that the scope is realistic and aligns with industry standards. Quantitative assessments (a), documentation (c), and predictions of scope changes (d) are not the primary roles of expert judgment in this process.

583. What input is essential for effectively defining the scope of a construction project for a new library?
a. Risk management plan
b. Requirements documentation
c. Quality metrics
d. Cost management plan

Answer: b. Requirements documentation. Explanation: Requirements documentation is critical when defining the scope of a construction project as it contains the conditions and capabilities that the project must meet or possess, specifically for a new library. This documentation ensures that the defined scope addresses all stakeholder requirements. A risk management plan (a), quality metrics (c), and a cost management plan (d) are important for other planning aspects but do not directly impact scope definition.

584. How does the market research technique benefit the Define Scope process in a project to launch a new consumer product?
a. It identifies the latest trends and consumer needs that can inform project scope
b. It provides a benchmark for future marketing strategies
c. It assists in determining the project's budget constraints
d. It defines the product's post-launch support strategy

Answer: a. It identifies the latest trends and consumer needs that can inform project scope. Explanation: Market research is valuable in the Define Scope process for a new consumer product as it helps identify current market trends and consumer preferences, which can directly influence the project's scope by ensuring the product meets real-world needs and has a competitive edge. Options b, c, and d, while relevant to broader project planning, do not directly influence the initial definition of project scope.

585. A project team is preparing the project scope statement for a new environmental sustainability initiative. Which of the following is NOT typically included in a project scope statement?
a. Project objectives
b. Product acceptance criteria
c. Detailed risk assessment
d. Project deliverables

Answer: c. Detailed risk assessment. Explanation: The project scope statement typically includes the project objectives, product acceptance criteria, and project deliverables to clearly define what the project will achieve and produce. A detailed risk assessment, however, is not typically part of the project scope statement; it is covered in the risk management plan.

586. During the development of a project scope statement for an IT system upgrade, which element ensures the project alignment with business goals?
a. Technical specifications
b. Project exclusions
c. Business case
d. Resource allocation

Answer: c. Business case. Explanation: The business case is a critical element in the project scope statement for an IT system upgrade as it justifies the necessity of the project and aligns it with strategic business goals. Technical specifications (a) detail the requirements for the system, project exclusions (b) clarify what is out of scope, and resource allocation (d) describes the resource requirements, but the business case directly connects the project to business objectives.

587. When finalizing the project scope statement for a construction project, what is the primary purpose of defining project boundaries?
a. To determine the project budget
b. To limit the scope and prevent scope creep
c. To identify key stakeholders
d. To schedule project phases

Answer: b. To limit the scope and prevent scope creep. Explanation: Defining project boundaries in the scope statement is crucial for setting clear limits to what the project will include, which helps prevent scope creep by making it easier to identify and reject requests or activities that are outside the agreed-upon project boundaries.

588. In a project scope statement for a new software development project, why is it important to include assumptions?
a. To provide a basis for estimating project costs and durations

b. To outline the project management approach

c. To list the project milestones

d. To describe the software's operational environment

Answer: a. To provide a basis for estimating project costs and durations. Explanation: Including assumptions in the project scope statement is important as they form the basis for planning project costs and durations. Assumptions are considered to be true for planning purposes and significantly influence how project estimates and schedules are developed.

589. Which component of the project scope statement can help in managing stakeholder expectations in a marketing campaign project?

a. Project deliverables

b. Change control process

c. Project constraints

d. Cost estimates

Answer: c. Project constraints. Explanation: Including project constraints in the scope statement helps manage stakeholder expectations by clearly defining what limits the project faces, such as budget, time, or resources. This transparency helps stakeholders understand the boundaries within which the project must operate.

590. What role does the project scope statement play during the project execution phase of a healthcare facility expansion?

a. It acts as a baseline to monitor and control project scope

b. It serves as a primary communication tool

c. It outlines the project closure criteria

d. It provides a detailed schedule

Answer: a. It acts as a baseline to monitor and control project scope. Explanation: During the project execution phase, the project scope statement serves as a baseline that helps the project team monitor and control the scope, ensuring the project remains aligned with its defined objectives and deliverables.

591. How should a project scope statement for a new mobile application development project address user acceptance criteria?

a. List all potential risks associated with user acceptance

b. Define what constitutes successful user acceptance of the application

c. Provide a timeline for user acceptance testing

d. Outline the marketing strategies for user acquisition

Answer: b. Define what constitutes successful user acceptance of the application. Explanation: Including user acceptance criteria in the project scope statement for a mobile application is crucial as it defines the conditions under which the application is considered accepted by users, which directly impacts the project's success and ensures alignment with user expectations.

592. For a large-scale renewable energy project, why is it important to clearly articulate project exclusions in the scope statement?
a. To enhance team communication
b. To facilitate the integration of technology
c. To prevent misunderstandings and manage stakeholder expectations
d. To comply with environmental regulations

Answer: c. To prevent misunderstandings and manage stakeholder expectations. Explanation: Clearly articulating project exclusions in the scope statement is crucial, especially in large-scale projects like renewable energy initiatives, as it helps prevent misunderstandings and manages expectations by defining what is not included in the project.

593. In preparing a project scope statement for a new academic building, which of the following should be included to ensure all necessary work is accounted for?
a. A list of potential vendors
b. Detailed descriptions of project deliverables
c. A generic risk management plan
d. Biographies of team members

Answer: b. Detailed descriptions of project deliverables. Explanation: Including detailed descriptions of project deliverables in the scope statement ensures that all necessary work required to complete the project is clearly understood and agreed upon, which is essential for planning and executing the project effectively.

594. When documenting lessons learned during the closure phase of an IT infrastructure upgrade, how should information from the project scope statement be utilized?
a. To evaluate the accuracy of the project deliverables
b. To confirm the project met its initial cost estimates
c. To assess whether the project deliverables met the scope criteria
d. To revise the scope statement for future projects

Answer: c. To assess whether the project deliverables met the scope criteria. Explanation: During the closure phase, information from the project scope statement should be used to assess whether the project deliverables met the initially defined scope criteria. This evaluation helps determine the project's success and informs lessons learned by comparing the planned outcomes with actual results.

595. What is the main benefit of having a culturally diverse project team?
a. increased conflict and communication challenges
b. reduced project costs and resource requirements
c. enhanced creativity, innovation, and problem-solving abilities
d. simplified project planning and decision-making processes

Answer: c. enhanced creativity, innovation, and problem-solving abilities. Explanation: The main benefit of having a culturally diverse project team is the enhanced creativity, innovation, and problem-solving abilities that come from bringing together people with different backgrounds, perspectives, and experiences. Cultural diversity can lead to a wider range of ideas, approaches, and solutions, as team members draw on their unique cultural knowledge and insights to tackle project challenges. Diverse teams are often better able to think outside the box, challenge assumptions, and generate novel solutions that may not have emerged in a more homogeneous group. While cultural diversity can sometimes lead to increased conflict or communication challenges, these issues can be effectively managed through inclusive leadership, cross-cultural training, and open communication.

596. Which of the following is not a key aspect of cultural diversity in project management?
a. national or ethnic background
b. age and generational differences
c. educational and professional qualifications
d. beliefs, values, and communication styles

Answer: c. educational and professional qualifications. Explanation: Educational and professional qualifications are not typically considered a key aspect of cultural diversity in project management. While education and experience can certainly shape an individual's perspective and approach to work, they are more closely related to skills and expertise than to cultural background. The key aspects of cultural diversity in project teams include differences in national or ethnic background, age and generational cohorts, beliefs and values, communication styles and preferences, and other cultural factors that influence how people think, behave, and interact. These cultural differences can have a significant impact on team dynamics, collaboration, and performance, and project managers need to be aware of and sensitive to these differences in order to effectively lead and manage diverse teams.

597. What is the first step in managing cultural diversity in a project team?
a. providing cross-cultural communication training for all team members
b. establishing clear project goals and performance expectations
c. recognizing and appreciating the cultural differences within the team
d. assigning team members to roles based on their cultural background

Answer: c. recognizing and appreciating the cultural differences within the team. Explanation: The first step in managing cultural diversity in a project team is recognizing and appreciating the cultural differences that exist within the team. This involves acknowledging that team members come from different cultural backgrounds and may have different values, beliefs, communication styles, and ways of working. By recognizing and valuing these differences, project managers can create an inclusive team environment that leverages diversity as a strength rather than a challenge. This recognition and appreciation should be communicated openly and consistently, setting the tone for respectful and collaborative interactions among team members. Providing cross-cultural training, establishing clear goals, and assigning roles are important steps in managing diversity, but they should be preceded by a fundamental acknowledgement and valuing of the cultural differences present in the team.

598. Which of the following is a best practice for fostering cross-cultural understanding and collaboration in a project team?

a. avoiding discussions about cultural differences to minimize conflict and discomfort
b. encouraging team members to adopt the majority culture's norms and practices
c. promoting open communication and dialogue about cultural perspectives and expectations
d. segregating team members based on cultural background to facilitate subgroup cohesion

Answer: c. promoting open communication and dialogue about cultural perspectives and expectations. Explanation: A best practice for fostering cross-cultural understanding and collaboration in a project team is promoting open communication and dialogue about cultural perspectives and expectations. This involves creating a safe and inclusive environment where team members feel comfortable sharing their cultural viewpoints, experiences, and concerns, and listening to and learning from others. By encouraging open and respectful dialogue, project managers can help team members to better understand and appreciate their cultural differences, identify potential sources of misunderstanding or conflict, and find common ground and shared values. This dialogue should be ongoing throughout the project lifecycle, as cultural dynamics can shift and evolve over time. Avoiding discussions about culture, enforcing majority norms, or segregating team members are counterproductive approaches that can lead to misunderstandings, resentment, and lost opportunities for learning and collaboration.

599. What is the role of the project manager in addressing cultural conflicts or misunderstandings within the team?
a. to act as a neutral mediator and facilitate a respectful resolution process
b. to identify the team member(s) at fault and enforce disciplinary action
c. to ignore minor cultural conflicts and focus on project goals and deliverables
d. to impose a predetermined set of cultural norms and expectations on the team

Answer: a. to act as a neutral mediator and facilitate a respectful resolution process. Explanation: The role of the project manager in addressing cultural conflicts or misunderstandings within the team is to act as a neutral mediator and facilitate a respectful resolution process. When cultural differences lead to conflicts, misunderstandings, or tensions within the team, the project manager should step in to help the parties involved to communicate openly, listen actively, and find a mutually acceptable solution. This involves creating a safe and non-judgmental space for dialogue, asking questions to clarify perspectives and needs, and guiding the team towards a resolution that addresses the underlying cultural issues and maintains positive working relationships. The project manager should remain neutral and objective, focusing on the problem rather than the people, and modeling respectful and inclusive communication. Ignoring conflicts, assigning blame, or imposing cultural norms are ineffective and potentially damaging approaches that can escalate tensions and undermine team morale and performance.

600. How can project managers leverage cultural diversity to enhance project innovation and outcomes?
a. by assigning team members to tasks that align with cultural stereotypes and expectations
b. by encouraging team members to suppress their cultural identities and conform to a uniform project culture
c. by creating opportunities for cross-cultural learning, collaboration, and synergy
d. by emphasizing cultural differences as a source of competition and motivation

Answer: c. by creating opportunities for cross-cultural learning, collaboration, and synergy. Explanation: Project managers can leverage cultural diversity to enhance project innovation and outcomes by creating opportunities for cross-cultural learning, collaboration, and synergy. This involves recognizing the unique strengths, perspectives, and ideas that team members from different cultural backgrounds bring to the project, and actively seeking ways to harness these diverse contributions. For example, project managers can create diverse subgroups or task forces to tackle complex problems, encourage team members to share cultural insights and best practices, and facilitate cross-cultural mentoring and knowledge-sharing. By fostering an inclusive environment that values and leverages cultural diversity, project managers can tap into a wider range of creative solutions, innovative approaches, and complementary skills that can drive project success. Assigning tasks based on stereotypes, suppressing cultural identities, or framing diversity as a source of competition are misguided strategies that fail to capitalize on the true benefits of cultural diversity in project teams.

601. What is the potential impact of cultural bias or stereotyping on project team dynamics and performance?
a. increased team cohesion and productivity
b. improved cross-cultural communication and understanding
c. reduced trust, collaboration, and engagement
d. enhanced problem-solving and decision-making abilities

Answer: c. reduced trust, collaboration, and engagement. Explanation: Cultural bias or stereotyping can have a negative impact on project team dynamics and performance by reducing trust, collaboration, and engagement among team members. When team members hold biased or stereotypical views about colleagues from different cultural backgrounds, they may make unfair assumptions, judgments, or attributions about their abilities, motivations, or behaviors. This can lead to a breakdown in communication, cooperation, and trust, as team members may feel disrespected, misunderstood, or marginalized. Stereotyping can also limit the exchange of ideas and perspectives, as team members may discount or dismiss contributions from colleagues they perceive as different or inferior. As a result, team morale, cohesion, and productivity can suffer, hindering project progress and outcomes. Project managers must actively identify and address cultural biases and stereotypes within the team, promoting a culture of respect, inclusion, and equal opportunity for all team members.

602. How can project managers promote cultural sensitivity and inclusivity in virtual or geographically dispersed teams?
a. by relying on written communication to minimize cultural misunderstandings
b. by adopting a "one size fits all" approach to team management and communication
c. by acknowledging and accommodating different cultural communication styles and preferences
d. by requiring all team members to speak a common language fluently

Answer: c. by acknowledging and accommodating different cultural communication styles and preferences. Explanation: Project managers can promote cultural sensitivity and inclusivity in virtual or geographically dispersed teams by acknowledging and accommodating different cultural communication styles and preferences. In virtual teams, cultural differences can be amplified by the lack of face-to-face interaction and nonverbal cues, making it more challenging to build rapport, trust, and shared understanding. To bridge these gaps, project managers should take the time to learn about and appreciate the cultural communication norms and expectations of team members, such as preferences for direct vs. indirect communication, formal vs. informal tone, or task-oriented vs. relationship-oriented interactions. They should also provide multiple communication channels and formats to accommodate different cultural preferences, such as written documents, audio or video calls, or visual aids. By flexibly adapting communication styles and tools to the cultural needs of the team, project managers can foster a more inclusive and effective virtual collaboration environment. Relying solely on written communication, adopting a uniform approach, or enforcing language requirements can exacerbate cultural differences and create barriers to full participation and engagement.

603. What is the significance of cultural intelligence (CQ) for project managers working in diverse or global project environments?
a. the ability to speak multiple languages fluently
b. the ability to memorize facts and figures about different cultures
c. the ability to adapt and function effectively in culturally diverse contexts
d. the ability to impose one's own cultural norms and expectations on others

Answer: c. the ability to adapt and function effectively in culturally diverse contexts. Explanation: Cultural intelligence (CQ) refers to the ability to adapt and function effectively in culturally diverse contexts. It is a critical competency for project managers working in diverse or global project environments, where they interact with stakeholders and team members from different cultural backgrounds. CQ involves a combination of cultural knowledge, awareness, and skills that enable project managers to navigate cultural differences, communicate effectively across cultures, and build positive relationships with culturally diverse partners. Project managers with high CQ are able to recognize and appreciate cultural differences, adapt their communication and leadership styles to different cultural contexts, and leverage cultural diversity for innovation and problem-solving. They are also better equipped to anticipate and mitigate potential cultural misunderstandings or conflicts that can impact project success. CQ is not about language proficiency, factual knowledge, or cultural imposition, but rather a strategic and adaptive approach to managing and thriving in culturally complex project environments.

604. What is the role of organizational culture in shaping project team culture and performance?
a. organizational culture has no impact on project team culture or performance
b. organizational culture should be ignored in favor of establishing a unique project team culture
c. organizational culture provides a broader context and set of values that influence project team culture and behaviors
d. organizational culture dictates a uniform set of norms and expectations for all project teams

Answer: c. organizational culture provides a broader context and set of values that influence project team culture and behaviors. Explanation: Organizational culture plays a significant role in shaping project team culture and performance by providing a broader context and set of values that influence team norms, behaviors, and expectations. Every organization has its own unique culture, which encompasses the shared assumptions, beliefs, values, and practices that guide how work is done and how people interact. This organizational culture sets the tone and framework within which project teams operate, and can have a strong impact on team dynamics, communication, decision-making, and performance. For example, an organizational culture that values innovation, risk-taking, and continuous learning may foster project teams that are more adaptable, creative, and open to new ideas. Conversely, an organizational culture that emphasizes hierarchy, control, and conformity may constrain project teams and limit their ability to respond to changing project needs. Project managers must be aware of and navigate the organizational cultural context in order to align project team culture with broader organizational goals and values, while also creating a team-specific culture that supports project success. Ignoring organizational culture, establishing a completely separate team culture, or enforcing a one-size-fits-all approach are not effective strategies for managing the complex interplay between organizational and project team cultures.

605. What is a conflict of interest in project management?
a. a disagreement between project team members about project goals or strategies
b. a situation where a project manager's personal or professional interests interfere with their ability to make objective decisions
c. a conflict between the project manager and the project sponsor about project scope or budget
d. a dispute between the project team and external stakeholders about project deliverables or timelines

Answer: b. a situation where a project manager's personal or professional interests interfere with their ability to make objective decisions. Explanation: A conflict of interest in project management refers to a situation where a project manager's personal, financial, or organizational interests interfere with their ability to make impartial and objective decisions in the best interest of the project. This can include personal relationships, financial investments, or competing professional commitments that create a real or perceived bias in the project manager's judgment or actions. Conflicts of interest can undermine trust, integrity, and fairness in project decision-making, and can lead to suboptimal outcomes or ethical breaches. Disagreements about project goals, conflicts with sponsors or stakeholders, or disputes about deliverables are not necessarily conflicts of interest, but rather normal challenges that project managers must navigate and resolve in the course of managing projects.

606. Which of the following is an example of a personal conflict of interest in project management?
a. a project manager's family member works for a company that is bidding on a project contract
b. a project manager has a financial stake in a company that could benefit from project decisions
c. a project manager volunteers for a non-profit organization that is not related to the project
d. a project manager has a strong personal belief or opinion about the project's objectives or approach

Answer: a. a project manager's family member works for a company that is bidding on a project contract. Explanation: A personal conflict of interest in project management arises when a project manager has a personal relationship or connection that could bias their decisions or actions related to the project. In this example, the project manager's family member working for a company that is bidding on a project contract creates a potential personal conflict of interest. The project manager may feel pressured to favor or select that company, even if it is not the best choice for the project, in order to benefit their family member. This personal connection can cloud the project manager's judgment and create the appearance of impropriety, even if no actual bias occurs. Having a financial stake in a project-related company is an example of a financial conflict of interest, while volunteering for an unrelated organization or holding strong personal beliefs are not necessarily conflicts of interest unless they directly impact project decisions.

607. What is the primary reason why conflicts of interest are problematic in project management?
a. they can lead to increased project costs and delays

b. they can create legal liabilities and reputational risks for the organization
c. they can undermine trust, integrity, and objective decision-making
d. they can demotivate and disengage project team members

Answer: c. they can undermine trust, integrity, and objective decision-making. Explanation: The primary reason why conflicts of interest are problematic in project management is that they can undermine trust, integrity, and objective decision-making. When project managers have personal, financial, or organizational interests that conflict with their project responsibilities, it can create real or perceived biases that call into question the fairness, transparency, and credibility of project decisions. Stakeholders may lose trust in the project manager's ability to act in the best interest of the project, leading to reduced cooperation, support, and buy-in. Team members may feel that decisions are being made based on favoritism or self-interest rather than merit or project needs, eroding morale and commitment. Compromised integrity and objectivity can lead to suboptimal project outcomes, as well as potential legal, financial, and reputational risks for the individuals and organizations involved. While conflicts of interest can sometimes result in increased costs, delays, or disengagement, the fundamental problem is the erosion of trust and integrity that undermines effective project management.

608. Which of the following is the best approach for project managers to prevent conflicts of interest?
a. avoid any personal or professional relationships with project stakeholders or team members
b. disclose any potential conflicts of interest and recuse oneself from related decisions
c. rely on personal integrity and judgment to manage conflicts of interest informally
d. establish a blind trust for any financial investments related to the project

Answer: b. disclose any potential conflicts of interest and recuse oneself from related decisions. Explanation: The best approach for project managers to prevent conflicts of interest is to proactively identify, disclose, and manage any potential conflicts in a transparent and formal manner. This involves carefully assessing one's personal, financial, and organizational interests and relationships, and identifying any situations that could create a real or perceived conflict with project responsibilities. Project managers should then disclose these potential conflicts to relevant stakeholders, such as the project sponsor, steering committee, or ethics officer, and work with them to develop appropriate mitigation strategies. In some cases, this may involve recusing oneself from certain decisions or actions related to the conflict, such as supplier selection or resource allocation. By being transparent and proactive in managing conflicts of interest, project managers can demonstrate their commitment to integrity, build trust with stakeholders, and ensure that project decisions are made objectively and in the best interest of the project. Avoiding all relationships, relying on personal judgment, or establishing blind trusts are not as effective or transparent in preventing conflicts of interest.

609. What should a project manager do if they become aware of a team member's conflict of interest?
a. ignore the conflict and trust the team member to manage it independently
b. immediately remove the team member from the project to avoid any potential bias
c. discuss the situation with the team member and jointly develop a plan to mitigate the conflict
d. report the team member to senior management for disciplinary action

Answer: c. discuss the situation with the team member and jointly develop a plan to mitigate the conflict. Explanation: If a project manager becomes aware of a team member's conflict of interest, the most appropriate action is to discuss the situation with the team member and jointly develop a plan to mitigate the conflict. This approach recognizes that conflicts of interest can arise unintentionally or unavoidably, and that the key is to manage them transparently and proactively. The project manager should have an open and non-judgmental conversation with the team member to understand the nature and extent of the conflict, as well as the team member's perspective and concerns. Together, they can then explore options for mitigating the conflict, such as reassigning certain tasks, recusing the team member from certain decisions, or implementing additional oversight or documentation. The goal is to find a solution that addresses the conflict while maintaining the team member's engagement and contribution to the project. Ignoring the conflict, removing the team member without due process, or escalating the issue to disciplinary action are not constructive or fair ways to handle the situation, and can damage trust and team morale.

610. How can organizational policies and procedures help to mitigate conflicts of interest in project management?
a. by prohibiting project managers from having any personal or professional relationships outside of work
b. by requiring project managers to disclose and divest any financial investments related to their projects
c. by establishing clear guidelines and processes for identifying, disclosing, and managing conflicts of interest
d. by assigning all project decisions to a committee to avoid individual conflicts of interest

Answer: c. by establishing clear guidelines and processes for identifying, disclosing, and managing conflicts of interest. Explanation: Organizational policies and procedures can play a key role in mitigating conflicts of interest in project management by establishing clear guidelines and processes for identifying, disclosing, and managing these situations. These policies should define what constitutes a conflict of interest, provide examples of common scenarios, and outline the expectations and responsibilities of project managers and team members in preventing and addressing conflicts. They should also specify the process for disclosing potential conflicts, such as filling out a standard form or meeting with a designated ethics officer, and the criteria and steps for evaluating and mitigating disclosed conflicts. By having a transparent and consistent framework for managing conflicts of interest, organizations can promote a culture of integrity, accountability, and trust in project management. Prohibiting all outside relationships, requiring divestment of all investments, or assigning all decisions to committees are not practical or effective solutions, as they do not address the root issue of identifying and managing conflicts in a case-by-case manner.

611. What is the role of the project sponsor in addressing conflicts of interest within the project team?
a. to investigate and verify all conflicts of interest reported by the project manager
b. to provide guidance and support to the project manager in managing conflicts of interest
c. to take disciplinary action against team members with conflicts of interest
d. to approve all project decisions to ensure they are not influenced by conflicts of interest

Answer: b. to provide guidance and support to the project manager in managing conflicts of interest. Explanation: The role of the project sponsor in addressing conflicts of interest within the project team is to provide guidance and support to the project manager in navigating these complex situations. As a senior leader and key stakeholder, the project sponsor can offer valuable perspective, resources, and backing to help the project manager identify, assess, and mitigate conflicts of interest in a manner that aligns with organizational policies and project objectives. This may involve providing advice on how to approach sensitive conversations with team members, escalating issues to higher-level management or ethics committees, or securing additional resources or oversight to manage conflicts effectively. The project sponsor should also reinforce the importance of integrity and transparency in project decision-making, and support the project manager in fostering a team culture that encourages open communication and proactive management of conflicts of interest. Investigating conflicts, taking disciplinary action, or approving all decisions are not typically direct responsibilities of the project sponsor, but rather functions that are carried out by the project manager, HR, or other designated parties according to established policies and procedures.

612. What is the potential impact of unaddressed conflicts of interest on project outcomes and success?
a. increased team collaboration and innovation
b. improved stakeholder trust and confidence in the project
c. decreased project costs and faster completion times
d. compromised project quality, efficiency, and reputation

Answer: d. compromised project quality, efficiency, and reputation. Explanation: Unaddressed conflicts of interest can have significant negative impacts on project outcomes and success. When conflicts of interest are not properly identified, disclosed, and managed, they can introduce bias, subjectivity, and misaligned priorities into project decision-making. This can lead to compromised project quality, as decisions may be made based on personal or external interests rather than technical merit or project requirements. Efficiency may also suffer, as team members may spend time and resources pursuing activities that benefit their own interests rather than optimizing project workflows and deliverables. Ultimately, the project's reputation and credibility may be damaged, as stakeholders lose trust in the integrity and fairness of the project management process. Unmitigated conflicts of interest can also expose the organization to legal, financial, and regulatory risks, further jeopardizing project outcomes. In contrast, proactively addressing conflicts of interest can enhance team collaboration, stakeholder confidence, and project performance by ensuring that decisions are made objectively and in the best interest of the project.

613. What is the difference between actual and perceived conflicts of interest in project management?
a. actual conflicts of interest are intentional, while perceived conflicts of interest are accidental
b. actual conflicts of interest involve financial interests, while perceived conflicts of interest involve personal relationships
c. actual conflicts of interest have a real impact on project decisions, while perceived conflicts of interest only appear to have an impact
d. actual conflicts of interest are more serious than perceived conflicts of interest

Answer: c. actual conflicts of interest have a real impact on project decisions, while perceived conflicts of interest only appear to have an impact. Explanation: The difference between actual and perceived conflicts of interest in project management lies in the real vs. apparent impact on project decisions. An actual conflict of interest exists when a project manager or team member has a personal, financial, or organizational interest that directly influences their ability to make objective and impartial decisions in the best interest of the project. For example, a project manager who owns stock in a company that is bidding on a project contract has an actual financial conflict of interest that could bias their selection decision. In contrast, a perceived conflict of interest exists when there is an appearance of bias or impropriety, even if no actual influence on decisions occurs. For example, a project manager who has a close friendship with a vendor may be perceived as favoring that vendor, even if the project manager remains objective in their dealings. Both actual and perceived conflicts of interest are serious concerns, as they can undermine trust, credibility, and the integrity of the project management process. Perceived conflicts can be just as damaging as actual conflicts, as they can create doubt and suspicion among stakeholders, even if no wrongdoing occurs. Project managers must be vigilant in identifying and managing both actual and perceived conflicts of interest to maintain the highest standards of ethics and professionalism.

614. How can project managers balance the need for transparency in disclosing conflicts of interest with the need for privacy and confidentiality?
a. by disclosing all conflicts of interest to all project stakeholders, regardless of relevance or sensitivity
b. by never disclosing any conflicts of interest to avoid violating privacy or confidentiality
c. by disclosing conflicts of interest only to the project sponsor and keeping all other information confidential
d. by carefully assessing each situation and disclosing conflicts of interest to the appropriate parties on a need-to-know basis

Answer: d. by carefully assessing each situation and disclosing conflicts of interest to the appropriate parties on a need-to-know basis. Explanation: Project managers must strike a delicate balance between transparency and privacy when disclosing conflicts of interest. On one hand, transparency is essential for building trust, demonstrating integrity, and ensuring that conflicts are properly identified and managed. Stakeholders have a right to know about any potential biases or competing interests that could affect project decisions and outcomes. On the other hand, project managers have a duty to protect sensitive personal, financial, or organizational information that may be involved in a conflict of interest situation. Disclosing such information too broadly could violate privacy rights, breach confidentiality agreements, or expose individuals to undue scrutiny or harm. To navigate this balance, project managers should carefully assess each situation and disclose conflicts of interest to the appropriate parties on a need-to-know basis. This means sharing relevant information with those stakeholders who have a legitimate interest in the conflict and can help to mitigate its impact, such as the project sponsor, ethics officer, or affected team members. The level of detail and scope of disclosure may vary depending on the nature and severity of the conflict, as well as applicable laws, regulations, and organizational policies. By being thoughtful and judicious in their approach to conflict of interest disclosure, project managers can uphold both the principles of transparency and the protection of privacy and confidentiality.

615. What is the first step in the ethical decision-making framework for project managers?
a. gather all relevant facts and information about the situation
b. identify and analyze the ethical issue or dilemma
c. consider the potential consequences of different actions
d. make a decision and implement the chosen course of action

Answer: b. identify and analyze the ethical issue or dilemma. Explanation: The first step in the ethical decision-making framework for project managers is to identify and analyze the ethical issue or dilemma. This involves recognizing that a situation involves ethical considerations and clearly defining the moral question or conflict at hand. Project managers must be attuned to the ethical dimensions of their work and proactively identify situations that may pose ethical challenges, such as conflicts of interest, confidentiality breaches, or misuse of resources. By clearly articulating the ethical issue, project managers can then gather relevant information, consider alternatives, and make a well-reasoned decision. Gathering facts, considering consequences, and implementing decisions are important subsequent steps in the framework, but the critical first step is to recognize and analyze the ethical issue itself.

616. Which of the following is not one of the key principles in the PMI Code of Ethics and Professional Conduct?
a. responsibility
b. respect
c. fairness
d. obedience

Answer: d. obedience. Explanation: Obedience is not one of the key principles in the PMI Code of Ethics and Professional Conduct. The four foundational values that inform the ethical conduct of project managers, according to the PMI Code, are responsibility, respect, fairness, and honesty. Responsibility involves taking ownership of decisions and being accountable for results. Respect involves showing high regard for ourselves, others, and project resources. Fairness involves making decisions and acting impartially and objectively. Honesty involves understanding the truth and acting in a truthful manner. While obedience to laws, regulations, and organizational policies is important, it is not one of the core ethical principles emphasized in the PMI framework.

617. What is the purpose of a project ethics charter or code of conduct?
a. to outline the project scope, deliverables, and success criteria
b. to establish the roles, responsibilities, and reporting structure of the project team
c. to provide guidance on acceptable behavior and ethical standards for the project
d. to identify and prioritize project risks and mitigation strategies

Answer: c. to provide guidance on acceptable behavior and ethical standards for the project. Explanation: The purpose of a project ethics charter or code of conduct is to provide clear guidance on acceptable behavior and ethical standards for all individuals involved in the project. This document sets forth the ethical principles, values, and expectations that should guide project decision-making and conduct, such as honesty, integrity, respect, and professionalism. It may also outline specific policies and procedures related to common ethical issues, such as conflicts of interest, confidentiality, and use of resources. By establishing a shared understanding of ethical conduct upfront, a project ethics charter helps to promote a culture of integrity, prevent misconduct, and provide a framework for addressing ethical challenges that may arise during the project. Project scope, team roles, and risk management are important elements of project planning but are typically addressed in separate documents, such as the project charter, responsibility assignment matrix, or risk register.

618. How can project managers create an environment that encourages ethical behavior and decision-making within the project team?
a. by focusing solely on meeting project objectives and deliverables, regardless of the means used
b. by providing ethics training and resources, and modeling ethical behavior in their own actions
c. by implementing strict penalties and punishments for any violations of ethical standards

d. by avoiding discussions of ethics to maintain team harmony and avoid conflicts

Answer: b. by providing ethics training and resources, and modeling ethical behavior in their own actions. Explanation: Project managers can create an environment that encourages ethical behavior and decision-making within the project team by providing ethics training and resources, and modeling ethical behavior in their own actions. This involves proactively educating team members about relevant ethical standards, principles, and practices, and providing ongoing guidance and support for navigating ethical challenges. Project managers should also lead by example, demonstrating a strong personal commitment to integrity, honesty, and ethical conduct in their own decision-making and interactions. By setting the tone at the top and creating a culture of openness, trust, and accountability, project managers can foster an environment where team members feel empowered and expected to act ethically. Focusing solely on results, implementing punitive measures, or avoiding ethical discussions altogether are counterproductive approaches that can lead to unethical behavior, erode team morale, and ultimately undermine project success.

619. What should a project manager do if they encounter an ethical dilemma that is not covered by existing policies or guidelines?
a. make a unilateral decision based on their personal moral principles
b. ignore the issue and focus on meeting project objectives
c. consult with trusted colleagues, mentors, or ethics experts to gain guidance and perspective
d. refer the matter to legal counsel and follow their advice without question

Answer: c. consult with trusted colleagues, mentors, or ethics experts to gain guidance and perspective. Explanation: If a project manager encounters an ethical dilemma that is not covered by existing policies or guidelines, the best course of action is to consult with trusted colleagues, mentors, or ethics experts to gain guidance and perspective. Ethical dilemmas are often complex, nuanced, and context-dependent, and may not have clear-cut answers. By seeking input from others who have relevant experience, expertise, or insight, project managers can gather different viewpoints, identify potential options and consequences, and make a more informed and reasoned decision. This consultation process may involve reaching out to peers within the organization, professional mentors, or subject matter experts in ethics or the specific domain related to the dilemma. The goal is not to find a quick fix or abdicate responsibility, but rather to engage in a thoughtful and collaborative process of ethical deliberation. Making unilateral decisions, ignoring the issue, or blindly following legal advice without consideration of broader ethical implications are not appropriate responses to novel or complex ethical challenges.

620. How can project managers balance competing ethical principles or stakeholder interests when making decisions?
a. by prioritizing the interests of the most powerful or influential stakeholders
b. by choosing the course of action that is least likely to cause conflict or controversy
c. by considering the potential consequences and choosing the option that does the greatest good and least harm
d. by deferring the decision to higher-level management or external authorities

Answer: c. by considering the potential consequences and choosing the option that does the greatest good and least harm. Explanation: Project managers can balance competing ethical principles or stakeholder interests when making decisions by carefully considering the potential consequences and choosing the option that does the greatest good and least harm for all involved parties. This approach, known as consequentialism or utilitarianism, seeks to maximize overall welfare and minimize negative impacts. When faced with ethical trade-offs or conflicting stakeholder needs, project managers should assess the short-term and long-term effects of each possible course of action on various stakeholder groups, as well as the project objectives and outcomes. They should strive to find a solution that respects the rights and interests of all concerned, while also advancing the greater good of the project and the organization. This may involve seeking win-win opportunities, making difficult compromises, or prioritizing certain principles or stakeholders based on a clear and justifiable rationale. Simply deferring to power dynamics, avoiding conflict, or abdicating responsibility are not ethically sound or professionally appropriate ways to navigate complex decision-making challenges.

621. What is the role of cultural differences and diversity in ethical decision-making for project managers?
a. cultural differences and diversity have no impact on ethical decision-making in project management
b. project managers should always defer to the dominant cultural norms and values of the organization or society
c. project managers should be aware of and sensitive to cultural differences, but make decisions based solely on universal ethical principles
d. project managers should consider cultural differences as one of many factors that can influence ethical perceptions and approaches

Answer: d. project managers should consider cultural differences as one of many factors that can influence ethical perceptions and approaches. Explanation: Cultural differences and diversity can play a significant role in ethical decision-making for project managers, and should be considered as one of many factors that can influence perceptions, values, and approaches related to ethics. Different cultures may have different norms, beliefs, and expectations regarding ethical behavior, communication, and decision-making, which can lead to misunderstandings, conflicts, or unintended consequences if not properly acknowledged and managed. Project managers should be aware of and sensitive to these cultural differences, and seek to understand and respect the cultural context in which they are operating. At the same time, they should not automatically defer to cultural relativism or abandon universal ethical principles in the face of cultural diversity. Rather, they should strive to find a balance between respecting cultural differences and upholding fundamental ethical standards, such as honesty, fairness, and responsibility. This may involve adapting communication and decision-making styles to fit cultural norms, while also clearly articulating and adhering to core ethical values. By considering cultural differences as one input among many in the ethical decision-making process, project managers can make more informed, inclusive, and culturally responsive choices that promote ethical conduct and project success.

622. What is the relationship between ethical decision-making and project success?
a. ethical decision-making is unrelated to project success and should be considered a separate concern
b. ethical decision-making is important, but should be subordinated to achieving project objectives and deliverables
c. ethical decision-making can contribute to project success by building trust, credibility, and long-term sustainability
d. ethical decision-making is the sole determinant of project success, regardless of other factors

Answer: c. ethical decision-making can contribute to project success by building trust, credibility, and long-term sustainability. Explanation: Ethical decision-making and project success are closely interrelated, and ethical conduct can contribute to positive project outcomes in several ways. First, making ethical decisions helps to build trust and credibility with stakeholders, including team members, clients, sponsors, and the wider community. When stakeholders perceive the project as being managed with integrity, transparency, and fairness, they are more likely to have confidence in the project's purpose, processes, and results. This can lead to increased buy-in, cooperation, and support, which are critical for project success. Second, ethical decision-making can enhance the long-term sustainability and value of project outcomes. By considering the broader social, environmental, and ethical implications of project decisions, managers can help to ensure that projects deliver not only short-term outputs, but also long-term benefits and positive impacts for stakeholders. Finally, ethical conduct can mitigate legal, financial, and reputational risks that can derail projects and damage organizational performance. While ethical decision-making is not the only factor in project success, and should not be pursued at the expense of other critical project management elements, it is an important enabler and safeguard for achieving successful project outcomes.

623. How can project managers effectively communicate and justify their ethical decisions to stakeholders?
a. by providing a detailed explanation of their personal moral philosophy and reasoning process
b. by emphasizing the potential negative consequences of alternative courses of action
c. by demonstrating how the decision aligns with organizational values, policies, and project objectives
d. by appealing to the emotions and personal interests of individual stakeholders

Answer: c. by demonstrating how the decision aligns with organizational values, policies, and project objectives. Explanation: Project managers can effectively communicate and justify their ethical decisions to stakeholders by demonstrating how the decision aligns with organizational values, policies, and project objectives. This approach focuses on the broader context and shared goals that should guide ethical conduct, rather than relying solely on personal moral beliefs or emotional appeals. When explaining an ethical decision, project managers should clearly articulate the relevant ethical principles, standards, or regulations that informed their choice, and how these align with the organization's stated values and commitments. They should also show how the decision supports the specific goals, deliverables, and success criteria of the project, and how it serves the best interests of the project stakeholders as a whole. By grounding ethical decisions in a clear and consistent framework of organizational and project priorities, managers can provide a persuasive and defensible rationale for their actions. This can help to build understanding, legitimacy, and support among stakeholders, even if some may disagree with the specific decision. Focusing too heavily on personal philosophy, negative outcomes, or individual interests can undermine the credibility and acceptability of ethical decisions, and may be seen as subjective, fear-mongering, or favoritism.

624. What steps can project managers take to continuously improve their ethical decision-making skills and practices?
a. rely solely on their personal intuition and experience to guide their ethical choices
b. avoid seeking feedback or input from others to maintain an appearance of confidence and authority
c. regularly review and reflect on their decisions, seek learning opportunities, and engage in ongoing dialogue and consultation
d. delegate ethical decision-making responsibilities to other team members or external experts

Answer: c. regularly review and reflect on their decisions, seek learning opportunities, and engage in ongoing dialogue and consultation. Explanation: To continuously improve their ethical decision-making skills and practices, project managers should regularly review and reflect on their decisions, seek learning opportunities, and engage in ongoing dialogue and consultation. Ethical decision-making is not a one-time event or a static set of rules, but rather an ongoing process of learning, growth, and adaptation. By taking the time to critically examine past decisions, identify strengths and weaknesses, and consider alternative approaches, project managers can gain valuable insights and refine their ethical reasoning and problem-solving abilities. They should also proactively seek out learning opportunities, such as ethics training, case studies, or mentoring, to expand their knowledge and skills in applying ethical principles to real-world situations. Engaging in regular dialogue and consultation with peers, experts, and stakeholders can provide fresh perspectives, challenge assumptions, and help to identify blind spots or biases in decision-making. By cultivating a habit of self-reflection, lifelong learning, and collaborative inquiry, project managers can continually sharpen their ethical acumen and make more sound and defensible decisions in the face of complex challenges. Relying solely on intuition, avoiding feedback, or delegating responsibility are not effective strategies for ethical growth and development.

625. What is the primary purpose of the PMI Code of Ethics and Professional Conduct?
a. to provide a framework for ethical decision-making and conduct in project management
b. to establish legal requirements for project managers to avoid liability and litigation
c. to promote the commercial interests and reputation of the project management profession
d. to ensure compliance with specific methodologies and best practices in project management

Answer: a. to provide a framework for ethical decision-making and conduct in project management. Explanation: The primary purpose of the PMI Code of Ethics and Professional Conduct is to provide a clear and consistent framework for ethical decision-making and conduct in the practice of project management. The Code articulates the values, principles, and standards that guide the behavior and actions of project management professionals, regardless of their specific roles, organizations, or cultural contexts. It serves as a moral compass and a shared foundation for navigating the complex ethical challenges that can arise in project work. The Code is not a legal document, a marketing tool, or a prescriptive methodology, but rather a set of aspirational and normative guidelines for upholding the integrity and accountability of the project management profession.

626. Which of the following is not one of the four foundational values outlined in the PMI Code of Ethics and Professional Conduct?
a. responsibility
b. respect
c. fairness
d. transparency

Answer: d. transparency. Explanation: Transparency is not one of the four foundational values outlined in the PMI Code of Ethics and Professional Conduct. The Code is built upon four key values: responsibility, respect, fairness, and honesty. Responsibility involves taking ownership of decisions and being accountable for results. Respect involves showing high regard for ourselves, others, and project resources. Fairness involves making decisions and acting impartially and objectively. Honesty involves understanding the truth and acting in a truthful manner. While transparency is an important ethical principle that is closely related to honesty and fairness, it is not explicitly identified as one of the core values in the PMI Code.

627. What does the value of "responsibility" in the PMI Code of Ethics and Professional Conduct require of project managers?
a. to prioritize their own interests and career advancement over project objectives
b. to accept full blame for any project failures or shortcomings, regardless of circumstances
c. to make decisions and take actions based on the best interests of the project and stakeholders
d. to avoid taking on challenging projects or roles that may pose risks or uncertainties

Answer: c. to make decisions and take actions based on the best interests of the project and stakeholders. Explanation: The value of "responsibility" in the PMI Code of Ethics and Professional Conduct requires project managers to make decisions and take actions based on the best interests of the project and its stakeholders. This means considering the needs, expectations, and well-being of all parties involved in or affected by the project, and striving to deliver value and benefits in an accountable and sustainable manner. Responsible project managers take ownership of their choices and outcomes, and proactively communicate and address any issues or concerns that may impact project success. They do not prioritize personal gain over project goals, avoid blame or accountability, or shy away from difficult challenges. Instead, they act as stewards and fiduciaries of the project resources and relationships entrusted to them, and make responsible decisions that balance competing interests and constraints.

628. How can project managers demonstrate the value of "respect" in their interactions with team members and stakeholders?
a. by ignoring or downplaying individual differences and perspectives to maintain harmony and agreement
b. by engaging in respectful and inclusive communication, and valuing the diversity and dignity of all individuals
c. by showing favoritism or leniency towards certain team members or stakeholders to gain their support
d. by avoiding direct confrontation or feedback, even when performance or behavior issues arise

Answer: b. by engaging in respectful and inclusive communication, and valuing the diversity and dignity of all individuals. Explanation: Project managers can demonstrate the value of "respect" in their interactions with team members and stakeholders by engaging in respectful and inclusive communication, and valuing the diversity and dignity of all individuals involved in the project. This means actively listening to and considering different viewpoints, experiences, and needs, and creating an environment where everyone feels heard, appreciated, and empowered to contribute their unique talents and perspectives. Respectful project managers use appropriate and professional language, avoid stereotypes or biases, and show empathy and understanding towards others. They also provide constructive feedback and address concerns or conflicts in a respectful and solution-oriented manner. Ignoring differences, showing favoritism, or avoiding difficult conversations are not respectful behaviors and can undermine trust, collaboration, and performance on the project team.

629. What is an example of how project managers can apply the value of "fairness" in their decision-making and problem-solving processes?
a. by making decisions based on personal preferences or relationships, rather than objective criteria
b. by consistently applying policies, procedures, and standards to all situations and individuals

c. by favoring efficiency and expediency over due process and stakeholder input
d. by avoiding transparency or documentation of decisions to maintain flexibility and control

Answer: b. by consistently applying policies, procedures, and standards to all situations and individuals. Explanation: An example of how project managers can apply the value of "fairness" in their decision-making and problem-solving processes is by consistently applying relevant policies, procedures, and standards to all situations and individuals involved in the project. Fairness requires that decisions are made based on impartial and equitable criteria, rather than personal biases, politics, or self-interest. Project managers should strive to establish clear and transparent decision-making frameworks that are grounded in the project objectives, stakeholder requirements, and organizational guidelines. They should also ensure that all team members and stakeholders have equal access to information, resources, and opportunities, and that any exceptions or variations are justified and communicated openly. Consistent and principled application of rules and standards helps to create a sense of fairness, predictability, and legitimacy in project decisions and outcomes.

630. How might the value of "honesty" influence a project manager's approach to communicating project status, risks, and issues?
a. by withholding or sugarcoating negative information to avoid causing alarm or disappointment
b. by exaggerating or overpromising project benefits and outcomes to secure support and resources
c. by providing accurate, timely, and complete information, even if it may be unwelcome or uncomfortable
d. by selectively sharing information with certain stakeholders to maintain power and control

Answer: c. by providing accurate, timely, and complete information, even if it may be unwelcome or uncomfortable. Explanation: The value of "honesty" in the PMI Code of Ethics and Professional Conduct would require a project manager to communicate project status, risks, and issues in an accurate, timely, and complete manner, even if the information may be unwelcome or uncomfortable for some stakeholders. Honesty means being truthful and transparent in all communications and dealings related to the project, and avoiding any form of deception, misrepresentation, or omission that could mislead or harm others. Project managers should strive to provide a clear and balanced picture of the project reality, including both positive and negative aspects, and proactively share any information that may impact stakeholder expectations, decisions, or actions. They should also create a culture of openness and trust, where team members and stakeholders feel safe to raise concerns or admit mistakes without fear of retaliation or blame. Withholding, exaggerating, or selectively sharing information are dishonest practices that can erode credibility, accountability, and alignment on the project.

631. What should a project manager do if they encounter a situation where two or more of the foundational values in the PMI Code of Ethics seem to be in conflict?
a. prioritize the value that is most commercially advantageous for the project or organization
b. choose the value that aligns with their personal beliefs or cultural norms
c. carefully analyze the situation and strive to find a resolution that upholds all relevant values to the greatest extent possible
d. ignore the conflict and make a decision based on expediency or political pressure

Answer: c. carefully analyze the situation and strive to find a resolution that upholds all relevant values to the greatest extent possible. Explanation: If a project manager encounters a situation where two or more of the foundational values in the PMI Code of Ethics seem to be in conflict, they should carefully analyze the situation and strive to find a resolution that upholds all relevant values to the greatest extent possible. Ethical dilemmas often involve competing principles or stakeholder interests that cannot be perfectly reconciled, but require a thoughtful and balanced approach. The project manager should consider the specific context and implications of the situation, and seek to identify options that maximize the overall alignment with the values of responsibility, respect, fairness, and honesty. This may involve finding creative solutions, making difficult trade-offs, or prioritizing certain values based on a clear and justifiable rationale. Simply defaulting to commercial, personal, or political considerations, or avoiding the dilemma altogether, are not ethically appropriate responses for a project management professional committed to the PMI Code.

632. How can adherence to the PMI Code of Ethics and Professional Conduct contribute to project success and stakeholder trust?
a. by ensuring strict compliance with all applicable laws and regulations, regardless of project outcomes
b. by providing a competitive advantage and enhancing the reputation of the project manager and organization
c. by fostering a culture of integrity, accountability, and professionalism that enables effective collaboration and performance
d. by shielding the project manager from any criticism or liability for project failures or challenges

Answer: c. by fostering a culture of integrity, accountability, and professionalism that enables effective collaboration and performance. Explanation: Adherence to the PMI Code of Ethics and Professional Conduct can contribute to project success and stakeholder trust by fostering a culture of integrity, accountability, and professionalism that enables effective collaboration and performance on the project. When project managers consistently demonstrate the values of responsibility, respect, fairness, and honesty in their actions and decisions, they set a positive tone and example for the entire project team. This helps to create an environment of mutual trust, open communication, and shared commitment to ethical conduct and excellence. Stakeholders are more likely to have confidence in the project and its leadership when they perceive a strong ethical foundation and consistency. Ethical behavior also helps to mitigate risks, conflicts, and issues that can arise from misaligned expectations, hidden agendas, or unethical practices. While compliance with laws and regulations is important, it is not the sole or primary benefit of ethical conduct. Similarly, while ethical reputation can enhance professional standing, it should not be pursued merely for competitive advantage. Ethical practice is not a guarantee of project success or a shield from accountability, but rather an enabler of the collaboration, performance, and trust needed for successful project outcomes.

633. What role do professional ethics play in the daily decision-making and conduct of project managers, beyond compliance with the PMI Code of Ethics?
a. professional ethics are only relevant in situations of clear legal or contractual breach
b. professional ethics should be considered as a separate and optional aspect of project management practice
c. professional ethics should inform and guide all aspects of project management practice, from strategic planning to interpersonal interactions

d. professional ethics are the sole responsibility of the project sponsoring organization or client, not the project manager

Answer: c. professional ethics should inform and guide all aspects of project management practice, from strategic planning to interpersonal interactions. Explanation: Professional ethics play a crucial and pervasive role in the daily decision-making and conduct of project managers, beyond mere compliance with the PMI Code of Ethics. Ethical considerations should inform and guide all aspects of project management practice, from strategic planning to interpersonal interactions. Every decision and action taken by a project manager has an ethical dimension and impact, whether related to project scope, resources, quality, communication, or stakeholder engagement. Project managers must constantly navigate complex issues and dilemmas that require sound ethical judgment and reasoning, based on a clear understanding of professional values, principles, and obligations. This includes not only adhering to the specific standards and rules outlined in the PMI Code, but also exercising personal moral courage and responsibility in the face of novel or ambiguous situations. Professional ethics are not a separate or optional aspect of project management, but rather a core and integral part of the discipline and the role. They cannot be delegated or compartmentalized, but must be actively embraced and applied by project managers in all their professional endeavors, as a reflection of their character, credibility, and commitment to the greater good of the project and the profession.

634. What is the main purpose of the PMI Code of Ethics and Professional Conduct?
a. to provide legal guidelines to protect PMP certified project managers
b. to establish a framework for ethical decision making and ensure a common set of values
c. to outline a comprehensive project management methodology
d. to promote the commercial interests of PMI and its members

Answer: b. to establish a framework for ethical decision making and ensure a common set of values. Explanation: The PMI Code of Ethics and Professional Conduct serves to establish a framework for ethical decision making and ensure that project management professionals operate under a common set of values, regardless of their specific roles or work environments. It does not provide legal protection, prescribe a project management methodology, or serve commercial interests.

635. Which of the following values is not one of the four foundational pillars of the PMI Code of Ethics?
a. responsibility
b. respect
c. fairness
d. integrity

Answer: d. integrity. Explanation: While integrity is an important ethical principle, it is not one of the four foundational values specifically outlined in the PMI Code of Ethics. The Code is built upon responsibility, respect, fairness, and honesty. Responsibility involves accepting ownership for decisions; respect involves showing high regard for self, others, and resources; fairness involves equal treatment and non-discrimination; and honesty involves understanding and acting consistently with the truth.

636. Under the PMI Code of Ethics, project managers have a duty to _____ if they believe a violation of the Code has occurred.
a. conceal the violation to protect the reputation of the project
b. report the violation to the appropriate authorities
c. confront the violator directly and demand an explanation
d. dismiss the violation if it did not cause harm to the project

Answer: b. report the violation to the appropriate authorities. Explanation: The PMI Code of Ethics requires project managers to report any suspected violations of the Code to the appropriate authorities, such as supervisors, PMI's Ethics Review Committee, or legal entities. Project managers have an ethical obligation to uphold the Code and ensure that violations are properly addressed, rather than concealing, confronting, or dismissing them based on personal judgment or project outcomes.

637. Which section of the PMI Code of Ethics addresses conflicts of interest?
a. Responsibility
b. Respect
c. Fairness
d. Honesty

Answer: c. Fairness. Explanation: The Fairness section of the PMI Code of Ethics specifically addresses conflicts of interest. It requires project managers to proactively identify, disclose, and resolve any potential or actual conflicts of interest that may affect their impartiality or objectivity in decision making. This includes personal, business, or financial relationships that could bias or compromise their professional judgment or actions.

638. How can project managers best demonstrate the value of respect in their interactions with team members and stakeholders?
a. by ignoring individual differences and treating everyone the same way
b. by engaging in open and inclusive communication and valuing diverse perspectives
c. by maintaining a strict hierarchy and expecting unquestioning obedience
d. by avoiding any personal or informal interactions to maintain professionalism

Answer: b. by engaging in open and inclusive communication and valuing diverse perspectives. Explanation: Project managers can best demonstrate respect by engaging in open and inclusive communication and valuing the diverse perspectives of team members and stakeholders. Respect involves recognizing the inherent worth and dignity of all individuals, regardless of their roles or backgrounds, and creating an environment of mutual understanding and trust. It requires active listening, empathy, and adaptation to different communication styles and needs, rather than ignoring differences, enforcing hierarchy, or avoiding personal connections.

639. According to the PMI Code of Ethics, which of the following is not an appropriate response to a conflict between two ethical principles?
a. seeking guidance from mentors or ethical advisors
b. prioritizing the principle that best serves the public good

c. choosing the principle that is most financially beneficial to the project
d. striving to find a solution that upholds both principles to the greatest extent possible

Answer: c. choosing the principle that is most financially beneficial to the project. Explanation: The PMI Code of Ethics does not endorse prioritizing financial benefits over ethical principles in the case of a conflict. When faced with a situation where two principles seem to be at odds, project managers should carefully analyze the context and implications, seek guidance from trusted advisors, and strive to find a resolution that upholds both principles to the greatest extent possible. If a true dilemma exists, they should prioritize the principle that best serves the overall public good and ethical responsibility, rather than narrow financial interests.

640. Under the value of responsibility, project managers have an obligation to:
a. take ownership of decisions and be accountable for outcomes
b. defer all decisions to the project sponsor or steering committee
c. prioritize their personal career goals over project objectives
d. avoid any decisions that involve uncertainty or risk

Answer: a. take ownership of decisions and be accountable for outcomes. Explanation: The value of responsibility in the PMI Code of Ethics requires project managers to take ownership of their decisions and be accountable for the resulting outcomes. This means having the courage and integrity to make principled choices, communicate them transparently, and accept the consequences, whether positive or negative. Responsible project managers do not defer decisions, prioritize personal interests, or avoid reasonable risks, but rather act as proactive and accountable stewards of project resources and objectives.

641. What is the relationship between the PMI Code of Ethics and the law?
a. the Code supersedes all legal requirements and takes precedence in case of conflict
b. the Code is a legal document that can be used as evidence in court proceedings
c. the Code is voluntary and aspirational, while the law is mandatory and enforceable
d. the Code only applies in countries where it has been formally adopted into legislation

Answer: c. the Code is voluntary and aspirational, while the law is mandatory and enforceable. Explanation: The PMI Code of Ethics is a voluntary and aspirational set of principles and standards that guide the behavior and decisions of project management professionals. It is not a legal document and does not supersede or replace applicable laws and regulations. Project managers are expected to comply with both the Code and relevant legal requirements, but the Code itself is not legally binding or enforceable. In contrast, laws are mandatory rules that are formally enacted and enforced by government authorities, and non-compliance can result in legal penalties or sanctions.

642.How can project managers contribute to fostering an ethical culture within their organizations?
a. by focusing solely on meeting project objectives and leaving ethical concerns to senior management
b. by modeling ethical behavior, encouraging open dialogue, and supporting ethical training and resources
c. by avoiding any discussions or reporting of ethical issues to maintain team harmony and trust
d. by prioritizing short-term financial gains over long-term ethical reputation and sustainability

Answer: b. by modeling ethical behavior, encouraging open dialogue, and supporting ethical training and resources. Explanation: Project managers can contribute to fostering an ethical culture within their organizations by consistently modeling ethical behavior in their own actions and decisions, encouraging open and respectful dialogue about ethical issues and concerns, and supporting ethical training and resources for their teams and stakeholders. By demonstrating a strong personal commitment to integrity, accountability, and professional values, project managers can inspire and influence others to uphold high ethical standards. They can create a safe and supportive environment for raising and addressing ethical questions or challenges, and advocate for the necessary resources and programs to build ethical awareness and competence throughout the organization.

643. What should a project manager do if they are pressured by a senior stakeholder to violate the PMI Code of Ethics?
a. comply with the request to avoid damaging important relationships or career prospects
b. seek guidance from trusted advisors and respectfully explain the ethical implications and risks
c. ignore the request and hope that the stakeholder will change their mind or forget about it
d. threaten to report the stakeholder to legal authorities or media outlets for attempted coercion

Answer: b. seek guidance from trusted advisors and respectfully explain the ethical implications and risks. Explanation: If a project manager is pressured by a senior stakeholder to violate the PMI Code of Ethics, they should first seek guidance from trusted advisors, such as mentors, colleagues, or PMI's Ethics Member Advisory Committee, to validate their concerns and explore potential response options. They should then respectfully and professionally explain to the stakeholder the specific ethical principles and standards that the request would violate, and the potential risks and consequences for the project, the organization, and the individuals involved. The project manager should try to find an alternative solution that meets legitimate business needs while upholding ethical obligations, and escalate the issue to higher authorities if necessary. Simply complying, ignoring, or threatening the stakeholder are not appropriate or effective ways to handle such a situation.

644. What is the primary purpose of the PMI Code of Ethics and Professional Conduct?
a. to provide legal protection for project managers in case of disputes or lawsuits
b. to establish a common set of values and standards for ethical behavior in project management
c. to prescribe specific project management methodologies and best practices
d. to promote the commercial interests of PMI and its certification holders

Answer: b. to establish a common set of values and standards for ethical behavior in project management. Explanation: The PMI Code of Ethics and Professional Conduct serves as a guide for project management professionals, establishing a shared framework of values, responsibilities, and standards for ethical conduct. It does not provide legal protection, prescribe specific methodologies, or promote commercial interests, but rather sets forth the ethical principles and expectations for the global project management community.

645. Which of the following is not one of the foundational values outlined in the PMI Code of Ethics and Professional Conduct?
a. responsibility
b. respect

c. fairness
d. transparency

Answer: d. transparency. Explanation: While transparency is an important ethical principle, it is not explicitly listed as one of the four foundational values in the PMI Code of Ethics and Professional Conduct. The Code is built upon responsibility, respect, fairness, and honesty. Transparency is inherent in these values, particularly honesty, but is not identified as a separate foundational value.

646. Under the value of "respect" in the PMI Code of Ethics, project managers have a duty to:
a. prioritize respect for authority over respect for individuals
b. show respect only to those stakeholders who have direct influence over the project
c. treat all stakeholders with dignity, courtesy, and sensitivity to cultural differences
d. maintain a strict hierarchy of respect based on organizational rank or position

Answer: c. treat all stakeholders with dignity, courtesy, and sensitivity to cultural differences. Explanation: The value of respect in the PMI Code of Ethics requires project managers to treat all project stakeholders, regardless of their role, background, or influence, with dignity, courtesy, and sensitivity to cultural differences. This includes team members, sponsors, customers, end-users, and the wider community affected by the project. Respect involves valuing diverse perspectives, fostering inclusivity, and avoiding discrimination or favoritism based on personal characteristics or organizational status.

647. What is the relationship between the PMI Code of Ethics and legal requirements?
a. the Code supersedes all legal requirements and takes precedence in case of conflict
b. the Code is a legally binding contract between PMI and its certification holders
c. the Code is voluntary and aspirational, while legal requirements are mandatory and enforceable
d. the Code only applies in countries where it has been formally adopted into legislation

Answer: c. the Code is voluntary and aspirational, while legal requirements are mandatory and enforceable. Explanation: The PMI Code of Ethics and Professional Conduct is a voluntary set of principles and standards that provide guidance for ethical behavior in project management. It does not replace or override legal requirements, which are mandatory and enforceable rules established by government authorities. Project managers are expected to comply with both the Code and all applicable laws and regulations, but the Code itself is aspirational and not legally binding.

648. In the context of professional responsibility, what is the primary role of the project manager in ensuring ethical conduct on the project?
a. to delegate all ethical oversight and accountability to the project sponsor or steering committee
b. to personally investigate and adjudicate any reported or suspected ethical violations
c. to model ethical behavior, foster an ethical culture, and ensure compliance with relevant standards and regulations
d. to prioritize project objectives over ethical considerations in case of conflicts or trade-offs

Answer: c. to model ethical behavior, foster an ethical culture, and ensure compliance with relevant standards and regulations. Explanation: As a professional, the project manager has a primary responsibility to model ethical behavior, foster an ethical project culture, and ensure compliance with relevant ethical standards and legal regulations. This involves leading by example, communicating ethical expectations, providing necessary training and resources, and proactively addressing any ethical concerns or issues that arise. The project manager should not delegate ethical accountability entirely, personally investigate or judge ethical violations, or sacrifice ethical principles for project expediency, but rather serve as an ethical steward and facilitator for the project and the team.

649. What should a project manager do if they encounter a situation that presents an ethical dilemma or conflict?
a. make a unilateral decision based on their personal moral intuition or preferences
b. ignore the dilemma and focus solely on meeting project objectives and deliverables
c. seek guidance from experts, consider multiple perspectives, and strive to find a solution that upholds relevant ethical principles
d. choose the course of action that is least likely to be discovered or challenged by others

Answer: c. seek guidance from experts, consider multiple perspectives, and strive to find a solution that upholds relevant ethical principles. Explanation: When faced with an ethical dilemma or conflict, the project manager should seek guidance from trusted advisors, such as mentors, colleagues, or PMI's Ethics Member Advisory Committee, to validate their concerns and explore potential response options. They should carefully consider the various stakeholder perspectives, values, and implications involved, and strive to find a resolution that upholds the relevant ethical principles and standards to the greatest extent possible. Making unilateral decisions, ignoring the dilemma, or choosing the path of least resistance are not professionally responsible approaches to navigating ethical challenges.

650. How can project managers contribute to promoting ethics and professional responsibility in the wider project management community?
a. by keeping their ethical practices and decisions confidential to avoid scrutiny or criticism
b. by participating in professional development, sharing lessons learned, and advocating for ethical standards and resources
c. by focusing solely on their own projects and avoiding engagement with broader industry initiatives or discussions
d. by competing with other project managers to demonstrate superior ethical performance and reputation

Answer: b. by participating in professional development, sharing lessons learned, and advocating for ethical standards and resources. Explanation: Project managers can contribute to promoting ethics and professional responsibility in the wider project management community by actively participating in professional development opportunities, such as training, conferences, or mentorship programs, to continuously improve their ethical knowledge and skills. They can also share their own experiences, challenges, and lessons learned with others, through informal networks, published articles, or conference presentations, to help build collective wisdom and support. Additionally, project managers can advocate for robust ethical standards, guidelines, and resources within their organizations and professional associations, to ensure that all practitioners have access to the necessary tools and frameworks for ethical decision-making and conduct.

651. What is the difference between personal and professional ethics in the context of project management?
a. personal ethics are irrelevant to project management, only professional ethics matter
b. personal ethics are more important than professional ethics, as they reflect individual character and integrity
c. personal and professional ethics are often in conflict and project managers must choose between them
d. personal and professional ethics should be aligned and integrated, with professional standards building upon personal values

Answer: d. personal and professional ethics should be aligned and integrated, with professional standards building upon personal values. Explanation: While personal ethics refer to an individual's moral principles and values, and professional ethics refer to the standards and expectations specific to a profession, the two should be aligned and integrated for project managers. Professional ethical standards, such as the PMI Code of Ethics, should not contradict or undermine personal ethical beliefs, but rather provide additional guidance and context for applying those beliefs in the project management domain. Project managers should strive to develop a strong personal ethical foundation, and then build upon that foundation with the specialized knowledge, skills, and obligations of their profession. Ethical conduct in project management should reflect a consistent and coherent integration of personal and professional values, rather than a compartmentalized or conflicting approach.

652. How can project managers handle situations where their professional ethical obligations conflict with organizational pressures or directives?
a. prioritize organizational loyalty and compliance over professional ethics to avoid risks to their job security or career prospects
b. resign from the project or organization immediately to avoid any involvement in unethical conduct
c. escalate the issue to higher authorities, legal counsel, or regulatory bodies for intervention and resolution
d. engage in respectful and principled dialogue with relevant stakeholders to find an ethical solution or compromise

Answer: d. engage in respectful and principled dialogue with relevant stakeholders to find an ethical solution or compromise. Explanation: When faced with situations where their professional ethical obligations conflict with organizational pressures or directives, project managers should first attempt to engage in respectful and principled dialogue with the relevant stakeholders, such as sponsors, executives, or team members. They should clearly articulate the specific ethical principles and standards at stake, the potential risks and consequences of unethical conduct, and the importance of finding a mutually acceptable solution that upholds both organizational goals and professional integrity. This dialogue should be approached with empathy, curiosity, and a collaborative mindset, rather than an adversarial or judgmental one. If a satisfactory resolution cannot be reached through dialogue, the project manager may need to consider escalating the issue to higher authorities, seeking legal or regulatory guidance, or, in extreme cases, resigning from the project or organization to maintain their ethical standards. However, these should be last resorts after sincere attempts at communication and problem-solving have been exhausted.

653. What role does professional development play in maintaining and enhancing ethical competence for project managers?
a. professional development is not necessary for ethical competence, as ethics are a matter of personal values and character
b. professional development is only useful for learning about new laws, regulations, or compliance requirements
c. professional development is essential for staying current with evolving ethical standards, best practices, and decision-making frameworks
d. professional development is only beneficial if it leads to formal certifications or credentials in ethics or compliance

Answer: c. professional development is essential for staying current with evolving ethical standards, best practices, and decision-making frameworks. Explanation: Professional development plays a crucial role in maintaining and enhancing ethical competence for project managers. As the field of project management evolves, so do the ethical challenges, expectations, and best practices associated with it. Regular participation in professional development activities, such as training, workshops, conferences, or self-study, allows project managers to stay informed about the latest developments in ethical standards, decision-making models, case studies, and resources. It provides opportunities to learn from the experiences and insights of other professionals, and to share one's own knowledge and perspectives. Professional development also supports continuous reflection, self-awareness, and growth in ethical reasoning and judgment, which are essential for navigating complex moral dilemmas. While personal values and character are important foundations for ethical behavior, ongoing professional development is necessary to translate those values into effective and responsible practice in the dynamic context of project management.

654. What is the primary purpose of using stakeholder engagement performance metrics in project management?
a. to identify and prioritize key project stakeholders
b. to assess the effectiveness of stakeholder engagement strategies and activities
c. to determine the level of authority and influence of each stakeholder
d. to forecast stakeholder reactions to project decisions and outcomes

Answer: b. to assess the effectiveness of stakeholder engagement strategies and activities. Explanation: Stakeholder engagement performance metrics are used to measure and evaluate the success of stakeholder engagement efforts throughout the project lifecycle. These metrics help project managers determine whether their engagement strategies and activities are effectively addressing stakeholder needs, expectations, and concerns, and contributing to overall project objectives. By tracking and analyzing engagement performance, project managers can identify areas for improvement, adjust their approaches, and demonstrate the value of stakeholder engagement to project sponsors and executives.

655. Which of the following is not a common stakeholder engagement performance metric?
a. stakeholder participation rate in project meetings and events
b. stakeholder response time to project communications and requests
c. stakeholder technical expertise and qualifications
d. stakeholder sentiment and satisfaction levels

Answer: c. stakeholder technical expertise and qualifications. Explanation: While stakeholder technical expertise and qualifications are important considerations in stakeholder analysis and management, they are not typically used as performance metrics for stakeholder engagement. Engagement metrics focus on measuring the quantity, quality, and outcomes of stakeholder interactions and relationships, rather than the inherent characteristics or capabilities of the stakeholders themselves. Common engagement metrics include participation rates, response times, sentiment scores, satisfaction levels, and feedback or issue resolution rates, among others.

656. How can project managers establish meaningful and measurable stakeholder engagement performance metrics?
a. by adopting a one-size-fits-all set of metrics used by other successful projects
b. by defining metrics that are easy to track, regardless of their relevance to project objectives
c. by aligning metrics with specific stakeholder engagement goals and desired outcomes
d. by selecting metrics that are likely to yield the most favorable results and impressions

Answer: c. by aligning metrics with specific stakeholder engagement goals and desired outcomes. Explanation: To establish meaningful and measurable stakeholder engagement performance metrics, project managers should start by clearly defining the specific goals and desired outcomes of their engagement efforts, in alignment with overall project objectives. These might include building trust and credibility, enhancing stakeholder buy-in and support, improving communication and collaboration, or reducing risks and issues. Once the goals are defined, project managers can identify metrics that directly measure progress and success in achieving those goals, such as stakeholder feedback scores, issue resolution rates, or stakeholder-initiated communication frequency. The metrics should be specific, measurable, achievable, relevant, and time-bound (SMART), and tailored to the unique needs and context of the project and its stakeholders.

657. What is the benefit of using both quantitative and qualitative stakeholder engagement performance metrics?
a. quantitative metrics are more objective and reliable than qualitative metrics
b. qualitative metrics are more comprehensive and insightful than quantitative metrics
c. using both types of metrics provides a more balanced and nuanced assessment of engagement effectiveness
d. quantitative and qualitative metrics are interchangeable and using both is redundant

Answer: c. using both types of metrics provides a more balanced and nuanced assessment of engagement effectiveness. Explanation: Quantitative stakeholder engagement metrics, such as participation rates or response times, provide objective and measurable data on the extent and efficiency of engagement activities. Qualitative metrics, such as stakeholder feedback comments or satisfaction ratings, provide subjective and contextual insights into the quality and impact of engagement efforts. Using both types of metrics in combination offers a more comprehensive and balanced assessment of engagement performance, as it captures both the tangible outputs and the intangible outcomes of stakeholder interactions. Quantitative metrics alone may miss important nuances and perceptions, while qualitative metrics alone may lack the precision and comparability needed for data-driven decision making. Together, they provide a richer and more reliable picture of engagement effectiveness.

658. How often should project managers review and report on stakeholder engagement performance metrics?
a. only at the end of the project, as part of the close-out process
b. at regular intervals throughout the project, based on the engagement plan and communication cadence
c. whenever a stakeholder raises a concern or complaint about the project
d. at random and unscheduled times, to avoid biasing stakeholder behavior or responses

Answer: b. at regular intervals throughout the project, based on the engagement plan and communication cadence. Explanation: Project managers should review and report on stakeholder engagement performance metrics at regular intervals throughout the project lifecycle, in alignment with the stakeholder engagement plan and the overall project communication cadence. This allows for continuous monitoring, assessment, and adjustment of engagement strategies and activities, based on real-time data and feedback. The frequency of review and reporting may vary depending on the project complexity, duration, and stakeholder needs, but should be often enough to identify and address any issues or opportunities in a timely manner. Waiting until the end of the project, reacting only to stakeholder complaints, or conducting random and unscheduled reviews are not effective or proactive approaches to managing engagement performance.

659. What is the role of stakeholder satisfaction surveys in measuring stakeholder engagement performance?
a. satisfaction surveys are the only reliable method for assessing stakeholder engagement
b. satisfaction surveys provide limited and subjective data that should not be used for decision making
c. satisfaction surveys are one of several tools that can provide valuable insights into stakeholder perceptions and expectations
d. satisfaction surveys are a legal requirement for all projects, regardless of their size or complexity

Answer: c. satisfaction surveys are one of several tools that can provide valuable insights into stakeholder perceptions and expectations. Explanation: Stakeholder satisfaction surveys are a common and useful tool for measuring stakeholder engagement performance, as they provide direct feedback from stakeholders on their experiences, opinions, and expectations related to the project. Surveys can help project managers understand stakeholder perceptions of communication, collaboration, responsiveness, and overall relationship quality, and identify areas for improvement or recognition. However, surveys are not the only or always the best method for assessing engagement, and should be used in combination with other metrics and tools, such as interviews, focus groups, or social media analysis. Surveys can be subject to response bias, low response rates, or misinterpretation, and should be designed and administered carefully to ensure validity and reliability. They are also not a legal requirement for all projects, but rather a recommended practice for gathering stakeholder feedback and fostering continuous improvement.

660. How can project managers use stakeholder engagement performance metrics to improve future projects and engagements?
a. by using metrics to compare and benchmark performance against other projects or industries
b. by using metrics to identify and reward high-performing team members or stakeholders
c. by using metrics to analyze trends, lessons learned, and best practices for stakeholder engagement
d. by using metrics to justify project decisions and deflect stakeholder criticism or blame

Answer: c. by using metrics to analyze trends, lessons learned, and best practices for stakeholder engagement. Explanation: Project managers can use stakeholder engagement performance metrics to continuously improve their approaches and outcomes in future projects by systematically analyzing the data and insights collected throughout the project lifecycle. This involves looking for patterns, trends, and correlations in the metrics that can reveal what engagement strategies, techniques, or behaviors are most effective in different contexts or with different stakeholder groups. It also involves documenting and sharing the key lessons learned, success stories, and best practices that emerge from the analysis, so that they can be replicated and scaled across other projects and teams. By using metrics as a feedback loop for learning and improvement, rather than just a scorecard for judgment or comparison, project managers can build a culture of stakeholder-centricity and engagement excellence that benefits the entire organization.

661. What are some potential challenges or pitfalls in using stakeholder engagement performance metrics, and how can project managers mitigate them?
a. metrics can be time-consuming and resource-intensive to collect and analyze, so project managers should use them sparingly
b. metrics can be misinterpreted or misused by stakeholders, so project managers should keep them confidential
c. metrics can be gamed or manipulated by team members, so project managers should rely on their intuition instead
d. metrics can be narrow or biased if not carefully designed and validated, so project managers should use multiple and diverse metrics

Answer: d. metrics can be narrow or biased if not carefully designed and validated, so project managers should use multiple and diverse metrics. Explanation: While stakeholder engagement performance metrics can provide valuable insights and accountability, they also pose some challenges and risks that project managers need to be aware of and mitigate. One key challenge is that metrics can be narrow, simplistic, or biased if they are not carefully designed, validated, and interpreted in context. For example, a high stakeholder response rate to a survey may not necessarily indicate high satisfaction or engagement if the survey questions are leading or the sample is skewed. To mitigate this risk, project managers should use multiple and diverse metrics that capture different aspects and perspectives of engagement, and triangulate the data to get a more holistic and reliable picture. They should also involve stakeholders in the design and validation of metrics, to ensure their relevance and credibility. Other potential challenges include the time and resources required for data collection and analysis, the potential for misinterpretation or misuse of metrics by stakeholders or team members, and the temptation to game or manipulate metrics for short-term gains. Project managers can mitigate these challenges by setting realistic expectations, communicating transparently, and using metrics as part of a larger system of stakeholder engagement and project governance.

662. How can project managers balance the need for standardized and consistent stakeholder engagement metrics with the need for flexibility and adaptability to different project contexts and stakeholder needs?
a. by using the same set of metrics for all projects, regardless of their size, complexity, or industry
b. by allowing each project team to create their own metrics, based on their preferences and assumptions
c. by establishing a core set of metrics that are aligned with organizational goals and values, while allowing for customization and innovation at the project level

d. by changing metrics frequently and randomly, to avoid predictability and complacency among stakeholders

Answer: c. by establishing a core set of metrics that are aligned with organizational goals and values, while allowing for customization and innovation at the project level. Explanation: To balance standardization and flexibility in stakeholder engagement metrics, project managers can work with their organizations to establish a core set of metrics that are aligned with overall goals, values, and best practices for stakeholder engagement. These core metrics should be based on industry standards, empirical research, and organizational experience, and should provide a consistent framework and language for measuring and communicating engagement performance across projects and portfolios. At the same time, project managers should have the flexibility to customize and adapt these core metrics to the specific needs, constraints, and opportunities of their projects and stakeholders. This may involve adding or modifying metrics that are relevant to the project domain, culture, or lifecycle, or experimenting with new metrics that can capture emerging trends or innovations in stakeholder engagement. The key is to strike a balance between consistency and creativity, rigor and responsiveness, so that metrics can serve as both a backbone and a catalyst for effective stakeholder engagement.

663. What role do stakeholder engagement performance metrics play in project governance and accountability?
a. metrics are a substitute for project governance and accountability, as they provide an objective measure of project performance
b. metrics are irrelevant to project governance and accountability, as they focus only on stakeholder perceptions and relationships
c. metrics are a key component of project governance and accountability, as they provide transparency and evidence of stakeholder engagement and value delivery
d. metrics are a hindrance to project governance and accountability, as they can be manipulated or misinterpreted by project managers

Answer: c. metrics are a key component of project governance and accountability, as they provide transparency and evidence of stakeholder engagement and value delivery. Explanation: Stakeholder engagement performance metrics play a critical role in project governance and accountability, as they provide tangible and verifiable evidence of how well the project is engaging and delivering value to its stakeholders. Metrics help to establish a clear and common understanding of what success looks like in terms of stakeholder satisfaction, collaboration, and impact, and enable project managers to demonstrate their progress and results to project sponsors, steering committees, and other governance bodies. By regularly reporting on engagement metrics, project managers can proactively identify and address any issues or risks that may affect stakeholder trust and support, and show how they are meeting their commitments and obligations to stakeholders. Metrics also help to hold project managers accountable for their engagement strategies and outcomes, and provide a basis for continuous improvement and learning. However, metrics are not a substitute for, or hindrance to, effective project governance and accountability, but rather a key enabler and complement to them. They should be used in conjunction with other governance mechanisms, such as project charters, progress reports, and stakeholder feedback sessions, to provide a comprehensive and balanced view of project performance and stakeholder engagement.

664. What is the main purpose of the Monitor Stakeholder Engagement process?

a. to identify project stakeholders and plan their engagement strategies
b. to manage stakeholder expectations and resolve any issues or conflicts
c. to assess the effectiveness of stakeholder engagement and adjust strategies as needed
d. to communicate project status and progress to stakeholders

Answer: c. to assess the effectiveness of stakeholder engagement and adjust strategies as needed. Explanation: The primary purpose of the Monitor Stakeholder Engagement process is to track and assess the effectiveness of stakeholder engagement strategies throughout the project lifecycle, and make necessary adjustments to ensure ongoing alignment and support. This process involves monitoring stakeholder relationships, evaluating engagement outcomes against planned objectives, and identifying areas for improvement or corrective action. While identifying stakeholders, managing expectations, resolving issues, and communicating progress are important aspects of stakeholder engagement, they are not the main focus of the monitoring process, which is more concerned with measuring and optimizing engagement performance.

665. Which of the following is not an input to the Monitor Stakeholder Engagement process?
a. project management plan
b. project documents
c. work performance data
d. stakeholder engagement strategy

Answer: d. stakeholder engagement strategy. Explanation: The stakeholder engagement strategy is not an input to the Monitor Stakeholder Engagement process, but rather an output of the Plan Stakeholder Engagement process. The key inputs to Monitor Stakeholder Engagement include the project management plan, which contains the stakeholder engagement plan and other relevant baselines; project documents, such as the stakeholder register, issue log, and lessons learned register; and work performance data, which provides information on the status and progress of stakeholder engagement activities. The stakeholder engagement strategy is the overarching approach and set of actions for engaging stakeholders, which is planned and documented separately from the monitoring process.

666. What is the primary tool or technique used in the Monitor Stakeholder Engagement process?
a. data analysis
b. decision making
c. communication skills
d. interpersonal skills

Answer: a. data analysis. Explanation: Data analysis is the primary tool and technique used in the Monitor Stakeholder Engagement process. This involves collecting, organizing, and evaluating data on stakeholder engagement activities, such as attendance at meetings, response rates to communications, or feedback scores from surveys. Data analysis techniques may include statistical analysis, trend analysis, or sentiment analysis, among others. The goal is to derive meaningful insights and metrics from the data that can inform decision making and continuous improvement of stakeholder engagement strategies. While decision making, communication skills, and interpersonal skills are important competencies for project managers, they are not specific tools or techniques of the Monitor Stakeholder Engagement process.

667. Which of the following is not a typical output of the Monitor Stakeholder Engagement process?
a. work performance information
b. change requests
c. project management plan updates
d. stakeholder engagement plan

Answer: d. stakeholder engagement plan. Explanation: The stakeholder engagement plan is not a typical output of the Monitor Stakeholder Engagement process, but rather an input that is part of the project management plan. The key outputs of this process include work performance information, which reports on the status and effectiveness of stakeholder engagement efforts; change requests, which may be needed to adjust engagement strategies or address stakeholder issues; and project management plan updates, which document any changes made to the stakeholder engagement plan or other related plans based on the monitoring results. Other project documents, such as the issue log or lessons learned register, may also be updated as outputs of this process.

668. What is the relationship between the Monitor Stakeholder Engagement process and the Manage Stakeholder Engagement process?
a. Monitor Stakeholder Engagement is a subset of Manage Stakeholder Engagement
b. Manage Stakeholder Engagement is a subset of Monitor Stakeholder Engagement
c. Monitor Stakeholder Engagement and Manage Stakeholder Engagement are independent processes
d. Monitor Stakeholder Engagement and Manage Stakeholder Engagement are interrelated and iterative processes

Answer: d. Monitor Stakeholder Engagement and Manage Stakeholder Engagement are interrelated and iterative processes. Explanation: The Monitor Stakeholder Engagement process and the Manage Stakeholder Engagement process are closely interrelated and iterative throughout the project lifecycle. Manage Stakeholder Engagement is focused on communicating and working with stakeholders to meet their needs and expectations, address issues, and foster appropriate engagement in project activities. Monitor Stakeholder Engagement, on the other hand, is focused on tracking and assessing the effectiveness of these engagement efforts, and making necessary adjustments based on performance data and feedback. The two processes inform and support each other in a continuous cycle of planning, execution, monitoring, and optimization of stakeholder engagement. Monitoring provides the data and insights needed to manage engagement effectively, while management provides the context and direction needed to monitor engagement meaningfully.

669. What is the main benefit of using data visualization techniques in the Monitor Stakeholder Engagement process?
a. to impress stakeholders with complex and colorful charts and graphs
b. to hide or obscure negative data points or trends from stakeholders
c. to make the data analysis process faster and easier for the project manager
d. to communicate complex engagement data in a clear and compelling way to stakeholders

Answer: d. to communicate complex engagement data in a clear and compelling way to stakeholders. Explanation: The main benefit of using data visualization techniques, such as charts, graphs, or dashboards, in the Monitor Stakeholder Engagement process is to communicate complex engagement data in a clear, concise, and compelling way to stakeholders. Visualization helps to transform raw data into meaningful patterns, trends, and insights that can be easily understood and acted upon by project managers and stakeholders alike. By presenting engagement data in a visual format, project managers can highlight key metrics, compare performance against benchmarks, and tell a persuasive story about the impact and value of their engagement efforts. Visualization is not about impressing stakeholders with flashy graphics, hiding negative results, or simplifying the analysis process, but rather about enhancing the transparency, accessibility, and impact of engagement monitoring and reporting.

670. How can project managers ensure that they are collecting relevant and reliable data for monitoring stakeholder engagement?
a. by relying solely on informal feedback and anecdotal evidence from stakeholders
b. by using a single data source or metric to measure engagement, such as attendance at meetings
c. by establishing clear and measurable engagement objectives, metrics, and data collection methods
d. by collecting as much data as possible, regardless of its quality or relevance to the project

Answer: c. by establishing clear and measurable engagement objectives, metrics, and data collection methods. Explanation: To ensure that they are collecting relevant and reliable data for monitoring stakeholder engagement, project managers should start by establishing clear and measurable objectives for their engagement efforts, in alignment with overall project goals and stakeholder needs. These objectives should be specific, achievable, and time-bound, and should define what success looks like in terms of stakeholder participation, satisfaction, or impact. Based on these objectives, project managers can then identify the key metrics and indicators that will be used to track progress and performance, such as response rates, sentiment scores, or issue resolution times. Finally, project managers should define the data collection methods and sources that will be used to gather accurate and consistent data on these metrics, such as surveys, interviews, or system logs. By taking a systematic and focused approach to engagement monitoring, project managers can avoid the pitfalls of relying on incomplete or biased data, using simplistic or irrelevant metrics, or collecting data for its own sake.

671. What is the role of the issue log in the Monitor Stakeholder Engagement process?
a. to document and track stakeholder complaints and grievances
b. to record and prioritize stakeholder requests for changes to the project scope or deliverables
c. to capture and communicate positive feedback and recognition from stakeholders
d. to identify and assess risks related to stakeholder engagement

Answer: a. to document and track stakeholder complaints and grievances. Explanation: The issue log is a key tool used in the Monitor Stakeholder Engagement process to document and track stakeholder complaints, concerns, or problems that may impact the project or the stakeholder relationship. The issue log provides a centralized and structured way to capture, categorize, and prioritize stakeholder issues, as well as to assign responsibility and deadlines for resolving them. By regularly reviewing and updating the issue log, project managers can proactively identify and address potential conflicts, misunderstandings, or dissatisfaction among stakeholders, before they escalate into major risks or disruptions. The issue log is not used to record change requests, positive feedback, or engagement risks, which are managed through separate processes and documents, such as the change log, lessons learned register, or risk register.

672. How can project managers use the results of stakeholder engagement monitoring to improve future projects and stakeholder relationships?
a. by using the results to assign blame or penalties to underperforming team members or stakeholders
b. by using the results to justify project decisions and deflect criticism or feedback from stakeholders
c. by using the results to identify best practices, lessons learned, and areas for improvement in stakeholder engagement
d. by using the results to compare and compete with other project managers or organizations

Answer: c. by using the results to identify best practices, lessons learned, and areas for improvement in stakeholder engagement. Explanation: Project managers can use the results of stakeholder engagement monitoring to continuously improve their approaches and outcomes in future projects by systematically analyzing and applying the insights and feedback collected throughout the project lifecycle. This involves looking for patterns, trends, and correlations in the monitoring data that can reveal what engagement strategies, tactics, or behaviors are most effective in different contexts or with different stakeholder groups. It also involves documenting and sharing the key lessons learned, success stories, and best practices that emerge from the analysis, so that they can be replicated and scaled across other projects and teams. By using monitoring results as a foundation for learning and improvement, rather than as a weapon for blame or justification, project managers can build a culture of stakeholder-centricity, accountability, and excellence that benefits the entire organization and its stakeholders over time.

673. What are some common challenges or barriers to effective stakeholder engagement monitoring, and how can project managers overcome them?
a. lack of time or resources for data collection and analysis, which can be addressed by automating and outsourcing monitoring activities
b. resistance or skepticism from stakeholders about the value or validity of engagement monitoring, which can be addressed by involving stakeholders in the design and interpretation of monitoring processes
c. inconsistent or conflicting data from different sources or metrics, which can be addressed by relying on a single, authoritative data point or metric
d. pressure from sponsors or executives to report only positive or favorable engagement results, which can be addressed by selectively disclosing or manipulating monitoring data

Answer: b. resistance or skepticism from stakeholders about the value or validity of engagement monitoring, which can be addressed by involving stakeholders in the design and interpretation of monitoring processes. Explanation: One common challenge or barrier to effective stakeholder engagement monitoring is resistance or skepticism from stakeholders about the value, validity, or purpose of monitoring activities. Some stakeholders may view monitoring as a burdensome or bureaucratic exercise that takes time and resources away from more important project work. Others may question the accuracy, relevance, or fairness of the monitoring data and metrics, or fear that the results will be used to judge or penalize them. To overcome these challenges, project managers should involve stakeholders in the design and interpretation of monitoring processes from the outset, to build trust, transparency, and ownership. This may include soliciting stakeholder input on the engagement objectives, metrics, and data collection methods, sharing monitoring results and insights regularly with stakeholders, and using the results to have constructive dialogues and drive joint action and improvement. By treating stakeholders as partners and co-creators in the monitoring process, rather than as passive subjects or recipients, project managers can increase stakeholder buy-in, participation, and satisfaction with engagement monitoring and its outcomes.

674. What is the primary purpose of an issue log in project management?
a. to document and track project risks and their potential impacts
b. to record and prioritize project change requests from stakeholders
c. to capture and monitor problems, concerns, or questions that arise during the project
d. to list and assign project tasks and deliverables to team members

Answer: c. to capture and monitor problems, concerns, or questions that arise during the project.
Explanation: The primary purpose of an issue log is to provide a centralized and structured way to document, track, and manage any problems, concerns, or questions that arise during the project lifecycle, and that require attention or resolution from the project team or stakeholders. Unlike a risk register, which focuses on potential future events, an issue log deals with current or actual issues that are already impacting the project. It is also distinct from a change log, which records requests for modifications to the project scope, schedule, or deliverables, and from a task list, which outlines the work to be performed by the team. The issue log helps project managers to proactively identify, prioritize, and resolve issues before they escalate into major conflicts or disruptions.

675. Which of the following is not a typical component of an issue log entry?
a. issue description and date identified
b. issue priority and category
c. issue owner and resolution due date
d. issue root cause and prevention plan

Answer: d. issue root cause and prevention plan. Explanation: A typical issue log entry includes a description of the issue, the date it was identified, its priority level (e.g., high, medium, low), its category or type (e.g., technical, financial, organizational), the person responsible for resolving it, and the target resolution date. It may also include additional details such as the stakeholders impacted, the current status, and any actions taken or decisions made. However, a root cause analysis and prevention plan are not usually part of the initial issue log entry, as they require a deeper investigation and may be documented separately once the issue is resolved. The focus of the issue log is on capturing and tracking the issue itself, rather than diagnosing its underlying causes or preventing future occurrences, which are important but distinct activities.

676. What is the main benefit of categorizing or grouping issues in an issue log?
a. to assign blame or responsibility for causing the issues
b. to prioritize the issues based on their level of urgency and impact
c. to identify patterns or trends in the types of issues occurring
d. to determine the appropriate resolution strategy for each issue

Answer: c. to identify patterns or trends in the types of issues occurring. Explanation: One of the main benefits of categorizing or grouping issues in an issue log is to identify patterns, trends, or commonalities in the types of issues that are occurring on the project. By analyzing the distribution and frequency of issues across different categories, such as technical, financial, organizational, or stakeholder-related, project managers can gain insight into systemic problems or risk areas that may require deeper attention or proactive management. For example, if a large number of issues are related to a particular vendor or deliverable, this may indicate a need to reassess the vendor relationship or the quality control processes. Categorization can also help with prioritization and resolution of issues, but its primary value is in providing a high-level view of the project's health and performance.

677. What is the role of the project manager in resolving conflicts that arise during the project?
a. to assign blame and punish the parties responsible for the conflict
b. to ignore or avoid the conflict in order to maintain harmony and positivity
c. to facilitate communication and negotiation between the conflicting parties
d. to escalate all conflicts to higher-level management for resolution

Answer: c. to facilitate communication and negotiation between the conflicting parties. Explanation: The role of the project manager in resolving conflicts that arise during the project is to facilitate open, respectful, and constructive communication and negotiation between the conflicting parties. Conflicts are a natural and inevitable part of project work, as stakeholders may have different goals, expectations, or personalities. The project manager's job is not to assign blame, avoid the issue, or escalate every disagreement, but rather to create a safe and productive space for the parties to express their concerns, explore their interests, and find mutually acceptable solutions. This may involve techniques such as active listening, reframing, brainstorming, and compromise. By modeling and promoting a collaborative and solutions-oriented approach to conflict resolution, the project manager can help to maintain trust, alignment, and momentum on the project.

678. Which of the following is not an effective strategy for preventing or minimizing conflicts on a project?
a. clearly defining and communicating project goals, roles, and expectations
b. fostering a culture of openness, respect, and psychological safety
c. ignoring or suppressing minor disagreements or tensions between stakeholders
d. regularly monitoring and addressing potential issues or risks proactively

Answer: c. ignoring or suppressing minor disagreements or tensions between stakeholders. Explanation: Ignoring or suppressing minor disagreements or tensions between stakeholders is not an effective strategy for preventing or minimizing conflicts on a project. In fact, it can have the opposite effect by allowing small issues to fester and escalate into larger, more disruptive conflicts over time. Effective conflict prevention strategies include clearly defining and communicating project goals, roles, and expectations upfront, to ensure that everyone is aligned and accountable; fostering a team culture of openness, respect, and psychological safety, where people feel comfortable raising concerns and admitting mistakes; and regularly monitoring and addressing potential issues or risks proactively, before they become full-blown conflicts. By creating a foundation of clarity, trust, and proactivity, project managers can reduce the likelihood and impact of conflicts and create a more resilient and high-performing team.

679. What is the first step a project manager should take when a conflict arises between two team members?
a. meet with each team member separately to gather information and perspectives
b. bring the team members together and force them to resolve their differences
c. escalate the conflict to the team members' functional managers for resolution
d. remove one or both team members from the project to eliminate the conflict

Answer: a. meet with each team member separately to gather information and perspectives. Explanation: The first step a project manager should take when a conflict arises between two team members is to meet with each team member separately to gather information and understand their perspectives on the situation. This allows the project manager to create a safe and confidential space for each person to express their concerns, feelings, and interests without fear of confrontation or judgment. It also helps the project manager to get a more complete and nuanced picture of the conflict, including its history, triggers, and impacts, which may not be apparent in a group setting. This individual fact-finding and rapport-building lays the groundwork for a more informed and productive joint conversation later on. Prematurely bringing the team members together, escalating the conflict, or removing team members are not recommended as initial steps, as they can exacerbate tensions and limit options for resolution.

680. What is the purpose of a conflict resolution plan in project management?
a. to outline the steps and strategies for resolving conflicts that may arise during the project
b. to assign blame and consequences for any conflicts that occur on the project
c. to identify and preempt all potential sources of conflict before the project begins
d. to document the results and lessons learned from previous conflicts on the project

Answer: a. to outline the steps and strategies for resolving conflicts that may arise during the project. Explanation: The purpose of a conflict resolution plan in project management is to proactively outline the steps, strategies, and resources that will be used to address and resolve any conflicts that may arise during the project lifecycle. The plan typically includes elements such as the project manager's role and responsibilities, the preferred conflict resolution methods (e.g., negotiation, mediation, arbitration), the escalation paths and decision-making authorities, and the communication and documentation protocols. By having a clear and agreed-upon plan in place, project managers can ensure that conflicts are handled consistently, efficiently, and effectively, and minimize their negative impacts on project outcomes. A conflict resolution plan is not designed to assign blame, eliminate all conflict, or document past conflicts, but rather to provide a roadmap for navigating future conflicts constructively.

681. What is the main difference between a win-win and a win-lose approach to conflict resolution?
a. a win-win approach results in a fair and mutually beneficial outcome, while a win-lose approach results in a clear victor and loser
b. a win-win approach is faster and easier to implement than a win-lose approach
c. a win-win approach is more appropriate for internal conflicts, while a win-lose approach is more appropriate for external conflicts
d. a win-win approach requires the involvement of a neutral third party, while a win-lose approach can be resolved directly by the conflicting parties

Answer: a. a win-win approach results in a fair and mutually beneficial outcome, while a win-lose approach results in a clear victor and loser. Explanation: The main difference between a win-win and a win-lose approach to conflict resolution lies in their intended outcomes and impacts on the relationship between the conflicting parties. A win-win approach aims to find a solution that satisfies the key interests and needs of all parties involved, and leaves everyone feeling heard, respected, and valued. It often requires creative problem-solving, compromise, and a focus on shared goals and long-term collaboration.

In contrast, a win-lose approach treats the conflict as a zero-sum game, where one party's gain is the other party's loss. It often involves aggressive tactics, power plays, and a focus on short-term victory at the expense of the relationship. While a win-lose approach may be quicker or easier in some cases, it can lead to resentment, retaliation, and further conflict down the road. In general, a win-win approach is preferred for fostering a positive and productive project environment, regardless of the type or scope of conflict.

682. How can project managers use active listening skills to help resolve conflicts?
a. by interrupting and correcting the conflicting parties when they express emotions or opinions
b. by offering advice and solutions based on the project manager's expertise and authority
c. by asking open-ended questions to clarify and validate the conflicting parties' perspectives
d. by taking notes and documenting the conflicting parties' statements for future reference

Answer: c. by asking open-ended questions to clarify and validate the conflicting parties' perspectives.
Explanation: Project managers can use active listening skills to help resolve conflicts by asking open-ended questions that clarify and validate the conflicting parties' perspectives, feelings, and needs. Active listening involves giving the speaker full attention, withholding judgment or advice, and using verbal and nonverbal cues to show interest and understanding. Open-ended questions, such as "Can you tell me more about why this is important to you?" or "How do you think this situation could be improved?" encourage the parties to share their experiences and ideas in their own words, and help the project manager to better understand the underlying issues and motivations. By creating a space for empathy and dialogue, active listening can help to defuse tensions, build trust, and find common ground for resolution. Interrupting, advising, or documenting are not active listening techniques and can actually hinder communication and problem-solving.

683. What is the role of a mediator in resolving conflicts on a project?
a. to investigate and determine the facts of the conflict
b. to facilitate communication and negotiation between the conflicting parties
c. to make a binding decision on how to resolve the conflict
d. to represent and advocate for one of the conflicting parties

Answer: b. to facilitate communication and negotiation between the conflicting parties. Explanation: The role of a mediator in resolving conflicts on a project is to facilitate communication and negotiation between the conflicting parties in an impartial and confidential manner. A mediator is a neutral third party who helps the parties to have a constructive dialogue, identify their interests and options, and reach a mutually acceptable agreement. Mediators do not investigate the facts, make decisions, or take sides, but rather use their process skills to create a safe and productive space for the parties to explore their differences and find their own solutions. Mediation can be an effective alternative to more formal or adversarial methods of conflict resolution, such as arbitration or litigation, especially when the parties have an ongoing relationship or need to maintain confidentiality. Project managers may act as mediators themselves or bring in an external mediator depending on the complexity and sensitivity of the conflict.

684. Which of the following is not one of the key interpersonal skills for effective project management?
a. active listening
b. emotional intelligence
c. technical expertise

d. conflict resolution

Answer: c. technical expertise. Explanation: While technical expertise is important for understanding and managing project requirements, it is not considered one of the key interpersonal skills for effective project management. Interpersonal skills focus on the ability to communicate, collaborate, and build relationships with project stakeholders. Active listening, emotional intelligence, and conflict resolution are all critical interpersonal skills that enable project managers to understand and respond to stakeholder needs, motivate and lead teams, and navigate complex social dynamics.

685. What is the main benefit of using active listening in project communication?
a. to demonstrate the project manager's authority and expertise
b. to gather information and perspectives from stakeholders
c. to persuade stakeholders to agree with the project manager's ideas
d. to minimize the time spent on communication and move quickly to action

Answer: b. to gather information and perspectives from stakeholders. Explanation: The main benefit of using active listening in project communication is to gather valuable information and perspectives from stakeholders, which can inform project planning, decision-making, and problem-solving. Active listening involves fully concentrating on the speaker, paraphrasing and reflecting their messages, and asking clarifying questions to ensure understanding. By creating a safe and receptive space for stakeholders to share their thoughts and experiences, project managers can gain a more complete and nuanced picture of the project context, risks, and opportunities, and build stronger relationships based on trust and respect. Active listening is not about asserting authority, persuading others, or minimizing communication, but rather about fostering open and meaningful dialogue.

686. Which of the following is an example of a nonverbal communication skill?
a. giving clear and concise written instructions
b. using technical jargon and acronyms
c. maintaining eye contact and an open posture
d. speaking in a loud and authoritative tone of voice

Answer: c. maintaining eye contact and an open posture. Explanation: Maintaining eye contact and an open posture is an example of a nonverbal communication skill, which involves using body language, facial expressions, and other visual cues to convey messages and build rapport. Nonverbal communication can reinforce or contradict verbal messages, and can have a powerful impact on how people perceive and respond to the communicator. In project management, effective nonverbal communication skills, such as nodding, smiling, and leaning forward, can demonstrate interest, empathy, and engagement with stakeholders, and can help to build trust and collaboration. Clear writing, technical language, and vocal tone are all important communication skills, but they are considered verbal rather than nonverbal.

687. What is the purpose of a project communication plan?
a. to outline the project's objectives, scope, and deliverables
b. to identify the project's stakeholders and their influence on the project
c. to define the project's budget, schedule, and resource requirements

d. to specify the project's communication goals, methods, and frequencies

Answer: d. to specify the project's communication goals, methods, and frequencies. Explanation: The purpose of a project communication plan is to provide a detailed roadmap for how project information will be shared, with whom, when, and through what channels, in order to meet the project's communication goals and stakeholder needs. The plan typically includes elements such as the communication objectives, target audiences, key messages, communication methods and frequencies, roles and responsibilities, and success metrics. By proactively planning and managing project communications, project managers can ensure that stakeholders receive timely, relevant, and accurate information, and can minimize misunderstandings, conflicts, and delays. A project communication plan is distinct from a project charter, stakeholder register, or project management plan, which focus on other aspects of project planning and management.

688. How can project managers adapt their communication styles to different project stakeholders?
a. by using the same communication approach for all stakeholders to ensure consistency
b. by assessing stakeholders' communication preferences and tailoring messages accordingly
c. by communicating more frequently with senior stakeholders and less frequently with junior ones
d. by avoiding communication with stakeholders who have opposing views or interests

Answer: b. by assessing stakeholders' communication preferences and tailoring messages accordingly. Explanation: Project managers can effectively adapt their communication styles to different project stakeholders by first assessing each stakeholder's communication preferences, such as their preferred methods, frequency, level of detail, and tone, and then tailoring their messages and delivery accordingly. This may involve using more formal or informal language, visual aids or data, high-level or granular information, and positive or neutral tone depending on the stakeholder's role, background, and expectations. By flexibly adjusting their communication approach to meet the diverse needs and styles of stakeholders, project managers can build stronger relationships, increase engagement and buy-in, and ensure that their messages are understood and acted upon. Using a one-size-fits-all approach, prioritizing senior stakeholders, or avoiding difficult stakeholders are not effective or appropriate communication strategies.

689. What is the main challenge of managing virtual or remote project teams?
a. building trust and rapport without face-to-face interactions
b. ensuring that team members have access to the necessary technology and tools
c. scheduling meetings across different time zones and locations
d. monitoring and controlling project progress and performance

Answer: a. building trust and rapport without face-to-face interactions. Explanation: The main challenge of managing virtual or remote project teams is building and maintaining trust, rapport, and a sense of connection among team members who may have little or no face-to-face interaction. In a virtual environment, project managers and team members lack the nonverbal cues, informal conversations, and shared experiences that help to foster relationships and collaboration in co-located teams. This can lead to misunderstandings, conflicts, and disengagement if not proactively addressed. While technology access, scheduling, and project control are also important considerations for virtual teams, they are typically easier to solve with the right tools and processes. Building a strong team culture and interpersonal bonds requires intentional and sustained effort, such as regular check-ins, team-building activities, and opportunities for social interaction and recognition.

690. What is the role of emotional intelligence in project management?
a. to manipulate stakeholders' emotions to gain their support and compliance
b. to suppress the project manager's own emotions to maintain a professional image
c. to recognize and respond appropriately to the emotions of self and others
d. to make decisions based solely on emotions rather than facts and logic

Answer: c. to recognize and respond appropriately to the emotions of self and others. Explanation: The role of emotional intelligence in project management is to enable project managers to effectively recognize, understand, and manage the emotions of themselves and others in order to build positive relationships, communicate effectively, and navigate complex social dynamics. Emotional intelligence involves skills such as self-awareness, self-regulation, empathy, and social awareness, which allow project managers to be attuned to the emotional states and needs of their team members and stakeholders, and to respond in a way that builds trust, rapport, and collaboration. Emotionally intelligent project managers are able to create a positive team climate, resolve conflicts constructively, and inspire and motivate others to achieve project goals. Emotional intelligence is not about manipulation, suppression, or irrationality, but rather about integrating emotions and reason to make sound decisions and build strong relationships.

691. What is the main difference between a stakeholder engagement plan and a project communication plan?
a. a stakeholder engagement plan focuses on building relationships, while a communication plan focuses on sharing information
b. a stakeholder engagement plan is developed before the project starts, while a communication plan is developed during project execution
c. a stakeholder engagement plan is the responsibility of the project sponsor, while a communication plan is the responsibility of the project manager
d. a stakeholder engagement plan and a project communication plan are interchangeable terms for the same document

Answer: a. a stakeholder engagement plan focuses on building relationships, while a communication plan focuses on sharing information. Explanation: The main difference between a stakeholder engagement plan and a project communication plan is their focus and purpose. A stakeholder engagement plan outlines the strategies and actions for identifying, analyzing, and involving stakeholders throughout the project lifecycle in order to build and maintain positive relationships, align expectations, and secure support for the project. It goes beyond just communicating information to actively collaborating with stakeholders and incorporating their input and feedback into project decisions. A project communication plan, on the other hand, focuses specifically on the goals, methods, and channels for disseminating project information to stakeholders in a timely and effective manner. It is a subset of the overall stakeholder engagement approach. Both plans are developed during project planning, owned by the project manager, and are complementary but distinct documents.

692. How can project managers use storytelling as a communication tool?
a. to entertain stakeholders and make project meetings more fun

b. to distract stakeholders from project issues and challenges

c. to make project data and information more engaging and memorable

d. to exaggerate project successes and downplay project failures

Answer: c. to make project data and information more engaging and memorable. Explanation: Project managers can use storytelling as a powerful communication tool to make project data, information, and messages more engaging, memorable, and impactful for stakeholders. Stories are a natural and universal way of conveying complex ideas, evoking emotions, and creating a shared sense of purpose and meaning. By using stories to frame project updates, lessons learned, or change initiatives, project managers can help stakeholders to better understand and relate to the project context, challenges, and outcomes. Effective storytelling involves using vivid language, concrete examples, and relatable characters to bring the project narrative to life and make it stick in the audience's minds. It is not about entertainment, distraction, or exaggeration, but rather about authentic and compelling communication that inspires and motivates action.

693. What is the impact of poor communication on project success?

a. increased stakeholder engagement and satisfaction

b. decreased team productivity and morale

c. enhanced project scope and quality

d. reduced project risks and issues

Answer: b. decreased team productivity and morale. Explanation: Poor communication can have a significant negative impact on project success by decreasing team productivity, morale, and collaboration. When project information is not shared clearly, consistently, or in a timely manner, team members may lack the direction, resources, or feedback they need to perform their tasks effectively. They may also feel uninformed, undervalued, or disconnected from the project goals and decision-making processes, leading to disengagement, frustration, and turnover. Poor communication can also lead to misunderstandings, errors, and conflicts among team members and stakeholders, which can further derail project progress and outcomes. Effective communication, on the other hand, is essential for aligning expectations, coordinating efforts, building trust, and fostering a positive team culture that drives project success.

694. What is the primary focus of the Manage Stakeholder Engagement process?

a. identifying and prioritizing project stakeholders

b. planning strategies for engaging stakeholders throughout the project

c. executing the stakeholder engagement plan to foster positive relationships

d. monitoring stakeholder relationships and adjusting engagement strategies

Answer: c. executing the stakeholder engagement plan to foster positive relationships. Explanation: The primary focus of the Manage Stakeholder Engagement process is to execute the stakeholder engagement plan, developed during the Plan Stakeholder Engagement process, in order to foster positive relationships with stakeholders. This process involves communicating and working with stakeholders to meet their needs and expectations, address issues as they occur, and encourage appropriate stakeholder involvement in project activities. Identifying stakeholders, planning engagement strategies, and monitoring relationships are part of other stakeholder management processes.

695. Which of the following is not an input to the Manage Stakeholder Engagement process?
a. stakeholder engagement plan
b. issue log
c. change requests
d. work performance reports

Answer: c. change requests. Explanation: Change requests are not a direct input to the Manage Stakeholder Engagement process. The main inputs are: the stakeholder engagement plan, which provides the planned strategies and actions for engaging stakeholders; the issue log, which documents any stakeholder concerns or problems that need to be addressed; and work performance reports, which provide information on project progress, status, and resource utilization relevant to stakeholder communication. Change requests, while they may result from stakeholder engagement activities, are typically an output of monitoring and controlling processes.

696. What is the purpose of the issue log in the context of managing stakeholder engagement?
a. to track and resolve stakeholder concerns or problems
b. to document formal project changes requested by stakeholders
c. to record stakeholder contact information and communication preferences
d. to prioritize stakeholders based on their power and interest in the project

Answer: a. to track and resolve stakeholder concerns or problems. Explanation: In the context of managing stakeholder engagement, the issue log is used to document, track, and resolve any concerns, problems, or disputes raised by stakeholders during the course of the project. It provides a centralized repository for capturing stakeholder issues, assigning responsibility for resolution, and monitoring progress towards closure. By proactively managing and communicating the status of issues, project managers can demonstrate responsiveness and build trust with stakeholders. The issue log does not capture change requests, stakeholder profiles, or prioritization, which are managed through other tools and techniques.

697. Which interpersonal skill is most critical for effectively managing stakeholder engagement?
a. active listening
b. technical expertise
c. time management
d. presentation skills

Answer: a. active listening. Explanation: Active listening is one of the most critical interpersonal skills for effectively managing stakeholder engagement. Active listening involves fully concentrating on, comprehending, and responding to what stakeholders are communicating, both verbally and nonverbally. It demonstrates respect, empathy, and openness to understanding stakeholder perspectives, needs, and concerns. By practicing active listening, project managers can build rapport, trust, and credibility with stakeholders, and gather valuable insights to inform project decisions and actions. Technical expertise, time management, and presentation skills, while important, are not as fundamental to building strong stakeholder relationships.

698. What is the main benefit of using a stakeholder engagement assessment matrix?
a. to evaluate the effectiveness of stakeholder communication activities
b. to assign roles and responsibilities for stakeholder management
c. to analyze the potential impact of project risks on stakeholders
d. to determine the appropriate level of stakeholder participation in project decisions

Answer: a. to evaluate the effectiveness of stakeholder communication activities. Explanation: The main benefit of using a stakeholder engagement assessment matrix is to evaluate the effectiveness of communication activities in engaging and satisfying stakeholders. The matrix typically compares current and desired levels of engagement for each stakeholder group, across dimensions such as awareness, support, and participation. By identifying gaps between actual and target engagement levels, project managers can assess the impact of their communication efforts and adjust their strategies accordingly. The engagement assessment matrix does not directly address stakeholder roles, project risks, or decision-making involvement, which are managed through other tools and techniques.

699. What is the difference between stakeholder management and stakeholder engagement?
a. stakeholder management focuses on communication, while stakeholder engagement focuses on collaboration
b. stakeholder management is the responsibility of the project manager, while stakeholder engagement is the responsibility of the project sponsor
c. stakeholder management is a one-time event, while stakeholder engagement is an ongoing process
d. stakeholder management and stakeholder engagement are interchangeable terms for the same process

Answer: a. stakeholder management focuses on communication, while stakeholder engagement focuses on collaboration. Explanation: While stakeholder management and stakeholder engagement are closely related, they differ in their focus and level of stakeholder involvement. Stakeholder management is a broader term that encompasses identifying, analyzing, planning, and controlling stakeholder relationships and communication throughout the project. Stakeholder engagement, on the other hand, is a subset of stakeholder management that emphasizes active stakeholder participation, dialogue, and collaboration in project activities and decisions. Engagement goes beyond one-way communication to foster two-way partnerships and shared ownership of project outcomes. Both stakeholder management and engagement are ongoing processes led by the project manager in collaboration with the project team and sponsor.

700. Which of the following is not a common communication method used in the Manage Stakeholder Engagement process?
a. interactive websites
b. social media platforms
c. stakeholder mapping
d. virtual meetings

Answer: c. stakeholder mapping. Explanation: Stakeholder mapping is not a communication method used in the Manage Stakeholder Engagement process, but rather an analytical technique used in the Identify Stakeholders process to assess and prioritize stakeholders based on their power, interest, and influence on the project. Common communication methods used to engage stakeholders include interactive websites, social media platforms, virtual meetings, in-person events, email newsletters, and printed materials. The choice of communication method depends on the stakeholder's preferences, communication plan, and project constraints.

701. How can project managers resolve conflicts or issues that arise during stakeholder engagement?
a. by avoiding or ignoring the conflict to maintain positive relationships
b. by accommodating all stakeholder requests to ensure their satisfaction
c. by collaborating with stakeholders to find mutually beneficial solutions
d. by competing with stakeholders to assert the project's priorities and authority

Answer: c. by collaborating with stakeholders to find mutually beneficial solutions. Explanation: Project managers can effectively resolve conflicts or issues that arise during stakeholder engagement by collaborating with stakeholders to find mutually beneficial solutions. Collaboration involves openly discussing the problem, exploring each party's interests and concerns, and brainstorming creative options that satisfy multiple needs. By approaching conflicts with a win-win mindset and a focus on shared goals, project managers can build consensus, trust, and long-term partnerships with stakeholders. Avoiding, accommodating, or competing with stakeholders may provide short-term relief but can lead to unresolved issues, resentment, and damaged relationships in the long run.

702. What is the role of the project sponsor in the Manage Stakeholder Engagement process?
a. to approve all stakeholder communication materials before distribution
b. to provide executive support and resources for stakeholder engagement activities
c. to directly communicate with all project stakeholders on behalf of the project manager
d. to resolve all stakeholder conflicts or issues without involving the project manager

Answer: b. to provide executive support and resources for stakeholder engagement activities. Explanation: The project sponsor plays a key role in the Manage Stakeholder Engagement process by providing executive support, resources, and guidance to enable effective stakeholder engagement. This may include securing budget and staffing for engagement activities, removing organizational barriers, and championing the project's value and benefits to senior stakeholders. The project sponsor also serves as an escalation point for significant stakeholder issues or decisions that exceed the project manager's authority. However, the project sponsor typically does not approve all communication materials, communicate directly with all stakeholders, or resolve all conflicts independently, as these are primary responsibilities of the project manager in collaboration with the project team.

703. What is a key output of the Manage Stakeholder Engagement process?
a. stakeholder register updates
b. project management plan updates
c. change requests
d. work performance information

Answer: d. work performance information. Explanation: A key output of the Manage Stakeholder Engagement process is work performance information, which includes data and reports on the status and effectiveness of stakeholder engagement activities. This information is used to communicate with stakeholders, assess engagement levels, and inform project decisions and adjustments. Other outputs may include stakeholder register updates, documenting new stakeholders or changes in stakeholder information; project management plan updates, reflecting changes to the stakeholder engagement plan or strategy; and change requests, proposing modifications to the project scope, schedule, or resources based on stakeholder feedback. However, work performance information is the most direct and specific output of the engagement management process.

704. What is the primary purpose of a stakeholder engagement assessment matrix?
a. to prioritize stakeholders based on their power and interest in the project
b. to assign roles and responsibilities for stakeholder communication
c. to evaluate the effectiveness of stakeholder engagement strategies
d. to identify potential risks and issues related to stakeholder management

Answer: c. to evaluate the effectiveness of stakeholder engagement strategies. Explanation: The primary purpose of a stakeholder engagement assessment matrix is to evaluate the effectiveness of the strategies and activities used to engage and communicate with project stakeholders. The matrix typically compares the current and desired levels of engagement for each stakeholder or stakeholder group, helping the project manager identify gaps and areas for improvement in their engagement approach. It is not used for prioritizing stakeholders, assigning roles, or identifying risks, which are addressed through other tools such as the power/interest grid, RACI matrix, and risk register.

705. Which dimensions are typically used to assess stakeholder engagement levels in the assessment matrix?
a. power, urgency, and legitimacy
b. interest, influence, and impact
c. awareness, support, and participation
d. communication frequency, method, and feedback

Answer: c. awareness, support, and participation. Explanation: The most common dimensions used to assess stakeholder engagement levels in the assessment matrix are awareness (stakeholder's knowledge and understanding of the project), support (stakeholder's level of backing or opposition for the project), and participation (stakeholder's active involvement in project activities and decision-making). These dimensions provide a comprehensive view of how well stakeholders are informed, aligned, and engaged with the project. Other dimensions such as power, urgency, legitimacy, interest, influence, impact, communication frequency, method, and feedback may be considered in the broader context of stakeholder analysis and planning but are not typically the primary focus of the engagement assessment matrix.

706. How are the desired levels of stakeholder engagement determined in the assessment matrix?
a. based on the project manager's personal preferences and experience
b. based on the available budget and resources for stakeholder management
c. based on the stakeholders' expectations and requests for involvement
d. based on the project's goals, requirements, and potential impact on stakeholders

Answer: d. based on the project's goals, requirements, and potential impact on stakeholders. Explanation: The desired levels of stakeholder engagement in the assessment matrix should be determined based on the specific needs and objectives of the project, rather than the project manager's preferences, available resources, or stakeholder demands alone. The project manager should consider factors such as the project's goals and deliverables, the requirements and expectations of key stakeholders, and the potential impact of the project on different stakeholder groups. By aligning the target engagement levels with the project's strategic priorities and stakeholder needs, the project manager can ensure that engagement efforts are focused, meaningful, and value-added.

707. What is the benefit of using a numeric rating scale in the stakeholder engagement assessment matrix?
a. to quantify the subjective aspects of stakeholder engagement
b. to compare engagement levels across different projects and organizations
c. to set precise targets and measure progress over time
d. to automate the process of analyzing and reporting engagement data

Answer: c. to set precise targets and measure progress over time. Explanation: A key benefit of using a numeric rating scale (e.g., 1-5 or 1-10) in the stakeholder engagement assessment matrix is the ability to set clear, measurable targets for desired engagement levels and track progress towards those targets over the course of the project. By assigning numeric values to the current and desired states of awareness, support, and participation, project managers can more easily identify gaps, prioritize engagement efforts, and demonstrate the impact of their strategies to stakeholders. While numeric ratings can help quantify subjective data, they are not intended to provide a definitive or universal measure of engagement that can be directly compared across projects or organizations. The specific rating scale and criteria should be tailored to the unique context and needs of each project.

708. How often should the stakeholder engagement assessment matrix be reviewed and updated?
a. once, at the beginning of the project
b. twice, at the midpoint and end of the project
c. regularly, based on the project's complexity and stakeholder dynamics
d. never, as the initial assessment is sufficient for the entire project

Answer: c. regularly, based on the project's complexity and stakeholder dynamics. Explanation: The stakeholder engagement assessment matrix should be reviewed and updated regularly throughout the project lifecycle, based on the complexity of the project and the dynamics of the stakeholder environment. For projects with a large number of stakeholders, frequent changes, or high levels of uncertainty, the matrix may need to be revisited monthly or even weekly to ensure that engagement strategies remain relevant and effective. For simpler projects with stable stakeholder relationships, a quarterly or bi-annual review may suffice. The key is to use the matrix as a living document that reflects the current state of stakeholder engagement and guides continuous improvement efforts, rather than a one-time or periodic exercise.

709. What is the relationship between the stakeholder engagement assessment matrix and the stakeholder engagement plan?
a. the assessment matrix is a component of the engagement plan

b. the engagement plan is a component of the assessment matrix
c. the assessment matrix and engagement plan are separate, unrelated documents
d. the assessment matrix and engagement plan are interchangeable terms for the same document

Answer: a. the assessment matrix is a component of the engagement plan. Explanation: The stakeholder engagement assessment matrix is typically a component or tool within the larger stakeholder engagement plan. The engagement plan outlines the overall approach, strategies, and activities for engaging and communicating with stakeholders throughout the project lifecycle. The assessment matrix is a specific tool used to evaluate the effectiveness of those engagement efforts and identify areas for improvement. The matrix helps to operationalize and measure the goals and objectives set forth in the engagement plan. While the two documents are closely related and should align with each other, they serve distinct purposes and are not interchangeable.

710. What are some common challenges or pitfalls in using the stakeholder engagement assessment matrix?
a. over-relying on numeric ratings without considering qualitative feedback
b. setting unrealistic or arbitrary target engagement levels
c. failing to regularly review and update the matrix based on changing project needs
d. all of the above

Answer: d. all of the above. Explanation: Some common challenges or pitfalls in using the stakeholder engagement assessment matrix include: a) over-relying on numeric ratings without considering qualitative feedback from stakeholders, which can lead to a false sense of precision or miss important nuances in engagement levels; b) setting unrealistic or arbitrary target engagement levels that are not grounded in the project's goals, resources, or stakeholder needs, which can lead to disillusionment or disengagement; and c) failing to regularly review and update the matrix based on changing project circumstances or stakeholder feedback, which can render the tool obsolete or disconnected from reality. To avoid these pitfalls, project managers should use the matrix as a starting point for deeper dialogue and analysis with stakeholders, set meaningful and achievable engagement targets, and treat the matrix as a dynamic tool that evolves with the project.

711. How can project managers use the results of the stakeholder engagement assessment matrix to inform their communication and engagement strategies?
a. by focusing communication efforts on stakeholders with the highest engagement levels
b. by reducing communication frequency for stakeholders who are already highly engaged
c. by tailoring communication methods and messages to the specific needs and preferences of each stakeholder group
d. by using a one-size-fits-all communication approach based on the average engagement level across all stakeholders

Answer: c. by tailoring communication methods and messages to the specific needs and preferences of each stakeholder group. Explanation: Project managers can use the results of the stakeholder engagement assessment matrix to inform their communication and engagement strategies by tailoring their approach to the specific needs, preferences, and engagement levels of each stakeholder group. For example, if the matrix reveals that a particular stakeholder group has low awareness of the project, the project manager may prioritize face-to-face meetings, detailed progress reports, and educational materials to increase their understanding and buy-in. If another group is highly supportive but has limited capacity for participation, the project manager may focus on providing concise updates and targeted requests for input at key decision points. The matrix helps project managers to segment their stakeholders and customize their engagement tactics accordingly, rather than using a blanket approach based on assumptions or averages.

712. What is the role of the project sponsor in relation to the stakeholder engagement assessment matrix?
a. to approve the matrix before it is used by the project team
b. to provide input and feedback on the engagement levels and targets for key stakeholders
c. to communicate the results of the matrix to all project stakeholders
d. to take over responsibility for stakeholder engagement from the project manager

Answer: b. to provide input and feedback on the engagement levels and targets for key stakeholders. Explanation: The project sponsor plays a crucial role in relation to the stakeholder engagement assessment matrix by providing strategic guidance, oversight, and support for stakeholder engagement efforts. As a key stakeholder and decision-maker, the project sponsor should be consulted in the development of the matrix to ensure that the engagement levels and targets align with the project's overall goals, priorities, and constraints. The sponsor can offer valuable insights into the expectations, concerns, and influence of high-level stakeholders, and help the project manager navigate complex organizational dynamics. While the sponsor should be kept informed of the results and progress of stakeholder engagement, they do not typically approve the matrix, communicate directly with all stakeholders, or take over responsibility for engagement from the project manager. The matrix remains a tool owned and used by the project manager and team, with the sponsor serving as a partner and advocate.

713. What is the difference between the current and desired engagement levels in the stakeholder engagement assessment matrix?
a. the current level represents the stakeholder's power, while the desired level represents their interest in the project
b. the current level represents the amount of communication sent to the stakeholder, while the desired level represents the amount of feedback received from the stakeholder
c. the current level represents the stakeholder's actual engagement at a given point in time, while the desired level represents the targeted or optimal engagement for the project's success
d. the current level is always lower than the desired level, as the goal is to continually increase engagement over the course of the project

Answer: c. the current level represents the stakeholder's actual engagement at a given point in time, while the desired level represents the targeted or optimal engagement for the project's success. Explanation: In the stakeholder engagement assessment matrix, the current engagement level refers to the stakeholder's actual or observed level of awareness, support, and participation at a specific point in the project lifecycle. This is based on data and feedback collected through various communication and monitoring channels. The desired engagement level, on the other hand, represents the ideal or targeted level of engagement that the project manager believes is necessary for the stakeholder to effectively contribute to and benefit from the project. This target is set based on the project's goals, requirements, and success criteria, as well as the stakeholder's role, influence, and expectations. The gap between the current and desired levels helps the project manager prioritize and tailor their engagement efforts. It is important to note that the desired level is not always higher than the current level, as in some cases, the project manager may seek to maintain or even reduce engagement for certain stakeholders, depending on the project's needs and constraints.

714. What is the primary objective of a stakeholder engagement plan?
a. to identify all project stakeholders and their contact information
b. to assign roles and responsibilities for stakeholder communication
c. to outline the strategies and actions for effectively engaging stakeholders
d. to evaluate the performance and satisfaction of project stakeholders

Answer: c. to outline the strategies and actions for effectively engaging stakeholders. Explanation: The primary objective of a stakeholder engagement plan is to define the approach, methods, and activities that will be used to effectively communicate with, involve, and manage the expectations of project stakeholders throughout the project lifecycle. The plan should align with the project's goals and requirements, and be tailored to the unique needs, interests, and influence of each stakeholder group. While identifying stakeholders, assigning roles, and evaluating performance are important elements of stakeholder management, they are not the main focus of the engagement plan itself.

715. Which of the following is not typically included in a stakeholder engagement plan?
a. stakeholder communication requirements
b. stakeholder engagement risks and issues
c. stakeholder performance metrics and targets
d. stakeholder contact information and preferences

Answer: d. stakeholder contact information and preferences. Explanation: Stakeholder contact information and preferences, such as names, titles, email addresses, and preferred communication methods, are typically captured in a separate document called the stakeholder register, rather than in the stakeholder engagement plan itself. The engagement plan focuses more on the strategic and tactical aspects of stakeholder engagement, such as the communication objectives, key messages, engagement activities, timeline, and success metrics. It may reference the stakeholder register as an input or companion document, but does not duplicate its contents.

716. When should the stakeholder engagement plan be developed?
a. during the initiating phase of the project
b. during the planning phase of the project
c. during the executing phase of the project
d. during the closing phase of the project

Answer: b. during the planning phase of the project. Explanation: The stakeholder engagement plan should be developed during the planning phase of the project, after the initial stakeholder identification and analysis has been completed. This allows the project manager to incorporate stakeholder inputs and expectations into the project scope, schedule, and resource planning, and to align the engagement approach with the overall project management plan. Developing the engagement plan too early, before

575

the project is fully defined, may result in misaligned or wasted efforts. Waiting until the executing or closing phases may be too late to proactively build stakeholder relationships and support.

717. Who is responsible for creating and implementing the stakeholder engagement plan?
a. the project sponsor
b. the project manager
c. the project management office (PMO)
d. the communications manager

Answer: b. the project manager. Explanation: The project manager is ultimately responsible for creating and implementing the stakeholder engagement plan, as part of their overall project management duties. While the project manager may delegate certain communication or engagement tasks to other team members, such as a communications manager or coordinator, they retain accountability for the effectiveness and outcomes of stakeholder engagement. The project sponsor, as a key stakeholder and decision-maker, should be consulted and informed throughout the engagement process, but does not typically lead the day-to-day engagement efforts. The PMO may provide templates, guidelines, or support for stakeholder engagement, but each project manager is responsible for tailoring the plan to their specific project needs.

718. What is the relationship between the stakeholder engagement plan and the communications management plan?
a. the stakeholder engagement plan is a subset of the communications management plan
b. the communications management plan is a subset of the stakeholder engagement plan
c. the stakeholder engagement plan and communications management plan are separate, unrelated documents
d. the stakeholder engagement plan and communications management plan are interchangeable terms for the same document

Answer: b. the communications management plan is a subset of the stakeholder engagement plan. Explanation: The communications management plan is typically a component or subset of the larger stakeholder engagement plan. The engagement plan takes a holistic view of stakeholder management, including identifying, analyzing, planning, and controlling stakeholder relationships and expectations. The communications management plan focuses specifically on the strategies, methods, and channels for information distribution and exchange with stakeholders, as part of the overall engagement approach. In some cases, the communications management plan may be a separate document that aligns with and supports the stakeholder engagement plan, but is not interchangeable with it.

719. Which of the following is not a common component of a stakeholder engagement plan?
a. stakeholder identification and analysis
b. communication goals and objectives
c. risk management strategies and contingency plans
d. engagement roles and responsibilities

Answer: c. risk management strategies and contingency plans. Explanation: While stakeholder engagement risks and issues may be identified and addressed at a high level in the stakeholder engagement plan, detailed risk management strategies and contingency plans are typically documented in a separate risk management plan, rather than in the engagement plan itself. The stakeholder engagement plan should focus on the specific elements related to stakeholder communication and involvement, such as stakeholder identification and analysis, engagement goals and objectives, communication methods and frequencies, key messages and content, roles and responsibilities, timelines and milestones, and success metrics and evaluation methods. Risk management is a related but distinct project management function that requires its own planning and control processes.

720. What is the purpose of defining clear roles and responsibilities in the stakeholder engagement plan?
a. to ensure that all stakeholders are equally involved in project decision-making
b. to limit the amount of communication and interaction with project stakeholders
c. to establish accountability and coordination for stakeholder engagement activities
d. to determine the appropriate compensation and recognition for stakeholder contributions

Answer: c. to establish accountability and coordination for stakeholder engagement activities. Explanation: The purpose of defining clear roles and responsibilities in the stakeholder engagement plan is to ensure that all stakeholder engagement activities are effectively planned, executed, and monitored, and that the right people are involved at the right times. By assigning specific roles and responsibilities, such as who will develop communication content, who will approve and distribute messages, who will facilitate meetings and events, and who will monitor and report on engagement outcomes, the project manager can establish clear accountability and coordination among the project team and stakeholders. This helps to avoid duplication of effort, gaps in communication, or conflicting messages, and ensures that engagement efforts are aligned with the project's goals and priorities. Roles and responsibilities should be based on each stakeholder's unique skills, influence, and level of involvement, rather than aiming for equal participation or limited interaction.

721. How can project managers ensure that the stakeholder engagement plan is effectively implemented and monitored?
a. by assigning all engagement responsibilities to a single team member
b. by communicating the plan to stakeholders once, at the beginning of the project
c. by regularly reviewing and updating the plan based on stakeholder feedback and project performance
d. by measuring success based solely on the number and frequency of communication activities

Answer: c. by regularly reviewing and updating the plan based on stakeholder feedback and project performance. Explanation: To ensure that the stakeholder engagement plan is effectively implemented and monitored, project managers should treat the plan as a living document that is regularly reviewed, updated, and communicated throughout the project lifecycle. This involves setting up processes and tools to track stakeholder engagement activities, such as communication logs, attendance records, and feedback surveys, and analyzing this data to assess the effectiveness and impact of engagement efforts. Project managers should also actively seek input and feedback from stakeholders on their communication needs, preferences, and satisfaction levels, and use this information to continuously improve the engagement approach. The plan should be flexible enough to adapt to changing project circumstances, risks, or stakeholder dynamics, while still maintaining consistency and alignment with the overall project objectives. Success should be measured not just by the quantity or frequency of engagement activities, but by the quality and outcomes of stakeholder relationships and project performance.

722. What is the difference between a stakeholder engagement plan and a stakeholder management strategy?
a. a stakeholder engagement plan focuses on communication tactics, while a stakeholder management strategy focuses on relationship-building
b. a stakeholder engagement plan is developed by the project manager, while a stakeholder management strategy is developed by the project sponsor
c. a stakeholder engagement plan is a short-term tactical document, while a stakeholder management strategy is a long-term strategic document
d. a stakeholder engagement plan and a stakeholder management strategy are interchangeable terms for the same document

Answer: c. a stakeholder engagement plan is a short-term tactical document, while a stakeholder management strategy is a long-term strategic document. Explanation: A stakeholder engagement plan and a stakeholder management strategy are related but distinct documents that serve different purposes in project management. A stakeholder engagement plan is a tactical document that outlines the specific communication and involvement activities that will be used to engage stakeholders throughout the project lifecycle. It is typically developed by the project manager during the planning phase and covers the duration of the project. A stakeholder management strategy, on the other hand, is a higher-level, longer-term document that defines the organization's overall approach to stakeholder relationship management, beyond the scope of a single project. It may be developed by senior management or the PMO, and includes elements such as stakeholder identification and prioritization criteria, engagement principles and protocols, and governance and decision-making structures. The stakeholder engagement plan should align with and support the stakeholder management strategy, but is more focused on the day-to-day execution of engagement activities within a specific project context.

723. What are some best practices for communicating and socializing the stakeholder engagement plan?
a. distributing the plan via email to all stakeholders, without any follow-up or discussion
b. presenting the plan to stakeholders in a formal, one-way communication session
c. involving key stakeholders in the development and review of the plan, and seeking their feedback and buy-in
d. keeping the plan confidential and sharing it only with the project team, to avoid creating unrealistic expectations among stakeholders

Answer: c. involving key stakeholders in the development and review of the plan, and seeking their feedback and buy-in. Explanation: To effectively communicate and socialize the stakeholder engagement plan, project managers should involve key stakeholders in the development and review of the plan, and actively seek their feedback and buy-in. This collaborative approach helps to ensure that the plan reflects the diverse needs, expectations, and constraints of different stakeholder groups, and that stakeholders feel heard and invested in the engagement process. Project managers can use a variety of communication methods, such as face-to-face meetings, workshops, webinars, or surveys, to present the plan and gather input from stakeholders. The plan should be communicated in clear, concise, and compelling language that highlights the benefits and value of effective stakeholder engagement, and addresses any concerns or objections that stakeholders may have. Sharing the plan via email or formal presentations, without any opportunity for dialogue or feedback, may lead to misunderstandings, resistance, or disengagement among stakeholders. Similarly, keeping the plan confidential or limited to the project team may create a sense of exclusion or mistrust among stakeholders, and limit the plan's effectiveness and impact.

724. What is the primary objective of the Plan Stakeholder Engagement process?
a. to identify all project stakeholders and their interests
b. to determine the communication and engagement needs of project stakeholders
c. to develop strategies for effectively engaging stakeholders throughout the project
d. to evaluate stakeholder satisfaction and engagement levels

Answer: c. to develop strategies for effectively engaging stakeholders throughout the project. Explanation: The primary objective of the Plan Stakeholder Engagement process is to develop strategic and tactical plans for effectively involving, communicating with, and managing the expectations of project stakeholders throughout the project life cycle. While identifying stakeholders, determining their needs, and evaluating their engagement levels are important activities, they are inputs or outputs of the process, rather than its main focus.

725. Which of the following is not a key input to the Plan Stakeholder Engagement process?
a. project charter
b. project management plan
c. stakeholder register
d. stakeholder engagement assessment matrix

Answer: d. stakeholder engagement assessment matrix. Explanation: The stakeholder engagement assessment matrix is not a key input to the Plan Stakeholder Engagement process, but rather an output of the Monitor Stakeholder Engagement process. The main inputs to Plan Stakeholder Engagement are the project charter, which provides high-level information about the project's purpose, objectives, and stakeholders; the project management plan, which includes relevant information from other planning processes; and the stakeholder register, which identifies and documents key project stakeholders and their characteristics.

726. Which tool or technique is used to analyze and prioritize project stakeholders based on their power, interest, and influence?
a. stakeholder mapping
b. power/interest grid
c. stakeholder engagement assessment matrix
d. communication requirements analysis

Answer: b. power/interest grid. Explanation: The power/interest grid is a tool used to analyze and prioritize project stakeholders based on their level of power (ability to influence project outcomes) and interest (concern or involvement in the project). Stakeholders are plotted on a matrix with power on the vertical axis and interest on the horizontal axis, creating four quadrants: high power/high interest, high power/low interest, low power/high interest, and low power/low interest. This visual representation helps project managers to identify key players, keep satisfied, keep informed, and monitor different stakeholder groups and tailor their engagement strategies accordingly. Stakeholder mapping is a more general term for identifying and analyzing stakeholders, while the stakeholder engagement assessment matrix and communication requirements analysis are used for other purposes in stakeholder management.

727. What is a key output of the Plan Stakeholder Engagement process?
a. stakeholder management strategy
b. stakeholder engagement plan
c. project team assignments
d. work performance reports

Answer: b. stakeholder engagement plan. Explanation: A key output of the Plan Stakeholder Engagement process is the stakeholder engagement plan, which documents the strategies, activities, and protocols for engaging and communicating with project stakeholders. The plan typically includes elements such as stakeholder analysis, communication methods and frequencies, key messages and topics, roles and responsibilities, and metrics for measuring engagement effectiveness. It serves as a roadmap for stakeholder management throughout the project life cycle. The stakeholder management strategy is a higher-level document that guides organizational approaches to stakeholder engagement, while project team assignments and work performance reports are related to project resource management and monitoring processes.

728. Which of the following is not a component of the stakeholder engagement plan?
a. stakeholder communication requirements
b. stakeholder engagement risks and issues
c. stakeholder performance evaluations
d. stakeholder engagement roles and responsibilities

Answer: c. stakeholder performance evaluations. Explanation: Stakeholder performance evaluations are not typically a component of the stakeholder engagement plan. The plan focuses on the strategies and activities for engaging and communicating with stakeholders, not on assessing their individual performance or contributions to the project. Common components of the stakeholder engagement plan include stakeholder communication requirements (information needs, methods, and frequencies), engagement risks and issues (potential challenges or barriers to effective engagement), and roles and responsibilities (who will plan, execute, and monitor engagement activities). Performance evaluations may be conducted as part of project human resource management or project closure processes, but are separate from the stakeholder engagement plan.

729. What is the purpose of a communication requirements analysis in the Plan Stakeholder Engagement process?
a. to determine the most cost-effective communication methods for the project
b. to identify the communication channels preferred by the project manager
c. to assess the communication skills and competencies of the project team
d. to document the information needs and preferences of project stakeholders
Answer: d. to document the information needs and preferences of project stakeholders. Explanation: The purpose of a communication requirements analysis in the Plan Stakeholder Engagement process is to gather and document the specific information needs, preferences, and expectations of project stakeholders. This includes identifying what information each stakeholder or stakeholder group requires,

how often they need it, in what format, and through which communication channels. The analysis helps project managers to tailor their communication and engagement approaches to the unique characteristics and interests of different stakeholders, rather than using a one-size-fits-all approach. It is not focused on cost-effectiveness, project manager preferences, or team competencies, but rather on understanding and meeting the communication requirements of stakeholders.

730. What is the relationship between the Plan Stakeholder Engagement process and the Identify Stakeholders process?
a. Plan Stakeholder Engagement is a predecessor to Identify Stakeholders
b. Identify Stakeholders is a predecessor to Plan Stakeholder Engagement
c. Plan Stakeholder Engagement and Identify Stakeholders are performed simultaneously
d. Plan Stakeholder Engagement and Identify Stakeholders are not related

Answer: b. Identify Stakeholders is a predecessor to Plan Stakeholder Engagement. Explanation: The Identify Stakeholders process is a predecessor to the Plan Stakeholder Engagement process in the project management life cycle. Identify Stakeholders, which is part of the initiating process group, involves identifying all individuals, groups, or organizations that may affect or be affected by the project, and documenting their characteristics, interests, and potential impact on project success. The output of this process, the stakeholder register, serves as a key input to Plan Stakeholder Engagement, which is part of the planning process group. Plan Stakeholder Engagement builds upon the stakeholder information gathered in Identify Stakeholders to develop specific strategies and plans for engaging and managing stakeholders throughout the project. The two processes are closely related and sequential, with Identify Stakeholders providing the foundation for effective stakeholder engagement planning.

731. What is the main benefit of involving stakeholders in the development of the stakeholder engagement plan?
a. to expedite the planning process and reduce the workload for the project manager
b. to ensure that the plan reflects the diverse needs and expectations of stakeholders
c. to transfer responsibility for stakeholder engagement to the stakeholders themselves
d. to eliminate the need for ongoing stakeholder communication and feedback

Answer: b. to ensure that the plan reflects the diverse needs and expectations of stakeholders. Explanation: The main benefit of involving stakeholders in the development of the stakeholder engagement plan is to ensure that the plan accurately reflects and addresses the diverse needs, expectations, and concerns of different stakeholder groups. By soliciting input and feedback from key stakeholders during the planning process, project managers can gain valuable insights into stakeholders' communication preferences, information requirements, and engagement goals. This collaborative approach helps to build trust, buy-in, and shared ownership of the engagement process, and reduces the risk of misunderstandings, conflicts, or disengagement later in the project. Involving stakeholders does not necessarily expedite the planning process, transfer responsibility for engagement, or eliminate the need for ongoing communication, but rather enhances the relevance, credibility, and effectiveness of the engagement plan.

732. How often should the stakeholder engagement plan be reviewed and updated?
a. once, at the beginning of the project

b. continuously throughout the project life cycle
c. only when major changes occur in the project scope or stakeholder landscape
d. once, at the end of the project during the closing process

Answer: b. continuously throughout the project life cycle. Explanation: The stakeholder engagement plan should be reviewed and updated continuously throughout the project life cycle, as part of the Monitor Stakeholder Engagement process. While the initial plan is developed during the planning phase, it should not be treated as a static or one-time document. As the project progresses, stakeholder needs, expectations, and engagement levels may change, new stakeholders may emerge, and the effectiveness of engagement strategies may vary. By regularly monitoring and assessing stakeholder engagement, project managers can identify areas for improvement and adapt the plan accordingly. This iterative approach helps to ensure that the engagement plan remains relevant, responsive, and aligned with the evolving project context and stakeholder dynamics. Reviewing the plan only at the beginning, end, or major milestones of the project may miss important opportunities for timely stakeholder communication and course correction.

733. What is the role of the project manager in developing the stakeholder engagement plan?
a. to independently create the plan without input from the project team or stakeholders
b. to delegate the planning responsibility to the project sponsor or steering committee
c. to facilitate a collaborative planning process with the project team and key stakeholders
d. to review and approve the plan developed by the project management office (PMO)

Answer: c. to facilitate a collaborative planning process with the project team and key stakeholders. Explanation: The role of the project manager in developing the stakeholder engagement plan is to facilitate a collaborative and inclusive planning process that involves the project team, key stakeholders, and other relevant experts or decision-makers. As the primary owner and driver of stakeholder engagement, the project manager is responsible for initiating and leading the planning effort, but should not work in isolation or simply delegate the task to others. Effective stakeholder engagement planning requires active participation, diverse perspectives, and shared ownership from multiple parties. The project manager's role is to create a structured yet flexible process for gathering input, building consensus, and documenting the agreed-upon strategies and actions in the engagement plan. This may involve activities such as conducting stakeholder interviews or surveys, facilitating planning workshops or meetings, drafting and revising the plan document, and communicating the final plan to all stakeholders. While the project sponsor, steering committee, or PMO may provide guidance, resources, or oversight for the planning process, the ultimate responsibility for developing and executing the stakeholder engagement plan lies with the project manager.

734. What is the purpose of a power/interest grid in stakeholder analysis?
a. to identify the communication preferences of each stakeholder group
b. to assess and prioritize stakeholders based on their influence and involvement in the project
c. to determine the appropriate engagement strategies for managing stakeholder expectations
d. to evaluate the performance and satisfaction levels of project stakeholders

Answer: b. to assess and prioritize stakeholders based on their influence and involvement in the project. Explanation: The primary purpose of a power/interest grid is to help project managers assess and prioritize project stakeholders based on their level of power (ability to influence project outcomes) and interest (concern or involvement in the project). By plotting stakeholders on a matrix with power on the vertical axis and interest on the horizontal axis, the grid creates four quadrants that categorize stakeholders as key players (high power, high interest), keep satisfied (high power, low interest), keep informed (low power, high interest), or minimal effort (low power, low interest). This visual representation allows project managers to quickly identify and focus on the most important stakeholders who require the most attention and engagement. The power/interest grid is used for stakeholder analysis and prioritization, not for determining communication preferences, engagement strategies, or performance evaluation, which are separate aspects of stakeholder management.

735. Which quadrant of the power/interest grid represents stakeholders who require the most active engagement and management?
a. high power, high interest (key players)
b. high power, low interest (keep satisfied)
c. low power, high interest (keep informed)
d. low power, low interest (minimal effort)

Answer: a. high power, high interest (key players). Explanation: The top-right quadrant of the power/interest grid, which represents stakeholders with high power and high interest in the project, requires the most active engagement and management from the project team. These "key players" have the ability to significantly influence project outcomes and are highly invested in the project's success or failure. Examples may include the project sponsor, key decision-makers, or major customers or users of the project deliverables. Project managers should prioritize frequent, personalized, and collaborative communication with these stakeholders to ensure their needs and expectations are met, their feedback is incorporated, and their support is maintained throughout the project. The other quadrants require varying levels of engagement, such as keeping satisfied (meet their needs, but don't bore with excessive communication), keeping informed (provide regular updates, but don't overwhelm), or minimal effort (monitor, but don't ignore completely), based on their relative power and interest levels.

736. What is a potential limitation or pitfall of relying solely on the power/interest grid for stakeholder analysis?
a. it may oversimplify the complex and dynamic nature of stakeholder relationships
b. it may overestimate the importance of stakeholders with high power and interest
c. it may underestimate the potential impact of stakeholders with low power and interest
d. all of the above

Answer: d. all of the above. Explanation: While the power/interest grid is a useful tool for initial stakeholder assessment and prioritization, relying solely on this framework may have several limitations or pitfalls. First, the grid may oversimplify the complex and dynamic nature of stakeholder relationships, which can shift over time and across different project issues or phases. Stakeholders may have varying levels of power and interest depending on the specific context, and their positions on the grid may change as the project evolves. Second, the grid may overestimate the importance of stakeholders with high power and interest, leading project managers to focus too much time and resources on managing these "key players" at the expense of other important stakeholders. Third, the grid may underestimate the potential impact of stakeholders with low power and interest, who may still have the ability to influence project outcomes indirectly or unexpectedly. To mitigate these limitations, project managers should use the power/interest grid as one of several tools for stakeholder analysis, and continually reassess and adapt their engagement strategies based on changing project and stakeholder dynamics.

737. What is the salience model of stakeholder analysis, and how does it differ from the power/interest grid?
a. the salience model prioritizes stakeholders based on their power, urgency, and legitimacy, while the power/interest grid focuses only on power and interest
b. the salience model is used for internal stakeholders, while the power/interest grid is used for external stakeholders
c. the salience model is a quantitative tool, while the power/interest grid is a qualitative tool
d. the salience model and the power/interest grid are interchangeable terms for the same framework

Answer: a. the salience model prioritizes stakeholders based on their power, urgency, and legitimacy, while the power/interest grid focuses only on power and interest. Explanation: The salience model is another framework for stakeholder analysis that prioritizes stakeholders based on three key attributes: power (ability to influence project outcomes), urgency (need for immediate attention or action), and legitimacy (perceived validity or appropriateness of stakeholder claims). According to this model, stakeholders who possess all three attributes (definitive stakeholders) require the highest priority and engagement, followed by those who possess two attributes (dominant, dangerous, or dependent stakeholders), and those who possess only one attribute (dormant, discretionary, or demanding stakeholders). The main difference between the salience model and the power/interest grid is that the salience model introduces the additional dimension of urgency, which reflects the time-sensitivity and criticality of stakeholder claims, and the dimension of legitimacy, which reflects the perceived validity or appropriateness of stakeholder claims. The power/interest grid focuses only on the dimensions of power and interest, which may not fully capture the dynamic and situational nature of stakeholder importance. The two models are complementary but distinct frameworks that can be used in combination or separately depending on the project context and stakeholder landscape.

738. How can project managers use the power/interest grid and salience model to develop effective stakeholder engagement strategies?
a. by focusing engagement efforts only on stakeholders with high power, interest, and salience
b. by ignoring or avoiding stakeholders with low power, interest, or salience
c. by treating all stakeholders equally regardless of their power, interest, or salience
d. by tailoring engagement approaches based on each stakeholder's unique combination of power, interest, and salience attributes

Answer: d. by tailoring engagement approaches based on each stakeholder's unique combination of power, interest, and salience attributes. Explanation: Project managers can use the insights gained from the power/interest grid and salience model to develop targeted and effective stakeholder engagement strategies that are tailored to each stakeholder's unique combination of power, interest, and salience attributes. For example, for key players or definitive stakeholders (high power, high interest, high salience), project managers may prioritize frequent, personal, and collaborative communication to build strong relationships and align project goals. For keep satisfied or dominant stakeholders (high power, low interest, high salience), project managers may focus on meeting their needs and expectations without overloading them with information. For keep informed or dependent stakeholders (low power, high interest, high salience), project managers may provide regular updates and opportunities for feedback while managing their expectations. For minimal effort or low salience stakeholders, project managers may monitor their potential influence while minimizing active engagement. The key is to use the stakeholder analysis frameworks as a starting point for developing customized engagement plans that balance the project's needs with the stakeholders' needs, rather than applying a one-size-fits-all or binary approach.

739. What is a common challenge in using the power/interest grid and salience model in practice?
a. the subjectivity and potential bias involved in assessing stakeholder attributes
b. the difficulty in obtaining accurate and complete information about all stakeholders
c. the need to continually update and adapt the frameworks as stakeholder dynamics change
d. all of the above

Answer: d. all of the above. Explanation: While the power/interest grid and salience model are valuable tools for stakeholder analysis, they can present several challenges in practical application. One common challenge is the subjectivity and potential bias involved in assessing stakeholder attributes such as power, interest, urgency, and legitimacy. These assessments often rely on the perceptions, experiences, and judgments of the project manager or team, which may be influenced by personal biases, assumptions, or blind spots. Another challenge is the difficulty in obtaining accurate and complete information about all project stakeholders, particularly for large, complex, or external stakeholders. Incomplete or outdated information can lead to misclassification or prioritization of stakeholders. A third challenge is the need to continually update and adapt the stakeholder analysis frameworks as project and stakeholder dynamics change over time. Stakeholder attributes and relationships are not static, and may shift in response to project events, external factors, or changing perceptions. Project managers must be proactive in monitoring and reassessing stakeholder dynamics and adjusting their engagement strategies accordingly. Overcoming these challenges requires a combination of stakeholder research, diverse perspectives, ongoing communication, and adaptive management approaches.

740. How can project managers validate and refine their stakeholder analysis using the power/interest grid and salience model?
a. by relying solely on their own perceptions and assumptions about stakeholders
b. by seeking input and feedback from the project team and the stakeholders themselves
c. by comparing the results of the power/interest grid and salience model to identify inconsistencies
d. by using the frameworks once at the beginning of the project and avoiding further changes

Answer: b. by seeking input and feedback from the project team and the stakeholders themselves. Explanation: To validate and refine their stakeholder analysis using the power/interest grid and salience model, project managers should actively seek input and feedback from multiple sources, particularly the project team and the stakeholders themselves. Involving diverse perspectives in the stakeholder assessment process can help to surface different insights, challenge assumptions, and build a more comprehensive and accurate picture of the stakeholder landscape. Project team members may have valuable knowledge or experience with specific stakeholders that the project manager lacks, while stakeholders can provide direct feedback on their own interests, concerns, and expectations. This collaborative approach to stakeholder analysis can also help to build trust, credibility, and buy-in for the project's engagement strategies. Relying solely on one's own perceptions, comparing the results of different frameworks, or avoiding ongoing refinement are not sufficient for ensuring the validity and relevance of stakeholder analysis over the course of the project.

741. What is a potential unintended consequence of using the power/interest grid and salience model for stakeholder analysis?
a. overemphasizing the importance of stakeholders with high power, interest, or salience at the expense of other stakeholders
b. underestimating the potential influence of stakeholders with low power, interest, or salience on project outcomes
c. creating an adversarial or transactional mindset towards stakeholder relationships
d. all of the above

Answer: d. all of the above. Explanation: While the power/interest grid and salience model are intended to help project managers prioritize and manage stakeholder relationships effectively, they can also have some unintended consequences if not used carefully. One potential consequence is overemphasizing the importance of stakeholders with high power, interest, or salience at the expense of other stakeholders who may still have valuable contributions or perspectives to offer. Focusing too narrowly on the "key players" or "definitive stakeholders" may lead to neglect or marginalization of other stakeholder groups. Another consequence is underestimating the potential influence of stakeholders with low power, interest, or salience on project outcomes, particularly through indirect or cumulative effects. Stakeholders who are initially classified as "minimal effort" or low salience may still have the ability to impact the project through their relationships, resources, or public opinion. A third consequence is creating an adversarial or transactional mindset towards stakeholder relationships, where stakeholders are seen as "boxes to be ticked" or "obstacles to be managed" rather than as partners or collaborators. The frameworks should be used to inform and enable genuine, mutually beneficial stakeholder engagement, not to manipulate or control stakeholders. Project managers must be mindful of these potential pitfalls and use the power/interest grid and salience model as part of a larger, more nuanced approach to stakeholder analysis and engagement.

742. How can project managers communicate the results of the power/interest grid and salience model analysis to project stakeholders?
a. by sharing the complete grid and model with all stakeholders to ensure full transparency
b. by providing a summary of the key findings and implications, tailored to each stakeholder group's needs and interests
c. by keeping the analysis confidential and sharing it only with the project sponsor and team
d. by avoiding any communication about the analysis to prevent stakeholder confusion or misinterpretation

Answer: b. by providing a summary of the key findings and implications, tailored to each stakeholder group's needs and interests. Explanation: When communicating the results of the power/interest grid and salience model analysis to project stakeholders, project managers should strike a balance between transparency and relevance. Sharing the complete grid and model with all stakeholders may be overwhelming, confusing, or even counterproductive, as some stakeholders may disagree with or misinterpret their classification or prioritization. Keeping the analysis entirely confidential may undermine trust and buy-in from stakeholders who expect to be informed and involved in the project's engagement approach. The most effective communication strategy is to provide a summary of the key findings and implications of the analysis, tailored to each stakeholder group's specific needs, interests, and communication preferences. This may involve highlighting the stakeholder's unique role, influence, and importance to the project, outlining the planned engagement activities and channels, and emphasizing the project's commitment to ongoing dialogue and collaboration. By framing the analysis results in terms of the stakeholder's perspective and the project's shared goals, project managers can build understanding, alignment, and ownership of the engagement process. The level of detail and format of the communication may vary depending on the stakeholder's salience and the project's communication plan, but should always be clear, concise, and purposeful.

743. What is the role of the project sponsor in the power/interest grid and salience model analysis process?
a. to independently conduct the stakeholder analysis without involving the project manager or team
b. to review and approve the analysis before it is shared with any other stakeholders
c. to provide input and validation of the analysis based on their knowledge of key stakeholders and organizational context
d. to be excluded from the analysis process to maintain objectivity and avoid bias

Answer: c. to provide input and validation of the analysis based on their knowledge of key stakeholders and organizational context. Explanation: The project sponsor plays a crucial role in the power/interest grid and salience model analysis process by providing strategic input, validation, and support based on their knowledge of key stakeholders and the broader organizational context. As a high-level champion and decision-maker for the project, the sponsor often has unique insights into the power dynamics, political landscape, and strategic priorities that shape stakeholder relationships and expectations. They can help the project manager to identify and assess key stakeholders, validate assumptions and classifications, and navigate complex or sensitive stakeholder issues. The sponsor's involvement in the analysis process also helps to ensure alignment between the project's stakeholder engagement approach and the organization's overall goals and values. However, the sponsor should not conduct the analysis independently or unilaterally approve it without the involvement of the project manager and team, who have more direct responsibility for stakeholder engagement. Nor should the sponsor be excluded from the process entirely, as their perspective and support are essential for effective stakeholder management. The ideal approach is a collaborative one, where the project manager leads the analysis process with input and validation from the sponsor and other key stakeholders, and communicates the results in a way that balances transparency and confidentiality.

744. What is the primary purpose of a stakeholder register in project management?
a. to document the communication preferences of project stakeholders
b. to assess the power and interest levels of project stakeholders
c. to identify and capture information about project stakeholders
d. to evaluate the performance and satisfaction of project stakeholders

Answer: c. to identify and capture information about project stakeholders. Explanation: The primary purpose of a stakeholder register is to identify and document relevant information about individuals, groups, or organizations that may affect or be affected by the project. The register typically includes details such as stakeholder names, titles, contact information, roles, interests, expectations, influence, and impact on the project. This information is used as an input for stakeholder analysis and engagement planning. The stakeholder register itself does not assess power and interest levels, document communication preferences, or evaluate stakeholder performance, which are separate components of the stakeholder management process.

745. Which of the following is not a typical component of a stakeholder register?
a. stakeholder name and contact information
b. stakeholder role and responsibility in the project
c. stakeholder communication preferences and frequency
d. stakeholder power and interest assessment

Answer: d. stakeholder power and interest assessment. Explanation: A typical stakeholder register includes basic information about each identified stakeholder, such as their name, title, organization, contact details, and role or responsibility in the project. It may also capture the stakeholder's key requirements, expectations, or concerns regarding the project outcomes and processes. Some registers may include additional details such as the stakeholder's communication preferences, engagement level, or potential impact on the project. However, the assessment of a stakeholder's power and interest levels is typically performed as part of a separate stakeholder analysis exercise, using tools such as the power/interest grid or salience model. The results of this analysis may be cross-referenced or linked to the stakeholder register, but are not usually documented directly within the register itself.

746. When should the stakeholder register be developed and updated?
a. once, at the beginning of the project planning phase
b. continuously throughout the project life cycle
c. once, at the end of the project during the closing phase
d. only when a new stakeholder is identified or an existing stakeholder's information changes

Answer: b. continuously throughout the project life cycle. Explanation: The stakeholder register should be developed as early as possible in the project life cycle, ideally during the initiation phase, and updated continuously throughout the project. The initial register is created by identifying and documenting all known stakeholders based on the project charter, business case, and other relevant documents or knowledge sources. As the project progresses, new stakeholders may emerge, existing stakeholders' information or status may change, and the project's stakeholder landscape may evolve. The project manager and team should regularly review and update the stakeholder register to ensure it remains accurate, complete, and relevant. This ongoing maintenance helps to inform stakeholder analysis, engagement planning, and communication management. Developing the register only once at the beginning or end of the project, or updating it only when a specific change occurs, may result in outdated or incomplete stakeholder information that hinders effective stakeholder management.

747. Who is responsible for maintaining and updating the stakeholder register?
a. the project manager
b. the project sponsor
c. the project management office (PMO)
d. the stakeholders themselves

Answer: a. the project manager. Explanation: The project manager is primarily responsible for maintaining and updating the stakeholder register throughout the project life cycle. As the overall leader and integrator of the project, the project manager has the central role in identifying, analyzing, and engaging stakeholders to achieve project objectives. This includes ensuring that the stakeholder register is accurate, complete, and up-to-date, and that it is used effectively to inform stakeholder management decisions and actions. The project manager may delegate certain stakeholder management tasks to other team members, but retains accountability for the overall process and outcomes. The project sponsor, PMO, and stakeholders themselves may provide input and feedback on the stakeholder register, but do not typically have direct responsibility for its maintenance and updates.

748. What is the main difference between the stakeholder register and the stakeholder engagement plan?
a. the stakeholder register identifies stakeholders, while the stakeholder engagement plan prioritizes them
b. the stakeholder register is an input to the stakeholder engagement plan
c. the stakeholder register is used for external stakeholders, while the stakeholder engagement plan is used for internal stakeholders
d. the stakeholder register and stakeholder engagement plan are interchangeable terms for the same document

Answer: b. the stakeholder register is an input to the stakeholder engagement plan. Explanation: The main difference between the stakeholder register and the stakeholder engagement plan is that the stakeholder register is an input to the development of the stakeholder engagement plan. The stakeholder register is a document that identifies and captures key information about project stakeholders, such as their names, roles, interests, and expectations. This information serves as a foundation for stakeholder analysis and engagement planning. The stakeholder engagement plan, on the other hand, is a document that defines the strategies, methods, and activities for effectively engaging and communicating with project stakeholders throughout the project life cycle. It is based on the analysis of the stakeholder register, as well as other inputs such as the project charter, requirements, and organizational factors. The engagement plan prioritizes stakeholders based on their power, interest, and other attributes, and outlines specific approaches for managing their expectations and involvement. While the two documents are closely related and iterative, they serve distinct purposes in the stakeholder management process.

749. What is the purpose of conducting a stakeholder analysis?
a. to identify all potential project risks and issues
b. to assess the feasibility and benefits of the project
c. to prioritize and understand stakeholder needs, interests, and influence
d. to assign project roles and responsibilities to stakeholders

Answer: c. to prioritize and understand stakeholder needs, interests, and influence. Explanation: The purpose of conducting a stakeholder analysis is to systematically gather and examine information about project stakeholders in order to prioritize their importance and understand their needs, interests, expectations, and potential influence on project outcomes. Stakeholder analysis involves assessing each stakeholder's power (ability to affect the project), interest (level of concern or involvement), and other relevant attributes, and using this information to develop targeted engagement strategies. The analysis helps project managers to identify key stakeholders who require the most attention and management, anticipate potential stakeholder reactions or risks, and tailor their communication and involvement approaches accordingly. Stakeholder analysis is not primarily focused on identifying project risks, assessing project feasibility, or assigning project roles, although it may inform these other project management processes.

750. Which of the following is not a common technique used in stakeholder analysis?
a. brainstorming and nominal group technique
b. interviews and focus groups
c. surveys and questionnaires
d. earned value analysis

Answer: d. earned value analysis. Explanation: Earned value analysis is not a common technique used in stakeholder analysis. Earned value analysis is a method for measuring project performance by comparing the planned work to the actual work completed and the actual costs incurred. It is used to track project progress, identify variances, and forecast future performance, but does not directly involve analyzing stakeholder attributes or needs. Common techniques used in stakeholder analysis include brainstorming and nominal group technique (to identify and prioritize stakeholders), interviews and focus groups (to gather in-depth information about stakeholder perspectives and expectations), and surveys and questionnaires (to collect broader feedback and data from a larger group of stakeholders). Other techniques may include document analysis, observation, and social network analysis, depending on the project context and stakeholder landscape.

751. How can project managers validate and refine their stakeholder analysis?
a. by relying solely on their own experience and judgment
b. by seeking input and feedback from the project team and stakeholders
c. by comparing the results of different stakeholder analysis techniques
d. by avoiding any changes to the initial stakeholder analysis to maintain consistency

Answer: b. by seeking input and feedback from the project team and stakeholders. Explanation: To validate and refine their stakeholder analysis, project managers should actively seek input and feedback from multiple sources, particularly the project team members and the stakeholders themselves. Stakeholder analysis is not a one-time or one-person exercise, but rather an ongoing and collaborative process that requires diverse perspectives and insights. Project team members may have valuable knowledge or experience with specific stakeholders that can help to verify or challenge the project manager's assumptions and assessments. Stakeholders can provide direct feedback on their own interests, expectations, and perceptions, which may reveal gaps or misalignments in the initial analysis. Engaging stakeholders in the analysis process can also help to build trust, credibility, and ownership of the project's engagement approach. While comparing the results of different analysis techniques and maintaining consistency are important considerations, they should not preclude the incorporation of new information or perspectives that can improve the accuracy and relevance of the stakeholder analysis over time. Relying solely on one's own judgment or avoiding any changes to the initial analysis can lead to blind spots, biases, or outdated information that hinders effective stakeholder management.

752. What are some common challenges or pitfalls in stakeholder analysis?

a. identifying and including all relevant stakeholders in the analysis
b. accurately assessing stakeholder power, interest, and influence levels
c. overcoming personal biases or assumptions about stakeholders
d. all of the above

Answer: d. all of the above. Explanation: Stakeholder analysis can present several common challenges or pitfalls that project managers need to be aware of and proactively address. One challenge is identifying and including all relevant stakeholders in the analysis, particularly those who may be less visible, vocal, or directly involved in the project, but still have the potential to impact or be impacted by its outcomes. Overlooking or excluding important stakeholders can lead to blind spots, resistance, or unintended consequences. Another challenge is accurately assessing stakeholder attributes such as power, interest, and influence, which are often subjective, context-dependent, and dynamic. Misclassifying or misinterpreting stakeholder attributes can result in misaligned engagement strategies or missed opportunities. A third challenge is overcoming personal biases, assumptions, or stereotypes about stakeholders, which can distort the analysis and lead to ineffective or even counterproductive stakeholder management approaches. Project managers must be self-aware, open-minded, and willing to challenge their own preconceptions when analyzing stakeholders. Addressing these challenges requires a combination of thorough research, diverse inputs, ongoing monitoring, and adaptive thinking.

753. How can project managers use the results of stakeholder analysis to inform project decision-making?
a. by prioritizing the needs and preferences of the most powerful stakeholders over other considerations
b. by making decisions that satisfy the largest number of stakeholders, regardless of feasibility or alignment with project objectives
c. by using stakeholder input to identify and evaluate alternative courses of action and their potential impacts
d. by delegating project decisions to stakeholders based on their level of interest and influence

Answer: c. by using stakeholder input to identify and evaluate alternative courses of action and their potential impacts. Explanation: Project managers can use the results of stakeholder analysis to inform project decision-making by incorporating stakeholder input and perspectives into the identification, evaluation, and selection of alternative courses of action. Stakeholder analysis provides valuable insights into the needs, expectations, concerns, and influence of different stakeholder groups, which can help project managers to anticipate potential reactions, risks, or opportunities associated with different project decisions. By considering stakeholder perspectives alongside other technical, financial, and organizational factors, project managers can make more informed and balanced decisions that optimize project outcomes and stakeholder satisfaction. However, this does not mean simply prioritizing the most powerful stakeholders' preferences, seeking to please the majority of stakeholders, or abdicating decision-making responsibility to stakeholders. Project managers must still exercise their professional judgment and leadership to make decisions that align with the project's objectives, constraints, and ethical principles, while taking stakeholder input into account. Effective decision-making requires weighing and integrating multiple sources of information, including stakeholder analysis, to find the best path forward for the project and its stakeholders.

754. What is the main output of the Identify Stakeholders process?
a. stakeholder management strategy

b. stakeholder engagement plan
c. stakeholder register
d. power/interest grid

Answer: c. stakeholder register. Explanation: The main output of the Identify Stakeholders process is the stakeholder register, which is a document that captures relevant information about individuals, groups, or organizations that may affect or be affected by the project. The stakeholder register typically includes details such as stakeholder names, contact information, roles, interests, expectations, influence, and potential impact on the project. The stakeholder management strategy and engagement plan are developed later in the Plan Stakeholder Engagement process, while the power/interest grid is a tool used for stakeholder analysis and prioritization, not an output of the identification process itself.

755. Which of the following is not an input to the Identify Stakeholders process?
a. project charter
b. procurement documents
c. enterprise environmental factors
d. stakeholder engagement assessment matrix

Answer: d. stakeholder engagement assessment matrix. Explanation: The stakeholder engagement assessment matrix is not an input to the Identify Stakeholders process, but rather an output of the Monitor Stakeholder Engagement process. The matrix is used to evaluate the effectiveness of stakeholder engagement strategies and activities throughout the project lifecycle. The key inputs to the Identify Stakeholders process are the project charter, which provides high-level information about the project's purpose, objectives, and key stakeholders; procurement documents, which may include contracts or agreements that identify external stakeholders; and enterprise environmental factors, such as organizational culture, structure, and policies that may influence stakeholder identification and expectations.

756. What is the primary purpose of the Identify Stakeholders process?
a. to prioritize stakeholders based on their power and interest in the project
b. to develop strategies for engaging and communicating with project stakeholders
c. to determine the communication preferences and requirements of project stakeholders
d. to identify and document all individuals and organizations that may affect or be affected by the project

Answer: d. to identify and document all individuals and organizations that may affect or be affected by the project. Explanation: The primary purpose of the Identify Stakeholders process is to identify and document all individuals, groups, or organizations that may affect, be affected by, or perceive themselves to be affected by the project or its outcomes. This includes both internal stakeholders, such as project team members, sponsors, and executives, and external stakeholders, such as customers, suppliers, regulators, and community groups. The process focuses on creating a comprehensive list of potential stakeholders and capturing key information about them, as a foundation for further analysis and engagement planning. It does not involve prioritizing stakeholders, developing engagement strategies, or determining communication preferences, which are addressed in subsequent stakeholder management processes.

757. When should the Identify Stakeholders process be conducted?
a. once, at the beginning of the project lifecycle
b. continuously throughout the project lifecycle
c. once, at the end of the project lifecycle
d. only when a new stakeholder is identified or an existing stakeholder's information changes

Answer: b. continuously throughout the project lifecycle. Explanation: The Identify Stakeholders process should be conducted continuously throughout the project lifecycle, starting from the initiating phase and extending through planning, executing, monitoring and controlling, and closing. While the initial stakeholder identification is typically done early in the project, based on the project charter and other initiating documents, the process should not be a one-time event. As the project progresses, new stakeholders may emerge, existing stakeholders' roles or interests may change, and the project's stakeholder landscape may evolve. Project managers should regularly review and update the stakeholder register to ensure it remains accurate, complete, and relevant. This iterative approach helps to inform ongoing stakeholder analysis, engagement, and communication management.

758. What is the role of expert judgment in the Identify Stakeholders process?
a. to replace the need for other stakeholder identification techniques
b. to assign stakeholders to specific roles and responsibilities in the project
c. to provide input and insight based on previous experience with similar projects or stakeholders
d. to validate the accuracy and completeness of the stakeholder register

Answer: c. to provide input and insight based on previous experience with similar projects or stakeholders. Explanation: Expert judgment is a tool and technique used in the Identify Stakeholders process to provide input, insight, and guidance based on the expert's previous experience with similar projects, stakeholders, or contexts. Experts may include senior managers, subject matter experts, stakeholder representatives, or external consultants who have relevant knowledge or perspective on the project's stakeholder landscape. Their judgment can help to identify potential stakeholders, assess their interests and influence, and anticipate their expectations or concerns. Expert judgment complements and informs other stakeholder identification techniques, such as brainstorming, interviews, or document analysis, but does not replace them entirely. It also does not involve assigning stakeholders to project roles or validating the stakeholder register, which are separate project management activities.

759. What is the difference between the project charter and procurement documents as inputs to the Identify Stakeholders process?
a. the project charter identifies internal stakeholders, while procurement documents identify external stakeholders
b. the project charter provides high-level information about key stakeholders, while procurement documents provide detailed information about contracted stakeholders
c. the project charter is an output of the Identify Stakeholders process, while procurement documents are an input
d. the project charter and procurement documents are interchangeable sources of stakeholder information

Answer: b. the project charter provides high-level information about key stakeholders, while procurement documents provide detailed information about contracted stakeholders. Explanation: The project charter and procurement documents serve different purposes as inputs to the Identify Stakeholders process. The project charter is a document that formally authorizes the existence of the project and provides high-level information about its purpose, objectives, scope, and key stakeholders. It is typically created by the project sponsor or initiator and serves as a starting point for stakeholder identification. Procurement documents, on the other hand, are contracts, agreements, or other legal documents that establish the relationship between the project and external stakeholders such as suppliers, vendors, contractors, or consultants. These documents provide more detailed information about the specific roles, responsibilities, deliverables, and terms and conditions of the contracted stakeholders. Together, the project charter and procurement documents help to identify both internal and external stakeholders, but at different levels of detail and formality.

760. What is the relationship between the Identify Stakeholders process and the Collect Requirements process?
a. Identify Stakeholders is a predecessor to Collect Requirements
b. Collect Requirements is a predecessor to Identify Stakeholders
c. Identify Stakeholders and Collect Requirements are not directly related
d. Identify Stakeholders and Collect Requirements are interchangeable processes

Answer: a. Identify Stakeholders is a predecessor to Collect Requirements. Explanation: The Identify Stakeholders process is a predecessor to the Collect Requirements process in the project management lifecycle. Identify Stakeholders, which is part of the initiating process group, focuses on identifying and documenting all individuals, groups, or organizations that may affect or be affected by the project. The output of this process, the stakeholder register, serves as an important input to the Collect Requirements process, which is part of the planning process group. Collect Requirements involves defining and documenting stakeholders' needs and expectations for the project deliverables and outcomes. By identifying and understanding the relevant stakeholders first, project managers can more effectively elicit, analyze, and prioritize their requirements. The two processes are closely related and sequential, with Identify Stakeholders setting the foundation for effective requirements management.

As we wrap up this journey through your CAPM Exam Prep, I hope you feel a surge of confidence, ready to tackle the challenges ahead. From the nitty-gritty of project scope statements to the intricacies of requirements documentation, we've covered a lot of ground together. Remember, this guide was designed not just to fill your head with knowledge but to equip you with the tools to think and act like a seasoned project manager.
Every chapter, every question was crafted to encourage your dreams of becoming a certified project manager. We've walked through various scenarios, unraveling complex concepts and transforming them into manageable, understandable parts. Perhaps there were moments that tested your resolve, sections that made you revisit your understanding, or topics that pushed you to connect dots in ways you hadn't before. That's all part of growing into the role you aspire to fill.
I know there might have been times when doubts crept in—maybe a tough chapter made you question your readiness. But remember, every professional faces setbacks. It's not just about how well you start but how strong you finish. Your perseverance is your greatest ally.
If fears about the exam linger, let's put them to rest right now. You are prepared. You've equipped yourself with knowledge and honed your critical thinking skills. As for those suspicions about the vastness of the

project management field, yes, it's broad and sometimes daunting, but it's also filled with opportunities for those who are well-prepared, like you.

Now, go ahead and give your best shot at the exam. Use this guide as your ally, revisit the questions that challenged you, and keep practicing. Success isn't just about passing the exam but about setting a strong foundation for your career in project management.

So, throw that proverbial rock at your challenges, break barriers, and open doors to new opportunities. Good luck, and remember, the path doesn't end here—it only begins. You've got this!

Made in the USA
Middletown, DE
19 September 2024

61123342R10329